FIRST YEAR
LATIN

FIRST YEAR LATIN

CHARLES JENNEY, JR.

ERIC C. BAADE

THOMAS K. BURGESS

PRENTICE HALL

Needham, Massachusetts   Englewood Cliffs, New Jersey

PROGRAM CONSULTANTS

Bernard Barcio
Carmel High School
Carmel, Indiana

Doris Kays
Foreign Language Consultant
Northeast ISD
San Antonio, Texas

Michael Mitchusson
Sherman High School
Sherman, Texas

Maureen O'Donnell
formerly of W.T. Woodson High School
Fairfax, Virginia

Grady L. Warren III
Northeast High School
Clarksville, Tennessee

STAFF CREDITS

PROJECT EDITOR:
Rita R. Riley

PRODUCT DEVELOPMENT:
Thomas Maksym

ART DIRECTOR:
L. Christopher Valente

TEXT DESIGNER AND PRODUCTION COORDINATOR:
Carol H. Rose

SENIOR DESIGNER:
Richard E. Dalton

PHOTO RESEARCHER:
Susan Van Etten

PHOTO COORDINATOR:
Katherine S. Diamond

PRODUCTION EDITOR:
Shyamol Bhattacherya

MANUFACTURING:
Roger Powers

COVER DESIGN:
John Martucci and L. Christopher Valente

MAPS:
Sanderson Associates

ILLUSTRATION:
Danielle Chlumecky

ISBN: 0-13-319328-4

2 3 4 5 6 7 8 9 9 97 96 95 94 93 92 91 90

A Simon & Schuster Company

(*page i*) Fresco from Pompeii
(*page ii*) Mosaic floor from Pompeii

ABOUT THE AUTHORS . . .

Charles Jenney, Jr., senior author, was graduated from Harvard University and did graduate work there as well as at the University of Toulouse in France and the American Academy at Rome. He taught at Belmont Hill School, Belmont, Massachusetts for fifty-four years serving not only as teacher, but as Head of the Latin Department, Director of Studies, and Assistant Headmaster.

Eric C. Baade received both his B.A. degree and Ph.D from Yale University and is currently the Chairman of the Department of Classics at Brooks School, North Andover, Massachusetts. He has co-authored many texts on Latin authors and on the teaching of Latin, and has had considerable teaching experience on both the high school and college levels. He has also conducted Archaeology Field Courses in Italy for both high school and college classes. In 1987 he received an award for the Massachusetts Classics Teacher of the year.

Thomas K. Burgess was graduated cum laude in Classics from Harvard University and received a Master of Philosophy in Classics at the University of London. He has taught Latin, Greek, Ancient History, and Roman Topography at St. Stephen's School in Rome, Italy and is presently a teacher of Classics at Brooks School, North Andover, Massachusetts.

The authors also acknowledge their indebtedness to their colleagues of the Brooks School faculty: William K. Poirot, Sally W. Morris, John H. Quirk, Jr., and Kathleen McDonnell, and also wish to express special gratitude to Maureen O'Donnell formerly of the W.T. Woodson High School, Fairfax, Virginia, in recognition of her service and devotion to the cause of Latin.

The authors dedicate this volume to the best of editors, Rita Riley.

CONTENTS

WHY STUDY LATIN?

I t is the beginning of the school year and the upper classmen in a local high school have planned various activities for the incoming Freshmen. Representatives of each subject area met during the last week of summer vacation and prepared their special welcome.

The members of the Latin Club decided that they would stress the advantages of studying Latin and show the new students how a knowledge of Latin could be used in all aspects of their student life.

The first part of their program was to sponsor a softball game between freshmen and sophomores. They hung banners and posters around the school to publicize the game. These were the banners that attracted the most attention:

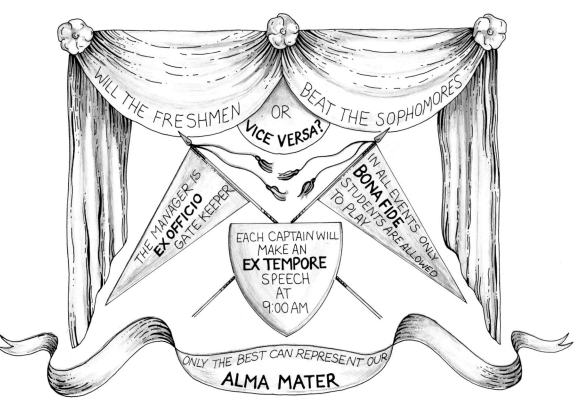

How many of these banners do you understand?

One of the problems that had to be solved very early in the school day was the open campus policy that had been in effect in the school system for the past two years. Although the program was very popular, it created a few administrative problems. Therefore, the school board wished to set up a series of meetings to see if the problems could be solved or if the program should be abolished. In reference to this, the Latin club prepared special brochures which were given to all students in preparation for the first meeting. The brochure read as follows:

RE: OPEN CAMPUS

If you don't agree with this proposal, set forth the PRO and CON(TRA) arguments with the members of the school board urging a REFERENDUM to the students.

Be careful! A single LAPSUS LINGUAE may spoil your case IN TOTO. You may use an effective A PRIORI argument, or say there is a PRIMA FACIE evidence that the open campus policy is a good thing; but if you fail to make your point, things remain in STATU QUO, the school board make their ULTIMATUM and the open campus policy makes its EXIT.

Do you understand this brochure?

After the softball game, the athletes and spectators were invited to a special luncheon—a Roman banquet prepared and served by members of the Latin Club. The waiters were dressed in togas, and the meal was fashioned after a typical Roman meal which is described in *First Year Latin*. The highlight of the event, however, was the speech delivered by the President of the Senior Class.

"I am here today to urge each one of you to be sure to register for the fine Latin program offered by this school. Some high-school students avoid Latin because it is considered to be difficult. This may be true, but the rewards that can be reaped from such a venture far outweigh any difficulty you may have trying to learn declensions and conjugations. There is no doubt that you can be educated and live your life without studying Latin, but so too can you fish on the bank of a stream without ever knowing the thrill of deep sea-fishing. Don't settle for too little. Don't let your world be too narrow. Know the fun of understanding expressions like "Herculean Labors," "The Midas Touch," "The Die is Cast," "Carpe Diem," "Caveat," and many other expressions which enliven and color our English language.

"Latin will be a great help to you in everything you study. In bookkeeping you won't confuse *debit* and *credit*, if you know their derivation. In mathematics you will know the meaning of *equation* and *integer*. In biology you will know what *auditory* and *duct* mean. In all the sciences you will find that many of the technical words come from Latin.

"But it is in English—the most everyday, practical study of all—that you will find Latin most useful. You will not misspell words like *separate, laudable, accommodate*, and so on, if you know Latin. Often without knowing it you will be using Latin words constantly. Half the words you speak or write, like *animal, radius*, and *conductor*, are exactly the same in both languages. Words like *timid, longitude*, and *vehicle*, have only slightly different endings. In your reading, a knowledge of Latin will often explain troublesome quotations and many references to mythology.

"Your French and Spanish teachers will like it much better if you have studied Latin first, for French and Spanish come from Latin and it will make their work and yours much easier.

"Lastly, Latin will make you a careful and accurate student. You will learn to reason things out and to express yourself in clear and correct English. You will read at first hand the literature of some of the world's greatest writers, which is so much better than reading it second hand in English, and you will obtain a background of culture which every successful person should have.

"I could go on ad infinitum but I will close by urging you to please think seriously about taking Latin. It disciplines the mind, promotes logical thinking, and develops a high power of concentration that will serve you all your life."

Verbum sat sapientī!

MAKING THE PIECES FIT

Welcome to the language of the ancient Romans! Think of learning Latin as working on a giant puzzle where you must make the pieces fit together to form a picture. To do this you must first become familiar with certain terms. Let's begin with three special terms: *inflection, declension,* and *conjugation.*

Both Latin and English are descendants of the parent language called Indo-European. It is characteristic of the older languages of this group (like Latin) to express the relationships of words to each other (syntax) by changes in the endings of the words rather than as in the younger languages (like English) by word order, prepositions, and auxiliary verbs. These changes in endings are called *inflection.* The inflection of nouns, adjectives, and pronouns is called *declension,* and that of verbs *conjugation.* We say that a noun, pronoun, or adjective is *declined* and a verb *conjugated.* A declension or a conjugation may also be the group of all words declined or conjugated in the same way as each other.

English words are inflected very little: a normal English verb has only three forms, e.g. *make, makes, made* (all other uses are dealt with by the use of such auxiliaries as *is, was, will, has, should,* and *might*). An English noun has four forms, e.g. *boy, boy's, boys, boys'*. A regular noun in Latin has twelve forms; a regular transitive verb has more than a hundred.

You will be working a lot with declensions and conjugations in Latin. But to do this correctly you will need to understand the other parts of the puzzle which are case, gender, and tense. Let's examine these, piece by piece.

CASE

A Latin noun has six cases; their basic uses are as follows:

1. The *Nominative* names the subject of the sentence, i.e. whatever the statement or question is about. The *boy* runs.
2. The *Vocative* is the case of direct address: Look, *Marcus!*
3. The *Genitive* enables a noun to qualify another noun in some way; most of its uses are represented in English by prepositional phrases with *of*: the gardens *of Caesar*; part *of the army*; love *of life*; a man *of great distinction*.
4. The *Dative* expresses the object indirectly affected by the action of a verb or by the quality of an adjective: I gave a book *to Lucius.* I gave *Lucius* a book. He did it *for his friend.* She is unfriendly *to my sister.* You are like *my father.*
5. The *Accusative* limits the action of the verb in various ways, i.e. it tells how far the action of the verb extends: She went *home.* I ran *a mile.* He saw *a bird.* We stayed *three days.*
6. The *Ablative* has three basic uses:
   a. Ablative Proper (separation: *from*): He comes *from New York.* She fainted *from hunger.* This book was written *by (i.e. comes from) Charles Dickens.*
   b. Instrumental/Circumstantial Ablative (instrument or circumstance: *with*): She listened *with great eagerness.* We dig *with shovels.* He came *with his father.* She is a woman *of (i.e. with) great influence.*
   c. Locative Ablative (location in space or time: *in, on, at*): *in Italy; in two days; on Thursday; at seven o'clock.*

GENDER

In English, gender is determined by sex: words naming males are nouns of the masculine gender, words naming females are nouns of the feminine gender, and words naming things are nouns of the neuter gender. In Latin, too, nouns naming males and females are masculine and feminine respectively, and many names of things are neuter. There are also, however, a great many names of things, inanimate objects, abstract qualities, actions, etc., which are not neuter, but masculine or feminine.

TENSE

A Latin verb has six tenses, one of which, the perfect, is used in two different ways. Here are the uses of the tenses:

PRESENT TENSES

The *present* describes an action as going on in the present, or as generally true: *He is sleeping. A rolling stone gathers no moss.* The *perfect* describes an action as completed by the present time: *We have come to see the city.*

PAST TENSES

The *perfect* is also used, like the English past tense, merely to state that an action took place in the past, without further qualifying it: *I arrived yesterday.* The *imperfect* describes an action as going on (not completed) at some time in the past. *When I arrived, he was leaving.* The *pluperfect* describes an action as already completed by some time in the past: *When I arrived, he had left.*

FUTURE TENSES

The *future* describes an action as taking place in the future: *He will refuse to go.* The *future perfect* describes an action as completed by some time in the future: *By this time tomorrow I shall have met my friend.*

These are the main pieces of the puzzle you will be working with as you learn Latin vocabulary and usage. Finally, you will need to say the words correctly. So the next step will be to develop proper speech patterns.

Proper Speech Patterns

If young Romans were to study English, they would first learn that the same vowels may have different sounds, for example:

a	fall	far	fat	fate	
ea	heart	heard	hear	head	
ou	tough	though	thought	through	thou

Then they would learn that there are two different sounds for the consonant *c,* as in *cat* and *cent,* and also for the letter *g,* as in *get* and *gem.*

Finally, when they learned that some English letters, both consonants and vowels, are often silent, they would probably be discouraged and complain to their teacher that Latin was much simpler. In Latin a vowel has only two sounds, short and long, the sound of a consonant seldom varies, and there are no silent letters. So you see, pronouncing Latin is easier than your native English. Before you use Latin orally, however, you must develop good habits of pronunciation. This involves becoming familiar with the alphabet, the pronunciation of individual vowels, diphthongs, and consonants, and the rules for syllabification. Once you are aware of these basic principles, the rest will come automatically through repetition and everyday use.

THE ALPHABET

The Latin alphabet is like the English, except that it has no *j* or *w*. *K* is used only in some archaic words, *y* and *z* only in words of Greek origin. The classification of letters as vowels or consonants is the same as in English, except that *i,* when it occurs between vowels or before a vowel at the beginning of a word, is a consonant. The letter *y* is always a vowel.

VOWELS

Each vowel in Latin has two sounds, long and short. The quantity of a vowel is indicated by a line (called a *macron,* plural *macra*) above it if it is long: short vowels are unmarked. The vowels are pronounced as follows:

LONG	SHORT
ā as in *father*	a as in *idea*
ā, fās, vās, hāc, pāx	ab, ac, ad, at, amat

LONG	SHORT
ē as in *obey*	e as in *bet*
ē, dē, nē, rēs, rēx, dēns	ex, et, nec, sed, vel, bene
ī as in *machine*	i as in *sit*
sī, sīc, quī, hī, dīc, vīdī	in, quis, dissimilis
ō as in *note*	o as in *omit*
dō, mōs, prō, nōn, ōrō	ob, mox, quot, tot, quod
ū as in *rule* (never as in pupil)	u as in *put*
tū, plūs, dūc, rūs, ūsū	sub, ut, dum, tuus, tumultus

The letter **y** is pronounced like the French *u* or the German *ü* (form the lips as if to say *oo,* but say *ee* instead).

syzygium

DIPHTHONGS

Latin has five principal diphthongs (combinations of two vowels to make a single sound), pronounced as follows:

ae like *aye*
prae, laetae, aegrae, aequae, aetās

au like *ow* in *now*
aut, aurum, laudō, paulō, gaudium

eu like *ay-oo,* said as one syllable
ceu, heu, Eurōpa, Teutonī

oe like *oy* in *joy*
poena, proelium, foedus, moenia

ui like *uee* in *queen*
huic, cui, hui

Four other diphthongs appear very rarely: **ai** (like *aye*), **ei** (as in *weigh*), **oi** (as in *oil*), and **ou** (as in *you*).

CONSONANTS

The consonants are pronounced as in English, with the following exceptions:

bs is pronounced *ps*
bt is pronounced *pt*
c is always hard, as in *came* (never soft, as in *city*)
ch as in *character*
g is always hard, as in *go* (never soft, as in *gem*)
gu before a vowel as in *anguish*

i (when used as a consonant) is like *y* in *youth*
ph as in *philosophy*
s as in *sit* (it never has the *z* sound, as in *busy*)
su before a vowel is often *sw*, as in *suave*
th is voiceless, as in *thick* (not voiced, as in *this*)
v is pronounced like *w*
z is like *dz* in *adze*

The letters **x** and **z** are called *double consonants* (as representing **ks** and **dz**). Every consonant must be sounded in pronouncing a Latin word; doubled consonants should not be run together but pronounced separately. **Addō** is **ad′dō,** not add′ō.

Pronounce the following words after your teacher:

arēna	cēnsus	Caesar	Cicerō
campus	pulchra	schola	iūs
chorus	silva	rosa	summās
iam	patientia	toga	Themis
terra	via	rēx	vōx
Athēnae	Galba	gēns	gesta

SYLLABICATION

More trouble for our Roman students learning English—English syllabication! The teacher puts the following pairs of words on the blackboard:

Rom-any	Ro-man
log-i-cal	lo-gi-cian
rat-i-fy	ra-tion-al

Notice how different the syllabication is in each pair. As the teacher tries to explain why this is so, the students wonder why English-speaking people have to have so many complicated rules. Their native Latin syllabication is simple and uniform.

Each Latin word has as many syllables as it has vowels or diphthongs; there are no silent letters. Consonantal **i** is not counted as a vowel, nor is **u** when it has the sound of English *w* after **g, q,** and sometimes **s.**

ae di fi′ ci um   du o dē vī gin ′ tī   gau′ di um
iu′ be ō   lin′ gua   per suā′ de ō   su′ us

The rules for the division of Latin words into syllables are:

1. A consonant between two vowels or diphthongs is pronounced with the following syllable:

dē' li gō   nu' me rus   o' cu lus   Trō iā' nus

EXCEPTION: The double consonants **x** and **z** go with the preceding syllable:

aux i' li um   gaz' a

2. In a group of two or more consonants, only the last consonant is pronounced with the following syllable.

dif fi cul' tas   tem pes' tas

EXCEPTIONS: a. A syllable cannot contain a doubled consonant.

ap pro pin' quō

    b. If the last consonant is **l** or **r**, preceded by **c, g, p, b, d,** or **t,** both these consonants may be pronounced with the following syllable.

a gri' co la or ag ri' co la   am' plus or amp' lus
pu' bli cus or pub' li cus

    c. **H** does not count as a consonant.

Co rin' thus

    d. The combinations **gu** (when it is pronounced *gw*), **qu,** and **su** (when it is pronounced *sw*), count as only one consonant each.

a' qua   an' guis   cōn suē' tus

Divide the following words into syllables:

APPLYING RULE **1**:

dominus	ager	animus	fāma	fuga	homō	nātūra
caput	dēsīderō	liber	casa	sexus	Cȳzicus	

APPLYING RULE **2**:

cōnsilium	annus	victōria	bellum	silva	oppidum
templō	prīnceps	puella	frātribus	fortūna	
sacrificābō	Dēiphobē	dīligentia	lychnus		

The last syllable of a Latin word is called the *ultima (last),* the next to last the *penult* (**paene-ultima,** *almost-last*), and the one before that the *antepenult* (**ante-paene-ultima,** *before-almost-last*).

QUANTITIES

Syllables are classified as long or short, depending on the length of time it takes to pronounce them. The Romans thought that it took twice as long to pronounce a long syllable as it did a short one. Since we are used to making such distinctions in length of syllables only in singing, it is difficult for us to reproduce this pronunciation; but we must learn to identify long syllables in order to accent words correctly.

1. A syllable which contains a long vowel or a diphthong is said to be long by nature. A short vowel before a consonant **i** becomes a diphthong and so is treated as long (as in **e′ ius, a li cu′ ius,** and **a′ iō**).
2. A syllable which ends in a consonant is said to be long by position.
3. Other syllables are short.

ACCENT

Imagine our Roman students learning a new vocabulary and coming across the words *object, present,* and *progress.* One of the students asks the teacher how to pronounce them, and she learns that you cannot tell how to accent the words correctly until they are used in a sentence. Imagine the class trying to read

> At *present* we *object* to the lack of *progress;* our *object* is to *present* the means by which we may *progress* more rapidly.

Once more they are struck by the greater simplicity of their native Latin, where accent, like pronunciation is uniform. There are only three simple rules for Latin accent:

1. A word of two syllables is accented on the first syllable.
2. In words of three or more syllables the accent is on the penult if it is long (either by nature or by position).
3. If the penult is short the accent falls on the antepenult.

    ca la′ mi tās   fa cul′ tās   ge′ nus   oc′ ci dō   oc cī′ do

One final exercise brings smiles to the faces of the Roman students. As they learn more and more English vocabulary, they are surprised and delighted to find out how like their native Latin much of it is. More than half of the English words they learn are derived from Latin, and many of them are identical in both languages.

You will be surprised and delighted too. Read the following Latin words, pronouncing them according to the rules you have just learned.

animal	dictātor	labor	toga
arēna	furor	minor	tūtor
cēnsor	genus	ōmen	ulterior
cēnsus	honor	pēnīnsula	victor
clāmor	horror	status	vīlla
cōnsul	inventor	terror	

As you study FIRST YEAR LATIN you will find that there are five main sections to each lesson: Forms, Syntax, Vocabulary, Practice, and Reading. The Forms you must memorize, Syntax shows you how the forms are used in a sentence, Vocabulary gives you new words to use, Practice gives you an opportunity to use what you have learned, and the Reading uses all the new elements in an interesting story.

An understanding of English grammar will be very helpful to you as you learn the principles of Latin grammar. If you feel you need to brush up on your English grammar, study aids are provided in the section entitled *English and Latin Grammar Compared* which is found at the beginning of the Appendix.

And now, let's begin the first lap of our journey to antiquity!

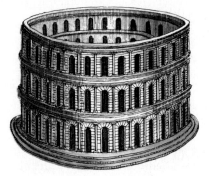

Italy and Sicily

Po R.

ETRURIA

Arretium •

Clusium •

Tiber R.

Tarquinii •

Veii •

Caere •

Fidenae •

Rome •

Ostia •

LATIUM

VOLSCI

SAMNIUM

Capua •

Cumae •

CAMPANIA

Pompeii •

VIA APPIA

Brundisium •

Crimisus •

Crotona •

ADRIATIC SEA

TYRRHENIAN SEA

CORSICA

SARDINIA

MEDITERRANEAN SEA

Segesta •

SICILY

Acis •

Syracuse •

IONIAN SEA

Carthage •

AFRICA

Malta

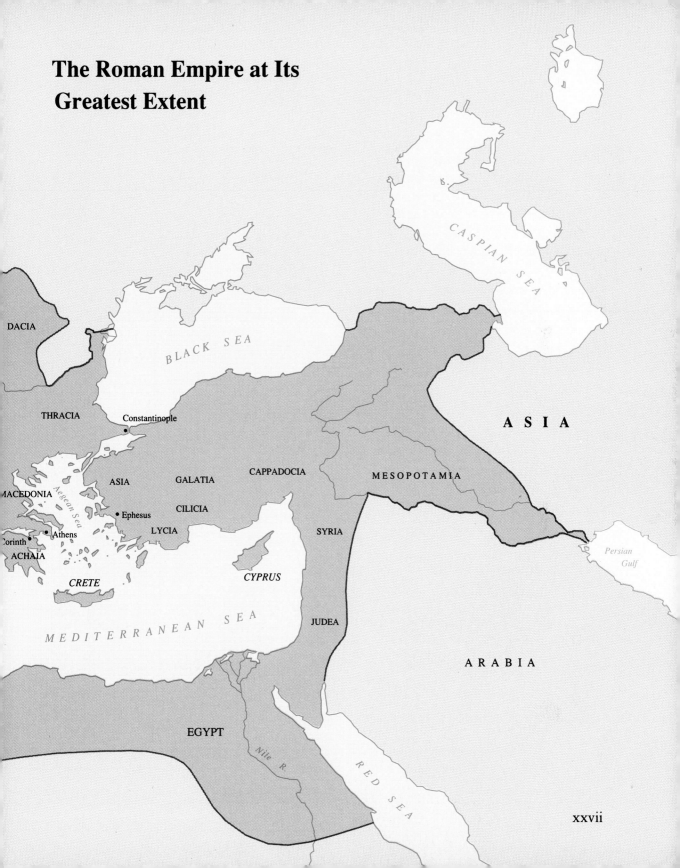

The Roman Empire at Its Greatest Extent

DACIA

BLACK SEA

THRACIA

Constantinople

ASIA

MACEDONIA

ASIA

GALATIA

CAPPADOCIA

MESOPOTAMIA

Aegean Sea

CILICIA

Ephesus

Corinth

Athens

LYCIA

SYRIA

ACHAIA

CYPRUS

CRETE

JUDEA

Persian Gulf

MEDITERRANEAN SEA

ARABIA

EGYPT

Nile R.

RED SEA

CASPIAN SEA

LESSON 1

First Declension: Nominative; Genitive; Ablative of Place Where

Fresco of Spring from a villa wall in Stabiae

YOUR HOUSE

The sizes and plans of Roman houses varied according to income and taste. They ranged from one-room apartments to elaborate mansions. Most people lived in large apartment buildings of five or six stories, often covering a whole city block (**īnsula**); in fact the term **īnsula** is sometimes used to refer to a large apartment building or tenement. These large buildings were built around a courtyard and sometimes had galleries and balconies. The apartments themselves varied from one to five rooms. The bottom floor of the complex was usually given over to shops (**tabernae** and **officīnae**). These shops sometimes had small living quarters attached, but most often the shop itself served for living quarters after closing time, with a sleeping-loft, reached by a ladder, above. Like many modern Italian shops, these were open across the whole front, and closed by a shutter (in which there was a door for the family) at night.

In the less elegant apartment buildings there was a common water supply (a fountain in the courtyard), as well as a communal latrine and laundry. In the more expensive buildings the apartments had running water and their own toilets, and the building itself might have an elaborate set of baths. A better apartment was also likely to have its own stairway to the street, instead of opening off the courtyard gallery, and might have windows and balconies looking into both the courtyard and the street. Such an apartment was called a horseback house (**domus equestris**) because it had a leg on each side. Still more elegant were the garden-apartment complexes, smaller buildings, each containing four identical apartments, set in their own grounds. The best examples of all of these apartment houses are found at Ostia, Rome's ancient port.

The houses of the more well-to-do were usually of two stories. There might be as many as eight or as few as one of these to an **īnsula**. They had

(Continued)

2

few external windows but rather looked inward on interior gardens. As in the large apartment buildings, the ground floor was usually edged with shops insulating the house inside from both heat and cold and street noise.

The mansions of the magnates, on the edge of the city, were set in their own grounds and were like small palaces, with other buildings and pavilions on the grounds.

The peristyle and garden of the House of the Vettii, Pompeii

ANCIENT ROME LIVES ON . . .

In what way do some modern apartment or condominium complexes resemble the large apartment buildings of ancient Rome?

FORMS

■ FIRST DECLENSION

Latin nouns are grouped together in different declensions. All nouns which use the same case endings belong to the same declension.

Nouns of the first declension may be recognized by the -ae ending of the genitive singular. First declension nouns are declined like **puella,** *girl.* The base of a first declension noun is found by dropping the -ae ending of the genitive singular; the endings are then added to this base. The genitive of **puella** is **puellae;** its base is **puell-.**

FIRST DECLENSION NOUNS

CASES			ENDINGS
		SINGULAR	
NOMINATIVE	puella	*a girl (the girl)*	**-a**
GENITIVE	puellae	*of a girl (the girl)*	**-ae**
DATIVE	puellae	*to (for) a girl (the girl)*	**-ae**
ACCUSATIVE	puellam	*a girl (the girl)*	**-am**
ABLATIVE	puellā	——	**-ā**
		PLURAL	
NOMINATIVE	puellae	*girls (the girls)*	**-ae**
GENITIVE	puellārum	*of girls (the girls)*	**-ārum**
DATIVE	puellīs	*to (for) girls (the girls)*	**-īs**
ACCUSATIVE	puellās	*girls (the girls)*	**-ās**
ABLATIVE	puellīs	——	**-īs**

1. Latin has no articles, no way of expressing, *a, an,* or *the;* so **puella** may be translated by *girl, a girl,* or *the girl,* according to the context.
2. Because of its many uses, no standard translation can be given for the ablative case.

SYNTAX

NOMINATIVE CASE

Nominative as Subject

The subject of a verb (i.e. the person, place, or thing about which something is said) is in the nominative case.

Predicate Nominative

A noun used with a linking verb to define or identify the subject is also in the nominative. Such a noun is called a predicate nominative, or predicate noun, or subjective complement.

> SUB.   PRED. NOM.
> Asia est prōvincia.
> *Asia is a province.*

GENITIVE OF POSSESSION

One of the uses of the genitive case is to show possession.

> agricolae vīlla
> *the farmer's farmhouse, the farmhouse of the farmer*
>
> agricolārum vīllae
> *the farmers' farmhouses, the farmhouses of the farmers*

The English translation of the genitive of possession uses *'s* or *s'*, or a prepositional phrase with *of*.

ABLATIVE OF PLACE WHERE

The ablative case is used with certain prepositions to answer the question *Where?*

> Agricola est in vīllā.
> *The farmer is in the farmhouse.*

VOCABULARY

When you learn a Latin noun you will need to know to which declension it belongs, what its base is, and its gender (masculine, feminine, or neuter). Therefore for each noun in the Vocabulary the nominative form, the genitive form, and the gender (*m.*, *f.*, or *n.*) are all included. The fact that the genitive of every noun in this Vocabulary ends in **-ae** tells us that they all belong to the first declension, and will be declined like **puella**. You can find the base to which the endings are added by dropping the **-ae**.

Be sure to learn the long marks (*macra*, singular *macron*) when you learn the words because the macron indicates that a vowel is long, and you need to know this for correct pronunciation.

BASIC WORDS

agricola, agricolae, m. *farmer*
fēmina, fēminae, f. *woman*
patria, patriae, f. *fatherland, native land*
prōvincia, prōvinciae, f. *province*
puella, puellae, f. *girl*
silva, silvae, f. *woods, forest*
terra, terrae, f. *earth, land*

via, viae, f. *way, road, street*
vīlla, vīllae, f. *farmhouse, villa*

est *is, there is*
sunt *are, there are*

in (preposition) *in, on*

Note: When **est** and **sunt** mean *there is* and *there are* they precede the subject.

Agricola est in vīllā. *The farmer is in the farmhouse.*
Est agricola in vīllā. *There is a farmer in the farmhouse.*

PROPER NAMES

Since proper nouns and the adjectives derived from them are the same, or almost the same, in English and Latin, you will not have to spend time memorizing them. For your convenience, however, a glossary is included in the Appendix, so that you will know their declension and (when it's not obvious) their gender.

■ LEARNING ENGLISH THROUGH LATIN

More than half of our English words come from Latin; so one of the great benefits of studying Latin is the opportunity to develop your English verbal skills. Each vocabulary in the text will be followed by a list of English words derived from the Latin words used in that lesson.

feminist	*one who wants women's rights equal to men's*
patriotic	*strongly supporting one's own country*
provincial	*limited in perspective; narrow; self-centered*
silvan *or* sylvan	*characteristic of woods or forests*
terrain	*a tract of land; ground*
via	*by way of*
villa	*a country house or estate*

The plan of one type of Roman house: a series of rooms grouped around a small open court, the **atrium.** One entered via the **fauces** to find a shallow pool, the **impluvium,** in the middle of the **atrium.** Bedrooms occupied the sides of the **atrium,** while clients waited in the **alae** for the master who worked in his office, the **tablinum.** A narrow corridor connected the house with the garden in the rear so that access was available if the **tablinum** was occupied.

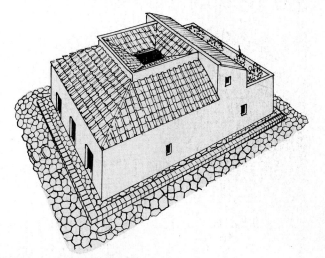

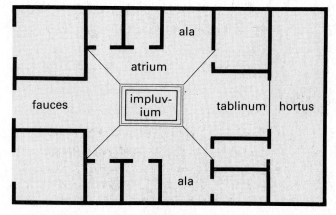

PRACTICE

A.   Fill in the blanks with the appropriate English words derived from the Latin words in this lesson:

1. He is so ___ that he salutes the flag whenever he sees it: his wife is such a ___ that she salutes it only if it's carried by a woman.   2. Send this letter ___ air mail.   3. Some Europeans think that American culture is backward and ___.   4. The ___ in this part of the country is flat and uninteresting: I want to find a ___ setting when I build my ___, where I can observe the wildlife of the forest.

B.   Using a dictionary, check the derivations of the verb *inter* and the noun *invoice*. From which words in this lesson are they derived?

C.   Change from singular to plural, keeping the same case:

1. viā   2. vīlla   3. silvam   4. fēminā   5. prōvinciam

D.   Change from plural to singular, keeping the same case:

1. agricolārum   2. puellae   3. viās   4. fēminārum   5. vīllās

E.   Decline the following nouns. When you do this aloud, remember the rules for placing the accent.

1. agricola   2. patria   3. terra

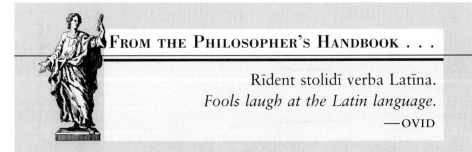

FROM THE PHILOSOPHER'S HANDBOOK . . .

Rīdent stolidī verba Latīna.
Fools laugh at the Latin language.
—OVID

Why study Latin? List four ways in which Latin can be a help to you in your future life. Prove the validity of this saying.

View of excavations of Roman garden apartments, Ostia

F.   Pronounce, and give the case(s) and number(s):

1. fēminīs   2. Eurōpa   3. puellae   4. patriā   5. silvās   6. vīllārum
7. viam   8. prōvinciā   9. Asia   10. terrae

G.   Give the following forms:

1. **Eurōpa** in the dative singular   2. **prōvincia** in the nominative plural
3. **terra** in the accusative plural   4. **vīlla** in the genitive singular   5. **fēmina**
in the ablative singular   6. **puella** in the dative plural   7. **Trōia** in the
nominative singular   8. **agricola** in the accusative singular   9. **patria** in
the genitive plural   10. **silva** in the ablative plural

H.   Translate into Latin:

1. The woman is in the farmhouse.   2. A woman is in the farmhouse.
3. There is a woman in the farmhouse.   4. The women are in the farmhouse.
5. There are women in the farmhouse.

I.   Pronounce, then translate into English:

1. Fēminae sunt in silvā.   2. Prōvincia est Asia.   3. Puellae in viā sunt.
4. Sunt fēminae in vīllā.   5. In Eurōpā sunt prōvinciae.   6. Viae sunt in
puellae patriā.   7. Prōvinciae Trōiae sunt in Asiā.   8. Agricolārum vīllae
in prōvinciā sunt.   9. Sunt viae in terrīs Eurōpae.   10. In agricolae terrā
sunt silvae.

J.   Translate into Latin:

1. Asia is a province.   2. There is a girl on the road.   3. The woman is
in the woods.   4. Troy is the girls' fatherland.   5. The provinces are in
Europe.   6. In Asia there are the lands of Troy.   7. The road is in the
province.   8. There are farmhouses on the farmer's land.   9. The woman's
farmhouse is in the forest.   10. There are roads in the provinces of Troy.

READING

Troy

Trōia est in Asiā. Trōiae prōvinciae in Asiā sunt. In prōvinciīs Trōiae sunt silvae. In Trōiae terrīs sunt agricolae: Trōia est patria agricolārum. In terrīs agricolārum sunt vīllae. Agricolārum fēminae sunt in vīllīs.

■ READING COMPREHENSION

1. Where is Troy?   2. Where are Troy's provinces?   3. Where are the forests?   4. Of whom is Troy the fatherland?   5. What are on the farmers' lands?   6. Where are the farmers' wives?

The ruins of ancient Troy, which flourished from circa 1800 to 1150 B.C. It was possibly this city that the Greeks destroyed.

LESSON 2

First Conjugation; Direct Object; Ablative of Accompaniment; Apposition

House of the Vettii, Pompeii—The Ixion Room. This room derives its name from the painting at the far right, showing Ixion being tied to his wheel.

THE ROOMS IN YOUR HOUSE

The rooms in Roman houses varied in size and arrangement according to the taste and wealth of the owner. However, there were certain arrangements which many houses had in common. In the homes of businessmen and politicians, parts of the house were open to the public. Visitors had to state their names to a doorkeeper (**ostiārius**) and give their names to a receptionist (**nōmenclātor**).

The main reception room (**ātrium**) often had two large side alcoves or wings (**ālae**) which served as secretaries' offices or waiting rooms. The atrium was lighted by a square opening (**compluvium**) in the center of the funnel-shaped roof, which might be supported by columns. Under this opening was a pool (**impluvium**) to catch the rain, and in the pool there sometimes was a fountain. Such pools often had one opening to a cistern, and one to the gutter of the street. When the rain began, the pool was allowed to drain into the street until it was clean; then a turn of the tap allowed the rainwater to be stored in the cistern. When the floors were scrubbed, all the dirty water could be swept into the **impluvium** and washed into the street.

The master's office (**tablīnum**) was a larger alcove opposite the front door. Here, if he was of an old family, he kept the death masks (**imāginēs**) of his ancestors. The **tablīnum** could be closed with curtains or shutters and used also as the master bedroom. Other bedrooms (**cubicula**) flanked the atrium on both sides.

Beyond the **tablīnum** there often was a large open courtyard, or peristyle, with flower beds and a pool or fountain. The peristyle was surrounded by a colonnade, and off the colonnade were more rooms and alcoves serving as dining rooms (**trīclīnia**), kitchen (**culīna**), toilet (**latrīna**), library, and rooms for a midday nap. Some really large houses had vegetable gardens or even a bit of pasture for a cow or two inside their walls. The most

(Continued)

luxurious ones also had private baths with saunas and hot tubs, heated by ovens which also baked the household bread.

In the atrium or peristyle, or both, there was often a small shrine (**aedicula**) or a chapel (**sacellum**) with paintings or statues of the household gods.

(*below*) Outdoor dining area of the House of Neptune and Amphitrite, Herculaneum. At night lamps were placed in the tragic and satyric masks.

ANCIENT ROME LIVES ON . . .

What would correspond, in a modern home, to the wax death masks in a Roman house?

Are there private dwellings today which are partly open to the public?

Romans could show their wealth by the amount of space they used on flower gardens, or by the number of rooms or single-function rooms in their house. Do people demonstrate their prosperity by these means today?

▰ FORMS ▰

▰ VERBS

Personal Endings

English shows the person and number of a verb by a pronoun subject (*I, we, you, he, she, it, they*). In Latin these are shown by the ending of the verb, called the personal ending because it indicates person. The personal endings of the active voice are as follows:

PERSONAL ENDINGS	SINGULAR		PLURAL	
1ST PERSON	-ō or -m	*I*	-mus	*we*
2D PERSON	-s	*you*	-tis	*you*
3D PERSON	-t	*he, she, it*	-nt	*they*

Principal Parts

You have seen that in order to have all the information you need about a noun you must learn its nominative, its genitive, and its gender. For verbs it will be necessary to learn the four Principal Parts; but just now you need only the first two, as shown in the Basic Words of the Vocabulary (e.g. **vocō, vocāre**). The first principal part is the dictionary form of a verb, the one under which it will be listed in a dictionary.

First Conjugation, Present Tense

Verbs are grouped into conjugations as nouns are into declensions. All verbs which have the same stem vowel belong to the same conjugation. All verbs whose present stem ends in -ā (e.g. **vocāre**) belong to the first conjugation, and are conjugated in the present active as follows:

FIRST CONJUGATION, PRESENT ACTIVE

		SINGULAR		PLURAL
1ST PERSON	vocō	*I call* *I am calling* *I do call*	vocāmus	*we call* *we are calling* *we do call*
2D PERSON	vocās	*you call* *you are calling* *you do call*	vocātis	*you call* *you are calling* *you do call*
3D PERSON	vocat	*he (she, it) calls* *he (she, it) is calling* *he (she, it) does call*	vocant	*they call* *they are calling* *they do call*

1. These forms are made by adding the personal ending to the present stem **vocā-**, which is found by dropping the **-re** from the second principal part.
2. The first principal part shows that the **-ā** of the stem is not used in the first person singular (**vocō**, not vocaō).
3. In any tense of a verb, a long vowel is shortened before the endings **-t** and **-nt.**
4. Notice that, in terms of English, a Latin verb is read backwards, giving first the name of the action and then the pronoun subject:

vocās = vocā- + -s   vocāmus = vocā- + -mus
call   you   call   we

5. The Latin verb has no special progressive or emphatic forms. Therefore **vocō** means *I call, I am calling,* or *I do call,* whichever sounds best in the sentence.

SYNTAX

■ AGREEMENT OF VERBS

A verb agrees with its subject in person and number.

Nauta nāvigat.   *The sailor is sailing.*
Nautae nāvigant.   *The sailors are sailing.*
Fēmina et puella nāvigant.   *The woman and the girl are sailing.*

16

ACCUSATIVE OF THE DIRECT OBJECT

One of the uses of the accusative case is to indicate the direct object of a verb.

> Poētās laudāmus. *We praise poets.*
> Rēgīnam puella spectat. *The girl looks at the queen.*

In each of these sentences the direct object is identified by its being in the accusative.

ABLATIVE OF ACCOMPANIMENT

Another use of the ablative case is with the preposition **cum,** *with,* to indicate accompaniment; in this use it is called the Ablative of Accompaniment.

> Agricola cum nautīs nāvigat.
> *The farmer is sailing with the sailors.*

(*left*) Atrium of The House of the Silver Wedding, Pompeii   (*right*) Atrium of The Samnite House, Herculaneum

The atrium of the House of Lucius Ceius
Secundus, Pompeii

APPOSITION

A noun used to describe another noun, or a pronoun, is said to be its appositive, or to be used in apposition with it. An appositive must refer to the same person or thing as the noun or pronoun to which it applies, and must also be in the same case. In Latin it usually follows its noun or pronoun.

> Hecuba rēgīna terram Graeciam spectat.
> *Queen Hecuba looks at the land [of] Greece.*

Notice that Latin does not use the genitive (*of*) for apposition, as English does in expressions like *the city of New York* or *the state of Indiana*.

VOCABULARY

BASIC WORDS

You will notice that most first-declension nouns are feminine. In fact, the only ones which are masculine are those which refer to males.

fābula, fābulae, f. *story*
familia, familiae, f. *household*
fīlia, fīliae, f. *daughter*
poēta, poētae, m. *poet*
rēgīna, rēgīnae, f. *queen*
vīta, vītae, f. *life*

amō, amāre *love, like*
habitō, habitāre *live, dwell*

laudō, laudāre *praise*
narrō, narrāre *tell, narrate*
vocō, vocāre *call*

cum (preposition used with the
   ablative) *with*

et (conjunction) *and* (adverb) *also, even*

■ LEARNING ENGLISH THROUGH LATIN

fabulous	*like a fable; imaginary, wonderful*
familiar	*closely acquainted*
habitation	*dwelling place*
laudatory	*expressing praise*
narrative	*story, tale*
poetic	*having the beauty of good poetry*
vital	*essential to life; indispensable*
vocation	*an impulse towards a certain career*

Translation Help

In order to translate a Latin sentence accurately, it is a good idea to establish the construction of each Latin noun to be sure of its place in the English sentence. The construction of a noun means its case and number and its use in the sentence.

EXAMPLE

Poēta cum Creūsā rēgīnae fīliā vītam in prōvinciā laudat.

poēta: nominative singular, subject of the verb **laudat**
Creūsā: ablative singular, ablative of accompaniment
rēgīnae: genitive singular, genitive of possession
fīliā: ablative singular, in apposition with (or appositive to) **Creūsā**
vītam: accusative singular, direct object of the verb **laudat**
prōvinciā: ablative singular, ablative of place where
The poet, with Creusa, the queen's daugher, praises life in the province.

═══ PRACTICE ═══

A. In the following sentences some of the English derivatives in the list above have been moved to the wrong sentences. Put them where they belong.

1. His *habitation* of his adventures was so *familiar* that I could hardly believe it. **2.** We have to have it to stay alive; it's really *laudatory*. **3.** *Vocation* is a *vital* way of saying "home"; are you *fabulous* with the word? **4.** He praised me very highly; his *narrative* remarks were almost embarrassing. **5.** His *poetic* is teaching.

B. Say which personal ending in Latin represents each of these pronouns in English:

1. he 2. we 3. I 4. it 5. you (*singular*) 6. they 7. she 8. you (*plural*)

C. Change from singular to plural or from plural to singular, keeping the same person:

1. habitat 2. amāmus 3. narrātis 4. laudās 5. vocant

D. Pronounce and translate:

1. amāmus 2. habitātis 3. laudās 4. narrō 5. vocant 6. habitat
7. narrant 8. vocāmus 9. amant 10. laudātis

Fresco from the summer dining room in the Empress Livia's country estate at Prima Porta showing an orchard garden—Terme Museum, Rome

E. Translate:

1. you (*plural*) praise   2. we love   3. I am calling   4. they are telling
5. you (*singular*) live   6. we are praising   7. they do call   8. you (*pl.*)
are living   9. he tells   10. you (*sing.*) are loving

F. Pronounce and translate:

1. Fēminās vocātis.   2. Aenēās patriam amat.   3. Cum fēminā puella est.
4. Rēgīna fābulam narrat.   5. Puella est agricolae fīlia.   6. Vītam agricolae
laudāmus.   7. Aenēās et Creūsa in Asiā terrā habitant.   8. In Eurōpae
silvīs sunt et viae.   9. Fābulam Trōiae amant poētae.   10. Fēmina cum
familiā in vīllā habitat.

G. Construe each noun (give number and case and explain the case) in the
sentences in F.

H. Translate these sentences. Keep in mind that Latin does not use possessive
adjectives (*my, our, your, his, her, its, their*) unless they are really necessary.

The woman loves her daughter.
Fēmina fīliam amat.

1. We praise the poets.   2. You (*sing.*) live in the province.   3. Poets tell
stories.   4. The farmer is calling the girls.   5. There is a road in the forest.
6. The woman and the farmer are on the road.   7. The girls love and praise
their native land.   8. The queen is with her daughter Creusa.   9. You
(*pl.*) like life in the land [of] Asia.   10. I live with my household in a
farmhouse.

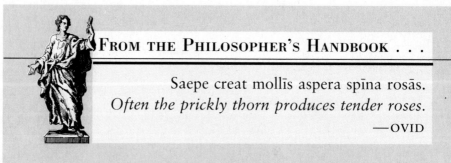

FROM THE PHILOSOPHER'S HANDBOOK . . .

Saepe creat mollīs aspera spīna rosās.
Often the prickly thorn produces tender roses.

—OVID

Can you apply this proverb to any of your experiences in school?

READING

Aeneas

Poēta narrat fābulam Aenēae. Aenēās cum fēminā Creūsā et familiā habitat in Asiā; Aenēae patria Trōia est. Hecuba est Trōiae rēgīna; Aenēae fēmina est Hecubae rēgīnae fīlia. Creūsam Aenēās amat et amat Aenēam Creūsa. Aenēās et Creūsa et Trōiam amant; vītam in patriā laudant. Laudant et terrās prōvinciārum Trōiae.

5

◼ READING COMPREHENSION

1. Where does Aeneas live?   **2.** With whom does he live?   **3.** What is the fatherland of Aeneas?   **4.** Who is Hecuba?   **5.** Who is Creusa?   **6.** How are they related to each other?

---

1. Aenēās: First declension men's names derived from the Greek language usually have **-ās** or **-ēs** instead of **-a** for a nominative singular ending.

LESSON 3

Sum; Expressions of Place; Questions

Detail from a Roman wall painting of Jason arriving at the court of Pelias—National Museum, Naples. The Romanized setting shows the simplicity of ancient furnishings.

YOUR FURNITURE

Many pieces of furniture which we consider essential in our homes today were not present in Roman homes, not even in homes of the upper classes. There were no rocking chairs, easy chairs, desks, or dressers, so we might think Roman furnishings were very meager. Basically, the furniture was limited to couches, beds, footstools, chairs, stools, benches, tables, sideboards, chests, and lamps. All but the heaviest pieces were portable and kept in storage until wanted.

The beds were for sleeping and the couches for dining, reading, and writing. They had the same name (**lectus**), and were different only in size: the dining couch was higher, and sometimes wider, than the bed, and was reached by means of a footstool (**scamnum**). Both were constructed of wood with legs sometimes made of or decorated with ivory. They had rope "springs," and were covered with mattresses, cushions, and coverlets, often elaborately embroidered. Both had a detachable raised piece (**fulcrum**) at one end which served as a head rest on a bed and an elbow rest on a couch; for Roman men not only lay down to eat, but also read and wrote reclining on the left side, with one knee drawn up to serve as a desk.

Dining tables were in two parts: the legs, which often stayed in place, and the tops (**mēnsae**), which were removed and changed with the courses. Wealthy people often had large collections of table tops, inlaid with exotic woods. Smaller decorative tables held vases, lamps, or figurines.

Seats (**sellae**) were of four kinds: stools and benches, and chairs with and without arms. On the whole, chairs were used more by women than men, who spent most of their time at home either standing or reclining.

23

Sarcophagus carved on the interior as a furnished room, showing shelves for vessels, a table, cupboards, and a bookcase—Rijksmuseum van Oudheden, Leiden

FORMS

THE VERB SUM

The present stem of **sum** keeps changing its form, but it takes the regular personal endings:

PRESENT TENSE OF SUM			
SINGULAR		**PLURAL**	
sum	*I am*	sumus	*we are*
es	*you are*	estis	*you are*
est	*he (she, it) is, there is*	sunt	*they are, there are*

SYNTAX

USES OF SUM

Sum is ordinarily used as a linking verb, connecting its subject with a predicate nominative or some other kind of subjective complement.

> Graecia est prōvincia.   *Greece is a province.*
> Graecia est in Eurōpā.   *Greece is in Europe.*

The third person of **sum,** when placed before its subject, is a predicative (not a linking) verb and means *there is* or *there are.*

> Est agricola in vīllā.   *There is a farmer in the farmhouse.*

A tripod and bowl shown on
a coin from southern Italy

◼ EXPRESSIONS OF PLACE

Accusative of Place to Which

The accusative is used with the prepositions **ad, in,** and **sub** to answer the question *Where [to]?*

Quō nāvigātis?   Ad Graeciam nāvigāmus.
  Where are you sailing [to]?   *We are sailing to Greece.*

Ablative of Place Where

The ablative is used with the prepositions **in** and **sub** to answer the question *Where [at]?*

Ubi estis? In Graeciā sumus.
  Where are you? We are in Greece.

Ablative of Place from Which

The ablative is used with the prepositions **ā (ab), dē,** and **ē (ex)** to answer the question *Where from?*

Unde nāvigātis?   Ā Graeciā nāvigāmus.
  Where are you sailing from?   We are sailing from Greece.

EXPRESSIONS OF PLACE—SUMMARY OF PREPOSITIONS

ā, ab[1] (preposition with the ablative)   *from, away from*
ad (preposition with the accusative)   *to, towards*
dē (prep. w. abl.)   *from, down from; about, concerning*
ē, ex[2] (prep. w. abl.)   *from, out of*
in (prep. w. acc. or abl.)
  into, onto, against (w. acc.); *in, on* (w. abl.)
sub (prep. w. acc. or abl.)
  to under, up to, to the foot of (w. acc.); *under, at the foot of* (w. abl.)

---

1. The form **ā** can be used only before a word beginning with a consonant (except *h*); **ab** may be used at any time.   2. The form **ē** can be used before a word beginning with *b, d, g,* consonant *i, l, m, n, r,* or *v*; otherwise **ex** is used.

■ QUESTIONS

To turn a statement into a question which has a yes-or-no answer, add the particle **-ne** to the end of the first word. The yes-or-no answer is expressed by repeating some part of the question.

Asiane est prōvincia?   *Is Asia a province?*
Est. *Yes.*   Nōn est. *No.*
Nōnne nāvigat ad Eurōpam Aenēās?   *Isn't Aeneas sailing to Europe?*
Nāvigat.   *Yes, he is.*   Nōn nāvigat.   *No, he isn't.*
Nōn ad Eurōpam.   *No, not to Europe.*

The particle **-ne** is an enclitic (from the Greek word for *leaning on*) and must be attached to the end of another word: **Asiane, nōnne.** When an enclitic has been attached to a word, the accent falls on the syllable before the enclitic, whether long or short.

If the question is not a yes-or-no question, it will not be introduced by a word with **-ne** attached, but by some interrogative pronoun, adjective, or adverb.

Quō nāvigātis? Ad Graeciam.   *Where are you sailing? To Greece.*

A marble table with decorative lion's head and claw legs, Herculaneum

VOCABULARY

When you learn a Latin preposition, it is important to learn whether it is used with the accusative case, the ablative case, or both. Some prepositions can be used with both cases, and the case with which they are used determines their meaning. For example, the prepositions **in** and **sub** can indicate either *place to which* or *place where*.

Be sure to learn both of the first two principal parts for each verb.

BASIC WORDS

dea, -ae, f. *goddess*
nauta, -ae, m. *sailor*

ambulō, ambulāre *walk*
nāvigō, nāvigāre *sail*
occupō, occupāre *seize*
spectō, spectāre *look at, watch*

sum, esse *be*

nōn (adverb) *not*
quō (interrogative adverb) *where [to]?*
  (relative adverb) *to which place, to which*

ubi (interrogative and relative adverb) *where [at]? where;* (adverbial conjunction) *when*
unde (interrogative adverb) *where from?* (relative adverb) *from which place, from which*

super (preposition with the accusative) *over, above*

Note: **Nōn** differs from other adverbs in that it may modify even nouns and pronouns. It is placed just before whatever it modifies. If the whole sentence or clause is negative it goes just before the verb.

> Aenēās ad Āfricam nōn nāvigat.
> *Aeneas isn't sailing to Africa.*

> Nōn Aenēās ad Āfricam nāvigat.
> *[Someone, maybe, but] not Aeneas is sailing to Africa.*

> Aenēās nōn ad Āfricam nāvigat.
> *Aeneas is sailing [somewhere, but] not to Africa.*

■ LEARNING ENGLISH THROUGH LATIN

amble	*to walk with a slow, easy gait*
ambulatory	*able to walk; not confined to a wheelchair*
nautical	*having to do with sailors or ships*
navigate	*to direct a ship or craft*
occupation	*that which chiefly engages one's time; seizure and control of a country*
spectator	*an onlooker; one who watches without taking an active part*

From Latin Prepositions:

absent	*being away*
demoted	*moved down*
exit	*way out*
subway	*an underground transportation system*
superman	*a superior person, greater or better than others*

▬ PRACTICE ▬

A. List as many English words as you can think of which begin with:

1. ex- (meaning *out*)   **2. sub-** (meaning *under*)   **3. super-** (meaning *over* or *above*)

B. Change from singular to plural or from plural to singular, keeping the same person:

1. sumus   2. ambulō   3. es   4. occupātis   5. sum   6. nāvigāmus   7. est
8. spectant   9. estis   10. vocās

C. Give person and number, and translate:

1. sum   2. ambulant   3. occupat   4. nāvigāmus   5. spectās   6. ambulātis   7. nāvigās   8. occupātis   9. spectāmus   10. estis

D. Give the construction of each numbered noun:

1. Agricolae¹ fīliās² vocāmus in vīllam.³   **2.** Fēminae⁴ cum puellīs⁵ ab Asiā⁶ nāvigant.   **3.** In Eurōpā⁷ est via⁸ ad Graeciam⁹ prōvinciam.¹⁰

E. Translate:

1. We are walking to the farmhouse.   2. Troy is in Asia.   3. He walks up to the forest.   4. We are sailing from Europe.

F. Translate:

1. Are you calling the farmer?   2. Where are they?   3. Is he looking at the farmhouse?   4. Where are you walking to?   5. Where are the sailors sailing from?

G. Read the Latin aloud and translate:

1. Ubi sumus? In Graeciā.   2. Fēminaene nautās spectant? Agricolās spectant.   3. Trōia ubi est? Sub terrā.   4. Nōnne laudat deam Helena rēgīna? Laudat.   5. Quō cum fīliā ab vīllā ambulās? Sub silvam.   6. Vīllamne agricolae occupant nautae? Nōn occupant.   7. Narratne poēta fābulam dē patriā? Narrat.   8. Nōnne ambulāmus ex Eurōpā ad Asiam? Nōn ad Asiam. 9. Deane sub terrā est? Nōn sub terrā, super terram.   10. Quō et unde cum nautīs nāvigātis? Ā Graeciā ad Asiam.

H. Translate:

1. Where is the farmer's daughter walking to? The farmhouse.   2. Is Queen Helen sailing from Greece to Asia? Yes, she is.   3. Isn't the goddess calling the women into the forest? Yes.   4. Is the farmer seizing the woman's farmhouse? No.   5. Where are you (*sing.*) sailing from? I am sailing from Europe.   6. Is the poet telling a story about a goddess? No.

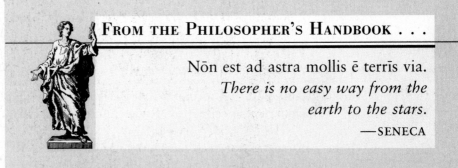

FROM THE PHILOSOPHER'S HANDBOOK . . .

Nōn est ad astra mollis ē terrīs via.
There is no easy way from the earth to the stars.
—SENECA

There were probably no spaceships in Seneca's time. What, then, do you think is the meaning of this statement?

READING

Helen of Troy

Poētae fābulam dē nautā Trōiae narrant. Dea Cytherēa nautam vocat ad Graeciam. Trōia in Asiā, Graecia in Eurōpā est. Nauta ad Graeciam nāvigat. In Graeciā est terra Lacōnica; Lacōnicae rēgīna Helena est. In Lacōnicā nauta Helenam rēgīnam spectat et amat. Rēgīnam occupat et cum rēgīnā ad Asiam nāvigat. Nauta et rēgīna habitant in Asiā. Creūsa, Aenēae fēmina, est nautae germāna.

5

READING COMPREHENSION

1. Who calls the sailor to Greece?   **2.** Where is Greece?   **3.** What land is in Greece?   **4.** Who is the queen of the land?   **5.** What happens when the sailor looks at the queen?   **6.** Who is this sailor?

Interior of an Athenian red-figured kylix showing Helen of Troy and King Priam—National Museum, Tarquinia

---

6. germāna, -ae, f: *sister*

LESSON 4

Second Declension; Predicate Accusative

A combination space heater and food warmer from the dining room of a house at Stabiae

YOUR FURNITURE: ACCESSORIES

What Roman furniture lacked in variety it made up for, in the finer houses, in beauty, especially as it was seen against a background of mosaic and marble floors, colorfully painted walls, carved woodwork, draperies, and curtains.

Storage pieces included chests (**arcae**) and cupboards (**armāria**). There were many kinds of chests, including iron-bound oak chests which served as safes, and fancy storage pieces with gilt-bronze hardware. They all had the form of large rectangular boxes with the lid on top. There were also cylindrical boxes (**scrīnia**) for storing books. Clothing, dishes, and food were stored in chests or in cupboards; some wealthy houses had rooms lined with shelves.

Lamps (**lychnī, lūcernae**) were beautiful but not very efficient, as they were fueled with third-pressing olive oil, which was watery and caused sputtering and smoke (the first two pressings were used for cosmetics and cooking respectively). Table lamps, floor lamps, and hanging lamps were made of bronze or iron, and often embellished with round or relief sculpture. For everyday use there were cheap, mass-produced terra-cotta lamps, carelessly glazed with metallic glazes to look like metal.

Roman houses (unless they had private baths) were not centrally heated. If you felt cold, you sent a slave for a portable heater, a bronze or iron pan on short legs, filled with glowing charcoal. Some of these were also designed to keep food warm at the table, and some even included water heaters, since the Romans liked to add hot water to their wine in cold weather. Braziers on taller legs served as altars for offerings made at meals.

(Continued)

The Romans were very fond of sculpture. In the atria and peristyles of fine houses, portrait busts and statues of gods and mythological figures abounded. Even a poor family might have one or two treasured works of this kind, perhaps on the lower shelf of the sideboard (**abacus**) on which food was displayed, or on the decorative bronze or marble table at the end of the **impluvium.**

(*below left*) Roman oil lamp   (*below right*) Modern reproduction of a Roman cupboard—Museo della Civiltà Romana, Rome

ANCIENT ROME LIVES ON . . .

Describe some modern lighting that is more beautiful than functional.

Although sculpture no longer abounds as in Roman times, what sort of art are you likely to find even in a modest home?

FORMS

SECOND DECLENSION

Nouns whose genitive singular ends in -ī belong to the second declension. They may be masculine, feminine, or neuter; but very few of them are feminine. Masculine nouns of the second declension end in -us or -er in the nominative singular; the few feminine nouns end only in -us; and neuter nouns end in -um. In the following declensions, amicus and ager are masculine and verbum is neuter.

SECOND DECLENSION NOUNS

SINGULAR				ENDINGS		
	MASC.	MASC.	NEUT.	MASC.		NEUT.
NOM.	amīcus	ager	verbum	-us	——	-um
GEN.	amīcī	agrī	verbī		-ī	
DAT.	amīcō	agrō	verbō		-ō	
ACC.	amīcum	agrum	verbum		-um	
ABL.	amīcō	agrō	verbō		-ō	

PLURAL				ENDINGS		
	MASC.	MASC.	NEUT.	MASC.		NEUT.
NOM.	amīcī	agrī	verba	-ī		-a
GEN.	amīcōrum	agrōrum	verbōrum		-ōrum	
DAT.	amīcīs	agrīs	verbīs		-īs	
ACC.	amīcōs	agrōs	verba	-ōs		-a
ABL.	amīcīs	agrīs	verbīs		-īs	

Two characteristics of the neuter are worth remembering:

1. Its nominative is always the same as the accusative.
2. In the plural these two cases will always end in -a.

In this declension, accordingly, the neuter differs from the masculine in the nominative singular and the nominative and accusative plural.

In terrīs Trōiae sunt agrī et oppida.
In Troy's lands there are fields and towns.
Agrōs et oppida spectant.
They are looking at the fields and towns.

SYNTAX

■ PREDICÁTE ACCUSATIVE

A verb of *making, naming,* or *choosing* may take, in addition to its direct object, a second accusative which we call the predicate accusative (or objective complement).

Fīliam vocō Helenam.　*I call my daughter Helen.*

Translation Help

You have seen that the order of words in a Latin sentence is likely to be quite different from the order of words in an English sentence. In English we learn the syntax from the word's position in the sentence. *The woman looks at the girl* does not mean the same thing as *The girl looks at the woman.*

In Latin, however, *The woman looks at the girl* can be expressed in six different ways.

Fēmina puellam spectat.　　Puellam spectat fēmina.
Fēmina spectat puellam.　　Spectat fēmina puellam.
Puellam fēmina spectat.　　Spectat puellam fēmina.

The most usual order for a Latin sentence is to begin with the subject and end with the verb, and whatever the verb needs to complete its meaning is put in between. Each variation from this order provides a different emphasis, but does not change the meaning of the sentence. That is why case endings are so important in Latin. From observing the case endings, it is very evident that, no matter what the order of the words, **fēmina** remains the subject and **puellam** the direct object of these sentences.

VOCABULARY

Notice that a noun ending in **-er** in the nominative may either keep the **-e** in the other cases (like **puer, puerī, m.**) or lose it (like **ager, agrī, m.**). You will know which kind of **-er** word you have by looking at the genitive.

A second declension noun whose base ends in **-i** has a genitive singular in **-ī** (not **iī**): **nūntius, nūntī, m.; auxilium, auxilī, n.** Therefore you will have to look at the nominative, and drop the **-us** or **-um**, to find the base. In such words the accent stays where it would be if both **i**'s were there: **auxi'lī.**

BASIC WORDS

ager, agrī, m. *field, territory*
amīcus, amīcī, m. *friend*
auxilium, auxilī, n. *help, aid*
bellum, bellī, n. *war*
lēgātus, lēgātī, m. *legate, envoy*
nūntius, nūntī, m. *message, news;*
  messenger
oppidum, oppidī, n. *town*
puer, puerī, m. *boy*
verbum, verbī, n. *word*
vir, virī, m. *man; husband; hero*

parō, parāre *prepare*
portō, portāre *carry, bring*

contrā (adverb) *on the contrary; on the other hand; in return* (prep. w. acc.) *against*

itaque (conjunction) *and so, therefore*

LEARNING ENGLISH THROUGH LATIN

agriculture	*the art of farming and cultivating the soil*
amicable	*friendly*
auxiliary	*giving help or aid, assisting*
belligerent	*showing a readiness to fight or quarrel*
contradict	*speak against, say the opposite of*
legate	*envoy or ambassador*
portable	*easily moved or carried*
puerile	*childish, immature*
virile	*manly*

Roman lantern—Museo della Civiltà Romana, Rome

▰▰ PRACTICE ▰▰▰▰▰▰▰▰▰▰▰▰▰▰▰

A. Here are some additional English words derived from the two verbs in the Vocabulary of this lesson. Fill in the missing letters and define the words:

1. – – – – ble   2. pre – – – – tion   3. im – – – –   4. irre – – – – ble
5. trans – – – – – tion   6. pre – – – – tory

B. Find the one noun in the Vocabulary of this Lesson whose base will make English words out of all of the following:

1. – – – – al   2. pro – – – –   3. – – – – iage   4. – – – – ose   5. – – – – atim

C. Name the gender of each of these second declension nouns:

1. ager   2. amīcus   3. verbum   4. oppidum   5. puer

D. Change from singular to plural, keeping the same case:

1. bellum   2. lēgātī   3. puer   4. auxiliō   5. amīcum

E. Change from plural to singular, keeping the same case:

1. verbīs   2. nūntiōrum   3. agrī   4. oppida   5. virōs

F. Give the following forms:

1. **ager** in the genitive singular   2. **auxilium** in the nominative plural
3. **lēgātus** in the nominative plural   4. **amīcus** in the dative singular
5. **bellum** in the accusative plural   6. **nūntius** in the accusative plural
7. **puer** in the ablative singular   8. **verbum** in the genitive plural   9. **oppidum** in the accusative singular   10. **vir** in the dative plural

G. Give the construction of the numbered nouns:

1. Agricola cum filiā¹ in villā² habitat.   2. Agricolae filia puella³ est, nōn fēmina⁵.   3. Filiam⁶ agricola⁷ vocat Helenam⁸.   4. Helena ex agrīs⁹ in oppidum¹⁰ ambulat.

H. Read the Latin aloud and translate:

1. Puer et puella verba parant.   2. Nūntius lēgātōs vocat in oppidum.
3. Puerī cum puellīs in agrīs ambulant.   4. Nūntius verba ad villam portat

This bronze oil lamp and glass cup are examples of the luxury styling of utilitarian objects.

ab agricolae amīcō.   5. Cum agricolā fīlia in agrīs est.   6. Bellumne parātis contrā patriam?   7. Nōnne estis puerōrum et puellārum amīcī?   8. Hecubae virum vocāmus Priamum.   9. Lēgātī nūntium dē bellō portant in agrōs. 10. Virī auxilium ad amīcōs in oppidum portant.

I. Translate:

1. The farmer's household lives in a farmhouse in the fields.   2. We do not like the town, and so we are walking in the forest.   3. Don't you call your daughter Helen?   4. The farmers are calling the boys and girls into the fields.   5. In the town there are envoys and messengers and sailors.   6. Are the men preparing war against the town?   7. The envoy of our native land is carrying a message about the war.   8. The woman is telling a story about a boy and his friends.   9. Do you like the messenger's words about the war with Greece?   10. The friends are carrying aid to the farmer in the fields.

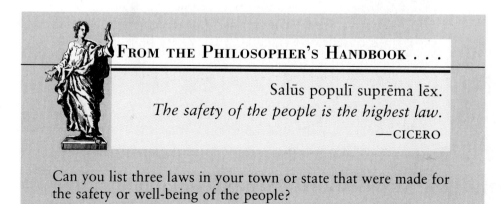

FROM THE PHILOSOPHER'S HANDBOOK . . .

Salūs populī suprēma lēx.
The safety of the people is the highest law.
—CICERO

Can you list three laws in your town or state that were made for the safety or well-being of the people?

READING

The Trojan War Begins

Helena in oppidō Trōiā habitat cum Trōiae nautā; itaque rēgīnam vocāmus "Helenam Trōiae." Nautam poētae vocant Alexandrum.

In Graeciā lēgātī ab Menelāō Helenae virō ad terrās et oppida nūntium portant: "Helena rēgīna ā Graeciā ad oppidum Trōiam in Asiam cum Alexandrō nāvigat!" Lēgātī vocant virōs Graeciae ad bellum contrā Trōiam. Graeciae virī bellum parant et ad Asiam nāvigant.

Priamus est vir Hecubae rēgīnae. Priamī lēgātī nūntium portant ad Trōiae prōvinciās. Lēgātōrum verba sunt "Virī Graeciae bellum parant in Trōiam et Asiam." Itaque virī prōvinciārum auxilium portant ad oppidum Trōiam.

▪ READING COMPREHENSION

1. Why is the queen called "Helen of Troy"?   **2.** What is the sailor's name? **3.** Who is Helen's husband?   **4.** Why did the envoys from Helen's husband call the men of Greece to war?   **5.** Who is Priam?   **6.** What message do his envoys carry to the provinces of Troy?

A heroic fight from the Trojan War depicted on an Etruscan burial urn, 2d c. B.C. Divinities on each side support the rival warriors.

---

4. in Asiam = *in Asia:* The Accusative of Place to Which is used here instead of the Ablative of Place Where because of the motion expressed in **nāvigat.**   **8. in Trōiam:** Remember that **in** with the accusative can also mean *against.*

REVIEW 1

=== **VOCABULARY DRILL** ===

A. Give the genitive, gender, and meaning of each of the following nouns:

ager	familia	patria	terra
agricola	fēmina	poēta	verbum
amīcus	✓fīlia	prōvincia	via
auxilium	lēgātus	puella	vīlla
bellum	nauta	puer	vir
dea	nūntius	rēgīna	vīta
fābula	oppidum	silva	

B. Give the second principal part and the meaning of each of the following verbs:

ambulō	laudō	occupō	spectō
amō	narrō	parō	sum
habitō	nāvigō	portō	vocō

C. Tell with which case or cases each of these prepositions is used, and give the meaning(s):

ā	contrā	ē	sub
ab	cum	ex	super
ad	dē	in	

D. Give the meaning of each of the following:

contrā (adverb)	et	nōn	ubi
itaque	-ne	quō	unde

LISTENING AND SPEAKING

In Town and Country

Lucius is a townsman and lives and works in his town. Marcus is a farmer and lives and works on a farm. As these two men meet and talk together, they realize that each prefers the life of the other.

LŪCIUS: Ubi, agricola[1], cum familiā habitās?

MĀRCUS: In agrīs sub silvā ad prōvinciam in vīllā habitō. Virī et puerī sumus agricolae.

LŪCIUS: Nōnne in oppidō habitās? Cur in oppidī viā es? Quō ambulās?

MĀRCUS: Nōn habitō. In oppidum ad Forum ambulō. Frūmentum[2] ad pistrīnum[3] cum amīcīs portō et vīnum[4] ad caupōnās[5] portāmus. Et amīcī sunt agricolae.

LŪCIUS: Amāsne vītam in oppidōrum viīs ubi sunt tabernae[6] et caupōnae et thermopōlia[7] in insulīs?

MĀRCUS: Vītam oppidanōrum amō et laudō. Verba poētārum dē agricolārum vītīs nōn amō. Poētae fābulās dē agricolārum vītā narrant sed vītam agricolae nōn amō. Est frūmentum in agrīs in prōvinciā sed est vīta in oppidī viīs. Itaque oppida laudō.

1. **agricola**—*When a person is called by name or addressed directly, the vocative case is used in Latin. For most nouns the vocative is identical with the nominative.*

2. **frūmentum, -ī, n.**—*grain*

3. **pistrīnum, -ī, n.**—*bakery, mill*

4. **vīnum, -ī, n.**—*wine*

5. **caupōna, -ae, f.**—*wine shop*

6. **taberna, -ae, f.**—*shop*

7. **thermopōlium, -ī, n.**—*snack bar*

In a reproduction of a funerary relief, cloth merchants in a market portico display their wares to customers—Museo della Civiltà Romana

LŪCIUS: Vītam in prōvinciā oppidānī contrā laudant. Agrōs et silvās spectant et terram laudant. Virī ex prōvinciīs auxilium ad oppida et ad patriam portant. Frūmentum dōnum deae, terrae et frūmentī rēgīnae, est. Super terram habitat dea et fēminās et virōs in agrīs spectat et laudat. Itaque vītam virōrum et familiārum in agrīs oppidānī amāmus.

A. Choose a partner and present an oral reading of the conversation between Lucius and Marcus.

B. Ask your partner the following questions.

1. Ubi habitat agricola?   2. Quō agricola frūmentum portat?
3. Amatne Mārcus verba poētārum?   4. Ubi vītam Mārcus amat?   5. Ubi habitat dea, terrae et frūmentī rēgīna?

Mosaic of a farmer at the plough— Cherchel, Algeria

TRACES OF ROMAN CIVILIZATION TODAY

Spain—Mérida

Mérida, Spain, located 213 miles southwest of Madrid, was founded in 25 B.C. on the orders of the Emperor Augustus. It was called "Emerita Augusta" and achieved great splendor under the Romans. It is today the largest Roman architectural site in Spain with its houses, baths, tombs, temples, bridges, aqueduct, theatre, and amphitheatre.

Fish mosaic

Roman theatre, 24 B.C. —one of the world's best examples

Perhaps the best preserved of these ruins are the theatre, aqueduct, and bridge. The theatre was built on the order of Augustus and held 5,000 spectators. The bridge was constructed of granite during the reign of Trajan, had 81 arches, and measured 2,575 feet in length. The aqueduct known as *Los Milagros* conveyed water to Mérida from a large Roman reservoir.

Many lovely mosaics can also be found at this site in the remains of Roman houses.

Los Milagros aqueduct

Roman bridge at Mérida

LESSON 5

Adjectives

Thermopōlium showing shelves for fresh fruit and vegetables—Ostia

YOUR KITCHEN

If we may judge by Pompeii and Ostia, many houses had no kitchens. Their inhabitants used braziers to cook on or to reheat food bought ready-cooked from the numerous "fast-food" restaurants (**thermopōlia**). The usual kind of **thermopōlium** was a small open-fronted shop (**taberna**) with a counter along the sidewalk. In this counter were sunk large pots in which food and drink could be kept hot. Some of the larger restaurants were not just "take-out" places, but had tables inside or in a garden behind, so that food could be eaten there instead of "to go."

In the homes of the wealthy, the ordinary kitchen (**culīna**) was small and open to the sky, with a raised hearth (**focus**) along one wall to serve as a stove. The pots and pans, most of which were made of coarse pottery, sat on small tripods, and hot coals of charcoal were raked under them. The number of coals determined the level of heat; a high heat was obtained by fanning them.

In these kitchens there was usually some crude painting, graffito, or talisman. Their purpose was to keep away the evil spirits which might otherwise get into the food and so enter the bodies of the diners.

Only the very wealthy had ovens. An oven was not in the kitchen: since it was used both for baking bread and for heating the air and water for private bath suites, it was located in the basement of the bath. Most people bought their bread from the bakery (**pistrīna**) or made it at home and sent it to the bakery to be baked, first stamping it with the family monogram to be sure of getting the same loaves back.

(*left*) A strainer, funnel,
and ladle for transferring
wine to smaller containers, Po~

(*above*) The kitchen, House of the Vettii, Pompeii,
showing cooking pots and utensils   (*left*) A glass
goblet from Pompeii

FORMS

ADJECTIVES

Adjectives are declined in all three genders. For adjectives of the first and second declensions, the masculine is declined like **amīcus, ager,** or **puer,** the feminine like **puella,** and the neuter like **verbum.**

FIRST AND SECOND DECLENSION ADJECTIVES

Adjectives ending in **-us**

	SINGULAR			PLURAL		
	MASC.	FEM.	NEUT.	MASC.	FEM.	NEUT.
NOM.	malus	mala	malum	malī	malae	mala
GEN.	malī	malae	malī	malōrum	malārum	malōrum
DAT.	malō	malae	malō	malīs	malīs	malīs
ACC.	malum	malam	malum	malōs	malās	mala
ABL.	malō	malā	malō	malīs	malīs	malīs

Adjectives ending in **-er** and retaining the **-e**

	SINGULAR			PLURAL		
	MASC.	FEM.	NEUT.	MASC.	FEM.	NEUT.
NOM.	miser	misera	miserum	miserī	miserae	misera
GEN.	miserī	miserae	miserī	miserōrum	miserārum	miserōrum
DAT.	miserō	miserae	miserō	miserīs	miserīs	miserīs
ACC.	miserum	miseram	miserum	miserōs	miserās	misera
ABL.	miserō	miserā	miserō	miserīs	miserīs	miserīs

(Continued)

Adjectives ending in **-er** and dropping the **-e**

	SINGULAR			PLURAL		
	MASC.	**FEM.**	**NEUT.**	**MASC.**	**FEM.**	**NEUT.**
NOM.	pulcher	pulchra	pulchrum	pulchrī	pulchrae	pulchra
GEN.	pulchrī	pulchrae	pulchrī	pulchrōrum	pulchrārum	pulchrōrum
DAT.	pulchrō	pulchrae	pulchrō	pulchrīs	pulchrīs	pulchrīs
ACC.	pulchrum	pulchram	pulchrum	pulchrōs	pulchrās	pulchra
ABL.	pulchrō	pulchrā	pulchrō	pulchrīs	pulchrīs	pulchrīs

SYNTAX

■ AGREEMENT OF ADJECTIVES

An adjective agrees with the noun it modifies in gender, number, and case. This is why a Latin adjective must have forms for all three genders, as well as for the cases and numbers.

Ager est magnus.   *The field is large.*
Via est magna.   *The road is large.*
Perīculum est magnum.   *The danger is great.*

Agrum magnum spectat.   *He looks at the large field.*
Viam magnam spectat.   *He looks at the large road.*

If one adjective modifies nouns in different genders, it is masculine plural if the nouns refer to persons; neuter plural if to things.

Silva et via magnae sunt.   *The forest and the road are large.*
Silva et ager magna sunt.   *The forest and the field are large.*

Fēminae et puellae sunt miserae.   *The women and girls are unhappy.*
Puerī et puellae sunt miserī.   *The boys and girls are unhappy.*

■ USES OF ADJECTIVES

Adjectives may be used in three ways: they may be attributive, predicative, or substantive.

An adjective which modifies a noun is either *attributive* or *predicative*.

1. An *attributive adjective* merely gives additional information about the noun it modifies; the sentence would still be a sentence without it.

> Agricola **miser** ambulat in **magnam** vīllam.
> *The **unhappy** farmer is walking into the **large** farmhouse.*

2. A *predicative adjective* (usually with the verb *to be*) makes a statement about the noun it modifies; if it is removed there is no sentence.

> Agricola **miser** est, sed vīlla est **magna**.
> *The farmer is **unhappy**, but his farmhouse is **large**.*

3. A *substantive adjective* has no noun to modify, but is used as a noun itself. It is translated according to its gender and number.

malus	*a bad **man***	malī	*bad **men**, the wicked*
mala	*a bad **woman***	malae	*bad **women***
malum	*a bad **thing***	mala	*bad **things**, evils*

This substantive use of the adjective is very common in Latin, but in English it is mostly restricted to certain plurals: "The good die young," "The poor you have always with you."

Silver tableware, Pompeii

VOCABULARY

When you learn a Latin adjective you learn all the nominative singular endings. This is necessary because you can't find the base from the masculine alone: for example, you wouldn't know whether **pulcher** drops the -e, like **ager**, or keeps it, like **puer**. The base is found by dropping the -a or the -um from the feminine or neuter ending.

BASIC WORDS

fuga, -ae, f. *flight, a running away, escape*

perīculum, -ī, n. *danger*

amīcus, amīca, amīcum *friendly*
ferus, fera, ferum *wild, savage*
inimīcus, inimīca, inimīcum *unfriendly, hostile*
magnus, magna, magnum *great, large*
malus, mala, malum *bad, evil, wicked*
miser, misera, miserum *poor, wretched, unhappy*

multus, multa, multum *much; (plural) many*

paucī, paucae, pauca (no singular) *few, a few*

pulcher, pulchra, pulchrum *beautiful, fine*

aedificō, -āre *build*

sed (conjunction) *but*

Note: The noun **amīcus, -ī, m.** which you have learned is in fact the adjective **amīcus, amīca, amīcum** used as a noun. In the same way **inimīcus, -ī, m.** means *enemy*.

LEARNING ENGLISH THROUGH LATIN

edify	*instruct or enlighten*
fugue	*(music) a composition in which one voice or instrument chases another*
magnify	*enlarge*
malice	*ill will, evil intent*
miser	*one who hoards money*
multiply	*increase in number*
paucity	*scarcity*
peril	*danger*
pulchritude	*beauty*

PRACTICE

A. Return the English derivatives to their proper sentences.

1. These moral teachings are meant to *magnify* you and free you from *fugue*. 2. The old *malice* thought of nothing but how to *edify* his wealth. 3. As long as we have the works of J. S. Bach we are not in *pulchritude* of suffering from the *peril* of *misers*. 4. She's not as beautiful as you said she was; you were just trying to *multiply* her *paucity*.

B. Change from singular to plural, keeping the same gender and case:

1. amīcā   2. ferī   3. mala   4. pulcher   5. inimīcam

C. Change from plural to singular, keeping the same gender and case:

1. multae   2. miserōs   3. magna   4. ferī   5. amīcārum

D. Change to feminine, keeping the same number and case:

1. malīs   2. pulchrī   3. inimīcōrum   4. miser   5. magnōs

E. Decline each noun with the adjective modifying it. Remember that although the two words will always be in the same gender, number, and case, their endings will not always be identical (e.g., **puer amīcus, agricolae malī**).

1. ager magnus   2. bellum ferum   3. fēmina amīca   4. nauta malus

F. Put each adjective into the correct form, and tell whether it is attributive, predicative, or substantive. Some of these sentences have more than one correct answer.

1. Poētae sunt (miser).   2. Cum puellā (pulcher) ambulat.   3. Dea fēminās spectat sed (malus) nōn amat.   4. (Āfricānus) in Āfricā habitant.   5. Ē (magnus) oppidō ambulat.   6. (Multus) (amīcus) auxilium portant. 7. Perīcula (paucī) sunt.   8. (Miser) agricolae vīlla nōn (magnus) est.

G. Translate:

1. The evil sailors are seizing the poor farmer's farmhouse.   2. Where do you live with your household? Where are you walking from?   3. The messenger's beautiful daughter loves the friend of the great envoy.   4. The wretched boy is walking out of the large town into the beautiful woods.

A bakery and flour mill at Pompeii, showing grain mills and a free-standing oven

FROM THE PHILOSOPHER'S HANDBOOK . . .

Nūllum magnum ingenium sine
mixtūrā dēmentiae fuit.
*There has not been any great talent without
an element of madness.*
—SENECA

This is a very thought-provoking observation. Select an extremely talented person from the past in any field of your choice and explain whether or not this saying applies to him or her. If so, in what way?

READING

Developing Reading Skills

In previous readings you have been given the meanings of unfamiliar words in the notes. To give you practice at looking up Latin words, they will now be listed only in the vocabulary in the back of the book. There are six unfamiliar words in this reading.

The Adventures of Dido

Ubi Graecī et Trōiānī in Bellō Trōiānō pugnant, Elissa, Poenōrum rēgīna, in magnō oppidō in Phoenīcā habitat. Elissae virum Sychaeum vocāmus. Elissa Sychaeum amat; sed rēgīnae germānus, vir malus, cum Elissae inimīcīs Sychaeum obtruncat. Itaque rēgīna fugam parat et cum Annā germānā et multīs amīcīs ā Phoenīcā ad Āfricam nāvigat, ubi magnum oppidum aedificat.   5
Poenī oppidum vocant Oppidum Novum. Oppidum Novum magnum et pulchrum est.

   Sed in Āfricā est magnum perīculum: ferī Āfricānī spectant Oppidum Novum in agrō Āfricānō; advenās Poenōs nōn amant. Itaque bellum parant contrā Elissam et amīcōs. Āfricānī multī, Poenī paucī sunt; miserae rēgīnae   10 perīculum est magnum.

■ READING COMPREHENSION

1. Who fought the Trojan War?   **2.** Who is the queen of the Phoenicians?
3. Who is her husband?   **4.** What happens to him?   **5.** When the queen leaves Phoenicia, where does she go and what does she do?   **6.** Why is the queen in grave danger?

---

1. Elissa or **Eliza:** better known by her nickname *Dido* ("Wanderer" in Phoenician)   **6. Oppidum Novum:** a translation into Latin of the Phoenician name of *Carthage*   **9. agrō Āfricānō:** When **ager** is modified by an adjective meaning *belonging to a nation, city,* or *town* it means *territory.*

LESSON 6

Vocative; Some Irregular Declensions; Formation of Adverbs

Roman mosaic showing the abundance of Mediterranean fish—National Museum, Naples

YOUR FOOD

The staple food of the early Romans was a kind of porridge which was baked into a cake or wafer on a griddle. Eventually this was replaced by bread, and bread, wine, and vegetables became the basic diet. Fruits, fish, and poultry, and sometimes meat, were added for special occasions. Vegetables, fruits, fish, poultry, and meat were bought at a central market (**macellum**); the staples, bread and wine, were sold at neighborhood shops.

The Romans ate many more varieties of fish and fowl than we do. They knew 150 kinds of edible fish; and they ate small songbirds, such as thrushes, as well as (on the tables of the wealthy) such exotic dishes as parrot, flamingo, and ostrich. On the other hand, they did not have rice, pasta, tomatoes, potatoes, sugar, corn, oranges, bananas, strawberries, raspberries, chocolate, coffee, tea, or distilled spirits. They did not use butter, preferring olive oil in their cooking; in the absence of sugar they used honey for sweetening. For lasagna-type dishes they used thin pancakes, since they had no pasta. They drank a great variety of wines, however, from all over the Roman world, nearly always mixing it with some proportion of water; drinking straight wine was not respectable.

We know a great deal about Roman cooking, since their chief cookbook has come down to us. The Roman cuisine was one of sauces, added to dishes cooked simply by boiling, broiling, or sautéing. These sauces were often highly spiced, and have strange (to us) combinations of sweet and salty or sour elements. Ubiquitous in their cuisine was the highly prized fish sauce called **garum** or **liquāmen,** which came at different prices depending on how long it had matured. It was made from the heads, bones, and entrails of fish, allowed to decompose in a strong brine, and tasted like anchovy paste or Chinese oyster sauce.

At dinner parties the presentation of food was as important as its taste.

(Continued)

57

One curious feature of the more elaborate dinners was the attempt on the part of the cooks to show their skill by making one food resemble another, such as a pig disguised as chicken, or cakes made to look like boiled eggs. Sometimes the dishes were prepared so elaborately that no one dared to ask for a portion without the host's lead. When this was not forthcoming, the same dish might appear untouched at a series of dinners.

(below) Funerary relief showing a dealer in poultry and vegetables. The monkeys are probably pets brought by sailors.

ANCIENT ROME LIVES ON . . .

Can you name some foods today that are shaped/disguised as other things?

Can you name some modern dishes that combine sweet and salty or sour flavors?

FORMS

VOCATIVE CASE

The vocative case is the case of direct address. It is normally not included in declensions because it is usually the same as the nominative. It is always like the nominative in the plural. But in the singular of second declension nouns which end in -us, and in the masculine singular of -us, -a, -um adjectives, the vocative is formed by adding -e to the base.

bone amīce   magne nūntie   lēgāte Trōiāne

1. Roman proper names which end in -ius, and fīlius, *son*, drop the -us and lengthen the i.

Vergilī   fīlī

These vocatives look just like the genitive, and, as with such genitives, the accent remains where it would be if the word ended in -ie: Vergi′lī, not Ver′gilī.
2. The adjective **meus, mea, meum** has an irregular masculine vocative singular **mī.**
3. Greek-derived first declension masculine names, like **Aenēās** and **Anchīsēs**, have a regular first-declension vocative like that of **puella: Aenēa, Anchīsa.**

SOME IRREGULAR DECLENSIONS

Deus, *god,* and **dea,** *goddess,* have some variant forms in the plural:

DECLENSION OF DEUS AND DEA

	SINGULAR	PLURAL		SINGULAR	PLURAL
NOM.	deus	deī, diī, dī		dea	deae
GEN.	deī	deōrum, deum		deae	deārum
DAT.	deō	deīs, diīs, dīs		deae	deābus
ACC.	deum	deōs		deam	deās
ABL.	deō	deīs, diīs, dīs		deā	deābus

To distinguish it from **fīlius, fīlia** also has **-ābus** instead of **-īs** in the dative and ablative plural: **fīliābus.**

■ FORMATION OF ADVERBS

Adverbs are normally made from adjectives of the first and second declensions by adding -ē to the base.

altē	*on high, deeply*
Graecē	*in Greek*
līberē	*frankly, freely*
longē	*far off, by far*
miserē	*wretchedly, desperately*
pulchrē	*beautifully, nicely*

Not all first and second declension adjectives have regularly formed adverbs. For example, the adverbs for *good* and *bad*, **bonus** and **malus,** are respectively **bene** and **male,** not bonē and malē, as we would expect.

══ SYNTAX ══

■ VOCATIVE CASE

The Vocative Case is used for speaking directly to someone. A noun or adjective in the vocative always denotes the person being spoken to. In English we show direct address by setting the words off with commas and placing them (usually) at the beginning or end of a clause.

> *Virgil, where are you walking to?*
> *Are you in the farmhouse, good friend?*
> *We are sailing to Asia, my son.*

In Latin the vocative comes not at the beginning or end of a clause, but just after the beginning, usually in the second or third place.

> Quō, Vergilī, ambulās?
> Esne, bone amīce, in vīllā?
> In Asiam, mī fīlī, nāvigāmus.

VOCABULARY

BASIC WORDS

deus, -ī, m. *god*

fīlius, fīlī, m. *son*

līberī, līberōrum, m. (pl.) *children*

servus, -ī, m. *slave*

altus, -a, -um *high, deep*

bonus, -a, -um *good*

līber, lībera, līberum *free*

longus, -a, -um *long*

meus, -a, -um *my, mine*

noster, nostra, nostrum *our, ours*

tuus, -a, -um *your, yours (one person's)*

vester, vestra, vestrum *your, yours
(more than one person's)*

bene (adverb) *well*

male (adverb) *badly, ill*

Notes: 1. A Roman **familia,** *household,* was made up of *slaves* and *free persons,* **servī** and **līberī.** Hence the Latin word for *children,* **līberī,** is merely the adjective **līber** used as a noun.

2. Possessive adjectives (**meus, noster, tuus, vester**) are not normally used when the fact of possession can be taken for granted. If they are used, they have an emphatic sense.

Cum fīliō ambulō. *I am walking with my son.*

Cum meō fīliō ambulō. *I am walking with my own son.*

FROM THE PHILOSOPHER'S HANDBOOK . . .

Dīs aliter visum.

It seemed otherwise to the Gods.

—VIRGIL

"Man proposes, God disposes . . ." "The best laid plans of mice and men . . ." Can you think of a situation in your life when the above quotation from Virgil's *Aeneid* would have been appropriate?

LEARNING ENGLISH THROUGH LATIN

altitude	*height above the earth or sea level*
benefit	*advantage, help*
bonus	*a payment above and beyond the required amount*
deity	*god or goddess*
filial	*of a son or daughter*
longevity	*long life*
malnutrition	*poor nourishment*
servile	*slave-like*

PRACTICE

A. Fill in the blanks with the derivatives in the above list and with the English translations of the Latin words from which they are derived:

1. A ___ manner is that of a ___, not a free person.   2. The ___ of anything is how ___ above sea level it is.   3. One who suffers from ___ is ___ nourished.   4. Everyone would agree that a ___ added to the salary is a ___ thing.   5. If you have received a ___ someone has done ___ by you.   6. A ___ duty is the duty of a ___ or ___ to his or her parents.

B. Give the vocatives, singular and plural, of the following:

1. bonus puer   2. miser agricola   3. fēmina pulchra   4. magna dea
5. nauta malus   6. vir ferus   7. puella amīca   8. meus fīlius   9. servus noster   10. rēgīna Āfricāna

C. Decline in the singular and plural (without the vocative):

1. deus noster   2. dea vestra

D. Give the adverbs of these adjectives:

1. altus   2. bonus   3. amīcus   4. inimīcus   5. līber   6. longus   7. malus
8. miser   9. pulcher

E. Translate:

1. Is your household large, good man? There are in my household many children and slaves.   2. I am a wretched slave, and so I am preparing flight far from the town into the forest.   3. The children and the slaves of our

household live in a friendly manner in a large farmhouse.   4. Messenger, are the wicked slaves seizing the poor farmer's farmhouses?   5. My son, do you praise the great gods and goddesses of our own fatherland?

F.   Read the Latin and translate:

1. Via longa est, itaque paucī nautae ab Āfricā ad Asiam nāvigant.   2. Est multum perīculum bellī, sed deī et deae auxilium ad patriam nostram portant.   3. Nautae in agrīs miserī sunt, et agricolae male nāvigant. 4. Inimīcī nostrī sunt malī et ferī, itaque fugam ā patriā parāmus.   5. Fābulam, mea fīlia, dē Aenēae fugā narrat poēta Vergilius.

G.   Construe each adjective in F. That is (1) give its gender, number, and case; (2) say whether it is used attributively, predicatively, or substantively; (3) if it is used attributively or predicatively, explain its gender, number, and case, and if it is used substantively explain its case.

EXAMPLE: Sentence 4: **Inimīcī:** masculine nominative plural; substantive; subject of the verb **sunt. Nostrī:** masculine nominative plural; attributive; agrees in gender, number and case with **inimīcī,** the substantive it modifies. **Malī** and **ferī:** masculine nominative plural; predicative; agree in gender, number and case with **inimīcī,** the substantive they modify.

Translation Help

Although there is a lot of variation possible in Latin word order, there are some rules. The most important of these is that ambiguity must be avoided.

Since the genitive goes with the nearest noun, common sense dictates that it not be placed between two nouns. Does **Servus agricolae agrōs spectat** mean *The farmer's slave is looking at the fields* or *The slave is looking at the farmer's fields?* Write **Agricolae servus** or **agrōs agricolae.**

In the same way, other cases and prepositional phrases must be placed where they cannot become attached to the wrong element. In the sentence **Servus in vīllā fēminam spectat,** who is in the farmhouse?

An adjective, however, provided that it can agree in gender, number, and case with only one noun in the sentence, may go anywhere. **Pulchrōs servus spectat agrōs** is an acceptable order: it emphasizes **pulchrōs:** *The slave is looking at beautiful fields.*

READING

The Story of the Aeneid

Longam fābulam dē Aeneā narrat poēta magnus Vergilius: Aenēās filius deae Cythereae est et Anchīsae Trōiānī. Post Bellum Trōiānum deī Anchīsam cum familiā vocant ad Hesperiam terram. Itaque Aenēās cum Anchīsā et filiō Ascaniō et amīcīs et servīs fugam parat et super altum nāvigat. Sed ā
5 viā longē ab Hesperiā errant et ad Elissae rēgīnae oppidum in Āfricam nāvigant.

   Bona rēgīna Aenēam cum amīcīs ad cēnam bene et amīcē vocat. In cēnā Aenēam interrogat de Bellō Trōiānō. Et ubi Aenēās fābulam narrat Elissa pulchrum virum Trōiānum miserē amat.

10 AENĒĀS: "Fābula, rēgīna, dē Bellō Trōiānō et dē nostrā viā super altum longa et misera est, et verba nōn bona sunt, sed līberē narrō."

◼ READING COMPREHENSION

1. Who are the parents of Aeneas?   2. Why must Aeneas' household leave their homeland?   3. Where are they supposed to go?   4. What happens on their journey?   5. What does Elissa want to learn from Aeneas? 6. What happens to Elissa as Aeneas tells his story?

A fourth-century B.C. coin from Carthage, Dido's **Oppidum Novum**

---

4. **Altum,** used as a neuter noun, means *the deep* (i.e. *the sea*).   8. **Ubi,** used as an adverbial conjunction, means *when.*

LESSON 7

Imperfect Tense; Future Tense;
Indirect Object; Dative of Reference

A mosaic showing an unswept floor covered with banquet leftovers.
Such decoration was popular on dining room floors to disguise the real debris.

YOUR MEALS

The Romans ate three meals a day. Breakfast (**ientāculum**) was very light and usually consisted of bread moistened with olive oil or wine, sometimes accompanied by fruit or cheese. Lunch (**prandium**) was also light, usually cold, and often composed of leftovers from the evening before. Dinner (**cēna**) was the substantial meal of the day. Because artificial lighting was poor, a dinner party might begin as early as 3:00 PM.

A dinner had three parts. It began with an appetizer course (**gustātiō**) of eggs, shellfish, salad, and the like, accompanied by **mulsum,** wine flavored with honey. The main part of the meal (**fercula**) was made up of an odd number of courses of fish, poultry, and occasionally meat, the chief dish of the meal being the middle one of the series. The meal ended with a dessert course (**secunda mēnsa** or **secundae mēnsae**) of fruits and sometimes pastry.

Wine was drunk during the **fercula** and the **secunda mēnsa.** If the host was serving some especially prized wine, it accompanied the dessert. Between these two courses there was a pause during which offerings of food or incense were made to the household gods.

The Romans reclined at meals, resting on the left elbow. Normally there were nine diners on three couches, but each person might have a small couch, or all might share one large semicircular couch at a round table. On arrival, each guest sat on his couch until a slave had removed his shoes and washed and dried his feet; this was considered the most degrading task a slave could do. Other slaves served from the open side of the table, often removing the entire table top and replacing it with another when courses were changed. Spoons were used for boiled eggs, soups, and stews, but there were no knives or forks at the table. Instead, a specially trained slave carved the food into bite-sized pieces, to be eaten with the fingers.

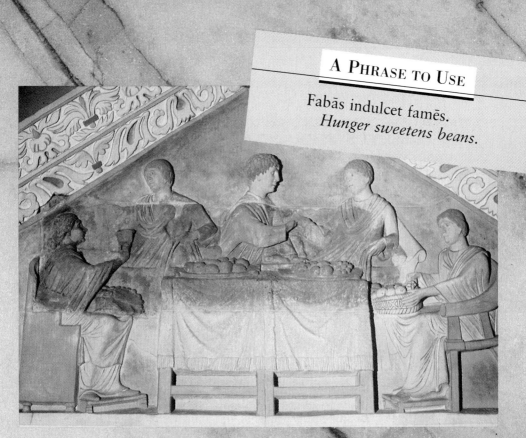

ANCIENT ROME LIVES ON . . .

What would a Roman family find
familiar about a modern dinner menu?

(*above*) A restored banquet scene: men
recline at the back while women sit at the
side, Trier, West Germany   (*right*) A
Roman family dinner: the husband
reclines while his wife sits conversing
with him; children and pets play below.

■ FORMS

■ PRESENT SYSTEM

Three tenses are formed on the present stem of a verb; they are the Present Tense, the Imperfect Tense, and the Future Tense. These three tenses belong to the Present System.

Remember that the present stem is found by dropping the **-re** from the second principal part of the verb. The present tense is formed by adding the personal endings directly to the present stem. The other tenses of the present system insert a tense sign between the present stem and the personal ending.

■ IMPERFECT TENSE

To form the imperfect tense, add the tense-sign **-bā-** to the present stem, and then add the personal endings **-m, -s, -t, -mus, -tis,** and **-nt,** shortening the ā of **-bā-** before **-m, -t,** and **-nt.**

IMPERFECT TENSE

SINGULAR		PLURAL	
vocā**bam**	*I was calling, I used to call*	vocā**bāmus**	*we were calling, we used to call*
vocā**bās**	*you were calling, you used to call*	vocā**bātis**	*you were calling, you used to call*
vocā**bat**	*he (she, it) was calling, he (she, it) used to call*	vocā**bant**	*they were calling, they used to call*

■ FUTURE TENSE

To form the future tense, add the tense-sign **-bi-** to the present stem of the verb, then the personal endings, **-ō, -s, -t, -mus, -tis,** and **-nt,** omitting the **-i** of **-bi-** before **-ō** and changing it to **-u** before **-nt.**

FUTURE TENSE			
SINGULAR		**PLURAL**	
vocā**bō**	*I shall call*	vocā**bimus**	*we shall call*
vocā**bis**	*you will call*	vocā**bitis**	*you will call*
vocā**bit**	*he (she, it) will call*	vocā**bunt**	*they will call*

SYNTAX

USE OF TENSES

Imperfect Tense

The imperfect tense (**imperfectum,** *incomplete*) describes an action as uncompleted by some time in the past. This can mean that the action is pictured as going on at some point in the past (as with the past progressive in English) or as repeated over a period of time in the past.

ACTION GOING ON:
Ōlim ad oppidum ambulābat.   *Once he was walking to town.*

ACTION REPEATED:
Saepe ad oppidum ambulābat.   { *He often used to walk to town.*
{ *He would often walk to town.*

The translation you choose will depend on the context.

Future Tense

The Latin future, like the future tense in English, merely states that an action will take place in the future.

Post ad oppidum ambulābit.   *He will walk to town later.*

DATIVE OF INDIRECT OBJECT

With verbs or other expressions of *giving, saying, showing,* and the like, the dative indicates to whom something is given, said, shown, etc. This use of the dative is called the Indirect Object. In English it has the preposition *to* or no preposition at all, depending on the word order.

Rēgīnae fābulam narrābat. $\begin{cases} \textit{He was telling a story to the queen.} \\ \textit{He was telling the queen a story.} \end{cases}$

Equum vocant dōnum deīs.   *They call the horse a gift to the gods.*

◼ DATIVE OF REFERENCE

The dative is also used with other verbs to show to whose advantage or disadvantage the action of the verb is performed. The English translation may use the preposition *for*, or no preposition at all.

Meō amīcō vīllam aedificant. $\begin{cases} \textit{They are building a farmhouse} \\ \quad \textit{for my friend.} \\ \textit{They are building my friend} \\ \quad \textit{a farmhouse.} \\ \textit{(They are building a farmhouse} \\ \quad \textit{to my friend's advantage.)} \end{cases}$

This dative may also be translated as if it were a genitive or an ablative of place from which.

Vīllam meō amīcō occupant. $\begin{cases} \textit{They are seizing the farmhouse} \\ \quad \textit{from my friend.} \\ \textit{They are seizing my friend's} \\ \quad \textit{farmhouse.} \\ \textit{(They are seizing the farmhouse} \\ \quad \textit{to my friend's disadvantage.)} \end{cases}$

A mosaic on a sidewalk in Ostia advertises the **thermopolium** of Fortunatus with the imperative, "Drink!"

VOCABULARY

BASIC WORDS

annus, -ī, m. *year*

dōnum, -ī, n. *gift*

equus, -ī, m. *horse*

porta, -ae, f. *gate*

somnus, -ī, m. *sleep*

lātus, -a, -um *wide, broad*

superō, -āre *surpass, overcome, defeat*

volō, -āre *fly, move swiftly, speed, rush*

ōlim (adv.) *once, at one time, at some time*

post (adv.) *afterward, behind*

saepe (adv.) *often*

per (prep. w. acc.) *through; (in oaths) by*

post (prep. w. acc.) *after, behind, in back of*

-que (enclitic conjunction) *and*

Notes: 1. The adverb of **lātus** is often used with the adverb of **longus** to mean *far and wide;* but the Romans say wide and far: **lātē longēque.**

2. The enclitic conjunction **-que** is a weaker kind of *and* than **et;** it is like the colloquial *'n'* we often hear used in English. It is usually used to connect things which are thought of together: **virī fēminaeque,** *men 'n' women,* **puerī puellaeque,** *boys 'n' girls.*

LEARNING ENGLISH THROUGH LATIN

annual — *yearly*

donation — *a gift or contribution*

equestrian — *pertaining to horses, horsemen, or horseback riding*

insuperable — *not able to be overcome, insurmountable*

latitude — *width, freedom from narrow restrictions*

portal — *doorway, gate, or entrance*

somnolent — *sleepy*

volatile — *explosive, unpredictable*

From Latin Prepositions:

perchance — *by chance, perhaps, accidentally*

postwar — *after the war*

PRACTICE

A. Find a slot in these two sentences for each of the English derivatives in this lesson.

1. He is allowed much ___ in choosing his seats at the ___ horse show, ___ because his ___ to the ___ Association was so large.   2. The ___ depression in France seemed ___, but the people were far from ___, and their ___ spirits soon brought them through the ___ of prosperity again.

B. Change to the imperfect tense, keeping the same person and number:

1. volant   2. portābō   3. amātis   4. aedificābit   5. superāmus

C. Change to the future tense, keeping the same person and number:

1. narrās   2. spectābātis   3. habitāmus   4. parābant   5. occupat

D. Conjugate in the present, imperfect, and future:

1. volō   2. portō   3. aedificō   4. superō   5. amō

E. Pronounce and translate each form:

1. narrāmus, spectābās, aedificābant   2. habitābimus, occupās, parābam
3. superābō, narrābunt, occupant   4. amābis, ambulō, volābāmus   5. laudat, ambulābit, portābātis   6. laudābitis, vocābat, nāvigātis

F. Construe each numbered noun (i.e. give its number and case and explain the case use):

1. Sunt multī līberī in agricolae vīllā.   2. Poētae fēminam pulchram vocant Helenam rēgīnam.   3. Puellīsne, mī filī, fābulam narrābis?   4. Nauta cum amīcīs ab Asiā ad Āfricam nāvigābat.   5. Equum puerō portābant.

G. Read the Latin and translate:

1. Ōlim in poētārum Graecōrum fābulīs equus altē super terrās volābat.
2. Nostrī ferōs Graecōs in bellō saepe superābant.   3. Per multās terrās longē ā meā patriā in Graeciam ambulābō.   4. Rēgīna pulchra Trōiānum spectat; post miserē amābit.   5. Virī fēminaeque cum filiīs filiābusque deōs deāsque nostrae patriae laudābunt.   6. Es servus miser, sed et meus amīcus es.   7. Deus lātē longēque super silvās agrōsque volābit.   8. Vestrī meōs agrōs paucōs inimīcē occupābant.

READING

Developing Reading Skills

In this reading there are more words which are not yet part of your active vocabulary, but you may not have to look them all up in the back of the book: intelligent guessing will tell you the meanings. Guessing can be based on English derivatives: it's not hard to guess what **victōria** (l. 7) means, and **vīcīnam** (l. 6) is easy if you know the word *vicinity*. Or it may be based on derivation from a word you have learned: **nāvigia** (l. 5) is not so hard if you remember **nāvigō**. Likewise, if you know **ē** and **volō** you know **ēvolō** (l. 11). Knowledge of the context may also help: if you know the story of the Trojan Horse you would know that **ligneum** (l. 4) means *wooden*.

The Trojan Horse

Aenēās rēgīnae et amīcīs fābulam dē Bellō Trōiānō narrābat: "Graecī bellum parābant contrā Trōiam et ad Asiam nāvigābant. Diū pugnābant, sed oppidum nōn occupābant. Dēnique, post multōs annōs, magnum equum ligneum aedificābant. Equum dōnum deae Minervae vocābant. Deinde ā nostrō oppidō nāvigābant quasi ad Graeciam; sed profectō nāvigia post īnsulam vīcīnam Tenedum cēlābant.   5

"Trōiānī laetī clāmābāmus, 'Nostra est victōria! Cum ferīs Graecīs nōn iam pugnābimus! Equus ligneus profectō est dōnum diīs nostrī oppidī,' et equum per oppidī portās portābāmus.

"Sed equus multōs Graecōs in uterō cēlābat. Itaque ubi Somnus oculōs   10
nostrōs caecābat, Graecī ex equī lignei uterō ēvolābant per oppidum et lātē longēque Trōiānōs obtruncābant. Sīc Trōiānōs superābant Graecī."

---

5. **profectō**: This adverb does not end in ē because it comes from the prepositional phrase **prō factō**, *for a fact*.   7. **Trōiānī**: In Latin, a noun may be the subject of a verb in the first or second person; in English we use apposition: *We Trojans* . . .   **Nostra est victōria** When a predicate adjective precedes the verb *to be*, the verb is used as a linking verb even if it precedes the subject: not *There is victory* . . . but *Victory is* . . .   8. Although **iam** by itself means *now* or *already*, with a negative it means *longer*: **nōn iam**, *no longer*.   10. **uterō**: By using the word *womb* to describe the hollow inside of the horse, Virgil presents the horse as giving birth to the destruction of the city.

Wall painting from Pompeii showing the wooden horse being drawn into Troy

■ READING COMPREHENSION

1. What did the Greeks build after many years of fighting with Trojans?
2. What did they call it?   **3.** What did they do then?   **4.** Why did the
Trojans shout "Nostra est victōria"?   **5.** How did the Greeks trick the
Trojans?   **6.** Why didn't the Trojans see what the Greeks were doing?

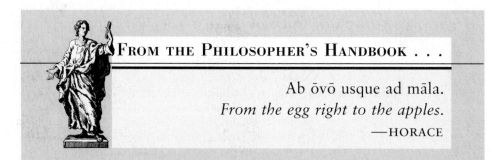

FROM THE PHILOSOPHER'S HANDBOOK . . .

Ab ōvō usque ad māla.
From the egg right to the apples.
—HORACE

Can you quote an English proverb that has the same meaning?
What does it mean?

LESSON 8

Imperfect and Future of Sum;
Ablative of Means or Instrument

The Pont du Gard, a famous Roman aqueduct in southern France

YOUR WATER SUPPLY

The development of good municipal water supplies was one of Rome's greatest contributions to the ancient world. Before the emergence of the Romans as a world power, most cities and towns relied upon natural springs and streams, wells, or rainwater collected in cisterns. Most people had to fetch their water from some central source, and contaminated water must have caused much disease.

With the coming of the Romans there was hardly any place of importance which did not have its aqueducts. These covered stone channels brought water often from great distances, tunneling straight through hills and crossing valleys on great arches of brick, masonry, or (from the first century B.C.) poured concrete. Another way of getting the water across valleys was by the inverted siphon, an achievement less spectacular but hardly less impressive when we remember that the water-tight pipe required had to be made by rolling and fusing sheets of lead.

An aqueduct carried water from some upland lake or river (**caput aquārum**) to a reservoir (**castellum**) from which it was distributed to its various destinations. The **castella** of smaller towns were simple, regulated by gravity and the size of pipe bores. Water for the public fountains was drawn off from the bottom, for the public baths above that, and for private use from the top of the reservoir. Hence in time of drought private users would be the first, and public fountains the last, to lose water. In cities where water was needed also for industrial purposes (as for the wool-processing industry at Pompeii) a more sophisticated system was used. The public fountains were supplied constantly, but the flow to baths, private houses, and the wool factories was regulated by adjusting gates so that the amount of water supplied depended on the time of day. More water went to the factories during working hours, to the baths in the afternoon, etc.

From the **castellum** the water was brought by gravity (by the use of

(Continued)

A PHRASE TO USE

Aqua profunda est quiēta.
Deep water is calm.
(Still waters run deep.)

inverted siphons) to various water towers, which were often disguised as triumphal arches or built into city gates. These towers provided the water pressure for adjacent buildings.

Within the house the flow of water was regulated by stopcocks and faucets much like ours. Public fountains, which normally ran night and day, could also be shut off in times of extreme drought by a tap worked by a special wrench.

(*below left*) Public fountain on a street in Pompeii   (*below right*) Garden fountain in The House of the Big Fountain, Pompeii

ANCIENT ROME LIVES ON . . .

What are the pros and cons of public fountains in modern society?

77

FORMS

IMPERFECT AND FUTURE OF SUM

The imperfect and future of **sum**, like its present, use normal endings; but the stem is **er-** and the tense signs do not have the **b** of **-bā-** and **-bi-**.

SUM: IMPERFECT TENSE

eram	*I was*		erāmus	*we were*
erās	*you were*		erātis	*you were*
erat	*he (she, it) was*		erant	*they were*
	there was			*there were*

SUM: FUTURE TENSE

erō	*I shall be*		erimus	*we shall be*
eris	*you will be*		eritis	*you will be*
erit	*he (she, it) will be*		erunt	*they will be*
	there will be			*there will be*

SYNTAX

ABLATIVE OF MEANS OR INSTRUMENT

The means by which, or the instrument with which, something is done is expressed by the ablative without a preposition. The means or instrument must not be a person. The English translation usually uses *with* or *by*, but it can also use any English preposition which in context implies *by means of*.

Deōrum auxiliō Graecōs superābimus.
   With (or by) the help of the gods we shall defeat the Greeks.
Fābulam paucīs verbīs narrābō.
   I shall tell the story in a few words.
Ad Asiam equō volābat.   *He was speeding to Asia on a horse.*

VOCABULARY

BASIC WORDS

caelum, -ī, n. *sky, heaven*
campus, -ī, m. *plain, meadow*
fortūna, ae, f. *fortune*
rēgnum, -ī, n. *kingdom, kingship*

convocō, -āre *call together, assemble*
exspectō, -āre *wait for, await*

ante (adv.) *before, earlier, in front*
cūr (interrogative adv.) *why?*

iam (adv.) *now, already;* nōn iam *no longer*
interim (adv.) *meanwhile, in the meantime*
nunc (adv.) *now, at this time*
tum or tunc (adv.) *then, at that time*

ante (prep. w. acc.) *before, in front of*
trāns (prep. w. acc.) *across*

Notes: 1. The plural of **caelum** is used very seldom by the Romans; when it is used it is masculine: **caelī, caelōrum.**
2. **Convocō** is only transitive: you can use it to say *He assembled the men,* but not *The men assembled.*

Part of the Emperor Hadrian's country villa at Tivoli

LEARNING ENGLISH THROUGH LATIN

celestial	*heavenly*
convoke	*call together; summon*
fortunate	*lucky*
interim	*the period of time between*

From Latin Prepositions:

| anteroom | *waiting room* |
| transparent | *able to be seen through; very clear; easily understood* |

PRACTICE

A. Use the following words in an English sentence:

1. transparent   2. convoke   3. interim   4. fortunate   5. celestial

B. Conjugate in the present, imperfect, and future, giving the meanings:

1. convocō   2. exspectō   3. sum   4. superō   5. volō

C. Choose the correct translation (or translations; there may be more than one) for each of the following forms:

1. **ambulābat:** he was walking, he will walk, he used to walk   2. **amābimus:** I shall love, we shall love, you were loving   3. **habitātis:** you were living, you are living, you live   4. **erunt:** they are, they were, they will be   5. **laudābās:** you are praising, you were praising, you will be praising   6. **narrō:** I tell, I am telling, I do tell   7. **nāvigābāmus:** you were sailing, we used to sail, we shall sail   8. **occupābit:** he used to seize, she will seize, he was seizing   9. **parābant:** he was preparing, he will prepare, they used to prepare   10. **portābitis:** we shall carry, they will carry, you will carry

D. Translate:

1. we are carrying   2. you used to prepare   3. I shall seize   4. they will sail   5. you (*pl.*) tell   6. we were praising   7. she will be   8. you (*sing.*) dwell   9. he used to like   10. we shall walk

E. Construe all the nouns and adjectives in the following sentence. To construe an adjective, give its gender, number and case, and tell whether it is used as an adjective or as a noun. If it is used as an adjective, tell what it modifies and say whether it is predicative or attributive. If it is used as a noun you construe it as a noun.

Cum bonīs amīcīs ex altā silvā equīs magnīs volābimus in lātōs campōs, ubi in magnā vīllā bene habitābimus.

F. Pronounce and translate:

1. Fēminae fortūna mala erat: virum malum miserē amābat.   **2.** Cūr in fugam līberōs vestrōs servōsque convocābitis?   **3.** Fābulamne, Vergilī, tuam dē Trōiānōrum fugā multīs verbīs ōlim narrābās?   **4.** Magnōrum patriae deōrum bonō auxiliō nostra mala superābāmus.   **5.** Rēgīnam patriae Hecubam līberē laudābimus; bona rēgīna est.   **6.** Interim fēmina amīca puerīs puellīsque fābulam longam bene narrābit.   **7.** Deī deaeque dē caelō dōna portābunt, itaque nunc post multōs annōs bonam fortūnam spectābis. **8.** Sub oppidī portā amīcōs exspectābam, et iam trāns campōs ad portam ambulant.   **9.** Aedificābantne, mī fīlī, paucī agricolae magnam vīllam in campō ubi ambulābās?   **10.** Post fugam ex perīculīs nautae līberī ad terram pulchram nāvigābunt, ubi erunt altae silvae et campī agrīque lātī.

Translation Help

When you translate a Latin sentence start with the verb, because it will usually lead you to other words which you can fit in as you go.

1. If the verb is transitive, look for the accusative of the direct object. There will certainly be one.
2. Whatever kind of verb it is, next look for a subject in the nominative case and the same number as the verb. There may not be one.
3. If the verb is one of *saying, giving,* or *showing,* look for a dative of the indirect object. There may not be one.
4. If the verb is one of *making, naming,* or *choosing,* look for a predicate accusative (objective complement). There may not be one.
5. If the verb is a linking verb, look for the subjective complement. There will certainly be one, but it will not necessarily be a predicate nominative. It could be a genitive or an ablative of place where.

When you have found the verb and everything which goes with it, everything else in the sentence will be some kind of adjectival or adverbial expression.

READING

Developing Reading Skills

Some words you probably won't have to look up in this reading are **gladius** (if you know what a gladiator was), **rēgia** (look at the context and think of the meanings of **rēgīna** and **rēgnum**), and **ruīna**. If you're interested in astronomy you probably already know what an **āra** is.

The Fall of Troy

Aenēās Elissae fābulam narrābat: "Nunc ferī Graecī in oppidō erant. Lātē longēque Trōiānōs gladiīs obtruncābant. Obtruncābant et Priamum in rēgiā ante deī āram, ubi cum Hecubā rēgīnā deōrum auxilium exspectābat. Tum occupābant Hecubam et ab ārā portābant captīvam. Deinde et Cassandram

5 Priamī Hecubaeque fīliam ante Minervae āram occupābant. Fēminās Trōiānās līberōsque ad castra captīvōs portābant, et virōs obtruncābant.

"Interim cum Anchīsā eram et Creūsā et Ascaniō, meō fīliō. In somnīs nūntium dē Trōiae ruīnā portābat umbra virī magnī, Priamī fīlī et Creūsae germānī: 'Ō malam fortūnam Trōiānōrum miserōrum! Ligneō equō Graecī

10 iam Trōiam occupant. Nunc Trōiānī spectābimus flammās ruīnāsque rēgnī nostrī. Cūr nōn volās ex oppidō?' Statim convocō familiam ad oppidī portam, et paucīs verbīs clāmō: 'Fugā volābimus trāns campōs in silvās, quō deī auxilium portant! Semper deōs amābāmus et verbīs dōnīsque laudābāmus, itaque de caelō Trōiānōs spectābunt. Deōrum auxiliō fugam

15 parābimus.' "

---

7. In somnīs: *In sleeps* is what the Romans often say when they mean *in a dream.* **8. virī magnī:** The great hero whose ghost came to Aeneas was Hector, Troy's mainstay in the war. **9. Ō malam fortūnam:** The Romans usually exclaimed in the accusative; this use is called the *Accusative of Exclamation.* **11–12. convocō, clāmō:** At moments of heightened emotion or excitement, Roman authors often use the present tense instead of a past. This use is called the *Historical Present.*

The body of the Trojan hero Hector being dragged around the walls of Troy—from a Hellenistic tomb at Tyre

READING COMPREHENSION

1. Once the savage Greeks were in the town, what did they do? **2.** What famous people fell victim to the Greeks? **3.** What did Aeneas dream? **4.** "Ō malam fortūnam Trōiānōrum miserōrum!" What did the shade of Hector mean by these words? **5.** What did Aeneas decide to do?

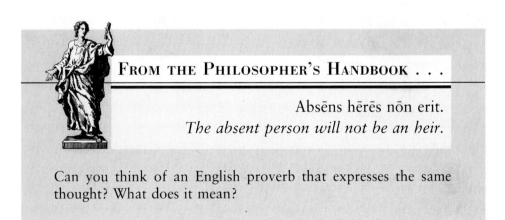

FROM THE PHILOSOPHER'S HANDBOOK . . .

Absēns hērēs nōn erit.
The absent person will not be an heir.

Can you think of an English proverb that expresses the same thought? What does it mean?

REVIEW 2

VOCABULARY DRILL

A. Give the genitive, gender, and meaning of these nouns:

annus	deus	fīlius	fuga	perīculum	rēgnum
caelum	dōnum	fortūna	līberī	porta	servus
campus	equus				

B. Give the other nominative forms, and the meanings, of these adjectives:

altus	ferus	līber	malus	multus	pulcher
amīcus	inimīcus	longus	meus	noster	tuus
bonus	lātus	magnus	miser	paucī	vester

C. Give the second principal part, and the meaning, of each verb:

aedificō	convocō	exspectō	superō	volō

D. Give the meaning of each preposition, and name the case(s) with which it is used:

ante	per	post	trāns

E. Give the meanings of these adverbs:

ante	iam	male	nunc	pulchrē	tum
bene	interim	miserē	ōlim	saepe	tunc
cūr	longē	nōn iam	post		

F. Give the meaning of the conjunctions **-que** and **sed.**

LISTENING AND SPEAKING

On The Farm

Lucius, like all townsmen, loves the life of the countryside. He asks Marcus to tell him about his farmhouse and his life in the fields.

LŪCIUS: Erisne diū, agricola, in nostrō oppidō? Nōn longē abest[1] hospitium[2] et crās ambulābis in agrōs ad vīllam tuam.

MĀRCUS: Non diū, amīce. Frūmentum ad farīnam[3] in pistrīnis[4] et vīnum in caupōnīs[5] virīs dabam et pecūniam post dabant. Nunc ex oppidī portīs ad vīllam meam volābō quod fēmina mea et līberī et familia pecūniam et nuntium dē vītā in oppidō exspectant.

LŪCIUS: Narrābisne, mī amīce, tuam vītam in terrā in agrīs et in vīllā?

MĀRCUS: Narrō. Mea vīlla est magna et pulchra. Parvulum[6] oppidum est. Sunt multī virī et fēminae in familiā. Virī in agrīs et in vīneīs[7] et in olīvētīs[8] lātē longēque hodiē labōrant. Fēminae et puellae in vīllā et in hortō[9] labōrant. Autumnō[10] familia in agrīs, brūmā[11] in vīllā labōrābit.

LŪCIUS: Cūr labōrābit familia autumnō?

MĀRCUS: Autumnō sunt multae operae[12] agricolārum. Frūmentum ex agrīs in horreum[13] portābimus. Et ūvās[14] ex vīneīs et olīvās[15] ex olīvētīs equī portābunt. Olīvas et ūvās prēlīs[16] dābimus. Ex olīvīs nostrīs est prīmae nōtae[17] oleum. Sūcus[18] uvārum in dōliīs[19] in cellā[20] diū stābit. Post annum vīnum bonum erit. Vīnum est sacrum dōnum Līberī,[21] deī vīnōrum!

A. Choose a partner. Read and translate the conversation for the class.

B. Answer the following questions in Latin.

1. Unde et quō Mārcus volābit? 2. Suntne paucī in familiā Mārcī? 3. Ubi virī lātē longēque labōrant? 4. Ubi labōrant fēminae et puellae? 5. Cūr sūcus uvārum in dōliīs in cellā diū stābit?

1. absum, abesse, āfuī, ——,—to be away
2. hospitium, -ī, n.—inn
3. farīna, -ae, f.—flour
4. pistrīnum, -ī, n.—flour mill, bakery
5. caupōna, -ae, f.—wine shop
6. parvulus, -a, -um—very little, tiny
7. vīnea, -ae, f.—vineyard
8. olīvētum, -ī, n.—olive grove
9. hortus, -ī, m.—garden
10. autumnus, -ī, m.—autumn
11. brūma, -ae, f.—the dead of winter
12. opera, -ae, f.—work, labor, service
13. horreum -ī, n.—barn, granary
14. ūva, -ae, f.—grape
15. olīva, -ae, f.—olive
16. prēlum, -ī, n.—press (for wine, etc.)
17. prīmae nōtae oleum—an oil of the first quality
18. sūcus, -ī, m.—juice
19. dōlium, -ī, n.—storage vats
20. cella, -ae, f.—storeroom
21. Līber, -ī, m.—Liber, a Roman name for Bacchus

85

TRACES OF ROMAN CIVILIZATION TODAY

United States—Washington, D.C.

Pierre Charles L'Enfant, a French engineer and architect, was commissioned by George Washington to design the new capital that was named in his honor. L'Enfant's plan is considered the country's outstanding achievement in municipal planning. The site of the Capitol Building was selected as the focal point with streets and avenues radiating from it like the spokes of a wheel.

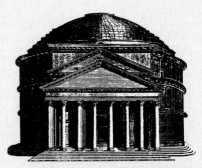

The Roman Pantheon

Washington, D.C.

So, although the plan of the city is due to this man's genius, much of the beauty of the architecture drew its inspiration from classical antiquity. For example:

The original model for the Capitol Building was the Roman Pantheon. The building shows the richness of early classical influence with its circular shape, roof dome, and rows of tall Corinthian columns. Even its interior, the Rotunda, shows a striking resemblance to the interior of the Pantheon.

The façade of Union Station is said to be based on the Arch of Constantine. Its vaulted passenger concourse is the largest room in the world and can hold 50,000 people.

The National Archives Building has many classical decorations including the "Guardians of the Portal," two figures in Roman armor.

The Supreme Court Building has an eight-columned portico in Corinthian style and a pediment with classical sculpture.

Pennsylvania Avenue has sometimes been called Washington's "Via Appia." Truly, ancient Rome lives on today in our beautiful capital city!

Capitol Rotunda

National Archives Building

Supreme Court Building

Union Station

Perfect Tense; Particles; Correlative Conjunctions

An allegorical figure of peace represented as a mother with two children—Ara Pacis, Rome

YOUR BIRTH AND INFANCY

When a baby was born, it was placed on the floor at the feet of its father, who recognized its legitimacy by picking it up. For the first eight days of its life it was thought to be vulnerable to evil spirits or the evil eye. Therefore the goddess Juno and the god Hercules were invoked to protect it. A couch for Juno and a table of food for Hercules were set up in the atrium. On the ninth day (**diēs lustricus**) the child, if male, was given a name, and a locket (**bulla**) containing charms against the evil eye was hung around his neck. Girls were not given names of their own, but were simply called by the family name in its feminine form.

The Romans in antiquity were unique in using family names. Just as we do, every Roman citizen had a given name (**praenōmen**) and a family name (**nōmen** or **nōmen gentīle**). There were only eighteen Roman first names, and since the same names recurred in the same family, there were soon many men with identical names. Hence, at least among the upper classes, a third name, the **cognōmen,** was added to distinguish one branch of a family from another. Some men had more than one **cognōmen,** e.g. **Pūblius Cornēlius Scīpiō Āfricānus Aemiliānus.** This man was adopted from the Aemilius family into the Scipio branch of the Cornelius family, and distinguished himself in Africa in the war against Carthage. A woman had her family name only; i.e., all of Scipio's adopted sisters, as well as all of his daughters, would have had the same name, Cornelia.

When a slave was freed, he adopted the **praenōmen** and **nōmen** of his master, keeping his own name as a **cognōmen.** Hence if P. Cornelius Scipio freed a slave named Syrus, his new name would be P. Cornelius Syrus.

A host of minor deities presided over the child both at its birth and during its growing stages. For example: Ossipaga strengthened its bones, and Carna put flesh on them. When it was weaned, Pota helped it learn to drink, then

(Continued)

A Phrase to Use

in locō parentis
in the place of a parent

Educa taught it to eat. Cuba was there when the baby was moved from a cradle to a bed. Additional household gods, Levana and Statanus, aided it to sit upright and to stand. Adeona was there when it began to walk to its parents, and Abeona assisted it to walk away from them. Fabulinus helped it to learn to talk.

None of these minor deities had any other function, so Roman parents could rest assured that their infant was well protected and cared for during every aspect of its growth.

(*below*) Sarcophagus of M. Cornelius Statius—Louvre Museum, Paris. The scene shows the education of a child from infancy to boyhood.

Ancient Rome Lives On . . .

How does our modern society underline the importance of a man's name over a woman's name?

FORMS

PRINCIPAL PARTS OF VERBS

As you learned in Lesson 2, a Latin verb has four principal parts. Of these, so far, you have been memorizing the first two, which give you the information you need to form the three tenses of the present system: the present, the imperfect, and the future. The other two principal parts will give you the stems for the other three tenses: the perfect, the pluperfect, and the future perfect. The four principal parts of **vocō** are:

vocō, vocāre, vocāvī, vocātum

All the verbs you have learned so far form their principal parts in the same way, except for **sum,** whose principal parts are **sum, esse, fuī, futūrus.**

PERFECT TENSE

The perfect active stem is found by dropping the -ī ending from the third principal part. The perfect stem of **vocō** is **vocāv-.** A special set of personal endings is added to this stem to form the active voice of the perfect tense.

PERSONAL ENDINGS, PERFECT ACTIVE

	SINGULAR	PLURAL
1ST PERSON	-ī	-imus
2D PERSON	-istī	-istis
3D PERSON	-it	-ērunt (*or* ēre)*

---

*The variant ending -**ēre**, although frequently used by Roman authors, will not appear in the Practice sections of this book.

The perfect tense is the only one of the six tenses which does not use the usual personal endings -**ō** or -**m, -s, -t, -mus, -tis,** and -**nt.**

PERFECT ACTIVE, FIRST CONJUGATION

vocāvī	*I have called* *I called* *I did call*	vocāv**imus**	*we have called* *we called* *we did call*
vocāv**istī**	*you have called* *you called* *you did call*	vocāv**istis**	*you have called* *you called* *you did call*
vocāv**it**	*he, (she, it) has called* *he, (she, it) called* *he, (she, it) did call*	vocāv**ērunt (-ēre)**	*they have called* *they called* *they did call*

PERFECT ACTIVE OF SUM

fuī	*I have been* *I was*	fuimus	*we have been* *we were*
fuistī	*you have been* *you were*	fuistis	*you have been* *you were*
fuit	*he, (she, it) has been* *he, (she, it) was*	fuērunt (-ēre)	*they have been* *they were*

SYNTAX

USES OF THE PERFECT TENSE

The perfect tense in Latin has the same meaning as two English tenses, the present perfect and the past. This is why each form is given three translations: *I have called* (present perfect), *I called,* and *I did call* (past). It is important to remember that these two English tenses are not interchangeable. Think of the difference between "I have come to see you" and "I came to see you." The first implies "and here I am," the second implies "at some time in the past." There are many sentences in the exercises in which either translation will do, but others will have adverbs or subordinate clauses which indicate that one or the other translation is more appropriate.

Ad oppidum modo ambulāvī.
I have just now walked to town.

Ad oppidum herī ambulāvī.
I walked to town yesterday (not *I have walked to town yesterday.*)

▇ INTERROGATIVE PARTICLES

A particle is a part of speech which cannot be translated by any particular word, but indicates what would be shown by punctuation or tone of voice in English.

1. You have already learned the enclitic particle **-ne,** which asks a yes-or-no question.

    Nāvigābisne ad Asiam?   *Will you sail to Asia?*

2. You have also seen that when **-ne** is attached to **nōn,** making **nōnne,** it asks a question which expects the answer *Yes.*

    Nōnne nāvigābis ad Asiam?   *Won't you sail to Asia?*

3. The particle **num,** which comes at the beginning of the sentence, expects the answer *No,* or expresses some surprise or indignation on the part of the speaker.

    Num nāvigābis ad Asiam?   *You won't sail to Asia, will you?*
    Surely you won't sail to Asia?

FROM THE PHILOSOPHER'S HANDBOOK . . .

Quōs amor vērus tenuit, tenēbit.
Those whom true love has held, it will
go on holding.
—SENECA

What does this mean? How can you apply it not only to personal relationships but also to other areas in your life?

4. The particle **utrum** is used when a question requires one answer or the other. In such a question *or* is expressed by **an**, *or not* by **annōn**.

> Utrum nāvigābis ad Asiam an Eurōpam?
> *Will you sail to Asia, or to Europe?*
> Utrum nāvigābis ad Asiam annōn?
> *Will you sail to Asia, or not?*

WAYS OF EXPRESSING *OR* IN LATIN

Aut is the usual word for *or* in statements, but when **aut** is used to connect questions it is best translated by *and*.

> Nāvigābisne ad Asiam? **aut** oppidane ibi spectābis?
> *Will you sail to Asia? **and** will you look at the towns there?*

Vel in statements means *or, or even, or possibly.* In questions it is used with **-ne** if the answer could be *yes* or *no*.

> Nāvigābis**ne** ad Asiam **vel** Eurōpam?
> *Will you sail to Asia or (possibly) to Europe?*

An and **annōn** are used with **utrum** if the question could not be answered by *yes* or *no*.

> **Utrum** nāvigābis ad Asiam **an** Eurōpam?
> *Will you sail to Asia, or to Europe?*

> **Utrum** nāvigābis ad Asiam **annōn**?
> *Will you sail to Asia, or not?*

■ CORRELATIVE CONJUNCTIONS

Aut . . . aut . . . and vel . . . vel . . . both mean *either . . . or . . .* (similarly et . . . et . . . means *both . . . and . . .*).

Aut ad Asiam **aut** ad Eurōpam nāvigābo.
  *I shall sail **either** to Europe **or** to Asia.*
Vel ad Asiam vel ad Eurōpam nāvigābō.
  *I shall sail **either** to Europe **or** possibly to Asia.*
Et ad Asiam et ad Eurōpam nāvigābō.
  *I shall sail **both** to Europe **and** to Asia.*

VOCABULARY

BASIC WORDS

īnsula, -ae, f. *island*
lingua, -ae, f. *tongue, language*
umbra, -ae, f. *shadow, shade, ghost*

parvus, -a, -um *little, small*

dō, dare, dedī, datum *give*
stō, stāre, stetī, statum *stand, stand still*

crās (adv.) *tomorrow*
herī (adv.) *yesterday*
hodiē (adv.) *today*
ibi (adv.) *there, in that place*
modo (adv.) *only, just; just now*

Note: Notice that **dō** and **stō** do not have the same kind of perfect stem as the other first conjugation verbs. **Dō** has **ded-** (instead of dāv-) and **stō** has **stet-** (instead of stāv-).

Dō is also irregular in that the -a of its stem is short except in the present active second person singular: **dās**, but **damus, datis, dabam, dabō**, etc.

LEARNING ENGLISH THROUGH LATIN

insulate *to detach from the rest; to separate*
isolate *to set apart from others; to place alone*
linguistic *pertaining to languages*
multilingual *speaking many languages*
procrastinate *to put off doing something to a future time; to postpone*
stable (adjective) *firm, steady*
status *position, rank, standing*

PRACTICE

A. Use an English dictionary which includes word derivations to answer these questions:

1. *Insulate* and *isolate* have very similar meanings and are derived from the same Latin word. What does the meaning of this Latin word have to do with the English meanings? Why are they spelled differently?   **2.** What connection does the meaning of *date* have with the meaning of **dō**? **3.** Explain the derivation of *dative* and *umbrella*.   **4.** *Stance, station, stable* (the noun, not the adjective), and *status* by derivation all mean *the act of standing;* how do they differ in their actual English meanings?

B. Pronounce and give both English translations (present perfect and past):

1. narrāvērunt   **2.** volāvī   **3.** ambulāvistis   **4.** portāvistī   **5.** spectāvimus **6.** parāvit

C. Name the tense, person, and number; then change to the perfect tense, keeping the same person and number:

1. aedificābās   **2.** exspectābimus   **3.** parant   **4.** erō   **5.** stābit **6.** occupābātis   **7.** convocās   **8.** dabāmus   **9.** superābunt   **10.** estis

D. Conjugate in the perfect active, giving both kinds of translation for each form:

1. exspectō   **2.** stō   **3.** convocō   **4.** dō   **5.** superō

E. Choose the correct translation(s):

1. volābat it flew, he was flying, she used to fly   **2. aedificāvistis** you built, you were building, you have built   **3. portābis** you carried, you were carrying, you will carry   **4. parāmus** we prepare, we used to prepare, we are preparing   **5. fuērunt** they will be, they were, they are   **6. occupāvī** he seized, I seized, he has seized   **7. nāvigābunt** they sailed, they sail, they will sail   **8. spectābō** I was looking at, I shall look at, I used to look at **9. ambulāvit** he walked, she walks, she has walked   **10. narrābās** you used to tell, you will tell, you told

F. Translate:

1. Are you praising the woman and her daughter?   **2.** Are you praising the woman, or her daughter?   **3.** Are you praising the woman or (possibly) her daughter?   **4.** You aren't praising the woman and her daughter, are you?   **5.** Aren't you praising the woman and her daughter?   **6.** Are you praising the woman, and do you love her daughter?

READING

The Departure from Troy

Vir Trōiānus Poenae rēgīnae fugam ex Trōiā narrābat: "Fuimus Trōiānī, fuit Trōia. Nunc ad oppidī portam ambulāvimus. Anchīsēs claudus erat et nōn bene ambulābat. Itaque Anchīsam claudum umerīs portābam, et parvus Ascanius Creūsaque post ambulābant. Iam ante portam stetimus, et fēminam meam exspectābam; sed ibi nōn erat Creūsa. Saepe clāmābam, 'Creūsa! Ubi,   5 Creūsa, es, aut quō ambulāvistī? Nōnne ambulābās cum familiā? Num dē viā errāvistī?' Rūrsus in oppidum volāvī, ubi in viīs perīcula multa et mala spectābam, sed Creūsam nōn spectāvī. Dēnique Creūsae umbram super terram spectāvī.

"Sōlātium miserō virō dedit: 'Bona Dea, Aenēa, tuam fēminam hīc in   10 Asiā servat. Deae famula semper erō. Sed cūr stās? Anchīsēs fīlium ad portam exspectat. Exspectat Trōiānōs et Hesperia, ubi nova fēmina, rēgīnae fīlia, erit tua.'

"Ā portā ad nāvigia ambulābāmus miserī. Nunc via nostra, nostra fuga, erat ad Hesperiam. Sed Hesperia ubi erat? Utrum in Eurōpā erat annōn?   15 Ignōrābāmus; sed interim ad Thrāciam super altum secundīs ventīs nāvigābāmus."

◼ READING COMPREHENSION

1. Describe the departure of Aeneas from Troy.   **2.** Why did he have to rush back to the town?   **3.** How did Creusa console her unhappy husband? **4.** "Exspectat Trōiānōs et Hesperia." What did Creusa foretell by these words?

---

1. fuimus, fuit: Since the perfect describes an action as completed, it can show that it is no longer taking place: *We no longer exist as Trojans; Troy no longer exists.*   **7. multa** et **mala:** In both Latin and English, adjectives may be connected by *and* or not: a *long wide plain* or *a long and wide plain.* However, English never uses *and* to connect *many* with another adjective; Latin always does.   **10. virō:** Remember that **vir** can mean *man, hero,* or *husband.* **Bona Dea:** *the Good Goddess* was probably the terrible goddess Cybele, also called the Great Mother. She was called *Good* to keep her from using her terrifying powers.

Roman mosaic showing a cat seizing a quail, with two ducks below

YOUR DAY

Because artificial lighting was poor, the Roman family rose at dawn. The father, if he was a person of importance, began the day by receiving his clients (**clientēs**) in the **tablīnum** and **ātrium.** This was called the **salūtātiō,** and was followed by the **dēductiō,** as the clients escorted him down to the Forum, the center for both business and politics. His importance would be shown by the number of clients which accompanied him. Every magnate was the protector (**patrōnus**) of a number of clients, poorer friends or freed slaves, whom he kept from starvation and represented in court if they were in trouble. In return they performed for him such services as they were capable of, including the **salūtātiō** and **dēductiō.** After his visit to the Forum the **patrōnus** was at leisure, or could deal with family affairs, in the afternoon. His wife, having laid out the day's work for the slaves (and even poor households had at least one slave), was free to spend the rest of the day in paying and receiving calls.

The children's day was spent in schooling and play. Roman children played with many of the same kinds of toys children use today: rattles (**crepundia**), stick horses, jacks (using knucklebones, **tālī**), dolls (**pūpae**), tops (**turbinēs**), hoops (**trochī**), and balls (**pilae**). The boys might also pretend to be gladiators or soldiers, sometimes with miniature weapons and armor. There is also evidence that children might have had small chariots, pulled by dogs or goats, for racing.

Simple games included "Odd or Even?" (**pār impār**), "How Many Fingers Do I Hold Up?" (**Bucca, bucca, quot sunt hīc?**), and **micātiō,** a game like the modern Italian mora. More sophisticated games, which were played by both children and adults, were called "Twelve Lines" (**duodecim scrīpta**) and "Little Bandits" (**latrunculī**). These were like backgammon and chess, respectively.

(Continued)

There were also ball games played rather like field hockey and soccer, and a three-cornered catch called **trigōn,** in which as many balls as possible were kept going at one time. All three players threw and caught with both hands, at a rapid pace. Of the two "officials" needed for the game, one kept score by counting dropped balls and the other picked them up and threw them back into the game.

(*below left*) Fresco showing a pet terrier, in The House of the Epigrams, Pompeii—National Museum, Naples   (*below right*) A dog collar with a tag advertising a reward for the dog's return

ANCIENT ROME LIVES ON . . .

How does a modern middle-class family's day differ from that of a Roman family?

FORMS

◼ PLUPERFECT TENSE

The Pluperfect Tense (called the Past Perfect in English) is formed by adding the tense-sign -erā- to the perfect stem, then adding the personal endings. The -ā of the tense-sign is shortened before -m, -t, and -nt.

PLUPERFECT ACTIVE, FIRST CONJUGATION

vocāv**eram**	*I had called*	vocāv**erāmus**	*we had called*
vocāv**erās**	*you had called*	vocāv**erātis**	*you had called*
vocāv**erat**	*he, (she, it) had called*	vocāv**erant**	*they had called*

◼ FUTURE PERFECT TENSE

The Future Perfect Tense is formed by adding the tense-sign -eri- to the perfect stem, and then the personal endings, dropping the -i of the tense-sign before -ō.

FUTURE PERFECT ACTIVE, FIRST CONJUGATION

vocāv**erō**	*I shall have called*	vocāv**erimus**	*we shall have called*
vocāv**eris**	*you will have called*	vocāv**eritis**	*you will have called*
vocāv**erit**	*he, (she, it) will have called*	vocāv**erint**	*they will have called*

A wicker tray and a toy clay horse—Royal Ontario Museum, Toronto

SYNTAX

USE OF THE PLUPERFECT AND FUTURE PERFECT

These two tenses have the same uses as the corresponding tenses in English.

The Pluperfect Tense represents an action as having already taken place at some point in the past.

> Nautās quod bene pugnāverant laudāvit.
> *He praised the sailors because they had fought well.*

Here the action of fighting took place before the action of praising.

The Future Perfect tense represents an action as already having taken place at some point in the future.

> Dōna dederitis ubi auxilium portābunt.
> *When they bring aid you will already have given the gifts.*

Here the action of giving will already have taken place before the action of bringing.

CLAUSES

In Latin every verb is considered to have its own clause. If a sentence has two verbs, then it has two clauses. These will be either two principal clauses, or one principal clause and one subordinate clause.

Two Principal Clauses

If a sentence has two principal clauses, they will be connected by a coordinating conjunction. That is, somewhere between the two verbs there will be a Latin word meaning *and, but, for, or,* or *nor.*

> Rēgīnam laudāmus, **nam** bona est.
> *We praise the queen, **for** she is good.*
> Rēgīnam laudāmus, **sed** bona nōn est.
> *We praise the queen, **but** she is not good.*

A rabbit sniffing figs, from a fresco in Herculaneum

COORDINATING CONJUNCTIONS

Meaning *and*:

atque or ac	*and* (emphatic), *and also, and even*
et	*and*
itaque	*and so*
-que	*and* (unemphatic), *'n'*

Meaning *but:*

at	*but, yet, but yet*
autem (postpositive)[1]	*but, but on the other hand, however*
sed	*but*

Meaning *for:*

enim (postpositive)	*for*
nam	*for*

Meaning *or:*

an	*or* (only in questions, with **utrum**)
aut	*or*
vel	*or, or even, or possibly*

Meaning *nor:*

neque or nec[2]	*nor*

One Principal Clause and One Subordinate Clause

In the following sentence there are two clauses, one principal and one subordinate.

Oppidum quō ambulās magnum est.
The town to which you are walking is large.

The principal clause is **Oppidum magnum est,** *The town is large.* This is a sentence, and can stand by itself. The subordinate clause, **quō ambulās,** *to which you are walking,* is not a sentence and cannot stand by itself. It is easy to recognize a subordinate clause: unlike a principal clause, it cannot stand by itself.

1. A postpositive conjunction never comes first in its clause; it usually comes second.   2. Neque (nec) . . . neque (nec) . . . means *neither . . . nor . . .*

**WORDS WHICH INTRODUCE
SUBORDINATE CLAUSES**

nisi	*if . . . not, unless*
quō	*to which place, to which*
quod	*because*
sī	*if*
ubi	*when, where*
unde	*from which place, from which*
ut	*as*

A Roman boy in a toga, 1st century A.D.

VOCABULARY

BASIC WORDS

amīcitia, -ae, f. *friendship*

āra, -ae, f. *altar*

dominus, -ī, m. *lord, master* (of slaves, of a nation, etc.)

frūmentum, -ī, n. *grain*

inopia, -ae, f. *need, lack*

locus, -ī, m. (*plural* loca, locōrum, n.) *place*

magister, magistrī, m. *master* (of a school or ship), *teacher, captain, steersman*

populus, -ī, m. *a nation, a people*

socius, -ī, m. *ally, comrade*

sacer, sacra, sacrum *sacred, holy; accursed*

nūntiō, -āre, -āvī, -ātum *announce, report*

pugnō, -āre, -āvī, -ātum *fight*

diū (adv.) *long, for a long time*

Notes: 1. **Populus** never means *people* as a plural of person. *Many people* is just **multī**; **multī populī** means *many peoples* (i.e., *many nations*).

2. **Pugnō** is intransitive in Latin: *We are fighting the men* must be translated **Cum virīs pugnāmus.**

■ LEARNING ENGLISH THROUGH LATIN

amity	*peaceful relations, friendship*
dominate	*to rule or control*
enunciate	*to speak clearly and distinctly*
locale	*a place; a setting for a story or play*
magisterial	*pertaining to a master, teacher, or other person in authority*
populace	*the common people; the masses*
pugnacious	*quarrelsome; ready to fight*
sociable	*enjoying the company of others, agreeable*

▬ PRACTICE ▬

A. Fill in the blanks with the correct form of one of the words from the list of English Derivatives:

1. He ____ his words so poorly that no one could understand him. 2. Her views were not accepted by the ____, so she was not elected. 3. The ____ of the comedy was a small village in southern France. 4. She ____ the whole meeting and wouldn't let anyone else speak. 5. He is so ____ that he is getting to be the class bully.

B. Show the connection of each of the following words to a Latin word in the lesson vocabulary:

1. location   2. popular   3. society

C. Translate:

1. pugnābit   2. fuerātis   3. ambulāverō   4. nāvigāvit   5. dō
6. nūntiāvimus   7. stābās   8. laudāverint   9. spectāverās   10. aedificābunt

D. Translate:

1. you (*sing.*) are carrying   2. we shall fly   3. they have lived   4. she had called together   5. I prepare   6. you (*pl.*) loved   7. I had called   8. you (*sing.*) will have awaited   9. we shall have told   10. he was seizing

E. You have now learned all of the six Latin tenses: present, imperfect, future, perfect, pluperfect, and future perfect. Conjugate these verbs in all six tenses, with meanings:

1. pugnō   2. sum   3. dō

F. Each of these sentences has two clauses. Separate the clauses and tell whether each clause is a principal clause or a subordinate clause:

1. Rēgīnam laudāmus quod bona est.   2. Rēgīnam laudāmus, nam bona est.   3. Rēgīnam nōn laudāmus nisi bona est.   4. Ut ad oppidum ambulābat, vīllās spectābat.   5. Ad oppidum ambulat ac vīllās spectat.   6. In agrōs ambulat ubi vīllās spectābit.   7. Nōn ambulātis, sed nāvigātis.   8. Neque ambulātis neque nāvigātis.   9. Utrum ambulābātis an nāvigābātis?   10. Aut ambulābitis aut nāvigābitis.

Translation Help

As the sentences in this book become longer and more complex, you will save time if you approach them systematically:

A. Count the verbs. This tells you how many clauses there are.

B. Separate the clauses, determining which are principal and which subordinate. Remember that a subordinate clause begins with the word (**nisi, quō, quod, ubi,** etc.) which introduces it and usually ends with its verb. Remember also that clauses may be nested one inside another in a way not usual in English.

C. Start with the verb of the principal clause (the first principal clause, if there are more than one). Determine its tense, voice, person, and number. Translate it. Determine whether it is transitive, intransitive, or a linking verb. If the verb is transitive,

   1. find its direct object (a noun in the accusative).
      a. if it is a verb of *giving, saying,* or *showing,* see if there is an indirect object (a noun in the dative).
      b. if it is a verb of *making, naming,* or *choosing,* see if there is an objective complement.
   2. see if there is an expressed subject (a noun in the nominative and in the same number as the verb).

   If the verb is a linking verb,

   1. see if there is an expressed subject,
   2. look for the subjective complement (most likely a predicate adjective or noun in the nominative, but possibly some other case, e.g. **Tēla sunt Aenēae,** *The weapons are Aeneas'*).

D. Finally, translate the adjectival and/or adverbial modifiers that make up the rest of the clause.

E. Apply the same techniques to each of the other clauses in turn.

READING

Developing Reading Skills

Guess at some of the unfamiliar words in this reading by thinking of *antique, gubernatorial* (what are gubernatorial elections?), *migrate, ramification, and sepulcher.* Have you studied chemistry? If so, you will know which element has the symbol *Au* and why.

The Bleeding Branches

Aenēās Trōiānōrum fugam ab Asiā ad Thrāciam narrābat: "Trōiānī cum Graecīs pulchrē pugnāverāmus, Graecī autem Trōiānōs superāverant. Nunc in Thrāciā erāmus, quō ab Asiā nāvigāverāmus. Thrāciae dominus socius populī Trōiānī diū erat, inter populōs enim erat amīcitia; itaque Polydōrus Priamī fīlius hūc ante bellum nāvigāverat cum multō aurō. Priamus Polydōrum 5
dominō Thrāciae mandāverat verbīs bonīs: 'Sī ferī Graecī Trōiam occupā-
verint, nōn occupābunt et aurum, nam meus fīlius aurum servābit salvum.'

"Ut locus bonus erat, 'Hīc,' clāmāvī, 'oppidum nostrum novum aedificābimus!' Portābant Trōiānī sacra dōna deīs, itaque āram aedificābam. Sed
ubi in virgulta unde rāmōs ad āram portābāmus ambulāveram, magnum 10
malum spectāvī: rāmī cruentī erant! Ibi erat et umbra miserī Polydōrī. Paucīs
verbīs miseram fābulam narrāvit: sacer Thrāciae dominus Polydōrum ob-
truncāverat atque aurum occupāverat. Virgulta in sepulcrō Polydōrī erant.

"Anchīsēs Trōiānōs convocāvit: 'Hīc nōn stābimus; ad Crētam nāvigābimus, patriam antīquam unde antīquī Trōiānī ad Asiam migrāvērunt. Deī 15
Trōiānōs ad Crētam vocant. Ibi oppidum nostrum aedificābimus.'

"Itaque ā Thrāciā ad Crētam magistrī nāvigia gubernābant."

---

4. erat: translate *had been* (not *was*); (False Pluperfect)   **6. occupāverint:** English uses the present in this kind of clause: *seize* (not *will have seized*).   **12. sacer Thrāciae dominus:** The accursed Lord of Thrace eventually paid the penalty for the robbery and murder. When Hecuba passed by on her way to Greece with her captor Ulysses, she scratched his eyes out.   **13. virgulta:** The thicket had grown up from the shafts of the spears with which Polydorus was killed.

Mosaic of a ship in harbor, with its gangplank extended to the harbor mole—
Museo della Civiltà Romana, Rome

■ READING COMPREHENSION

1. Where did Aeneas sail to from Asia?   **2.** Who had sailed there previously?
3. What had been entrusted to this person?   **4.** What did Aeneas discover
when he was building an altar?   **5.** What sad story did this reveal?
6. Where did Anchises decide to go to build the new town?

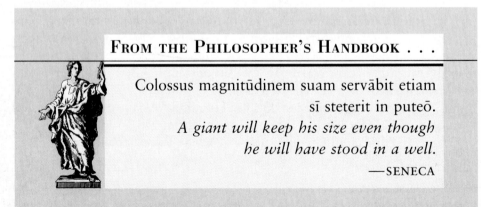

FROM THE PHILOSOPHER'S HANDBOOK . . .

Colossus magnitūdinem suam servābit etiam
sī steterit in puteō.
*A giant will keep his size even though
he will have stood in a well.*
—SENECA

What is your interpretation of this saying? Can you cite a specific
example?

LESSON 11

Passive Voice; Present System;
Ablative of Personal Agent

Roman mosaic showing the school of Plato in Athens—National Museum, Naples

YOUR EDUCATION

There were no free schools, but parents who could afford it paid for elementary education for both boys and girls. It began with reading, writing, and arithmetic. Roman history was taught through literature, and the study of Greek language and literature was also begun early. The children of the wealthy might be taught at home by tutors (often Greek slaves). Some of the great houses of Pompeii have schoolrooms where we can see scratched on the walls alphabets, both Latin and Greek, tags from Virgil, geometric figures, complaints about the difficulty of Cicero, and insults directed at the tutor.

There were also schools (**lūdī**), held by individual teachers in hired halls or in the open air. A child was accompanied to school by a personal slave, the **paedagōgus,** who would keep him from harm, carry his books and notebooks, and sometimes supervise his studies.

The pages (**pāginae**) of books (**librī, volūmina**) were glued side by side to form a long strip which was rolled from one roller to another as one passed from page to page. Notebooks (**tabellae, pugillārēs**) were small wooden frames filled with wax which could be written on by a **stilus,** a stick or metal rod pointed at one end and flattened at the other (for erasures).

For an equivalent to our high schools, upper-class boys aged twelve to fifteen were sent to schools run by Greek teachers to learn rhetoric. Girls of the same class might pursue the study of Greek and Latin literature with tutors at home.

There were no official educational requirements for the teacher, who was always male. He might be a slave or freedman of the proprietor of the school, or he might be in business for himself. The teachers were strict disciplinarians and practiced corporal punishment.

Upper-class boys destined for a political career continued their education longer than girls, and went to "college" by attaching themselves to some

(Continued)

well-known orator to learn oratory and law. If they planned to become writers, they might also be sent to Athens or Rhodes to learn philosophy. Music and athletics, the core of Greek education, were considered unnecessary, even unsuitable, for good Romans. Upper-class boys, however, did learn horseback riding and sword-fighting.

(below left) Pompeian fresco showing Paquius Proculus and his wife with notebook, stilus, and book
(below right) A stylus and writing tablet

ANCIENT ROME LIVES ON . . .

Why does it take us longer to finish our formal education than it did the Romans?

FORMS

PASSIVE VOICE, PRESENT SYSTEM

In the present system (present, imperfect, and future) the passive voice is conjugated like the active voice, but with a different set of personal endings.

PERSONAL ENDINGS, PASSIVE

	SINGULAR	PLURAL
1ST PERSON	-or, -r	-mur
2D PERSON	-ris, (-re)	-minī
3D PERSON	-tur	-ntur

1. The ending **-or** is used in the passive where the ending **-ō** is used in the active. The ending **-r** is used in the passive where the ending **-m** is used in the active.
2. The 2d singular endings **-ris** and **-re** are used interchangeably; **-ris** is more common.

Vocō is conjugated as follows in the passive voice of the present system.

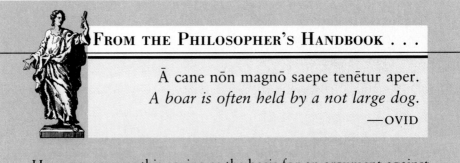

FROM THE PHILOSOPHER'S HANDBOOK . . .

Ā cane nōn magnō saepe tenētur aper.
A boar is often held by a not large dog.

—OVID

How can you use this saying as the basis for an argument against inferiority complexes?

PRESENT PASSIVE, FIRST CONJUGATION

vocor	*I am called*	vocāmur	*we are called*
	I am being called		*we are being called*
vocāris (-re)	*you are called*	vocāminī	*you are called*
	you are being called		*you are being called*
vocātur	*he, (she, it) is called*	vocāntur	*they are called*
	he, (she, it) is being called		*they are being called*

IMPERFECT PASSIVE, FIRST CONJUGATION

vocābar	*I was being called*	vocābāmur	*we were being called*
vocābāris (-re)	*you were being called*	vocābāminī	*you were being called*
vocābātur	*he, (she, it) was being called*	vocābantur	*they were being called*

FUTURE PASSIVE, FIRST CONJUGATION

vocābor	*I shall be called*	vocābimur	*we shall be called*
vocāberis (-re)	*you will be called*	vocābiminī	*you will be called*
vocābitur	*he, (she, it) will be called*	vocābuntur	*they will be called*

Notice that in the future passive the **-bi-** tense sign is changed to **-be-** before **-ris** and **-re.**

SYNTAX

■ VOICES

In Latin, as in English, verbs have two voices, the active voice and the passive voice. The active voice shows that the subject of the verb performs the action of the verb. The passive voice shows that the subject receives the action. In other words the direct object of an active verb becomes the subject when the verb is passive:

> Fābulam narrat.
> *He is telling a story.*
> Fābula narrātur.
> *A story is being told.*

Intransitive verbs, and the verb **sum,** which do not take direct objects, are not normally used in the passive.

ABLATIVE OF PERSONAL AGENT

With an active verb the person by whom the action is performed is the subject, and is expressed by the nominative. With a passive verb the person by whom the action is performed is expressed by the ablative with the preposition **ā** or **ab,** since the Romans thought of the action as coming *from* the agent.

> Poēta fābulam narrat.
> *The poet is telling a story.*
> Fābula ā poētā narrātur.
> *A story is being told by the poet.*

You can remember that the Ablative of Personal Agent needs three p's: a passive, a person, and a preposition. This will keep you from confusing the ablative of personal agent with the ablative of means.

> Ā deīs servābitur.   *She will be saved by the gods.*
> Deōrum auxiliō servābitur.
> *She will be saved by the help of the gods.*

PREDICATE NOMINATIVE WITH PASSIVE VERBS

A verb of *making, naming,* or *choosing* (which may take a predicate accusative when it is active) may take a predicate nominative when it is passive.

ACTIVE: Fīliam vocābat Helenam.
           He used to call his daughter Helen.
PASSIVE: Fīlia vocābātur Helena.
           The daughter used to be called Helen.

VOCABULARY

BASIC WORDS

cōpia, -ae, f. *supply; plenty; opportunity*
fāma, -ae, f. *rumor, report; reputation*
īra, -ae, f. *anger, rage*
tēlum, -ī, n. *weapon, spear*

laetus, -a, -um *joyful, glad*
novus, -a, -um *new*
parātus, -a, -um *ready, prepared*

clāmō, -āre, -āvī, -ātum *shout*

dēmōnstrō, -āre, -āvī, -ātum
  point out, show
labōrō, -āre, -āvī, -ātum *toil,*
  suffer, be in difficulties
līberō, -āre, -āvī, -ātum *free, set*
  free
servō, -āre, -āvī, -ātum *save;*
  keep, guard

rūrsus (adv.) *back; again*
semper (adv.) *always; continually; still*

LEARNING ENGLISH THROUGH LATIN

copious	*plentiful, abundant*
demonstrable	*capable of being shown or proved*
elaborate (verb)	*to develop in great detail*
exclamation	*an abrupt, forceful utterance; an outcry*
irate	*angry*
liberate	*to set free, release*
novice	*a person new to a particular activity*
reservation	*something set aside and kept until called for; a limiting condition—"I have reservations about this procedure."*

PRACTICE

A. Write an original sentence that uses two or more words from the above list of English derivatives.

B. Find these English derivatives:

1. Check your dictionary and find more derivatives which come from **dēmōnstrō.** Show how they are related in meaning to **dēmōnstrō.**   **2.** What other derivatives can you find that come from **clāmō**? The English forms of the stems will be *-claim* and *clama-*. (You will find the list of prefixes in the Appendix helpful.) **3.** What is the relation of the English word *reservation* to the Latin **servō**? What other derivatives can you find from this word? Remember to look for forms in *-serve, -serva-,* and *-servat-,* and to check your list with a dictionary to be sure that your words are in fact derived from **servō**.

C. Change from passive to active, keeping the same tense, person, and number, translating both the passive and the active form:

1. exspectāberis   **2.** spector   **3.** laudābāminī   **4.** servābātur
5. līberābimur

D. Choose the correct translation(s) for these verb forms:

1. occupābat she was seized, she was seizing, she seized   **2. amāberis** you will be loved, you were loving, you were being loved   **3. portātis** you are carried, you are carrying, you carry   **4. dēmōnstrābor** I was pointing out, I shall be pointed out, I was being pointed out   **5. parāris** he is being prepared, you were prepared, you are being prepared   **6. laudābimur** we shall be praised, we shall praise, we used to be praised   **7. līberāminī** you were freed, you are freed, you are freeing   **8. exspectābantur** they were awaiting, they were awaited, they were being awaited   **9. servābāmur** it was saved, we were being saved, we were saving   **10. spectābāris** you are being looked at, you were being looked at, you were looking at

E. Change from active to passive, keeping the same tense, person, and number, and translating both the active and the passive:

1. portābimus   **2.** parant   **3.** occupās   **4.** demonstrābātis   **5.** amābit

F. Conjugate the following verbs in the present system, active and passive, with meanings:

1. servō   **2.** dō   **3.** līberō

G. Translate:

1. With savage tongue the Greek is shouting evil words about the reputation of our good queen.   **2.** Good slave, won't the wild horses in your master's meadows be looked at by many people?   **3.** Meanwhile news about the farmers' flight from the fields was being long awaited.

Relief showing a school for secretaries and notaries—National Museum, Ostia. Education, even of the wealthy, had vocational goals.

READING

Developing Reading Skills

You know the verb **volō** and the prepositions **dē, ā,** and **ad.** Therefore, you know the meanings of **dēvolō, āvolō,** and **advolō.** The meaning of **domina** also is easy to determine from a Latin word which you have learned.

English derivatives will help you to guess at the meanings of **mōnstrum, pestilentia, rapidē,** and **dēvorō.**

Are you familiar with the English words *frustrate* and *dire?* If so, you can guess at the meanings of **frūstrā** and **dīrus.**

The Harpies

Fugam Trōiānōrum Aenēās semper narrābat: "In Crētā laetī oppidum aedificāvimus, sed frustrā. Caelī īra in populum Trōiānum ā deīs semper dēmōnstrābātur, nam frūmentī inopiā pestilentiāque labōrābāmus. Tum in meīs somnīs deī Trōiae dē caelō volāvērunt atque auxilium dedērunt, viam
5 enim ad Ītaliam dēmōnstrāvērunt: 'Ītalia vocātur Hesperia; in Ītaliā Trōia nova ā Trōiānīs aedificābitur.'

"Ut super altum ergō nāvigābāmus, magnā procellā ad īnsulam portābāmur ubi Harpȳiae, mōnstra dīra et fera, habitābant. Feminae foedae erant, at magnīs ālīs volābant. Atque ut cēnam parābāmus dē caelō dēvolāvērunt et
10 cibum rapidē occupāvērunt et tum altē āvolāvērunt. Rūrsus cibum parāvimus rūrsusque advolāvērunt Harpȳiae, parātī autem erāmus, nam tēla occupāvē-rāmus. Diū cum Harpȳiīs pugnābāmus at dēnique mōnstra in fugam nostrīs tēlīs dabantur. At īram ut āvolābant dēmōnstrāvērunt, et mala verba fātidica ā Harpȳiārum dominā clāmābantur: 'In Ītaliam nāvigābitis, sed magnā
15 inopiā ante labōrābitis itaque et mēnsās vestrās dēvorābitis.' "

An archaic Greek depiction of the legend of Phineus. The head and winged figure on the right are two harpies, Ocypele and Aello—590 B.C., Delphi

■ READING COMPREHENSION

1. Why was the Trojans' joy on Crete short-lived?   **2.** What did the gods of Troy reveal to Aeneas in a dream?   **3.** Who were the Harpies?   **4.** How did they harass the Trojans?   **5.** What prophetic words did the Harpies hurl at the Trojans?

---

7. īnsulam: This was one of the Strophades, the islands to which the Argonauts had chased the Harpies from the palace of King Phineus.   **12. in fugam ... dabantur:** In fugam dō is an idiom meaning *I put to flight*.   **13. fātidica:** As supernatural creatures, the Harpies could foresee the future.

LESSON 12

Passive Voice, Perfect System; Imperative Mood

A fresco from Herculaneum showing the dressing of a bride

YOUR WEDDING

The most elaborate Roman wedding ceremony was called **cōnfarreātiō,** *spelt-cake-sharing.* The spelt cake (**farreum**) was an unleavened wafer, the Romans' most primitive form of bread. The ceremony began on the evening before the wedding in the bride's home, where she dedicated her childhood clothes and toys to the **Larēs,** the gods she would be leaving behind when she left her home.

In the morning a spear-point was used to part the bride's hair into six tresses, which were fastened around her head with strips of white wool (**vittae**). She was then dressed in a white seamless tunic, girded at the waist with a special knot called **nōdus Herculeus** (*knot of Hercules*), and saffron-dyed veil (**flammeum**), hair-net, and shoes (saffron was the Roman wedding-color).

The guests then assembled in the atrium of the bride's house to witness the sacrifice of a sow or ewe. The bride and groom sat on two seats covered with a single sheepskin, broke and ate the spelt-cake, and joined hands while the contract was read and witnessed by ten witnesses, who affixed their seals to copies of the contract. The bride then spoke the words, **Ubi tū Gāius, ego Gāia** (*Where you are Gaius, I am Gaia*). There followed good wishes and congratulations, and the wedding-feast, at which the sacrificial animal was eaten. This lasted until dusk.

As soon as the evening star appeared, the bride, pretending reluctance or fear, was snatched from her mother's arms and escorted to the groom's house by children singing a wedding hymn, matrons of honor, men carrying torches, and maids of honor (**prōnubae**) carrying a distaff and spindle, symbols of her new duties. Nuts, cakes, and coins, which were symbols of wealth and fertility, were scattered among the bystanders. Songs were sung insulting the newlyweds (to ward off the evil eye and the envy of the gods).

(Continued)

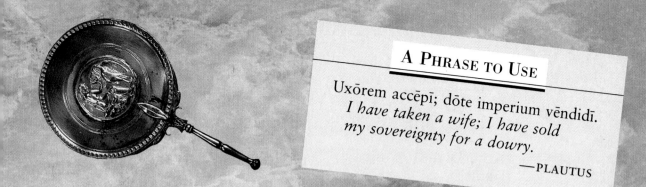

A PHRASE TO USE

Uxōrem accēpī; dōte imperium vēndidī.
*I have taken a wife; I have sold
my sovereignty for a dowry.*

—PLAUTUS

At the groom's door the torches were extinguished and thrown to the spectators, who scrambled for them as lucky charms. The bride anointed the door with oil and hung strips of white wool on the doorposts, then was lifted over the threshold by the men so that she would not stumble as she entered (an inauspicious omen). The groom put the bride in charge of his household by offering her a pitcher of water and a brazier of burning coals. He then retired to the **tablīnum,** to which the matron of honor escorted his new wife as the guests withdrew.

(top) A mirror from Pompeii showing Leda and the swan
(left) A Roman cameo of Iphigenia in Tauris
(below right) Sarcophagus showing a bride and groom joining hands

ANCIENT ROME LIVES ON . . .

Which wedding customs do we get from the Romans?

FORMS

PASSIVE VOICE, PERFECT SYSTEM

For the passive of the perfect, pluperfect, and future perfect you use the fourth principal part of the verb, in the nominative case, along with the present, imperfect, and future of **sum.**

PERFECT PASSIVE, FIRST CONJUGATION

vocātus, -a, -um sum	*I have been called, was called*
vocātus, -a, -um es	*you have been called, were called*
vocātus, -a, -um est	*he, (she, it) has been called, was called*
vocātī, -ae, -a sumus	*we have been called, were called*
vocātī, -ae, -a estis	*you have been called, were called*
vocātī, -ae, -a sunt	*they have been called, were called*

FROM THE PHILOSOPHER'S HANDBOOK . . .

Perfer et obdūrā; dolor hic tibi prōderit ōlim.
*Be patient and tough; some day this pain will
be useful to you.*

—OVID

Suffering builds character. Have you ever met anyone who has triumphed over suffering and become a better person?

PLUPERFECT PASSIVE, FIRST CONJUGATION

vocātus, -a, -um eram	*I had been called*
vocātus, -a, -um erās	*you had been called*
vocātus, -a, -um erat	*he, (she, it) had been called*
vocātī, -ae, -a erāmus	*we had been called*
vocātī, -ae, -a erātis	*you had been called*
vocātī, -ae, -a erant	*they had been called*

FUTURE PERFECT PASSIVE, FIRST CONJUGATION

vocātus, -a, -um erō	*I shall have been called*
vocātus, -a, -um eris	*you will have been called*
vocātus, -a, -um erit	*he, (she, it) will have been called*
vocātī, -ae, -a erimus	*we shall have been called*
vocāti, -ae, -a eritis	*you will have been called*
vocātī, -ae, -a erunt	*they will have been called*

IMPERATIVE MOOD

The verb forms you have learned so far have been those of the Indicative Mood, used to make statements and ask questions. The Imperative Mood is used for giving commands.

The Imperative Mood has both numbers (singular and plural) and both voices (active and passive), but only two tenses, the present and the future, and two persons, 2d and 3d (the 3d only in the future).

Present Imperative

The present imperative active 2d person singular is regularly the same as the present stem: **nāvigā,** *sail.* The plural adds **-te** to the singular, **nāvigāte,** *sail.* The singular form is used when one person is addressed, the plural when more than one person is addressed.

Fābulam, poēta, līberīs narrā.	*Tell the children a story, poet.*
Fābulās, poētae, līberīs narrāte.	*Tell the children stories, poets.*

The present imperative passive 2d person singular uses the ending **-re** and is like the second principal part. The plural is the same as the indicative, ending in **-minī**.

> Cōnfīrmāre, mī amīce.　　*Be encouraged, my friend.*
> Cōnfīrmāminī, meī amīcī.　　*Be encouraged, my friends.*

PRESENT IMPERATIVES

PRESENT ACTIVE, FIRST CONJUGATION

	SINGULAR		PLURAL	
2D PERSON	vocā	*call*	vocāte	*call*

PRESENT PASSIVE, FIRST CONJUGATION

	SINGULAR		PLURAL	
2D PERSON	vocāre	*be called*	vocāminī	*be called*

PRESENT ACTIVE OF SUM

	SINGULAR		PLURAL	
2D PERSON	es	*be*	este	*be*

Future Imperative

The future tense of the imperative is used for commands to be carried out later or at all future times. It is common in laws and instructions, but rare elsewhere, and it will not be used in the practice exercises in this book. Its forms can be found in the Appendix.

SYNTAX

AGREEMENT OF THE PERFECT TENSES PASSIVE

In the passive of the perfect system the fourth principal part must agree with the subject in gender, number, and case.

Puer vocātus est.   *The boy has been called. The boy was called.*
Puellae vocātae erant.   *The girls had been called.*
Vocātus sum.   *I have been called. I was called.*
Vocāta sum.   *I have been called. I was called.*

VOCABULARY

BASIC WORDS

anima, -ae, f. *breath, life, soul*
animus, -ī, m. *spirit, mind, soul;* (plural)
  morale
aqua, -ae, f. *water*
cōnsilium, -ī, n. *plan; advice, counsel*

captīvus, -a, -um *captive*
foedus, -a, -um *foul, filthy, horrible,*
  detestable
grātus, -a, -um *pleasing, welcome;*
  grateful
vērus, -a, -um *true, real*

cōnfīrmō, -āre, -āvī, -ātum
  strengthen; establish; encourage
iuvō, iuvāre, iūvī, iūtum *help, assist;*
  delight, please, gratify

circum (prep. w. acc.) *around* (adv.)
  around, round about
inter (prep. w. acc.) *among, between*
prope (prep. w. acc.) *near* (adv.) *nearby;*
  nearly

mox (adv.) *soon*

Notes: 1. **Anima** and **animus** both come from a root meaning *wind* or *breath*. The **anima** animates; animals and humans have **anima**. Animals do not have **animus**, which is what enables humans to think.
2. **Captīvus** is often used in the masculine or feminine as a noun.

LEARNING ENGLISH THROUGH LATIN

aquatic   *growing, living, or done on the water*
captivate   *to capture the attention or the affection of*
circumference   *the line bounding a circle; the distance around*
confirmation   *proof, the act of establishing as true*
gratify   *to give pleasure or satisfaction to*
magnanimous   *noble; quick to overlook injury or insult*
verify   *to prove or test the truth of*

▰▰ PRACTICE ▰▰

A. Complete the following sentences with the correct form of one of the derivatives from this lesson:

1. Although upset with the referee's call, the team was ___ and congratulated the winners.   2. I need these measurements. What is the ___ of the table?   3. When the professor had ___ all her findings, he gave her an A on her report.   4. Your prompt attention to this matter is very ___ to me.   5. I do like to swim, but on the whole I don't enjoy ___ sports.   6. I was so ___ by the music that I didn't hear anyone come in.   7. It was a relief to the scientist to receive a ___ of his findings.

B. A synopsis of a verb is a list of all its forms in a given person, number, and voice. The order is always the same: all indicative tenses, present, imperfect, future, perfect, pluperfect, future perfect; and present imperative (if the synopsis is in the 2d person).

SYNOPSIS, VOCŌ, SECOND PERSON SINGULAR, ACTIVE

PRESENT INDICATIVE	vocās
IMPERFECT INDICATIVE	vocābās
FUTURE INDICATIVE	vocābis
PERFECT INDICATIVE	vocāvistī
PLUPERFECT INDICATIVE	vocāverās
FUTURE PERFECT INDICATIVE	vocāveris
PRESENT IMPERATIVE	vocā

Give the following synopses:

1. **iuvō** in the 1st singular, passive
2. **sum** in the 2d singular, active
3. **dēmōnstrō** in the 3d singular, passive
4. **labōrō** in the 1st plural, active
5. **servō** in the 2d plural, passive

Ribbed blue glass bowl from Pompeii—National Museum, Naples

C. Match each form of **iuvō** in column A with its correct translation(s) in column B:

A	B
1. iūvistī	a. you had been helped
2. iūvistis	b. you are helped
3. iūta eris	c. you will have been helped
4. iūtus erās	d. you had helped
5. iuvābis	e. you will help
6. iuvābās	f. you helped
7. iūveris	g. help
8. iuvāris	h. you were helping
9. iūverās	i. you have helped
10. iuvā	j. you will have helped

D. Find in column B the verb which is in the same tense, person, and number as each verb in column A, and translate both forms:

A	B
1. cōnfirmātae erātis	a. cōnfirmāminī
2. cōnfirmāverint	b. cōnfirmāveritis
3. cōnfirmāvimus	c. cōnfirmābāris
4. cōnfirmābis	d. cōnfirmātī erāmus
5. cōnfirmābitur	e. cōnfirmābit
6. cōnfirmātus est	f. cōnfirmāvit
7. cōnfirmābās	g. cōnfirmātī sumus
8. cōnfirmāverāmus	h. cōnfirmāberis
9. cōnfirmāte	i. cōnfirmāverātis
10. cōnfirmātī eritis	j. cōnfirmātae erunt

E. Pronounce and translate, and tell whether each of the verbs is the verb of a principal clause or of a subordinate clause:

1. Parātī ad bellum erāmus, deōrum autem auxiliō ē bellō servātī sumus.
2. Cūr equī ferī spectābantur ā parvīs puellīs in lātīs campīs quō cum magistrō ambulāverant?   3. Aut ibi stāte, puerī, in locō ubi estis aut īram magistrī exspectāte.   4. Sī fāma vēra est, magnum malum est: dominī fīliī tēlīs pugnābant prope silvam.   5. Servī quod miserī erant et in agrīs silvīsque diū familiae labōrābant (false perfect; translate *had been toiling*) ā dominō bonō līberātī erant.

Translation Help

Translating from one language into another is not simply transferring words, one at a time, from one language to the other. For example, you cannot simply translate an English preposition into Latin, since the same English preposition may represent two or more completely different Latin constructions:

He is on the road.   ABLATIVE OF PLACE WHERE
He fled on a horse.   ABLATIVE OF MEANS
The master subdued the slave with a word.   ABLATIVE OF MEANS
The master walked with his friends.   ABLATIVE OF ACCOMPANIMENT
They were saved by their good fortune.   ABLATIVE OF MEANS
They were saved by their friend.   ABLATIVE OF PERSONAL AGENT

Before translating prepositions, think of the questions that are being answered. Does the phrase answer the question *where, by what means, along with whom, by whom,* etc.? This will tell you what construction to use.

F.   Translate:

1. She told the story in the farmhouse.   2. She told the story in a few words.   3. He had been helped by the gods.   4. He had been helped by the aid of the gods.   5. They rushed to the farmhouse on horses.   6. They rushed to the farmhouse on the island.   7. We are fighting with weapons. 8. We are fighting with the Harpies.

READING

Developing Reading Skills

There are some unfamiliar words in this reading that you may not have to look up, if you know the English words *miracle, nomination,* and *benign.* If you know what *inevitable* means you can probably guess at ēvītō also.

Friends and Monsters

Aenēās Elissam fābulā iuvābat: "Ab Harpȳiārum īnsulā ad Hadriam nāvigāvimus, unde ad Ēpīrum mīrā fāmā vocātī sumus: captīvī Trōiānī Andromacha et Helenus dominī Ēpīrī nōminātī erant! Iuvābāmur quod grāta fāma erat vēra; mox Andromacha nostrōs ad rēgiam benīgnē vocāvit, ubi Anchīsae Ascaniōque dōna multa et magna dedit. Helenus Andromachae vir erat   5
fātidicus nōtus, itaque animōs nostrōs vērīs verbīs cōnfirmābat atque grātum cōnsilium dē viae perīculīs dedit: 'Ad Hesperiam nāvigātōte circum īnsulam Siciliam, nam inter Ītaliam Siciliamque sunt dīra mōnstra. Hinc mōnstrum nautās ex nāvigiō occupat; hinc ut aquae ā secundō mōnstrō vorantur nāvigia pessum dantur. Fretum ergō ēvītātōte et nāvigātōte circum Siciliam.   10
Ēvītātor et Sicilianum mōnstrum Polyphēmus; multōs enim virōs Graecōs iam dēvorāvit.'

"Sīc nāvigābāmus ergō ut cōnsilium ab Helenō datum erat. Sed ut prope Siciliam nāvigābāmus ā miserō nautā ad ōram vocātī sumus: 'Servāte, Trōiānī, miserum Graecum! Cum Ithacae dominō ad Siciliam nāvigāvī, sed   15
in nostrā fugā ubi Polyphēmus multōs sociōs dēvorāverat et a nostrīs caecātus est ab amīcīs errāvī; itaque cum dominō ab īnsulā nōn nāvigāvī.' Ut miser clāmābat Polyphēmus ad ōram ambulāvit, mōnstrum dīrum foedum magnum caecum. Statim nāvigāvimus ab īnsulā; Graecum servāvimus et nāvigiīs nostrīs portābāmus.   20

"Post Anchīsēs, heu, animam exspīrāvit; sepulcrum in Siciliā est. Tum ad tuum, rēgīna, rēgnum in Āfricam magnā procellā portātī sumus."

▪ READING COMPREHENSION

1. What amazing (but true) rumor brought Aeneas to Epirus?   **2.** What welcome did the Trojans get at the palace?   **3.** Why did Helenus, the soothsayer, want Aeneas to sail around Sicily?   **4.** Who was Polyphemus?
5. Why did the unfortunate Greek sailor call to the Trojans for help?

---

7. nāvigātōte: future imperative (see Appendix)   **8. mōnstra:** Scylla and Charybdis. Scylla snatched six sailors from passing ships with her six heads. But the ships which sailed along the other side of the strait were sucked down by Charybdis, who made a huge whirlpool by drinking in the waters of the sea. **Hinc ... hinc ...:** literally *from here ... from here ...* Translate *from one side ... from another side ....*   **10. pessum dantur:** literally, *are given downward,* an idiom for *are destroyed* **ēvītātōte, nāvigātōte:** future imperatives (see Appendix)   **13. Sīc ... ut ...,** *just as*   **18. dīrum foedum,** etc.: Roman writers sometimes omit a series of conjunctions.

REVIEW 3

VOCABULARY DRILL

A. Give the genitive, gender, and meaning of each of these nouns:

amīcitia	cōnsilium	inopia	magister
anima	cōpia	īnsula	populus
animus	dominus	īra	socius
aqua	fāma	lingua	tēlum
āra	frūmentum	locus	umbra

B. Give the other nominative singular forms, and the meanings, of these adjectives:

captīvus	laetus	parātus	sacer
foedus	novus	parvus	vērus
grātus			

C. Give the other three principal parts, and the meanings, of these verbs:

clāmō	dō	līberō	servō
cōnfirmō	iuvō	nūntiō	stō
dēmōnstrō	labōrō	pugnō	sum

D. Give the meaning of each preposition, and name the case(s) with which it is used:

circum	inter	prope

E. Give the meanings of the following adverbs:

crās	hodiē	rūrsus	semper
diū	ibi	modo	sī
circum	prope	mox	ut
herī	quod	nisi	

LISTENING AND SPEAKING

A Business Call

Marcus explains that the owner of his farmhouse, Gnaeus Mucius,[1] has a big house in town. He describes the business call he made to this house.

LŪCIUS: Num rūrsus,[2] Mārce, ad agrōs nunc ambulās? Diū in oppidō labōrābās itaque nunc fessus[3] es.

MĀRCUS: Hodiē ambulābō. Herī in parvō hospitiō eram, sed hodiē familia mē[4] exspectat. In agrōs cum pecūniā ambulābō.

LŪCIUS: Multam pecūniam reservāvistī quod multum vīnum et frūmentum ad tabernās portābās.

MĀRCUS: Nunc nōn multam pecūniam portō, nam herī pecūniam dominō vīllae meae dedī. Dominus vīllae nōn sum. Dominus Gnaeus Mūcius est, et prope[5] habitat.

LŪCIUS: Estne domus[6] Mūciī magna?

MĀRCUS: Est. Herī ad Mūciī domum ambulāvī et ostia[7] pultāvī.[8] Servus ostia spectat. Servum ostiārium vocāmus. Ostiārius viam ad ātrium dēmōnstrābat. In ātriō impluvium aquae plēnum[9] et in impluviō erat fonticulus[10] pulcher.

LŪCIUS: Utrum Mūcius in ātriō an in tablīnō erat?

MĀRCUS: In tablīnō erat cum multīs negōtiīs.[11] In ālīs diū multī agricolae dominum exspectābant. Dēnique[12] pecūniam dominō dedī. Bonus vir dominus est! Herī multīs cēnam[13] dedit et magnum aprum[14] gustābāmus.[15]

LŪCIUS: Ubi erant domina et līberī? Utrum cum Mūciō in tablīnō erant annōn?

MĀRCUS: Nōn erant in tablīnō. Domina Lūcrētia in culīnā erat et servōs et cēnam spectābat. Līberī in peristȳlō[16] cum servō erant. Servus magister est et discipulī[17] līberī sunt.

LŪCIUS: Bona est vīta dominī et dominae in domō magnā! Diū labōrō in pistrīnā meā et nōn sunt multī servī. Sūper pistrīnam cum fēminā habitō. Locus parvus est, sed miserī nōn sumus, etsī[18] in oppidō habitāmus.

Give a summary in Latin of Marcus' visit to the home of Gnaeus Mucius.

1. Gnaeus Mūcius— *Gnaeus is a* praenōmen; *Mucius is a* nōmen
2. rūrsus, adv.—*back, again*
3. fessus, -a, -um— *weary, tired*
4. mē—*me*
5. prope, adv.— *nearby*
6. domus (part 4th and part 2nd declension) -ī, f.— *house*
7. ostium, -ī, n.—*door*
8. pultō, -āre, -āvī, -ātum—*knock on, strike*
9. plēnus, -a, -um— *full*
10. fonticulus, -ī, m.—*a small fountain*
11. negōtium, -ī, n.— *business*
12. dēnique (adv.)— *finally*
13. cēna, -ae, f.—*dinner*
14. aper, aprī, m.—*wild boar*
15. gustō, -āre, -āvī, -ātum—*taste, eat*
16. peristȳlum, -ī, n.—*a peristyle*
17. discipulus, -ī, m.— *pupil, student*
18. etsī, adv.—*even if*

TRACES OF ROMAN CIVILIZATION TODAY

Morocco—Volubilis

Roman Mosaic

Because of Morocco's strategic location, its civilization has been shaped by successive eras of migration and imperial conquest. It is located on the land and sea routes from the Mediterranean to the Atlantic and on the crossroad between Europe and Africa.

Volubilis

Ancient Chella near Rabat

In prehistoric times it was overrun by the ancestors of the Berbers who probably migrated from the Middle East. In 1100 B.C. first the Phoenicians and later the Carthaginians established settlements there. In 25 B.C. the Romans made Juba II king of an area that extended from Rabat (present-day capital) to eastern Algeria, a region called Mauretania. Plagued by Berber rebellions, western Mauretania, called Mauretania Tingitanis because of its capital Tangier, became a Roman province in 42 A.D. Unfortunately, most traces of this important Roman period have perished but there are some notable vestiges in an area called Volubilis.

The Vandal invasion of 429 A.D. severed the Roman tie and for the next century Morocco was under Byzantine control.

If you were to continue studying the molding of Morocco's culture and civilization, you would proceed from the Roman era, through the Arab conquest, through the period of French and Spanish control and finally, to its independence and constitutional monarchy.

Roman Gateway

Roman Arch

133

Third Declension Nouns: Masculine, Feminine; Dative With Adjectives

Wall painting: portrait of a girl holding wax tablets and a stylus—National Museum, Naples

THE ROLE OF WOMEN

Roman women were legally second-class citizens. A Roman woman was not given a name of her own, but was called by the feminine form of her father's family name: e.g., all daughters of a Tiberius Claudius would be called Claudia. (They might, however, be numbered: Claudia Prima, Claudia Secunda, etc.). Her full name included the name of her husband or father in the genitive (of possession) to show to whom she belonged; for she remained her father's property until she was married, when she became the property of her husband. The names of the other two Roman forms of marriage, **emptiō** (*purchase*) and **ūsus** (*usufruct*) make the wife's position as a chattel clear. The power of a father over a daughter or a husband over a wife was called **manus.**

A woman could not vote, hold office, make a will, sign a contract, or represent herself in court. The chief duty of a good Roman wife was to supervise the female slaves at their morning tasks of spinning, weaving, sewing, and embroidery. She could then receive or make social calls on other matrons during the afternoon. At dinner parties, she dined with the wives of her husband's guests in a separate dining room.

The legal position of women, however, is belied by their real political and economic powers. History is full of examples of Roman women who played very important roles, always through their influence on their fathers, husbands, or brothers. Since political and business alliances were usually sealed by intermarriage of the families involved, upper-class women wielded considerable power; some even managed, by legal fictions, to acquire limited legal rights. During many reigns, especially those of the Julio-Claudians and the Severi, the women of the imperial family exercised much control over the entire Roman Empire.

135

A PHRASE TO USE

Lānam fēcit, domī mānsit.
(Epitaph of a good wife)
She did her wool; she stayed at home.

ANCIENT ROME LIVES ON . . .

Do any of the Roman attitudes towards women still survive today in our country? elsewhere?

(*above*) Portrait of a provincial woman, 2nd century A.D.—Archeological Museum, Florence   (*right*) Wall painting: an upper-class woman spinning

■ FORMS

■ MASCULINE AND FEMININE NOUNS OF THE THIRD DECLENSION

Nouns and adjectives of the third declension can be recognized by the genitive singular ending -is.

Masculine and feminine third declension nouns are declined like **frāter, frātris,** m., *brother,* and **soror, sorōris,** f., *sister.*

THE THIRD DECLENSION, MASCULINE AND FEMININE

	SINGULAR		ENDINGS
NOM.	frāter	soror	——
GEN.	frātris	sorōris	-is
DAT.	frātrī	sorōrī	-ī
ACC.	frātrem	sorōrem	-em
ABL.	frātre	sorōre	-e

	PLURAL		ENDINGS
NOM.	frātrēs	sorōrēs	-ēs
GEN.	frātrum	sorōrum	-um
DAT.	frātribus	sorōribus	-ibus
ACC.	frātrēs	sorōrēs	-ēs
ABL.	frātribus	sorōribus	-ibus

1. The vocative is the same as the nominative.

2. The rule for finding the base is the same in this declension as in the others: remove the genitive singular ending (in this declension -is).

3. There is no standard nominative singular ending.

▬▬ SYNTAX ▬▬

▪ DATIVE WITH ADJECTIVES

The dative case has two basic uses in Latin. One use is with verbs and the other with adjectives. An example of its use with verbs is the Dative of the Indirect Object. When it is used to complete or extend the meaning of adjectives it is called the Dative with Adjectives.

The following adjectives are often used with a noun in the dative case.

amīcus, -a, -um	*friendly*
cārus, -a, -um	*dear*
fīnitimus, -a, -um	*adjacent, neighboring*
grātus, -a, -um	*pleasing, welcome; grateful*
idōneus, -a, -um	*suitable*
inimīcus, -a, -um	*unfriendly, hostile*
nōtus, -a, -um	*known, well-known*
propinquus, -a, -um	*near, close*
vīcīnus, -a, -um	*near, neighboring*

An aristocrat of the mid-empire, Empress Julia Domna— Capitoline Museum, Rome

Poenī Āfricānīs fīnitimī sunt.
The Carthaginians are adjacent to the Africans.

Poenī Trōiānīs amīcī sunt.
The Carthaginians are friendly to the Trojans.

If, however, these adjectives are used as nouns, they will have the genitive rather than the dative:

Poenī fīnitimī Āfricānōrum sunt.
The Carthaginians are the Africans' neighbors.

Poenī amīcī Trōiānōrum sunt.
The Carthaginians are the Trojans' friends.

VOCABULARY

BASIC WORDS

amor, amōris, m. *love*

flamma, -ae, f. *flame*

frāter, frātris, m. *brother*

māter, mātris, f. *mother*

nepōs, nepōtis, m. or f. *grandson, granddaughter*

pater, patris, m. *father*

soror, sorōris, f. *sister*

cārus, -a, -um *dear, expensive*

fīnitimus, -a, -um *adjacent, neighboring;* (as noun) *neighbor* (on a map)

idōneus, -a, -um *suitable*

nōtus, -a, -um *known, well-known*

propinquus, -a, -um *near, close;* (as noun) *kinsman, relative*

vīcīnus, -a, -um *near, neighboring;* (as noun) *neighbor* (in a neighborhood)

Note: As adjectives, **fīnitimus, propinquus,** and **vīcīnus** appear to mean about the same; but if you look at their meanings when they are used as nouns, you will see that there are different shades of meaning here.

Princess Zenobia of Palmyra, 3rd century A.D.— National Museum, Damascus

LEARNING ENGLISH THROUGH LATIN

amorous	*loving*
charity	*an act or feeling of good will*
fratricide	*the killing of a brother or sister; one who has killed a brother or sister*
inflammatory	*likely to cause a fire; likely to arouse excitement or violence*
maternity	*motherhood*
nepotism	*favoritism shown to a relative, especially the placing of a relative in a desirable position*
paternal	*fatherly*
propinquity	*nearness in time, place, or relationship*
sorority	*a group of women joined by a common interest*
vicinity	*the state of being near or close by; neighborhood*

PRACTICE

A. Fill the blanks with the appropriate derivatives from the above list:

1. He was the boss' son, but so hard up that we didn't know whether his getting the job was ___ or ___ ___. **2.** Cain was the first ___; he committed ___ when he killed Abel. **3.** At the university a new ___ house was built in close ___ to the museum. **4.** There was so much noise coming from the athletic field that no one could study anywhere in the ___. **5.** The rabble-rouser made another ___ speech.

B. Change the number, keeping the same case:

1. frātris **2.** patre **3.** sorōrum **4.** nepōtem **5.** mātrī **6.** amor

C. Give the following forms:

1. Dative singular: **amor, frāter, soror** **2.** Nominative plural: **māter, nepōs, amor** **3.** Accusative singular: **pater, māter, flamma** **4.** Genitive plural: **soror, nepōs, frāter** **5.** Ablative plural: **nepōs, pater, servus**

D. Pronounce and translate:

1. Pater tuus inimīcus meī frātris est. **2.** Sicilia propinqua est et Āfricae et Ītaliae. **3.** Vīlla vestra est vīcīna nostrae. **4.** Sorōris meae vīcīnus est amīcus lēgātī. **5.** Lēgātī māter amīca est propinquō meō.

E. Decline, singular and plural:

1. cāra soror   2. amor idōneus   3. nepōs nōta

F. Translate:

1. He is friendly to Dido.   2. He is Dido's friend.   3. He is close to his granddaughter.   4. He is his granddaughter's kinsman.   5. Juno is unfriendly to Venus.

G. Pronounce and translate:

1. Ut vīta vestrae mātris bona erat vērē vocāta est Fortūnae fīlia.   2. In perīculīs animī Poenōrum cōnfīrmātī sunt, exspectābant enim auxilium deum Carthāginī amīcōrum.   3. Aut servōs, male domine, hodiē līberā aut fugae cōpiam miserīs parābimus.   4. Et propinquī nostrae familiae et amīcī sociīque ad vīllam ambulābunt, nam ā patre convocātī sunt.   5. Nisi fīnitimī populī pulchra dōna rēgīnae dederint, amīca fīnitimīs nōn erit.

H. Translate:

1. The broad plains to which we are walking are suitable for horses.   2. The Greek captive was known to the messenger, for he had once given many gifts to the messenger's granddaughter.   3. My son, the gods and goddesses friendly to the fatherland will have been praised in the Latin language by a great poet.   4. Neither to my sister nor to my brother was the news about our father's exile welcome.   5. Yesterday the legate's slaves were fighting for a long time on the plain with men unfriendly to their master, but afterwards they were defeated.

READING

Developing Reading Skills

There are unfamiliar words here which you won't have to look up if you know the English words *compute*, *dissimulate* (or *dissemble*), *excite*, *false*, *locate*, and *simulate*. Also, **amīcitia** and **inimīcus** help with **inimīcitia**.

Juno and Venus Conspire

Trōiānī procellā ad oppidum Carthāginem portātī sunt. Procellam excitāverat dea Iūnō rēgīna caelī; nam Iūnō Aenēae Trōiānīsque semper inīmica, Dīdōnī Poenīsque semper amīca erat. Atque nunc ad deam Venerem Aenēae mātrem advolat. Inimīcitiam dissimulat simulatque amīcitiam: "Tuum Aenēan amātō
5   Dīdō mea et in rēgnō Pūnicō servātō. Hīc semper habitantō Trōiānī; dabō meum oppidum Carthāginem Trōiānīs tuīs." In fātidicō animō autem putābat, "Sī Aenēās Trōiānīque in Ītaliā oppidum aedificāverint, ōlim Bellum Pūnicum in Carthāginem parābunt Rōmānī. Sīn autem ad Ītaliam nōn nāvigāverint sed hīc habitābunt, Dīdōnī auxilium bonum dabunt contrā
10   Āfricānōs Poenīs inimīcōs. Fātīs quidem vetor, at temptābō." Sīc putābat quod Dīdō Poenīque Iūnōnī cārī erant.

Iūnōnis cōnsilium Venerī grātum est, sīc enim Aenēās fīlius cārus interim tūtus erit. Itaque Cytherēa Iūnōnī auxilium dat. Ascanium occupat Venus et cum nepōte in caelum volat; interim in terrā in Ascaniī locō fīlium
15   Amōrem, Aenēae frātrem, collocat. Dīdō parvum Ascanium amābat itaque misera Amōrem, falsum Ascanium, in gremiō collocāvit. Ut amor ā gremiō in animum volāvit, ubi flammās excitāvit, rēgīna Aenēam miserē amāvit. Atque Dīdōnem, quod bona pulchraque erat, amāvit vir Trōiānus.

Ā Trōiānīs Poenī, ā Poenīs Trōiānī, iuvābantur: Trōiānī in Poenōrum
20   oppidō habitābant atque cum Poenīs bellum in ferōs Āfricānōs parābant.

◼ READING COMPREHENSION

1. How did the Trojans arrive at Carthage?   **2.** What proposal did Juno make to Aeneas' mother?   **3.** What were her real thoughts behind this proposal?   **4.** How did Venus help Juno in her plan?   **5.** Why did Aeneas love Dido?

---

4. Aenēan: First declension names derived from the Greek often have **-ān** or **-ēn** in the accusative singular (so also **Anchīsēn**). **amātō:** future imperative (see Appendix)   **5. servātō, habitantō:** future imperatives (see Appendix)   **15. Amōrem:** In the Aeneid Virgil charmingly describes how much fun the mischievous Amor has taking off his wings, putting on his disguise, practising Ascanius' walk, etc.

LESSON 14

Third Declension Neuter Nouns;
Objective Genitive

Fragment of a sarcophagus showing the Emperor Gordianus III, circa 238 A.D.

THE TOGA

Men who were citizens of Rome were permitted (and on some occasions required) to wear the toga, which was an Etruscan variation of the Greek himation. The himation was a simple rectangle, usually about two yards by four in size. The middle of one long side was placed under the right arm, and the two ends were thrown over the left shoulder, one from in front and one from behind. The weight of cloth on the left arm made it inconvenient for military wear; yet, shortened, it would have been hard to wear, since it was the weight of cloth front and back that kept it from falling off. The Etruscans invented the toga by cutting off two of the himation's corners, so that it was long enough to stay in place, but much reduced in weight. The Romans adopted this trapezoidal garment, calling it a toga. The fact that the toga was originally a military uniform explains why its use was restricted to Roman citizens, since citizenship originally depended on service in the army.

The toga was always made of white wool. A young boy's toga had a purple stripe along its edge (**toga praetexta**). This was replaced by a plain white toga (**toga virīlis**) when he came of age. A purple stripe was also worn by the wealthy class called the Knights (**Equitēs**), and a broader one by men of senatorial rank. Since the king had worn an entirely purple toga, the stripes no doubt represented the sharing of his imperium among all the **Patrēs.** The purple-bordered toga was changed for a plain white one (**toga candida**) when a noble was running for office—hence our word *candidate.*

In time the toga grew in size, still keeping its trapezoidal shape. Eventually a double version was developed, two trapezoids (one a little narrower than the other) joined along their long sides and folded over on this line before being wrapped around the body. Part of the inner trapezoid was then pulled out over the outer one at the breast, forming the fold called the **sinus.** In its largest form the toga was a formal garment, requiring a good deal of

(Continued)

A PHRASE TO USE

Cēdant arma togae.
Let arms yield to the toga.

time and trouble to drape properly; then its use began more and more to be restricted to special occasions.

Early in the republic the toga, as it grew larger, ceased to be a military uniform and became the official dress of a civilian citizen. As late as the first century B.C. we find the younger Cato still wearing the single toga (**toga exigua**), but he deliberately dressed in an old-fashioned way to show his conservatism. The garment reached its fullest size in the times of the Antonines. In the late empire it shrank to a small trapezoidal cape held on by a long band, and was worn only by the Consuls, and only when they were giving the starting signal for the chariot races. A full-sized toga, again all of purple, was worn by the later emperors.

(*below*) The Emperor Titus wearing the full imperial style toga

ANCIENT ROME LIVES ON . . .

What garments do we have whose shape and use have been modified over time?

What garments in our society have a merely symbolic use?

NEUTER NOUNS OF THE THIRD DECLENSION

Third declension neuters are declined like masculine and feminine nouns, with the standard exceptions which apply to neuters of all declensions: the nominative and accusative are identical, and in the plural always end in **-a.**

The base, as always, is found by dropping the genitive ending.

Many neuter nouns of the third declension end in:

1. **-men** (base **-min-**), like **nūmen, nūminis,** n., *nod*
2. **-us** (base **-or-**), like **decus, decoris,** n., *ornament*
3. **-us** (base **-er-**), like **mūnus, mūneris,** n., *duty*

NEUTER NOUNS OF THE THIRD DECLENSION

				ENDINGS	
	SINGULAR	PLURAL		SINGULAR	PLURAL
NOM.	nūmen	nūmina		——	-a
GEN.	nūminis	nūminum		-is	-um
DAT.	nūminī	nūminibus		-ī	-ibus
ACC.	nūmen	nūmina		——	-a
ABL.	nūmine	nūminibus		-e	-ibus
	SINGULAR	PLURAL		SINGULAR	PLURAL
NOM.	decus	decora		mūnus	mūnera
GEN.	decoris	decorum		mūneris	mūnerum
DAT.	decorī	decoribus		mūnerī	mūneribus
ACC.	decus	decora		mūnus	mūnera
ABL.	decore	decoribus		mūnere	mūneribus

SYNTAX

OBJECTIVE GENITIVE

When a noun is the name of an action, it may be accompanied by a noun in the genitive telling who or what receives the action. Because this person or thing would be the direct object if the action noun were a verb, we call this use the Objective Genitive.

> Puellam amō.
> *I love the girl.* (**Puellam** is the direct object.)
> meus amor puellae
> *my love for the girl* (**Puellae** is an objective genitive.)

1. You will have to decide whether a genitive is possessive or objective on the basis of the context: **Dīdōnis amor** could mean either *Dido's love (for someone)* or *(someone's) love for Dido.*
2. The objective genitive differs from all other genitives in that it cannot always be translated with *of*. An example is *my love for the girl;* another is **fuga malōrum,** *a flight from evils.*

Translation Help

The "normal" order of words in a Latin sentence with an intransitive verb is *Subject, Verb.* If the verb is transitive the order is *Subject, (Indirect Object), Direct Object, (Predicate Accusative), Verb.* With the verb *to be* the order is *Subject, Subjective Complement, Verb.*

A word displaced from its normal position becomes emphatic, the more so as its distance from its usual place increases.

Hence the sentence **Vīllam fēmina spectat** means *The woman is looking at the farmhouse,* but the sentence **Pulchram meus amīcus amat puellam,** since the adjective is as far as it can be from the noun it modifies, really means something like *The girl my friend loves is beautiful.* In other words, the adjective use can be changed from attributive to predicative by moving it.

In deciding on the placement of words for emphasis, remember to avoid ambiguity and never to place a word of the principal clause inside a subordinate clause.

VOCABULARY

BASIC WORDS

auctor, auctōris, m. *founder, author*
cupīdō, cupīdinis, f. *longing, desire*
cūra, -ae, f. *care, anxiety*
decus, decoris, n. *ornament, honor, glory;* (plural) *honorable exploits*
grātia, -ae, f. *pleasantness; influence; gratitude*
imperium, -ī, n. *command, empire*
laus, laudis, f. *praise, fame, glory*

memoria, -ae, f. *memory*
mūnus, mūneris, n. *duty; funeral; gift; gladiatorial show*
nūmen, nūminis, n. *nod; divine will, divine spirit, divinity*
pectus, pectoris, n. *breast, heart*
timor, timōris, m. *fear*
virtūs, virtūtis, f. *manliness, worth, courage*

Notes: 1. **Grātia** in the ablative, following an objective genitive, means *for the sake:* **Iovis grātiā,** *for the sake of Jupiter, for Jupiter's sake.*
2. The different meanings of **mūnus** come from the idea of *duty.* A **mūnus** is the kind of gift you feel you owe in gratitude. The funeral is what the living owe to the dead. Gladiatorial shows were given as part of a funeral celebration.
3. Roman religion was nuministic: everything, even qualities and inanimate objects, was felt to be able to express its will in some way.

LEARNING ENGLISH THROUGH LATIN

curator	*one in charge of a museum or library*
fatalistic	*accepting everything as inevitable*
imperial	*pertaining to an empire, majestic*
mercurial	*quick, changeable, fickle*
numinous	*deeply spiritual, divine, supernatural*
remuneration	*pay, reward, compensation*
virtuosity	*great technical skill in the fine arts (especially music)*

PRACTICE

A. Choose five words from the English derivative list above and use each one in a sentence which shows that you understand its meaning.

B. Show the relationship of the English words *gracious, jovial, memorial, timorous,* and *virtual* to Latin words in the Vocabulary. Look up the meaning of any word you do not know.

C. Give the number and case(s):

1. laudibus   2. nūminum   3. timōrēs   4. virtūtī   5. pectore   6. mūnera
7. decoris

D. Change the number, keeping the same case:

1. auctōrum   2. virtūs   3. cūram   4. pectorī   5. cupīdinis   6. timōre
7. imperia   8. memoriās   9. decus   10. laudum   11. nūmina   12. grātiā

E. Decline **pectus laetum** in the singular and plural.

F. Translate the following examples of the objective genitive, using the English preposition which makes the construction clearest: *of, for, from, over,* etc.

1. cūra līberōrum   2. memoria amīcitiae   3. auctor nostrae fortūnae
4. amor fēminae   5. grātia (meaning *gratitude* here) mūneris   6. fuga
perīculōrum   7. cupīdō laudis   8. laus puellae   9. timor nūminum
10. imperium terrārum

G. Translate:

1. For the sake of honor you are preparing war against the Greeks, but are the authors of your dangers the Greeks or the divine wills of the gods?
2. As the year has been good for the farmers they will walk to the holy place in the fields, where they will show the good gods their gratitude for the great supply of grain.

H. Pronounce and translate:

1. Laetī oppida spectāmus, vītam in vīllā autem laudāmus, agrōrum amor enim animōs nostrōs occupāvit.   2. Magnum erat imperium Rōmānum, atque ā magnīs poētīs memoria Rōmānōrum virtūtum linguīs et Graecā et Latīnā servāta est.   3. Quod in somnīs anima cārī patris Anchīsae bonum cōnsilium Aenēae dederat et viam ad Ītaliam dēmōnstrāverat animī Trōiānōrum decoris amōre mox cōnfīrmātī sunt.   4. Agrōrum, campōrum, silvārum, aquārum sunt nūmina unde dōna multa et bona Populō Rōmānō parāta sunt, itaque mūnera nūminibus grāta ad loca deīs deābusque sacra Rōmānī saepe portant.

READING

Developing Reading Skills

From their English derivatives you can learn the meanings of **agitō**, **cessō** (think of *incessant*), **glōria**, and **īrātus**. If the English word *mutable* means *able to be changed* and *mutation* means *a change in form*, what would the Latin verb **mūtō** mean?

A Jealous Rival Stirs up Trouble

Laetus in Dīdōnis rēgnō Aenēās cum Trōiānīs habitābat, laetus cum Poenīs oppidum novum aedificābat. Magnus rēgīnae amor pectus occupāverat: nec iam pietās nec virtūs, nec Fātōrum imperia nec nūmina deōrum in animō erant.

5   Iarbās rēx Āfricānōrum Dīdōnis amōre miserē agitātus est, at rēgīna rēgem nōn amāvit. Itaque amor in īram mutātus est atque propter īram bellum in Poenōs parābat. Iarbae fāma dē Dīdōnis amōre nuntiāta est: nunc rēgīna Aenēam amābat! Rēx fīlius Iovis erat, itaque rēx ad āram deī advolāvit et auxilium postulāvit: "Ubi nunc, ō mī pater et meī rēgnī auctor, est tuus
10   amor Iarbae? Dīdōnī locum in meīs terrīs dedī oppidō idōneum, sed grātiam multōrum bonōrum nōn dēmōnstrāvit rēgīna. Atque modo nāvigāvit ad Elissae rēgnum Trōiānus hospes, vērus Veneris fīlius, nōn vir—virum sine virtūte nōn vocō virum vērum. Tum Cupīdō frātrem iūvit—et nunc Aenēās in oppidō Carthāgine habitat, novus rēgnī dominus! Nisi tuum fīlium iuvābis,
15   frūstrā ad tuās ārās Āfricānī portāmus mūnera sacra."

Statim Iuppiter īrātus Mercurium vocat: "Rapidē advolā, fīlī, in Āfricam, et ad Veneris fīlium imperium Fātōrum et meum portā: statim nāvigātō in Hesperiam, quō Fāta Trōiānōs vocant. In Āfricā cessat, fēminae captīvus, nam antīqua cupīdō bonae fāmae et decoris et laudis et glōriae cum Anchīsae
20   memoriā cūrāque Ascaniī ā virō āvolāvit. Statim nāvigātō, statim!"

---

17. nāvigātō: future imperative (see Appendix)   **19. decoris et laudis et glōriae:** Be careful not to translate *glory, glory, and glory*. These words have different meanings in Latin and you must distinguish them in your translation.

A bronze depiction of Mercury from Roman Germany

READING COMPREHENSION

1. How did his new life in Dido's kingdom affect Aeneas?   **2.** Who was the rival of Aeneas?   **3.** Why did this rival go to Jupiter for help?   **4.** How did Jupiter react, and what message did he send to Aeneas?

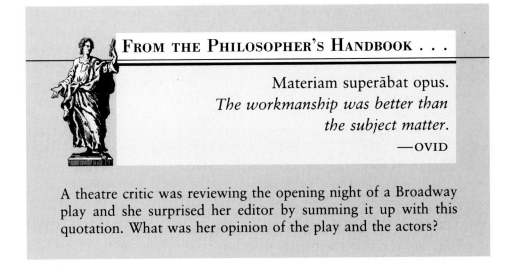

FROM THE PHILOSOPHER'S HANDBOOK . . .

Materiam superābat opus.
*The workmanship was better than
the subject matter.*
—OVID

A theatre critic was reviewing the opening night of a Broadway play and she surprised her editor by summing it up with this quotation. What was her opinion of the play and the actors?

LESSON 15

Third Declension Adjectives; Adverbs; Ablative of Specification

A Roman fresco showing a well dressed lady decanting perfumes—Terme Museum, Rome

YOUR CLOTHING

The toga was originally a military uniform. Since in the early days female camp followers had worn togas given to them by the soldiers, its use was forbidden to respectable women. When it became too voluminous for military use it was replaced by the **sagum,** a short cloak held in place by a safety-pin (**fibula**) on the right shoulder. Commanders wore a larger, purple-dyed version called a **palūdāmentum.**

Because of its military origins, the toga was also the mark of a Roman citizen. It had to be worn at all religious ceremonies, including plays, races, and gladiatorial games, and whenever the citizen was exercising his rights, as at elections and official meetings. It was also worn at very formal dinner-parties. A citizen had to wear his toga when he paid his morning call on his patron (no doubt a relic of the days when the **salūtātiō** represented a military muster of dependents in uniform).

The toga in classical times was always worn over the tunic (**tunica**), the basic garment of both men and women. This was a white woolen garment with a neck- and arm-holes, with or without sleeves. It reached the ankles, but men pulled it up through the belt to calf-length, or above the knees for active work. The tunic was worn alone by slaves and workmen, and by men of any class in the privacy of the home: it was the "shirt-sleeves" of the Romans.

Women wore the tunic (sometimes colored) ankle length, tied with a **cingulum** at the waist and a **strophium** under the bosom. Over the tunic matrons wore the **stola,** a more voluminous garment with shoulder straps; when girt up it reached the ground. Over this, outdoors, they wore a himation (**palla**).

For informal dinner-parties men wore the **synthesis** ("ensemble"), a colored tunic with a harmonizing himation (**pallium**). The **palla** was more elaborate than the **pallium,** with such embellishments as embroidery and fringes.

(*above*) A young girl in formal dress—Louvre Museum, Paris   (*right*) Military regalia and dress: the emperor at a sacrifice in the Campus Martius—2nd century relief reworked from the Arch of Constantine

FORMS

THIRD DECLENSION ADJECTIVES

Adjectives of the third declension are divided into three groups, those of one termination, those of two terminations, and those of three terminations.

Adjectives of One Termination

Adjectives of one termination have the same form for the nominative singular of all three genders. All third declension adjectives which do not end in -er or -is in the masculine nominative singular are adjectives of one termination. Some of these have regular third declension endings; but most of them have a stem ending in -i, which changes some of the endings. **Pār** (*equal*) is an example of these. Notice that its ablative singular, and genitive and accusative plural, in all genders, and its neuter nom. plural show the -i of the stem.

DECLENSION OF ONE-TERMINATION ADJECTIVES

| | SINGULAR | | PLURAL | |
	M. & F.	NEUT.	M. & F.	NEUT.
NOM.	pār	pār	parēs	paria
GEN.	paris	paris	parium	parium
DAT.	parī	parī	paribus	paribus
ACC.	parem	pār	parīs	paria
ABL.	parī	parī	paribus	paribus

Adjectives of Two Terminations

Adjectives which end in -is in the masculine nominative singular are adjectives of two terminations. Two-termination adjectives are all i-stems, like **pār**, and show the -i of the stem in the ablative singular, and genitive and accusative plural, in all genders, and the neuter nominative plural. An example is **omnis**, *all*. **Omnis** is called an Adjective of Two Terminations because (since it has a separate form for the neuter) it has two different endings in the nominative singular.

DECLENSION OF TWO-TERMINATION ADJECTIVES

| | SINGULAR | | PLURAL | |
	M. & F.	NEUT.	M. & F.	NEUT.
NOM.	omnis	omne	omnēs	omnia
GEN.	omnis	omnis	omnium	omnium
DAT.	omnī	omnī	omnibus	omnibus
ACC.	omnem	omne	omnīs	omnia
ABL.	omnī	omnī	omnibus	omnibus

Adjectives of Three Terminations

Adjectives of three terminations have separate forms for the masculine, feminine, and neuter in the nominative singular. They all end in **-er** in the masculine nominative singular. Some, like **celer,** *swift,* retain the -e of this ending in the other forms; while others, like **ācer,** *sharp,* drop it. They are all i-stems.

DECLENSION OF THREE-TERMINATION ADJECTIVES

| | SINGULAR | | | PLURAL | | |
	MASC.	FEM.	NEUT.	MASC.	FEM.	NEUT.
NOM.	celer	celeris	celere	celerēs	celerēs	celeria
GEN.	celeris	celeris	celeris	celerium	celerium	celerium
DAT.	celerī	celerī	celerī	celeribus	celeribus	celeribus
ACC.	celerem	celerem	celere	celerīs	celerīs	celeria
ABL.	celerī	celerī	celerī	celeribus	celeribus	celeribus
NOM.	ācer	ācris	ācre	ācrēs	ācrēs	ācria
GEN.	ācris	ācris	ācris	ācrium	ācrium	ācrium
DAT.	ācrī	ācrī	ācrī	ācribus	ācribus	ācribus
ACC.	ācrem	ācrem	ācre	ācrīs	ācrīs	ācria
ABL.	ācrī	ācrī	ācrī	ācribus	ācribus	ācribus

Third-declension adjectives sometimes end in -ēs in the accusative plural. This form is not used in this book.

◼ FORMATION OF ADVERBS

Adverbs made from third declension adjectives are formed by adding **-iter** to the base. This is the accusative singular of the noun **iter, itineris,** n., *way.*

| celeriter | *in a swift way, swiftly* |
| ācriter | *in a fierce way, fiercely* |

▰▰ SYNTAX ▰▰

◼ ABLATIVE OF SPECIFICATION

The ablative is used, without a preposition, to answer the question *With respect to what?* This use is known as the Ablative of Specification. The preposition *in* is usually used to translate this construction into English. However, when the Ablative of Specification is used with the adjective **dīgnus,** *worthy,* the English uses the preposition *of.*

Nostrōs virtūte superant.
 They surpass our men in courage. (with respect to courage)
Hecuba nōmine modo rēgīna est.
 Hecuba is queen only in name. (with respect to the name)
Aenēās laude dīgnus est.
 Aeneas is worthy of praise. (with respect to praise)

A noble family in imperial garb—Ara Pacis, Rome

VOCABULARY

Because adjectives of one termination have only one nominative singular form, the nominative and genitive singular will be given in the Vocabularies so that you may find the base. You will know that they are not nouns by their meaning and because no gender is given.

Notice that **celer** keeps the -e in its base, whereas **ācer** drops it. Every third declension adjective of three terminations is declined like one or the other of these. You can tell which by looking at the feminine nominative singular to see if the -e is kept or dropped.

BASIC WORDS

iter, itineris, n. *route, way; journey*
multitūdō, multitūdinis, f. *large number, number, multitude*
nōmen, nōminis, n. *name*

ācer, ācris, ācre *sharp, fierce, keen*
celer, celeris, celere *swift*

dīgnus, -a, -um *worthy*
ingēns, ingentis *huge, vast*
memor, memoris *mindful, remembering*
omnis, omne *all; every*
pār, paris *equal*
similis, simile *like, alike*
vetus, veteris *old*

Notes: 1. The adjective **memor** is used with an objective genitive.

> Memorēs mortis este. *Be mindful of death.*

2. **Omnēs,** used substantively, may be translated *everyone,* and **omnia** *everything.*
3. The adjective **pār,** like **fīnitimus, idōneus, propinquus,** and **vīcīnus,** often requires a Dative with Adjectives.

> Poenī parēs Trōiānīs virtūte nōn erant.
> *The Carthaginians were not equal to the Trojans in courage.*

Like the others, too, it is used with a genitive when it is a substantive.

> Poenī parēs Trōiānōrum virtūte nōn erant.
> *The Carthaginians were not the equals of the Trojans in courage.*

4. **Similis** often uses the genitive of a person, the dative of a thing.

> Meum oppidum simile tuō est. *My town is like yours.*
> Meus frāter similis tuī est. *My brother is the like of yours.*

5. **Vetus** is not an i-stem, and is declined like 3 declension nouns.

■ LEARNING ENGLISH THROUGH LATIN

accelerate	*to increase the speed of*
acrid	*sharp, bitter, irritating to taste or smell*
inveterate	*firmly established over a long period of time; deep-rooted*
multitudinous	*great in number, extent, or variety*
nominal	*in name only; very small compared to normal expectations*
omnivorous	*eating any sort of food; taking in everything indiscriminately*
par	*on equal or common standing (as in "on a par with")*
simile	*a figure of speech in which one thing is likened to another*

▰ PRACTICE ▰

A. Derivatives

1. A different form of the word *accelerate* is used in reference to automobiles. What is this word and what is its connection with a Latin word in this lesson?   **2.** What connection does the word *dignity* have with a Latin word in the Vocabulary of this lesson?   **3.** Give an example of a simile in English. How does the meaning of the English word relate to the Latin word? **4.** Use the word *omnivorous* in an English sentence.   **5.** Can you show the relationship between the English words *inveterate* and *veteran*? From what Latin word are they derived?

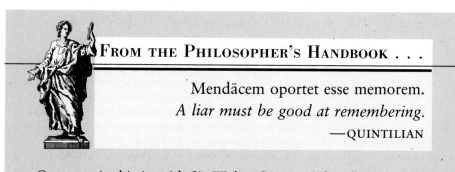

FROM THE PHILOSOPHER'S HANDBOOK . . .

Mendācem oportet esse memorem.
A liar must be good at remembering.
—QUINTILIAN

Can you tie this in with Sir Walter Scott's "Oh, what a tangled web we weave when first we practise to deceive?" How do they both tell us about the danger of not being truthful and honest?

B. Which adjectives in the Vocabulary are adjectives

1. of one termination?   2. of two terminations?   3. of three terminations?

C. Each of the following adjectives could be in more than one gender, number, and/or case. Give all the possibilities for each:

1. celeris   2. omnīs   3. dīgnīs   4. similīs   5. celere   6. omne   7. similia
8. ācrī   9. omnis   10. simile   11. celerīs   12. similium   13. omnibus
14. ācris   15. ācre   16. celerī   17. vetere   18. memorī   19. ācrīs
20. parium   21. memor   22. ingentī   23. pār   24. memorēs   25. vetus

D. Decline:

1. omne nōmen   2. pār multitūdō   3. timor celer

E. Pronounce, translate, then rewrite the sentence according to the indicated changes:

1. Omnēs deī populī nostrī sunt laude dīgnī. (Replace **deus** with **nūmen.**)
2. Omnēs memorēs fāmae nostrae, quod magna est, semper erunt. (Replace **fāma** with **nōmen.**)   3. Decus meum tuō simile est. (Replace **decus** with **laus.**)   4. Ad terram multitūdine virōrum parem vestrae nāvigāveram. (Replace **terra** with **oppidum.**)   5. Longam viam ad oppidum nūntiō dēmōnstrāvī. (Replace **via** with **iter.**)

F. Translate:

1. Your son is like my brother in courage.   2. Your native land is like my town in language.   3. Love is like a flame in the heart.   4. Helen is like Venus in reputation.   5. Our mothers are alike in soul.

READING

Developing Reading Skills

English words which might assist you in guessing unknown words in this reading are *ingratitude* and *vestment*.

The End of the Affair

Ubi Mercurius imperia Iovis Fātōrumque portāverat Aenēās timōre nūminum occupātus est. Trōiānōs convocāvit: "Ad lītus properāte, virī, et omnia fugae idōnea parāte, mox enim nāvigābimus. Omnia autem clam parātōte, nam imperia deōrum Dīdōnī nōn grāta erunt. Et quamquam Poenōs virtūte superāmus, Poenī nostrōs multitūdine virōrum superant." 5

Interim ācribus cūrīs animus Aenēae labōrat. Elissam miserē amat, at amor rēgīnae cum deum timōre, cum pietāte, cum decoris cupīdine in pectore pugnat. Atque quōmodo Elissae imperia Iovis nūntiābit?

Mala fāma autem ad Dīdōnem iam advolāverat: Trōiānī ad lītus proper-ābant atque fugam parābant. Īra cum amōre in rēgīnae pectore 10 pugnābat. Īrāta ad virum Trōiānum volāvit, et ācribus verbīs Aenēam vocāvit: "Ubi nunc, Aenēa, est tuus amor Dīdōnis? Trōiānōs tuōs servāvī iūvīque ubi ā dīs aquārum in altō paene pessum datī erātis. Dominus in meō rēgnō vocāris. Num nunc, ingrāte, ā meō oppidō nāvigābis? Scīlicet vir es dīgnus cūrā Fātōrum!" Nec stetit nec Aenēae verba exspectāvit, sed īrātē 15 rūrsus in rēgiam ambulāvit.

Trōiānī iam fugam parāverant, iam nāvigiīs celeribus super altum nāvi-gābant. Statim nāvigāverant, itaque nōn omnia tēla Aenēae vestīmentaque in nāvigiīs erant.

Tum Dīdō Annam sorōrem advocāvit: "Memoria sacrī Trōiānī et amōris 20 foedī pessum dator. Aedificābō magnum rogum quō tēla Aenēae vestīmen-taque portābō. Ibi omnia, vestīmenta et tēla cum amōris ingrātī memoriā, ignī dabuntur et flammīs vorābuntur!"

◼ READING COMPREHENSION

1. What great conflict did Aeneas have? **2.** How did Dido react when she heard the news of the departure? **3.** What did she decide to do? **4.** Why did Aeneas order his men to make their preparations in secret?

---

3. parātōte: future imperative (see Appendix) **14. Scīlicet** (adv.), *of course, certainly, to be sure,* is usually a signal that the speaker is being sarcastic or speaking ironi-cally. **21. dator:** future imperative (see Appendix) **22. memoriā:** Dido's bonfire is a kind of witchcraft, aiming magically to destroy all memory of Aeneas by destroying his possessions in a mock funeral.

LESSON 16

Third Declension I-Stem Nouns; Partitive Expressions

The Emperor Tiberius wearing the civic crown—Vatican Museum

OTHER FASHIONS

A felt cape (**lacerna**), safety-pinned on the right shoulder, served as a raincoat or overcoat. For travel a large cloak (**paenula**) with a hood (**cucullus**) was worn.

Indoors, both men and women wore leather sandals (**soleae**) with a narrow strap around the ankle and another between the toes. Outdoors, **calceī** were worn. These were sandals fastened with broad straps which covered the foot, so that they were more like shoes than sandals. Senators' sandals had longer broad straps which wound up the leg, making something like boots. These were black, with a small ivory crescent at the ankle. Magistrates wore red **calceī**, women white or colored ones. Soldiers wore hobnailed boots (**caligae**) of leather; peasants wore wooden shoes (**sculpō-neae**) or, like other poor people, went barefoot. The wealthier ladies got about in litters, and so had no special outdoor footgear.

Fashions did not really change very much among the Romans, as they do with us. The one thing that did vary a good deal, however, was hair style, especially among upper-class women. Much use was made of hot curling irons, dyes and bleaches, and false hair-pieces. For these, blonde hair taken from the heads of captive German women was especially popular. Ladies' hair styles began to become fantastically elaborate toward the end of the first century of our era. Some wealthy women even had their portraits carved with a detachable hairpiece so that after they were dead new pieces could be carved as the styles changed. In this way the portrait would never be out of fashion.

During most of the Republican period and during the early Empire, men were short-haired and clean-shaven, although fashionable young men might cultivate carefully trimmed beards. A full beard was the mark of a philosopher. From the reign of the emperor Hadrian, hair was worn longer and beards, fashionable in the early Republic, came back into fashion.

A PHRASE TO USE

Calvō turpius est nihil comātō.
*Nothing is uglier than a bald man
with hair (i.e. a man who combs
his few remaining hairs to try to
hide his baldness)*

—MARTIAL

ANCIENT ROME LIVES ON . . .

Why do you suppose modern
clothing styles change so rapidly and
ancient Roman styles changed so
slowly?

(*above left*) Gold earrings from Greco-Roman
Sicily—Archeological Museum, Syracuse
(*above*) Bracelets in the form of a writhing
snake were popular with both men and
women.   (*left*) Roman onyx cameo with
the Imperial Eagle. Such a jewel may well
have adorned an important official or his
wife in the high Empire.

FORMS

THIRD DECLENSION I-STEM NOUNS

A group of third declension nouns add **-ium** (instead of **-um**) to the base in the genitive plural and are called i-stem nouns. I-stem nouns include the following:

Masculine and Feminine

1. Most nouns ending in **-is** or **-ēs** (and a few in **-er**) in the nominative and having the same number of syllables in the genitive singular.

   nāvis, nāvis, f.   *ship*
   caedēs, caedis, f.   *slaughter, murder*
   imber, imbris, m.   *rainstorm, shower*

2. Nouns ending in **-ns** or **-rs** in the nominative singular.

   parēns, parentis, m. or f.   *parent*   mors, mortis, f.   *death*

3. Nouns of one syllable in the nominative singular whose base ends in two or more consonants.

   arx, arcis, f.   *citadel, castle*   urbs, urbis, f.   *city*

DECLENSION OF MASCULINE AND FEMININE I-STEM NOUNS

	SINGULAR	PLURAL	ENDINGS	
NOM.	nā**vis**	nā**vēs**	—	**-ēs**
GEN.	nā**vis**	nā**vium**	**-is**	**-ium**
DAT.	nā**vī**	nā**vibus**	**-ī**	**-ibus**
ACC.	nā**vem**	nā**vīs**	**-em**	**-īs**
ABL.	nā**ve**	nā**vibus**	**-e**	**-ibus**
NOM.	mors	mor**tēs**	arx	arc**ēs**
GEN.	mor**tis**	mor**tium**	arc**is**	arc**ium**
DAT.	mor**ti**	mor**tibus**	arc**ī**	arc**ibus**
ACC.	mor**tem**	mor**tīs**	arc**em**	arc**īs**
ABL.	mor**te**	mor**tibus**	arc**e**	arc**ibus**

1. Masculine and feminine i-stem nouns sometimes end in -ī in the ablative singular and in -ēs in the accusative plural. These endings will not be used in this text.
2. However, a very few i-stems always have -ī in the ablative singular, and even have an accusative singular in -im. Vīs, vīs, f., *force,* is the only such noun to appear in the vocabularies of this text. It also has an irregularly formed base in the plural.

DECLENSION OF VĪS, VĪS,. F., *FORCE*

	SINGULAR	PLURAL
NOM.	vīs	vīrēs
GEN.	vīs	vīrium
DAT.	vī	vīribus
ACC.	vim	vīrīs
ABL.	vī	vīribus

Neuter

Neuter nouns ending in -e, -al, or -ar in the nominative singular are i-stem nouns.

mare, maris, n.   *sea*

These nouns, like third declension adjectives, end in -ī in the ablative singular and -ia in the nominative and accusative plural. As with all i-stems, the genitive plural ends in -ium.

Roman woven leather sandal from Italy

DECLENSION OF NEUTER I-STEM NOUNS

	SINGULAR	PLURAL	ENDINGS SINGULAR	PLURAL
NOM.	mare	maria	——	-ia
GEN.	maris	marium	-is	-ium
DAT.	marī	maribus	-ī	-ibus
ACC.	mare	maria	——	-ia
ABL.	marī	maribus	-ī	-ibus

SYNTAX

PARTITIVE EXPRESSIONS

The Genitive of the Whole (Partitive Genitive)

A word which implies a part or portion of a whole person, thing, or group may be used with a genitive to indicate the whole. This genitive is called the Genitive of the Whole (or Partitive Genitive). The English translation of this genitive always uses the preposition *of*.

> Pars urbis occupāta est.   *Part of the city has been seized.*
> Multae nāvium ad īnsulam nāvigant.
>   *Many of the ships are sailing to the island.*
> Multitūdō nāvium ad īnsulam nāvigat.
>   *A large number of ships is sailing to the island.*

Many phases made up of a noun of quantity with a partitive genitive in Latin are translated as a noun with an adjective in English. Some of these nouns of quantity are:

> nihil, nihilī, n.   *nothing*
> parum, n.   *too small an amount, too little*
> plūs, plūris, n.   *a larger amount, more*
> satis, n.   *a sufficient amount, a sufficient number, enough*

> nihil aquae   *nothing of water* = *no water*

parum frūmentī
  too small an amount of grain = too little grain
plūs vīrium   *a larger amount of strength = more strength*
satis amōris   *a sufficient amount of love = enough love*

These nouns are defective, which means that they do not have all the forms which other nouns have. They have no plural, and are declined as follows in the singular:

DECLENSION OF DEFECTIVE NOUNS OF QUANTITY

NOM.	nihil	parum	plūs	satis
GEN.	nihilī	——	pluris	——
DAT.	——	——	——	——
ACC.	nihil	parum	plūs	satis
ABL.	nihilō	——	plūre	——

Partitive Ablative of Place from Which

The partitive idea with **paucī,** and sometimes **multī,** is expressed by the ablative with **dē** or **ex (ē).**

Paucī dē nautīs ad īnsulam nāvigant.
  Few (or A few) of the sailors are sailing to the island.
Multae ē nāvibus ad īnsulam nāvigant.
  Many of the ships are sailing to the island.

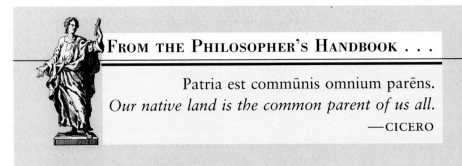

FROM THE PHILOSOPHER'S HANDBOOK . . .

Patria est commūnis omnium parēns.
Our native land is the common parent of us all.
—CICERO

What does this mean to you as an American?

Partitive Adjectives

Some adjectives already contain a partitive idea in their meaning, and so they do not need either a genitive or an ablative to express it. Some of these adjectives are:

extrēmus, -a, -um	*end of*	omnis, -e	*all of*
īmus, -a, -um	*bottom of*	reliquus, -a, -um	*rest of*
medius, -a, -um	*middle of*	summus, -a, -um	*top of*

Ad extrēmum oppidum ambulō. *I'm walking to the end of the town.*
Nāvis est in īmō marī. *The ship is at the bottom of the sea.*
In mediā silvā stat. *She is standing in the middle of the forest.*
Omnēs nāvēs ad īnsulam nāvigant.
  All of the ships are sailing to the island.
Ascanium et reliquōs puerōs spectāvī.
  I looked at Ascanius and the rest of the boys.
Arx est in summā urbe. *The citadel is at the top of the city.*

VOCABULARY

BASIC WORDS

All of these nouns are i-stems:

amnis, amnis, m. *river*
arx, arcis, f. *citadel, castle*
caedēs, caedis, f. *slaughter, murder*
hostis, hostis, m. *enemy*
ignis, ignis, m. *fire*
imber, imbris, m. *rainstorm, shower*
mare, maris, n. *sea*

mors, mortis, f. *death*
nāvis, nāvis, f. *ship*
parēns, parentis, m. or f. *parent*
pars, partis, f. *part, share; role*
urbs, urbis, f. *city*
vīs, vīs, f. *force, violence;* (plural) vīrēs, vīrium, f. *strength*

Notes: 1. **Hostis** means a *public enemy,* an enemy of the state, **inīmicus** (used as a noun), *a personal enemy.*
The normal English translation of the plural of **hostis** is by the collective singular *enemy.*

Ubi sunt hostēs? *Where are the enemy?*

Hostis is always used in the plural when more than one person is meant.
2. **Magna pars** usually means *the large part,* i.e. *the majority.*

■ **LEARNING ENGLISH THROUGH LATIN**

annihilate	*to destroy completely*
hostility	*a feeling of ill will; antagonism*
ignite	*to set fire to*
immortal	*living forever, deathless*
partial	*favoring one side more than another; prejudiced*
participant	*one who shares with others in some activity*
urban	*characteristic of a city*
urbane	*courteous in a smooth, polished way*
vim	*strength, energy*

A decorative safety pin or **fibula** with which early Roman men and women held up their garments

■ **PRACTICE** ■

A. Derivatives

1. The words *paraffin*, *plural*, *plus*, and *satisfy* are derived from the defective nouns of quantity which you learned in this lesson. What is the connection of each one with the Latin? **2.** Both *urban* and *urbane*, though seemingly different in their definitions, are derived from the same Latin word. Show the relationship. **3.** How many other English words can you find that are derived from the same Latin word as *immortal*? **4.** A different form of the word *ignite* is used in reference to automobiles. What is this word and what is its connection with a Latin word in this lesson? **5.** What connection do the words *naval* and *submarine* have with Latin words in the Vocabulary of this lesson?

B. Tell which rule for identifying i-stems applies to each noun in the Vocabulary.

C. Give the case(s) and number(s):

1. ignem   2. amnis   3. vim   4. arcis   5. nāvīs   6. caedēs   7. parentibus
8. hostī   9. maria   10. imbrium

D. Change the number, keeping the same case:

1. partīs   2. urbī   3. mors   4. ignem   5. amne   6. caedis   7. nāvium
8. parentēs

E. Decline:

1. urbs similis   2. parēns vetus   3. ingēns mare   4. pār multitūdō

F. Translate:

1. a few of the parents   2. a large number of the parents   3. part of the parents   4. the rest of the parents   5. many of the parents   6. all of the parents   7. no slaughter   8. enough slaughter   9. more slaughter   10. too little slaughter

G. Read the Latin and translate:

1. Propinquus meus plūs cupīdinis laudis iam dēmōnstrāverat, itaque reliquōs virtūte superāvit.   2. Utrum trāns amnem ā lātīs campīs sub silvam ubi plūs umbrae grātae erit an circum agrōs in oppidum ad summam arcem ubi semper multitūdō fēminārum est crās ambulābimus?   3. Ante bellum multitūdō nāvium populī nostrō inimīcī celeriter super mare nāvigābat, nunc autem post bellum in īmō marī est.   4. Si dī omnēs vestrō populō īram longam diū dēmōnstrant, num erit equus celer satis dōnī et mūnus nūminibus grātum?   5. Cūr post multōs inōpiae annōs deī nostrae fortūnae auctōrēs plūs frūmentī modo dedērunt?

H. Translate:

1. For the sake of friendship a few of the allies were helping our men yesterday, but they gave too little help.   2. In a few of the lands there are both plenty and want, for there is either enough grain but no water or more water but too little grain.

READING

Developing Reading Skills

Now that you have been working with derivatives, you should be able to determine the meanings of the following words used in this reading: **fūnus, fūneris,** n.; **magicus, -a, -um; vestis, vestis,** f.; **audāx, audācis** (What does *audacious* mean?); **vulnerō, -āre, -āvī, -ātum; dolor, dolōris,** m.; and **mortuus, -a, -um.**

Italy at Last!

Elissa ingentem rogum vocāverat fūnus magicum amōris vel dīs īnferīs
sacrum mūnus; sed erat mors in tristī rēgīnae animō. Itaque Dīdō ante āram
Iūnōnis steterat et "In extrēmā vītā, Iūnō," clāmābat, "in mediā morte tuum
nūmen vocō: dēhinc nihil amīcitiae estō inter Poenōs et Trōiānōs, impium
5   populum: semper hostēs suntō gentēs nostrae, semper pugnantō nepōtēs et
prōlēs." Tum rēgīna in summō rogō cum Aenēae vestibus et gladiō reliquīsque
tēlīs stetit; tum virtūtem audācem dēmōnstrāvit: Aenēae gladium occupāvit
et suum pectus vulnerāvit et animam exspīrāvit.

Interim in mediō marī Aenēās cum Trōiānīs ad Siciliam celeriter nāvigābat.
10 Spectābat lītus Āfricae ubi flammae, ut ignis ācer rogum in arce occupāvit,
ad caelum volābant. Timor dolorque Trōiānī pectus miserē occupāvit.

Tum ad Siciliam in rēgnum amīcī Acestae, ubi Anchīsēs animam exspī-
rāverat, Trōiānī nāvigāvērunt. Acestēs fīlius erat Segestae Trōiānae fēminae
(ad Siciliam ante nāvigāverat Segesta, fugā perīculōrum bellī Trōiānī) et
15 Crīmīsī, nūminis amnis Siciliānī. Ibi, ut Trōiānī fūneris mūnera animae patris
Anchīsae dabant, pars fēminārum "Satis terrārum spectāvimus," pūtāvit,
"mariumque satis; urbs nostra hīc aedificātor!" Tum ignem in nāvīs
portāvērunt, unde nāvēs flammīs occupātae sunt. At Iuppiter, ubi ab Aeneā
vocātus erat, imbrem magnum dē caelō dedit, itaque pars nāvium servāta
20 est.

Rūrsus in marī Trōiānī nāvigābant; dē fēminīs paucae cum virīs nāvigāverant, multae autem in Acestae rēgnō steterant. Dēnique Aenēās ad oppidum
Cūmās in Italiam nāvigāvit.

■ **READING COMPREHENSION**

1. Describe the end of Dido.   **2.** What did Aeneas see as he was sailing
toward Sicily?   **3.** What did the women do during the funeral games of
Anchises?   **4.** What did Jupiter do?

---

1. īnferīs: Appropriately the Gods Below, Dis, Proserpina, and Hecate, were gods of both
magic and death.   **4. estō:** future imperative (see Appendix)   **5. suntō, pugnantō:** future
imperatives (see Appendix) **semper ... prōlēs:** Dido's curse came true in the Punic Wars
between Carthage and Rome, the descendant of Troy.   **11. occupāvit:** A singular verb may
be used with a double subject if the two parts of the subject are thought of as making one
idea: *an emotion part fear, part grief, seized ...*   **17. aedificātor:** future imperative (see
Appendix)

A water numen, perhaps Oceanus. The Romans envisaged the numina of the
oceans and rivers such as the Crimisus in Sicily as divinities with human form—
Capitoline Museum, Rome

Translation Help

Most Latin words have several meanings in English, but only one of them is
likely to be appropriate to a particular context. By choosing the wrong
translations from a large Latin dictionary it is possible to translate the famous
opening words of Caesar's Commentaries, *All Gaul is divided into three parts* as
Every Gaul is quartered into three halves.

Which is the better translation of this sentence?

Puella post parentium mortem, et cārae mātris et patris clārī, dolōre ācrī in
pectore occupāta est; sed ubi sacra mūnera nūminibus dederat ā deīs iūta est et
animīs cōnfīrmāta est et magnam virtūtem dēmōnstrāvit; tum vērō grāta cūrae
caelī erat.

1. After the death of her parents, both her dear mother and her famous father,
   the girl was seized by sharp grief in her heart; but when she had given sacred
   gifts to the divinities she was helped by the gods and was stengthened in her
   spirits and showed great courage; then in truth she was grateful for the care of
   heaven.
2. After the death of her parents, both her expensive mother and her clear father,
   the girl was seized by shrill pain in her chest; but where she had given
   accursed gladiatorial games to the nods she was delighted from the gods and
   was established in minds and pointed out big manliness; then by means of a
   real thing she was welcome of the anxiety of the sky.

REVIEW 4

A. Give the genitive, gender, and meaning of the following nouns. (If the noun is defective, say which forms it does and doesn't have.):

amnis	frāter	māter	nōmen	propinquus
amor	grātia	memoria	nūmen	satis
arx	hostis	mors	parēns	soror
auctor	ignis	multitūdō	pars	timor
caedēs	imber	mūnus	parum	urbs
cupīdō	imperium	nāvis	pater	vīrēs
cūra	laus	nepōs	pectus	virtūs
decus	mare	nihil	plūs	vīs
flamma				

B. Give the other nominative singular forms for adjectives of two and three terminations, and the genitive for adjectives of one termination, plus meanings:

ācer	extrēmus	ingēns	omnis	similis
cārus	fīnitimus	medius	pār	summus
celer	idōneus	memor	propinquus	vetus
dīgnus	īmus	nōtus	reliquus	vīcīnus

═══ DRILL ON FORMS ═══

Decline:

1. īmus amnis   2. parēns vetus   3. mare ingēns   4. vīs celer   5. omne nūmen

174

LISTENING AND SPEAKING

Morning Comes Early

Life was not always easy for the Romans. They worked long hours, sometimes starting before dawn. The women took charge of the household and the shopping. Marcus and Lucius are both very grateful that their wives are so dependable.

MĀRCUS: Salvē,[1] Lūci, mī amīce! Esne fessus? Māne[2] est. Nōnne diū in cubiculō erās?

LŪCIUS: In pistrīnā meā, Mārce, multō māne labōrāvī. Pistor[3] sum et pistōrēs in furnīs[4] pānem[5] multum torrent.[6] Est servus sōlus[7] in pistrīnā, itaque ante prīmam lūcem[8] multum iam labōrāverāmus.

MĀRCUS: Nōnne uxor[9] tua in pistrīnā labōrat?

LŪCIUS: Nōn in pistrīnā sed in aedium culīnā labōrat. Nunc meam uxorem exspectō, nam māne in Forum cum vīcīnīs et fīnitimīs ambulāvit, et mox obsōnium[10] rūrsus portābit.

MĀRCUS: Sunt fēminae in viā prope tabernam. Nōnne uxor est pallā roseā[11] et stolā croceā[12] amicta?[13]

LŪCIUS: Est; Horātia vocātur. In Forum ambulāvit et holera[14] comparāvit, nam prandium nostrum iūs[15] holerum cum pāne novō ex furnō meō erit. Horātia bona coqua[16] est sed sōla in culīnā labōrat, quod nōn est serva in culīnā. Sed ubi uxor tua hodiē est?

MĀRCUS: In vīllā meā mānsit. Hodiē multī virī in agrīs sunt et multae servae in vīllā labōrant. Mox fēminae lānās[17] et tunicās nēbunt.[18] Uxor mea, nōmine Tullia, vīllam et servōs cūrat. Fēlīx[19] vir sum, quod fēmina fīda vīllam et servōs spectat ubi in oppidō cum negōtiīs sum!

LŪCIUS: Etiam mea fīda est; sumus virī fēlīcēs!

Choose two Romans and two interpreters. The Romans ask and answer the questions and the interpreters translate.

1. Ubi Lūcius multō māne labōrāvit? **2.** Utrum uxor Lūcī in cūlīnā an in pistrīnā labōrat? **3.** Quō Horātia ambulāvit? **4.** Cur uxor Mārcī, nōmine Tullia, in vīllā mansit? **5.** Cūr Mārcus et Lūcius virī fēlīcēs sunt?

1. salvē—'hello'
2. māne (adv.)—*early*
3. pistor, -is, m.—*flour miller, baker*
4. furnus, -ī, m.—*oven*
5. pānis, pānis, m.—*bread*
6. torreō, torrēre, torruī, tōstum—*bake*
7. sōlus, -a, -um,—*alone, sole*
8. lux, lūcis, f.—*light*
9. uxor, -is, f.—*wife*
10. obsōnium, -ī, n.—*food, provisions*
11. roseus, -a, -um—*pink, reddish*
12. croceus, -a, -um—*yellow, saffron*
13. amictus, -a, um—*dressed, clad*
14. holus, -eris, n.—*vegetable*
15. iūs, iūris, n.—*soup*
16. coquus, -i, m. or coqua, -ae, f.—*cook*
17. lāna, -ae, f.—*wool*
18. nēo, nēre, nēvi, nētum—*to spin*
19. fēlīx, fēlīcis—*lucky, fortunate*

Portugal—Conimbriga

I n 201 B.C. Carthage was defeated by the Romans in the Second Punic War. Rome gained the right to the Iberian Peninsula as part of the peace settlement. Gradually they conquered the peoples on the peninsula and by the time of Christ they had completed their conquest of what is now Portugal.

Mosaic from
House of the Fountains

Conimbriga: House of the Fountains

Conimbriga

However, conquest by the Romans was often a benefit to the people of the area. For example, they did much to build up Portugal. They established a network of roads and founded new cities. Latin, the language used by the Romans, became the basis for both the Portuguese and Spanish languages.

The origin of the name Portugal came from the Roman name of the port and city of the present day Porto, **Portus Cale.**

The Roman town of Conimbriga, founded in the second century B.C., is famous for its well-preserved Roman ruins—town walls, an aqueduct, fountains, baths, and mosaics.

Roman temple of Diana from 2nd century A.D.

LESSON 17

Second Conjugation; Ablative of Separation

Women exercising at the Palaestra—a Roman mosaic from the Imperial Villa at
Piazza Armerina, Sicily

YOUR ENTERTAINMENT: PUBLIC BATHS

The great public baths (**thermae**) were a uniquely Roman institution. Other cities, Pompeii, for example, had public baths, but the huge establishments, as much community centers as bathing establishments, began at Rome in the time of Augustus. From Rome they spread to all parts of the empire. Some of the best preserved are in North Africa.

The bath was a public park. Within its outer walls and surrounding its buildings were promenades, avenues of trees, flower gardens, park benches, and pavilions (**exedrae**) to sit in, which were cooled in the summer and heated in cold weather.

The bath was a public health club. In the bath building proper there were cold, warm, and hot rooms (**frigidāria, tepidāria,** and **caldāria**). The latter two were heated by hot air channels (**hypocausta** or **suspēnsūrae**) beneath the floors and in the hollow walls. In these rooms were cold, warm, and hot plunge baths (**solia**) and small pools (**piscīnae**). Usually there was a large swimming pool (**nātātiō**), open to the sky and surrounded by porticos. There were open-air courts (**palaestrae**) for wrestling and ball games. There were rooms (**unctōria**) for massage and private calisthenics. Trainers, coaches, masseurs, and medical advisers were available. Outdoors there were often running tracks (**stadia**).

The bath was a place for continuing education and entertainment. There were halls (**scholae**) where traveling lecturers gave talks on serious or amusing subjects, or authors read aloud their latest works. Most baths had public libraries (**bibliothēcae**), usually one for Greek and one for Latin literature. The baths were also art museums, since the buildings and grounds were decorated with antique or modern statuary and paintings.

The bath, like a modern mall, was also a restaurant complex and shopping center. Its outer walls were lined with restaurants and shops.

(Continued)

A PHRASE TO USE

Mēns sāna in corpore sānō
A sound mind in a sound body
—JUVENAL

A huge staff of public slaves manned the bath, providing a constant supply of clean towels and looking after the heating system.

The variety of activities offered at the public baths explains why the Romans could spend so much time there. Many were earnestly interested in improving their minds as well as their bodies. The usual hour for actual bathing was between two and three, but the establishment remained open from noon to sunset. It was the emperors' boast that there were so many public baths (925 by the time of Constantine) in Rome that the whole population (at its height perhaps a million people) could be using them at the same time.

(*below*) Ancient Roman thermal bath, Bath, England

ANCIENT ROME LIVES ON . . .

The similarities between ancient Roman baths and modern health clubs are obvious. What differences are there?

FORMS

SECOND CONJUGATION

As you recall, the present stem of a verb is found by dropping the -re from the second principal part. The Second Conjugation includes verbs whose present stem ends in -ē. The tenses are formed in exactly the same way as in the first conjugation, except that the stem vowel is not dropped in the present indicative first person singular.

In the first conjugation the principal parts of the majority of verbs end in -ō, -āre, -āvī, -ātum. In the second conjugation the majority of verbs ends in -eō, -ēre, -uī, -itum. You will notice the exceptions as you meet them in the Vocabularies.

PRESENT SYSTEM OF THE SECOND CONJUGATION, INDICATIVE

ACTIVE		PASSIVE	
SINGULAR	PLURAL	SINGULAR	PLURAL
PRESENT			
habeō	habēmus	habeor	habēmur
habēs	habētis	habēris (-re)	habēminī
habet	habent	habētur	habentur
IMPERFECT			
habēbam	habēbāmus	habēbar	habēbāmur
habēbās	habēbātis	habēbāris (-re)	habēbāminī
habēbat	habēbant	habēbātur	habēbantur
FUTURE			
habēbō	habēbimus	habēbor	habēbimur
habēbis	habēbitis	habēberis (-re)	habēbiminī
habēbit	habēbunt	habēbitur	habēbuntur

SECOND CONJUGATION IMPERATIVES

PRESENT
ACTIVE

habē	habēte

PASSIVE

habēre	habēminī

For the Future Imperative see Appendix.

Public toilets outside the Forum baths at Ostia

PERFECT SYSTEM OF THE SECOND CONJUGATION, INDICATIVE

ACTIVE		PASSIVE	
SINGULAR	PLURAL	SINGULAR	PLURAL
PERFECT			
habuī	habuimus	habitus, -a, -um sum	habitī, -ae, -a sumus
habuistī	habuistis	habitus, -a, -um es	habitī, -ae, -a estis
habuit	habuērunt (-ēre)	habitus, -a, -um est	habitī, -ae, -a sunt
PLUPERFECT			
habueram	habuerāmus	habitus, -a, -um eram	habitī, -ae, -a erāmus
habuerās	habuerātis	habitus, -a, -um erās	habitī, -ae, -a erātis
habuerat	habuerant	habitus, -a, -um erat	habitī, -ae, -a erant
FUTURE PERFECT			
habuerō	habuerimus	habitus, -a, -um erō	habitī, -ae, -a erimus
habueris	habueritis	habitus, -a, -um eris	habitī, -ae, -a eritis
habuerit	habuerint	habitus, -a, -um erit	habitī, -ae, -a erunt

SYNTAX

ABLATIVE OF SEPARATION

With a verb of separation, when no motion is implied, *from* is expressed by the ablative without a preposition. We call this use the Ablative of Separation. The preposition *from* (or, with certain verbs, no preposition) is used for the English translation.

Servum timore līberāvimus.   *We freed the slave from fear.*

When separation is not implied by the verb, the preposition **sine**, *without*, is used with the ablative.

Sine aquā sumus.   *We are without water.*

Note: When motion from, rather than separation, is implied, *from* is expressed by the Ablative of Place From Which with the preposition **ā, ab.**

Servum ā dominō līberāvimus.   *We freed the slave from his master.*

If advantage or disadvantage, rather than either separation or motion from is implied, the dative of reference is used to express the *from* idea.

Bona virō occupāvērunt.
They seized the goods from the man (i.e. to the disadvantage of the man).

Similarly, these sentences may be translated

We kept the enemy from the city. Hostīs urbe prohibuimus. Hostīs ab urbe prohibuimus. Hostīs urbī prohibuimus.

FROM THE PHILOSOPHER'S HANDBOOK . . .

Stultum est timēre quod vitāre nōn potes.
It is foolish to fear that which you cannot avoid.
—PUBLILIUS SYRUS

Philosophers and psychologists spend a lot of time thinking about fear. How could this proverb help us on our way to banishing it from our lives?

VOCABULARY

BASIC WORDS

careō, carēre, caruī, _____ *lack* (with ablative of separation)

habeō, habēre, habuī, habitum *have, hold; consider*

iaceō, iacēre, iacuī, iacitum *lie, be situated*

maneō, manēre, mānsī, mānsum *stay, remain, last*

teneō, tenēre, tenuī, tentum *hold, grasp*

timeō, timēre, timuī, _____ *fear, be afraid*

videō, vidēre, vīdī, vīsum *see*; (passive) *seem*

prae (prep. w. abl. of place where) *before, ahead of; in comparison with*

prō (prep. w. abl. of place where) *before, out in front of; for (on behalf of, in exchange for, in proportion to)*

Notes: 1. The Romans never used the fourth principal part of **careō** or **timeō**.
2. *Consider* as a meaning of **habeō** comes from its meaning *hold*, as in *We hold (consider) these truths to be self-evident.*
3. **Timeō** may be used with a dative of reference in addition to, or instead of, a direct object.

Perīculum timeō. *I fear danger.*
Perīculum fīliō timeō. *I fear danger for my son.*
Fīliō timeō. *I am afraid for my son.*

LEARNING ENGLISH THROUGH LATIN

adjacent — *positioned or lying next to something*
caret — *mark used in writing to indicate where something is to be added (∧)*
permanence — *the quality of lasting indefinitely without change*
prohibition — *order forbidding something to be done*
retention — *ability to remember or keep in mind*
tenable — *able to be held, defended, or maintained*
timid — *lacking self-confidence; easily frightened*
visible — *able to be seen*

A decorative border of birds and leaping dolphins from an Etruscan tomb

Building Vocabulary

Your Latin vocabulary can be increased by learning compounds of the basic words in the lesson vocabulary. For example, notice these compounds of the verbs **habeō** and **teneō**:

From **habeō** (**habeō** in compounds becomes **-hibeō** or **-beō**):
praebeō, praebēre, praebuī, praebitum
   (hold in front) offer
prohibeō, prohibēre, prohibuī, prohibitum
   (hold out in front) hold off, keep away; prohibit

From **teneō** (**teneō** in compounds becomes **-tineō**):
contineō, continēre, continuī, contentum   *hold together, restrain*
retineō, retinēre, retinuī, retentum   *hold back*
sustineō, sustinēre, sustinuī, sustentum   *hold up, withstand*

PRACTICE

A.   Derivatives

   1. Why do people get permanent waves? From what Latin words does the expression come?   2. Give synonyms for *timid, visible,* and *adjacent.*
3. Write an original sentence using two or more of the derivatives in the list in this lesson.   4. Other commonly used words which are derived from **teneō** are *content, tenant,* and *tenement.* Look up their definitions in a dictionary and show their relation to **teneō.**

B.   Pronounce and translate the following sentences. Then substitute **praebeō** for **dō,** and **videō** for **spectō:**

   1. Ā populō rēgī laus dabātur.   2. Puerī magistrum spectāvērunt.   3. Dōnum amīcō dabimus.   4. Nōnne spectāverātis hostīs?   5. Multa bona ā nūminibus data sunt.   6. Miser caedem sociōrum spectāverō.   7. Lēgātōne auxilium dās?   8. Ubi āram spectāverāmus sacra deīs dedimus.   9. Omnēs nāvēs nostrae hostibus dabuntur.   10. Nisi mūnera dederitis deī perīcula nostra nōn spectābunt.

C. Give the person, number, voice, and tense of the following verb forms, pronounce, and translate:

1. tenēbar   2. praebēbant   3. vidēris   4. vīderis   5. timēbimus
6. vidēmus   7. praebēbiminī   8. manēbat   9. vidēberis   10. carēbunt

D. Translate:

1. we were lying   2. I shall be held   3. I am being restrained   4. she fears   5. you (*pl.*) are held up   6. you (*sing.*) used to be restrained   7. it will hold up   8. they are holding back   9. we lacked   10. be held (*pl.*)

E. Give the following synopses (indicative and, where applicable, imperative) with meanings:

1. **careō** in the 1st singular active   2. **iaceō** in the 2d singular active
3. **praebeō** in the 3d singular passive   4. **prohibeō** in the 1st plural passive
5. **maneō** in the 2d plural active   6. **teneō** in the 3d plural passive

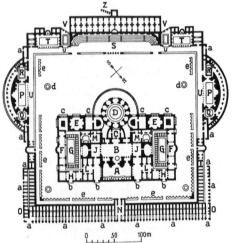

A plan and model of the Baths of Caracalla, Rome. The vast hot baths and pools were fed by an aqueduct and reservoirs which held more than 80,000 liters of water.

N Main Entrance
a Shops
Q Nymphaea
P Rooms opening on colonnade
R Heated Rooms
T Libraries (Greek and Latin)
S Stadium
V Water Tanks
z Aqueduct

b Entrances to the baths
L Dressing Rooms
A Nātātiō
B Central Hall
C Tepidarium
D Caladarium
G Palaestrae
F Exedrae
c and E Lecture Halls

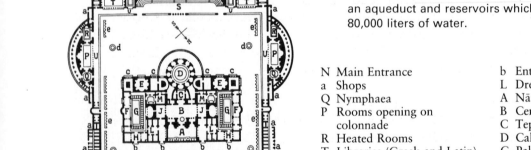

READING

Developing Reading Skills

Use your knowledge of Latin and English to determine the meanings of the following: **exemplum, -ī,** n.; **immortālitās, immortālitātis,** f.; **immemor, immemoris; permaneō, -ēre, permānsī, permānsum; sōl, sōlis,** m.; and **taurus, -ī,** m.

English derivatives will help you to determine the meanings of the following: **ardeō, -ēre; ārsī, ārsum** (*ardent, arson*); **iuvenis, -is,** m. or f. (*juvenile*).

The Temple at Cumae

In oppidō Cūmīs Sibylla nōmine Dēiphoba habitābat in templō ubi erat deī Apollinis magna aedēs. Apollō, quod puellam Dēiphobam ōlim amābat, Sibyllae prō amōre dederat dōnum immortālitātem. Deus autem immemor quod amōre ardēbat et Aurōrae exemplum memoriā nōn tenēbat secundum dōnum Dēiphobae nōn dedit: Sibylla nōn mānsit semper iuvenis. Itaque 5 nunc erat parvula vetula, per multōs enim annōs vīta et anima miserae veterī iam permānsit.

Apollinis aedēs ā nōtō Daedalō aedificāta erat. Ā Mīnōe Crētae rēge Labyrinthō cum Īcarō filiō retentus erat, unde tamen fugam parāverat: per caelum modo fuga patēbat, itaque pennās cērā miscuit et sīc alās fugae 10 idōneās parāvit. Ubi parātī erant volāvērunt et pater et filius; sīc ā Labyrinthō et ferō inimīcōque dominō līberātī sunt. Sed ut Īcarus patris cōnsilī immemor prope sōlem altē volāvit cēra tabuit et mors in mediō marī īnfēlīcem puerum mox occupāvit. Pater ut filium nōn iam vidēbat diū prope mortis locum

---

2. **Dēiphobam:** Word order is important here: **Dēiphobam puellam** would mean *the girl Deiphobe;* **puellam Dēiphobam** means *Deiphobe as a girl* or *Deiphobe when she was a girl.* 4. **exemplum:** Aurora had gained immortality for her lover Tithonus, but had forgotten to include eternal youth. Tithonus grew so old and withered that he was eventually changed into a grasshopper or cicada. **memoriā teneō,** *I hold by memory = I remember* 6. **parvula:** The suffix **-ulus, -ula, -ulum** is called a diminutive suffix. It adds the meaning *little* to the word. 7. **permānsit:** Remember that when a verb with two subjects is singular it may mean that the two subjects are parts of a single idea.

A Renaissance depiction of the fall of Icarus, Pieter Breugel, 16th century

15   manēbat "Īcare!" que clāmābat, tum tristis ad Siciliam, deinde ad oppidum
Cūmās volāvit, ubi in summā arce novam aedem decore mīram Apollinī
aedificāvit, nam grātiam salūtis deō salvātōrī dēmōnstrābat. Aedis in portā
caelāvit fābulam dē foedō mōnstrō Mīnōtaurō, virō ingentī cum taurī capite.
Mīnōtaurus in Labyrinthō habitābat, ubi Mīnōis imperiō līberōs Atticōs, et
20   puerōs et puellās, dēvorābat. Sed Thēseus vir Atticus iūtus est ab Ariadnā
Mīnōis fīliā pulchrā, ac sīc Mīnōtaurum obtruncāvit et iuvenēs servāvit.

     Reliquam fābulam et de fugā per caelum Daedalus caelāvit, sed ut Īcarī
figūram caelābat pater cūrā dolōreque occupātus est itaque cessāvit.

     Nunc Aenēās cum fīdō amīcō Achāte ad Sibyllam in templum celeriter
25   ambulābat.

▨ READING COMPREHENSION

1. What gift did Apollo bestow on Deiphobe?   **2.** What gift did he forget
to give her?   **3.** How did Daedalus escape from the Labyrinth, where he
was held by Minos, King of Crete?   **4.** What happened to his son Icarus?
5. How did Daedalus show his gratitude for his escape?   **6.** What was the
Minotaur? Who destroyed it?

LESSON 18

Third Conjugation; Ablative of Manner

An actor in royal costume ready to go on stage—wall painting from Herculaneum

YOUR ENTERTAINMENT: THEATRE

Dramatic performances (**lūdī scaenicī**) formed part of the religious festivals (**lūdī**) of Rome. By and large, the Roman taste was for farce rather than comedy, melodrama rather than tragedy. Above all a Roman audience liked a spectacular effect.

The native Italian drama consisted of slapstick and rude repartee among comically masked actors, interspersed with dances. The characters were probably stock types and the "theatre" a booth at the fair.

In the Third Century B.C. Greek drama was first translated and then imitated, but it was not until 145 B.C. that the first theatre, a temporary wooden structure, was built. Before this time spectators had to bring their own seats, or stand. The first permanent theatre was built by Pompey in 55 B.C. It was followed by the theatres of Balbus and Marcellus (the latter built by Augustus) in 13 B.C. These were the only permanent theatres at Rome; temporary wooden ones were still erected as the need arose.

Late republican and early imperial productions were lavish. At the opening of Pompey's theatre, in a tragedy about Agamemnon, the booty of Troy was brought on stage loaded on 600 mules (according to Cicero, but he may have exaggerated; the Romans said 600 as we might say a million). Under Nero, in a play called *The Fire,* (**Incendium**) a house was erected on stage, furnished, and then actually burnt down. To add realism to the acting, the actors were allowed to keep anything they rescued from the blaze. Occasionally condemned criminals might take part in dramatic performances and actually be killed on stage. In spite of these spectacular effects the Romans soon lost interest in the drama and turned more and more to comic opera (**mīmī**) and ballet (**pantomīmī**).

All of these forms of entertainment produced their popular stars. We know the names of many actors, singers, and dancers. There were even fan clubs: on the wall of an inn at Pompeii we find scribbled a notice of a

(Continued)

190

A PHRASE TO USE

Ars grātiā artis
Art for art's sake

meeting of men calling themselves **Fanāticī Actiānī Anicētiānī,** fans of Actius Anicetus (an actor very popular at Pompeii).

(*below*) A reconstruction model of the Theatre of Marcellus—Museo della Civiltà Romana, Rome

ANCIENT ROME LIVES ON . . .

What modern films/movies would an ancient Roman enjoy? How do you think a Roman would react to a film/movie you have seen recently?

▰ FORMS ▰

◼ THIRD CONJUGATION

Verbs whose present stem ends in a consonant or a -u belong to the Third Conjugation. They may be recognized by the fact that the second principal part ends in -ere (not -ēre, as in the Second Conjugation). Their present stem is found not by dropping the -re of the second principal part but by dropping the -ō of the first principal part. Thus the present stem of the verb pōnō, pōnere, posuī, positum, *put, place*, is pōn-.

Theatre mask of a Satyr—Scala Museum, Milan

Present Tense, Indicative Mood

Because adding the personal endings directly to a stem ending in a consonant would cause problems of pronunciation, a vowel (i, e, or u) is added to the stem before most of the personal endings.

THIRD CONJUGATION, PRESENT INDICATIVE

ACTIVE		PASSIVE	
SINGULAR	PLURAL	SINGULAR	PLURAL
pōnō	pōn*i*mus	pōnor	pōn*i*mur
pōn*i*s	pōn*i*tis	pōn*e*ris (-re)	pōn*i*minī
pōn*i*t	pōn*u*nt	pōn*i*tur	pōn*u*ntur

Imperfect Tense, Indicative Mood

The tense sign for the imperfect is **-ēbā-** (not **-bā-**, as in the first two conjugations).

THIRD CONJUGATION, IMPERFECT INDICATIVE

ACTIVE		PASSIVE	
SINGULAR	PLURAL	SINGULAR	PLURAL
pōnēbam	pōnēbāmus	pōnēbar	pōnēbāmur
pōnēbās	pōnēbātis	pōnēbāris (-re)	pōnēbāminī
pōnēbat	pōnēbant	pōnēbātur	pōnēbantur

A marble decoration from the theatre at Ostia portraying a character mask

Future Tense

The tense sign for the future is **-ē-** (**-a-** in the first person sing.), not **-bi-**.

THIRD CONJUGATION, FUTURE INDICATIVE

ACTIVE		PASSIVE	
SINGULAR	PLURAL	SINGULAR	PLURAL
pōnam	pōnēmus	pōnar	pōnēmur
pōnēs	pōnētis	pōnēris (-re)	pōnēminī
pōnet	pōnent	pōnētur	pōnentur

The Perfect System

The tenses of the perfect system are formed in exactly the same way as in the first two conjugations.

THIRD CONJUGATION, PERFECT INDICATIVE

	ACTIVE		PASSIVE
SINGULAR	PLURAL	SINGULAR	PLURAL
posuī	posuimus	positus, -a, -um sum	positī, -ae, -a sumus
posuistī	posuistis	positus, -a, -um es	positī, -ae, -a estis
posuit	posuērunt (-ere)	positus, -a, -um est	positī, -ae, -a sunt

---

THIRD CONJUGATION, PLUPERFECT INDICATIVE

	ACTIVE		PASSIVE
SINGULAR	PLURAL	SINGULAR	PLURAL
posueram	posuerāmus	positus, -a, -um eram	positī, -ae, -a eramus
posuerās	posuerātis	positus, -a, -um erās	positī, -ae, -a eratis
posuerat	posuerant	positus, -a, -um erat	positī, -ae, -a erant

---

THIRD CONJUGATION, FUTURE PERFECT INDICATIVE

	ACTIVE		PASSIVE
SINGULAR	PLURAL	SINGULAR	PLURAL
posuerō	posuerimus	positus, -a, -um erō	positī, -ae, -a erimus
posueris	posueritis	positus, -a, -um eris	positī, -ae, -a eritis
posuerit	posuerint	positus, -a, -um erit	positī, -ae, -a erunt

THIRD CONJUGATION, PRESENT IMPERATIVES

	ACTIVE		PASSIVE	
SINGULAR	PLURAL		SINGULAR	PLURAL
pōne	pōnite		pōnere	pōniminī

The Future Imperative can be found in the Appendix.

Strolling musicians in comedy—Villa of Cicero, Pompeii

SYNTAX

■ THE ABLATIVE OF MANNER

The manner in which an action is performed is expressed by the ablative case with or without the preposition **cum**. If the noun expressing the manner is not modified by an adjective, **cum** must be used.

> Verba cum cūrā parāvit.   *He prepared his words with care.*

If the noun is modified by an adjective, the **cum** may be omitted; if it is included the word order must be *adjective,* **cum,** *noun:*

> Verba magnā cūrā parāvit. ⎫
> Verba magnā cum cūrā parāvit. ⎭   *He prepared his words with great care.*

VOCABULARY

■ BASIC WORDS

dolor, dolōris, m. *pain, grief*
dux, ducis, m. *leader*
gaudium, -ī, n. *joy*
homō, hominis, m. *or* f. *human being, person,* (plural) *people*
rēx, rēgis, m. *king*

cēdō, cēdere, cessī, cessum *move, yield*
dūcō, dūcere, dūxī, ductum *lead*
mittō, mittere, mīsī, missum *let go, send*
petō, petere, petīvī, petītum *aim at, seek, attack*
pōnō, pōnere, posuī, positum *put, place, lay down*
regō, regere, rēxī, rēctum *rule*

Notes: 1. Cēdō is often construed with a dative of reference and sometimes an ablative of specification.

> Herculī cēdō.   *I yield to Hercules.*
> Herculī virtūte cēdō.   *I yield to Hercules in courage.*

When it means *move* it is construed with the Accusative of Place to Which:

> Ad āram cēdō.   *I move towards the altar.*

2. Dūcō does not add the **-e** in the present active imperative second person singular, which is **dūc.** This is also true of its compounds.

Translation Help

There are three Latin constructions which are normally translated into English using the preposition *with*:

1. The Ablative of Accompaniment (*with = accompanied by*)

   Cum sociīs hostīs superābimus.
      We shall overcome the enemy with our allies (= accompanied by our allies).

2. The Ablative of Means or Instrument (*with = by means of*)

   Deum auxiliō hostīs superābimus.
      We shall overcome the enemy with the help (= by means of the help) of the gods.

3. The Ablative of Manner (could be replaced by an adverb)

   Magnā cum laude hostīs superābimus.   *We shall overcome the*
   Magnā laude hostīs superābimus.   *enemy with great glory (= very gloriously).*

The word order *adjective-**cum**-noun* is invariable in the Ablative of Manner; but when any preposition is used with a noun which is modified by an adjective, several arrangements of the words are possible:
in māgnā silvā   in silvā magnā   magnā in silvā   silvā in magnā

FROM THE PHILOSOPHER'S HANDBOOK . . .

Culpam poena premit comes.
Punishment closely follows crime as its companion.
—HORACE

What evils in our society today are a threat to teenagers? How could this quotation help them to be wary of falling into their trap?

LEARNING ENGLISH THROUGH LATIN

accessible	*easy to approach or enter; obtainable*
deduce	*to reason from known facts*
dolorous	*very sorrowful; sad; mournful*
homicide	*manslaughter; murder*
homunculus	*little man; dwarf*
rectitude	*uprightness of character; strict honesty*
regalia	*emblems of kingship; splendid clothes; finery*
viaduct	*long bridge, supported on towers, over valleys and gorges*

Building Vocabulary

1. Compounds of **cēdō:**

   accēdō, accēdere, accessī, accessum   *go to, go toward, approach*
   discēdō, discēdere, discessī, discessum   *go away, depart*

2. Compounds of **dūcō:**

   dēdūcō, dēdūcere, dēdūxī, dēductum   *lead down, escort*
   ēdūcō, ēdūcere, ēdūxī, ēductum   *lead out, raise up*

3. Compounds of **mittō:**

   āmittō, āmittere, āmīsī, āmissum   *let go away, lose*
   committō, committere, commīsī, commissum
       combine; entrust (w. direct and indirect object)

4. A compound of **pōnō:**

   compōnō, compōnere, composuī, compositum   *collect, arrange, quiet*

PRACTICE

A. Derivatives

1. Make English derivatives of **cēdō** by inserting *cede, ceed,* or *cess:* ac____,
ac____, pro____, pro____, re____, re____, suc____, suc____ **2.** Make English
derivatives of **dūcō** by inserting *duce* or *duct:* aque____, in____, in____,
pro____, pro____ion, re____, re____ion **3.** Make English derivatives of **mittō**

by inserting *mit* or *miss:* ___ion, com___, com___ion, sub___, sub___ion, trans___, trans___ion   **4.** Give the definitions of the words you formed in 1, 2, and 3.

B. Pronounce, give tense, voice, mood, person, and number, and translate:

1. ēdūcēbar   2. āmittēbant   3. rēgeris   4. rēxeris   5. committēmus
6. petimus   7. pōnēminī   8. compōnēbat   9. dūcēris   10. dūceris

C. Translate:

1. we were moving   2. I shall be led   3. I am being let go   4. she seeks
5. you (*pl.*) are placed   6. you (*sing.*) used to be ruled   7. it will approach
8. they are going away   9. we led down   10. be raised up (*pl.*)

D. Give the following synopses, indicative and imperative, with meanings:

1. **cēdō** in the 1st singular active   2. **accēdō** in the 2d singular active
3. **dūcō** in the 3d singular passive   4. **mittō** in the 1st plural passive
5. **discēdō** in the 2d plural active   6. **dēdūcō** in the 3d plural passive

E. Pronounce and translate:

1. Itinera inter Āfricae urbīs oppidaque sunt longa et viae paucae, et magnō perīculō hominēs ibi ambulant.   2. Multā cum grātiā mūnera deīs fortūnae meae auctōribus quod satis imbris frūmentīs idōneī herī mīsērunt laetus hodiē praebēbō.   3. Post mortem ubi hominēs vītam vel animam āmīsērunt umbrae malōrum ā Mercuriō convocantur ac per lātum iter magnō cum dolōre ad īmum Dītis rēgnūm in loca nōmine Tartarum ambulant quō ā deō dūcuntur, ubi semper retinēbuntur neque līberābuntur.

READING

Developing Reading Skills

The following English words will help you to guess at some of the unfamiliar words in this reading: *animal, cause, form, inane, lunar, malignant, move, obscure, oracle, respond, spectacle, temporary, vacuum.*

The Golden Bough

Ut Aenēās diū stābat et aedis portam formā mīram spectābat, Sibylla "Nōn spectācula, Aenēa, tempus poscit," clāmāvit, "sed, sī ōrācula petis, mūnera sacra deō Apollinī grāta! Post ad aedem accēde." Tum, ubi Trōiānī sacra in ārā posuerant, Dēiphoba Aenēam in aedem dūxit, ubi ōrācula deī ducī
5 Trōiānō dedit: "Maris perīculīs iam labōrāvistī, sed terrae perīcula magna dīraque manent. Bella, horrida bella videō! Causa bellī secunda Helena erit; erit et secundus Achillēs."

Ad Apollinis verba Aenēās "Ad bella iam parātus sum," Sibyllae respondit, "sed ante ad Dītis rēgnum accēdam, ubi Anchīsēs cārus parēns fīlium
10 exspectat. Nōnne illūc dēdūcar, ut Orpheus vel Pollūx, ut Thēseus vel Herculēs? Omnēs parēs, omnēs deum prōlēs sumus, dīgnī auxiliō tuō." Dēiphobae respōnsum "Illūc" erat "nōn dēdūcēris, ō Veneris fīlī, nisi ante aureum rāmum in silvā petīveris et hūc portāveris, mūnus pulchrae Prōserpinae."

15 Aenēās ut in silvam discēdēbat geminās columbās vidit, avīs Venerī deae sacrās. Māter columbās ad fīlium mīserat dūcēs. Itaque Aenēam dūcēbant, et mox in silvā aureum rāmum magnō gaudiō vīdit occupāvitque dē arbore ac ad Sibyllam portāvit. Deinde cum Dēiphobā ante ārās sacra mūnera Hecatae Prōserpinaeque dedit atque Dītī, multa animālia nigra. Statim
20 magnō cum fragōre silvae campīque omnēs mōvēbantur et vīsum est iter per terram ad Dītis rēgnum, quō Dēiphoba Aenēam dēdūcēbat. Incēdēbant obscūrī sub nocte per umbram perque aedīs Dītis vacuās et inānia rēgna, pariter ut per incertam lūnam malignā sub lūce est iter in silvīs, ubi caelum condidit umbrā Iuppiter.

READING COMPREHENSION

1. What do the oracles of the god have to say to the Trojan leader? **2.** What does Aeneas want to do before going to war? **3.** What condition must Aeneas fulfill before he can accomplish this desire? **4.** How is he helped in his quest? **5.** Describe the journey of Aeneas and the Sybil.

---

6. Helena: The second Helen (i.e. a wife from a foreign land) will be Lavinia, a Latin princess. The second Achilles will be Aeneas' great adversary Turnus, whose rage at losing Lavinia to Aeneas will resemble that of Achilles at the loss of Briseis. **10. Orpheus, etc.:** These heroes all went alive to the Lower World and returned: Orpheus to retrieve his bride Eurydice; Pollux to change places daily with his dead brother Castor; Theseus in an attempt to kidnap Proserpina for his friend Pirithous; and Hercules to bring the dog Cerberus to the Upper World. **19. nigra:** Black animals were the proper sacrifices for the Gods below.

LESSON 19

Third Conjugation—iō Verbs;
Dative of Possession

Mosaics of charioteers wearing the colors of the four teams—Terme Museum, Rome

YOUR ENTERTAINMENT: CHARIOT RACING

Chariot races (**lūdī circēnsēs**), like theatrical performances, were held in honor of various gods; but they also provided entertainment which was immensely popular with all classes of Romans. A day of racing began with a parade (**pompa**) led by the magistrate giving the games, riding in a triumphal chariot and dressed in triumphal costume: scarlet tunic, wide-bordered toga, golden crown, and ivory sceptre. Then came images of the gods with their priests, and then a marching band. After the procession the presiding magistrate sat in his box, and the musicians took their places on the two towers (**oppida**), above the starting gates (**carcerēs**). When the magistrate signaled the start by dropping his handkerchief, the gates were opened and the race began. The chariots, usually four in number and with four horses each, made seven laps (about four and a half miles) around the central barrier (**spīna**). The laps were marked by seven wooden eggs, one of which was removed after each lap, and seven bronze dolphins, one of which was turned over after each lap.

The two center horses of the **quadrīga** were harnessed to the chariot pole, the outside ones tied directly to the chariot. The left-hand horse, the one on the inside rounding the turning posts (**mētae**), was considered the most important. Because of the difficulty of controlling four horses at once, the driver (**aurīga**) had the reins tied around his waist. He carried a knife to cut them so as not to be dragged if the chariot should smash into the barrier or overturn. The chariot was light and tipped easily, and there was great danger of its going over at the turns; the driver had to keep it balanced with movements of his body. As the chariots began their last lap a chalk line was drawn across the end of the course, and the first chariot to cross it was the winner.

In Greece chariot racing had been a rich man's sport, since each team was owned, and its charioteer hired, by an individual. But at Rome chariot

(Continued)

racing was engaged in by joint-stock companies, each of which had its own distinctive color worn by its charioteers. Teams and charioteers were hired from these companies (**factiōnēs**) by the government or the giver of the games. The two original factions were the *Reds* and the *Whites*. At the beginning of the imperial period the *Blues* and the *Greens* were added. The *Greens* were backed by the emperor and the mob, the *Blues* by the senatorial aristocracy, the *Reds* and the *Whites* by opposition parties. Toward the end of the third century the *Whites* joined the *Greens* and the *Reds* the *Blues*, leaving only the *Blues* and the *Greens*.

(*below left*) Cupid riding a chariot—fresco from the House of the Vettii, Pompeii   (*below right*) Relief from the tomb of a circus magistrate depicting a chariot race

FORMS

THIRD CONJUGATION -iō VERBS

A few important verbs of the third conjugation have present stems ending in -i. An example is **capiō, capere, cēpī, captum,** *take.* With both **pōnō, pōnere,** and **capiō, capere,** the second principal part tells you that the verbs belong to the third conjugation. The first principal part of each tells you that **capiō** is an i-stem and that **pōnō** is not (remember that the present stem in the third conjugation is found by dropping the -ō from the first principal part).

The short -i of the stem is changed to short -e in the second principal part, the present passive indicative second person singular, and the present active and passive imperative second person singular. The present active and passive indicative third person plural insert a -u between the stem and the ending. In all other forms these -iō verbs follow the normal rules for conjugating verbs: stem + tense sign + ending. The tense signs for the imperfect (-ēbā-) and future (-a-, -ē-) are the same as for **pōnō.**

Cameo: **Victoria** in a chariot

Present System

THIRD CONJUGATION -io VERBS, PRESENT INDICATIVE

ACTIVE		PASSIVE	
SINGULAR	PLURAL	SINGULAR	PLURAL
capiō	capimus	capior	capimur
capis	capitis	caperis (-re)	capiminī
capit	capiunt	capitur	capiuntur

THIRD CONJUGATION -iō VERBS, IMPERFECT INDICATIVE

ACTIVE		PASSIVE	
SINGULAR	PLURAL	SINGULAR	PLURAL
capiēbam	capiēbāmus	capiēbār	capiēbāmur
capiēbās	capiēbātis	capiēbārīs (-re)	capiēbāminī
capiēbat	capiēbant	capiēbātur	capiēbantur

THIRD CONJUGATION -iō VERBS, FUTURE INDICATIVE

ACTIVE		PASSIVE	
SINGULAR	PLURAL	SINGULAR	PLURAL
capiam	capiēmus	capiar	capiēmur
capiēs	capiētis	capiēris (-re)	capiēminī
capiet	capient	capiētur	capientur

Perfect System

The tenses of the perfect system are formed in exactly the same way as in all other Latin verbs.

THIRD CONJUGATION -iō VERBS, PRESENT IMPERATIVES

ACTIVE		PASSIVE	
SINGULAR	PLURAL	SINGULAR	PLURAL
cāpe	cāpite	cāpere	cāpiminī

The Future Imperative can be found in the Appendix.

■ SYNTAX

■ DATIVE OF POSSESSION

The dative case is used with the verb **sum** to show possession. The possessor is put into the dative. The thing possessed is the subject of the verb *to be* and is in the nominative.

> Puerō equus est.   *A horse is to the boy = The boy has a horse.*

Similarly, **dēsum, dēesse, dēfuī, dēfutūrus,** *be missing, be lacking* (a compound of **sum**), is used with the dative of possession to show lack of possession.

> Puerō equus dēest.
> *A horse is lacking to the boy = The boy does not have a horse.*

The dative of possession has no particular emphasis, as opposed to the genitive of possession, which emphasizes the possessor.

> Equus puerī est.   *The horse is the boy's.*

A final way of expressing possession is the use of the verb **habeō,** *have, hold*. This stresses the physical fact of possession.

> Puer equum habet.   *The boy has (possesses, holds) a horse.*

■ VOCABULARY

■ BASIC WORDS

anguis, anguis, m. or f. (i-stem) *snake*
carmen, carminis, n. *song, poem*
herba, -ae, f. *grass*
lēx, lēgis, f. *law, rule*
uxor, uxōris, f. *wife*

aspiciō, aspicere, aspexī, aspectum *look at, behold, see*
respiciō, respicere, respexī, respectum *look back at; (of a god) look with favor upon*

capiō, capere, cēpī, captum *take, capture*
faciō, facere, fēcī, factum *make, do*

dēnique (adv.) *finally, at last, at length*
paene (adv.) *almost*
statim (adv.) *immediately, at once*

Notes: 1. **Cōnsilium capiō** is an idiom meaning *I form (or make) a plan.*
2. **Faciō** is like **dūcō** in the present active imperative 2d person singular: **fac.** Its compounds, however, keep the **-e.**
   Faciō may have an adverb instead of a direct object when it means *do* in the sense of *act.*

   Fac amīcē.   *Act in a friendly manner = Be friendly.*

LEARNING ENGLISH THROUGH LATIN

confection   *any kind of candy or sweet preparation*
defective   *imperfect, faulty*
deficient   *lacking in some essential, incomplete*
efficacious   *effective, having the intended result*
facile   *easy; requiring little effort*
herbaceous   *having the nature of herbs*
incipient   *just beginning to exist; in the first stage*
legitimate   *lawful, reasonable*
uxorious   *submissive to or doting on one's wife*

Building Vocabulary

Compounds of **capiō**, which becomes **-cipiō, -cipere, -cēpī, -ceptum:**

accipiō, accipere, accēpī, acceptum   *receive*
excipiō, excipere, excēpī, exceptum   *take out, catch*
incipiō, incipere, incēpī, inceptum   *begin* (transitive)
praecipiō, praecipere, praecēpī, praeceptum
   receive in advance; instruct, teach (w. direct and indirect object)
recipiō, recipere, recēpī, receptum   *take back, accept*

Compounds of **faciō**, which becomes **-ficiō, -ficere, -fēcī, -fectum:**

cōnficiō, cōnficere, cōnfēcī, cōnfectum   *finish, accomplish; use up, weaken*
dēficiō, dēficere, dēfēcī, dēfectum   *fail, run out, be deficient*
efficiō, efficere, effēcī, effectum   *produce, effect, make*
interficiō, interficere, interfēcī, interfectum   *destroy, kill*

Other derivatives of **faciō:**

facilis, -e *easy*   difficilis, -e   *difficult, hard*

PRACTICE

A. Fill in the blanks with the appropriate English derivatives:

1. I went to the candy store to buy some ___ for the party. 2. Fortunately the doctor said it was only an ___ cancer and could be cured. 3. The treatment was so ___ that the patient was completely cured. 4. The new carburetor in my car must be ___; the gas is not flowing properly. 5. He has such a ___ wit that he is the life of the party.

B. Write an original sentence using two or more of the English derivatives from the list in this lesson.

C. *Effective* and *efficient* are, like *efficacious*, derived from **efficiō**; they all have approximately the same meaning. Precisely how do these three words differ in meaning?

D. Change the voice, keeping the same person, number, tense, and mood:

1. accipite 2. interficior 3. efficiēbat 4. cōnfectae sumus 5. recēperāmus
6. praecipientur 7. incepta erunt 8. excipis 9. facere 10. capitis

E. Pronounce, give person, number, voice, tense, and mood, and translate:

1. respiciēbar 2. incipiēbant 3. caperis 4. cēperis 5. interficiēmus
6. recipimus 7. efficiēminī 8. efficiēbat 9. efficiēris 10. efficeris

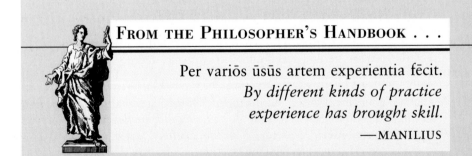

FROM THE PHILOSOPHER'S HANDBOOK . . .

Per variōs ūsūs artem experientia fēcit.
*By different kinds of practice
experience has brought skill.*
—MANILIUS

Can you apply this proverb to the various activities in your Latin class? Can you apply it to other activities in your daily life?

F.   Translate:

1. we were looking at   2. I shall be weakened   3. I am being looked back at   4. she fails   5. you (*pl.*) are received   6. you (*sing.*) used to be   7. it will approach   8. they are effecting   9. we accepted   10. do (*sing.*)

G.   Give the following synopses, indicative and imperative, with meanings:

1. **accipiō** in the 1st singular passive 2. **cōnficiō** in the 2d singular passive 3. **excipiō** in the 3d singular active   4. **dēficiō** in the 1st plural active 5. **aspiciō** in the 2d plural passive   6. **praecipiō** in the 3d plural active

H.   Translate:

1 & 2. The man has a wife. [2 ways]   3 & 4. The man does not have a wife. [2 ways]   5. He taught his wife the Latin language.

READING

The Lower World

Vergilius poēta ubi fābulam dē Aenēae fugā incipiēbat auxilium ā Mūsā, sed ubi dē Dītis rēgnō ā deīs īnferīs, petīvit. Deum auxiliō omnia sub terrā aspexit et in fābulā narrāvit.

Aenēās ut cum Sibyllā duce ad Orcī līmen accessit mala nūmina vīdit Cūrārum Morbōrumque et Famis Egestātisque, terribilium formārum. Hīc   5 erant et Mors et Labor et Somnus Mortis frāter, tunc malōrum Gaudiōrum et dēnique Bellī Caediumque ferōrum animae. Aspiciēbantur et mōnstra, Centaurī Scyllaeque biformēs et centumgeminus Briareus ac bēlua Lernae Chimaeraque, Gorgonēs Harpȳiaeque et forma tricorporis Gēryonis umbrae. Aenēās pugnam incipiēbat, sed virō Sibylla "Nōn vēra" praecēpit "mōnstra   10 sunt, sed mōnstrōrum umbrae omnēs."

Tum ad locum accessērunt ubi Acherōn amnis in Cocȳtum fluit propinquus Stygiae palūdī. Hīc multitūdō animārum virōrum fēminārumque et puerōrum puellārumque in rīpā stābat. Mūnera sepulcrī frūstrā exspectābant, nam

---

1. **Mūsā:** Poets customarily began important works or parts of works by invocations to one or more of the Muses.   5. **Cūrārum,** etc.: These words are capitalized to show personification: *of Cares and Diseases, of Famine and Poverty.*

The many monsters of the underworld were primarily of Greek invention. This 6th century vase shows the Chimaera, part lion and part goat, with a snake for a tail. Note the baby beneath!

15   hominēs sī sepulcrō carent trāns amnem nōn prōcēdunt. Portitor Charōn,
deus hominī veterī foedōque similis, ubi aureum rāmum aspexerat Aenēam
Sibyllamque trāns amnem nōn celeriter portāvit, ubi Cerberus canis trīceps
portam servābat. Anguēs ingentī Cerberō prō iubā erant. Dēiphoba autem
offam medicātam ācrī canī praebuit et Cerberum ubi offam vorāverat somnus
20   occupāvit.

Trāns amnem ad locum accessērunt ubi iūdex Mīnōs Crētae rēx mortuōs
iūdicat. Locō fīnitimī erant Campī Luctuōsī, quō hominēs accēdunt ubi
dolōre amōris cōnfectī sunt. Hīc per altās silvās campōsque lātōs errant
ambulantque tristēs et post mortem. Nunc inter miserās umbrās fēminārum
25   Aenēās aspexit formam nōtam.

▪ READING COMPREHENSION

1. What evil spirits did Aeneas see on the threshold of Orcus?   **2.** What are some of the monsters found in the Kingdom of Dis?   **3.** What was the multitude of souls doing on the river bank?   **4.** Describe Cerberus.   **5.** How did Aeneas and Deiphobe get past Cerberus?   **6.** Who judges the dead?

LESSON 20

Fourth Conjugation; Review of Conjugations and Case Uses

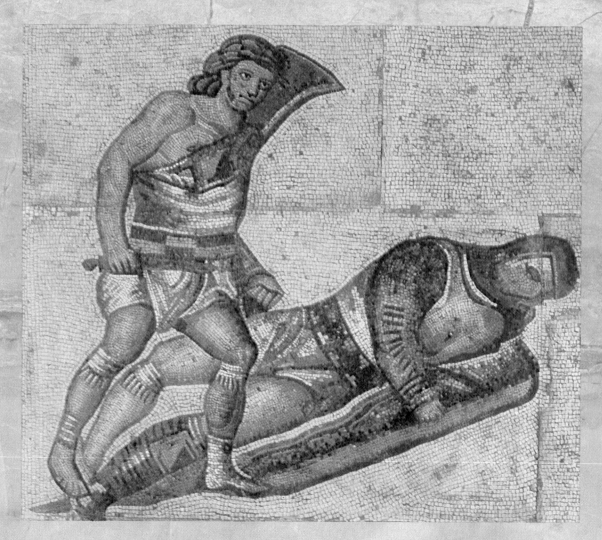

Mosaic of gladiatorial combat—Villa Borghese, Rome. A **Samnis** in a **galērus** and armed with a **spatha** has laid a **Hoplomachus** low.

YOUR ENTERTAINMENT: GLADIATORS

Gladiatorial games (**mūnera**) were first held by the Etruscans; prisoners of war were made to fight to the death, at the funeral of a general. The Romans found it useful and interesting to observe the armament and fighting styles of their enemies, and so they maintained the custom, substituting trained slaves or professional gladiators when there were no prisoners. The chief kinds of gladiators were: Samnite (**Samnis**), armed with a visored helmet with a plume, a broad belt, a greave on the left leg only (the left leg would be exposed when he knelt behind his shield), a neck protector (**galērus**) on his left shoulder to protect his neck from side blows of a sword, a broad two-edged sword (**spatha**) without a point, and a tall curved rectangular shield (**scūtum**); Thracian (**Thrāx**), with a helmet and two greaves, a small round shield (**parma**), and a curved sword (**sīca**); Charioteer (**Essedārius**), fighting from a light two-wheeled British chariot with two horses; Gaul (**Myrmillō**, so called from the name of a fish which was represented on his helmet), with helmet, sword, and shield; Net-man (**Retiārius**), armed only with neck protector, fishing net, and trident; Pursuer (**Secūtor**), like the Samnis but without the neck protector; Noose-man (**Laqueārius**), armed with only a lasso and a curved piece of wood; Two-dagger-man (**Dimachaerus**), with a dagger in each hand; Armor-fighter (**Hoplomachus**), fully-armed and with a breastplate and visored helmet; and Safe-walker (**Andābata**), armed to the point of invulnerability but with a helmet that covered his face so that he was blind.

If a gladiator found himself at the mercy of his opponent, he raised a finger to show that he surrendered. It was then up to the giver of the games (**ēditor mūnerum**) to decide whether or not he was to be killed. The killing of a gladiator cost the **ēditor** money, so his impulse must usually have been to spare him. Since his aim was popularity, however, he usually let himself be guided by the wishes of the people, who waved handkerchiefs if they

(Continued)

212

wanted the fallen gladiator spared. If they wanted him killed they displayed upturned thumbs (**pollicēs versī**), the symbol of the *coup de grace*, a sword-thrust through the throat. A man who had fought bravely would usually be spared. After a number of victories a gladiator might be retired at the demand of the audience. He was then presented with a wooden sword, which signified that, though still a slave, he no longer had to fight in the arena unless he wished to. He might end his days teaching other gladiators; if he was willing to fight, he might be able to buy his freedom or be set free by popular acclamation.

(*below left*) A Roman gladiator's shortsword or dagger—Pompeii
(*below right*) A Roman gladiator's processional helmet—Pompeii.
Such full-dress headgear was worn in the prefight procession only.

ANCIENT ROME LIVES ON . . .

How do fans feel today about fights and injuries at sporting events?

How would the ancient Romans react to our sports uniforms?

FORMS

FOURTH CONJUGATION

A verb whose present stem ends in -ī belongs to the Fourth Conjugation. As in the first and second conjugations, the present stem is found by dropping the -re from the second principal part. The tense signs are the same as those of the third conjugation. In fact, fourth conjugation verbs are exactly like third conjugation -iō verbs except in the second principal part and some forms of the present tense.

The principal parts of most verbs of the fourth conjugation end in -iō, -īre, -īvī, -ītum but, as always, there are exceptions. **Audiō, audīre, audīvī, audītum,** *hear,* is a typical fourth conjugation verb.

Present System

FOURTH CONJUGATION, PRESENT INDICATIVE

ACTIVE		PASSIVE	
SINGULAR	PLURAL	SINGULAR	PLURAL
audiō	audīmus	audior	audīmur
audīs	audītis	audīris (-re)	audīminī
audit	audiunt	audītur	audiuntur

FOURTH CONJUGATION, IMPERFECT INDICATIVE

ACTIVE		PASSIVE	
SINGULAR	PLURAL	SINGULAR	PLURAL
audiēbam	audiēbāmus	audiēbar	audiēbāmur
audiēbās	audiēbātis	audiēbāris (-re)	audiēbāminī
audiēbat	audiēbant	audiēbatur	audiēbantur

FOURTH CONJUGATION, FUTURE INDICATIVE

ACTIVE		PASSIVE	
SINGULAR	PLURAL	SINGULAR	PLURAL
audiam	audiēmus	audiar	audiēmur
audiēs	audiētis	audiēris (-re)	audiēminī
audiet	audient	audiētur	audientur

FOURTH CONJUGATION, PRESENT IMPERATIVES

ACTIVE		PASSIVE	
SINGULAR	PLURAL	SINGULAR	PLURAL
audī	audīte	audīre	audīminī

The Future Imperative can be found in the Appendix.

Perfect System

The tenses of the perfect system are formed in exactly the same way as in the other three conjugations.

Relief depicting a gladiatorial combat—Terme Museum, Rome

■ REVIEW OF CONJUGATIONS

PRESENT SYSTEM

	1ST PRINCIPAL PART	2D PRINCIPAL PART	STEM VOWEL	STEM VOWEL FOUND BY REMOVING	IMPERFECT TENSE SIGN	FUTURE TENSE SIGN
FIRST	-ō	-āre	ā	**-re** from 2d princ. part	-bā-	-bi- (-b-, -bu-)
SECOND	-eō	-ēre	ē	**-re** from 2d princ. part	-bā-	-bi- (-b-, -bu-)
THIRD	-ō	-ere	-	**-ō** from 1st princ. part		
	-iō		i		-ēbā-	-ē- (-a-)
FOURTH	-iō	-īre	ī	**-re** from 2d princ. part	-ēbā-	-ē- (-a-)

PERFECT SYSTEM

In all conjugations the perfect stem (used for the perfect active) is always found by removing the **-ī** from the third principal part; and the participial stem (used for the perfect passive) is found by removing the **-um** from the fourth principal part. The personal endings and the tense sign for the pluperfect and future perfect are the same in all conjugations.

■ SYNTAX

■ REVIEW OF CASE USES

Reference is provided to each mention of the construction, which will be found in the *Syntax* section of the lesson whose number is given. Additional references are marked with an **F** if the mention occurs in the *Forms* section, with an **H** for *Translation Help*, with a **V** for *Vocabulary Notes*, and with an **R** for *Reading Footnotes*.

The Nominative Case names or makes a statement about the subject of a verb.

Subject	1 2H 7R 8H 10H 16R
Predicate Nom. (Subjective Complement)	1 8H 10H 11
Appositive	2

The Vocative Case is used for direct address.

Direct address	6
Appositive	2

The Genitive Case shows possession, denotes the whole of which a part is mentioned, or tells who or what receives the action of a noun or adjective.

Genitive of Possession	1 2H 6H 13 15V 19
Partitive Genitive (Gen. of the Whole)	6H 16
Objective Genitive	6H 14 14V 15V
Appositive	2

Relief with **bestiāriī** in combat. The magistrates watch from the officials' box—La Scala Museum, Milan

The Dative Case indicates the indirect object of a verb or shows to whose advantage or disadvantage the action is performed, is used to complete the meaning of an adjective, or is used as a subjective complement with the verb *to be* to show possession.

Dative of Indirect Object	7 8H 10H
Dative of Reference	7 17 17V 18V
Dative with Adjectives	13 15V
Dative of Possession	19
Appositive	2

The Accusative Case limits the action of a verb, as the direct object, as a second accusative with verbs of making, naming, or choosing, and to answer the question *where to?*

Accusative of the Direct Object	2 2H 8H 10H 19V
Predicate Acc. (Objective Complement)	4 8H 10H
Accusative of Place to Which	3 4R 11R 18V
Appositive	2

The Ablative Case was originally only the *from* case (ablative means *taking away*). Then it took over the functions of two other cases: the *with* case (called Instrumental-Circumstantial), and the *in-on-at* case (called Locative). Hence the Ablative Case has three distinct functions:

The Ablative Proper expresses the idea *from*.

Ablative of Separation	17
Ablative of Place from Which	3 17
Partitive Ablative of Place from Which	16
Ablative of Personal Agent	11 12H
Appositive	2

The Instrumental-Circumstantial Ablative expresses the idea *with*.

Ablative of Means or Instrument	8 12H 14V 17R 18H
Ablative of Specification	15 18V
Ablative of Accompaniment	2 2H 10V 12H 18H
Ablative of Manner	18 18H
Appositive	2 2H

The Locative Ablative expresses the idea *in, on,* or *at*.

Ablative of Place Where	1 2H 3 12H
Appositive	2

VOCABULARY

BASIC WORDS

aurum, -ī, n. *gold*

gēns, gentis, f. *family, clan; nation*

pius, -a, -um *loyal, dutiful*

tristis, -e *mournful, grim*

aperiō, aperīre, aperuī, apertum *open, uncover, make known*

audiō, audīre, audīvī, audītum *hear, listen to*

errō, -āre, -āvī, -ātum *wander, stray; be wrong*

misceō, -ēre, -uī, mixtum *mix*

mōveō, -ēre, mōvī, mōtum *move*

mūtō, -āre, -āvī, -ātum *change, exchange*

reperiō, reperīre, repperī, repertum *find, discover*

veniō, venīre, vēnī, ventum *come*

Notes:

1. **Pius** means specifically *loyal to the gods, members of one's own family, or a guest or host.* Loyalty to these was the only commandment of the Roman gods, and a breach of this loyalty the only sin.

2. **Misceō** is followed either by two direct objects or by a direct object and either an ablative of means or an ablative of accompaniment.

> Frūmentum et aquam miscēbat.   *He was mixing grain and water.*

> Frūmentum cum aquā miscēbat. ⎫
> Frūmentum aquā miscēbat.   ⎬ *He was mixing grain with water.*

FROM THE PHILOSOPHER'S HANDBOOK . . .

Gladiātor in arēnā cōnsilium capit.
The gladiator is making his plan in the arena.

—SENECA

Now that you have learned about the role of the gladiators in Roman culture, can you figure out the significance of this saying?

■ **LEARNING ENGLISH THROUGH LATIN**

aperture	*opening, hole, gap*
audible	*loud enough to be heard*
audit	*periodic checking of accounts to verify their correctness*
err	*to wander, go astray; to be wrong or mistaken*
erroneous	*mistaken, wrong*
genteel	*having or showing good taste and refinement*
impious	*lacking respect or reverence*
mutation	*change in form, nature, or quality*

Building Vocabulary

Note these compounds of **veniō**:

conveniō, convenīre, convēnī, conventum   *come together*
inveniō, invenīre, invēnī, inventum   *come upon, find*
perveniō, pervenīre, pervēnī, perventum
    come all the way, arrive
(**Inveniō** usually means *to find accidentally,*
    reperiō *to find by searching.*)

■ PRACTICE ■

A.   Derivatives

1. There are several English words derived from the Latin verb **errō**. Look in your dictionary for the definitions of *erratum, errant,* and *erratic.*   **2.** The Latin verb **audiō** also has several English derivatives. Find five of its derivatives in your dictionary and give the meaning of each.   **3.** Check your dictionary for the differences in meaning of *genteel, gentile,* and *gentle.* How are they related to the Latin **gēns?**

B.   Change the voice, keeping the same person, number, tense, and mood:

1. audītī erunt   **2.** inveniam   **3.** miscuerātis   **4.** reperiēbāris   **5.** mōtī sumus   **6.** mūtat

C.   Change the number, keeping the same tense, voice, and mood:

1. perveniēs   2. errābāmus   3. apertum erat   4. conveniō   5. vēnistis
6. mixta erunt

D.   Give tense, voice, mood, person, and number, and translate:

1. capiet   2. caret   3. aperiet   4. cēdet   5. mūtāminī   6. audiēminī
7. miscēminī   8. petēminī   9. dūc   10. fac

E.   Translate:

1. they are making   2. we mix   3. we were being moved   4. it will be
5. you (*pl.*) will be led   6. they will come   7. you (*pl.*) were being changed
8. she is wrong   9. you (*sing.*) were uncovering   10. I was being found

Translation Help

Latin word order, as we have seen, is determined by two factors, achieving the right emphasis and avoiding ambiguity. Other rules of word order:

Nōn—always goes just before the word it modifies; in front of the verb if the whole clause is negative.
Ablative of Manner—adjective-**cum**-noun.
Populus Rōmānus—always together and in that order.
Vocative and postpositive conjunctions—may not come at the beginning of a clause.

The position of an appositive affects its meaning:
Alexander rēx rēgnum bene rēxit.
   King Alexander ruled the kingdom well.
Rēx Alexander rēgnum bene rēxit.
   Alexander, while king, ruled the kingdom well.
   As king, Alexander ruled the kingdom well.

When a sentence begins with a subordinate clause whose subject is the same as some noun in the principal clause, that noun is usually placed at the beginning:
Fīliō ut ex urbe discēdēbat rēx aurum commīsit.
   As his son was leaving the city the king entrusted the gold to him.
Rēx ut ex urbe discēdēbat fīliō aurum commīsit.
   As the king was leaving the city he entrusted the gold to his son.

READING

Encounters with the Dead

Inter fēminārum īnfēlīcium umbrās in Campīs Luctuōsīs Dīdō errābat silvā in magnā. Forma rēgīnae nōn clāra erat, sed vidēbātur ut lūna nova per nūbīs vidētur. Pius Aenēās dēmīsit lacrimās dulcīque amōre Elissam appellābat: "Īnfēlīx Dīdō, vērus nūntius ergō vēnerat? Fūneris heu causa fuī? Per
5 sīdera iūrō, per superōs et nūmina īmā sub terrā, invītus, rēgīna, tuō dē lītore cessī." Plūs verbī incipiēbat, sed Dīdō verba nōn audiēbat, nec mōvēbātur. Dēnique discessit atque inimīca refūgit in nemus umbriferum, coniunx ubi pristinus rēgīnae respondet cūrīs aequatque Sychaeus amōrem.

Dēnique Sibylla Aenēam in locum dūxit quō bellō clārī post mortem
10 cēdunt. Hīc et amīcōs et hostīs invēnit, sed morte miserē mūtātī erant. Graecōrum animae ut virum Trōiānum aspexērunt magnō cum timōre fūgērunt, Trōiānōrum autem ad Aenēam convēnērunt et multa et dē bellō et dē fugā perīculōrum rogābant. Ut verba Aenēae audiēbant, Dēiphoba "Cūr stās?" clāmāvit, "Hīc locus est ubi via finditur: pars Dītis magnī sub
15 moenia tendit, iter nostrum ad Campōs Elysiōs; pars malōrum exercet poenās et ad impia Tartara mittit."

Itaque Aenēās, ubi loca sacra in īmō Erebō quō discēdunt malī et ubi in aeternum continentur aspexerat, cum duce Sibyllā ad Campōs Elysiōs pervēnit, ubi inter bonōrum animās cārī patris Anchīsae umbram dēnique
20 repperit. Fīliō multās animās dēmōnstrāvit vītae in terrā ante mortem nōn memorīs, Lēthaeā enim aquā mūtātī sunt et nihil memoriā tenēbant. Ubi Aenēās animārum nōmina rogāvit, pater "Nunc umbrae sine nōmine sunt," respondit, "sed ōlim prōlēs tuī erunt, ducēs tuae gentis." Et fāta Populī Rōmānī fīliō aperuit.

■ READING COMPREHENSION

1. What did Aeneas say to Dido when he saw her in the Land of the Dead?
2. What was Dido's reaction?   3. How did the souls of the Greeks and Trojans react to Aeneas' visit?   4. Whom did Aeneas find in the Elysian fields?   5. How did the water of Lethe affect souls?

---

8. **coniunx ubi = ubi coniunx:** If no ambiguity could result, a word which belongs to a subordinate clause may be brought outside the clause for emphasis.

REVIEW 5

LESSONS 17–20

VOCABULARY DRILL

A. Give the genitive, gender, and meaning of these nouns:

anguis	dolor	gaudium	homō	rēx
aurum	dux	herba	lēx	uxor
carmen	gēns			

B. Give the other nominative singular form(s) and the meanings of these adjectives:

facilis	difficilis	pius	tristis

C. Give the other three principal parts and the meanings of these verbs:

accēdō	compōnō	efficiō	misceō	recipiō
accipiō	cōnficiō	errō	mittō	rēgō
āmittō	contineō	excipiō	mōveō	reperiō
aperiō	conveniō	faciō	mūtō	respiciō
aspiciō	dēdūcō	habeō	perveniō	retineō
audiō	dēficiō	iaceō	petō	sustineō
capiō	dēsum	incipiō	pōnō	teneō
careō	discēdō	interficiō	praebeō	timeō
cēdō	dūcō	inveniō	praecipiō	veniō
committō	ēdūcō	maneō	prohibeō	videō

D. Tell with which case or cases the prepositions **prae** and **prō** are used and give the meanings.

E. Give the meanings of the adverbs **dēnique, paene,** and **statim.**

223

LISTENING AND SPEAKING

Holidays in Town

1. **festīnō, -āre, -āvī, -ātum**—*to hasten, hurry*

2. **feriae, ārum, f. pl.**—*holidays*

3. **ineptus, -a, -um**—*foolish*

4. **Flōrālia, -ium, n. pl.**—*the Floralia, festival of Flora, a goddess of spring and flowers*

5. **flōs, flōris, m.**—*flower*

6. **ēversus, -a, -um**—*overturned*

7. **vulnerātus, -a, -um**—*wounded*

8. **amphitheātrum, -ī, n.**—*amphitheater*

9. **duumvir, -ī, m.**—*a duumvir, the town version of a consul*

10. **Cornēlius, -ī, m.**—*Cornelius*

11. **imperātor, -is, m.**—*general*

12. **invītātus, -a, -um**—*invited; guest*

13. **speciōsus, -a, -um**—*handsome, beautiful*

14. **Celadus, -ī, m.**—*Celadus*

15. **suspīrium, -ī, n.**—*sigh (here 'heartthrob')*

16. **nūgae, -ārum, f. pl.**—*trifles, excl. 'nonsense!'*

17. **nūbo, -ere, nupsī, nuptum**—*to be married to*

*It's festival time and Gnaeus Mucius and his wife Lucretia have been invited to attend the games and a gladiatorial show in honor of a famous general. Listen to the conversation between Lucretia and Apollonia, her maid (**ancilla**), as preparations are being made for the games.*

LŪCRĒTIA: Apollōnia, ancilla mea, ubi es? Festīnā;[1] meam pallam et stolam croceam petō. Ubi posuistī?

APOLLŌNIA: In armāriō, domina, sunt. Hodiē et crās erunt feriae.[2] Quō cēdēs? Utrum in vīllā manēbis annōn?

LŪCRĒTIA: Cūr, puella inepta,[3] stolam croceam petō? Cum virō Mūciō in oppidum ad lūdōs accēdam. Festīnā, nam vir iam parātus est!

APOLLŌNIA: Utrum, domina, lūdōs circēnsīs an mūnera vidēbis? equōs celerīs quadrīgāsque et aurīgās fortīs amō.

LŪCRĒTIA: Hodiē, ut Flōrālia,[4] lūdī Flōrae deae flōrum[5] sacrī, sunt, lūdōs circēnsīs spectābimus, nam vir equōs celerīs amat. Multa autem perīcula in lūdīs sunt, nam in Circō ad mētās multās quadrīgās ēversās[6] et aurīgās vulnerātōs[7] saepe vīdī.

APOLLŌNIA: Vidēbisne etiam in amphitheātrō[8] gladiatōrēs?

LŪCRĒTIA: Crās, Apollōnia, ā Liciniō, duumvirō[9] urbis, mūnera magna in Cornēlī[10] imperātōris[11] honōrem dabuntur; et Mūcius, vir meus, invītātus[12] Licinī erit.

APOLLŌNIA: Amāsne, domina, mūnera? Gladiatōrēs autem amō; sunt speciōsī[13] pulchrīque. Fēminae gladiātōrem Thrācem Celadum[14] suspīrium[15] puellārum vocāmus!

LŪCRĒTIA: Fābulās, nugās![16] Num mūnera et gladiatōrēs amās? Thrācēs et Retīariī et omnēs gladiatōrēs servī malī sunt. Sī gladiatōrēs semper spectābis, numquam virō bonō nūbēs![17] Mūneribus sunt perīcula et vulnera et mortēs. In amphitheātrō autem nōn gaudium sed dolor semper reperītur.

APOLLŌNIA: Cūr ergō, domina, lūdōs spectās? Cūr in vīllā nōn manēs?

LŪCRĒTIA: Nōn modo bona uxor Mūciī, sed etiam bona invītāta Licinī erō. Virī mūnera et lūdōs nōn semper spectant, et fēminae ā virīs saepe spectantur. Multīs enim feminīs grātum est. Pallam novam gemmāsque[18] geram et multās amīcās amīcōsque vidēbō. Ubi soleās meās posuistī?

18. gemma, -ae, f.— *jewel, gem*

A. Choose a partner and present an oral reading of the conversation.

B. Answer the following questions in Latin.

1. Cūr Lūcrētia stolam croceam petēbat? 2. Ubi sunt multa perīcula? 3. Amantne fēminae gladiātōrem Celadum? 4. Cūr Lūcrētia in amphitheātrō semper dolōrem reperit? 5. Cūr fēminae mūnera spectant?

A mosaic of gladiatorial combat from Bignor, Sussex, England. An **Andābata** or **Hoplomachus** squares off against a **Retiārius.**

United States—Universities

Seal of Harvard University,
Cambridge, Massachusetts

Throughout the United States, our colleges and universities abound with traces of Roman civilization. The language of the Romans can be seen in college seals, which are often reproduced on furniture, glassware, banners, t-shirts, yearbooks, and alumni magazines.

Roman architecture is very prevalent on the college campus. Buildings with domes, columns, arches, and other aspects of Roman architecture are commonplace.

University of Virginia

Texas A&M University

Seal of Wellesley College,
Wellesley, Massachusetts

University of California,
Berkeley

Shades of the Circus Maximus and the Colosseum can be found in the modern football stadium. Many classes adopt Latin proverbs or sayings for their class mottos.

Visit a college or university in your area and make a list of all the traces of Roman civilization you find there.

Yale University,
New Haven, Connecticut

Memorial Stadium,
University of Texas,
Austin, Texas

Roman Colosseum

LESSON 21

Numerals 1–20; Genitive and Ablative of Description

A Gallo-Roman **raeda** transporting passengers. Note the hoof protectors which the horses wear.

YOUR TRANSPORTATION

Transportation for the Romans was slow by our standards: travel by mule-drawn cart would have averaged 5 MPH. They were, however, able to provide for all their travel needs by a variety of vehicles.

For ordinary passengers there were six different types of vehicles. Two-passenger mule-drawn two-wheelers could be hired outside the gates of cities and at various points along the major roads. A driver would be hired with one of them (**cisium**), but the other (**essedum**), being more solid and steady, if a little slower, could be driven by anyone. A still slower, more comfortable, four-wheeled mule-drawn cart (**carrūca**) with a cover had room in it to recline or even sleep. The fourth cart (**raeda**), also four-wheeled and mule-drawn, was much larger and had several seats; it could carry a large party with their luggage. The smaller four-wheeled **pīlentum** was used by ladies calling on friends who lived a short distance out of town; for men there was a litter (**basterna**) carried by two mules.

For freight there were at least three kinds of wagons. The **carrus** had removable sloping sides and two large spoked wheels. The **plaustrum,** used for transporting farm produce, was built more sturdily with solid wheels. The heavy-duty **sarrācum,** used for amphorae of wine, building-blocks, and other heavy items, was very solid with four much smaller wheels. Freight wagons were drawn by oxen, or sometimes by donkeys.

Other types of Roman road transport were the army truck (**clabulāre**), an open four-wheeled wagon with wickerwork sides used to transport troops, and a closed-in padded four-wheeled cart (**arcera**) used as an ambulance for the transport of sick or aged people.

ANCIENT ROME LIVES ON . . .

Cite similarities between ancient Roman
systems of transport and ours.

(*above left*) An ornamental essedum
used for a cult procession of Jupiter
and the Dioscurii—Italy, 3rd c. A.D.
(*below*) An ox-drawn plaustrum on a
mosaic from a Roman imperial
hunting lodge—Piazza Armerina

FORMS

NUMBER WORDS

There are several kinds of number words:

CARDINAL NUMBERS: one, two, three, etc.
ORDINAL NUMBERS: first, second, third, etc.
DISTRIBUTIVE NUMBERS: one by one, two by two, three by three, etc.
MULTIPLICATIVE NUMBERS: single, double, triple, etc.
NUMERAL ADVERBS: once, twice, thrice, etc.

Of these the cardinals and ordinals are most frequently used.

NUMERALS, 1—20

ROMAN NUMERALS	CARDINAL NUMBERS		ORDINAL NUMBERS	
I	ūnus, -a, -um	1	prīmus, -a, -um	1st
II	duo, -ae, -o	2	secundus, -a, -um	2d
III	trēs, tria	3	tertius, -a, -um	3d
IIII, IV	quattuor	4	quartus, -a, -um	4th
V	quīnque	5	quīntus, -a, -um	5th
VI	sex	6	sextus, -a, -um	6th
VII	septem	7	septimus, -a, -um	7th
VIII	octō	8	octāvus, -a, -um	8th
VIIII, IX	novem	9	nōnus, -a, -um	9th
X	decem	10	decimus, -a, -um	10th
XI	ūndecim	11	ūndecimus, -a, -um	11th
XII	duodecim	12	duodecimus, -a, -um	12th
XIII	tredecim	13	tertius, -a, -um decimus, -a, -um	13th
XIIII, XIV	quattuordecim	14	quartus, -a, -um decimus, -a, -um	14th
XV	quīndecim	15	quīntus, -a, -um decimus, -a, -um	15th
XVI	sēdecim	16	sextus, -a, -um decimus, -a, -um	16th
XVII	septendecim	17	septimus, -a, -um decimus, -a, -um	17th
XVIII	duodēvīgintī	18	duodēvīcēsimus, -a, -um	18th
XVIIII, XIX	ūndēvīgintī	19	ūndēvīcēsimus, -a, -um	19th
XX	vīgintī	20	vīcēsimus, -a, -um	20th

1. The forms IV, IX, XIV, and XIX were used for IIII, VIIII, XIIII, and XVIIII in inscriptions, since they were quicker to carve and took up less space.
2. Ordinal numbers are regular adjectives of the first and second declensions.
3. Most of the cardinal numbers in Latin are indeclinable: they do not change their form to agree with different genders or cases.

> Quattuor puerī puellīs dōna dedērunt.
> *Four boys gave gifts to the girls.*
> Puerī dōna dedērunt quattuor puellīs.
> *The boys gave gifts to four girls.*
> Puerī puellīs dedērunt quattuor dōna.
> *The boys gave four gifts to the girls.*

Declension of Ūnus, Duo, and Trēs

1. The first three cardinals are, however, declined. **Ūnus** belongs to the pronoun declension, which has **-īus** in the genitive singular (instead of **-ī, -ae, -ī**) and **-ī** in the dative singular (instead of **-ō, -ae, -ō**).

DECLENSION OF ŪNUS

	MASC.	FEM.	NEUT.
NOM.	ūnus	ūna	ūnum
GEN.	ūnīus	ūnīus	ūnīus
DAT.	ūnī	ūnī	ūnī
ACC.	ūnum	ūnam	ūnum
ABL.	ūnō	ūnā	ūnō

2. **Duo** is irregular in its declension. **Ambō,** *both,* is declined in the same way as **duo.** They are the only two adjectives in the language which do not have **-a** in the neuter nominative and accusative plural.

DECLENSION OF DUO AND AMBŌ

	MASC.	FEM.	NEUT.	MASC.	FEM.	NEUT.
NOM.	duo	duae	duo	ambō	ambae	ambō
GEN.	duōrum	duārum	duōrum	ambōrum	ambārum	ambōrum
DAT.	duōbus	duābus	duōbus	ambōbus	ambābus	ambōbus
ACC.	duōs	duās	duo	ambōs	ambās	ambō
ABL.	duōbus	duābus	duōbus	ambōbus	ambābus	ambōbus

3. **Trēs** is a regular third-declension adjective.

DECLENSION OF TRĒS

	MASC. & FEM.	NEUT.
NOM.	trēs	tria
GEN.	trium	trium
DAT.	tribus	tribus
ACC.	trīs	tria
ABL.	tribus	tribus

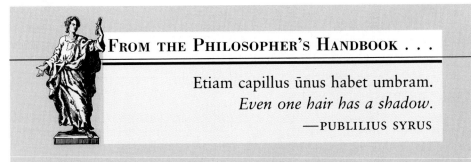

FROM THE PHILOSOPHER'S HANDBOOK . . .

Etiam capillus ūnus habet umbram.
Even one hair has a shadow.
—PUBLILIUS SYRUS

Think of someone you know who unexpectedly exerted a special influence on your life. Show how the experience reflects the above proverb.

■ PARTITIVE EXPRESSIONS WITH NUMERALS

The Partitive Ablative of Place from Which is used with cardinals, the Genitive of the Whole (Partitive Genitive) with ordinals.

Duo ex fīliīs iam virī sunt.
Two of my sons are already men.

Fīliōrum prīmus et secundus iam virī sunt.
The first and second of my sons are already men.

■ GENITIVE AND ABLATIVE OF DESCRIPTION

Quality may be denoted by either the genitive or ablative.

Vir magnae virtūtis. ⎫
Vir magna virtūte. ⎭ *A man of great courage.*

The Genitive of Description and the Ablative of Description are interchangeable. They are used when in English a noun of quality (e.g., *courage*) is modified by an adjective (e.g., *great*). When a noun of quality is not modified by an adjective (as in the phrase *a man of courage*), simply translate **vir fortis,** *a brave man.*

VOCABULARY

■ BASIC WORDS

altitūdō, altitūdinis, f. *height, depth*
forma, -ae, f. *form, shape; beauty*
lātitūdō, lātitūdinis, f. *width, breadth*
longitūdō, longitūdinis, f. *length*
mōns, montis, m. (i-stem) *hill, mountain*

nēmō, nēminis, m. (no plural) *no one, nobody*

fortis, -e *brave*

LEARNING ENGLISH THROUGH LATIN

ambidextrous	*able to use both hands with equal ease*
ambiguous	*having two or more possible meanings; not clear*
ambivalence	*simultaneous conflicting emotions towards a person or thing* (e.g., *love and hatred*)
formality	*the observation of prescribed customs or rules*
fortitude	*the strength to bear misfortunes patiently*
prime	*principal, main, first in importance*
saturnine	*sluggish, gloomy, morose*
tertiary	*of the third rank, order, formation, etc.*
tricolor	(noun) *a flag having three colors in large areas;* (adj.) *having three colors*

PRACTICE

A. Derivatives

1. The ancient Roman year began with the month of March. Which months of our calendar reflect, in their names, this way of counting?   **2.** In the revised calendar of the Romans, the month named after the god Janus was put first. Why is this appropriate?   **3.** Explain the following expressions: **a)** The actress is in her prime. **b)** The program is scheduled for prime time. **c)** a prime advantage **d)** The banks post their prime interest rates. Which Latin number gives these expressions their meanings?   **4.** The second largest planet in the solar system is named after a Roman god. Which is it? Why are personalities described as *jovial, saturnine,* or *mercurial*?   **5.** Some English words for height, width, and length are derived from Latin nouns. Give both the English and the Latin forms.

B. Count from one to twenty in Latin.

C. Count from first to twentieth in Latin.

D. Decline:

1. ūna forma   2. duo montēs   3. trēs pedēs

E. Give the Roman numeral, cardinal and ordinal adjectives for each item:

1. five   **2.** nine   **3.** six   **4.** eight   **5.** ten   **6.** eighteen   **7.** eleven
8. seventeen   **9.** twelve   **10.** nineteen

F.   Pronounce and translate:

1. Trīs montīs ingentī magnitūdine aspeximus.   **2.** Duōbus dē quattuor līberīs multa praecepta sunt.   **3.** Quartus quīnque ducum homo magnae virtūtis est.   **4.** Mūnera duodecim nūminibus, sex deīs sexque deābus, praebita sunt.   **5.** Ūnī ex agricolīs multum, secundō autem et tertiō nihil dedērunt.

READING

Developing Reading Skills

Determine the meanings of the following from the English derivatives: **hospes, hospitis,** m.; **mātrimōnium, -ī,** n.; **ōrāculum, -ī,** n.; **virgō, virginis,** f.; **externus, -a, -um; promittō, -ere, prōmīsī, prōmissum.**

Determine from your knowledge of Latin: **superus, -a, -um.**

Eating Tables

Rēx vetus Laurentiōrum Latīnus vocātus est. Latīnus fīlius erat Faunī fātidicī deī, Sāturnī nepōtis. Rēgī fīliī dēerant; Latīnus autem et Amāta uxor ūnam fīliam habuērunt nōmine Lavīniam, pulchram virginem septendecim annō-rum. Amāta Lavīniam fīliam Rutulōrum prīncipī in mātrimōnium prōmīserat. Turnus (nam ita vocātus est prīnceps) vir magnā virtūte erat et laude dignus et Amātae grātus cārusque. At Latīnus Turnum nōn magnī faciēbat

5

---

6. nōn magnī faciēbat: The genitive of nouns and adjectives of quantity is used with **sum** and **faciō** to indicate indefinite value:

Servus parvī est.   *The slave is of little value.*
Vīlla magnī est.   *The farmhouse is of great value.*
Tuum cōnsilium plūris faciō.   *I consider your advice worth more.*
Tua verba nihilī faciō.   *I consider your words worth nothing.*

This use is called the Genitive of Indefinite Value.

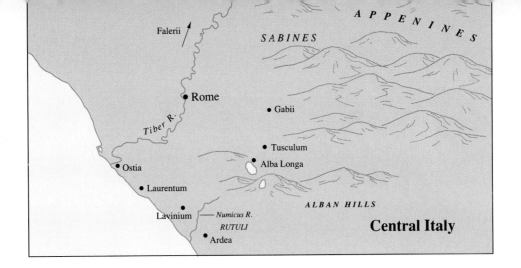

Central Italy

quod verba fātidica audīverat ubi ōrāculum Faunī parentis fāta praecipiēbat: "Nihilī, mī fīlī, fac mātrimōnium Latīnum, Lavīniae tuae veniet enim vir externus. Per hospitem nōmen nostrum ad caelum volābit atque nepōtēs nostrī omnīs populōs lātō imperiō regent." Latīnō ergō Rutulus prīnceps   10
vir magnae grātiae nōn erat.

Interim Aenēās quīnque amnīs Erebī relīquerat et trāns sextum, flūmen magnā lātitūdine, portābātur ad superās terrās. Deinde cum sociīs ad Latium octō nāvibus nāvigāvit. Ut in lītore cēnābant, locō ubi mēnsae dēerant, cibum in pānibus prō mēnsīs posuērunt. Ut pānis post cēnam vorābant,   15
parvus Ascanius tum clāmāvit: "Heus, etiam mēnsās consūmimus?" Statim verba foedae Harpȳiae in Aenēae animum vēnērunt cum paucīs verbīs fātidicīs Anchīsae parentis et laetus clāmāvit, "Pervēnimus, dēnique pervēnimus in Hesperiam terram, ubi urbem novam aedificābimus!"

Deinde Aenēās centum fortīs lēgātōs, virōs etiam bonō cōnsiliō, ad Latīnī   20
oppidum Laurentum mīsit, ut interim reliquī Trōiānī castra in lītore mūniēbant. Latīnus rēx, homō bonī animī, lēgātōs Trōiānōs amīcē accēpit et in rēgiam, ubi in mediīs propinquīs et sociīs amīcīsque stābat, convocāvit, nam ōrāculī memor semper erat et verba dē fīliae mātrimōniō memoriā tenēbat.

◼ READING COMPREHENSION

1. Why didn't Latinus hold Turnus in high esteem as a son-in-law?   **2.** Why did little Ascanius say, "Heus, etiam mēnsās consūmimus?"   **3.** What did this statement mean to Aeneas?   **4.** How did King Latinus receive the Trojan envoys? Why?

---

8. Nihilī: genitive of indefinite value   **15. pānibus:** These were large round, flat unleavened loaves.

LESSON 22

Cardinal and Ordinal Numbers 21–1000;
Genitive of Measure; Ablative of Price

A street of Pompeii. Notice the corner posts at the intersection to slow down
the wagons entering the main road.

TRAFFIC AND ACCOMMODATIONS

Did you know that Roman cities had to have traffic restrictions? For example, wheeled traffic was not allowed in the cities between sunrise and 4:00 PM. This ruling was to ensure the safety of pedestrians. Deliveries had to be made in the evening or at night. At intersections, corner posts kept wagons from turning too tightly and damaging the buildings; or there were raised pedestrian crossings with gaps an axle-length apart for the same purpose. To eliminate through traffic most cities had a ring-road just inside or just outside the walls. This was the long way around, and at Pompeii the manure-truck drivers must have been in the habit of taking a short cut, for we find a notice on one of the houses near the north gate: **Stercorārī, ad mūrum prōgredere. Sī prē⟨n⟩sus fueris poena⟨m⟩ patiāre neces⟨s⟩e est. Cavē.** *Manure-truck driver, go along by the wall. If you get caught you will have to pay the penalty. So look out.*

Vestal virgins and women of the imperial family were exempted from the wheeled-traffic rule, and could ride in a light two-wheeled mule-drawn gig, the **carpentum.** Other wealthy people used the litter (**lectica**) or sedan-chair (**sella**). Tall slaves carried the poles of the litter on their shoulders, lifting the occupant above the crowd. The litter could be closed with a cover and side curtains for privacy; the occupant rode in a reclining position and could even sleep. The sedan-chair was carried lower, its poles slung from the slaves' shoulders by straps.

Travel accommodations were poor. Most country inns were dirty and there was danger from both fire and robbers. Many wealthy people maintained little houses (**mānsiōnēs**) where they could put up for the night. In the cities the custom of guest-friendship (**hospitium**) made up for the lack of good hotels. By this custom, families in different cities made permanent arrangements for putting each other up. This is why the Latin word **hospes** can be translated either *guest* or *host.* It really means *guest-friend.*

239

ANCIENT ROME LIVES ON . . .

"Road closed to traffic 2–5," "Deliveries made in the rear." Why would a Roman driver find these signs perfectly understandable?

What alternatives to hotels do we have, as the Romans had guest-friendship and **mānsiōnēs**?

(*above*) The excavated main street of Herculaneum; the raised sidewalks offered protection to pedestrians from dust and mud   (*left*) Wall painting: woman giving water to a traveler—House of the Dioscuri, Pompeii

FORMS

■ CARDINAL AND ORDINAL NUMBERS, 21–1000

Cardinal multiples of ten from twenty to a hundred are indeclinable adjectives; ordinals are regularly declined.

ROMAN NUMERALS	CARDINAL NUMBERS		ORDINAL NUMBERS	
XXX	trīgintā	30	trīcēsimus, -a, -um	30th
XXXX, XL	quadrāgintā	40	quadrāgēsimus, -a, -um	40th
L	quīnquāgintā	50	quīnquāgēsimus, -a, -um	50th
LX	sexāgintā	60	sexāgēsimus, -a, -um	60th
LXX	septuāgintā	70	septuāgēsimus, -a, -um	70th
LXXX	octōgintā	80	octōgēsimus, -a, -um	80th
LXXXX, XC	nōnāgintā	90	nōnāgēsimus, -a, -um	90th
C	centum	100	centēsimus, -a, -um	100th

1. The forms XL and XC were used for XXXX and LXXXX in inscriptions because they took up less space.

2. To form numbers beyond twenty, Latin simply combines the adjectives as in English: **105** (**CV**) is either *one hundred five* (**centum quīnque**) or *one hundred and five* (**centum et quīnque**). *Twenty-one* is **vīgintī ūnus** and *twenty-first* is **vīcēsimus prīmus**.

> Centum ⟨et⟩ septuāgintā ūnus Rōmānī cum centum ⟨et⟩ nōnāgintā duōbus Graecīs pugnābant.

> *A (One) hundred ⟨and⟩ seventy-one Romans were fighting with a (one) hundred ⟨and⟩ ninety-two Greeks.*

Cardinal multiples of a hundred from two hundred to nine hundred, and their ordinals, are regularly declined. The cardinal for one thousand is indeclinable; the ordinal for thousandth is declined.

ROMAN NUMERALS	CARDINAL NUMBERS		ORDINAL NUMBERS	
CC	ducentī, -ae, -a	200	ducentēsimus, -a, -um	200th
CCC	trecentī, -ae, -a	300	trecentēsimus, -a, -um	300th
CCCC	quadringentī, -ae, -a	400	quadringentēsimus, -a, -um	400th
D	quīngentī, -ae, -a	500	quīngentēsimus, -a, -um	500th
DC	sescentī, -ae, -a	600	sescentēsimus, -a, -um	600th
DCC	septingentī, -ae, -a	700	septingentēsimus, -a, -um	700th
DCCC	octingentī, -ae, -a	800	octingentēsimus, -a, -um	800th
DCCCC	nōngentī, -ae, -a	900	nōngentēsimus, -a, -um	900th
M	mīlle	1000	mīllēsimus, -a, -um	1000th

DISTRIBUTIVES, MULTIPLICATIVES, AND ADVERBS

Distributive numbers also are regular adjectives of the first and second declensions: **singulī, -ae, a** (*one at a time, one by one, one each*), **bīnī, -ae, -a** (*two at a time, two by two, two each*), **trīnī, quaternī, quīnī**, etc.

Multiplicatives are third declension adjectives and have the suffix **-plex, -plicis: simplex, simplicis** (*single, simple*), **duplex, duplicis** (*double, twofold*), **triplex, quadruplex, quīnquiplex**, etc.

Adverbs which answer the question *how often?* are **semel** (*once*), **bis** (*twice*), **ter** (*thrice, three times*), **quater** (*four times*), **quīnquiēns,** (*five times*), **sexiēns, septiēns, octiēns, noviēns, deciēns**, etc.

SYNTAX

GENITIVE OF MEASURE

Definite measurements, using numerals, are expressed by the genitive.

> amnis decem pedum   *a ten-foot river (a river of ten feet)*

With the Genitive of Measure the dimension (length, width, height, depth) is specified by an ablative of specification.

amnis quīnque pedum altitūdine	*a river five feet in depth* *a river five feet deep* *a five-foot-deep river*
amnis quīnquāgintā pedum lātitūdine	*a river fifty feet in width* *a river fifty feet wide* *a fifty-foot-wide river*
amnis quīngentōrum pedum longitūdine	*a river 500 feet in length* *a river 500 feet long* *a 500-foot-long river*

ABLATIVE OF PRICE

With verbs of buying, selling, and exchanging, the price or means of payment is put in the ablative case.

Agrum ducentīs quīnquāgintā aureīs ēmit.
He bought the field for 250 gold pieces.
Agrum magnā pecūniā vēndidit.
He sold the field for a large sum of money.

Agrum vīllā mūtāvit.
Agrō vīllam mūtāvit. } *He exchanged the field for a farmhouse.*

VOCABULARY

BASIC WORDS

avis, avis, f. (i-stem) *bird*
fātum, -ī, n. *fate*
pecūnia, -ae, f. *money, sum of money*
pēs, pedis, m. *foot*
saeculum, -ī, n. *age, generation, century*

aureus, -a, -um *golden, of gold;* (as substantive) aureus, -ī, m. *aureus (a gold coin), gold piece*
secundus, -a, -um *following; second; favorable*

emō, -ere, ēmī, emptum *buy*
vēndō, -ere, vēndidī, vēnditum *sell*

Note: As a unit of measure, **pēs ūnus** = 11.65 of our inches.

Building Vocabulary

1. In compounds **emō** means *take*:

   dēmo, -ere, dēmpsī, dēmptum   *take away, subtract*
   eximō, -ere, exēmī, exemptum
     take out, exempt (w. abl. of separation)
   prōmo, -ere, prōmpsī, prōmptum   *take forth, bring forth*

2. Similarly **dō**, in compounds, means *put*:

   addō, -ere, addidī, additum
     put to, add (w. direct object and indirect object)
   condō, -ere, condidī, conditum
     put together, collect, found [a city]; *bury, conceal*
   prōdō, -ere, prōdidī, prōditum   *put forth, betray*

■ LEARNING ENGLISH THROUGH LATIN

aviary	*a cage or building for housing birds*
aviculture	*the raising and care of birds*
exemption	*a release from obligation or legal requirement*
expedient	(adj.) *advantageous, convenient, suited*
pecuniary	*of or involving money*
pedestal	*the foot or bottom support of a column, pillar, statue, etc.*
pedestrian	(noun) *one who goes on foot*
secular	*relating to worldly things as opposed to religious things*
vendor	*one who sells, seller*

▬ PRACTICE ▬

A. Fill in the blanks with appropriate English words derived from the Latin words in this lesson.

1. When the movers brought in the furniture, they broke the ___ of the lamp.   **2.** The traffic light has two signals: one for vehicles and one for ___.   **3.** If you don't return your library books on time, it will be considered a ___ offense and you will have to pay a fine.   **4.** Medical expenses and real estate taxes are two big ___ on one's income tax return.   5. I enjoy visiting the zoological gardens. My favorite place is the ___ because I am very interested in ___.   6. Many composers wrote both sacred and ___ music.   7. The solution may not be what is right and just, but what is ___ for his purpose.   8. It is interesting to see the ___ displaying their wares at the flea market.

B. Count in Latin, giving cardinal numbers and Roman numerals:

1. from two to twenty by twos   2. from twenty-one to fifty-one by threes   3. from one hundred to one hundred and fifty by fives   4. from three hundred to five hundred by tens   5. from one hundred to one thousand by fifties

C. Give the ordinal numerals for each of the numbers in B.

D. Pronounce and translate:

1. centum et vīgintī duōrum hominum   2. cum trecentīs sexāgintā quīnque nautīs   3. mīllēsimum quīntum decimum oppidum   4. centēsima et ūndēvīcēsima avis   5. quadringentārum trīgintā ūnīus fēminārum   6. in septimā decimā urbe   7. ex mīlle octingentīs septuāgintā tribus nāvibus   8. ducentēsimus ūndecimus annus   9. ad vīcēsimum secundum oppidum   10. quadrāgintā trēs nepōtēs

---

Translation Help

Latin writers are very reluctant to use the same word twice in a sentence, unless for a special rhetorical effect. This is true even when the word would have appeared in a different form.

> Virī multa tēla, puer ūnum modo portābat.
> *The men were carrying many weapons, the boy only one.*

Here the missing words, **portābant** and **tēlum**, do not have the same form as the **tēla** and **portābat** in the sentence.

Notice also that Latin tends to leave the verb out the first time it should appear and put it in later, whereas the English sentence puts it in the first time and omits it afterwards. Latin treats the other parts of speech in the same way as English.

E. Translate:

1. We saw seven hundred and twenty-three birds.   2. We saw the seven hundred and twenty-third bird.   3. The leader came with one thousand four hundred and sixty-two men.   4. There are eighty-one mountains in the land.   5. The eighty-first mountain is of great height.   6. There are eight hundred and one mountains in the land.   7. The eight hundred and first mountain is of great height.   8. The fields of thirty-five farmers were taken by the enemy.   9. The fields of three hundred and fifty farmers were taken by the enemy.   10. The three hundred and fifty-first farmer kept his field.

F. Fill in the blanks:

1. Sī ā trecentōs sēdecim nāvibus ducentōs nōnāgintā octō dēmpserimus, erunt ___ nāvēs.   2. Ad quīnque campōs adde quattuordecim; nunc sunt ___ campī.   3. Quīnquiēns duodecim lēgēs sunt ___ lēgēs.   4. Ā septendecim tēlīs dēme decem; tum quattuor adde; nunc erunt ___ tēla.   5. Ā quater novem saeculīs vīgintī tria dēme; tum erunt ___ saecula.

G. Pronounce and translate:

1. iter mīlle nōngentōrum nōnāgintā novem pedum longitūdine   2. ad arcem ducentōrum quīnquāgintā ūnīus pedum altitūdine   3. ex campō sescentōrum sexāgintā sex pedum lātitūdine   4. in monte magnae altitūdinis   5. trāns amnem trīgintā trium pedum altitūdine

H. Translate:

1. We saw a twenty-two-foot-deep river.   2. The enemy had a citadel one hundred and thirty-three feet high.   3. He bought a seventy-four-foot-wide field for forty-one gold pieces.   4. The citadel is a one hundred and ninety-seven-foot hill.   5. We live on a street nine hundred and seventy-eight feet long.

I. Translate:

1. Dido founded a city in Africa, Aeneas in Italy.   2. My father has many friends, yours only three.   3. In the city there are twelve triple gates, in the town two double ones.   4. My son has sailed to Asia five times, my daughters just twice.   5. We give no gifts to the king, but many to the gods.

READING

Developing Reading Skills

Here are familiar Latin words which will help with some unfamiliar ones: **bene, faciō, homō, labōrō, mōveō, post, pugnō.**

English words which may help: *dubious, introvert, matrimony, mental, moo, pacify, prolific, promise, semicircle, vestige.*

Hercules and Cacus

Latīnus per Aenēae lēgātōs rēgī Trōiānō pācem cum Laurentiīs mātrimōni-
umque Lāvīniae fīliae amīcē praebuit, atque Trōiānīs singula dōna addidit
centum equōs, Aenēae autem dōnum duplex, duōs equōs acrīs, ambōs prōlem
Sōlis equōrum. Equōs mīrōs magnā pecūniā ā Circā Sōlis fīliā ēmerat.

At Iūnō, semper Aenēae Trōiānīsque inimīca, saevā īrā commōta est et   5
Furiam ad Amātam mīsit Latīnī uxōrem mātremque Lāvīniae, ubi anguem
in rēgīnae pectore posuit, deinde ad Turnum Rutulōrum ducem, ubi flammās
in animum immīsit; dēnique in Trōiānōs āvolat. Itaque Ascanius cervum
mansuētum interfēcit cārum Silviae fīliae pastōris prīmī Latīnī rēgis. Silviae
frātrēs cum Ascaniī sociīs pugnāvērunt, unde bellum inter Trōiānōs Latīn-   10
ōsque inceptum est.

Bellī sociōs igitur Aenēās petēbat et ad Palātium montem (posteā ūnum
ex septem montibus urbis Rōmae) ambulāvit, ubi Evandrum rēgem invēnit.
Evander auxilium prōmīsit, tum Aenēam ad āram magnam Herculī sacram
Tiberī amnī propinquam dūxit ibique ūnum dē Herculis duodecim labōribus   15
rēx rēgī praecēpit:

"Memoriam beneficiōrum semper servāmus, ut vidēbis, itaque āram
posuimus magnā cum grātiā Herculis auxilī, multīs enim perīculīs ab Iovis

---

1. per ... lēgātōs: Persons cannot be used for the ablative of means or instrument; instead
per with the accusative is used. This use is called secondary agency.   **16. rēx rēgī:** This is
a Latin way of saying *one king to the other.*

Hercules clad in his lion skin
—Greek bronze

20 fīliō exemptī sumus. Hīc in spēluncā habitābat Cācus mōnstrum ingēns sēmihomō, fīlius Vulcānī deī. Herculēs veniēbat ab Gēryonis īnsulā unde sexāgintā et trecentās bovēs agēbat, et ut ad locum nostrum accessit prope amnem somnō superātus est. Herculī ut dormiēbat Cācus nōnāgintā ex bōbus dēmpsit caudīsque in spēluncam trāxit ibique condidit. Sīc vestīgia omnia nōn intrō sed ex spēluncā tendēbant. Herculēs ut nōnāgintā nōn 25 repperuit damnumque mente nōn comprehendit cum reliquīs bōbus dūbius in animō discēdēbat, ubi bovēs in spēluncā mūgīvērunt itaque Cācum prōdidērunt. Herculēs post magnam pugnam ingentem montem in Cācum iniēcit et sīc mōnstrum cōnfēcit."

Et fābulā et amīcitiā Evandrī Trōiānī iūtī sunt.

READING COMPREHENSION

1. What gifts did Latinus offer to Aeneas? Where did he get them?   **2.** What does "Iunō . . . Furiam ad Amātam mīsit" mean?   **3.** What did Evander teach Aeneas?   **4.** Who was Cacus?   **5.** How did Cacus trick Hercules?   **6.** How was his trick discovered?   **7.** What happened to Cacus?

---

20. fīlius Vulcānī: A story of a giant son of the god of fire who lived in a mountain cave may have been an early way of accounting for the activity of volcanos.   **Gēryonis:** The Tenth Labor of Hercules was to bring back the cattle of Geryon. As Geryon's island was near Spain, Hercules passed through Italy on his way back to Greece.

LESSON 23

Demonstratives

A Roman road near Vetulonia in Etruria

ROADS

Not the least of Rome's contributions to western civilization was the paved road. Rome's road-building was first begun in response to military needs but, once they were built, Roman roads served the purposes of trade, communication, and even pleasure trips.

You have often heard the expression, "All roads lead to Rome." This was literally true in antiquity, since the mileage, marked by milestones (**mīliāria**), was measured throughout the empire from the Golden Milestone (**Mīliārium Aureum**) set up by Augustus in the Forum. Its base is still visible, and distances in Italy are still measured from it. Movement from one part of the Roman Empire to another was unrestricted, and travel was relatively easy over a vast network of roads which eventually stretched out from Mesopotamia to Lisbon, from upper Egypt to the north of England, altogether nearly 100,000 miles.

This elaborate network began with Rome's need to move armies within Italy itself. It was started in 312 B.C. by Appius Claudius, who oversaw the construction of the Appian Way (**Via Appia**), which connected Rome with Capua. The **Via Appia** was later extended to Brundisium, Italy's chief port for traffic with Greece. The network was continued until almost any part of Italy could be reached by one of the great roads; then it was extended to the provinces. These routes (and in some cases even the pavements) are still in use today.

Roman road-building took little account of the terrain. The roads for the most part were quite straight, crossing valleys on arched bridges and cutting through hills by man-made terraces, cuts, or tunnels. On marshy ground the road was laid on rafts. When the cuts, bridges, and rafts had been made, the route of the road was marked by parallel ditches 15 to 20 feet apart. The earth was then dug out from between the ditches (road-building was done by soldiers as part of their basic training) and the excavation leveled.

(Continued)

A mortar **pavīmentum** of sand and lime was then laid. On top of this went the **statūmen,** a layer of large flagstones, then the **rūdus,** a layer of lime-and-gravel concrete. The next layer, the nucleus, was also concrete, this time made of dirt, lime, and pieces of brick. On top went the **summum dorsum** or **summa crusta,** the final pavement, made of polygonal blocks of flint or basalt. The large polygonal stones of the pavement were fitted so closely together that the joints were invisible. Where flint or basalt was unavailable the pavement was of concrete or rammed flint gravel. The center of the road was made a little higher than the edges, for drainage. The depth of all these strata was 5 to 10 feet.

(*below left*) Roman remains at Timgad, Algeria, showing a triumphal arch and roadway   (*below right*) Houses flanking a street in Herculaneum

ANCIENT ROME LIVES ON . . .

What improvements, if any, have we made in road-building since the second century B.C.?

FORMS

DEMONSTRATIVES

The demonstratives are so called because they point out a person, object, or place. There are demonstrative adjectives, which are also used as pronouns, and demonstrative adverbs.

The demonstrative adjectives are **is**, *this, that (the one spoken of)*, **hic**, *this [here]*, **iste**, *that [near you]*, and **ille**, *that [there]*. The demonstrative pronominal adjectives are declined, like **ūnus**, in the pronoun declension, with -ius in the genitive singular and -i in the dative singular.

DECLENSION OF IS, EA, ID

	SINGULAR			PLURAL		
	MASC.	FEM.	NEUT.	MASC.	FEM.	NEUT.
NOM.	is	ea	id	eī	eae	ea
GEN.	eius	eius	eius	eōrum	eārum	eōrum
DAT.	eī	eī	eī	eīs	eīs	eīs
ACC.	eum	eam	id	eōs	eās	ea
ABL.	eō	eā	eō	eīs	eīs	eīs

The demonstrative adverbs of this adjective are: **ibi**, *here, there, in this place, in that place*; **eō**, *[to] here, [to] there, to this place, to that place*; and **inde**, *from here, from there, from this place, from that place.*

Paving stones on the Via Appia. The hard lava stone of the nearby Alban Hills made flat pavers for the major routes into Rome.

DECLENSION OF HIC, HAEC, HOC

| | | SINGULAR | | | PLURAL | |
	MASC.	FEM.	NEUT.	MASC.	FEM.	NEUT.
NOM.	hic	haec	hoc	hī	hae	haec
GEN.	huius	huius	huius	hōrum	hārum	hōrum
DAT.	huic	huic	huic	hīs	hīs	hīs
ACC.	hunc	hanc	hoc	hōs	hās	haec
ABL.	hōc	hāc	hōc	hīs	hīs	hīs

The adverbs of **hic, haec, hoc** are: **hīc**, *here, in this place;* **hūc**, *[to] here, to this place;* and **hinc**, *from here, from this place.*

DECLENSION OF ISTE, ISTA, ISTUD

| | | SINGULAR | | | PLURAL | |
	MASC.	FEM.	NEUT.	MASC.	FEM.	NEUT.
NOM.	iste	ista	istud	istī	istae	ista
GEN.	istīus	istīus	istīus	istōrum	istārum	istōrum
DAT.	istī	istī	istī	istīs	istīs	istīs
ACC.	istum	istam	istud	istōs	istās	ista
ABL.	istō	istā	istō	istīs	istīs	istīs

The adverbs of **iste** are: **istīc**, *there near you, in that place of yours;* **istūc**, *[to] there near you, to that place of yours;* and **istinc**, *from there near you, from that place of yours.*

DECLENSION OF ILLE, ILLA, ILLUD

| | SINGULAR | | | PLURAL | | |
	MASC.	FEM.	NEUT.	MASC.	FEM.	NEUT.
NOM.	ille	illa	illud	illī	illae	illa
GEN.	illīus	illīus	illīus	illōrum	illārum	illōrum
DAT.	illī	illī	illī	illīs	illīs	illīs
ACC.	illum	illam	illud	illōs	illās	illa
ABL.	illō	illā	illō	illīs	illīs	illīs

The adverbs of **ille** are: **illīc,** *there, in that place;* **illūc,** *[to] there, to that place;* and **illinc,** *from there, from that place.*

1. **Hic . . . hic . . .** can mean *one . . . another . . .*

> Ambō discēdunt, hic ad Asiam, hic ad Āfricam.
> *They are both leaving, one for Asia, one for Africa.*

2. **Ille** can mean *the former* and **hic** *the latter.*

> Et meus frāter et tuus discēdunt, hic ad Asiam, ille ad Āfricam.
> *Both your brother and mine are leaving, the latter for Asia, the former for Africa.*

3. **Iste** can also mean *that . . . of yours.*

> Iste frāter male fēcit.   *That brother of yours has behaved badly.*

4. A demonstrative pronominal adjective normally precedes the word it modifies. When **ille** comes after the word it modifies, it means *that famous, that well-known.*

▰ SYNTAX ▰

▰ USES OF DEMONSTRATIVE ADJECTIVES

A demonstrative adjective follows the same rules as other adjectives. If it modifies a noun it must agree with it in gender, number, and case. If it does not modify a noun, it becomes a pronoun, just as other adjectives, when they have no noun to modify, become nouns. **Is, hic, iste,** and **ille** can all be used as third person personal pronouns (*he, she, it, they*). As pronouns, demonstratives are translated according to gender and number.

> Hae puellae spectant illōs puerōs.
> *These girls [here] are looking at those boys [there].*

> Hic illam spectat. }
> Ille hanc spectat. } *He is looking at her.*

These last two sentences do not mean exactly the same thing in Latin: the first means *he (this man here)* is looking at *her (that woman there)*, the second *he (that man there)* is looking at *her (this woman here)*.

VOCABULARY

BASIC WORDS

arma, -ōrum, n. (no singular) *arms*
castra, -ōrum, n. (no singular) *camp*
tempus, temporis, n. *time*

clārus, -a, -um *clear; bright; famous*
iuvenis, iuvenis (no neuter) *young*
mīrus, -a, -um *amazing, wonderful*

tālis, -e *such, of such a kind*
tantus, -a, -um *so great, so large*
tot (indecl. adj.) *so many*

ergō (adv.) *therefore, consequently, then*
iterum (adv.) *again, a second time*
totiēns (adv.) *so often*

Notes:
1. **Arma** refers to both defensive and offensive arms, **tēla** only to offensive weapons. When **arma** and **tēla** are used together, **tēla** refers only to missile weapons.
2. **Arma** and **castra** are always plural in Latin, but **castra** is translated as singular in English.

> Haec castra sunt.   *This is the camp.*

   For numbers with plural nouns of this kind, distributives are used: **bīna castra,** *two camps,* **quīna arma,** *five sets of arms.*
3. Used as a noun, **iuvenis** means *young man* or *young woman.*
4. **Iterum** and **rūrsus** (short for **reversus**) both mean *again*: **iterum** in the sense of *a second time,* **rūrsus** in the sense of *going back.*

◼ LEARNING ENGLISH THROUGH LATIN

armistice	*a truce by mutual agreement*
contemporaneous	*happening in the same period of time*
extemporaneous	*done or spoken without preparation*
pro tem	*for the time being, temporarily*
reiterate	*say or do repeatedly*
retaliate	*return like for like; get even*
tantamount	*equal, equivalent*
temporal	*limited by time; pertaining to worldly affairs*

▦ PRACTICE

A. Derivatives

1. Other words which are derivatives of the Latin words in this lesson are *clarion, clarify, juvenile,* and *miraculous.* Give the meaning of each word and identify its Latin origin. **2.** Exactly how does *contemporary* differ from *contemporaneous* in meaning?

B. Give gender(s), number(s), and case(s):

1. id, huius, istum, ille **2.** huic, istō, iste, illōrum **3.** eius, istī, illa, illīs
4. eō, hoc, illud, hārum **5.** eī, hī, istae, illīus **6.** eae, hae, istōrum, illī
7. ea, hōrum, istīs, illum **8.** eōrum, hīs, is, illud **9.** eīs, ista, hic, illae
10. haec, hōc, istud, istīus

C. Decline:

1. hoc tempus **2.** ista iuvenis **3.** illud saeculum **4.** is mons **5.** haec avis

D. Give the adverbs for each adjective which express *at, to,* and *from:*

1. iste **2.** hic **3.** is **4.** ille

E. Pronounce and translate:

1. Hoc est illīus oppidum. **2.** Istī haec praebuimus. **3.** Cur ille istam spectat? **4.** Istud huic da. **5.** Eius frāter par huic tuō virtute est.

F. Translate:

1. Her brother loves his sister. **2.** These men here will take that camp of yours. **3.** We came to that city. **4.** Give it to him. **5.** She saw their slaves.

G. Pronounce and translate:

1. Eōrum castra in illō monte sunt. **2.** Sī istōs hostīs superāveritis, omnia et arma et tēla vestrīs ab eīs dabuntur. **3.** Ista puella nōn pulchra est prae hāc. **4.** Deus Poenōrum malus, noster bonus est, itaque huic mūnera, illī autem nihil praebēmus. **5.** Omnēs fēminae ad arcem accessērunt, hae ā vīllīs, hae ab omnibus urbis partibus.

H. Translate:

1. My brother is your brother's friend, but the former is good and the latter bad. **2.** Two envoys left the city; one carried good news, the other bad. **3.** This city is wretched; that one is beautiful. **4.** In Asia we saw a city; that city was beautiful. **5.** There are two sets of arms here; is this one, or that one, pleasing to you?

========================= **READING** =========================

Developing Reading Skills

English words which may help: *arboreal, clang, expulsion, impel, miracle, signal, triumph,* and *tuba.*

New Allies, New Attacks

Etrūscī in Asiā ōlim habitāverant, unde in Ītaliam iter longum difficileque fēcerant; eō tempore ubi Aenēās in Latium pervēnit eōrum rēx Mezentius ille erat. Is rēx autem ut vir summā crūdēlitāte saevitiāque erat ā gente

5

Etrūscā ēiectus erat. Iuvenem Pallantem Evandrī fīlium Etrūscī rēgem post dēligēbant; hoc autem vātēs sacer prohibuit aperuitque fāta hīs verbīs: "Nēminī Italōrum trāditōte tantum rēgnum." Itaque Evander Aenēae praecēpit: "Ut iam rēx es Trōiānōrum, sīc dux Etrūscōrum estō; ad castra Etrūsca cum Pallante accēde; ibi ubi ducem novum petunt omnēs magnō cum gaudiō talem virum recipient."

10

Trōiānus dubius erat, at subitō mīrum signum ā Cytherēā mātre eī datum est: et fulmen vīsum est et Etrūscus tubae per caelum mūgīvit clangor. Dēnique in caelō aspexērunt omnēs arma clāra et formā mīra. Haec arma Venus Vulcānī uxor ā virō accēperat et mox fīliō trādidit. Clipeus praecipuē mīrābilis erat, nam in eō deus decora Rōmānōrum ā temporibus Rōmulī

15

Remīque usque ad Augustī triumphum ēnarrāvit. Aenēās ergō sīc fēcit ut Evander monuerat: ad Etrūscōs accessit et hōs fēcit sociōs et amīcōs populī Trōiānī.

Interim Turnus cum Latīnīs castra Trōiānōrum oppugnābat et ut castrīs ā Trōiānīs prohibēbātur ad nāvīs cum igne accessit. Quod arborēs autem

20

unde eae nāvēs factae erant in Īdā monte Magnae Mātrī sacrō steterant dea timōre commōta est et ad Iovem properāvit, ubi illud ab eō poposcit: "Dē flammīs, fīlī, meās arborēs servā!" et hic respondit: "Cōnfīrmāre, māter; servābuntur atque in Nymphās mūtābuntur." Et statim, ut Turnus Latīnīque magnō timōre mīrāculum aspiciēbant, omnis nāvis Nympha maris facta est.

25

Hae Nymphae novae eō ubi Aenēās Pallāsque cum novīs sociīs ad Latium nāve Etrūscā nāvigābant accessērunt et dē castrōrum perīculō illum monuērunt ac nāvīs impulērunt. Turnus interim clāmābat: "Sine nāvibus hostēs nunc fugae cōpiā carent!" et semel et iterum Latīnōs contrā Trōiāna castra dūxit.

■ READING COMPREHENSION

1. Who was Mezentius?   2. Why was Pallas not chosen king?   3. What wonderful sign was granted to Aeneas?   4. Describe the shield.   5. Explain the following: Dē flammīs, fīlī, meās arborēs servā.   6. How was this accomplished?

---

6. **trāditōte**: future imperative (see Appendix). So also **estō** in line 7.   15. **sīc fēcit**: remember that **faciō** with an adverb may be intransitive and mean *act* or *behave*.   21. **illud**: Latin usually uses **illud** or **illa** to refer to what is to come; English uses *this* rather than *that*.   26. **illum**: *the former*, i.e. Aeneas, not Pallas

LESSON 24

Kinds of Clauses

Harbor view from Stabiae—National Museum, Naples

SEA TRAVEL

Sea travel was much less comfortable and more dangerous than travel by land. The Romans were not by nature or inclination good sailors, and had so little understanding of shipbuilding that in order to build a fleet for the First Punic War they had to copy a grounded Carthaginian warship. Their merchant shipping was carried on by other nationalities. The Romans had many superstitions about sea travel: for example, they would cut neither their hair nor their nails while on a voyage, for fear of bad luck.

The two chief kinds of ships were warships (**nāvēs longae**) and freight and passenger ships (**nāvēs onerāriae**). Speed and maneuverability were the chief requirements for the warships. They relied more on oars than on sails, and under battle conditions did not even carry masts. Military ships had either three or five banks of oars; the former kind was called **trirēmis,** the latter **quīnquerēmis.** A quinquereme was about 120 feet by 17, and carried 300 sailors and rowers, 120 soldiers, and 20 officers. Warships had to put ashore to allow the men to sleep or to eat a substantial meal.

A **nāvis onerāria** was 70 to 80 feet long by 18 to 20 feet wide. It was decked, with a cabin aft, and carried passengers as well as freight. It carried perhaps 50 tons of cargo. These merchant ships relied primarily on their sails, and could make 70 to 90 miles a day. Their masts, unlike those of warships, were permanently fixed: a vertical mainmast amidships, carrying a large square or trapezoidal sail and a small triangular sail above it, and a slanted mast forward carrying a jib. Three-masted vessels were rare. Merchant ships were not very seaworthy, and ordinarily made only coasting voyages, and then only between mid-March and early October.

Roman trade routes covered the Mediterranean and Black Seas, the north Atlantic coast of Africa, the English Channel, the Red Sea, the Persian Gulf, and the Indian Ocean.

ANCIENT ROME LIVES ON . . .

Describe some of the sea-going vessels we have now, and show how they differ according to their purpose.

(*above left*) **A corbīta**, a small two-masted coaster—Roman Carthage, 200 A.D.
(*above right*) **Faber Nāvalis**, fleet carpenter shown in the process of building a boat—funerary relief
(*below*) Wall painting of a sea battle and warships—House of the Vettii, Pompeii

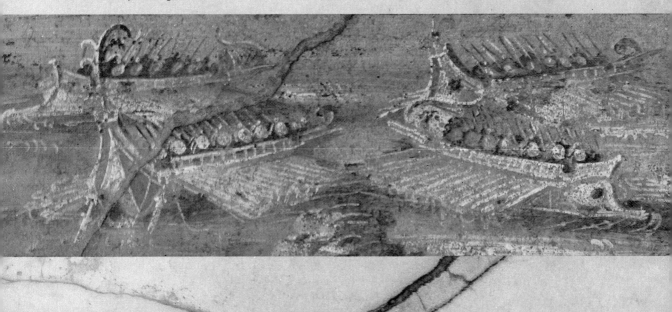

SYNTAX

KINDS OF CLAUSES

Every verb is contained in a clause; clauses are either principal or subordinate. The subordinate clauses used so far have been of five different kinds, relative, temporal, causal, conditional, and comparative.

Relative Clauses

Relative clauses are clauses which serve as adjectives. The demonstrative adjective **is, ea, id** often identifies the noun which is modified by a relative clause. Relative clauses are introduced by the following relative adverbs:

ubi	*where, at which place*
quō	*to which place, to which*
unde	*from which place, from which*

Stābō in eō locō **ubi** stās.
　I shall stand in that place where you are standing.
Accēdam ad **eum** locum **quō** accēdis.
　I shall go to that place to which you are going.
Veniam ex eō locō **unde** venis.
　I shall come from that place from which you are coming.

These relative clauses of place may also modify the demonstrative adverbs **ibi,** *there,* **eō,** *[to] there,* and **inde,** *from there.*

Ibi stābō **ubi** stās.
　I shall stand in that place where you are standing.
Eō accēdam **quō** accēdis.
　I shall go to that place to which you are going.
Inde veniam **unde** venis.
　I shall come from that place from which you are coming.

The pairs **ibi** and **ubi, eō** and **quō,** and **inde** and **unde** are called correlatives.

Temporal Clauses

Temporal clauses are adverbial clauses which answer the question *When?* They may be introduced by the following adverbial conjunctions:

ubi	*when*	postquam	*after*
cum	*when*	simul atque (ac)	*as soon as*
ut	*as*		

The demonstrative adverb **tum**, *then, at that time,* is correlative with **cum.**

> Eum vīdistī **ubi** ē vīllā discēdēbat.
> *You saw him when he was leaving the farmhouse.*
> Eum vīdistī **ut** ē vīllā discēdēbat.
> *You saw him as he was leaving the farmhouse.*
> Eum **tum** vīdistī **cum** ē vīllā discēdēbat.
> *You saw him at that time when he was leaving the farmhouse.*
> Eum vīdistī **postquam** ē vīllā discessit.
> *You saw him after he left the farmhouse.*
> Eum vīdistī **simul atque** ē vīllā discessit.
> *You saw him as soon as he left the farmhouse.*

Causal Clauses

Causal clauses are adverbial clauses answering the question *Why?* They may be introduced by the following adverbial conjunctions:

ut	*as*	quia	*because*
quod	*because*	quoniam	*since, because*

Ut aqua dēest, hinc discēdēmus.
> *As there is no water, we shall leave this place.*
Hōc fēcit **quia** eam amāvit.   *He did this because he loved her.*

Conditional Clauses

Conditional clauses answer the question *On what condition?* They are introduced by the following adverbial conjunctions:

sī	*if*	etsī	*even if*
nisi	*if not, unless*	sīn	*but if*
sīve (seu) ... sīve (seu) ...	*whether ... or ...*		

Sī ille hūc vēnerit discēdam.   *If he comes here, I shall leave.*
Sīve ille nunc **seu** post hūc vēnerit discēdam.
> *Whether he comes here now or later, I shall leave.*

Notice that a future or future perfect in the conditional clause is usually translated by a simple present in English.

Comparative Clauses

Comparative clauses, which express a comparison, are introduced by the following adverbial conjunctions:

ut	*as* (when actions are being compared)
quam	*as* (when qualities are being compared)

Adverbs which are correlative with **ut** are **sīc** and **ita,** *so, in such a manner.* **Sīc** and **ut** are sometimes written as one word, **sīcut,** *just as, just as if.*

> Is hoc sīc (ita) facit **ut** ea facit.   *He does this just as she does.*

Adverbs which are correlative with **quam** are **tam** and **ita,** *so, to such a degree.* **Tam** and **quam** are sometimes written as one word, **tamquam,** *just as, just as if.*

> Is **tam** (ita) laetus est **quam** ea est.   *He is as happy as she is.*

The verb may be omitted from a comparative clause.

> Is hoc sīcut ea facit.   *He does this just as she does.*
> Is laetus est tamquam ea.   *He is as happy as she is.*

VOCABULARY

BASIC WORDS

corpus, corporis, n. *body*
ōs, ōris, n.   *mouth, face*
virgō, virginis, f.   *girl, maiden*

gravis, -e *heavy, serious*
vīvus, -a, -um *alive, living*

iaciō, -ere, iēcī, iactum   *throw*
vinciō, -īre, vinxī, vinctum   *tie, bind*
vincō, -ere, vīcī, victum   *conquer*
vīvō, -ere, vīxī, victum   *live, be alive*

etiam (adv.) *even, yet, still, also*
quoque (adv.)   *also, too*
tamen (adv.)   *nevertheless, yet, still*

-ve (enclitic conj.)   *or, or possibly*

Notes: 1. It is easy to confuse the verbs **vinciō, vincō,** and **vīvō,** and the verbs **iaceō** and **iaciō,** with each other. Note the differences carefully.
2. *To live,* in the sense of *to dwell,* is **habitāre;** in the sense of *to be alive,* **vīvere.**
3. **Quoque** comes after whatever word it goes with.

> Is quoque ad illōs veniet.   *He, too, will come to them.*

Building Vocabulary

Note the following compounds of **iaciō:**

adiciō, -ere, adiēcī, adiectum   *throw to, add*
coniciō, -ere, coniecī, coniectum   *throw together, hurl*
ēiciō, -ere, ēiēcī, ēiectum   *throw out*
iniciō, -ere, iniēcī, iniectum   *throw in, into, on, onto*
trāiciō, -ere, trāiēcī, trāiectum   *throw across; pierce*

■ LEARNING ENGLISH THROUGH LATIN

aggravate	*to make worse or more serious*
conjecture	*a prediction based on guesswork*
corporeal	*bodily, of the body*
corpus delicti	*the material evidence of the fact that a crime has been committed*
gravity	*seriousness; heaviness*
invincible	*unable to be overcome*
trajectory	*the path taken by a thrown or projected object*
victuals	*food*
vivacious	*full of life and animation*

▬ PRACTICE ▬

A.   Derivatives

1. Look in your dictionary under *viv-* and list three English words, with their meanings, that have to do with *being alive* or *lively*.   **2.** List three English words that are derived from the Latin *corpus*. Consult your dictionary if necessary.   **3.** Give a synonym for the word *invincible*.   **4.** What does *osculation* mean, and from which Latin word in this lesson is it derived? Remember that the suffix *-culus* means *small*.   **5.** Give one English word that is derived from each of the following compounds of **iaciō: adiciō, ēiciō, iniciō.** The stem will be the prefix plus *-ject-*.

B. Tell which kind(s) of subordinate clause can be introduced by each of the following:

1. cum   2. etsī   3. nisi   4. postquam   5. quam   6. quia   7. quō
8. quod   9. quoniam   10. seu   11. sī   12. simul ac   13. simul atque
14. sīn   15. sīve   16. ubi   17. unde   18. ut

C. Give the correlative adverb(s) for each of these relative adverbs:

1. unde   2. quō   3. quam   4. ubi   5. ut (comparative)

A view of an island sanctuary from Pompeii with a pleasure boat sailing by and a commercial vessel in the foreground—National Museum, Naples

D. Identify each clause as principal or subordinate, name the subordinate clauses, pronounce, and translate:

1. Ita fac ut ille facit, sīc enim bene faciēs. **2.** Urbs unde vēnistis magna, sed nōn clāra est prae nostrā. **3.** Utrum hīc manēbit an eō accēdet ubi bona vīta eum exspectat? **4.** Multī nostrōrum, nisi deus imbrīs mīserit, mortī cēdent, nam parum aquae habēbimus. **5.** Puella quia aurum ibi quō herī accessit invēnit ā mātre laudāta est. **6.** Sīve hunc servum vēndideritis sīve retinēbitis, nōn bene faciētis; cūr eum nōn līberātis? **7.** Hic puer tum cum parvus etiam erat perīculum ducī nūntiāvit itaque patriam servāvit. **8.** Ut ā vīllā excēdēbam avīs tam pulchrās vīdī quam ante in silvā aspexeram. **9.** Sī hominēs nūminibus multa dederint hī illōs respicient, sīn ārae mūneribus carēbunt populus inopiā nōn līberābitur. **10.** Ūnī ex lēgātīs, ut homo magnā virtūte erat, magna pecūnia praebita est, ille autem eam nōn recēpit.

Translation Help

Each separate clause is easy to translate if you start from the verb and go on from there; but sometimes it is not easy to distinguish the clauses from each other, especially as subordinate clauses are often nested one inside another.

EXAMPLE: **Tū sī eō quō ego postquam pecūniam accipiam et ex urbe discēdam ambulābō crās accesseris mē in vīllā meā inveniēs.** It is well to remember that in Latin usually, and in this text always, a subordinate clause will end with its verb. Begin by counting the verbs; this will tell you the number of clauses. Here there are five: **accipiam, discēdam, ambulābō, accesseris,** and **inveniēs.** Next see which of the verbs are introduced by subordinating words (see Drill B.) These are subordinate clauses; all the words that are left outside of them belong to the principal clause. Two verbs joined by a coordinating conjunction are in the same kind of clause, whether principal or subordinate. The clauses in the example are:

PRINCIPAL CLAUSE:	Tū mē in vīllā meā inveniēs
	You will find me in my own farmhouse
CONDITIONAL CLAUSE:	sī eō crās accesseris
	if tomorrow you come to that place
RELATIVE CLAUSE:	quō ego ambulābō
	to which I shall walk
TEMPORAL CLAUSE 1:	postquam pecūniam accipiam
	after I receive the money
TEMPORAL CLAUSE 2:	et ex urbe discēdam.
	and leave the city.

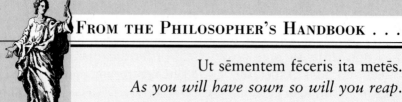

FROM THE PHILOSOPHER'S HANDBOOK . . .

Ut sēmentem fēceris ita metēs.
As you will have sown so will you reap.
—CICERO

This is a proverb that you have probably heard many times, and its meaning seems quite obvious. However, think of it in relation to your life in school—your friends, your studies, your extra-curricular activities—and its effect on your adult life. How will what you "sow" now affect your life ten years from now?

READING

Developing Reading Skills

Words which may help in determining the meanings of unfamiliar Latin words: *condition, et cetera, include, invulnerable, pacify, rupture,* and *victor.*

The Belt of Pallas

Tum cum Aenēās etiam in marī erat Turnus cum sociīs Latīnīs castra Trōiāna oppugnābat et ubi Trōiānī decoris cupīdine occupātī sunt et portam castrō-rum aperuērunt intrāvit; tum cum porta iterum clausa erat Turnus ūnus sine reliquīs sociīs inclūsus et paene captus est. Etsī magnā cum virtūte 5 pugnābat, pār tamen tot hostibus nōn erat atque tandem postquam in Tiberim dēsiluit per amnem nāvit et ad sociōs et ad salūtem.

Aenēās Pallāsque ubi cum Etrūscīs pervēnērunt auxilium Trōiānīs dedērunt, et Latīnī cēdēbant et fūgērunt. Sed victōria dolōre mixta est, nam
Pallās, postquam cum Lausō Mezentī fīliō pugnāvit, ā Turnō interfectus
erat. Pallantī iuvenī fuerat cingulum aureum mīrā formā; hoc eius corporī   10
cēpit Turnus et habēbat servābatque.

Deinde Mezentius (nam Etrūscus contrā Etrūscōs cēterōs tamen prō Turnō
ille rēx pugnābat) ab Aeneā vulnerātus et paene cōnfectus est, sed Lausus
patrem clipeō servāvit. At pius iuvenis postquam Mezentium ē proeliō ēdūxit
ab Aeneā interfectus est; cārī fīlī corpus ad parentem portātum est. Vetus   15
Mezentius simul atque hoc vīdit equō in proelium volāvit, ubi Aeneam
petēbat. Mezentius cum Aeneā ubi eum repperit fortiter pugnāvit; ab hōc
tamen cōnfectus est ille. Mors et patris et fīlī Aeneam trīstem fēcit, nam ille
etsī malus erat filium sīc amāverat ut Aenēās Ascanium et hic erat pulcher
et iuvenis et fortis tamquam Pallās fuerat.   20

Postquam hōc secundō quoque proeliō Latīnī superātī et paene victī sunt
animī eīs dēficiēbant, et Trōiānī Latīnīque pacem effēcērunt illā condīciōne:
"Pugnantō ducēs ambō; victor rēx duōrum populōrum vocātor." Sed Iūturna
dea, Turnī soror, mortem frātrī timuit et Rutulīs clāmāvit: "Num prō
omnibus, Rutulī, pugnābit Turnus ūnus? Nisi eum iūveritis virī nōn iam   25
vocābiminī!" Itaque tum cum pugna inter ducēs singulōs iam incepta erat
pācem rūpērunt Rutulī et lātē longēque cum Trōiānīs pugnābant, sed hī illōs
vincēbant.

Tandem Aenēās cum Turnō convēnit. Ubi rēgēs diū et ācriter pugnābant
cecidit hic et ab illō victus est. Aenēās misericordiā paene mōtus est, at   30
simul atque cingulum Pallantis aspēxit īrā occupātus est et Rutulum interfēcit.

READING COMPREHENSION

1. How did Turnus escape the Trojans?   **2.** What did Turnus take from
Pallas after he killed him?   **3.** What were the peace terms between the
Trojans and the Latins?   **4.** Why did the Rutulians break the treaty?
5. What made Aeneas lose his pity for Turnus?

---

22. illā: Latin often uses **ille** for what is to follow; in English we use *this*. **23. Pugnantō:**
future imperative (see Appendix). So also **vocātor**.   **27. pugnābant:** use the false pluperfect
in English: *had been fighting*

REVIEW 6

■■■ VOCABULARY DRILL ■■■

A. Give the genitive, gender, and meaning of the following nouns:

altitūdō	castra	lātitūdō	ōs	saeculum
arma	corpus	longitūdō	pecūnia	tempus
aureus	fātum	mōns	pēs	virgō
avis	forma	nēmō		

B. Give the meaning of each indeclinable adjective; give the nominative and genitive singular, and the meaning, of each adjective of one termination; give the other nominative singular (or plural) forms, and the meanings, for the others.

ambō	fortis	iste	quīnī	tantus
aureus	gravis	iuvenis	quīnquiplex	tot
bīnī	hic	mīrus	simplex	trīnī
clārus	ille	quadruplex	singulī	triplex
duplex	is	quaternī	tālis	vīvus

C. Give the other three principal parts, and the meanings, of these verbs:

addō	dēmō	iaciō	prōmō	vinciō
adiciō	ēiciō	iniciō	trāiciō	vincō
condō	emō	prōdō	vēndō	vīvō
coniciō	eximō			

D. Give the meanings of these adverbs:

cum	hūc	istinc	quoniam	sīn
eō	ibi	istūc	quoque	sīve
ergō	illīc	ita	seu	tam
etiam	illinc	iterum	sīc	tamen
etsī	illūc	postquam	simul ac	tamquam
hīc	inde	quam	simul atque	tōtiens
hinc	istīc	quia		

LISTENING AND SPEAKING

Make Haste Slowly

Livius, a freedman, is walking to the city and sees Marcus on the road with oxen and cart. Marcus gives him a lift, and they discuss the transportation problems of the day.

LĪVIUS: Heus,[1] agricola, quō plaustrō tuō accēdis?

MĀRCUS: Multās amphorās[2] oleī et vīnī in urbem portāmus, et crās laterēs[3] ab laterāriīs emām et rūrsus ex urbe ad vīllam portābimus.

LĪVIUS: Habēsne locum in plaustrō fessō viatōrī?

MĀRCUS: Hīc, mī amīce, multa et gravia onera sunt, et bovēs[4] labōrant, sed semper est locus amīcō.

LĪVIUS: Grātiās, Mārce, agō.[5] Longum et difficile pedibus ad urbem iter est. Bovēs autem validī[6] sunt; etsī plaustrum nōn celeriter trahent,[7] ad urbem tamen sine negōtiō accēdēmus.

MĀRCUS: Cūr in urbem ambulābās?

LĪVIUS: Nūntium dē dominō meō ad amīcum in urbem portō. Heu,[8] via difficilis plaustrō est! Vidē illum dīvitem in lectīcā. Facile iter lectīcā est, quod dominus ab octō servīs validīs portātur!

MĀRCUS: Modus itinerum dominō facilis sed nōn celer est. Cisia et essedā vēlōcia[9] sunt, sed onera gravia cisiō et essedō nōn portantur. Onera autem plaustrō āut sarrācō lentē[10] portāmus.

LĪVIUS: Cūr prope mare nōn habitāmus? Ibi nāvēs onerāriae bona nostra ūtiliter[11] et celeriter portābunt.

MĀRCUS: Mare, Līvī, et ventōs timeō. Et nāvēs nōn celerēs sunt, nam saepe in mare nōn excēdent quod ventī malī semper reflant.[12] Vītam prope mare nōn amō.

LĪVIUS: Vēra, Mārce, dīcis. Nunc cum bōbus lentē festīnāmus!

1. **Heus** (interjection)—*Hey*
2. **amphora, -ae, f.**—*amphora (a 2-handled large jar used for transporting goods)*
3. **later, -eris, m.**—*brick (-ārius, -ī, m.—brickmaker)*
4. **bōs, bovis, m. or f.**—*ox, cow* (dat./abl. pl. **bōbus**)
5. **grātiās agō, agere, ēgī, āctum**—*to give thanks, to thank*
6. **validus, -a, -um**—*strong (physically)*
7. **trahō, trahere, trāxī, trāctum**—*to pull, haul, drag*
8. **Heu** (interjection)—*alas*
9. **vēlox, vēlōcis**—*swift, speedy*
10. **lentē** (adv.)—*slowly*
11. **ūtiliter** (adv.)—*usefully, advantageously*
12. **reflō, -āre, -āvī, reflātum**—*blow back, blow contrary*

Divide the class into two teams. An Interrogator will ask members of their teams the following questions in any order. Each student who fails to answer correctly must sit down. At the end of a specified time the team with the greater number of students standing wins.

1. Quō Mārcus agricola plaustrō accēdit? **2.** Quid portat plaustrum? **3.** Quōmodo dominus facile iter facit? **4.** Quot servī lectīcam dominī portat? **5.** Cūr Mārcus vītam prope mare nōn amat?

TRACES OF ROMAN CIVILIZATION TODAY

North Africa—Algeria

Timgad: Arch of Trajan

Algeria, a republic in the northwestern section of Africa, is, after Sudan, the second largest country in the continent, and is a land of striking contrast and differences. Seven-eighths of the land is predominated by the bleak Saharan landscape, a startling contradiction to the rest of the region which is reminiscent of Mediterranean Spain, Italy, and France.

Djemila

In the early days of its history, the regions along the Algerian coast were affiliated with Carthage, but the interior and the mountains and plains were under Berber control and independent of Carthage. In 146 B.C. Carthage was destroyed and three centuries of Roman occupation of Algeria began. However, the Romans also occupied mostly coastal regions and coexisted with Berber monarchies in the mountains and plains. In the 400's A.D., the Romans were replaced by the Vandals, who maintained coastal garrisons for the next hundred years. During the sixth century, the Byzantine emperor, Justinian I, hoped to restore the Roman Empire and drove the Vandals from North Africa. However, his control proved to be too weak and he was, in turn, overwhelmed by the first Arab invaders.

And so, the Roman era was forever ended. However, traces of its prosperous three-hundred year reign can still be found in such cities as Timgad (ancient Thamugadi) and Djemila (ancient Cuicul).

Timgad: View of the Forum

Djemila: Gateway and Arch of Caracalla

Djemila: The Capitoline

273

Roman fresco from Pompeii showing a country shrine and a shepherd bringing a ram to sacrifice—National Museum, Naples

YOUR RELIGION: THE NŪMINA

Roman religion was originally nuministic, based on a belief in **nūmina,** the divine spirits present in every object and even in abstractions. There were separate **nūmina** of the door, the hinge, the lintel, and the threshold; of cattle-, horse-, and sheep-breeding; of the planted seed, the sprouted seed, and the growing plant—in short, of everything. There was, for example, a divinity called Limus, the **nūmen** of a sidelong glance.

These **nūmina** were not gods: having no personality or mythology, they were simply presences which could feel resentment and bring punishment on those who offended them. The Romans were not even sure whether one of the most important state deities, Pales, was male or female. Worship consisted of bribing the **nūmina** to do no harm. If a farmer had to cut down a grove of trees, he sacrificed a pig to the **nūmen** of the grove. If the pig proved to be deformed internally, it meant that the **nūmen** did not accept the sacrifice, and another pig would have to be slaughtered. Only the skin, fat, and bones had to be given to the **nūmen** by being burned; the farmer and his family and neighbors could eat the rest.

The **nūmina** were thought of as watching for even the tiniest breach of contract, for which they would take revenge. Hence the rituals had to be exactly right, and could never be varied. Even an unaccustomed sound could spoil the rite, and so silence was enjoined on the worshippers with the words **Favēte linguīs,** and the celebrant covered his head with a fold of his toga to keep from hearing outside sounds. Some of the ritual actions, prayers, and hymns which had been passed down orally from antiquity were totally incomprehensible to later Romans, but they went on being repeated anyway, for fear that some alteration might offend the **nūmina.**

Even after Roman religion had arrived at a more sophisticated stage with the development of the idea of personal gods, the worship of the **nūmina** played an important role in both state and private religion. A Roman's day

(Continued)

A PHRASE TO USE

Nīl sine nūmine
*Nothing without a numen (i.e. do
nothing without considering the
god's will)*

must have been full of small ritual acts, like our superstitious practices of touching wood or throwing spilt salt over our shoulders.

(*below right*) Statue of a patrician in priestly garb, from the early Empire—Borghese Gallery, Rome (*below left*) Statue of a Vestal Virgin in the House of the Vestals, Roman Forum. The remains of the Temple of Antoninus and Faustina (now a Christian Church) stand behind.

ANCIENT ROME LIVES ON . . .

What resemblance do today's superstitions have to the worship of the **nūmina**?

FORMS

PERSONAL PRONOUNS

The pronouns for the first and second persons are **egō**, *I*, **nōs**, *we*, **tū**, *you (sing.)*, and **vōs**, *you (pl.)*. For the personal pronoun of the third person (*he, she, it, they*) Latin uses the demonstratives **is, hic, iste,** and **ille.**

DECLENSION OF THE PERSONAL PRONOUNS

	FIRST PERSON		SECOND PERSON	
	SINGULAR	PLURAL	SINGULAR	PLURAL
NOM.	ego	nōs	tū	vōs
GEN.	meī	nostrum, nostrī	tuī	vestrum, vestrī
DAT.	mihi	nōbīs	tibi	vōbīs
ACC.	mē	nōs	tē	vōs
ABL.	mē	nōbīs	tē	vōbīs

The **Suovetaurīlia**: a sacrifice of a bull, ram, and boar to the God Mars. Altar of Domitius Ahenobarbus—Louvre, Paris

◼ REFLEXIVE PRONOUNS

The first and second person reflexive pronouns (*myself, ourselves, yourself, yourselves*) are like the personal pronouns, but lack a nominative. The third person reflexive pronoun (*himself, herself, itself, themselves*) is **suī, sibi, sē, sē.** It is the same in the singular and in the plural.

DECLENSION OF THE REFLEXIVE PRONOUNS

	FIRST PERSON		SECOND PERSON		THIRD PERSON	
	SING.	PL.	SING.	PL.	SING.	PL.
GEN.	meī	nostrum, nostrī	tuī	vestrum, vestrī	suī	suī
DAT.	mihi	nōbīs	tibi	vōbīs	sibi	sibi
ACC.	mē	nōs	tē	vōs	sē (sēsē)	sē (sēsē)
ABL.	mē	nōbīs	tē	vōbīs	sē (sēsē)	sē (sēsē)

▬▬ SYNTAX ▬▬

◼ AGREEMENT OF PRONOUNS

The substantive for which a pronoun stands is called its antecedent. In Latin, as in English, a pronoun must agree with its antecedent in gender, number, and person. It takes its case, as a noun does, from its use in the sentence. We follow this rule automatically in English.

Helen seemed happy when I saw her.   Helena ubi **eam** vīdī laeta vīsa est.

But *it* in English may have to be rendered by masculine or feminine, or plural, forms in Latin.

Sī anguis ad nōs accedit **eum** timēmus.
If a snake comes near us we fear it.
Ut avis volābat **eam** spectāvī.
As the bird was flying I watched it.
Sī castra posuerint **ea** capiēmus.
If they pitch a camp we shall take it.

The antecedent of the reflexive pronoun is the subject of the clause in which it is found.

Mē laudō.	*I praise myself.*
Tē laudās.	*You praise yourself.*
Is sē laudat.	*He praises himself.*
Ea sē laudat.	*She praises herself.*
Nōs laudāmus.	*We praise ourselves.*
Vōs laudātis.	*You praise yourselves.*
Sē laudant.	*They praise themselves.*

◼ USES OF THE PERSONAL AND REFLEXIVE PRONOUNS

1. When different personal pronouns are used together, the first person takes precedence over the second, and the second over the third, both in word order and in determining the person of the verb.

   Ego et tū discessimus. ⎫
   Ego et vōs discessimus. ⎭ *You and I left.*

   Tū et eī discessistī. ⎫
   Vōs et eī discessistī. ⎭ *You and they left.*

2. The genitive of the personal and reflexive pronouns is not used to show possession. Instead we use the possessive adjectives.

meus, -a, -um	*my, mine, my own*
noster, nostra, nostrum	*our, ours, our own*
tuus, -a, -um	*your, yours, your own*
vester, vestra, vestrum	*your, yours, your own*

   suus, -a, -um ⎧ *his, his own*
               ⎪ *her, hers, her own*
               ⎨ *its, its own*
               ⎩ *their, theirs, their own*

3. **Suus** is used only when it means *belonging to the subject.* Otherwise *his, her, hers, its, their,* and *theirs* are translated by the genitive of **is, hic, iste,** or **ille.**

Suum aurum servat.	*He guards his (own) gold.*
Eius aurum servat.	*He guards his ⟨someone else's⟩ gold.*

4. In the genitive plurals the **-ī** forms are used for the objective genitive, the **-um** forms for the partitive genitive (genitive of the whole).

   Multī vestrum nostrī memorēs erant.   *Many of you remembered us.*
   Pārs nostrum nostrō timōre vestrī mōta est.
   Part of us were moved by our fear of you.

5. The accusative of the reflexive pronouns is used with the preposition **inter** to express the reciprocal pronouns *one another* and *each other*.

> Inter nōs pugnāmus.
> *We are fighting with each other (one another).*
> Dōna inter vōs dabitis.
> *You will give gifts to each other (one another).*
> Inter sē amant. *They love each other (one another).*

6. In the ablative of accompaniment, the preposition **cum** is attached to the end of personal and reflexive pronouns: **mēcum, nōbīscum, tēcum, vōbīscum, sēcum.**

7. In **fugam dō** with a reflexive object means *take to flight*.

> Mē in fugam dedī. *I took to flight.*

ACCUSATIVE OF EXTENT OF SPACE

The accusative case, without a preposition, is used to answer the question *How far?* In this use it is called the Accusative of Extent of Space.

> Quīngentōs pedēs ambulābit. *He will walk five hundred feet.*
> Oppidum ab amne nōngentōs pedēs iacet.
> *The town lies nine hundred feet from the river.*

EXPRESSIONS OF TIME

Accusative of Duration of Time

The accusative case, without a preposition, is used to answer the question *How long?* In this use it is called the Accusative of Duration of Time.

> Eam trīs hōrās exspectāvimus. *We waited for her for three hours.*

Ablative of Time When

The ablative case, without a preposition, is used to answer the question *When?* In this use it is called the Ablative of Time When.

> Quartā hōrā veniet. *He will come at the fourth hour.*

Ablative of Time Within Which

The ablative case, without a preposition, is used to answer the question *Within what period?* In this use it is called the Ablative of Time Within Which.

> Quattuor hōrīs veniet. *He will come within four hours.*

Ablative of Degree of Difference

The ablative case, without a preposition, is used to answer the question *By how much?* In this use it is called the Ablative of Degree of Difference.

> Multīs ante annīs vēnit.
>> *He came many years ago (before by many years).*
> Multīs post annīs vēnit.
>> *He came many years later (afterwards by many years).*

In these sentences **ante** and **post** are used as adverbs and should not be confused with the prepositions **ante** and **post,** used with the accusative.

> Post multōs annōs vēnit.   *He came after many years.*

VOCABULARY

BASIC WORDS

cīvis, cīvis, m. or f. (i-stem) *citizen*
fors, (defective; abl. forte) f. *chance, luck*
hōra, -ae, f. *hour*
lītus, lītoris, n. *seashore, coast*
nātūra, -ae, f. *birth, nature*
nox, noctis, f. (i-stem) *night*
sanguis, sanguinis, m. *blood*

cēterī, -ae, -a *the other, the rest (of)*
fēlix, fēlīcis *lucky, successful, happy*
fugiō,-ere, fūgī, fugitum *flee, flee from*
inquam (defective verb) *say*
quidem (postpositive adv.) *in fact; to be sure, at any rate;* nē . . . quidem *not even*

Notes:
1. When **cīvis** is modified by a possessive adjective (**meus, noster, tuus, vester, suus**) it means *fellow-citizen.*
2. **Hōra:** For the Romans an hour represented one-twelfth of the time between sunrise and sunset, or between sunset and sunrise. For convenience we count from six to six, so that **quartā hōrā** = *at ten o'clock.*
3. **Cēterī** (like **reliquus, medius, summus,** etc.) contains the *of* idea and so does not need a genitive.

> Cēterī cīvēs hoc nōn fēcērunt.
>> *The rest of the citizens did not do this.*

4. **Fugiō** is one of a few Latin verbs which may be either transitive or intransitive.

> Fugiō.   *I am fleeing.*   Tē fugiō.   *I am fleeing from you.*

(Continued) 5. **Inquam** has only four commonly used forms:

inquam	*I say (said)*		
inquis	*you say (said)*		
inquit	*he (she, it) says (said)*	inquiunt	*they say (said)*

It is used only to introduce direct quotations and is always placed after the first word, or first few words, of the quotation.

Magister "Crās" inquit "vōs nōn vidēbō."
The teacher said, "I shall not see you tomorrow."

7. The word modified by **nē . . . quidem** comes between them.

Nē Alexander quidem tālia fēcit.   *Not even Alexander did such things.*

LEARNING ENGLISH THROUGH LATIN

et cetera	*and the rest, and so forth*
felicity	*great happiness; bliss*
fortuitous	*happening by good luck*
fugitive	*one who flees from danger or justice*
nocturnal	*happening, or active, in the night*
sanguinary	*bloodthirsty; accompanied by much bloodshed*
supernatural	*not attributable to natural forces*

FROM THE PHILOSOPHER'S HANDBOOK . . .

Ignōscitō saepe aliīs, numquam tibi.
Forgive others often, yourself never.

Why would today's psychologists dispute the second part of this proverb? Do you think it is important to forgive yourself? Why or why not?

PRACTICE

A. Derivatives

1. Name and define three English words that are derived from the Latin **cīvis**. **2.** Two derivatives of the Latin **modus** are *modify* and *module*. Check their meanings with a dictionary and explain their relation to **modus**. **3.** Other derivatives of **sanguis** are *sanguine, sanguineous,* and *sanguinolent.* What do they mean?

B. Decline orally:

1. ego **2.** nōs **3.** tū **4.** vōs

C. Decline orally in full the first, second, and third person reflexive pronouns.

D. Change the number of these pronouns, keeping the same case:

1. tū **2.** suī **3.** mihi **4.** vestrī **5.** nostrum **6.** sē **7.** tibi **8.** sibi **9.** ego **10.** tuī

E. Match the sentence in column **A** with the correct translation(s) in **B**:

	A		**B**
1.	Eam timet.	a.	He fears him.
2.	Sibi timent.	b.	She fears him.
3.	Illam timet.	c.	They fear for themselves.
4.	Sibi timet.	d.	They fear him.
5.	Eum timet.	e.	He fears her.
6.	Illum timent.	f.	She fears for herself.
7.	Istam timet.	g.	He fears himself.
8.	Sē timet.	h.	He fears for himself.
9.	Hunc timet.	i.	She fears her.
10.	Huic timent.	j.	They fear for her.
		k.	She fears herself.
		l.	They fear for him.

F. Translate the English words into Latin:

1. *He and I* ambulābimus *with you (pl.).* **2.** *She* dedit *it to me.* **3.** *They* portābunt *us with them.* **4.** *He* amat *his* mātrem. **5.** *He* amat *her* mātrem.

READING

Developing Reading Skills

English words derived from or related to unfamiliar words in this reading: *augment, conception, hospitality, rapacious.*

The Adventures of Anna

Tum cum et Aenēās ab urbe discesserat et Dīdō sē interfēcerat Carthāgō et rēge et rēgīnā carēbat. Tribus post annīs invāsērunt Africānī rēgnum ita sine duce atque Iarbās rēx postquam rēgiam occupāvit in soliō sēdit et sēcum "Nunc ego," inquit "misera Dīdō, istūc mē recēpī unde totiēns ā tē ēiectus
5   sum." Ut Poenī hūc et illūc fugiēbant Anna Elissae soror partem cīvium convocāvit et cum hīs ūnā nāve ad Melitam īnsulam nāvigāvit, ubi rēx omnīs hospitiō accēpit. At tertiō annō postquam Anna hūc pervēnit Pygmaliōn frāter cum multīs nāvibus ad īnsulam nāvigāvit ad Melitaeque rēgem accessit sorōremque bellō petīvit. Rēx Annae "Nōs nōn sumus" inquit "ad bellum
10 cum tot hostibus parātī; tū ergō hinc fuge!" Iterum in marī fugam petīvit Anna et tandem ad lītora Latīna forte pervēnit.

    Iam pius Aenēās rēgnō fīliāque Latīnī auctus erat, populōsque miscuerat duōs. Hic ōlim cum in lītore cum Achāte amīcō ambulābat Annam aspēxit sēcumque putāvit, "Cūr illa in agrum Latīnum vēnit?" et clāmāvit Achātēs,
15 "Anna est!" Anna magnō timōre commōta est et rūrsus fugam incipiēbat, at Aenēās "Manē tū;" inquit "hīc nōmine grāta tuō, grāta sorōris, eris, nam memorēs sumus tot beneficiōrum vestrōrum. Ad rēgiam tē dūcam, ubi nōbīscum habitābis." Ibi Annam Lāvīniae commīsit tālibus verbīs: "Hanc tibi, cāra uxor, trādō pietātis grātiā, haec enim mē auxiliō iuvābat ubi inopiā
20 omnium labōrābam."

---

3. sēcum: with verbs of thinking and saying the Romans used *with myself, yourself, himself,* etc., where we would say to *myself, yourself,* etc.   **4. ego:** Even though the verb alone tells us person and number, the pronoun subject may be expressed for emphasis or to contrast with another subject.   **16. nōmine . . . tuō:** *on your own account*

Water nymph on a
marine monster,
cover of a silver
jewelry box—Taranto
Archeological
Museum

Lāvīnia omnia promīsit sed sēcum putābat, "Mē ergō nōn amat vir meus sed hanc Poenam," et īram in pectore concēpit. Inimīcitiam tamen dissimulāvit et Annae amīca vīsa est. At nocte in somnīs umbra Dīdōnis ad sorōrem accessit et monuit, "Hinc fuge tū, locum fuge hunc tristem; rēgīna tibi mortem parat." Misera discessit ex rēgiā Anna et per agrōs errābat.　25 Dēnique forte in Numīcium amnem cecidit et aquīs rapta est. Aenēās ubi cum suīs miseram petēbat animam Annae aspexit et tālia ex eā audīvit: "Ā Numīciō deō in deam mūtāta sum. Ego Nympha huius amnis facta sum; vōs mihi sacra mūnera datōte; sīc semper fēlīcēs eritis."

Post Rōmānī Annam in numerō deum suōrum habuērunt.　30

READING COMPREHENSION

1. Who was Anna?　2. Why did she have to leave Malta?　3. What plans did Aeneas have for Anna after he found her?　4. Why did Anna leave the palace?　5. What happened to her?

---

29. datōte: future imperative (see Appendix)

A famous wall fresco from Pompeii of Diana, goddess of the hunt—National Museum, Naples

YOUR RELIGION: THE GODS

As farmers were gathered into communities, the numina which were of concern to the whole community were worshipped communally; hence the numina of the sky, of marriage, of industry and agriculture, of the communal hearth, etc., became more important than the little local numina, which were still worshipped with a thousand little ritual acts primarily within the family. When the Romans met the Etruscans they learned to visualize the more important numina in human form; and from the Greeks of southern Italy they also heard the stories about their doings, which we call myths. The more important numina became gods, and other gods, hitherto unheard of, were imported from Etruria, Greece, and the Near East. Twelve gods formed a kind of heavenly Senate, the "gods who agree with each other" (**deī cōnsentēs**). These were grouped in male-female pairs: Jupiter (god of the sky, king and father of gods and men) and Juno (his wife and sister, goddess of women and marriage); Neptune (brother of Jupiter, god of bodies of water) and Minerva (daughter of Jupiter, goddess of trades, arts, and crafts, and of wisdom in war); Mars (son of Jupiter and Juno, god of the growing grain and of war) and Venus (goddess of female beauty and love); Apollo (son of Jupiter, god of light, male beauty, disease, and music) and Diana (his twin sister, goddess of wild nature, virginity and fertility, and childbirth); Vulcan (son of Juno, god of destructive fire and of the fire of the forge) and Vesta (goddess of the fire on the hearth); Mercury (son of Jupiter, god of the dead, of heralds, of profit, and of thieves and merchants) and Ceres (sister of Jupiter, goddess of fertility and crops).

Of these six male gods, Jupiter was identified with the Greek Zeus, the Libyan Ammon, and the Teutonic Thor; Neptune with the Greek Poseidon; Mars with the Greek Ares; Apollo was imported from the Greeks, keeping his original name; Vulcan was identified with the Greek Hephaestus; Mercury was imported from the Greeks, and his name changed from Hermes (he

(Continued)

was later identified with the Egyptian Thoth and Teutonic Odin). Of the goddesses, Juno was identified with the Greek Hera and sometimes the Levantine Astarte; Minerva with the Greek Athena; Venus with the Greek Aphrodite and sometimes with Astarte; Diana with the Greek Artemis and sometimes with Astarte; Vesta (an important numen to the Romans) with the minor Greek goddess Hestia; and Ceres with the Greek Demeter.

(*below right*) An early depiction of Minerva, and (*below left*) one from the Empire (note the wolf with Romulus and Remus on her shield)

ANCIENT ROME LIVES ON . . .

From the names of which gods are the following words derived, and what do they mean: *cereal, jovial, junoesque, martial, mercurial, vulcanize, volcano?*

≡ FORMS ≡

■ THE RELATIVE PRONOUN AND ADJECTIVE; THE INTERROGATIVE ADJECTIVE

The relative pronoun (*who, which, that*), the relative adjective (*which*), and the interrogative adjective (*which?*) are all declined in the same way.

RELATIVE PRONOUN AND ADJECTIVE; INTERROGATIVE ADJECTIVE

	SINGULAR			PLURAL		
	MASC.	FEM.	NEUT.	MASC.	FEM.	NEUT.
NOM.	quī	quae	quod	quī	quae	quae
GEN.	cuius	cuius	cuius	quōrum	quārum	quōrum
DAT.	cui	cui	cui	quibus	quibus	quibus
ACC.	quem	quam	quod	quōs	quās	quae
ABL.	quō	quā	quō	quibus	quibus	quibus

This follows the pronoun declension, with **-ius** in the genitive singular, **-i** in the dative singular, and a **-d** ending in the neuter nominative and accusative singular.

Other relative and interrogative adjectives to learn are:

quālis, -e *of what kind;* **tālis . . . quālis** *such . . . as*
quantus, -a, -um, *how big, how large, how much;* **tantus . . . quantus** *as big (as large, much) . . . as*
quot (indeclinable) *how many;* **tot . . . quot** *as many . . . as*
quotiēns (adv.) *how often;* **totiēns . . . quotiēns** *as often . . . as*

■ THE INTERROGATIVE PRONOUN

The interrogative pronoun (*who? what?*) is the same as the interrogative adjective except for some forms in the singular.

THE INTERROGATIVE PRONOUN

	SINGULAR		PLURAL		
	M. & F.	NEUT.	MASC.	FEM.	NEUT.
NOM.	quis	quid	quī	quae	quae
GEN.	cuius	cuius	quōrum	quārum	quōrum
DAT.	cui	cui	quibus	quibus	quibus
ACC.	quem	quid	quōs	quās	quae
ABL.	quō	quō	quibus	quibus	quibus

The preposition **cum** is normally attached to the relative and interrogative pronouns, as it is to the personal and reflexive: **quōcum, quācum, quibuscum.**

Puella quācum ambulās pulchra est.
The girl with whom you are walking is beautiful.

■ SYNTAX ■

■ AGREEMENT OF THE RELATIVE PRONOUN

Like all other pronouns, the relative pronoun must agree with its antecedent in gender, number, and person, while its case is determined by its use in its own clause.

Hae sunt fēminae quās vīdimus.　　*These are the women whom we saw.*

Note that **quās** is feminine plural to agree with its antecedent **fēminae**. It is accusative plural because it is used as the direct object in its own clause.

Hī sunt eī quōrum urbem vīdimus.
These are the people whose city we saw.

Quōrum is masculine plural to agree with its antecedent **eī** and is genitive because of its possessive use in its own clause.

Ego quī prīmā hōrā discessī septimā perveniam.
I who left at the first hour will arrive at the seventh.

Quī is masculine singular and first person (as the form of **discessī** tells us) to agree with its antecedent **ego.** It is nominative because it is the subject of its own clause.

THE RELATIVE WITHOUT AN ANTECEDENT

The demonstrative antecedent of the relative pronoun, adjective, or adverb is often omitted, and must be supplied.

> Quod facitis mē nōn iuvat.
> *That which you are doing does not please me.*
> Quī bene vīvit fēlīx erit.
> *He who lives well will be happy.*

THE RELATIVE PRONOUN AS A CONJUNCTION

Normally, of course, the relative pronoun introduces a relative clause. It may, however, also introduce a principal clause, in which case it serves as a conjunction + a demonstrative: **qui = et is, quae = et ea, quod = et id.**

> Erant ignēs in hostium arce, quōs simul
> atque vīdī ad amīcōs nūntium mīsī.
> *There were fires on the enemy citadel, and as*
> *soon as I saw them I sent a message to my friends.*

USE OF THE INTERROGATIVE PRONOUN

The interrogative pronoun is used to ask questions. The English equivalents are as follows: NOM., *Who? What?* GEN., *Whose?* DAT. *To whom? For whom? To what? For what?* ACC. *Whom? What?* ABL. *Whom? What? With what?*

> Quis hoc fēcit?   *Who did this?*
> Quī hoc fēcērunt?   *Who (Which ones) did this?*
> Quis cīvium hoc fēcit?   *Which of the citizens did this?*
> Quis cīvis hoc fēcit?   *Who, being a citizen, did this?*
> Quid cōnsilī cēpit?   *What plan did he form?*

Note the use of the partitive genitive with interrogative pronouns. It is especially common with **quid.**

■ USE OF THE INTERROGATIVE ADJECTIVE

Compare these sentences with those above:

Quī cīvis hoc fēcit?   *Which (What) citizen did this?*
Quī cīvēs hoc fēcērunt?   *Which (What) citizens did this?*
Quod cōnsilium cēpit?   *Which (What kind of) plan did he form?*

═══ VOCABULARY ═══

■ BASIC WORDS

aedēs, aedis, f. (i-stem) *temple;*
   (pl.) aedēs, aedium, f. *house*
aetās, aetātis, f. *age; lifetime*
caput, capitis, n. *head*
imāgō, imāginis, f. *image, likeness,*
   portrait, statue
mēns, mentis, f. (i-stem) *mind*
modus, -ī, m. *measure, degree; manner,*
   way

absum, abesse, āfuī, āfutūrus *be away,*
   be absent, be distant
ardeō, -ēre, ārsī, ārsum *burn*
   (intransitive)
colō, -ere, coluī, cultum *cultivate;*
   worship
legō, -ere, lēgī, lēctum *pick; read*
relinquō, -ere, relīquī, relīctum *leave*
   behind, leave, abandon
trādō, -ere, trādidī, trāditum *hand over,*
   hand down

Notes:
1. **Puer octō annōrum aetāte,** *an eight-year-old boy* < a boy of eight years with respect to age (gen. of measure, abl. of specification)

2. The phrases **quem ad modum** (*to which degree*) and **quō modō** (*in which way*) are often run together to make the adverbs **quōmodo** and **quemadmodum,** both meaning *how* or *as.*

   Quemadmodum (*or* quōmodo) hoc facis?   *How do you do this?*
   Sīc (*or* ita) hoc fac quemadmodum (*or* quōmodo) ego faciō.
   Do this just as I do.

3. **Relinquō** and **discēdō** both mean *leave,* but the former is transitive, the latter not:

   Urbem relīquit. ⎱
   Ex urbe discessit. ⎰ *He left the city.*

Building Vocabulary

Note the following compounds of **legō**:

colligō, -ere, collēgī, collēctum   *collect*
dēligō, -ere, dēlēgī, dēlēctum   *pick out, choose*
dīligō, -ere, dīlēxī, dīlēctum   *prize, love, feel affection for*

The Verospi Jupiter—Pio Clementino Museum, Vatican

Translation Help

Another way to discover which clauses are principal and which subordinate is to look carefully at the words that lie between the verbs. If between the verbs there is a coordinating conjunction, the verbs are in the same kind of clause. If there is a subordinating word, then the second verb is in a subordinate clause. If there is neither a coordinating conjunction nor a subordinating word, then the first verb is in a subordinate clause. Note the following examples:

Ad oppidum ambulābimus et frūmentum emēmus.
Ad oppidum ambulābimus ubi frūmentum emēmus.
Sī ad oppidum ambulābimus frūmentum emēmus.

■ LEARNING ENGLISH THROUGH LATIN

aetat. or aet.	*an abbreviation (for **aetāte**) meaning aged (a specific number of years), at the age of*
ardent	*intense in feeling; enthusiastic or zealous*
decapitate	*behead; cut off the head of*
derelict	*(adj.) neglectful of duty*
	(n.) a destitute person rejected by society
edifice	*a large, imposing building*
illegible	*unable to be read*
quidnunc	*an inquisitive, gossipy person; a busybody*
relinquish	*surrender, abandon, let go*

From the Philosopher's Handbook . . .

Quī nōn prōficit, dēficit.
The one who does not advance falls behind.

How does this saying apply to your study of Latin? Can you ever stand still in any of your school subjects? Can this motto also be applied to your interests outside of school? Explain.

PRACTICE

A. Derivatives

1. Name two English words derived from the Latin **absum.** 2. *Cult, cultivate,* and *culture* are all derivatives of the Latin **colō.** Look up their meanings in a dictionary and show their relationship to the Latin. 3. What is the antonym of *illegible?* 4. Show the relationship of the English words *capital, captain,* and *chapter* to the Latin **caput.** 5. Write one original sentence using at least two of the derivatives in this lesson.

B. Give all possible genders, numbers, and cases for each of these forms of the relative pronoun:

1. cui 2. cuius 3. quā 4. quae 5. quem 6. quī 7. quibus 8. quō 9. quod 10. quōrum

C. Give all possible genders, numbers, and cases for each of these forms of the interrogative pronoun:

1. cui 2. cuius 3. quae 4. quārum 5. quem 6. quī 7. quibus 8. quid 9. quō 10. quōrum

D. Fill the blanks with interrogative pronouns or adjectives from the list below, then translate each sentence. More than one answer may be possible for each sentence.

1. ___ oppida vīdistī? 2. ___ deōrum aedēs in arce sunt? 3. ___ imāginem dēmōnstrāvit? 4. ___ cum discēdēs? 5. ___ dēlēgērunt?

cui cuius quā quae quam quārum quās quem quibus quid quō quōrum quōs

E. Pronounce and translate:

1. Quotiēns illīus ad aedīs accessistis? 2. Quōmodo iter tam difficile conficient? 3. Quid pecūniae nōbīs est? 4. Quī hīc in oppidī viīs clāmābant? 5. Quemadmodum deae imāginem ex aurō faciēmus?

F. Translate:

1. Which poem will you read a part of? 2. What kind of king began this war? 3. Whose children were shouting? 4. How large a mountain did you walk around? 5. To how many gods did they offer gifts?

G. Fill in the blanks with the appropriate relatives from the choices given:

1. ___ ad oppidum venit totiēns frūmentum emit. (quālia, quot, quotiēns)
2. Nōn ante tālem urbem vīdī ___ haec est. (quālia, quālis, quanta)   3. Tot aureōs servāvī ___ āmīsī (quod, quot, quotiēns).   4. Alba Longa tanta erat ___ Lāvīnium (quālis, quantum, quem).   5. Id oppidum ___ vīdī magnum erat (quem, quod, quot).

H. Pronounce and translate:

1. Ubi sunt sociī quibuscum urbem relīquistis?   2. Quī fēlīx nōn semper laetus, quī miser nōn semper tristis est.   3. Is cui pecūnia trādita est homō est aetāte annōrum circā quīnque et trīgintā.   4. Tum memor mātris meae factus sum, cuius simul atque imāgō in mentem vēnit illinc discessī. 5. Sunt bīnae aedēs in hāc viā, quārum hae centum et vīgintī pedēs, illae dūcentōs istinc absunt.

I. Translate:

1. That is the house to which I sent the gift.   2. The boy to whom I taught the Latin language is sixteen years old.   3. Are these the weapons with which you fought?   4. Those men whose morale was strengthened did not leave the city.   5. The enemies to whom our leader yielded were few.

The infant Jupiter seated on the Amalthean goat—coin of Valerian II, 253–255 A.D.

READING

The Kings of Alba Longa

Post Bellum Latīnum Aenēās cum populō suō ex oppidō Laurentō migrāvit et urbem condidit quam ab uxōris nōmine Lāvīnium vocāvit. Tribus post annīs Aenēās ad caelum portātus et deus factus est. Ut Ascanius Iūlusve fīlius Aenēae tum puer erat cum patrem āmīsit Lāvīnia noverca cīvīs diū

prō illō rēgēbat. Post duōs et vīgintī annōs autem ille vīsus est omnibus vir 5
magnā virtūte et tālī animō quālis fortī parentī fuerat, et tam dīgnus laude;
itaque, ut ager Lāvīnius prō hominum multitūdine satis nōn iam erat et
cōpia frūmentī dēficiēbat, cīvium partem ad montem eī locō in quō Rōma
hodiē stat propinquum dēdūxit et ibi novum oppidum, Albam Longam
nōmine, condidit. Pius iuvenis tot cīvīs quot sēcum ēdūxerat relīquit Lāvīniae 10
cārae novercae, quae ita rēgīna facta est et cīvibus Lāvīniīs multōs annōs
lēgēs dabat. Alba Longa nōn modo multitūdine hominum sed etiam magnitūdine agrī tanta mox erat quantum Lāvīnium. Pācem multōs annōs haec
duo oppida inter sē servāvērunt.

    In silvā forte Iūlī uxor fīlium virō genuit, unde illī nōmen Silviō datum 15
est, quod nōmen per saecula mānsit et omnibus quoque rēgibus quī altō ā
sanguine auctōris gentis, fīlī Veneris, vēnērunt trāditum est. Multīs post
annīs nōmen gentis Silviae mūtātum est quae ex eō tempore Iūlia ab Iūlī
clārō nōmine vocāta est; sīc Iūlius Caesar ille Venerem deam vocābat
genetrīcem suam. Tredecim post saeculīs hominum Numitor Silvius Albam 20
Longam rēgēbat. Quem postquam frāter, Amūlius nōmine, quī imperī
cupīdine mōtus erat, ē rēgnō vī ēiēcit, hīc, homō ācris saevitiae, rēx in frātris
locō factus est. Addidit scelerī scelus: nōn modo frātris fīliīs caede vītam
dēmpsit, sed etiam sorōrem eōrum, Rhēam Silviam vel Īliam nōmine,
Vestālem dēlēgit, sēcum enim "Sīc" inquit "quōmodo erunt aut fīliī virginī 25
aut frātrī nepōtēs? Imperium semper meum et meōrum erit."

    At hoc cōnsilium foedum Fāta mīrīs modīs vetābant: nam Mars, nūmen
frūmentī et armōrum, Rhēae Silviae amōre captus est et haec fīliōs geminōs
deō genuit. Rhēa quoniam Vestālis erat capitis condemnāta est, atque prōlēs
duplex in aquās Tiberis amnis iniecta est. 30

![] READING COMPREHENSION

1. What city did Aeneas found after the Latin War? How did it get its name?
2. What city did Ascanius found? **3.** What crimes were committed by
Amulius? **4.** Why did he choose Rhea Silvia as a Vestal? **5.** How did
the Fates forbid his ugly plan?

---

15. Silviō: Latin usually makes the name an appositive to the person named, not to the noun
nōmen. **20. saeculīs hominum** = *generations* **25. Vestālem:** The six Vestal Virgins, who
tended the sacred hearth of Rome in the temple of Vesta, were not allowed to marry. **29. capitis:**
the Genitive of the Penalty, an idiomatic use of the genitive with verbs of condemning or
acquitting:

        Eum capitis condemnāvērunt.   *They condemned him to death.*

LESSON 27

Other Adjectives of the Pronoun Declension; Universal Pronoun, Adjectives, and Adverbs

The Emperor Domitian reluctantly sets out for war assisted by Mars and Minerva (left) and sent by the goddess Rōma and the old man and the youth representing **Senātus Populusque Rōmānus**— Vatican Museum

YOUR RELIGION: OFFICIAL CULTS

Jupiter, Juno, and Minerva were the three chief gods of the state, worshipped in every community which had earned the title of Colony of Rome. They are called the Capitoline Triad, since their chief temple stood on the Capitoline Hill. Later, as a pledge of allegiance, the deified emperors had to be worshipped. These gods did not demand love or even belief from their worshippers, but only worship. The other major gods had priesthoods to carry on their worship, which did not require public participation; but the Roman calendar was full of feasts in honor of minor **nūmina**, whose functions and nature were often not understood by their worshippers. Of the 365 days of the Julian calendar more than 160 were full or partial religious holidays, often celebrated with plays, races, and fairs.

The basic form of worship was animal sacrifice. The victim was decked out and brought to the altar; if it struggled or tried to escape, the sacrifice was considered unsuccessful. With his head veiled, and accompanied by a flute player, to keep him from hearing distracting sounds, the priest read the necessary prayers, calling the god by all of his names to make sure of getting the right one. He was careful not to change a word, even one unintelligible to him. He then sprinkled the victim's head with salt mixed with spelt and wine, and cut its throat.

The Romans read the will of the gods in the flight patterns of wild birds and the eating habits of tame ones, and from the time and direction of lightning and thunder. From the Etruscans they had learned also how to read omens in the internal organs of sacrificial animals. For more specific answers they could turn to the Sibylline Books, books of prophecy written by the Cumaean Sibyl and sold to King Tarquin II, or send embassies to Greek oracles, especially that of Apollo at Delphi.

The body governing religious practices at Rome was the College of Pontiffs

(Continued)

(**Collegium Pontificum**), made up of the Pontifices ("Bridge-Builders"), so called because they consecrated the **iānī**, magical bridges over the magical boundary of the city (**pōmērium**). The group was presided over by the **Pontifex Maximus**, and included also the **Rēx Sacrificulus**, who dealt with some of the sacrifices which the kings had performed, and the three highest **Flāminēs**, those of Jupiter (**Flāmen Diālis**), Mars (**Flāmen Martiālis**), and Quirinus, the deified Romulus (**Flāmen Quirīnālis**). The 6 **Vestālēs** celebrated the rituals of Vesta. The 15 **Flaminēs** were the priests supervising the worship of individual gods. The wives of the **Pontifex Maximus** and the **Flāmen Diālis** also had priestly functions. The children who attended the priests at sacrifices were called **Camillī** and **Camillae**. The College of Augurs (**Augurēs**) was in charge of the reading of the auspices (**auspicia**) in the behavior of birds and the lightning and thunder. The 60 **Haruspicēs** (originally Etruscans) read the omens in the entrails of sacrificed animals.

(*below*) Marcus Aurelius with head veiled and accompanied by a flute player officiating at a sacrifice in front of the Temple of the Capitoline Triad

ANCIENT ROME LIVES ON . . .

What are the means through which modern people try to find out the future? Are there any similarities between these and those of ancient Rome?

FORMS

OTHER ADJECTIVES OF THE PRONOUN DECLENSION

Īdem

The adjective **īdem, eadem, idem,** *the same, this same, that same,* is **is, ea, id** with the particle **-dem** attached. Some changes in spelling make pronunciation easier.

DECLENSION OF IDEM

	SINGULAR			PLURAL		
	MASC.	FEM.	NEUT.	MASC.	FEM.	NEUT.
NOM.	īdem	eadem	idem	eīdem	eaedem	eadem
GEN.	eiusdem	eiusdem	eiusdem	eōrundem	eārundem	eōrundem
DAT.	eīdem	eīdem	eīdem	eīsdem	eīsdem	eīsdem
ACC.	eundem	eandem	idem	eōsdem	eāsdem	eadem
ABL.	eōdem	eādem	eōdem	eīsdem	eīsdem	eīsdem

The adverbs are **ibidem,** *in the same place,* **eōdem** *to the same place,* and **indidem,** *from the same place.*

Fighting cocks were the symbols of Mercury, whose caduceus, money-bag, and wand lie on the table. Mosaic from Pompeii —National Museum, Naples

Ipse

The intensive adjective **ipse, ipsa, ipsum,** *myself, ourselves, yourself, yourselves, himself, herself, itself, themselves,* is declined like **iste** and **ille** except that it has **-um** and not **-ud** in the neuter nominative and accusative singular.

DECLENSION OF IPSE

	SINGULAR			PLURAL		
	MASC.	FEM.	NEUT.	MASC.	FEM.	NEUT.
NOM.	ipse	ipsa	ipsum	ipsī	ipsae	ipsa
GEN.	ipsīus	ipsīus	ipsīus	ipsōrum	ipsārum	ipsōrum
DAT.	ipsī	ipsī	ipsī	ipsīs	ipsīs	ipsīs
ACC.	ipsum	ipsam	ipsum	ipsōs	ipsās	ipsa
ABL.	ipsō	ipsā	ipsō	ipsīs	ipsīs	ipsīs

Nūllus, Sōlus, Tōtus, Ūllus

Nūllus, -a, -um, *no, none, not any,* sōlus, -a, -um, *alone,* tōtus, -a, -um, *whole,* and ūllus, -a, -um, *any,* are declined exactly as ūnus, -a, -um is.

Alter, Neuter, Uter

Alter, altera, alterum, *the other (of two), the second,* neuter, neutra, neutrum, *neither,* and the interrogative adjective uter, utra, utrum, *which? (of two),* are also declined in the pronoun declension, with genitive and dative singular in -īus and -ī: alterīus, neutrīus, and utrīus; and alterī, neutrī, and utrī.

Alius

Alius, alia, aliud, *other, another,* ends (like ille and iste) in -ud in the neuter nominative and accusative singular. It has no genitive singular.

DECLENSION OF ALIUS

	SINGULAR			PLURAL		
	MASC.	FEM.	NEUT.	MASC.	FEM.	NEUT.
NOM.	alius	alia	aliud	aliī	aliae	alia
GEN.	____	____	____	aliōrum	aliārum	aliōrum
DAT.	aliī	aliī	aliī	aliīs	aliīs	aliīs
ACC.	alium	aliam	aliud	aliōs	aliās	alia
ABL.	aliō	aliā	aliō	aliīs	aliīs	aliīs

1. To express possession, use the possessive adjective **aliēnus, -a, -um,** *another's, someone else's.* For the partitive or objective genitive, use the genitive of **alter, alterīus.**

> Id pecūniā aliēnā ēmit. *He bought it with someone else's money.*
> Amōre alterīus mōtus est. *He was motivated by love for another.*

2. The adverbs of **alius** are **aliter,** *otherwise, else,* **alibi,** *at another place,* *elsewhere,* **aliō,** *to another place, elsewhere,* **aliunde,** *from another place,* and **aliās,** *at another time.*

UNIVERSAL PRONOUN, ADJECTIVES, AND ADVERBS

Adding an enclitic particle **-que** (not to be confused with the **-que** that means *and*) makes any interrogative universal.

> **quisque, quidque** *each one*
> **quīque, quaeque, quodque** *each*
> **uterque, utraque, utrumque** *each [of two]*
> **ubique** *everywhere*
> **undique** *from everywhere, on all sides*

SYNTAX

USE OF IPSE

Although **ipse** has the same English translations as the reflexive pronouns, it is intensive and not reflexive.

REFLEXIVE		INTENSIVE	
Mē laudō.	*I praise myself.*	Ipse eum laudō.	*I myself praise him.*
Sē laudat.	*He praises himself.*	Ipse mē laudat.	*He himself praises me.*

An easy test helps in translating from English into Latin: if the sentence has the same sense when the -self word is removed, the word to be used is **ipse.**

IDIOMATIC USES OF ALIUS AND ALTER

If **alius** or **alter** is used twice in the same case, it has special meanings:

> alius . . . alius *one . . . another*
> aliī . . . aliī *some . . . others*

> alter ... alter   *the one ... the other*
> alterī ... alterī   *the ones ... the others*

Aliī in aedibus habitant, aliī in vīllā.
Some live in a city house, others in a farmhouse.
Duae fīliae mihi sunt, quārum altera Helena, altera Anna vocātur.
I have two daughters, one of whom is called Helen, the other Anna.

If alius is used twice, but in different cases, or with one of its adverbs, the sentence must be translated twice.

> Alius aliud petit.   *One seeks one thing, another another.*
> Aliī aliō ambulant.   *Some walk to one place, others to another.*

VOCABULARY

BASIC WORDS

coniunx, coniugis, m. or f. *spouse, wife, husband*

flūmen, flūminis n. *stream*

oculus, -ī, m. *eye*

sōl, sōlis, m. *sun*

studium, -ī, n. *eagerness, enthusiasm; study, hobby*

aeternus, -a, -um *eternal, everlasting*

plēnus, -a, -um *full*

versō, -āre, -āvī, -ātum *keep turning; occupy, (passive) be employed*

vertō, -ere, versī, versum *turn*

deinde (adv.) *then, next; henceforth, hereafter, thereafter*

igitur (adv.) *therefore*

apud (prep. w. acc.) *among, at the house of, in the presence of, in the works of*

Note: **Plēnus** is construed with either the genitive of the whole or the ablative of means.

> Flūmen aquae plēnum est.   *The stream is full of water.*
> Flūmen aquā plēnum est.   *The stream is filled with water.*

LEARNING ENGLISH THROUGH LATIN

conjugal   *referring to the relation between husband and wife*
flume   *a narrow gorge or ravine with a stream running through it*
oculist   *one who deals with functions and diseases of the eye*
replenish   *furnish a new supply*

Priestly duties: **flamines** in pointed skull caps lead a procession—Ara Pacis, Rome

sempiternal	*everlasting, perpetual, eternal*
solar	*produced by or coming from the sun*
solstice	*the time at which the sun is either at its farthest north or its farthest south of the equator*
ubiquitous	*seeming to be present everywhere at the same time; omnipresent*
versatile	*competent in many things; able to turn easily from one occupation to another.*

PRACTICE

A. Look up the meanings of the following words and show their relation to **vertō:** *converse; inverse; reverse.*

B. Explain the meaning of each italicized word and show its Latin origin:

1. My appointment with the *oculist* is for next Thursday. 2. I am going to the supermarket to *replenish* my food supply. 3. Although he did not major in Accounting, he is so *versatile* that the firm offered him the job anyway. 4. The house is very modern and even has *solar* heating. 5. In the Northern Hemisphere the summer *solstice* falls on June 21st or 22d. 6. The dandelion is a *ubiquitous* spring nuisance.

C. Name all the words which you have learned which are declined in the pronoun declension (-īus, or -ius in the genitive singular and -ī in the dative singular).

D. Give all possible genders, numbers, and cases for each form:

1. alium   2. alterīus   3. eadem   4. ipsa   5. nūllae   6. quīque   7. sōlī   8. tōtō   9. utrīque   10. utrīs

E. Give the following forms:

1. The neuter nominative singular of **is, quis, alius**   2. The masculine genitive singular of **iste, nūllus, uter**   3. The feminine dative singular of **hic, ūnus, neuter**   4. The neuter accusative singular of **ille, uterque, ipse**   5. The feminine ablative singular of **quī, ūllus, quisque**   6. The masculine nominative plural of **īdem, quīque, sōlus**   7. The feminine dative plural of **alter, is, quis**

F. Translate:

1. of the other eye   2. fear of another   3. another's enthusiasm (*nom.*)   4. of the sun itself   5. at the same time   6. to the only man (*dat.*)   7. of the entire city   8. for each one   9. each eye (*acc.*)   10. each citizen (*acc.*)

G. Translate the *-self* word with the proper form of the intensive or reflexive:

1. He offered the gift *himself*.   2. He offered the gift *to himself*.   3. They *themselves* taught Latin.   4. They taught *themselves* Latin.

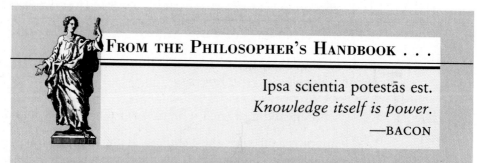

FROM THE PHILOSOPHER'S HANDBOOK . . .

Ipsa scientia potestās est.
Knowledge itself is power.
—BACON

List five ways in which knowledge could be a powerful force in your everyday life.

READING

Developing Reading Skills

The following words will help you in guessing the meanings of unfamiliar words: *adolescent, celebrate, cupidity, diurnal, divide, Gemini, mammal, nude, opus, otiose, pastoral,* and *predatory.*

Romulus and Remus

Amūlī imperiō geminī fīliī Martis et Īliae in Tiberim amnem iniectī erant. Forte eō tempore aqua flūminī dēficiēbat quod ergō parum celeriter fluēbat, itaque parvulī ad rīpam undīs portātī sunt, ubi lūpa quae suam prōlem āmīserat eōs invēnit et eīs mammās praebuit. Mīrīs igitur modīs ē morte exemptī sunt. Magister rēgiī pecoris, Faustulus nōmine, simul atque geminōs   5

Faustulus discovering the twins Romulus and Remus being suckled by the wolf— from the Arca Casari, Vatican Museum

cum lūpā aspexit utrumque portāvit ad Accam Lārentiam coniugem suam. Post puerōs quibus nōmina Rōmulō et Remō data erant Faustulus et Lārentia sīcut cārōs fīliōs suōs ēdūxērunt.

Geminī iuvenēs postquam aetās adolēvit cūrae pecoris sē dēdidērunt, sed non huic operī sōlī: quotiēns ōtium, postquam tōtum opus dīurnum confēc- ērunt, eīs erat sē in vēnātiōne quoque versābant. Deinde, quoniam nunc et fortēs et validī hōc studiō factī erant et alter alterī par virtūte vīribusque erat, aliās cum lātrōnibus quī tōtō agrō Latīnō versābantur pugnābant et praedae partem capiēbant quam cēterīs pastōribus dīvidēbant. Multī aliī iuvenēs, cupidī et tālis praedae et decoris, undique convēnērunt, itaque geminī mox factī sunt ducēs tōtīus multitūdinis illōrum.

Ōlim hōs iuvenēs, ubi nūdī cum nūllīs armīs Lupercālia celebrābant, lātrōnēs quibus praedam pastōrēs occupāverant vīcērunt et partem iuvenum, quī aliī aliō fugiēbant, cēpērunt tenēbantque captīvōs. Rōmulus ipse cum parte suōrum sē in fugam dedit, Remum autem cēterōsque pastōrēs lātrōnēs vīnxērunt et ad Numitōrem dēdūxērunt. "Hunc lātrōnem, domine," inquiunt "excēpimus ut ex tuīs agrīs praedam portābant et tibi nunc trādimus; sed alter, huius geminus, nōs fūgit." At Numitor, ut Remum aspiciēbat, sēcum pūtābat, "Nōnne hic iuvenis, homō huius aetātis, sī ūnus dē geminīs duōbus est, meus nepōs quem āmīsī est?" Eōdem tempore pervēnit Faustulus et Numitōrī omnia dē utrōque geminō aperuit.

Rōmulus et Remus ergō suōs et Numitōris virōs ad rēgiam dūxērunt, ubi Rōmulus Amūlium interfēcit. Hōc modō Numitor rēgnum unde ā frātre ēiectus erat iterum accēpit.

READING COMPREHENSION

1. How were the twin sons of Mars and Ilia saved from the river Tiber? 2. Who was Faustulus? 3. How did the twin boys live during their childhood? 4. What happened at the feast of Lupercus? 5. What thoughts went through Numitor's mind when he saw Remus? 6. How did Numitor recover his kingship?

---

13. tōtō agrō: the Ablative of Place Where, when the noun is modified by tōtus, -a, -um, often omits the preposition: tōtā urbe, *all over the city* 15. praedae et decoris: The adjective cupidus, -a, -um, *desirous*, is construed with the objective genitive, not the dative with adjectives. 17. Lupercālia: the festival of the god Lupercus, at which young men stripped themselves for a footrace 27. suōs et Numitōris: The genitive of possession may be joined to a possessive adjective by a coordinating conjunction, since both express possession.

LESSON 28

Indefinite Pronouns and Adjectives

Fresco from the **Larārium** of the House of the Vettii, Pompeii. The **genius** is flanked by two **Larēs,** each pouring wine from a **rhyton** into a small wine bucket, or **situla.**

YOUR RELIGION: PERSONAL WORSHIP

The chief gods among the countless **nūmina** of the household were the **Genius** of the head of the family, the **Lār** or **Genius Locī**, and the **Penātēs**. The **Genius**, a guardian spirit, was thought to resemble the man whom he protected (every man had a Genius and every woman a Juno) and to mediate with the other gods on the family's behalf. The **Lār** was the guardian of a particular place, and was left behind if the family moved. By a special exception, Aeneas was allowed to bring his **Lār** from Troy to Rome, and from the time of Augustus each household in Italy had two **Larēs**, the second being the **Lār** of Troy. A **Lār** is represented as a youth in a girt-up tunic and high boots, dancing as he pours some liquid from a drinking-horn into a small bucket. He may also be represented as a crested or bearded serpent. The **Penātēs** ("dwellers in the store-cupboard") watched over the prosperity of the family, and were whatever gods or heroes the individual family head might choose. We find amongst the **Penātēs** gods of commerce and trade and patrons of cities and guilds, as well as a number of foreign gods, particularly those of Egypt and the Middle East.

Public gods were also worshipped privately, as we learn from the votive offerings placed in their temples. Because of the contractual nature of their religion, the Romans used vows (**vōta**) where we would use prayers. A vow is the promise of some kind of gift or sacrifice to be made to the god only after a particular favor had been granted. If the god did not grant the wish, the promised payment would not be made. If he did, the vow had to be fulfilled scrupulously or the votary would risk the future enmity of the god he had cheated. When the vow had been paid, a commemorative tablet (**stēla**) was set up at the votary's expense, with inscriptions or depictions of the granting of the vow, or by a replica of the part of the body which the god had healed. The priests of the god kept a file of vows and checked periodically to make sure they were paid.

Dō ut dēs.
I give so that you will give.

(*right*) A Roman family votive stele, dedicated to Saturn, god of the harvest, recording the payment of a pig— Djemila, Algeria   (*below*) The **nūmen** of the **Lār**: a bearded snake who wards off evil from the household. The rich vegetation symbolizes its protection of the bounty of the earth—House of the Vettii, Pompeii

ANCIENT ROME LIVES ON . . .

To whom does modern man make "vows"?

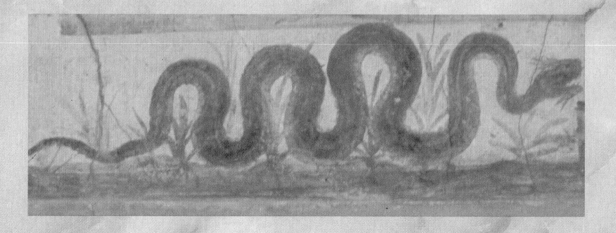

▬ FORMS ▬

■ INDEFINITE PRONOUNS AND ADJECTIVES

Indefinite pronouns and adjectives are used to indicate that some person or thing is meant, without specifying which one. They are formed from the interrogative pronoun **quis, quid**, and its adjective **quī, quae, quod**.

Aliquis and Aliquī

The indefinite pronoun **aliquis, aliquid** means *someone, anyone, something, anything*. The adjective **aliquī, aliqua, aliquod** means *some* or *any*.

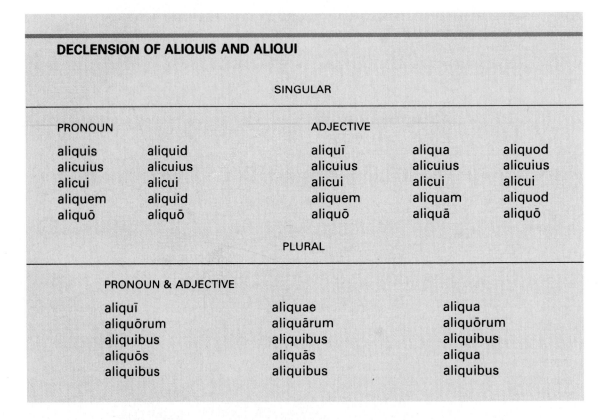

DECLENSION OF ALIQUIS AND ALIQUI

SINGULAR

PRONOUN		ADJECTIVE		
aliquis	aliquid	aliquī	aliqua	aliquod
alicuius	alicuius	alicuius	alicuius	alicuius
alicui	alicui	alicui	alicui	alicui
aliquem	aliquid	aliquem	aliquam	aliquod
aliquō	aliquō	aliquō	aliquā	aliquō

PLURAL

PRONOUN & ADJECTIVE		
aliquī	aliquae	aliqua
aliquōrum	aliquārum	aliquōrum
aliquibus	aliquibus	aliquibus
aliquōs	aliquās	aliqua
aliquibus	aliquibus	aliquibus

Quis and Quī

The indefinite pronoun **quis, quid** (*anyone, anything, someone, something*) and the indefinite adjective **quī, qua, quod** (*any*) are declined like **aliquis** and **aliquī** without the **ali-**.

Quisquam

The indefinite pronoun **quisquam, quidquam** (*anyone, anything*) is the interrogative (not the indefinite) pronoun **quis, quid** with **-quam** attached. You have already learned the declension of its adjective **ūllus, -a, -um.**

The Indefinite Relative Pronoun and Adjective

The indefinite relatives mean *whoever, whatever, whichever.* The pronoun is **quisquis, quidquid,** the adjective **quīcumque, quaecumque, quodcumque.** You can easily remember these because **quisquis** is simply the interrogative pronoun **quis** doubled and **quīcumque** is the interrogative adjective **quī, quae, quod** with **-cumque** attached.

Quīdam

The indefinite pronoun **quīdam, quiddam** and its adjective **quīdam, quaedam, quoddam** mean *someone, a certain person, something, a certain thing, some, certain.*

DECLENSION OF QUIDAM (PRONOUN AND ADJECTIVE)

SINGULAR

PRONOUN		ADJECTIVE		
quīdam	quiddam	quīdam	quaedam	quoddam
cuiusdam	cuiusdam	cuiusdam	cuiusdam	cuiusdam
cuidam	cuidam	cuidam	cuidam	cuidam
quendam	quiddam	quendam	quandam	quoddam
quōdam	quōdam	quōdam	quādam	quōdam

PLURAL

PRONOUN & ADJECTIVE		
quīdam	quaedam	quaedam
quōrundam	quārundam	quōrundam
quibusdam	quibusdam	quibusdam
quōsdam	quāsdam	quaedam
quibusdam	quibusdam	quibusdam

To sum up, remember the following four rules. Indefinite adjectives and adverbs are made from interrogatives by:

1. adding **ali-** or **alic-** (e.g. **aliquantus, -a, -um,** *some, any,* **alicubi,** *somewhere, anywhere*)
2. adding **-quam** (e.g. **quōquam,** *to somewhere, to anywhere*)
3. doubling (e.g. **quamquam,** *however*)
4. adding **-cumque** (e.g. **quāliscumque, quālecumque,** *of whatever kind*)

▬ SYNTAX ▬

■ USES OF INDEFINITE PRONOUNS, ADJECTIVES AND ADVERBS

1. For *someone, anyone, something, anything, some,* or *any:*
   a. **quis** and **quī** are used after **num** and in conditional clauses; otherwise **aliquis** and **aliquī** are used.
   b. **quisquam** and **ūllus** are used in negative statements.

2. For *some* or *someone:*
   a. **aliquis, quis,** and **quisquam** mean *someone* (as opposed to *no one*), *someone or other, anyone at all.*
   b. **quīdam** means *someone I know of.*

3. For *whoever, whatever, whichever:*
   quisquis and **quīcumque** introduce indefinite relative clauses.

   > Aliquis quī hoc fēcerit errābit.
   > *Someone (anyone) who does this will be wrong.*
   > Sī quis hoc fēcerit errābit.
   > *If someone (anyone) does this, he will be wrong.*
   > Sī quīdam hoc fēcerit errābit.
   > *If someone (a certain person) does this, he will be wrong.*
   > Nec quisquam quī illud fēcerit errābit.
   > *Nor will someone (anyone) who does that be wrong.*
   > Quisquis hoc fēcerit errābit.
   > *Whoever does this will be wrong.*

Quīdam, like **paucī** and the cardinal numbers, is construed with a partitive Ablative of Place from Which, not the partitive genitive (genitive of the whole).

> Quaedam dē fēminīs discessērunt.　　*Some of the women have left.*

VOCABULARY

BASIC WORDS

hospes, hospitis, m. or f. *stranger; guest-friend, guest, host*

moenia, -ium, n. (i-stem) *fortifications, walls*

sēdēs, sēdis, f. (i-stem) *seat; (pl.) residence*

signum, -ī, n. *sign, signal; (military) standard*

vestis, vestis, f. (i-stem) *garment, clothing; (pl.) clothes*

posterus, -a, -um *subsequent, following; (substantive) posterī, -ōrum, m. posterity, descendants*

posterum, -ī, n. *the future*

claudō, -ere, clausī, clausum *shut, close*

currō, -ere, cucurrī, cursum *run*

expōnō, -ere, exposuī, expositum *put out, expose, explain*

sedeō, -ēre, sēdī, sessum *sit*

circā (prep. w. acc.) *around, about, at the side of; (adv.) about, round about, approximately*

quandō (inter. adv.) *when?*

Building Vocabulary

In compounds **claudō** becomes -**clūdō**:

inclūdō, -ere, inclūdī, inclūsum *shut in*

exclūdō, -ere, exclūdī, exclusum *shut out*

LEARNING ENGLISH THROUGH LATIN

cloister	*a place of religious seclusion, such as a monastery or convent*
divest	*to free of something unwanted*
expound	*to set forth point by point, to state in detail*
investiture	*the conferring of an office or special authority, with appropriate symbols, robes, etc.*
posterity	*all succeeding generations; future mankind*
sedentary	*keeping seated most of the time*
vestibule	*a small entrance hall or room*

Translation Help

If you find, in translating English to Latin, that you have forgotten a word and have to look it up in the English Vocabulary, be sure to check the word also in the Latin Vocabulary. This is important because otherwise you may miss some essential information. For example, suppose that in the sentence *They are leaving the city* you have written **urbem** but can't remember the word for *leave*. If you look up *leave* you will find both **discēdō** and **relinquō**. You must then look them both up in Latin, where you will find that **discēdō** means *depart, go away, leave*, and **relinquō** means *leave, leave behind, abandon*. Therefore **discēdō** cannot be used with a direct object; hence you must either use **relinquunt** or else change **urbem** to **ex urbe**.

The Latin section will also give you the number of the Lesson in which the word first appears. You may need to refer to this Lesson for further important information (e.g. in *He was instructing them*, the *them* must be dative, not accusative).

═══ PRACTICE ═══

A. Explain the meanings of the italicized words in the following sentences and state from which Latin word each comes:

1. I listened to the politician *expounding* on his views for more than an hour. 2. The millionaire had *divested* himself of his stocks before the stock market crash. 3. The athlete did not like the office job; it was too *sedentary*. 4. Because the house has no *vestibule*, the living room gets cold in winter. 5. The artist wished to paint a masterpiece for *posterity*.

B. The following words are derivatives of Latin words in this lesson. Show the connection of each with its Latin word: *exposition; hospitality; session.*

C. Give the following forms:

1. The feminine nominative singular of **quisquis, aliquī, quīdam** (adj.)
2. The masculine genitive singular of **quīcumque, quīdam** (pron.), **quisquam**
3. The neuter dative singular of **aliquis, quīdam** (adj.), **ūllus** 4. The masculine accusative singular of **quisquis, aliquis, quīcumque** 5. The

feminine ablative singular of **quis, quī, quīdam** (adj.)   6. The feminine nominative plural of **aliquī, quīdam** (pron.), **quis**   7. The neuter genitive plural of **quīdam** (pron.), **aliquis, quisquam** (adj.)   8. The masculine dative plural of **quis, aliquī, quidam** (pron.)   9. The neuter accusative plural of **aliquis, quīdam** (adj.), **quis**   10. The feminine ablative plural of **quīdam** (pron.), **quīcumque, aliquis**

D.   Pronounce and translate:

1. Miser sum, nec quidquam mihi dās; da mihi aliquid.   2. Sī quis hoc fēcerit errābit.   3. Quisquis hoc fēcerit errābit.   4. Quidquid hic fēcerit errābit.   5. Num quid malī fēcistī?   6. Ille sī quandō hoc fēcerit errābit. 7. Quōquō accessit laetus erat.   8. Ubicumque habitāvit laetus erat. 9. Alicubi in terrīs maribusve id reperiam.   10. Nisi quō istinc accesseritis in perīculō eritis.

READING

Developing Reading Skills

English words which will help:

asylum, discriminate, equestrian, fugitive, intervene, legation, ludicrous, munition, mural, pauper, society, and *valley.*

The Founding of Rome; Marriage by Kidnapping

Postquam Numitōrī rēgnum Albānum iterum commissum est Rōmulum Remumque cupīdo alicuius novī cēpit, itaque in eīs locīs ubi expositī et eductī erant urbem condidērunt. Ager Albānus enim multitūdinī Albānōrum Latīnōrumque dēficiēbat, ad quam pastōrēs quoque additī erant. Omnēs igitur, "Parva Alba Longa," pūtābant, "parvum Lāvīnium erit prae tantā urbe quantam condēmus."

5

Sed deinde intervēnit avītum malum imperī cupīdō, atque inde foedum
certāmen, quoniam ambō geminī eādem aetāte erant nec aetās ergō ūllum
discrīmen fēcit, itaque iuvenēs quōs uterque dūcēbat inter sē alterī cum
alterīs pugnābant. Postquam Rōmulus cum suīs moenia in Palātiō incēpit
Remus frātrem ludēbat quia mūrī novī tam parvī erant et ludībriō eōs
trānsiluit; deinde ab īrātō Rōmulō quī illa verba quoque adiēcit, "Sīc deinde
quīcumque alius trānsiliet moenia mea," interfectus est. Deinde mūnītiō
Palātī confecta est, in quā Forum quoque inclūsum est. Quod magnitūdō
novae urbis, quae Rōma ā nōmine eius ā quō condita erat vocāta est, plēna
hominibus nōn erat, Rōmulus dux, quī sē rēgem nunc vocābat et lēgēs suīs
dabat, in Capitōliō asylum aperuit, quō pauperēs fugitīvīque ex fīnitimīs
populīs undique conveniēbant. Hōc modō nova urbs mox magna facta est.

At urbī, quamquam magnae, nūllae fēminae erant et Rōmānī igitur
uxōribus carēbant. Tum Rōmulus ex cōnsiliō centum Patrum quōs Senātōrēs
dēlēgerat lēgātōs circā vīcinās gentīs mīsit, quī societātem cōnubiumque
novō populō petēbant. Nusquam autem benīgnē lēgātiō audīta est, nam
fīnitimī novam urbem in mediō sibi et posterīs timēbant. "Cūr" inquiunt
"fēminīs quoque asylum nōn aperiētis? Sīc enim dēnique pār cōnubium
vōbīs erit."

Postquam lēgātī trīstēs illinc rūrsus vēnērunt Rōmulus īrātus "Nōbīs
tamen" sēcum putābat "coniugēs vī reperiēmus fēminās aliēnās" cōnsili-
umque ergō cēpit quō vocāvit fīnitimōs Sabīnōs ad Cōnsuālia, quōs lūdōs
Neptūnō equestrī, cui nōmen Cōnsō quoque datum erat, praebēbat. Hic
Cōnsus nūmen erat flūminis quod sub terrā conditum erat illīc ubi equī
celerēs in certāmine currēbant. Tum cum illūc hospitēs convēnerant et in
herbā in utrōque monte Palātiō et Aventīnō sedēbant unde vallem in quā
aliquot post saeculīs Circus aedificātus est aspiciēbant, omnēs Rōmānī, quī
ut Rōmulus praecēperat tēla in vestibus cēlāverant, quōdam signō virginēs
Sabīnās, quisque coniugem sibi, statim occupāvērunt.

READING COMPREHENSION

1. Why did Romulus and Remus want to found a new city? **2.** How did
Remus enrage Romulus, and what did Romulus do? **3.** What was the
name of the new city? **4.** How did Romulus find citizens for the new city?
5. What was the chief problem for the new citizens? **6.** How was it solved?
7. What is the Consus?

---

12. "Sīc deinde, etc.": Romulus' words, here quoted from Livy (a Roman historian, 59 B.C.–
16 A.D.), pronounce a formal curse on future invaders. **20.** ex cōnsiliō: ē, ex often means
on the basis of

VOCABULARY DRILL

A. Give the genitive, gender, and meaning of these nouns:

aetās	flūmen	imāgō	moenia	posterī	signum
caput	fors	lītus	natūra	posterum	sōl
cīvis	hōra	mēns	nox	sanguis	studium
coniunx	hospes	modus	oculus	sēdēs	vestis

B. Give the genitive and meaning of each pronoun:

ego nōs tū vōs

C. Give the other nominative singular forms, and the meanings, of these pronouns:

aliquis	quis (interrogative)	quisque
quī	quis (indefinite)	quisquis
quīdam	quisquam	

D. Give the other nominative singular (or plural) forms, and the meanings, of these adjectives:

aeternus	nūllus	quīque
aliēnus	plēnus	quot
aliquantus	posterus	quotcumque
aliquī	quālis	quotquot
aliquot	quāliscumque	sōlus
alius	quantus	suus
alter	quantuscumque	tōtus
cēterī	quī (relative)	ūllus
fēlīx	quī (interrogative)	uter
īdem	quī (indefinite)	uterque
ipse	quīcumque	
neuter	quīdam	

LISTENING AND SPEAKING

A Country Thanksgiving

Gnaeus Mucius and his family, while at their country house, make preparations to observe the holidays sacred to the god Terminus, the ancient god of the boundaries of farms.

1. candidus, -a, -um—
   white
2. Terminus, -ī, m.—
   the god *Terminus*
3. VII Kal. Mart.—*23 February*
4. Terminālia, ium, n. pl.—*the festival of Terminus*
5. fīnis, fīnis, m.—*end, (in plural = "boundaries")*
6. fundus, -ī, m.—*farm, country property*
7. tūtēla, -ae, f.—*protection*
8. lapis, lapidis, f.—*stone*
9. cella, -ae, f.—*room, sanctuary of a temple*
10. saxum, -ī, n.—*rock*
11. pertinax, pertinācis—*stubborn, tenacious*
12. tacitus, -a, -um,—*silent*
13. lignum, -ī, n.—*wood, log*
14. carbō, carbōnis, m.—*charcoal* (candens, -entis—*glowing*)
15. mel, mellis, n.—*honey*
16. agnus, -ī, m.—*lamb*
17. caro, carnis, f.—*meat*
18. canō, -ere, cecinī, cantum—*sing*

GNAEUS: Omnia vestimenta candida[1], servī, in cubicula portāte et Lūcrētiae uxorī et līberīs dāte, nam hōdie feriās sacrās deō Terminō[2] in agrīs habēmus!

TĪTUS: Cuius feriās, pater? Quī deus est Terminus et cūr nōn in vīllā in ātriō ad aediculam sacra facimus?

GNAEUS: Hōdie, fīlī, VII Kal. Mart.[3] est; hae feriae Terminālia[4] ab hominibus vocantur. Terminus deus vetus fīnium[5] fundōrum[6] est cui Numa, secundus Rōmanōrum rēx, sacra pia ōlim condidit.

TĪTUS: Ubi, pater, habitat deus?

GNAEUS: Habitat in caelō cum reliquīs deīs, sed in tūtēlā[7] lapidēs[8] terminālīs fundōrum tenet. Est etiam in aedis Iōvis Optimī Maximī cellā[9] in urbe Rōmā antīquum et vetus saxum[10] deī Terminī, quod Terminus locum nōn mōvit ubi rēx Ētruscus aedem Iōvis aedificāvit.

TĪTUS: Terminus deus fortis et pertinax[11] erat! Sed cūr omnis familia in agrōs accēdet? Fessus sum itaque non cēdam.

GNAEUS: Tacitus[12] estō, Tīte! Omnēs in agrīs cēdēmus, quod omnēs sacra deō faciēmus. Est mūnus nōn modo patrī et mātrī sed etiam fīliō et fīliae. Sunt autem mūnera servīs. Venīte, Lūcrētia uxor et Mūcia fīlia. Excēdimus!

MŪCIA: Quid, pater, faciam? Estne etiam mūnus puellae?

GNAEUS: Est vērō, Mūcia! Prīmum omnēs super deī lapidem flōrēs pōnēmus. Deinde āram lignīs[13] et saxīs faciam. Māter Lūcrētia ignem et carbōnēs[14] candentīs in ollā portat et ignem accendet. Tum, Tīte, ter in ignem frūmentum iaciēs et tū, Mūcia, mel[15] et vīnum deō dabis.

TĪTUS: Festīnāte omnēs! Videō lapidem Terminālem. Mox sacra omnēs agēmus. Quid, pater, servī facient?

GNAEUS: Post prīma sacra, sacrificium agnō[16] servōrum auxiliō faciam. Deinde super ignem carnem[17] pōnēmus et omnēs, pater māterque et līberī servīque, et canēmus[18] et cēnābimus.

A. Choose a group of two boys and one girl to act out the above conversation between Gnaeus, his son, Titus, and his daughter, Mucia.

B. Formulate a question for each of the following statements.

1. Terminus vetus deus fīnium fundōrum est.   2. Omnis familia sacra deō Terminō in agrīs ad lapidem Terminālem facient.   3. Numa, secundus Rōmanōrum rēx, sacra Terminō instituit.   4. Mūcia, fīlia Gnaeī, mel et vīnum deō dabit.
5. Super lapidem Terminālem familia flōrēs pōnent.

A rural shrine in an idyllic landscape; a fresco from Pompeii—National Museum, Naples

Turkey—Istanbul

Istanbul is the largest city in Turkey and is the only city in the world located on two continents—Asia and Europe. It has always been an important city and has a fascinating history.

People probably lived in the Asian part of Istanbul as early as 3000 B.C. Greek colonists founded a city called Byzantium during the mid-600's B.C. It later became

View from park
of Hagia Sophia

Hagia Sophia

Mosaic showing Constantine and Justinian

cially noted for its great interior height and space. Rare and costly building materials were brought from many parts of the Roman Empire for its construction. The walls are marble-lined with many colors and designs, and are decorated with a variety of mosaics, portraits of rulers, and beautiful religious paintings. It was built as a Christian cathedral, was used as a mosque when the Turks conquered Constantinople, and is now a museum.

The Ottoman Turks conquered Constantinople in 1453 A.D. and it was then that the name became Istanbul.

part of the Roman Empire and in 324 A.D. the Roman Emperor Constantine chose it as his capital and changed its name to Constantinople, City of Constantine. This became official in 330 A.D.

In 395 A.D. the Roman Empire split into two sections—the West Roman Empire and the East Roman Empire. Constantinople remained the capital of the East Roman Empire (also called the Byzantine Empire). In 532 A.D. during the reign of the Emperor Justinian, anti-government riots destroyed much of the city. Justinian undertook to rebuild it and it was at this time that Hagia Sophia (also called Santa Sophia) was built.

Hagia Sophia is a Greek phrase meaning Holy Wisdom. The structure is one of the finest examples of Byzantine architecture ever built. The floor plan is oblong and over the center is a great dome. It is espe-

Interior of dome section

323

Worried family members at a sick girl's bedside

YOUR HEALTH: THE CABBAGE CURE

Until the second century B.C. Roman medicine was essentially folk medicine. An example of it has been preserved for us in the elder Cato's *On Farming* (**Dē Agrī Cultūrā**), written circa 160 B.C., on the healing powers of cabbage. Here is one of his medicines:

"Wild cabbage has very great powers. You should dry it and grind it up quite small. If you want to purge someone, he shouldn't eat the day before. The next morning before he eats anything, give him the ground cabbage and four ladles of water. Nothing else purges so well and without danger and, let me tell you, it's good for the body. You'll cure people you had no hope of curing.

"This is how you treat someone who wants to be cured by this method: Give him this in water for seven days. When he wants to eat, give him roast meat. If he doesn't want to eat, give him cooked cabbage and bread, and let him drink a mild wine, diluted. He should bathe seldom, but be rubbed with oil. Anyone who has been treated in this way will enjoy good health for a long time, and he won't catch any disease unless it's his own fault.

"And if someone has a sore, either infected or new, sprinkle this wild cabbage with water and apply it; you will cure him. And if the wound has closed, push it in in a pellet. If it won't take a pellet, make a solution, put it into a bladder, attach a reed to the bladder, and squeeze; it will go into the closed wound; this will quickly cure him.

"And if there is a growth inside your nose put dried ground wild cabbage in your hand and bring it to your nose and sniff as hard as you can; the growth will fall out within three days. And when it does, still do the same for some days, to disinfect the roots of the growth.

"If you don't hear very well with your ears, grind the cabbage with wine, squeeze out the juice, and drop it lukewarm into your ear; you will soon realize that your hearing has improved."

(*right*) Roman false teeth set in gold bridges. Such devices were expensive and obviously beyond the means of Lucius Vibius (above), whose funeral monument shows only the results of the extractor's skill.

FORMS

FOURTH DECLENSION

Nouns whose genitive singular ends in -ūs belong to the fourth declension. Masculine and feminine nouns, like **ūsus, ūsūs,** m., *use, usefulness,* or **manus, manūs,** f., *hand, band (of men),* end in **-us** in the nominative singular. Neuters, like **cornū, cornūs,** n., *horn, wing (of an army),* end in **-ū.**

DECLENSION OF MANUS AND CORNŪ

	SING.	PL.	ENDINGS		SING.	PL.	ENDINGS	
NOM.	manus	manūs	-us	-ūs	cornū	cornua	-ū	-ua
GEN.	manūs	manuum	-ūs	-uum	cornūs	cornuum	-ūs	-uum
DAT.	manuī	manibus	-uī	-ibus	cornū	cornibus	-ū	-ibus
ACC.	manum	manūs	-um	-ūs	cornū	cornua	-ū	-ua
ABL.	manū	manibus	-ū	-ibus	cornū	cornibus	-ū	-ibus

1. There are no fourth-declension adjectives.

2. **Domus** and **manus** are the only fourth-declension feminine nouns which are used very frequently. Most **-us** nouns of the fourth declension are masculine, and most of these are made from the fourth principal parts of verbs: e.g. **cursus, cursūs,** m., *a running, course,* is from the fourth principal part of **currō.**

3. There are very few fourth-declension neuter nouns.

Domus

Domus, domūs, f., *home, house,* has forms of both the second and the fourth declension.

DECLENSION OF DOMUS

	SING.	PL.		ENDINGS	
NOM.	domus	domūs		-us	-us
GEN.	domūs	domuum		-ūs	-uum
DAT.	domuī	domibus		-uī	-ibus
ACC.	domum	domōs		-um	-ōs
ABL.	domō	domibus		-ō	-ibus

SYNTAX

◼ DATIVE OF PURPOSE

The dative of a few nouns is used to show what the noun serves as, its purpose or its result.

> Hoc auxiliō praebet.   *He offers this as (for) an aid.*

Only six of the nouns in the Vocabularies of this book are commonly used as datives of purpose:

auxiliō	*as (for) an aid, help*	impedīmentō	*as (for) a hindrance*
cordī	*for a heart, dear*	salūtī	*as (for) a salvation*
cūrae	*for a care (or worry)*	ūsuī	*as (for) a use (or advantage)*

◼ DOUBLE DATIVE

The dative of purpose is usually coupled with a dative of reference. This construction is called the double dative.

> Hoc mihi auxiliō est.   *This serves as a help to me.*
> Hoc mihi impedīmentō est.   *This acts as a hindrance to me.*
> Quod dīs cordī est mox faciētur.
> *That which is dear to the gods will be done soon.*

Fīlius patrī cūrae erat. { *The son was a worry to his father.*
The father was worried about his son.

Ea fortūna nōn modo ūsuī sed etiam salūtī nōbīs erat.
That piece of luck was not only advantageous to us, it even saved us.

DOUBLE ACCUSATIVE

Rogō, -āre, -āvī, -ātum, *ask, ask for,* and **doceō, -ēre, -uī, doctum,** *teach,* may have a direct object of the person, a direct object of the thing, or both.

Rēgem rogāvit.   *He asked (questioned) the king.*
Pecūniam rogāvit.   *He asked for money.*
Rēgem pecūniam rogāvit.   *He asked the king for money.*
Vōs doceō.   *I teach you.*
Linguam Latīnam doceō.   *I teach the Latin language.*
Vōs linguam Latīnam doceō.   *I teach you the Latin language.*

In the passive, either the person or the thing may be the subject; the other remains in the accusative as a retained direct object.

Rēx pecūniam rogātus est. } *The king was asked for money.*
Pecūnia rēgem rogāta est.

Vōs linguam Latīnam docēminī. } *You are taught the Latin language.*
Vōs lingua Latīna docētur.

FROM THE PHILOSOPHER'S HANDBOOK . . .

Dente lupus, cornū taurus petit.
The wolf attacks with his fang, the bull with his horn.
—HORACE

Everyone has a special way of attacking problems. How do you attack the problems that beset you?

VOCABULARY

BASIC WORDS

cor, cordis, n. *heart*
cornū, -ūs, n. *horn; wing (of an army)*
cursus, -ūs, m. *running, course*
domus, -ūs, f. *home*
impedīmentum, -ī, n. *hindrance*
manus, -ūs, f. *hand; band (of men)*
mīlia, -ium, n. (plural only) *thousands*
passus, -ūs, m. *pace*

salūs, salūtis, f. *health, welfare, safety, salvation*
ūsus, -ūs, m. *use, usefulness, advantage; habit, practice*

doceō, -ēre, -uī, doctum *teach, inform*
rogō, -āre, -āvī, -ātum *ask, ask for*

Notes:

1. Since **mīlia** is a noun it cannot modify a noun as the adjective **mīlle** does, but must be used with a Partitive Genitive.

   > Mīlle cīvēs et tria mīlia servōrum hīc habitant.
   > *One thousand citizens and three thousand slaves live here.*

   But to express the partive idea the Partitive Ablative of Place from Which must be used.

   > Duo mīlia ex nostrīs quattuor mīlia hostium vīcērunt.
   > *Two thousand of our men conquered four thousand enemies.*

2. A **passus**, *pace*, was a measure of distance. There were five feet to a pace and a thousand paces to a mile.

   > Domus mea decem pedēs ā tuā abest.
   > *My house is ten feet away from yours.*
   > Domus mea decem passūs ā tuā abest.
   > *My house is ten paces (fifty feet) away from yours.*
   > Vīlla mea mīlle passūs ā tuā abest.
   > *My farmhouse is a mile away from yours.*
   > Vīlla mea decem mīlia passuum ā tuā abest.
   > *My farmhouse is ten miles away from yours.*

3. **Salūtem alicui dō** means *I greet someone.* The salutation, complimentary close, and signature of a Roman letter were all contained in the first sentence, e.g. **Titō suō Spurius salūtem dat**, *Spurius greets his dear Titus (Dear Titus, . . . Yours truly, Spurius).*

■ LEARNING ENGLISH THROUGH LATIN

abrogate *cancel or repeal by authority; annul*
arrogant *full of self-importance and unwarranted pride*
derogatory *belittling, tending to lessen or detract*
domestic *having to do with home or housekeeping*
impediment *an obstacle; anything that interferes*
prerogative *an exclusive right; a superior advantage*
salubrious *promoting health or welfare*
usury *the practice of lending money at excessive interest*

PRACTICE

A. Match the following words with their synonyms from the above derivatives:

1. privilege   2. hindrance   3. wholesome   4. disparaging   5. haughty
6. abolish

B. Look up the meanings of the following words and explain their derivation from Latin words in this lesson:

1. manipulate   2. interrogation   3. salutary   4. domicile
5. indoctrination

C. Decline in full:

1. ūsus nūllus   2. utra domus   3. ūllum cornū

D. Give the number(s) and case(s) of each form:

1. cornū   2. cursūs   3. domuī   4. manuum   5. passum   6. salūs
7. ūsibus   8. domūs   9. cornua   10. domōs

E. Change from singular to plural, keeping the same case:

1. cornūs   2. cursuī   3. domum   4. manus   5. passū   6. salūs
7. cursus   8. domuī   9. manum   10. domō

F. Which of the six datives of purpose fills the blank for each English sentence?

Hoc ___ nōbīs erat.   1. This is what saved us.   2. We were concerned about this.   3. This worked to our advantage.   4. We wanted this very much.   5. This is what helped us.   6. This held us up.   7. This was dear to our hearts.   8. This came in handy for us.   9. We had to take care of this.   10. This got in our way.

G.   Pronounce and translate:

1. Mīlle domūs ūnō sōlō annō aedificātae erunt.   2. Tria mīlia domuum ūnō sōlō annō aedificāta erunt.   3. Duo mīlia ex hīs domibus post vēndita erunt.   4. Mīlle nāvibus ad Asiam Graecī nāvigāvērunt.   5. Quot mīlibus nāvium Poenī ad Siciliam nāvigāvērunt?

H.   Translate:

1. A thousand citizens were killed.   2. Three thousand citizens were killed.
3. Three thousand of the citizens were killed.   4. He gave six thousand gold pieces to two thousand citizens.   5. We ran a mile, but you walked eighteen miles.

I.   Pronounce and translate these sentences. Then rewrite them with the same meaning, but in the active voice:

1. Lēgēs patriae vōbīs ā magistrō praecipiēbantur.   2. Vōs lēgēs patriae ā magistrō docēbantur.   3. Lēgēs patriae ā magistrō docēbāminī.   4. Aurum ex vōbīs ā magistrō petēbātur.   5. Aurum vōs ā magistrō rogābātur.
6. Aurum ā magistrō rogābāminī.   7. Magistrō ā vobis aurum dabātur.
8. Rēx ā populō dēlectus es.   9. Rēx ā populō vocātus es.   10. Rēx ā populō factus es.

READING

Developing Reading Skills

Latin words which will help you to determine the meaning of unfamiliar words:
geminus, iaciō, narrō, petō, prōdō, socius, vulnerō.

English words: *anular, congest, deject, desist, impetus, laevose, narration, perfidy, ponderous, vulnerable.*

The traitress Tarpeia being stoned to death. A frieze from the Basilica Aemilia—The Forum, Rome

Two Influential Women

Sabīnī quibus fēminās Rōmānī cēperant postquam ad oppida sua rūrsus fūgērunt ad urbem Rōmam iterum, nunc tamen ad bellum parātī, convēnērunt et ācrem impetum in Rōmānōs faciēbant. Id quod illīs ūsuī auxiliōque erat, hīs autem magnō impedīmentō, arcem in Capitōliō tenēbant, quam illō modō cēperant.

Arx Sp. Tarpēiō, cui ducī commissa erat, cūrae erat, cuius fīlia virgō forte Vestālis erat. Ea igitur extrā arcis moenia per Forum ambulāverat ad quandam fontem unde aquam sacrīs idōneam rūrsus ad arcem portābat. Ad

---

3. Id: A noun or pronoun which is in apposition to a whole idea, not just a single word, is in the accusative. This use is called the Accusative in Apposition with a Clause.   **4. illō:** here, as often, **ille** refers to what is coming, *"the following"*

quam postquam T. Tatius Sabīnōrum rēx amīcē accessit puellam suōrum
10   admissiōnem in arcem rogāvit. Quia magna pars autem Sabīnōrum aureās
armillās magnī ponderis brācchiō laevō gemmātīsque magnā formā ānulōs
habēbat, Tarpēia "In arcem" inquit "vōs dūcam sī mihi quod in sinistrīs
manibus habētis dederitis." Sīc compositum est, sed mīlitēs ut per arcis
portam posterā nocte veniēbant scuta illī miserae prō aureīs dōnīs conger-
15   ēbant et sīc īnfēlīcem interfēcērunt, poenam prōditiōnis. Deinde aliquot
saecula locus prōditiōnis poenae quoque locus erat: nam quī patriam
prōdiderant dē Rūpe Tarpēiā dēiciēbantur.

Apud alium auctōrem aliam narrātiōnem saepe invenīmus; sīc sunt duae
fābulae dē Tarpēiā, quārum altera eam perfidam patriae, altera Tatiō, habet.
20   Apud quōsdam enim auctōrēs quamquam puellae verba "quod in sinistrīs
manibus habētis" eadem sunt ipsīus nātūra longē ā prōditiōne abest. Nam
tum cum Sabīnī ergō armillās ānulōsque, ut putābant, illī prōmīsērunt perque
deōs hoc iūrāvērunt puella dolōsa scuta prō aureīs dōnīs poposcit. Sīc in
arcem sine scutīs acceptī itaque mox interfectī sunt ā Rōmānīs quī arcem
25   servābant.

Rōmānī Sabīnīque in Forō diū et ācriter inter sē pugnābant cum Hersilia
Rōmulī uxor cēterās Sabīnās inter duōs exercitūs ēdūxit, quae "Dē istā
caede" clāmābat "dēsistite vōs quī utrīque nōbīs cordī estis! Num interficiētis
filiārum coniugēs, coniugum patrēs? Sī adfīnitās inter vōs, sī cōnubium vōs
30   nōn iuvat, in nōs vertite īrās; nōs causa bellī, nōs vulnerum ac caedium virīs
ac parentibus sumus. Quōmodo vīvēmus sine alterīs vestrum aut viduae aut
orbae?" Haec verba Hersiliae reliquārumque Sabīnārum salūtī omnibus
erant, nam sīc mīrō modō bellum compositum est. Duo populī mixtī sunt
et uterque rēx, et Rōmulus et Tatius, ambōs rēgēbat. Rēgnum duplex
35   cōnsociant; imperium omne pōnunt in urbe Rōmā, quae ita magnitūdine
gemīnātur.

READING COMPREHENSION

1. What advantage did the Sabines have as they prepared for war on Rome?
2. What are the two versions of the story of Tarpeia?   3. Who was Hersilia?
4. How did she settle the war?   5. Who ruled after the war was over?

---

10. autem: in narrative, sometimes has a loosely connective function, like *now* in English:
Now, because most of the Sabines ...   **15. poenam:** accusative in apposition with a
clause   **26. pugnābant:** *had been fighting* (False Perfect)   **31. alterīs:** alter can mean *either
one, the one or the other*

LESSON 30

Fifth Declension; Locative; Supine; Special Place Constructions

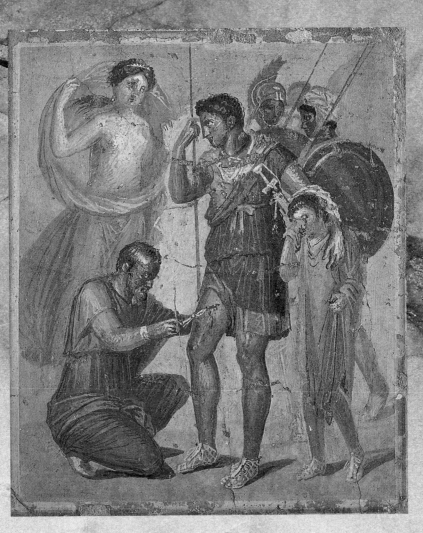

Pompeian wall painting showing the treatment of the wounded Aeneas. The doctor and surgical instruments are contemporary with the early Empire.

YOUR HEALTH: AESCULAPIUS

know this

I n 293 B.C. there was a plague in Rome so serious that the Senate ordered that the Sibylline Books be consulted. The fifteen priests in charge of the books discovered that the Greek god of healing, Asclepius, whom the Romans called Aesculapius, should be brought to Rome. The ambassadors who were sent to his temple at Epidaurus in the Peloponnesus were given a snake embodying the god, which they brought back to Rome. As the barge they were using was being towed up the Tiber, the snake slipped from the barge and swam to the Tiber Island. The temple was built there, on the spot which the god himself had chosen. With the coming of Christianity St. Bartholomew took over both the temple and its hospital, and St. Bartholomew's church and hospital stand there today. Aesculapius also had a small shrine in the Forum.

To be healed by Aesculapius, one had to make appropriate sacrifices and then spend the night sleeping in the temple precinct (the process was called **incubātiō**, *sleeping in*). The god would appear in a dream, inquire about the disease, and then prescribe for it. Some cures were simply common sense: an overweight person would be told to eat less. Others, such as cures of paralysis or blindness, were more impressive, and must represent the faith-healing of psychosomatic disorders.

We know about hundreds of cures from the votive tablets set up at the god's shrines, especially Epidaurus. Aesculapius was a sympathetic god: one of the tablets tells how a child, in his dream, impulsively offered the god his toys, which the god accepted as more valuable than the purse of gold which the child's father had provided.

Aesculapius was depicted as a kindly-looking, bearded middle-aged man, accompanied by a dog and leaning on a staff around which a serpent is entwined. The modern symbol for medicine, a wand with two serpents,

(Continued)

came from the confusion of the staff of Aesculapius with the Caduceus of Mercury. Aesculapius' daughter, the goddess Salus (*Health*), was usually worshipped along with him.

(*below left*) Aesculapius treating a victim of a snake bite—a Greek relief, 4th c. B.C.   (*below right*) A votive plaque thanking Aesculapius for the cure of deafness, 4th c. B.C.

ANCIENT ROME LIVES ON . . .

What role is belief in the physician thought to play in modern medicine?

FORMS

FIFTH DECLENSION

Nouns ending in -ēs, -ēī (or -eī) in the nominative and genitive singular belong to the fifth declension. They are declined like **diēs, diēī,** m., *day,* or **rēs, reī,** f., *thing.*

DECLENSION OF DIĒS AND RĒS

					ENDINGS	
	SING.	PL.	SING.	PL.	SING.	PL.
NOM.	diēs	diēs	rēs	rēs	-ēs	-ēs
GEN.	diēī	diērum	reī	rērum	-ēī, -eī	-ērum
DAT.	diēī	diēbus	reī	rēbus	-ēī, -eī	-ēbus
ACC.	diem	diēs	rem	rēs	-em	-ēs
ABL.	diē	diēbus	rē	rēbus	-ē	-ēbus

1. The -e of the stem is short in the genitive and dative singular when it comes after a consonant. It is always short in the accusative singular.
2. All fifth-declension nouns are feminine, with the single exception of **diēs** and its compounds. There are no neuters and no adjectives.
3. Only **diēs** and **rēs** are declined in full; the other fifth-declension nouns have only the nominative and accusative in the plural.

LOCATIVE CASE

Certain nouns of the first three declensions have, in addition to the usual cases, an additional case, called the locative. It is exactly like the dative except in the singular of the second declension, where it is like the genitive. Nouns which have a locative include:

1. The proper names of cities, towns, and small islands:

> 1ST DECLENSION EXAMPLES: Rōmae, Athēnīs
> 2D DECLENSION EXAMPLES: Lāvīnī, Vēiīs
> 3D DECLENSION EXAMPLES: Carthāginī, Sardibus

2. The following nouns:

> domus, -ūs, f., *home*: LOCATIVE: domī, *at home*
> humus, -ī, f., *ground, soil*: LOCATIVE: humī, *on the ground*
> rūs, rūris, n., *countryside, country place*: LOCATIVE: rūrī, *in the country, at one's country place*

SUPINE

The supine is the fourth principal part of the verb, declined in the fourth declension, but only in the accusative and ablative singular. The verb **sum** has no supine.

DECLENSION OF SUPINES

						ENDINGS
ACC.	vocātum	habitum	positum	captum	audītum	-um
ABL.	vocātū	habitū	positū	captū	audītū	-ū

Two bleeding cups and an open case of surgical instruments—from the Aesculapieion in Roman Athens

SYNTAX

◼ SPECIAL PLACE CONSTRUCTIONS

Nouns which have the locative case express place relationships differently from other nouns. They use the locative to express place where, the accusative without a preposition to express place to which (this construction is called the Accusative of Limit of Motion), and the ablative without a preposition to express place from which.

The ruins of the Temple of Apollo Sosianus, Rome. Aesculapius's father, Apollo, was likewise revered for his healing powers. This temple was originally dedicated in 433 B.C. after a severe plague.

PLACE CONSTRUCTIONS

	NOUNS WITHOUT A LOCATIVE	NOUNS WITH A LOCATIVE
PLACE WHERE	In vīllā est. *He is in the farmhouse.* In Ītaliā habitāmus. *We live in Italy.*	Domī est. *He is at home.* Rōmae habitāmus. *We live at Rome.*
PLACE TO WHICH	Ad vīllam venit. *He comes to the farmhouse.* In Ītaliam venimus. *We are coming to Italy.*	Domum venit. *He comes home.* Rōmam venimus. *We are coming to Rome.*
PLACE FROM WHICH	Ex vīllā venit. *He comes from the farmhouse.* Ab Ītaliā venimus. *We are coming from Italy.*	Domō venit. *He comes from home.* Rōmā venimus. *We are coming from Rome.*

USES OF THE SUPINE

The supine, whether accusative or ablative, is always translated by the English present active infinitive, *to call, to have, to place, to take, to hear.* Each of its cases has only one use.

The accusative of limit of motion is used with verbs of motion to indicate purpose. The accusative supine of a transitive verb takes a direct object.

Urbem spectātum vēnit.   *He has come to look at at the city.*
                           (*He has come towards looking at the city.*)

The ablative is used as an ablative of specification with certain adjectives. It does not take a direct object.

Hoc nōn modo foedum vīsū sed etiam audītū est.
   This is ugly not only to see, but even to hear.
Quid bonum erit factū?
   What will be a good thing to do?
Hoc facile est inceptū, difficile confectū.
   This is easy to begin, but difficult to finish.

VOCABULARY

BASIC WORDS

diēs, -eī, m. *day*

faciēs, -eī, f. *appearance; face*

fidēs, -eī, f. *faith, trust, belief*

humus, -ī, f. *ground, earth, soil*

rēs, reī, f. *thing, affair, fact*

rūs, rūris, n. *country, countryside;*
country place

speciēs, -eī, f. *sight, appearance, show;*
kind

spēs, -eī, f. *hope, expectation*

publicus, -a, -um *public, belonging to*
the people (populus)

rūsticus, -a, -um *of the country, of*
farming

Notes: 1. **Fidēs** can also mean *trustworthiness, pledge, safe-conduct, protection.* With the preposition **in,** in either the accusative or ablative, it means *under the protection.*

> Dianae sumus in fidē. *We are under the protection of Diana.*
> Graecī in fidem populī Rōmānī vēnērunt.
> *The Greeks came under the protection of the Roman People.*

2. **Rēs** almost never can be translated *thing,* which is nevertheless the only English word which comes close to covering its wide range of meanings, which include *circumstances, reality, property, benefit, lawsuit, business, art,* and *science.* Some idioms which illustrate its meanings:

> rēs publica *republic, commonwealth*
>
> dē rē rūsticā *about the business (science, art) of farming*
>
> rēs novae *revolution, political change*
>
> rēs secundae *favorable circumstances, prosperity*
>
> carmen dē rērum nātūrā *a poem about the nature of the universe*
>
> rē vērā *in actual fact, really*
>
> ex tuā (meā, suā, etc.) rē
> *to your (my, his, her, their, etc.) own advantage*
>
> summa rēs
> *(sometimes abbreviated to* **summa***) sum-total, the bottom line*
>
> omnibus rēbus *in all respects*
>
> Fac tuam rem. *Mind your own business.*

▪ LEARNING ENGLISH THROUGH LATIN

bonafide	*without dishonesty, fraud, or deceit*
diurnal	*daily, in the daytime*
exhume	*dig out of the earth*
fidelity	*faithful devotion to duty or obligations*
inhume	*bury (a dead body)*
rebus	*a puzzle consisting of pictures, letters, signs, etc., which taken together suggest a word or phrase*
rusticate	*(1) to live or stay in the country, to live a rural life*
	(2) to suspend from a university
	(3) to use rough-looking wood or stone on a building
superficial	*shallow, not profound*

▬ PRACTICE

A. Restate each of the following sentences using a derivative from the list in this lesson. The new sentence may mean the same or the opposite.

1. Her disloyalty to the school amazed her peers.   2. The student made a very profound study of the Trojan War.   3. His nocturnal visits to the abandoned farmhouse puzzled his neighbors.   4. I prefer to live in the city, or "to urbanize", as my friends say.   5. This is an authentic document which proves that I am right.

B. Decline:

1. fēlīx diēs   2. rēs bona

C. Convert from singular to plural, keeping the same case(s):

1. fidem   2. spēs   3. diēī   4. rē   5. speciēs

D. Convert from plural to singular, keeping the same case(s):

1. diēbus   2. faciēs   3. rērum   4. fidēs   5. speciēs

E. Give all possible cases and numbers for each noun:

1. rūs   2. cornū   3. Vēiīs   4. rēs   5. rūrī   6. manūs   7. Carthāginī
8. diēī   9. Rōmae (*sing.* only)   10. humī

F. Translate, using the supine:

1. I have come to see you.   2. This is difficult to do.   3. The news was sad to hear.   4. Did they go away to fight?   5. She went to seek water.

G. Translate:

1. To Rome, from Carthage, at Lavinium, (to) home   2. from the country, in our country, to Italy, from the city   3. In Sardis, to Veii, in Greece, to the city   4. from Europe, in Sicily (a large island), from our country, to the country   5. in Athens, from Laurentum, to Carthage, at Veii   6. from Rome, in Crotona, to Athens, from home

H. Pronounce and translate:

1. Uterque poēta clārus carmen nōtum fēcit, alter dē rērum nātūrā, alter dē rē rūsticā; utrīus legēs?   2. Sī prō eā rē quam ēmeris nihil dabis ex tuā rē nōn faciēs, nam rē vērā fidem omnibus rēbus āmīseris, nec iam quisquam tibi ūllam rem vendet.   3. Nē in rēbus secundīs quidem quīdam dē nostrīs cīvibus reī publicae fidem praebent, semper autem rēs novās petunt.

Translation Help

So far you have been analyzing Latin sentences before translating them, first separating the clauses and then looking for the verbs and the constructions which go with them. You should now begin trying to read them as the Romans did, fitting in each word as it appears. Since Latin word order is so different from English, this is not easy at first, but will become so with practice. In approaching the first sentence in the reading, *The End of the First Reign,* your thoughts would go something like this:

Sabīnī, nom. pl. (not gen. sing., since there's no noun with it): *The Sabines*

quī, masc. nom. pl. (agrees in gender, number, person with **Sabīnī**; subject of the relative clause): *who*

fēminās, accusative: (who did something to) *women*

petītum, supine: (no, who went somewhere) *to seek women*

Rōmam, accusative (not direct object: **vēnerant** is intransitive): *to Rome*

vēnerant: *had come to Rome*

The Sabines who had come to Rome to seek their women . . .

READING

Developing Reading Skills

English words which may help: *community, concord, consecration, conspectus, contend, dense, deposit, election, just, justice, mortal, nimbus, opinion, sacrifice, salutation, salute, serene, silence, solemn, sublime, tempest, tranquil,* and *turbid.* Latin words: **cor, cursus, faciō, ponō, mors, sacer,** and **salus.**

The End of the First Reign

Sabīnī quī fēminās petītum Rōmam vēnerant post ūnum proelium sōlum in pāce fidēque populī Rōmānī Rōmae mānsērunt. Inde nōn modo commūne sed concors etiam rēgnum duōbus rēgibus Rōmulō Tatiōque fuit. Post aliquot annōs autem quīdam propinquī rēgis T. Tatiī lēgātīs Laurentium vim praebuērunt, et ubi Laurentēs sē in Tatī fidē posuerant remque suam huic 5 commīsērunt, apud Tatium grātia suōrum iūstitiam superāvit. Igitur illōrum poenam in sē vertit, nam Lāvīnī, postquam ad sollemne sacrificium eō vēnit, concursū Laurentium interfectus est. Eam rem nōn tantā cum īrā quantā dignum erat audīvit Rōmulus, sīve quod societātī rēgnī fidēs dēest, seu quia caedem Tatī iūstam habēbat. 10

Nōn multīs post annīs vītam mortālem dēposuit Rōmulus ipse mīrō modō. Nam ut in Campō contiōnem habēbat subita tempestās cum imbre et magnō frāgōre tonītribusque dēnsō rēgem operuit nimbō et cōnspectum eius contiōnī dēmpsit, nec deinde in terrīs Rōmulus fuit. Mīlitēs, quibus rēx semper cordī fuerat, postquam ex tam turbidō diē serēna et tranquilla lūx sōlis rūrsus 15 vēnit, ubi vacuam sēdem rēgiam vīdērunt, etsī ā Patribus quī prope rēgem steterant timor compōnēbātur quī "Rēx" inquiunt "sublīmis—mīrābile dictū!—raptus procellā est," tamen velut orbitātis metū plēnī trīste aliquod tempus silentium tenuērunt. Deinde postquam paucī ex eā multitūdine salūtātiōnem incēpērunt deum deī fīlium rēgem parentemque urbis Rōmānae 20 tōta manus iuvenum Rōmulum salūtāvit et novum deum precibus pācem rogābant et "Nōs respice, pater," clāmābant "et in fidem tuam recipe!"

Fuērunt tum quoque aliquī quibus alia opīniō fuit: rēx, pūtāvērunt, Patrum manibus discerptus erat, quī deinde partīs corporis eius domum sub vestibus

Model of an Iron Age hut.
Archaeological finds on the Palatine
have established the existence of
these structures dating to the time
of Romulus.

25   portāverant. Rōmulus enim nōn tam grātus Patribus quam iuvenibus cīvibus
fuerat, quī etsī armīs nēminī cessit fīnitimāsque gentīs et Fīdēnātēs et Vēientēs
vīcerat novam urbem tamen totiēns perīculīs bellī exposuerat.

    Rōmulus post mortem vel consecrātiōnem nūllum filium relīquit, id quod
ēlectiōnem novī rēgis difficilem facit. Nam Rōmānī prīscī et quī Sabīnī
30   fuērunt dē rēgnō verbīs contendunt alterī cum alterīs, quoniam neutrī rēgem
aliēnum, nec Rōmānī Sabīnum nec Sabīnī Rōmānum, recipient. Dēnique
autem invenitur quīdam vir Numa Pompilius nōmine, Sabīnus quidem at
tamen homō tam bonus tantāque pietāte quantā nēmō alius, sīve Rōmānus
seu Sabīnus, quem duplex populus rēgem dēligit.

◼ READING COMPREHENSION

1. What happened to King Titus Tatius?   **2.** What was the reaction of
Romulus?   **3.** What are the two versions of the death of Romulus?   **4.** Why
was Romulus unpopular with the city fathers?   **5.** Why was the choice of
a new king difficult?   **6.** Who was finally chosen?

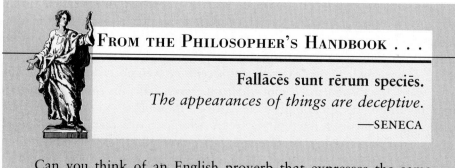

FROM THE PHILOSOPHER'S HANDBOOK . . .

Fallācēs sunt rērum speciēs.
The appearances of things are deceptive.
—SENECA

Can you think of an English proverb that expresses the same
sentiment? What does it mean?

LESSON 31

Ferō; Dative with Compound Verbs

A medical professor giving an anatomy lesson—fresco from the Hypogeum on the Via Latina, Rome

YOUR HEALTH: SCIENTIFIC MEDICINE

The Romans developed folk medicine and religious medicine themselves, but they were taught theoretical medicine by the Greeks. The father of medicine, the Greek Hippocrates (469–399 B.C.), was the first to separate medicine from philosophy. The first Greek doctors came to Rome as slaves, who either treated only the master's family or went into general practice, with the master collecting the profits. But in 46 B.C. Julius Caesar granted freedom and Roman citizenship to all doctors then practicing in Rome. The status of doctors rose thereafter until Galen, the most influential of the ancient physicians, could call himself the friend of Emperor Marcus Aurelius.

Ailments were classified strictly by their symptoms: the most commonly mentioned "diseases" are the cough (**tussis**) and the fever (**fēbris**)—there were three temples of the goddess Febris in Rome. Other ailments were the sore throat (**angina**), the foot pain (**podagra**), and skin eruptions (**lepra**). It is sad to think that sufferers from acne, psoriasis, eczema, and impetigo were treated as lepers because of this kind of classification.

Most doctors believed that diseases were caused by an imbalance of the four liquids (**hūmōrēs**) of the body; blood, phlegm, black bile (**melancholia**), and yellow bile (**cholē**). Individuals were characterized as sanguine, phlegmatic, melancholy, or choleric, according to the mixture (**temperāmentum**) of the humors. We still use these adjectives, and still speak of being in a bad or good humor, and of having one or another kind of temperament.

Surgery, performed without anesthetics, used instruments like modern ones, except that they were larger and made of bronze. Scalpels, forceps, scissors, hypodermic needles, and screws for raising sunken parts of fractured skulls have been found in archaeological excavations.

Free public hospitals, first for soldiers and then for the general public, were established during the Empire.

A PHRASE TO USE

Ars longa, vīta brevis.
The science is long; a lifetime is short.

—HIPPOCRATES

ANCIENT ROME LIVES ON . . .

How does the development of a modern doctor's career resemble the history of doctors in Rome?

(*left*) Frieze of an oculist treating a patient—Church of Saint Victor, Ravenna   (*above and right*) Surgical tools from ancient Rome and Pompeii

FORMS

■ FERŌ

The verb **ferō, ferre, tulī, lātum,** *bear, bring, take,* is irregular in that its last two principal parts do not use the same root as the first two.

It is also unlike other third-conjugation verbs in that it does not, in many of its forms, insert a vowel between the stem and the ending to make pronunciation easier. This can be seen in the second principal part, which adds **-re** to the stem instead of **-ere.**

PRESENT INDICATIVE OF FERŌ

	ACTIVE		PASSIVE	
	SINGULAR	PLURAL	SINGULAR	PLURAL
1ST PERSON	ferō	ferimus	feror	ferimur
2D PERSON	fers	fertis	ferris (ferre)	feriminī
3D PERSON	fert	ferunt	fertur	feruntur

PRESENT IMPERATIVES OF FERŌ

	ACTIVE		PASSIVE	
	SINGULAR	PLURAL	SINGULAR	PLURAL
2D PERSON	fer	ferte	ferre	feriminī

The Future Imperative can be found in the Appendix.

The other tenses are regular, formed in the same way as those of other third-conjugation verbs.

■ SYNTAX

■ DATIVE WITH COMPOUND VERBS

Many verbs compounded with the following prefixes may take an indirect object, which will complete the meaning of the prefix, rather than that of the verb itself.

ad-	*to, towards*	ob-	*to meet; in opposition*
ante-	*before*	post-	*behind, after*
circum-	*around*	prae-	*ahead of, in front of*
con-	*together; forcibly*	pro-	*for; forth*
in-	*in, on, against*	sub-	*under; up; to the aid of*
inter-	*between; to pieces*	super-	*upon; over and above*

Is mihi adest.   *He is here for me* (lit. *He is towards me*).
Cēterīs malīs dolor accessit.
   To the rest of the evils grief was added (lit. *Grief came to . . .*).
Hostibus instābant.
   They were pressing the enemy (lit. *They were standing on the enemy*).
Hic illī praestat.
   This man is better than that one (lit. *This man stands ahead of that one*).
Id tibi prōderit.
   It will be profitable for you (lit. *It will be for you*).

If the verb is transitive it will take a direct object as well.

Cēterīs malīs mors ducis dolōrem adiēcit.
   The death of the leader added (lit. *threw*) *grief to the rest of the evils.*
Portīs vim attulērunt.
   They applied (lit. *brought*) *force to the gates.*
Nōmen novum iuvenī impōnent.
   They will give the young man (put on the young man) *a new name.*
Ignīs aedibus intulērunt.
   They set the house on fire (They brought fires onto the house).
Amīcitiam nōbīs ostendite.
   Show us friendship (Stretch friendship out towards us).
Mūnera eīs praebuit.
   He offered them gifts (He held gifts in front of them).

The main thing to remember is this: when the prefix of a verb seems to need something to complete its meaning you should look for a dative.

VOCABULARY

BASIC WORDS

metus, -ūs, m. *fear, dread*

versus, -ūs, m. *a turning; a verse [of poetry] a line [of prose]*

adsum, adesse, adfuī, adfutūrus *be present; (w. dat.) be present at, be present to help*

ferō, ferre, tulī, lātum *bear, bring, take; relate*

impōnō, -ere, imposuī, impositum (w. acc. & dat.) *put in, put on*; (w. dat.) *deceive*

īnstō, -āre, institī, ____ (w. dat.) *stand in, stand on; follow closely, press*

ōstendō, -ere, ōstendī, ōstentum *display, show*

praestō, -āre, praestitī, praestitum (w. dat.) *stand before, excel*

prōmittō, -ere, prōmīsī, prōmissum *send forth*; (w. dat.) *promise*

prōsum, prōdesse, prōfuī, prōfutūrus (w. dat.) *be useful, be advantageous, be profitable*

A 13th century A.D. Italian fresco shows Hippocrates and Galen—Agnani Cathedral. The renown of ancient medical authors survived even the Dark Ages.

Building Vocabulary

Notice the following compounds of **ferō**:

adferō, adferre, attulī, allātum *bring up*; (w. dat.) *bring to, report*
auferō, auferre, abstulī, ablātum *carry off, steal*
cōnferō, cōnferre, contulī, collātum *bring together, collect*; (w. dat.) *compare*
īnferō, īnferre, intulī, illātum *carry onward*; (w. dat). *bring upon, inflict*
referō, referre, rettulī, relātum *bring back, report back*
tollō, tollere, sustulī, sublātum *lift up, raise, remove*

Notes:

1. Notice that when a prefix is attached to a verb its spelling may be changed to make pronunciation easier. This process is called *assimilation*.

   in + posuī > imposuī
   ad + tulī > attulī
   ab + ferō > auferō
   in + lātum > illātum

2. Some compounds of **ferō** have idiomatic uses:

   Cōnferō with a reflexive object means *betake oneself, proceed, go:* **Domum sē contulērunt.** *They went home.*
   Bellum alicui īnferō means *I make war on someone.*
   Signa īnferunt (*They carry the standards onward*) means *They advance to the attack.*
   Pedem referō means *I go back, I return, I give ground.*
   Grātiam alicui (dat. of reference) **referō** means *I show gratitude to someone.*

LEARNING ENGLISH THROUGH LATIN

collate	*to gather together in proper order; to compare facts*
defer	*to yield to the wishes of another*
deference	*courteous regard or respect*
dilatory	*slow or late in doing things; causing delay*
imposition	*application by authority; unwelcome obtrusion*
infer	*to conclude from something known or assumed; to draw as a conclusion*
ostensibly	*apparently, seemingly*
promissory	*containing a promise; stipulating conditions*

▰ PRACTICE ▰

A. Explain the meaning of each of the following sentences:

1. Increased spending has required the imposition of new taxes this year.
2. The author was dilatory in sending his manuscript to the publisher.
3. The lengthy report was collated by the secretary.   4. I will defer to your superior knowledge and vast experience.   5. Even though I would rather not go, I will attend the meeting out of deference to my colleagues.
6. Ostensibly they were embarrassed, but I feel that they knew from the beginning.   7. The insurance policy contained a promissory warranty.
8. Am I therefore to infer that I am in danger of failing this course?

B. There are many English words formed from the compounds of **ferō**. Give the meanings of the following English words and show how the prefix of each word influences the meaning.

1. circumference   2. conference   3. reference   4. transferral

C. Pronounce, give tense, voice, mood, person, and number, and translate:

1. adeste   2. īnstābās   3. prōfuimus   4. ablātī erant   5. īnfer   6. tollet
7. attulistī   8. confertur   9. sublātus eris   10. rettulerint

D. Translate:

1. they will be profitable   2. I am borne   3. she will have excelled   4. you (*pl.*) were brought to   5. I shall have brought together   6. you (*sing.*) were being brought back   7. you (*sing.*) are being borne   8. take away (*pl.*)   9. they had lifted   10. it had been brought in

E. Give the following synopses, indicative and (where applicable) imperative, with meanings:

1. **adferō** in the first person singular passive   2. **auferō** in the second person singular active   3. **cōnferō** in the third person singular passive   4. **īnferō** in the first person plural active   5. **referō** in the second person plural passive   6. **tollō** in the third person plural active

F. Translate:

1 & 2. They are here to help us. (*2 ways*)   3. They followed us closely.
4. They are better than we.   5. They deceived us.

READING

Developing Reading Skills

Helpful English words: *art, augment, bellicose, benign, cause, civil, convivial, discipline, dissimilar, divine, egregious, indicator, inject, initial, institute, military, pacify, piety, prefect, prolific, reign, repudiate, sacerdotal, satisfaction, transfer, tyrant,* and *valid.*

Helpful Latin words: **bellum, bene, cīvis, dō, faciō, ferō, iaciō, mors, pius, prae, rēgnum, sacer, satis, similis, trāns,** and **uterque.**

Peace and War

Prīmī duo ex rēgibus nōn iam aderant Rōmānīs. Alter, dē quō apud Q. Ennium clārum poētam versum legimus "Ō Tite tūte Tatī, tibi tanta, tyranne, tulistī!" mortuus erat; alter, deī Martis fīlius, ipse in caelum translātus et deus factus erat. Quōrum in locō Numa Pompilius, homō ēgregiā pietāte, reī Rōmānae nunc rēx secundus (nam Tatius in numerō rēgum nōn habētur)   5
praeerat, quī multīs modīs Rōmānīs proderat, praecipuē novīs lēgibus quibus velut iterum urbem condidit tantamque pāce quantam bellō Rōmulus fēcit. Iānum in Forō indicem pācis bellīque fēcit, dē quō "Hic aperiētur" inquit "quotiēnscumque cīvēs in armīs erunt, totiēns autem claudētur quotiēns pāx cum omnibus circā populīs facta erit." Bis deinde post Numae rēgnum ad   10
initium Augustī prīncipātūs clausus est, semel post Pūnicum prīmum bellum, iterum post bellum quod Augustus M. Antōniō Cleopātraeque rēgīnae intulit, tum cum pācem terrā marīque fēcerat. Numa multitūdinis animīs fortibus quōs metus hostium disciplīnaque mīlitāris ante continuerat metum deōrum nunc iniēcit. Multa templa aedīsque sacrās fēcit praefēcitque sac-   15
erdōtēs cuique deōrum atque sīc novōs modōs īnstituit quibus dī colēbantur.

---

2. tūte: a strengthened form of **tū**   **8. Iānum:** Besides being the name of the god, a Janus is also a magical bridge over the magical boundary of a city. When its gates are closed the magic is retained, so that the **imperium** may be taken in and out of the city. Open, they allow the magic to escape, so that enemies cannot bring their **imperium** in.   **13. terrā marīque:** This idiom, *by (on) land and sea,* is usually without the preposition, like a locative.

(*left*) A bronze imperial coin showing the double-faced Janus (*right*) A coin from the reign of Nero showing the temple of Janus with its doors closed during a rare outbreak of peace

Hōc modō cīvium mentīs ā rē mīlitārī ad rēs dīvīnās vertit. Ita duo deinceps rēgēs, alius aliā viā, ille bellō, hic pāce, cīvitātem auxērunt. Rōmulus septem et trīgintā rēgnāvit annōs, Numa trīs et quadrāgintā. Urbs tum valida et
20 bellī et pācis artibus erat.

Numae morte Tullus Hostīlius, homō animī ferī et bellicōsī, rēx tertius dēlectus est. Hic nōn modo Numae dissimilis erat sed etiam Rōmulō ipsī praestābat decorum bellī cupīdine. Tantus deōrum metus quantum Numa cīvium animīs iniēcerat Tullō grātus nōn erat, nam decorī impedīmentō fuit.
25 Undique ergō causās bellī petīvit quās illō modō repperit. Quīdam rūsticī Albānī Rōmānīs, Rōmānī Albānīs pecora auferēbant. Utrimque lēgātī ferē sub idem tempus rēs repetītum missī sunt. Rōmānī celeriter, at segniter Albānī rem fēcērunt. Hī enim tum modo cum illī Albam rem repetītum accesserant et ab Albānō duce iam audītī erant, quī illīs satisfactiōnem
30 repudiāvit, Tullum, quī hōs benignē accēperat et in convīvium vocāverat, pecora quae ablāta erant rogāvērunt. Quibus Tullus "Referte" inquit "haec verba rēgī vestrō: Quia populus tuus prīmus satisfactiōnem repudiāvit et lēgātōs dīmīsit, nōs dī magnī respicient nōbīsque auxiliō erunt ad id bellum quod nunc in trīcēsimum diem indīcō." Tristēs Rōma discēdunt et haec
35 nūntiant domum Albānī, et bellum utrimque ācriter parābātur cīvīlī simile bellō, prope inter parentēs fīliōsque, Trōiānam utramque prōlem, quoniam Lāvīnium ab Trōiā, ab Lāvīniō Alba, ab Albānōrum sanguine rēgum oriundī Rōmānī erant.

■ READING COMPREHENSION

1. How was Numa Pompilius good for the Romans?   **2.** What is the Janus?
3. How did Numa turn the minds of the citizens from war?   **4.** Who succeeded Numa?   **5.** What was he like?

---

27. sub + acc. with expressions of time means *towards* or *just before*.   **34. in trīcēsimum diem:** Remember that in + acc. often means *for*.

LESSON 32

Eō; Dative with Intransitive Verbs;
Impersonal Passives

Silver cup from the Boscoreale Treasure showing skeletons and a tripod and bowl. Such cups were meant to remind their wealthy owners of their mortality—Louvre, Paris

FUNERAL CUSTOMS

When a Roman of good family died, the body was washed, dressed in the dead man's robes of office, and laid out on a bed in the atrium, its feet toward the door. A branch of cypress was hung outside the door. During the mourning period the bereaved family did not wash, comb their hair, or change their clothes. Some families kept special mourning garments (**vestēs pullae**) made of undyed, unbleached wool and occasionally artificially tattered and soiled.

On the day of the funeral, the body was carried to the Forum, where a close relative pronounced a eulogy (**laudātiō**) on the dead man, naming his chief accomplishments. These might also be written on signs, or depicted in paintings, carried in the funeral procession. The corpse was escorted outside the city walls by a band of musicians, hired female mourners singing dirges (**nēniae**), and hired actors wearing the wax masks of the dead man's ancestors (normally displayed in the **tablīnum** of the house) and dressed in their official garments. In this way it was shown that the continuity of the family was not affected by individual deaths, and reminded the mourners that the dead man had gone to join his forebears.

The heir carried a torch to light the funeral pyre, which was piled with offerings and anointed with perfumed oil. When the fire had burned out, the bones were collected, washed with wine, and placed in an urn. The urn or coffin, if the body was to be inhumed rather than cremated (both customs were used), was then placed in the family tomb. Some days later the heir swept death out of the house with a special broom.

Poorer people might belong to a funeral club, paying annual dues to a fund from which the funerals were paid for. Each club had its own large tomb with niches for the funeral urns. Such a tomb was called a dove-cote (**columbārium**) from the appearance it presented with its rows of niches for the urns.

(Continued)

Once a year everyone visited the family or club tomb for a picnic, at which food and wine were also given to the dead. Some family tombs have a dining room over the urn chamber with a hole in the floor through which offerings could be dropped.

(*below right*) Roman mosaic from Pompeii of a skeleton as a servant—National Museum, Naples   (*below left*) A Roman tombstone inscription—Lateran Museum, Vatican

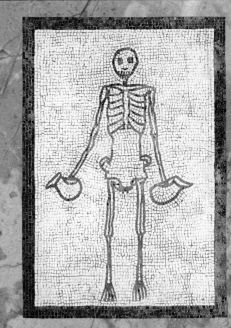

ANCIENT ROME LIVES ON . . .

Some anthropologists assume that the Romans' offerings of food mean that they believed that the dead needed to eat. What would future anthropologists say about our custom of putting flowers on graves? In what other ways do our funeral customs compare with those of the Romans?

TERRA PARENSTIBIFORTVNATAECOMMISIMVS
OSSA QVAETANGISMATRESPROXVMITATE
TVOS NVLLVMCONVSINCVMBASSPERETEFVMBRACINIS

FORMS

EŌ

Eō, īre, iī (īvī), **itum, go,** is an irregular verb which is used very frequently in Latin. Its stem is **e-** before vowels and **i-** before consonants. It belongs to the fourth conjugation, but its imperfect and future are like those of the first and second conjugations.

Although eō is intransitive, most of its compounds—e.g. **adeō, adīre, adiī (adīvī), aditum,** *go to, approach*—are transitive and so have a passive.

PRESENT ACTIVE INDICATIVE OF EŌ; PRESENT PASSIVE OF ADEŌ

eō	īmus	adeor	adīmur
īs	ītis	adīris (-re)	adīminī
it	eunt	adītur	adeuntur

IMPERFECT AND FUTURE ACTIVE OF EŌ; PASSIVE OF ADEŌ

IMPERFECT		FUTURE		IMPERFECT		FUTURE	
ībam	ībamus	ībō	ībimus	adībar	adībāmur	adībor	adībimur
ībās	ībātis	ībis	ībitis	adībāris	adībāminī	adīberīs	adībiminī
ībat	ībant	ībit	ībunt	adībātur	adībantur	adībitur	adībuntur

PRESENT ACTIVE IMPERATIVES OF EŌ; PRESENT PASSIVE OF ADEŌ

ī	īte	adīre	adīminī

The Future Imperative can be found in the Appendix.
The perfect tenses of eō are, as in all verbs, regular.

SYNTAX

DATIVE WITH INTRANSITIVE VERBS

Certain verbs with the following meanings take an indirect object in Latin (instead of a direct object, as in English):

believe	distrust	harm	oppose	please	spare
command	envy	help	pardon	resist	threaten
displease	favor	obey	persuade	serve	trust

The following are the most commonly used of these verbs which take the dative:

> cōnsulō, -ere, cōnsuluī, cōnsultum
>   *take counsel for, consult the interests of*
> crēdō, -ere, crēdidī, crēditum   *believe*
> faveō, -ēre, fāvī, fautum   *favor*
> invideō, -ere, invīdī, invīsum   *envy*
> noceō, -ēre, -uī, -itum   *harm*
> parcō, -ere, pepercī, pārsum   *spare*
> pāreō, -ēre, -uī, -itum   *obey*
> placeō, -ēre, -uī, -itum   *please*
> serviō, -īre, -īvī, -ītum   *serve*

Two of these verbs may also be used transitively, with accusative direct objects: **crēdō** when it means *entrust*, and **cōnsulō** when it means *consult*.

> Tibi crēdidī.   *I believed you.*
> Tibi pecūniam crēdidī.   *I entrusted the money to you.*
> Tibi dē hāc rē cōnsuluī.   *I consulted your interests in this matter.*
> Tē dē hāc rē cōnsuluī.   *I consulted you about this matter.*

Timeō may also be used either transitively or intransitively.

IMPERSONAL PASSIVES

Intransitive verbs are used in the third person singular passive to indicate that an action takes place, without specifying the subject. In the perfect system the verb is treated as though the subject were neuter. Impersonal passives cannot be translated literally.

Ad summum montem perveniētur.
The top of the mountain will be arrived at (not *It will be arrived to the top of the mountain*).

Diū et ācriter pugnātum est.
Fighting went on long and fiercely or *The fighting was long and fierce*.

The intransitive verbs which take an indirect object must be used impersonally in the passive.

Tibi crēdō.   *I believe you.*   Tibi crēditur.   *You are believed.*

Eī nōn nocēbant.   *They were not harming him.*

Eī nōn nocēbātur.
He was not being harmed or *No harm was being done to him.*

Vidētur may be used impersonally to mean *It seems best.*

Dīs aliter vīsum est.
The gods decided otherwise (*It seemed best otherwise to the gods*).

VOCABULARY

BASIC WORDS

These are all compounds of eō.

abeō, abīre, abiī (abīvī), abitum   *go away*

adeō, adīre, adiī (adīvī), aditum   *go to, approach* (transitive)

obeō, obīre, obiī (obīvī), obitum   *go to, go to meet, take part in* (transitive)

pereō, perīre, periī (perīvī), peritum   *perish, be lost*

praetereō, praeterīre, praeteriī (praeterīvī), praeteritum   *go by* (transitive)

redeō, redīre, rediī (redīvī), reditum   *go back, come back, return*

subeō, subīre, subiī (subīvī), subitum   *go under, go up to* (transitive)

trānseō, trānsīre, trānsiī (trānsīvī), transitum   *go over, go across* (transitive)

Note: Some of these compounds are transitive, even though eō itself is not. Those that are transitive take a direct object (not a dative with compound verbs, as you would expect).

■ LEARNING ENGLISH THROUGH LATIN

consultation	*a meeting to plan or discuss something*
credible	*believable, reliable*
invidious	*giving offense, inciting ill-will*
parsimonius	*stingy, miserly*
placebo	*a harmless preparation given to patients to humor them; something done to win the favor of another*
placid	*tranquil, calm, quiet*
subservient	*serving in a subordinate capacity; submissive*
transient	*temporary, staying for only a short time*

A Roman mosaic table top showing a skull and butterfly representing the human soul on the wheel of fortune. A carpenter's level above shows that in death the king's robe and sceptre are not above the beggar's cane, pack, and ragged cloak—National Museum, Naples.

PRACTICE

A. Fill in each blank with an appropriate derivative from this lesson.

1. The staff has special arrangements for the ___ population at the resort.
2. One group was given the new medication, the other a ___. 3. I consider that an ___ comparison, and will no longer listen to what you have to say.
4. He will never run out of money because he is so ___. 5. She is so nice to deal with because she has such a ___ temperment. 6. It really is a ___ explanation and not a lame excuse. 7. The valedictorian of the senior class is aiming for the stars and will never accept a ___ position. 8. My Latin teacher wants to have a ___ with me about the final examination.

B. Change from plural to singular, giving the meaning before and after the change:

1. abeunt   2. adīmur   3. perītis   4. rediimus   5. praeterībuntur   6. īte
7. subībant   8. obiērunt   9. trānseuntur   10. perierint

C. Change the voice, giving the meaning before and after the change:

1. obit   2. subīs   3. trānsiit   4. adītis   5. praeterīs   6. obīmur
7. subeunt   8. trānsītur   9. aditae sunt   10. obīminī

Translation Help

Just as one Latin word often has several English meanings, so a single English word may include concepts which are quite separate in Latin. This is another reason why it is important, when you look up an English word in the back of the book, to check its Latin translations: to make sure you choose the correct one. Suppose, for example, that in translating *He gave me still more money* you find that you have forgotten the Latin for *still*. The meanings given in the English-Latin Vocabulary are **etiam, semper,** and **tamen.** When you look these up in the Latin-English Vocabulary you find that **etiam** means *still* and *even*, **semper** means *still* and *always*, and **tamen** means *still* and *nevertheless*. In the context of the sentence *even more money* makes sense, whereas *always more money* and *nevertheless more money* don't; therefore the correct word is **etiam.**

D. Change to the present tense, giving the meaning before and after the change:

1. abībunt 2. periistī 3. obitum est 4. redībātis 5. subita erunt
6. transībō 7. aditī erātis 8. praeterībāris 9. redierāmus 10. ieris

E. Give the following synopses, with meanings:

1. **adeō** in the 1st person singular passive 2. **eō** in the 2d person singular active 3. **obeō** in the 3d person singular passive 4. **abeō** in the 1st person plural active 5. **praetereō** in the 2d person plural passive 6. **redeō** in the 3d person plural active

F. Pronounce and translate:

1. Abī, male, in malam rem. 2. Mortem bellō ōbiit. 3. Perībunt in marī omnēs et omnia. 4. Urbs adībitur. 5. Ad urbem accēdētur.

Roman tombs along the Appian Way. Such monuments lined the routes leading out of the capital.

G. Translate:

1. I shall return home tomorrow.   2. In a few hours the river will have been crossed.   3. Everything has passed me by.   4. We were going up to the citadel.   5. They are going from Lavinium to Rome.

H. Pronounce and translate:

1. Rōmānīs Albānī favent.   2. Rōmānīs ab Albānīs fautum est.   3. Mihi ā tē invidētur.   4. Nōbīs nocēbās.   5. Semper eīs pārēbātur.   6. Istīs nōn crēdētur.   7. Eī timuimus.   8. Eum timuimus.   9. Rōma adītur.   10. Rōmā abītur.

I. Translate:

1. You were consulted.   2. Your interests were consulted.   3. The city was arrived at.   4. The city was approached.   5. Many will be spared. 6. This pleases us.   7. They will serve us.   8. They will be served by us. 9. Do you envy me?   10. She will not be harmed.

J. Translate:

Still more danger is approaching us, but still we do not leave Rome; for we are still waiting for you and taking counsel for your safety, since for the sake of friendship we will not leave you alone there.

READING

Developing Reading Skills

Latin words which will help in determining the meaning of unfamiliar words: **clāmō, cupīdō, currō, cursus, ferus, imperium, memor, mittō, mors, pār, prae, pugnō, speciēs, sum, super, ūnus, uterque, vertō,** and **vincō.**

English words which will help: *case, cause, cognate, colloquial, concurrent, diction, disparity, expire, federal, ferocious, ferrous, integral, impetus, interval, material, rationale, segregate, spatial, specious, spoils, stimulate, tardy, universal, versus, victor, victory,* and *vulnerable.*

The Horatii and the Curiatii

Ut Rōmānī Albānīs bellum īnferēbant, atque utrīque suōs in aciem ēdūcēbant, lēgātus quem Albānī praemīserant colloquium inter ducēs prōposuit. Quī ubi convēnerant Albānus "Huius bellī" inquit "causa rē vērā nōn est rēs quae ablāta est, id quod tū, Tulle, prae tē fers. Sī vēra, nōn modo dictū speciōsa, dicta erunt, cupīdō imperī duōs cognātōs vīcīnōsque populōs ad arma stimulat. Dē illō pugnātur: utrī nostrum utrīs servient? Sī quam dīiūdicātiōnem sine proeliō invēnerimus nostrīs parcēmus quī aliter mortem obībunt." Placet rēs Tullō, quamquam et animō et spē victōriae cupidus bellī est. Dēnique igitur ratiō initur cui et Fortūna ipsa praebuit māteriam. Forte in utrōque tum exercitū sunt trigeminī frātrēs nec aetāte nec vīribus disparēs, quōrum alterī Horātiī, alterī Cūriātiī vocantur, hī Albānī, illī Rōmānī. Foedus initur hīs lēgibus: trigeminī ferrō pugnābunt prō suā quisque patriā, et ibi imperium erit undecumque victōria fuerit et cuiuscumque populī cīvēs eō certāmine vīcerint is alterī populō cum bona pāce imperitābit.

Duo exercitūs utrimque prō castrīs humī sedent. Inde trigeminī utrīque arma capiunt et in medium inter duās aciēs prōcēdunt. Tum cum signum datur trīnī iuvenēs gladiōs stringunt et pugnātum concurrunt. Prīmō concursū duo Horātiī mortem obeunt et super alium alius cadunt, ad quōrum cāsum Albānī magnō gaudiō conclāmant. Forte tertius Horātius integer fuit, ut ūniversīs sōlus nēquāquam par, sīc adversus singulōs ferox. Tribus Cūriātiīs autem vulnera illāta erant quibus tardī erant. Ergō ille sē in fugam dat, itaque hōc modō hōs sēgregat sīcut quisque vulnere labōrat. Iam aliquantum spatiī ex eō locō ubi pugnātum est fūgerat cum respicit et videt magna intervalla quibus hostēs veniunt, ex quibus ūnus ipsī īnstat. In eum magnō impetū rediit et superāvit et victor secundam pugnam statim petēbat. Ut tertius Cūriātius auxilium frātrī adferēbat—nec procul aberat—et secundum cōnficit. Superest tertius, sed hic fessum cursū fessum vulnere corpus vix trahit, nec ergō diū pugnātur. Hunc Horātius interficit et victōriam aufert.

Ut ex pugnā Rōmam redībat ac prae sē ferēbat trigemina spolia, obitus est ā sorōre, cui ūnus ex Cūriātiīs cordī fuit. Horātia ubi super umerōs frātris vestem spōnsī vīdit quam ipsa confēcerat solvit comam et flēbiliter nōmine spōnsum mortuum vocāvit. Mōvit ferōcī iuvenī animum dolor sorōris in victōriā suā tantōque gaudiō publicō. Itaque gladium strīnxit et virginem trāiēcit et ut misera vitam exspīrābat "Abī hinc cum immātūrō amōre ad spōnsum," inquit, "immemor frātrum mortuōrum vīvīque, immemor patriae! Sīc ītō quaecumque Rōmāna lūgēbit hostem."

---

4. prae sē ferre = *to display, offer as a pretext*   31. solvit comam: *as a sign of mourning*
36. ītō: future imperative (see Appendix)

A Graeco-Roman relief from Tyre, Phoenicia, showing a heroic battle. Roman writers envisioned the Horatii and Curiatii in such terms.

■ READING COMPREHENSION

1. What was said at the conference between the Roman and the Alban leaders? **2.** What system was decided upon to avoid a battle? **3.** What were the rules of the duel? **4.** How did Horatius achieve his victory? **5.** How did Horatius treat his sister? Why?

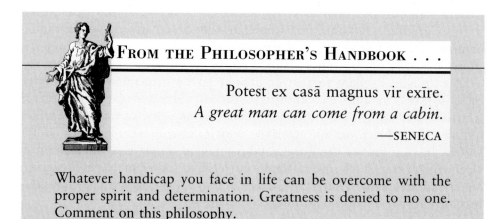

FROM THE PHILOSOPHER'S HANDBOOK . . .

Potest ex casā magnus vir exīre.
A great man can come from a cabin.
—SENECA

Whatever handicap you face in life can be overcome with the proper spirit and determination. Greatness is denied to no one. Comment on this philosophy.

REVIEW 8

VOCABULARY DRILL

A. Give the genitive, gender, and meaning of these nouns:

cor	domus	impedīmentum	passus	speciēs
cornū	faciēs	manus	rēs	spēs
cursus	fidēs	metus	rūs	ūsus
diēs	humus	mīlia	salūs	versus

B. Give the other nominative singular forms, and the meanings, of these adjectives:

publicus   rūsticus

C. Give the other principal parts, and the meanings, of these verbs:

abeō	crēdō	īnstō	pereō	referō
adeō	doceō	invideō	placeō	rogō
adferō	eō	noceō	praestō	serviō
adsum	faveō	obeō	praetereō	subeō
auferō	ferō	ōstendō	promittō	tollō
cōnferō	impōnō	parcō	prōsum	trānseō
cōnsulō	īnferō	pāreō	redeō	

D. Translate:

1. In rē rūsticā versātur.   2. Spem rērum secundārum habēmus.   3. Tūne rē vērā hoc fēcistī?   4. Sī dūcentās et vīgintī duās rēs duōbus mīlibus addideris, quid erit summa rēs?   5. Meam rem faciēbam.   6. Prō rē publicā pugnāte.   7. Rērum novārum cupīdine mōtus est.   8. Carmen dē rērum natūrā legam.   9. Ex vestrā rē hoc fēceritis.   10. Tibi omnibus rēbus praestō.

LISTENING AND SPEAKING

The Roman Flu

Titus, the son of Gnaeus Mucius, is ill. Gnaeus summons a Greek doctor who examines the patient and recommends that he go to the Temple of Aesculapius on the Tiber Island for a cure. The whole household is upset! Listen!

1. trepidus, -a, -um—*nervous, fearful*
2. aeger, aegra, aegrum—*sick*
3. forsan (adv.)—*perhaps, maybe*
4. medicāmentum, -ī, n.—*medicine*
5. tussis, -is, f.—*cough*
6. amābō—*"please"*
7. incidō, incidere, incidī, _____,—*to fall upon, befall*
8. immō (adv.)—*no*
9. asper, aspera, asperum—*rough*
10. siccus, -a, -um—*dry*
11. calor, -is, m.—*heat*
12. frīgus, -oris, n.—*cold*
13. morbus, -ī, m.—*disease*
14. Ecce nōs—*Here we are!*
15. commendō, -āre, -āvī, -ātum—*introduce*
16. Avē—*Good morning, greetings*
17. fēbris, -is, f.—*fever*
18. hiems, hiemis, f.—*winter*
19. contactus, -ūs, m.—*contact, touching*
20. vulgō, -āre, -āvī, -ātum—*to spread*

LŪCRĒTIA: Heu, Apollōnia, Mūcium in cubiculum statim vocā. Festīnā.

APOLLŌNIA: Statim, domina, eum vocō. Estne domī aliquid malī? Trepida[1] vidēris!

LŪCRĒTIA: Tītus noster aeger[2] est. Forsan[3] Mūcius aliquod medicāmentum[4] bonum ad tussim[5] habēbit.

APOLLŌNIA: Venī, domine, venī, amābō![6] Tītus tuus aeger est.

MŪCIUS: Heus, fīlī, quid tibi incidit?[7] Num dolor tibi est?

TĪTUS: Immō,[8] pater, vērō male mihi est. Est mihi tussis et aspera[9] et sicca.[10] Tōtam noctem nōn modo calōrem[11] sed etiam frīgus[12] sentiēbam, itaque nihil dormiēbam.

MŪCIUS: Hīc domī nōn satis medicāmentī est, sed apud Ūlpium, fīnitimum nostrum, est Graecus, quī medicus dīcitur. Ego exībō et hūc eum adducam.

TĪTUS: Grātiās tibi, pater, agō. Salūtem enim bonam cupiō quod morbōs[13] nōn amō!

MŪCIUS (*who returns with the doctor*): Ecce[14] nōs. Tibi, Lūcrētiae, medicum Graecum nōmine Agamemnōnem commendō.[15]

LŪCRĒTIA: Avē,[16] medice. Dabisne nōbīs auxilium?

AGAMEMNŌN: Quōmodo, puer, tū tē sentīs? Plānē tussim gravem et fēbrim[17] malam habēs.

TĪTUS: Vērō male, magister, mihi est. Māne vix spīritum ducēbam.

AGAMEMNŌN: Hōs diēs multī similī morbō labōrant, nam eā hieme[18] pestilentia urbī incidit quī morbus hīc celeriter contactū[19] in hominēs vulgātur.[20] Puerum, Mūcī, autem ad Aesculāpī aedem in īnsulam Tīberīnam portābō. Ibi et incubātiō et medicāmenta multa magnō auxiliō fīliō tuō erunt.

LŪCRĒTIA: Num, Mūcī, huius Graecī bonum est cōnsilium? Tītus domō in incubātiōnem forās nōn exībit! Domī, Tīte, manē!

AGAMEMNŌN: Animōs tuōs, domina, tranquīllā,[21] amābō! Tītus tuus nōn modo medicāmentīs sed etiam quiēte dē tussī mox sānābitur,[22] nam modo duōbus diēbus incubātiōnis egēbit.[23] Mox domum in plēnā salūte redībit.

21. tranquillō, -āre, -āvī, -ātum—*to calm*

22. sānō, -āre, sānāvī, sānātum—*to cure*

23. egeō, egēre, eguī, ____,—*to need*

A. Select a team of three boys and two girls to give a presentation of this selection.

B. Answer the following questions. Then use the answers to the questions to give a summary in Latin of Titus' illness.

1. Quid domī Mūcī incidit?   2. Cūr Mūcius domō exit?
3. Quōmodo medicus Graecus vocātur?   4. Quō medicus Graecus Tītum portābit?   5. Habetne Lūcrētia hoc cōnsilium Graecī bonum?

The Tiber Island in the model of Rome—Museo della Civiltà Romana. The buildings on the left housed the sick, while the snakes sacred to Aesculapius resided in the temple on the right.

TRACES OF ROMAN CIVILIZATION TODAY

France—Arles and Nîmes

Arles is a city in southeastern France, located in the Camargue plain where the Rhone divides to form its delta. The old quarter with its narrow winding streets is surrounded by Roman and medieval ramparts. Around the first century B.C., Arles had become the capital of Roman Gaul.

La Tour Magne

The Amphitheatre at Arles

La Maison Carrée

The city we see today was built for the most part out of stones of the immense Roman monuments from the Age of Augustus. One of the outstanding Roman remains in Arles is a large amphitheatre still used for bullfights and fairs.

Nîmes is another town in southern France famous for Roman remains. The central and oldest part of the town is encircled by a boulevard along the sites of the old fortifications and it is here that most of the remains are located. La Maison Carrée is a Roman temple dedicated to the adopted sons of Augustus and dates from the beginning of the Christian era. It houses a collection of sculpture and classical fragments. La Tour Magne is the oldest monument in Nîmes. It was used as a watchtower and subsequently turned into a fortress. Nearby is the reservoir from which the water carried by the Roman aqueduct, Pont du Gard, was distributed throughout the town.

Le Pont du Gard

373

Deponent and Semideponent Verbs; Objective Genitive with Verbs

Cupids as goldsmiths—from the Red Triclinium in the House of the Vettii, Pompeii

BUSINESS AND INDUSTRY

Rome was at first a nation of farmers, the men producing the raw materials and the women turning them into food and clothing. But the farmers had to spend more and more time as soldiers or as statesmen, as the government grew to fit the growing empire, and large-scale trade and manufacturing enterprises replaced the village- or cottage-based operations. Roman industry, crafts, and trades had the same great variety as ours. Almost any kind of modern industry, craft, or trade can be matched in antiquity.

The chief difference between our times and theirs lies in the failure of the Romans to develop a machine-based economy, for they had no industrial revolution to answer the ever-growing demand for manufactured goods. They had the technology: the principle of the steam engine was understood, and numerous hydraulic devices had been developed. But these were thought of essentially as amusing toys, and were not applied to production methods.

The institution which inhibited and replaced machine technology was that of slavery. In the long run the machine would probably have been more economical than the slave. The upkeep of slaves was expensive, since they had to be maintained through the unproductive years of extreme youth and old age. Cato advised selling a slave while he would still bring a good price and before his maintenance costs grew too high; for when a slave was granted freedom, his former master had some obligation to support him. Nevertheless, because of the abundant supply of slave labor, there was no immediate pressure to develop more efficient methods of production. Consequently the Romans had nothing we would recognize as a factory. The place of the factory was held by large slave workshops (**ergastēria**), or more often by the guilds of free proprietors of small slave-run workshops, who banded together to standardize their output, fix prices, and market their wares.

(*above*) A relief from the tomb of the Haterii showing the construction of an elaborate tomb. Slaves power the sprocket wheel of the **machina tractōria** as it erects an obelisk. (*right*) The grape harvest: slaves treading on the grapes, the first step in wine making—a mosaic floor, Merida, Spain

FORMS

DEPONENT VERBS

Deponent verbs are passive in form but active in meaning. They are called deponent because they have *laid aside* or *put down* (**dēpōnō, -ere, deposuī, depositum**) their passive meanings. Since there is no perfect active form, a deponent verb has only three principal parts. The third principal part shows the supine stem.

DEPONENT VERBS

1ST CONJUGATION:	moror, morārī, morātus sum *delay*
2D CONJUGATION:	vereor, verērī, veritus sum *stand in awe of; fear*
3D CONJUGATION:	oblīvīscor, oblīvīscī, oblītus sum *forget*
3D I-STEM:	patior, patī, passus sum *endure, experience; allow*
4TH CONJUGATION:	potior, potīrī, potītus sum *get possession of*

1. A deponent verb may be recognized in the Vocabulary by its **-or** ending.
2. Note that the second principal part ends in **-rī** except in the third conjugation, where it ends in **-ī**.

Slaves pressing olives—mosaic from Saint Romain en Galle, 3rd c. A.D.

SEMIDEPONENT VERBS

A few verbs are deponent only in the perfect system. These are called semideponent, and may be recognized by the third principal part.

gaudeō, gaudēre, gāvīsus sum *rejoice*

SYNTAX

CASE USAGE WITH DEPONENT VERBS

Direct Object of Deponent Verbs

In spite of its passive form, a transitive deponent verb takes a direct object.

Mē ab itinere morātus est. *He delayed me on (lit. from) my way.*
Nōnne deōs verēbiminī? *Will you not fear the gods?*
Fortiter mala patere! *Endure evils bravely!*

Ablative of Means with Deponent Verbs

Five deponent verbs are construed with an ablative of means rather than a direct object. They are:

fruor, fruī, fructus sum *enjoy*
fungor, fungī, functus sum *perform*
potior, potīrī, potītus sum *get possession of*
ūtor, ūtī, ūsus sum *use*
vēscor, vēscī, —— *feed upon*

Aedibus potīta erat. *She had gotten possession of the house.*
Meā pecūniā ūtēbāris. *You were using my money.*

OBJECTIVE GENITIVE WITH VERBS

Potior sometimes takes an objective genitive instead of an ablative of means. It is always construed with the genitive in the idiom **Rērum potior,** *I get (or have) control of the situation.*

Post bellum Caesar rērum potītus est. *After the war Caesar took charge.*

The genitive is also used with verbs of remembering and forgetting.

Vestrī meminērunt. *They remember you.*
Aenēāsne rēgīnae oblīvīscētur? *Will Aeneas forget the queen?*

VOCABULARY

BASIC WORDS

fruor, fruī, fructus sum   *enjoy*
fungor, fungī, functus sum   *perform, finish*
gaudeō, gaudēre, gāvīsus sum   *rejoice*
meminī, meminisse, ___   *remember*
moror, morārī, morātus sum   *delay*
oblīvīscor, oblīvīscī, oblītus sum   *forget*

patior, patī, passus sum   *endure, experience; allow*
potior, potīrī, potītus sum   *get possession of*
ūtor, ūtī, ūsus sum   *use*
vereor, verērī, veritus sum   *stand in awe of; fear*
vēscor, vēscī, ___   *feed upon*

Notes: 1. The second prinicpal part of **meminī** will be explained in the next Lesson.
2. Although **meminī** has forms of the perfect system only, it has the meanings of the present system.

Tuī meminī.   *I remember you.*
Tuī memineram.   *I remembered you.*
Tuī meminerō.   *I shall remember you.*

3. For the imperative of **meminī** the future imperative forms are used (see Appendix).

Mementō meī!   }
Mementōte meī! }   *Remember me!*

LEARNING ENGLISH THROUGH LATIN

defunct	*no longer existing; dead or extinct*
fruition	*a coming to fulfillment; realization*
function	*the performance required of an object or activity*
gaudeamus	*merrymaking, especially of college students (from the first word of a medieval student song)*
gaudy	*bright and showy but lacking in taste*
memento	*anything serving as a reminder; a souvenir*
moratorium	*an authorized delay or stopping of a specified activity*
oblivious	*unmindful or forgetful*
utility	*usefulness; the quality of being useful*

▰ PRACTICE ▰

A. Explain the meaning of each sentence:

1. The client was completely oblivious to the judicial proceedings.   2. Why are electricity, gas, and the telephone called public utilities?   3. The project the staff was working on so long is now defunct.   4. The new house was lovely, but the furnishings were really gaudy.   5. What is the function of that apparatus on your kitchen counter?   6. The financially troubled company declared a moratorium on raises and hiring.   7. My diploma is the fruition of four years of study and hard work.   8. My bookcase is full of mementos of my travels.

B. Change the following from singular to plural:

1. morābitur   2. passus erās   3. ūtere   4. vēscētur   5. fruor   6. gavīsus erit   7. fungēbāris   8. oblītus sum   9. verēris   10. potīre

C. Give the following synopses, indicative and (for the second person) imperative:

1. **oblīvīscor** in the 2d person plural   2. **vereor** in the 1st person singular
3. **gaudeō** in the 3d person singular   4. **meminī** in the 2d person plural

---

FROM THE PHILOSOPHER'S HANDBOOK . . .

Praeceptōrēs suōs adulēscens
venerātur et suspicit.
*Young people respect and look up
to their teachers.*
—SENECA

We meet many teachers in our lives who are not necessarily in the schoolroom. Think of such a person in your life whom you respect and look up to. How has she or he influenced your life?

5. potior in the 3d person plural   **6. moror** in the 2d person singular
7. fruor in the 1st person plural

D.   Give the English, and identify the form:

1. vēsciminī   **2.** ūsae erant   **3.** patiēmur   **4.** morātus est   **5.** meminerō

E.   Give the Latin, and identify the form:

1. she will have rejoiced   **2.** you (sing.) were enjoying   **3.** perform (sing.)
4. they will forget   **5.** I shall get possession of

F.   Pronounce and translate:

1. Alius armīs et castrīs gaudet, alius vītā rūsticā fruitur.   **2.** Paucīs post diēbus ille morte functus est.   **3.** Quotiēns hūc pervenītur totiēns suī quisque dolōris meminit.   **4.** Magnā virtute istōs metūs patere, et fidēs tua salūtī tibi erit.   **5.** Sī diū morāberis mūneribus male fungēris, sīn tempore bene ūsus eris omnia efficiēs.

G.   Choose the word which will correctly complete each sentence, then pronounce and translate:

1. ___ memineris. (nostrum, nostrī, nōbīs, nōs)   **2.** ___ adībunt. (urbis, urbī, urbem, urbe)   **3.** ___ ūsae sunt. (pecūniae, pecūniam, pecūniā, pecūniārum)

READING

Developing Reading Skills

Latin words which will help in determining the meanings of new words: **bellum, bene, caelum, circum, dīgnus, dō, ducō, facilis, faciō, familia, ferō, fugiō, humus, inter, iuvō, novus, nūntius, ōs, pōnō, rēgnum, sēdeō, stō, sum,** and **volō.**

English words which will help; *adjutant, ample, apt, augment, augury, bellicose, benefit, celestial, cogitation, conciliate, conspicuous, divine, equity, faculty, familiar, heir, honor, human, humility, indignity, induce, ingress, institute, irate, married, migrate, morbid, nativity, novelty, pestilence, potent, private, prodigy, region, reign, religion, sedition, testament,* and *tutor.*

The King is Dead—
Long Live the King!

Haud ita multō post pestilentiā labōrātum est. Rēx ferus et bellicōsus, quī
ante deōrum oblītus erat, nunc mūtātus est et nūmina verēbātur. Sed Tullus
ut sacrīs Iovis fungēbātur sīve verbīs seu rēbus errāvit, itaque ā deō, quī
īrātus est, fulmine ictus est et cum domō suā ārsit. Tullus magnā gloriā bellī
5 rēgnāvit annōs duōs et trīgintā.

Post hunc Ancus Mārcius, Numae ex fīliā nepōs, rērum potītus est. Hic
vir, aequitāte et religiōne avō similis, Rōmulī etiam meminerat; sīc igitur
bellō fruēbātur ut sacrīs deōrum gāvīsus est. Latīnōs bellō domuit, urbem
ampliāvit, et eī nova moenia circumdedit. Ad Tiberis ostia urbem condidit,
10 Ostiamque vocāvit. Vīcēsimō quartō annō imperī morbō obiit.

Tum cum Ancus Rōmae rēgnābat quīdam Lucumō, vir impiger et dīvitiīs
potēns, Tarquiniīs Rōmam commigrāvit. Inductus erat cupīdine ac spē magnī
honōris cuius Tarquiniīs (nam ibi quoque peregrīnā stirpe oriundus erat)
facultās nōn fuerat. Dēmarātī Corīnthiī fīlius erat, quī ob sēditiōnēs profugus
15 Tarquiniīs cōnsēderat. Post mortem patris dīvitis hērēs Lucumō tōtā pecūniā
Dēmarātī fruēbātur, quae dīvitiae ut animōs eī faciēbant sīc uxor Tanaquil,
quae Tarquiniīs summō in locō nāta erat, auxit. Haec fēmina superba nōn
facile rēs humilīs patiēbātur, sed coniugī, quod peregrīnus erat, nūlla honōris
spēs Tarquiniīs fuit. Quam indīgnitātem quia aequō animō nōn ferēbat,
20 "Hīc," inquit, "mī marīte, nōn morābimur, sed Rōmam nōs conferēmus,
ubi honōre magnō in novā urbe nōn exclūdēris."

Rēs ergō sustulērunt et ēmigrābant Rōmam. Ad Iāniculum forte ventum
erat. Ibi eī, ut in carpentō cum uxōre sedēbat, aquila pilleum abstulit, et
postquam altē ēvolāvit, capitī aptē reposuit. Accēpit id augurium laeta
25 Tanaquil, perīta, ut vulgō Etrūscī, caelestium prōdigiōrum mulier. Virum
complexa est et "Excelsa et alta" inquit "spērā, nam ea avis quae ex eā
regiōne caelī et eius deī nūntia vēnit sustulit quod humānō capitī superpositum
erat deinde dīvīnitus eīdem reddidit. Ūtere ergō hāc fortūnā quam deus tibi
dedit." Hās spēs cogitātiōnēsque sēcum portābant ut in urbem ingressī sunt,
30 ubi domum ēmērunt et L. Tarquinium Prīscum ēdidērunt nōmen. Rōmānīs
cōnspicuum eum novitās dīvītiaeque faciēbant; et ipse fortūnam benignō
adloquiō beneficiīsque (nam ita pecūniā suā ūtēbātur) adiuvābat, multōs

---

10. obiit: obeō (with **mortem** understood) means *to die;* hence our word *obituary.*
19. aequō animō: *with level mind = with equanimity.*   **25. prōdigiōrum:** objective genitive
with the adjective **perīta.**   **27. eius deī:** the eagle was the bird of Jupiter.

An Etruscan lord passes his lady a favor at a banquet. Etruscan ladies, like Tanaquil, reclined at table as their husbands' equals—Tomb of the Leopards, Tarquinia

enim sibi sīc conciliāvit. Dēnique in rēgiam quoque dē eō fāma perlāta est. Mox in familiāris amīcitiae adductus est iūra, et nōn modo publicīs sed etiam prīvātīs cōnsiliīs intererat; postrēmō tūtor etiam līberīs rēgis testāmentō 35 īnstitūtus est.

▦ READING COMPREHENSION

1. Why did Jupiter become angry with Tullus? How did he show his anger?
2. Describe the reign of Ancus Martius.   **3.** Who was Lucumo? Why did he come to Rome?   **4.** How did Tanaquil interpret the omen of the eagle?
5. How did the Romans receive Lucumo?

Forms of the Infinitive;
Subjective and Objective Infinitive

Amphorae used for transporting wine, recovered from a sunken merchantman—Civic Museum, Alberga

IMPORT–EXPORT TRADING

In the late Republic and early Empire great fortunes could be made in the import-export business. This trading could be engaged in by individuals with capital, by the great commercial families, or by joint stock companies with capital invested by shareholders. These large businesses, family-run or shareholder-controlled, had branch offices in every part of the empire and indeed well beyond its borders. We know for example that in the first century B.C. at least 80,000 Roman citizens were living in the various kingdoms of Asia Minor, and a large number also in Numidia. Hoards of Roman coins have been found in what is now Vietnam, where Romans and Chinese must have maintained offices for the selling of silk, which was immensely popular in the early Empire—so popular that it caused a serious gold shortage.

Members of the social-political-economic class we call the Knights (**Equitēs**), families which had acquired their wealth slowly and carefully over generations, amassed huge fortunes safely by diversifying their investments. Investors with less capital who were willing to gamble went in for more risky speculations, with dramatic profits and losses. Freed slaves, especially, having no conservative family traditions to inhibit them, made and lost huge fortunes overnight, so that "freedman's wealth" became proverbial.

A quick response on the part of an importer to the changing fads and fashions of conspicuous waste could make a fortune, especially if he could be the first to meet the demand. He had to act before the market was flooded or the fickle wealthy turned to some new craze, and prices would fall. Fabrics for clothing, wines, and foodstuffs were the most likely fields for speculation.

Banking practices kept pace with the expansion of big business. Banks maintained foreign branches, and there were ancient equivalents of checking accounts, bank loans, and business insurance.

ANCIENT ROME LIVES ON . . .

How would a Roman importer apply today's economic principle of "supply and demand"?

(*above*) A **sestertius** from the reign of the Emperor Nero showing Neptune regarding Rome's recently renovated port, Ostia
(*left*) A mosaic on the walkway in front of the shipping agency for trade between Ostia and Narbona in southern Gaul—Portico of Corporations, Ostia   (*below*) A view of part of the Portico of Corporations, a building containing many shipping agencies that connected Rome with all parts of the Mediterranean

FORMS

FORMS OF THE INFINITIVE

The present active infinitive is the second principal part of the verb.

vocāre	*to call*
habēre	*to hold*
pōnere	*to place*
capere	*to take*
audīre	*to hear*
esse	*to be*

The present passive infinitive is formed like the second principal part of deponent verbs.

morārī	*to delay*	vocārī	*to be called*
verērī	*to fear*	habērī	*to be held*
oblīvīscī	*to forget*	pōnī	*to be placed*
patī	*to endure*	capī	*to be taken*
potīrī	*to get possession of*	audīrī	*to be heard*

Remember that, while the present passive infinitive of the other conjugations ends in **-rī**, that of the third ends in just **-ī**.

The perfect active infinitive is formed by adding **-isse** to the perfect stem.

vocāvisse	*to have called*	cēpisse	*to have taken*
habuisse	*to have held*	audīvisse	*to have heard*
posuisse	*to have placed*	fuisse	*to have been*

The perfect passive infinitive is the fourth principal part with **esse**.

morātum esse	*to have delayed*
veritum esse	*to have feared*
oblītum esse	*to have forgotten*
passum esse	*to have endured*
potītum esse	*to have gotten possession of*
vocātum esse	*to have been called*
habitum esse	*to have been held*
positum esse	*to have been placed*
captum esse	*to have been taken*
audītum esse	*to have been heard*

The future active infinitive is the fourth principal part with **-ūr-** inserted, sometimes with **esse.**

morātūrum [esse]	*to be about to delay*
veritūrum [esse]	*to be about to fear*
oblītūrum [esse]	*to be about to forget*
passūrum [esse]	*to be about to endure*
potītūrum [esse]	*to be about to get possession of*
vocātūrum [esse]	*to be about to call*
habitūrum [esse]	*to be about to hold*
positūrum [esse]	*to be about to place*
captūrum [esse]	*to be about to take*
audītūrum [esse]	*to be about to hear*
futūrum [esse] or fore	*to be about to be*

Fore is an irregular alternative form for the future active infinitive of **sum.**

SYNTAX

SUBJECTIVE AND OBJECTIVE INFINITIVES

The infinitive is a verbal noun; that is, it is neither a verb nor a noun, but something in between. Like a verb, it has tense and voice, and will take a direct object if it is active and transitive. Like a noun, it can be the subject or the direct object of a verb. As a noun it is always neuter singular. It is sometimes translated by the English infinitive or gerund:

Amō carmina legere.
  I like to read poems. I like reading poems.

Mihi placet carmina legere.
  Reading poems pleases me. It pleases me to read poems.

Carmina legere mihi grātum est.
  It is pleasant for me to read poems. Reading poems is pleasant to me.

Mē carmina legere docuit.
  He taught me to read poems.

Timeō domum sōlus īre.
  I fear going home alone. I am afraid to go home alone.

Aedīs aedificāre incipient.
  They will begin to build a house. They will begin building a house.

VOCABULARY

BASIC WORDS

coepī, coepisse, coeptum (perfect system only) *began*

cōnstituō, -ere, cōnstituī, constitūtum *establish; decide*

cupiō, -ere, cupīvī, cupītum *want, desire*

dēbeō, -ēre, -uī, -itum *owe; ought*

dēsinō, -ere, dēsiī, dēsitum *stop, cease*

optō, -āre, -āvī, -ātum *choose, wish for; wish*

properō, -āre, -āvī, -ātum *hasten*

temptō, -āre, -āvī, -ātum *test; try*

numquam (adv.) *never*

umquam (adv.) *ever*

Notes: 1. The choice of a translation for some verbs depends on whether the direct object is an accusative or an objective infinitive.

Oppidum cōnstituērunt.   *They established a town.*
Oppidum condere cōnstituērunt.   *They decided to found a town.*

Pecūniam mihi dēbēs.   *You owe me money.*
Pecūniam mihi dare dēbēs.   *You ought to give me money.*

2. You will often find īnstituō, -ere, īnstituī, īnstitūtum used instead of cōnstituō, with the same meanings.

The expansion of trade: a funerary relief from Germany showing the transfer of money to a bank or business, 2nd c. A.D.

▪ LEARNING ENGLISH THROUGH LATIN

constitute	*to set up, establish, give a certain function to*
cupidity	*avarice, greed*
institution	*establishment; something established*
opt	*to make a choice*
option	*something that can be chosen; a choice*
tempt	*to try to persuade or induce; to attract*
temptation	*an enticement; something that tempts*

▬ PRACTICE ▬

A. Fill in the blanks with a word from the derivative list in this lesson.

1. The dentist had two ___: to pull the tooth or do a root canal procedure.
2. Twelve months ___ a year.   **3.** I will not succumb to that ___.   **4.** The ___ of the Roman Republic dates from the expulsion of the Tarquins.   **5.** I ___ out of this organization.

B. Other derivatives from this vocabulary are *debit, co-opt, constituent,* and *constitution.* Look up their meanings in a dictionary and show their relation to Latin.

C. Give the tense and voice of these infinitives, pronounce, and translate:

1. meminisse   2. crēdere   3. veritum esse   4. ūsūrum esse   5. tollī
6. abiisse   7. āfutūrum esse   8. morārī   9. relātum esse   10. adesse

D. Give the following infinitives:

1. The present active of **pereō** and **īnferō**   2. The present passive of **patior** and **potior**   3. The perfect active of **faveō** and **īnstō**   4. The perfect passive of **oblīvīscor** and **cōnferō**   5. The future active of **fruor** and **claudō**

E. Pronounce and translate:

1. Timēbat perīculīs sē expōnere.   2. Grātum est rēbus secundīs ūtī.
3. Carmina tam clārī poētae audīre amābam.   4. Suōs cīvīs aurum iterum rogāre cōnstituerat.   5. Dēsine istī virginī sōlī placēre temptāre.

F. Pronounce and translate:

1. Nēmō eī cui deī favent umquam invidēre dēbet.   2. Quī tantam imāginem nōnāgintā sex pedum altitūdine cōnstituērunt?   3. Amīcō quī vīllam quadringentīs aureīs eī vēndiderat pecūniam dēbuit.   4. Herba in campō simul atque igne excepta est ācriter ardēre coepit.

G. Translate:

1. Why do they want to harm you?   2. Age has taught us to live well. 3. He wished to be profitable to the republic.   4. When will we begin to enjoy rural life?   5. Have you been taught to read verses?

Translation Help

As your Latin vocabulary and translation ability grow, more unfamiliar words are added to the Readings, to ensure that your ability to determine the meanings of new words will keep pace with your other skills. When you come across an unfamiliar word in translating Latin into English, don't be in too much haste to look it up; that can be a waste of time. First see if you can't arrive at the meaning on the basis of knowledge you already have. In the last reading, for example, there was a sentence in which only half of the words had been given in the lesson vocabularies: **Ibi eī, ut in *carpentō* cum uxōre sedēbat, *aquila pilleum* abstulit, et postquam altē *ēvolāvit,* capitī *aptē reposuit.* How many of the other six did you look up? How many did you really have to look up? If you worked out the syntax of the sentence you could see that it meant *There, as he was sitting in the ____ with his wife, a ____ took his ____ away from him, and after it ____ on high, ____ it ____ly on his head.*

Since you knew from the context that Tarquin and Tanaquil were traveling from Tarquinii to Rome, you would know that **carpentō** must be a vehicle holding at least two people; and you might remember from Lesson 21 that a **carpentum** is in fact a light two-wheeled cart suitable for women. Knowing both **ē** and **volō**, you would know that **ēvolāvit** means *flew out;* hence the **aquila**, if it flew high up, must be some kind of bird. You know **pōnō**, and what **re-** means, so you knew that the **aquila** *re*placed the **pilleum** on his head; **pilleum** must mean some kind of hat. The English word *apt* would help you with **aptē**. In the end the only word you really needed to look up was **aquila**: and if you were willing to wait and see what the context would tell you about it, a footnote told you even what that meant.

READING

Developing Reading Skills

Some of the unfamiliar words in this reading are made from these words which you know: **circum, cīvis, clāmō, compōnō, cursus, dūcō, faciō, iaciō, pareō, rēx, servus, -spiciō, teneō, veniō,** and **vertō.**

Some of these English derivatives may help in determining others:

adolescent, appellate, belligerent, clamor, conciliate, contumely, create, dormitory, dubious, educate, erect, extinguish, ferocious, ferrous, intent, matrimony, obstreperous, oration, persuade, portend, possess, prodigy, pupil, secret, sequential, tumult, tumultuous, tutor, vestibule, vociferate, and *vulnerable.*

A Stolen Kingship;
A Head on Fire

Post Ancī mortem L. Tarquinius, nunc rēgis līberōrum tūtor, properāvit comitia convocāre. Deinde sub tempus quō cīvēs rēgem dēlectum veniēbant Ancī fīliōs vēnātum dīmīsit. Ambitiōsē rēgnum petīvit et apud comitia ōrātiōnem habuit quā sibi populum conciliāvit. Sīc in pupillōrum locō rēgnō potītus est. Quod Senātum facere amīcum sibi cupīvit, Senātōribus quōs Rōmulus creāverat centum aliōs addidit, hominēs quōs sibi pecūniā conciliāverat. Multa bella fēlīciter gessit, ac multōs agrōs quōs hostibus dēmpsit agrō Rōmānō adiēcit. Cloācam sub terrā condidit; templum in Capitōliō īnstituit et aedem aedificāre coepit. Eō tempore in rēgiā prōdigium vīsū ēventūque mīrum fuit: servae fīliō cui Ser. Tulliō fuit nōmen, ut dormiēbat, caput ārsit multōrum in cōnspectū. Servōs quī flammam aquā exstinguere temptābant Tanaquil rēgīna retinuit, nām prōdigiōrum perīta sēcum "Tāle prōdigium" putābat "sine nūmine nōn ēvēnerit." Mox cum somnō et flamma abiit. Rēgīna virum in secrētum abdūxit et "Ōlim" inquit "hic puer praesidiō

___

4 **ōrātiōnem habēre** = *to deliver a speech*

rēbus nostrīs dubiīs erit." Rēgī persuāsum est, nam semper ēvenit quod dīs   15
cordī est. Dēhinc Servius coeptus est habērī velut rēgis et rēgīnae fīlius et
cum līberīs rēgiīs ēducārī, cui postquam adolēvit rēx fīliam suam in
matrimōnium dedit. Ancī fīliī duo igitur quibus Tarquinius rēgnum abstulerat
īrātī sunt et rēs novās cupere coepērunt, spem enim imperī post mortem
rēgis obtinuerant; "Sed nunc" inquiunt "in eādem cīvitāte post centēsimum   20
ferē annum rēgnum quod Rōmulus, deī fīlius deus ipse, tenuit, quod rēgnum
nōbīs dēbētur, servus servae fīlius possidēbit." Ferrō igitur eam arcēre
contumēliam cōnstituunt. Ex pastōribus duo ferōcēs dēliguntur ad facinus,
quī in vestibulō rēgiae tumultuōsē speciē rixae in sē omnīs apparitōrēs rēgiōs
convertunt; inde, ubi ambō rēgem appellābant clāmorque eōrum penitus in   25
rēgiam pervēnerat, adductī ad rēgem sunt. Ibi uterque vōciferārī et certātim
alter alterī obstrepere incipit; Lictōris iussū tandem obloquī dēsinunt; ūnus
rem ex compositō ōrdītur. Ut intentus in eum sē rēx tōtus vertēbat, alter
secūrim sustulit et in caput dēiēcit. Hoc tēlum in vulnere relinquit et ambō
sē forās ēiciunt. Clāmor inde concursusque undīque populī. Tanaquil inter   30
tumultum rēgiam claudit, arbitrōs ēicit. Deinde Servium vocat et "Tuum
est," inquit "Servī, sī vir es, rēgnum, nōn eōrum quī aliēnīs manibus tam
malum facinus fēcēre. Ērige tē deōsque ducēs sequere quī ōlim ubi caput
igne dīvīnō circumfundēbant hoc portendērunt!"

■ READING COMPREHENSION

1. How did Lucius Tarquin get possession of the kingship?   **2.** What did
he do during his kingship?   **3.** What was the amazing sign in the palace?
4. How did Queen Tanaquil interpret the sign?   **5.** Describe the death of
L. Tarquinius Priscus.   **6.** What did Queen Tanaquil say to Servius?

---

28. ex compositō = *by prearrangement*. **rem ordīrī** = *to begin to present a case*   **rēx
tōtus:** Latin often uses an adjective modifying the subject where English would use an adverb:
not *the entire king* but *the king . . . entirely*.   **33. fēcēre:** The ending **-ēre** is sometimes used
instead of **-ērunt**.

LESSON 35

Possum; Infinitive Phrase;
Complementary Infinitive

Via Biberatica in the famous Market of Trajan, Rome

MANUFACTURING

In the Roman world, with its good roads and harbors, and its lack of trade barriers, the market for manufactured goods was very big. The fine red pottery of Arretium, greenware from Gaul, the bronzes of Campania, Italian glassware and mass-produced terra-cotta lamps, Egyptian paper, Pergamene parchment, the dyed woolen cloth of the Levant, Chinese silk, wares from everywhere were distributed to the farthest corners of the empire.

There were various centers to which wholesale dealers would go to inspect various products. The great Markets of Trajan at Rome were one such; but Rome must have been an important wholesale center even before the time of Trajan. A small dealer in iron objects at Pompeii had on the wall of his little shop a list of eight market towns, seven places near Pompeii plus Rome. No doubt the ironmongers' guild of Pompeii would send samples to Rome for exporters and foreign importers to inspect.

Rome was certainly not the only center of this kind. Wholesale buyers of processed woolen cloth must have flocked to Pompeii to view samples in the great cloth-processors' hall there. This hall, facing on the Forum, was a colonnaded courtyard surrounded by dozens of large show windows, with offices for representatives of the various houses. The Square of the Corporations at Ostia was a similar construction, a park and temple precinct surrounded by a colonnade, off which opened many small offices. Here various guilds and large trading corporations could install their representatives.

ANCIENT ROME LIVES ON . . .

If an ancient Roman merchant visited a modern wholesale center, what would be familiar or unfamiliar to him?

(*above*) The Forum of Julius Caesar: a row of shops is visible behind the columns of the double colonnade. **Fora** such as this were like the elaborate malls of today. (*right*) Frieze of a knife seller displaying his wares to a customer. His display case could be broken down into portable units and moved from town to town.

FORMS

POSSUM

The verb **possum, posse, potuī, ___,** *be able, can,* is **sum** with the prefix **pos-** or **pot-** (from **potis,** *able*), so its conjugation is as follows:

CONJUGATION OF POSSUM

PRESENT		IMPERFECT		FUTURE	
possum	possumus	poteram	poterāmus	poterō	poterimus
potes	potestis	poterās	poterātis	poteris	poteritis
potest	possunt	poterat	poterant	poterit	poterunt

PERFECT		PLUPERFECT		FUTURE PERFECT	
potuī	potuimus	potueram	potuerāmus	potuerō	potuerimus
potuistī	potuistis	potuerās	potuerātis	potueris	putueritis
potuit	potuērunt	potuerat	potuerant	potuerit	potuerint

There are no imperatives.

SYNTAX

ACCUSATIVE SUBJECT AND SUBJECTIVE COMPLEMENT OF AN INFINITIVE

The subject, and hence also the subjective complement, of an infinitive are in the accusative case. The perfect passive and future active infinitives agree with the subject in gender and number. We call an infinitive with subject accusative an infinitive phrase. The infinitive phrases in the examples on page 398 are **mē abīre, tē hoc facere, puerōs domum īre, Lūcium esse amīcum meum, tē hoc fēcisse,** and **sē fore amīcum meum.**

INFINITIVE PHRASE

Some verbs *must* be followed by an infinitive phrase, i.e. an infinitive with subject accusative. One of these is **iubeō, -ēre, iussī, iussum,** *order.*

> Mē abīre iussit.   *He ordered me to go away.*

Other verbs *may* take infinitive phrases as their objects.

> Tē hoc facere cupit.   *She wants you to do this.*
> Puerōsne domum īre patientur?   *Will they allow the boys to go home?*
> Lūcium esse amīcum meum optō.   *I wish Lucius to be my friend.*

Remember that some of these verbs may also take objective infinitives.

> Hoc facere cupit.   *She wants to do this.*
> Lūcī esse amīcus optō.   *I wish to be Lucius' friend.*)

The English infinitive phrase cannot always be used to translate a Latin infinitive phrase.

> Tē hoc fēcisse gaudet.   *She is glad that you have done this.*
> Puerōs domum īre prohibēbunt.   *They will prevent the boys from going home.*
> Lūcius sē fore amīcum meum promittit.   *Lucius promises to be my friend.*

COMPLEMENTARY INFINITIVE

Some verbs need an infinitive to complete their meaning. These verbs are called modal verbs, and the infinitive which they govern is called the complementary infinitive. The modal verbs used in this book are **audeō, -ēre, ausus sum,** *dare,* **possum, posse, potuī, ___,** *be able, can,* and **soleō, -ēre, solitus sum,** *be accustomed, do usually.*

> Hoc facere audeō.   *I dare to do this.*
> Hoc facere possum.   *I am able to do this. I can do this.*
> Hoc facere soleō.   *I am accustomed to doing this. I usually do this.*

Many verbs which govern an infinitive phrase need a complementary infinitive instead when they are passive.

> Abīre iussus sum.   *I was ordered to go away.*
> Puerī domum īre prohibēbuntur.   *The boys will be prevented from going home.*

Some intransitive verbs may take a complementary infinitive. Three such verbs which you should learn are **cessō, -āre, -āvī, -ātum,** *pause, hesitate,*

dubitō, -āre, -āvī, -ātum, *doubt, hesitate,* and **valeō, -ēre, -uī, -itum**, *be well, be strong.*

Discēdere $\left.\begin{array}{l}\text{cessāvit.}\\ \text{dubitāvit.}\end{array}\right\}$ *He hesitated to leave.*

Stāre nōn valeō.   *I am not strong enough to stand.*

VOCABULARY

BASIC WORDS

audeō, -ēre, ausus sum *dare*	iubeō, -ēre, iussī, iussum *bid, order*
cessō, -āre, -āvī, -ātum *pause, hesitate*	iūrō, -āre, -āvī, -ātum *swear*
cogō, -ere, coēgī, coactum *collect* (w. acc.); *compel* (w. inf. phrase)	soleō, -ēre, solitus sum *be accustomed, do usually*
doleō, -ēre, -uī, -itum *suffer pain* (intrans.); *cause pain* (w. dat.); *lament* (w. acc.); *be sorry* (w. inf. phrase)	spērō, -āre, -āvī, -ātum *expect; hope, hope for*
dubitō, -āre, -āvī, -ātum *doubt, hesitate*	valeō, -ēre, -uī, -itum *be strong, be well*

Notes: 1. Verbs of *hoping, promising,* and *swearing* are not followed by an objective infinitive, as in English, but by an infinitive phrase.

Mē hoc factūrum spērō.   *I hope to do this.*
Mē hoc factūrum prōmittō.   *I promise to do this.*
Mē hoc factūrum iūrō.   *I swear to do this.*

2. In the imperative **valeō** means *farewell, goodbye.*

A blacksmith at the forge, from Roman Britain, 3rd c. A.D.

■ LEARNING ENGLISH THROUGH LATIN

audacious	*bold or daring; fearless*
audacity	*brazen boldness; insolence*
cessation	*a ceasing or stopping*
cogent	*compelling*
desperate	*lacking hope; reckless of consequences*
indubitably	*undoubtedly; without question*
invalidate	*to make null or void*
valiant	*characterized by courage or valor*

▬ PRACTICE ▬

A. Rewrite each of the following sentences replacing one of the words with a synonym from the English derivatives listed in this lesson.

1. She did not sign the contract, so it was nullified. 2. He had the temerity to criticize his boss. 3. I feel I must comply; these are convincing arguments. 4. The figure skaters will unquestionably win a gold medal. 5. The mountain climbers faced the challenge with a courageous spirit. 6. The board voted for the termination of the project. 7. Our present situation is hopeless.

B. Pronounce, identify, and translate:

1. potuērunt 2. poterunt 3. poterātis 4. potuerātis 5. potuerō 6. poterō 7. posuistis 8. potuistis 9. possumus 10. potueris

Frieze: wool merchants displaying their cloth—Museo della Civiltà Romana, Rome. Pompeii contained a wool dealers' market which attracted buyers from Italy and the provinces.

C.   Rewrite, with the verb in the passive:

EXAMPLE:
     Hostīs cogēmus fugere.
     Hostēs ā nōbīs fugere cogentur.

1. Cīvīs servōs esse coēgit.   2. Rēx aliēnōs urbem praeterīre iussit.
3. Virginem prōhibuerant mentem mūtāre.   4. Vōs abīre iubēbō.   5. Nostrī
hostīs urbem adīre prōhibēbant.

D.   Pronounce and translate:

1. Aurum cupiō.   2. Aurum humō tollere cupiō.   3. Tē aurum humō
tollere cupiō.   4. Sē vīllam tot aureīs vēndidisse gaudēbat.   5. Sē vīllam
aureīs tam paucīs vēndidisse dolēbat.   6. Iūrat sē frātrem repertūram.
7. Spērābant sē ad castra quattuor hōrīs perventūrōs.   8. Prōmīserat sē
nōn diū domī morātūrum.   9. Valētisne tēla conicere?   10. In silvīs nocte
errāre solet.

E.   Translate: Note that two of these English infinitives are not translated by
Latin infinitives.

1. We ought to stand in awe of the gods.   2. They dared to betray their
fatherland.   3. He hesitated to go away from home.   4. We have come
here to see you.   5. This bird is no longer able to fly.   6. They decided
to run to the shore.   7. Had you hesitated to cross the stream?   8. The
news was wonderful to hear.   9. He will not allow you to perish.   10. It
pleased the horses to feed upon the grass.

F.   Identify the use of each infinitive in the sentences you have just translated
in part E.

G.   Pronounce and translate:

1. Sī rēgem et propinquōs discēdere ex urbe cogere temptāverimus, ab eīs
quī illī favent cogēmur ipsī abīre.   2. Quia dare tōtam pecūniam quam
frātrī dēbuērunt nōn potuērunt hic īrā in illōs mōtus est.   3. Quis inimīcōs
quī mihi nocēre cupiunt mē petere prōhibēbit?   4. Sedēre sub sōle ante
aedīs nec domō discēdere solēbat, nam nē ad vīcīnōs quidem ambulāre
valēbat.   5. Cūr cessās patriae servīre? Verērisne mortis faciem aspicere,
vel spērās tē in aeternum vīctūrum?

READING

Evil Begets Evil

Ut Tarquinius moribundus iacet Tanaquil nēminem rēgiam inīre patitur, per altam fenestram autem populum adloquitur iubetque bonō animō esse. "Rēgem," inquit "quī nōn graviter vulnerātus est, paucīs diēbus valitūrum spērō. Vōs ipsum mox vīsūrōs prōmittō; interim vōs iubet Ser. Tulliō parēre,

5   quī omnibus rēgis officiīs fungētur." Sīc ubi paucīs post diēbus mors rēgis populō aperta est cīvēs omnēs Serviō parēre solitī sunt, quī igitur sine ūllō negōtiō rēx dēlectus est. Tullius spērāvit Tarquinī fīliōs tālem inimīcitiam sibi nōn ostentūrōs esse quālem Ancī fīliī Tarquiniō, itaque duās fīliās suās iuvenibus rēgiīs, Lūciō atque Arruntī Tarquiniīs, in mātrimōnium dedit.

10   Servius cēnsum īnstituī iussit quō omnīs cīvīs variīs ordinibus distribuit. Dehinc bellī pācisque mūnera et officia nōn viritim, ut ante, sed prō habitū pecūniārum cuique commissa sunt: sīc dīvitēs multam, parvam pauperēs, potentiam grātiamque in rē publicā habuērunt. Eō tempore mīlia octōgintā cīvium cēnsa sunt, in quō numerō nōn inclūduntur quī pecūniae inopiā

15   arma ferre prohibitī sunt. Ad eam multitūdinem urbs quoque amplificāta est: rēx addidit duōs montīs, Quirīnālem Vīminālemque; inde deinceps auxit Esquiliās, ibique ipse habitābat, nam spērābat sē hōc modō dīgnitātem locō adiectūrum. In monte Aventīnō ingentem aedem Diānae cōnstituit, quam deam ut omnēs Latīnī colēbant, urbs Rōma nunc caput rērum omnibus

20   Latīnīs facta est.

---

19. caput rērum = *the capital*

Servius iam ūsū haud dubiē rēgnō potītus erat, sed eī ab ūnō ex fīliīs L. Tarquinī Prīscī invīsum est. Hic L. Tarquinius, homō animō audācī ferōcīque, frātrem habuerat Arruntem Tarquinium, mītis ingenī iuvenem. Hīs duōbus, ut ante dictum est, duae Tulliae rēgis fīliae nūpserant, et ipsae longē dispārēs mōribus, altera mītis, altera ferox. Forte duo violentia ingenia matrimōniō 25 nōn iuncta erant, sed ferox uxor mītī marītō, ferōcī marītō mītis uxor datae erant. Dolēbat ferox Tullia nihil māteriae in virō neque ad cupiditātem neque ad audāciam esse; coepit tōta in alterum Tarquinium āvertī eumque mīrārī, eum virum vocāre ac vērum fīlium rēgiī sanguinis. Contrahit celeriter similitūdō eōs, ut saepe accidit—malum malō aptum est—sed initium 30 malōrum ā fēminā ortum est. Ea aliēnum virum sēcrētīs sermōnibus adīre solēbat, in quibus nūllīs verbōrum contumēliīs dē virō ad frātrem, dē sorōre ad virum, parcēbat. Celeriter adulēscentem suae temeritātis implēvit, quī cupere suā uxōre sē līberāre et alteram Tulliam in mātrimōnium dūcere coepit. 35

READING COMPREHENSION

1. What did Queen Tanaquil say to the populace? **2.** How did Servius help the rich and hurt the poor? **3.** How did Servius enlarge the city? **4.** How would you describe the two sons of L. Tarquinius Priscus? **5.** How did the beginning of evil come from the evils of the younger Tullia?

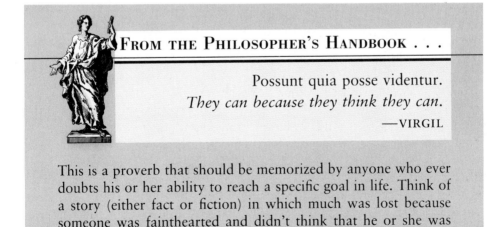

FROM THE PHILOSOPHER'S HANDBOOK . . .

Possunt quia posse videntur.
They can because they think they can.
—VIRGIL

This is a proverb that should be memorized by anyone who ever doubts his or her ability to reach a specific goal in life. Think of a story (either fact or fiction) in which much was lost because someone was fainthearted and didn't think that he or she was able.

---

33. temeritātis: partitive or objective genitive with verbs of *filling* and *emptyin*

LESSON 36

Indirect Statements; Tenses of the Infinitive

The construction of the Colosseum was a large government project, seen here
as it appeared circa 200 A.D.—Museo della Civilità Romana, Rome

GOVERNMENT CONTRACTS

Not surprisingly, government contracts were an important part of big business in Roman times. These were awarded to the highest bidder by the Censors, a board of two who were elected every five years from men who had held the consulate. The government contracts for military equipment and for public works were much like ours; in addition there were contracts for the government monopolies on mining, salt production, public welfare, and the collecting of taxes. The tax contracts, invariably awarded to joint-stock companies of Knights, enabled the government to start the fiscal year with money in hand, leaving it to the company with the highest bid to collect enough money over and above the taxes due to reimburse itself for the bid, to pay dividends to shareholders, and to pay its employees, the **publicānī**. By the time the cost of these necessary profits had been passed down to the taxpayer, the tax was very much higher than the amount the government had actually collected. This made the publicans even more unpopular than tax collectors usually are.

The public welfare contracts chiefly involved the distribution of free or affordable grain to the urban poor. As the empire grew it included in its boundaries areas which were more efficient wheat producers than Italy, especially Sicily, the Black Sea countries, and Egypt. Free trade made it impossible for the Italian small holders to compete, especially as many farms had fallen into disrepair while their proprietors were on military service. The farmers sold their holdings and migrated to the towns, where their military and agricultural skills were not much in demand. The small holdings were combined into large ranches (**lātifundia**), raising sheep in the south and cattle in the north. Wool and leather were, of course, much in demand for the equipping of the armies. Italy is perfectly adapted for ranching, offering as it does upland pastures for summer and winter grazing in the plains. Even the production of wine and oil became big business, as the

(Continued)

405

small vineyards and olive groves were combined into large, efficiently run estates.

Hence as the home grown supply of grain dwindled the number of urban unemployed who had to be fed grew. Beginning in the second century B.C. attempts were made to halt this vicious cycle, usually agrarian legislation which took the land which was technically state owned from the hands of the wealthy proprietors and divided it among the urban poor as small farms. Similar laws awarded small farms, by way of pension, to discharged soldiers. But economic forces, combined with the lack of agricultural skills on the part of both urban proletariat and discharged soldier, guaranteed that the holdings would soon find their way back into the hands of the big businessmen. The little place in the country sounded very good to the city slum dweller or soldier on duty, but the hard realities of farming always proved less attractive than idleness in the city, where **pānēs et circēnsēs** were available. Attempts were also made, especially by the Flavian emperors, to provide employment in the city. The Colosseum, though a marvel of engineering, was deliberately built by old-fashioned, less efficient methods in order to provide more work. Vespasian is even said to have bought and suppressed a labor saving invention, a new kind of crane which would replace some manpower. But a little income for work always seemed less desirable than a little income for nothing. In the end the existence of a large number of urban unemployed seemed so much a matter of course that Constantine, when he founded Constantinople as an eastern capital, took half of Rome's mob to stock its empty streets and alleys.

ANCIENT ROME LIVES ON . . .

What social issues so prevalent in modern times were just as prevalent in Ancient Rome?

SYNTAX

INDIRECT STATEMENTS

A statement which is not quoted directly, with quotation marks, but is reported indirectly, is called an indirect statement. In English an indirect statement may be either an infinitive phrase or a clause introduced by *that*.

They report this to be true.   *They report that this is true.*

In Latin, however, an indirect statement is always an infinitive phrase and never a clause.

Id vērum esse nūntiant.

Unless the infinitive is used impersonally, the accusative subject must always be expressed.

Ad summum montem ante noctem perventum esse dīxērunt.
They said that the mountain-top had been arrived at before night.
Sē ad summum montem ante noctem pervēnisse dīxērunt.
They said that they had arrived at the mountain-top before night.

A Publican engaged in the unpopular task of tax collecting, 2nd c. A.D.—Germany

■ TENSES OF THE INFINITIVE

The tenses of verbs are called absolute tenses because they refer to real time, past, present, or future. The tenses of infinitives are relative tenses, and tell only whether the action takes place before (perfect tense), during (present tense), or after (future tense) the action of the verb.

Id vērum esse nūntiant.   *They report that this is true.*
Id vērum fuisse nūntiant.   *They report that this has been true.*
Id vērum futūrum esse (fore) nūntiant.   *They report that this will be true.*
Id vērum esse nūntiāvērunt.   *They reported that this was true.*
Id vērum fuisse nūntiāvērunt.   *They reported that this had been true.*
Id vērum futūrum esse (fore) nūntiāvērunt.
     They reported that this would be true.

If you have trouble deciding on the tense of the verb in English, begin by translating literally: e.g., *They reported this to be (to have been, to be about to be) true.*

■ VERBS GOVERNING INDIRECT STATEMENTS

Besides verbs of *saying*, verbs of *informing, thinking, knowing,* and *perceiving* may also take indirect statements.

Id vērum esse meminerāmus.   *We remembered that this was true.* (knowing)
Id vērum esse vīdērunt.   *They saw that this was true.* (perceiving)
Id vērum esse audiō.   *I hear that this is true.* (perceiving)
Id vērum esse crēdunt.   *They believe that this is true.* (thinking)
Mē id vērum esse docuit.   *He taught me that this was true.* (informing)

All of the verbs in this lesson can govern indirect statements. Verbs of *saying*: **dīcō, negō**; of *informing*: **moneō, scrībō**; of *thinking*: **exīstimō, putō**; of *knowing*: **nōscō, sciō**; of *perceiving*: **cernō, sentiō**.

■ PRONOUNS IN INDIRECT STATEMENTS

A reflexive pronoun in an indirect statement refers back to the nominative subject of the verb governing the indirect statement, not to the accusative subject of the indirect statement.

Virgō eum sibi nocuisse dēmōnstrāvit.
The girl pointed out that he had harmed her.

Hence a first person subject in a direct statement is represented by a reflexive pronoun in an indirect statement.

"Hoc" inquit "ego faciam."	*She said, "I shall do this."*
Sē hoc factūram dīxit.	*She said that she would do this.*

Note the following conversions of the second person pronoun:

Mihi "Tū errāvistī" inquit.	*She said to me, "You were wrong."*
Mē errāvisse mihi dīxit.	*She said to me that I had been wrong.*
Tibi "Tū errāvistī" inquit.	*She said to you, "You were wrong."*
Tē errāvisse tibi dīxit.	*She said to you that you had been wrong.*
Eī "Tū errāvistī" inquit.	*She said to him, "You were wrong."*
Eum errāvisse eī dīxit.	*She said to him that he had been wrong.*

Translation Help

Since the use of infinitives in Latin is on the whole quite different from their use in English, it is important to remember a few important points:

1. When you see an infinitive in a Latin sentence which you are about to translate, decide immediately how it is going to fit into the sentence: Is it used as subject, object, complementary infinitive, or the infinitive of an infinitive phrase? Otherwise you may come to the end of your translation and find that although your sentence makes sense you have an infinitive left over. For example, in the sentence **amīcum in lītore stāre vīdī**, if you begin by finding the verb and an accusative to be its object, you will end up with *I saw my friend on the shore* instead of I *saw that my friend was standing on the shore.*

2. Latin infinitives often cannot or should not be translated by English infinitives. A subjective or objective infinitive will often sound better as an English gerund. **Tē vidēre mihi placet.** *Seeing you pleases me.* An indirect statement translated literally usually makes impossible English. *If I see him I'll tell him I saw you*, literally translated from the Latin, would be *If I shall have seen him I shall say to him myself to have seen you.*

3. English infinitives often cannot be translated by Latin infinitives. None of the infinitives in these sentences could be translated by a Latin infinitive: *This is to be done quickly. This book is interesting to read. I came to see you. He made me do it.* Remember that a Latin infinitive used with a verb has only four uses, and so, if the English infinitive use is not one of those, there will not be an infinitive in Latin. The Latin infinitive is never used as an adjective or an adverb, or to express purpose.

VOCABULARY

BASIC WORDS

cernō, -ere, crēvī, crētum *or* certum
   perceive, determine
dīcō, -ere, dīxī, dictum   *say*
exīstimō, -āre, -āvī, -ātum   *suppose,*
   consider
moneō, -ēre, -uī, -itum   *warn, advise*
negō, -āre, -āvī, -ātum (w. acc.)   *deny,*
   refuse; (w. indir. statement) *say . . . not*

nōscō, -ere, nōvī, nōtum   *come to know,*
   find out, learn
putō, -āre, -āvī, -ātum   *think*
sciō, -īre, -īvī, -ītum   *know*
scrībō, -ere, scrīpsī, scrīptum   *write*
sentiō, -īre, sēnsī, sēnsum   *feel, perceive*

Notes: 1. Most verbs of *saying* or *perceiving*, etc. used in the passive, require a
complementary infinitive instead of an indirect statement.

   Pulchra esse dīcitur.   *She is said to be beautiful.*
   Pulchra esse exīstimātur (putātur).   *She is thought to be beautiful.*

2. The alternative fourth principal part of **cernō** is used as an adjective, **certus,**
-a, -um, *sure, certain.* **Mihi certum est,** *for me it is definite = I have decided.*

3. **Negō** makes an indirect statement negative.

   Hostīs ad urbem accēdere negāvit.
   He said that the enemy were not approaching the city.

4. The negative of **sciō** is not **nōn sciō** but **nesciō, -īre, -īvi, ____.**

5. Since **nōscō** means *come to know*, its perfect **nōvī** (*I have come to know*)
means *I know*. The same is true of its compound **cognōscō.**

LEARNING ENGLISH THROUGH LATIN

abnegation	*self-denial; a giving up of rights*
admonish	*to caution against specific faults; warn gently*
cognoscente	*an expert; a person with special knowledge in a particular field*
contradict	*to state the opposite of what someone has said*
dictum	*a formal statement or pronouncement*
nescient	*ignorant; lacking knowledge*
omniscient	*knowing all things*
premonition	*a forewarning, foreboding*

PRACTICE

A. Show the relationship of the English words to the given Latin words:

1. diction, edict, predict: **dīcō**   2. consent, sentient, sentiment: **sentiō**
3. negation, negative **negō**

B. Using the list of prefixes and suffixes in the Appendix, see how many English words you can find which are derived from:

1. **putō** (forms in *-pute* and *putat-*)   2. **scrībō** (forms in *-scribe* and *script-*)

C. Pronounce and translate:

1. Legere linguam Latīnam ā patre doctus sum.   2. Ab hostibus coactī erātis pecūniam aliāsque rēs eīs adferre.   3. Illa urbs dīcitur ā cīvibus magna esse.   4. Dux hostīs adīre signō monitus est.   5. Domō abīre inopiā prohibēberis.   6. Omnēs ā rēge iussī sunt in Forum convenīre.   7. Ea mihi vidētur pulchra esse.   8. Hic homō ab omnibus fortiter pugnāvisse exīstimātur.   9. Līberī ā magistrō docēbantur Asiam longē abesse.   10. Hostēs ā Senātōribus putantur ā patriā discessūrī esse.

D. Rewrite the sentences in C with the verb in the active voice, making the necessary changes in case uses and pronouns, and changing the infinitive construction if necessary.

> Pater linguam Latīnam legere mē docuit.

E. Change from direct to indirect statements (infinitive phrases), remembering to replace forms of **inquam** with forms of **dīcō** or **iubeō**, and to change the pronouns where necessary.

> Eī "Ad oppidum tuum" inquit "discēdam."
> Eī dīxit sē ad eius oppidum discessūrum (discessūram).

1. Putābāsne, "Hae aedēs magnae sunt"?   2. Herī amīcīs "Valēte" inquit.
3. Mihi "Tuō cōnsiliō" scrīpsit "ūtar."   4. Graecī clāmābant "Hostēs victī sunt; urbs est nostra!"   5. "Crās" inquit "Rōmā discēdam."

F. Change from indirect to direct, remembering to replace forms of **dīcō** and **iubeō** with forms of **inquam**, and to change the pronouns where necessary.

> Mihi dīxērunt sē meī oblītōs esse.
> Mihi "Tuī" inquiunt "oblītī sumus."

1. Dīcit sē Rōmam itūram. **2.** Cūr putāvistī tuōs equōs esse bonōs? **3.** Patrem valēre iussī. **4.** Mihi tē mē vidēre cupere scrīpsistī. **5.** Rēgem urbem relinquere dēbēre clāmābunt.

G. Pronounce and translate:

1. Quoniam iste iuvenis clārus tam celeriter quam avis volat currere solēbat eum exīstimāvistis ā nūllīs cursū vincī posse. **2.** Dīcēbat ille nōs dēbēre vīvere et aliōs vīvere patī, nec cuiquam sīve cīvī nostrō sīve hospitī aut impedīmentō esse aut īnstāre aut nocēre, modo sīc enim omnīs posse vītā fēlīcī fruī. **3.** Meīs oculīs vīdī (mīrum vīsū!), at tamen vērum esse nōn crēdidī, deam ipsam mihi adesse tālī fōrmā quālī illa eius imāgō aurea, atque audīvī eam dīcere mē dēbēre deinde amīcō meō invidēre dēsinere. **4.** In aeternum nōs et posterī nostrī meminerimus, nec umquam oblīvīscēmur, vōs fortem ducem nostrum domō exēmisse et nōbīs abstulisse et vinxisse et interfēcisse et in terrā condere etiam prohibuisse ac caput manūsque eius in castrōrum moenibus exposuisse et istīc humī avīs ferās corpore et sanguine eius vēscī passōs esse.

H. Translate:

I have learned by chance that some of the enemy who are making war on us have passed by our camp and crossed the seventy-foot-wide river and are at this moment (**nunc iam**) coming up here to the city.

READING

Developing Reading Skills

Familiar Latin words which will help with unfamiliar ones: **animus, auctor, circum, clāmō, dīgnus, eō, ex, faveō, prae, pāreō, parō,** and **rēx.** English derivatives which will help you to guess intelligently: *approbation, authority, clamor, grade, indignity, necessity, nuptials, onerous, prepare, regal, respond, suffrage, vacuum,* and *vocal.*

A Palace Coup

L. Tarquinius et Tullia secunda quoniam nōn modo amōre inter sē sed etiam
rēgnī cupīdine occupātī erant, cōnstituērunt duplicī caede sē coniugibus
līberāre. Tum ubi domōs vacuās novō mātrimōniō fēcerant iunctī sunt
nuptiīs quās Servius nec prohibēbat nec probābat. Tum vērō in diēs perīculum
et senectūtī Tullī et rēgnō crēscēbat. Iam enim coepit ab scelere ad aliud   5
spectāre mulier scelus, nec nocte nec diē virum conquiēscere patī. Saepe eī
dīcēbat sē frūstrā frātrem eius, suum maritum, eum frūstrā sorōrem suam,
eius uxōrem, interfēcisse, eum enim ipsum esse frātris similem ignāviā.
Negāvit eī, ut patrī eius, peregrīnum rēgnum occupāre necesse esse; dīxit
deōs eum Penātīs patriōsque et patris imāginem et domum rēgiam et in   10
domō rēgāle solium et nōmen Tarquinium creāre vocāreque rēgem. "Mementō" inquit "mē et caput parentis et rēgnum fēcisse dōtāle, tē ergō exigere
dōtis opēs dēbēre."

Tarquinius igitur quōs pater Senātōrēs creāverat ambitiōsē circumībat et
monēbat eōs patris suī beneficiōrum memorīs sibi favēre dēbēre. Dōnīs   15
iuvenēs sibi conciliābat. Postrēmō, ut iam tempus idōneum esse vīsum est,
ipse et quī eī favēbant in Forum cum armīs inrūpērunt. Ibi in rēgiā sēde prō
Cūriā sēdit et Patrēs in Cūriam per praecōnem cītārī iussit. Convēnēre
extemplō, aliī quia iam ante ad hoc praeparātī erant, aliī quia sibi vim
cēterōrum timēbant. Apud quōs Tarquinius ōrātiōnem habuit Servium,   20
ipsum servum servaeque fīlium, post mortem indīgnam parentis suī nōn, ut
ante, per comitia suffrāgiumve populī, nōn Senātōrum auctōritāte, muliebrī
dōnō rēgnum occupāvisse. Cēnsum īnstituisse; pauperibus favisse; dīvitibus
pecūniās occupāvisse et onera omnia tōtīus reī publicae imposuisse.

Huic ōrātiōnī Servius, quī trepidō nūntiō generum suum in soliō sedēre   25
excītātus est, intervēnit. Statim ā vestibulō Cūriae magnā vōce "Quid hoc,"
inquit, "Tarquinī, reī est? Quā tū audāciā vocāre ausus es Patrēs aut in sēde
sedēre meā?" Ubi ille ferōciter ad haec respondet sē patris suī tenēre sēdem,
sē fīlium rēgis rēgnī hērēdem esse, clāmor ab utrīusque fautōribus orītur, et
concursus undique populī in Cūriam. Tum Tarquinius necessitāte iam etiam   30
ipsā coactus est dīrum facinus facere, quī, ut rēgī et aetāte et vīribus multō
praestābat, medium arripuit Servium et ē Cūriā extulit et dē Cūriae gradibus

---

4. in diēs: an idiom meaning *from day to day, from one day to the next*   18. per praecōnem:
per with the accusative is used when a person becomes a means or instrument Convēnēre:
the ending -ēre is an alternative for -ērunt   32. medium . . . Servium: *seized the middle of
Servius = seized Servius around the waist.*

414

The interior of the imperial Curia, 3rd c. A.D. Roman kings ruled from a far smaller structure.

35

humum dēiēcit. Inde Senātōrēs coactum in Cūriam rediit. Vērum est quod scrīpsit Ennius, "Amīcus certus rē incertā cernitur": fūgērunt rēgis appāritōrēs atque comitēs. Ipse prope exanimis sine rēgiō comitātū domum sē recipere temptābat.

READING COMPREHENSION

1. What crimes did Lucius Tarquin and the second Tullia commit? **2.** What complaints did Tullia make to her husband? **3.** Why did Tullia feel that it was not necessary for her husband to seize a foreign kingdom? **4.** How was Tarquin able to summon the Senators? **5.** What did Tarquin do to Servius?

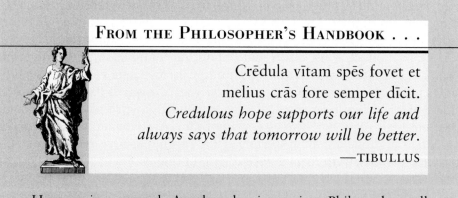

FROM THE PHILOSOPHER'S HANDBOOK . . .

Crēdula vītam spēs fovet et
melius crās fore semper dīcit.
*Credulous hope supports our life and
always says that tomorrow will be better.*
—TIBULLUS

Hope springs eternal. Another day is coming. Philosophers all through the ages have provided sayings to encourage us to carry on and not give up even though the road is long. Are we misled by such sayings?

REVIEW 9

VOCABULARY DRILL

A. Give the other nominative singular forms, and the meaning, of **certus**.

B. Give the other principal parts and the meaning of each verb:

audeō	dēsinō	iubeō	optō	sentiō
cernō	dīcō	iūrō	patior	spērō
cessō	doleō	meminī	possum	temptō
coepī	dubitō	moneō	potior	ūtor
cōgō	exīstimō	moror	properō	valeō
cognōscō	fruor	negō	putō	vereor
cōnstituō	fungor	nesciō	sciō	vēscor
cupiō	gaudeō	nōscō	soleō	
dēbeō	īnstituō	oblīvīscor	scrībō	

C. Give the meanings of the adverbs **numquam** and **umquam**.

D. Give the following meanings:

1. Cōgō with an accusative object; with an infinitive phrase.   **2. Cōnstituō** with an accusative object; with an objective infinitive.   **3. Dēbeō** with an accusative object; with an objective infinitive.   **4. Doleō** with no object; with a dative of reference; with an accusative object; with an infinitive phrase.   **5. Patior** with an accusative object; with an infinitive phrase.

DRILL ON FORMS

Give the following synopses in the indicative and (where possible) the imperative:

1. fruor in the first person singular   **2. possum** in the third person singular
3. gaudeō in the third person plural   **4. ūtor** in the first person plural

LISTENING AND SPEAKING

Bargaining for Bricks

Marcus has come to the brick factory to buy bricks for a new barn he is planning to build. There are bricks for a bargain price at the brick factory, but there is also Livia who knows how to settle accounts!

1. **lībertus, -ī, m.—** *freedman*

2. **pretium, -ī, n.—** *price*

3. **patrōnus, -ī, m.—** *patron*

4. **lātifundium, -ī, n.—** *a large estate, big farm*

5. **cūro, -āre, -āvī, ātum—***care for, take care of*

6. **cotīdie (adv.)—***daily*

MĀRCUS: Heus, līberte[1], hicne est locus ubi laterēs emere possum?

GLYCO: Ad officīnam ipsam, agricola, vēnistī. Hīc laterēs omnis generis facimus. Quālis cupis? Mūrō idonēōs?

MĀRCUS: Laterēs mūrō idonēōs petō sed pretiō[2] magnō nōn emō.

GLYCO: Fēlix eris! Hīc sunt laterēs pretiō parvō, nam laterāriae dominī sunt Quintus Iūlius et uxor. Quintus Iūlius patrōnus[3] meus est, et ergō nōmine Quintus Iūlius Glyco sum.

MĀRCUS: Nōmen Quintī Iulī cognōvī, nam quīdam eum dominum lātifundī[4] prope fundum meum esse dīcunt. Tenetne etiam ille dīves officīnās in urbe?

GLYCO: Tenet aliquās, sed dominus Iulius lātifundium et agrōs cūrat.[5] Uxōrī autem suae laterāria cūrae est. Cotīdiē[6] uxor nōmine Līvia

(*below*) **Opus reticulatum**, a network of stones set in concrete—House of Livia, Rome   (*left*) A mason's tools—Archeological Museum, Aquileia

cum duōbus servīs in officīnam venit. Fēmina vulpes[7] est, quod omnis pecūniae ratiōnem habēre cupit. Mēhercule[8] ecce illa!

LĪVIA: Heus, Glyco, cūr in portā stās et garrīs?[9] Nōnne tibi labōrēs sunt? Mementō, labor omnia vincit!

GLYCO: Est, domina, mihi labor quod hic agricola laterēs emere cupit.

LĪVIA: Bene, tū et servī auxilium agricolae dāte, ut ego tuās ratiōnēs officīnae inspiciō.

GLYCO: Quot laterēs, agricola, cupiēbās? Quid aedificābis?

MĀRCUS: Novum horreum aedificābō et multī laterēs mihi dēsunt. Mīlle laterēs emam, sī nimium[10] oneris bōbus nōn erunt.

GLYCO: Nimium ponderis erit itaque dīmidiam[11] partem tibi vendam.

LĪVIA: Nōnne habitās, agricola, prope fundōs nostrōs? Cūr, Glyco, quīngentōs laterēs in agricolae plaustrō servī nōn impōnunt et alteram dīmidiam partem in sarrācō nostrō, nam crās sarrācum in agrōs ad vīllam nostram exībit.

GLYCO: Statim, domina, faciō. Mīlle laterēs centum et mīlle sestertiīs[12], pretiō parvō, vendō. Heus, servī, quīngentōs laterēs in agricolae plaustrō impōnite!

MĀRCUS. Euge,[13] sunt mihi ūndecim aureī. Grātiās vōbīs agō. Valē, domina; valē et tū, Glyco.

LĪVIA: Valē, agricola. Euge, Glyco, ratiōnes tuae ad nummum[14] conveniunt. Hōdie fabrīs[15] et tibi mercēdēs[16] dabō. Reliqua pecūnia lūcrum Iūliīs erit!

7. vulpes, -is, m. + f.—*fox, vixen*

8. mēhercule (interj.)—*by Hercules!*

9. garriō, -īre, -īvī, ītum—*to chatter*

10. nimium, -ī, n.—*too much*

11. dīmidius, -a, -um—*half*

12. sestertius, -ī, m.—*a silver coin*

13. euge (interj.)—*bravo*

14. nummus, -ī, m.—*penny, coin*

15. faber, fabrī, m.—*worker, laborer*

16. merces, mercēdis, m.—*wages, pay*

A. After an oral presentation of the dialogue, be prepared to tell how many bricks Marcus buys, how much he pays for them, and how they will be delivered to his farm.

B. Answer the following questions in Latin.

1. Quid Mārcus agricola emere cupit?   2. Quis patrōnus Glycōnis est?   3. Cui ratiōnēs officīnae cūrae sunt? 4. Quotiēns Līvia in officīnam venit?   5. Cūr Līvia sarrācum in agrōs crās exitūrum dīcit?

TRACES OF ROMAN CIVILIZATION TODAY

Yugoslavia—Split

Detail of the forecourt

Split, in the center of the Yugoslav Adriatic coast, has a two-thousand year history that has left its mark on the whole area. One of the most outstanding Roman emperors, Diocletian, came from this area. He was born in humble circumstances in about 245 A.D. and his official name was Gaius Aurelius Valerius Diocletianus. The army was his path to greatness. He began his career as an ordinary soldier but quickly advanced to general, and finally to emperor of the greatest empire of his age. In fact he was proclaimed emperor by his troops in 284 A.D. He was responsible for many reforms in government, military and economic affairs, which prolonged the life of the Roman Empire. He abdicated of his own free will and in about 300 A.D. built a vast place where he intended to spend his last days and then be buried in the monumental mausoleum that he erected for himself.

Defensive Tower

Model of Diocletian's Palace

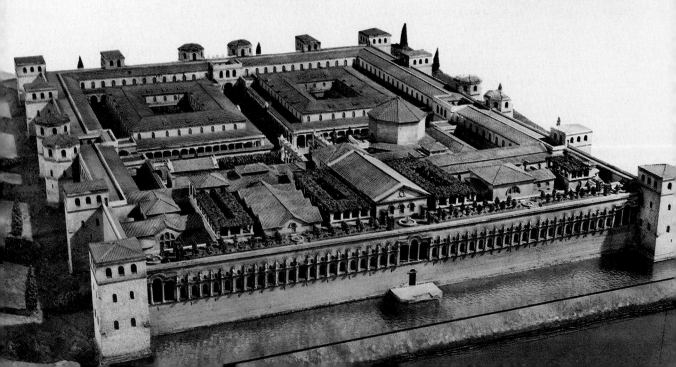

Interior view of the Mausoleum

Forecourt of the Palace

Split

After his death in 313 A.D., the palace became state property and served as a prison for dethroned Roman emperors. In 614 A.D. when the town was destroyed by warlike tribes from the north, the inhabitants found shelter in the Palace and founded a new town there in which there was room for 3,000 to 4,000 people. This new town was first called Spaleteum but the name was later changed to Split.

The palace was built of white stone and had gigantic proportions. Its sides were 215 by 180 metres long and it covered an area of 30,000 square meters. It was both a summer residence and a fortress built in the manner of Roman military camps. The southern side, overlooking the sea, looked like a luxurious Roman villa. The other three sides, forever threatened by the warlike tribes from the north, were fortified with strong ramparts and defended by sixteen square and octagonal towers.

Four gates led to the palace. The north gate, called the Golden Gate, was the main and most richly decorated of the four. It was built in the shape of a Roman triumphal arch and the whole wall was richly decorated with niches in which sculptures used to stand.

The Mausoleum, an octagonal building once surrounded by a covered area with granite and marble columns above which used to be a stone-coffered vault, is partly preserved.

All in all, the Palace is one of the most famous, most monumental and best preserved examples of Roman architecture.

LESSON 37

Comparison of Adjectives

Interior of the Pantheon (138 A.D.), showing the marble floor, concrete dome, and oculus

ARCHITECTURE

The Romans' technological contributions to the art and science of architecture are inestimable. They were the inventors of the arch and its variations, the barrel vault, cross vault, annular vault, and dome, and were also the first to develop poured concrete construction. Early Roman architecture was of the simplest, most utilitarian kind, plain buildings of baked or (more often) unbaked brick. The arch and its variations were the products not of architects, but of engineers, a solution to the problem of spanning spaces wider than post-and-lintel construction can cover. The use of vaults to support the seats enabled the Romans to build theatres and race courses not merely into hillsides, in the Greek way, but anywhere they wanted them. They could also, with vaults, raise their temples on high, artificial platforms instead of seeking natural heights. Triumphal statues were also given high, vaulted (not solid) bases, which eventually developed into the uniquely Roman, elaborately decorated triumphal arch. It is clear that they thought of the arch and vault as utilitarian, not beautiful, since in the actual temples they built false rectangular doorways inside their arches and hung false flat ceilings from the vaulted roofs. With the development, early in the first century B.C., of poured concrete construction it became much easier to decorate the undersides of vaulted and domed roofs with coffering or the "pumpkin-dome" pattern, and the Romans became aware of the aesthetic possibilities of their utilitarian invention.

Except for the round temples, which presumably developed from the round hut, the Romans seem to have taken their basic temple design from the Etruscans, but to have modified it with details taken from the Greeks. A Greek temple was designed to be viewed from any direction, and more often on a level or even from above: a Roman temple was typically designed to be seen from below and strictly from the front. Most Roman temples were

(Continued)

provided with forecourts of one kind or another which prevent them from being approached except from the front.

The Romans used all types of columns and entablatures except the Doric, to which they preferred the Tuscan. The Doric appears only in conjunction with other orders. Best of all they liked the Corinthian and the Composite, the first a Greek variation on the Ionic, the second a Roman invention.

(*below left*) The Ionic style: The Temple of Portunus (a numen of the Tiber Port) near the Forum Boarium in Rome, 2nd c. B.C.
(*below right*) The Triumphal Arch of the Emperor Titus, 81 A.D.

ANCIENT ROME LIVES ON . . .

What buildings do you know of that reflect Roman architecture?

FORMS

COMPARISON OF ADJECTIVES

Besides gender, number, and case, adjectives have another attribute, which we call degree. The three degrees of an adjective are the *positive* (e.g. *long*), *the comparative* (e.g. *longer*), and *the superlative* (e.g. *longest*). To compare an adjective is to give its three degrees (*long, longer, longest*). In English the usual suffixes for the comparison of an adjective are *-er* (comparative) and *-est* (superlative). In Latin they are **-ior** and **-issimus,** and are added to the base of the adjective.

| longus | longior | longissimus |
| *long* | *longer* | *longest* |

| gravis | gravior | gravissimus |
| *heavy* | *heavier* | *heaviest* |

| fēlīx | fēlīcior | fēlīcissimus |
| *lucky* | *luckier* | *luckiest* |

ADJECTIVES ENDING IN -ER

Adjectives which end in **-er** in the masculine nominative singular have normal comparatives, but for the superlative they add **-rimus** to the masculine nominative singular (not **-issimus** to the base). This is true whether they are first and second or third declension adjectives, and whether or not the -e is part of the base.

| miser | miserior | miserrimus |
| *wretched* | *more wretched* | *most wretched* |

| pulcher | pulchrior | pulcherrimus |
| *beautiful* | *more beautiful* | *most beautiful* |

| celer | celerior | celerrimus |
| *swift* | *swifter* | *swiftest* |

| ācer | ācrior | ācerrimus |
| *sharp* | *sharper* | *sharpest* |

ADJECTIVES ENDING IN -ILIS

Most adjectives ending in **-ilis** are compared in the usual way, but there are six which form the superlative by adding **-limus** to the base:

facilis	facilior	facillimus
easy	*easier*	*easiest*
difficilis	difficilior	difficillimus
difficult	*more difficult*	*most difficult*
gracilis	gracilior	gracillimus
thin	*thinner*	*thinnest*
humilis	humilior	humillimus
low	*lower*	*lowest*
similis	similior	simillimus
like	*more like*	*most like*
dissimilis	dissimilior	dissimillimus
unlike	*more unlike*	*most unlike*

DECLENSION OF THE COMPARATIVE

The comparative is a third declension consonant-stem. Unlike positive adjectives of the third declension, it does not have the **-i** in the ablative singular, the genitive plural, the neuter nominative and accusative plural, or the masculine and feminine accusative plural.

DECLENSION OF THE COMPARATIVE

	SINGULAR		PLURAL	
	MASC. & FEM.	NEUT.	MASC. & FEM.	NEUT.
NOM.	longior	longius	longiōrēs	longiōra
GEN.	longiōris	longiōris	longiōrum	longiōrum
DAT.	longiōrī	longiōrī	longiōribus	longiōribus
ACC.	longiōrem	longius	longiōrēs	longiōra
ABL.	longiōre	longiōre	longiōribus	longiōribus

■ DECLENSION OF THE SUPERLATIVE

The superlative is an adjective of the first and second declensions.

DECLENSION OF THE SUPERLATIVE

SINGULAR

	MASCULINE	FEMININE	NEUTER
NOM.	longissimus	longissima	longissimum
GEN.	longissimī	longissimae	longissimī
DAT.	longissimō	longissimae	longissimō
ACC.	longissimum	longissimam	longissimum
ABL.	longissimō	longissimā	longissimō

PLURAL

	MASCULINE	FEMININE	NEUTER
NOM.	longissimī	longissimae	longissima
GEN.	longissimōrum	longissimārum	longissimōrum
DAT.	longissimīs	longissimīs	longissimīs
ACC.	longissimōs	longissimās	longissima
ABL.	longissimīs	longissimīs	longissimīs

FROM THE PHILOSOPHER'S HANDBOOK . . .

Simia quam similis, turpissima bestia, nōbīs!
How like us is that very ugly beast the monkey!
—CICERO

What do you think Cicero meant by this exclamation?

■ PARTITIVE GENITIVE WITH THE COMPARATIVE OR SUPERLATIVE

The partitive genitive is often used with a comparative or superlative.

Iūlia est altior puellārum.   *Julia is the taller of the ⟨two⟩ girls.*
Iūlia est altissima puellārum.   *Julia is the tallest of the girls.*

■ COMPARATIVE WITH QUAM

Quam is used after a comparative, like *than* in English, to join the two words which are being compared. The Latin usage differs from the English in that the word following **quam** must be in the same case as the word with which it is being compared.

GEN.   GEN.
Nūllīus virginis pulchriōris quam illīus meminī.
I remember no maiden more beautiful than she.

DAT.   DAT.
Rēgī multō clāriōrī quam tibi pāret.
He obeys a king much more famous than you.

When two qualities are being compared, both adjectives are in the comparative degree.

Vīllam altiōrem quam lātiōrem vīdī.
I saw a farmhouse taller than ⟨it was⟩ wide.

Quam may be used with **ante** and **post** to mean *earlier than* and *later than.*

Domō ante discessit quam eō pervenīre poteram.
He left home earlier than I could get there.

■ ABLATIVE OF DEGREE OF DIFFERENCE WITH THE COMPARATIVE OR SUPERLATIVE

The ablative of degree of difference is often found with a comparative or superlative.

Iūlia est multō altior quam Tullia.   *Julia is much taller than Tullia.*
Iūlia est multō altissima puellārum.   *Julia is much the tallest of the girls.*

(*top*) The Flavian Amphitheatre, 80 A.D. (better known as the Colosseum). Following a convention of Roman architecture, the higher up a column appears, the higher its architectural order. (*bottom*) The Five Orders of Roman Architecture: Tuscan, Doric, Ionic, Composite, and Corinthian

THE FIVE ANTIENT ORDERS OF ROMAN ARCHITECTURE.

Tuscan   Doric   Ionic   Composite   Corinthian

VOCABULARY

BASIC WORDS

exercitus, -ūs, m. *army*

genus, generis, n. *birth; offspring; kind*

mīles, mīlitis, m. *soldier*

plēbs, plēbis, f. *the multitude, the common people*

proelium, -ī, n. *battle*

dissimilis, -e *unlike*

gracilis, -e *thin, slim, scrawny*

humilis, -e *low, humble*

nōbilis, -e *well-known; noble*

adversus (prep. w. acc.) *against*

LEARNING ENGLISH THROUGH LATIN

adversity	*misfortune, trouble*
degenerate	*deteriorate, depreciate*
generate	*to bring into being, produce*
humility	*absence of pride or pretentiousness*
ignoble	*dishonorable, base, mean*
militia	*an army composed of citizens rather than professional soldiers*
plebeian	*vulgar, coarse, common*
regenerate	*(adj.) renewed, restored*

A corner of the ruins of the Emperor Hadrian's villa at Tibur (now Tivoli) showing the functional and decorative use of the arch

PRACTICE

A. Using derivatives in this lesson, restate the following sentences to express the exact opposite:

1. The soldier's arrogance was not acceptable in the eyes of his superiors.
2. She had much good fortune during her long life.   3. The deed was considered most praiseworthy.   4. The situation ameliorated as time went on.   5. In ancient Rome they would have been considered patrician.
6. The speech given at assembly killed the spark of hope the students needed.

B. Pronounce and translate:

1. Haec via longissima omnium est.   2. Haec via longa est.   3. Haec via longior quam illa est.   4. Ūter frātrum humilior est?   5. Quī frāter humilis est?   6. Quis frātrum humillimus est?   7. Quī frāter nōbilissimus est?
8. Tēlum ācrius quam meum invēnī.   9. Tēlum in castrīs ācerrimum invēnī.
10. Tēlum ācre invēnī.

C. Compare these adjectives:

1. amīcus   2. fortis   3. gracilis   4. līber   5. sacer

D. Decline **mare altius** and **via longior.**

E. Translate:

1. I am more like you than he.   2. I am more like you than him.
3 **and** 4. He is more like me than you (this sentence has two meanings in English; translate both).   5. He is more like me than unlike you.

F. Pronounce and translate:

1. Hārum puellārum altera fortior, altera amīcior est; ūtram pulchriōrem habēs?   2. Quae est pulcherrima eārum avium omnium?   3. Ācerrimum tēlum, multō ācriōrem quidem quam tuum, coniēcit.   4. Caesar mihi etiam inimīcior quam tibi, sed Mārcō inimīcissimus est.   5. Quis miserior est quam ego, miserrima in hāc terrā?

G. Translate:

1. That brother of yours is most unlike M. Brutus, "the noblest Roman of them all." 2. I envy a person more fortunate than that one. 3. I have forgotten girls more beautiful than Julia. 4. This poem was written by a poet more famous than our father. 5. I have never seen anyone thinner than your sister.

H. Pronounce and translate:

1. Soror mea et faciē et corporis altitūdine tuae nōn dissimilis, similior est autem Lūcī; sed illīus Senātōris uxōrī simillima est. 2. Num ūllīus fīliae mēns potest esse foedior quam Tulliae, quae cōnsilium cēpit quō pater ipsīus et rēgnum et vītam āmīsit? 3. Negāvit sē illīus urbium grātissimae iam meminisse; quōmodo oblīvīscī poterat locī tantō pulchriōris quam cēterōrum? 4. Iste amīcus — foedum vīsū! — gracilior est quam corpus alicuius quī mortem multīs ante annīs obiit. 5. Quī nostrum exercitum dūcit nōbilissimus ducum nostrōrum, corde tamen humillimus omnium est.

READING

Developing Reading Skills

Familiar Latin words which will help with the unfamiliar ones in this reading: **auctor, cēdō, dō, dominus, ferus, fugiō, habeō, iaciō, iubeō, mīles, moneō, pater, pōnō, praetereō, rēx, stō,** and **vocō.**

English derivatives which will help: *admonition, appellation, authority, cohort, conciliate, consequent, dire, domination, example, ferocious, fraud, gladiator, grade, inhibit, inhuman, lento, militia, paternal, preternatural, querulous, reign, sepulcher, succeed, tumult,* and *vehicle.*

Wicked Street

Ser. Tullius postquam dē Cūriae gradibus ā L. Tarquiniō dēiectus est ut sine
rēgiō comitātū domum sē cōnferēbat ab eīs quī ab Tarquiniō eum consecūtum
missī erant interfectus est. Crēditur, quia ā cēterō scelere nōn abhorret,
admonitū Tulliae id factum esse. Carpentō certē in Forum invecta est, ubi
ēvocāvit virum ē Cūriā rēgemque prīma appellāvit. Ā quō ubi sē ex   5
tantō tumultū domum recipere iussa est ā Forō ad Esquiliās vehēbātur; sed
ut ad summum Cӯprium Vīcum perventum est, ubi carpentum ad dextram
in Urbium Clīvum vertī dēbuit, cōnstitit pavidus atque inhibuit frēnōs is quī
iūmenta agēbat, corpusque Servī humī iacēre dominae ōstendit. Foedissimum
et inhūmānissimum inde trāditur scelus, quō Tullia per patris corpus carpentum   10
ēgisse fertur, partemque sanguinis ac caedis paternae cruentō vehiculō

A contemporary view of **Clīvus Scaurī** on the Caelian Hill in Rome suggests the
atmosphere of the streets traversed by Tullia in her blood spattered **carpentum**.

rettulisse ad Penātīs suōs virīque suī. Via ubi hoc dīrissimum scelerum commissum est deinde Vīcus Scelerātus vocāta est.

15 Ser. Tullius rēgnāvit annōs quattuor et quadrāgintā, rēx et aequior multō et mitior quam is quī eī successit. Inde enim L. Tarquinius rēgnāre coepit, cui Superbō cognōmen ingenium ferox indidit, quia socerum gener sepelīrī prōhibuit — nam Rōmulum quoque nōn sepultum esse crūdēliter dīcēbat — ducēsque Patrum quōs Servī rēbus fāvisse crēdēbat interfēcit. Et quod deinde ab sē ipsō adversus sē exemplum capī posse sciēbat, cohorte rēgiā

20 corpus circumsaepsit; neque enim ad iūs rēgnī quidquam praeter vim habēbat, quoniam neque populī iussū neque auctōritāte Patrum rēx factus erat. Nunc quoque sīc rēgnābat quomodo rēgnō potītus erat; nam sine cōnsiliīs vel nōbilium vel plēbis omnia sōlus faciēbat.

L. Tarquinius Superbus ut domī crūdēlī dominātiōne sīc mīlitiae fraude

25 et dolō rēs ēgit. Nam tum cum bellum lentius quam spērāverat cum Gabiīs incēperat illud cōnsilium iniit: fīlius Sextus Tarquinius trānsfūgit ex compositō Gabiōs ubi patris in sē saevitiam crūdēlissimam querēbātur. Iam Superbum ab aliēnīs in suōs vertisse superbiam; sē quidem inter tēlā et gladiōs patris sē in fugam dedisse nec quidquam usquam sibi tūtum esse

30 nisi apud hostīs L. Tarquinī crēdidisse. Cīvēs Gabīnī eum magnō studiō recēpērunt, nam exīstimāvērunt eum sibi ūsuī adversus patrem fore. Nōbilīs iuvenēs sibi sīc conciliāvit; mox dux exercitūs Gabīnī factus est, quem aliquot proeliīs fēlīciōribus quam eīs quibus ante pugnātum erat adversus L. Tarquinium dūxit, atque aliquotiēns mīlitēs Rōmānōs etiam vīcit. Dēnique

35 Sex. Tarquinius tum cum Gabiīs et nōbilibus et plēbī grātior quam ducēs Gabīnī factus erat ex suīs ūnum Rōmam ad patrem mīsit rogātum: "Quid nunc facere dēbeō?"

▮ READING COMPREHENSION

1. Why did the driver of Tullia's carriage stop in panic?   2. According to tradition, what did Tullia do?   3. How long did Servius Tullius reign? 4. How did Tarquin the Proud conduct his domestic and foreign policies? 5. What was his relationship to his son Sextus?   6. What did Sextus do?

---

18. **rēbus:** rēs, either singular or plural, can mean *side* or *party*   24. **mīlitiae:** locative, *on military service* (as opposed to **domī**, *at home*); **Domī** and **mīlitiae** can also mean *in domestic policy* and *in foreign policy,* respectively

LESSON 38

Irregular Comparisons; Ablative of Comparison; Implied Comparison

The Circus Maximus in its final state during the Roman Empire, from the model of imperial Rome in 300 A.D.—Museo della Civiltà Romana, Rome

THE CIRCUS MAXIMUS

The name for a racetrack, used for both chariot races (**lūdī circēnsēs**) and gladiatorial shows (**mūnera gladiātōria**), was **circus**. Of the various **circī** at Rome, the Circus Maximus was the oldest and the largest. The valley of the little stream later called Consus was the scene of the races at which the Sabine women were abducted by Romulus and his men. A formal racecourse was laid out here by the first Etruscan king of Rome, Tarquinius Priscus. In its earliest version, seats for the spectators were probably merely cut into the turf of the valley-side. Later these were replaced with stone, and when more seating became necessary the higher tiers were raised on vaults, some of which gave access to stairs leading to the upper seats, while others were used as shops or other commercial enterprises. Eventually the Circus Maximus reached a size of 350′ x 1800′, and could seat 385,000. There were two monumental gates to the racing area. The one in the curved eastern end, the **Porta Triumphālis**, was used only when the triumphal procession of a victorious general passed through the Circus on its way to the Forum. The one in the flat western end of the Circus was surmounted by the box where the giver of the games sat, and flanked by the starting gates, the **carcerēs**. At the corners at this end were two towers, the **oppida**, where sat the musicians who accompanied the parades and the fighting or racing (as the electronic organ plays for modern basketball games). In the middle of the north side part of the imperial palace on the Palatine projected in the form of a two-storied pavilion, the box for the emperor and his family. The **mētae**, the markers for the turns at each end of the course, were three columns on a semicircular base. The **mētae** were connected by the **spīna**, a wall 4′ high and 12′ wide. In the center of the **spīna** was the underground altar of Consus, the god of the stream which had been buried to make room for the Circus. It was uncovered on his festivals in August and December. Near it was an obelisk of Ramses II,

(Continued)

434

brought from Egypt. Also on the **spīna** were numerous small temples, fountains, and statues (notable among them one of Victoria). The lap markers were seven large wooden eggs in egg cups, one of which was removed after each lap, and seven bronze dolphins, one of which was turned over after each lap. The dolphin was the symbol of Neptune, creator of the horse; the egg, of the horse tamers Castor and Pollux.

(*below*) The ruins of the Circus of the Emperor Maxentius on the Via Appia. The **oppida** flank the **carcerēs**.

ANCIENT ROME LIVES ON . . .

What similarities are there between a modern race track and the Circus Maximus?

FORMS

IRREGULAR COMPARISONS

In both English and Latin there are adjectives which form the comparative and superlative degrees irregularly. Examples in English are *bad, worse, worst, far, farther, farthest, good, better, best.* The most common irregular comparisons in Latin are the following:

POSITIVE	COMPARATIVE	SUPERLATIVE
bonus, -a, um *good*	melior, -ius *better*	optimus, -a, -um *best*
dexter, -tra, -trum *handy*	dexterior, -ius *handier*	dextimus, -a, -um *handiest*
īnferus, -a, -um *below*	īnferior, -ius *lower*	īnfimus, -a, -um (īmus, -a, -um) *lowest*
magnus, -a, -um *great*	maior, maius *greater*	maximus, -a, -um *greatest*
malus, -a, -um *bad*	peior, peius *worse*	pessimus, -a, -um *worst*
multī, -ae, -a *many*	plūrēs, plūra *more*	plūrimī, -ae, -a *most*
parvus, -a, -um *small, little*	minor, minus *smaller, less*	minimus, -a, -um *smallest, least*
posterus, -a, -um *following*	posterior, -ius *latter, later*	postrēmus, -a, -um (postumus, -a, -um) *last*
superus, -a, -um *above*	superior, -ius *higher*	suprēmus, -a, -um (summus, -a, -um) *highest*
vetus, veteris *old*	vetustior, -ius *older*	veterrimus, -a, -um *oldest*

There are also some adjectives which are lacking one of the degrees, like ___, *former, foremost* or ___, *upper, uppermost* in English.

POSITIVE	COMPARATIVE	SUPERLATIVE
iuvenis, -is *young*	iunior *younger*	___
senex, senis *old*	senior *older*	___

POSITIVE	COMPARATIVE	SUPERLATIVE
multus, -a, -um *much*	——	plūrimus, -a, -um *most*
——	prior, prius *former*	prīmus, -a, -um *first, foremost*
——	propior, -ius *nearer*	proximus, -a, -um *nearest, next*
——	potior, -ius *preferable*	potissimus, -a, -um *most important*
——	ulterior, -ius *farther*	ultimus, -a, -um *farthest*

1. **Plūrēs** is unlike the other comparatives in having a genitive in **-ium** instead of **-um**.
2. **Iuvenis** (which has no neuter) and **senex** (which is used only in the masculine) are not i-stems. Their missing superlatives are supplied by the idioms **minimus nātū**, *smallest to be born, youngest,* and **maximus nātū**, *biggest to be born, eldest.*
3. The missing comparative of **multus** is supplied by the noun **plūs** with a partitive genitive.

> Nōbīs attulērunt plūs auxilī et plūra dōna.
> *They brought us more help and more gifts.*

SYNTAX

ABLATIVE OF COMPARISON

When the noun which is compared with another noun is in the nominative or accusative, *than* may be expressed by the ablative without a preposition instead of **quam** with a nominative or accusative. This construction is called the ablative of comparison.

Iuvenem celeriōrem quam Lūcium numquam vīdī. Iuvenem celeriōrem Lūciō numquam vīdī.	*I have never seen a young man swifter than Lucius.*
Perīculum est maius quam omnēs spērāvērunt. Perīculum est maius spē omnium.	*The danger is greater than everyone hoped.*

■ IMPLIED COMPARISON

The comparative and superlative are sometimes used with no specific comparison in mind and may be translated with *too* or *rather* (comparative) and *most* or *very* (superlative).

Haec via lātior est $\left.{\text{illā.} \atop \text{quam illa.}}\right\}$ *This road is wider than that one.*

Haec via lātior est.   *This road is* $\left.{\text{too} \atop \text{rather}}\right\}$ *wide.*

Fēlīcissimī hominum erāmus.   *We were the happiest of men.*

Fēlīcissimī erāmus.   *We were* $\left.{\text{most} \atop \text{very}}\right\}$ *happy.*

═══ VOCABULARY ═══

■ BASIC WORDS

aciēs, -ēī, f. *sharp edge; straight line; line of battle.*
numerus, -ī, m. *number; group*
vōx, vōcis, f. *voice*

caecus, -a, -um *blind; invisible*
dexter, dextera, dexterum (or dextra, dextrum) *on the right; handy, skillful*

īnferus, -a, -um *below*
senex, senis (masculine only) *old*
sinister, sinistra, sinistrum *on the left*
superus, -a, -um *above*

nāscor, -ī, nātus sum *be born*

Notes: 1. When **dextra** and **sinistra** appear in the feminine with no noun to modify, they modify **manus** understood, and mean *right hand* and *left hand*. *On the right* and *on the left* are expressed by the ablative of place from which with **ā, ab.**

Aliī ā dextrā, aliī ā sinistrā stābant.
Some were standing on the right, some on the left.

2. The positives of **īnferus** and **superus** appear most often used substantively in the plural:

īnferī, -ōrum, m.   *the gods below (gods of the Lower World)*
superī, -ōrum, m.   *the gods above (heavenly gods)*

A chariot race of **quadrigae,** from a fresco from Pompeii—National Museum, Naples

LEARNING ENGLISH THROUGH LATIN

ambidextrous	*able to use both hands with equal ease*
ameliorate	*become better, improve*
dexterous	*adroit; having skill in the use of the hands or body*
nascent	*coming into being, being born*
pejorative	*making worse; disparaging, derogatory*
renascence	*rebirth; new life, strength or vigor*
senility	*mental deterioration due to old age*
vociferous	*clamorous; loud and noisy in making one's feelings known*

Translation Help

You will have noticed that, with some exceptions, Latin nouns and adjectives have few English meanings but verbs have many. This is because verbs tend to be general, and nouns and adjectives specific, in their meanings. Hence the verb usually comes at or near the end of the sentence, since its precise meaning depends on its subject, object, and other words which precede it. When you look up an unfamiliar verb, therefore, be sure to look at the entire entry, note all the meanings, and determine whether the verb needs anything to complete its meaning (e.g., a direct object, a dative, a complementary infinitive).

In the reading *Villainy and Revolt*, in the clause **postquam vim ā Sextō sibi factam esse aperuit,** it would be a mistake merely to note that the basic meaning of **aperiō** is *open*, since *after she opened violence to have been done to her by Sextus* makes no sense in English.

▬ PRACTICE ▬

A. Use what you have learned in this lesson to explain the following sentences:

1. The twins were very different in temperament: one was an optimist and the other a pessimist. **2.** The politician was very pleased with his plurality. **3.** The greatest hindrance to her success is her inferiority complex. **4.** Her insurance policy covered all prenatal care. **5.** Dextral and sinistral are antonyms. **6.** What is the maximum amount of money I can spend? **7.** Examine your priorities.

B. Irregular comparisons are made easier to remember by the fact that so many of the comparatives and superlatives are used as English words with no change in spelling. *Junior, ulterior,* and *optimum* are three examples; find 10 others in this lesson.

C. Fill in each missing degree, or say if it does not exist:

	POSITIVE	COMPARATIVE	SUPERLATIVE
1.	——	potior	——
2.	——	——	ultimus
3.	multī	——	——
4.	——	dexterior	——
5.	——	——	īmus
6.	parvus	——	——
7.	——	maior	——
8.	——	——	postrēmus
9.	vetus	——	——
10.	——	senior	——
11.	——	——	postumus
12.	malus	——	——
13.	——	melior	——
14.	——	——	īnfimus
15.	iuvenis	——	——
16.	——	prior	——
17.	——	——	suprēmus
18.	multus	——	——
19.	——	propior	——
20.	——	——	summus

Rounding the **metae,** a charioteer wrapped in his reins approaches the turn.
Another has fallen, and a leader disappears in the background—Louvre, Paris

D.   Translate:

1. This land is very full of good things, but its mountains are too high.
2. Whatever that is, its body is rather huge and its horns are very sharp.
3. He showed me a very swift stream on the right and a rather wide forest
on the left.   4. I am sorry that that rather large serpent is feeding upon
those very beautiful maidens.   5. We were most happy, and never too
serious.

E.   Pronounce and translate:

1. Iūlia est gracilis, quā Lūcrētia etiam gracilior est, at Iūnia est longē
gracillima.   2. Eī trēs fīliī sunt, quōrum Mārcus iūnior Lūciō, sed Sextus
omnium minimus nātū est.   3. Bonum nōn semper est hominem pessimīs
esse meliōrem.   4. Dixit sē ad ultimum lītus nāvigāvisse, nos autem multō
ulterius modo crēvimus.   5. Bonō dominō servīre potius est quam malō,
sed eī quī servus est omnium potissimum est perīre.

F.   Translate:

1. This old man is older than you, but my father is the oldest of you all.
2. If anything is lower than the gods below, it ought to be very low.
3. Give us more horses and more grain.   4. Your town is old; our town is
far older; which is the oldest of the towns of Latium?   5. We worship a
god greater than yours, the greatest in fact of all gods.

441

(*left*) A 5th c. A.D. ivory diptych of a chariot race under the supervision of the Emperor—Christian Museum, Brescia. In the Christian Empire, chariot teams even came to stand for various theological tenets and beliefs. (*below*) A reconstructed view of the Circus Maximus in Rome as it may have looked in the late Empire

FROM THE PHILOSOPHER'S HANDBOOK . . .

Ā bōve maiōre discit arāre minor.
*A younger ox learns how to plow from
an older one.*

The United States is fast becoming a nation of senior citizens. How can this be an advantage to those of you who are young?

READING

Developing Reading Skills

Familiar Latin words which will tell you the meanings of unfamiliar ones in this reading: **ambulō, annus, dē, diū, ē, ex, in, invideō, mittō, mōveō, soleō, līber, pugnō, sub, super, ut,** and **vel.**

English derivatives which will help: *annual, calamity, cause, coerce, conspectus, create, deliberate, dubious, emit, expulsion, false, horticulture, incriminate, injury, invidious, insolent, judicial, liberty, manifest, married, odious, potency, respond, response, secret, sequence,* and *tacit.*

Villainy and Revolt

Sex. Tarquinius, trium fīliōrum L. Tarquinī minimus nātū, quī summam grātiam apud Gabīnōs patris hostīs consecūtus erat, Gabiīs ūnum ex suīs Rōmam ad patrem mīserat consilium rogātum. Huic nūntiō quia dubiae fideī vidēbātur nihil vōce respōnsum est; rēx velut dēlīberābundus in hortum aedium trānsit quō eum nūntius fīlī sequitur; ibi inambulāvisse tacitusque 5 summa papāverum capita dīcitur baculō dēcussisse. Nūntius dolet sē nihil, ut putat, respōnsī accēpisse Gabiōsque redit; ea quae ipse dīxit quaeque vīdit refert: seu īrā, seu odiō, seu ingenī superbiā nūllam eum vōcem ēmīsisse. Sextus simul atque ea cognōverat quae pater quamquam tacitus manifestē tamen praecipiēbat coepit submōvēre ducēs et nōbilium et plēbis, multōs 10 crīmine falsō iūdiciōque, plūrīs caede secrētā. Plurimī sē in fugam dabant quod invidiam aliquidve peiōris timēbant. Dēnique Sextus ubi hōc modō rērum Gabiīs potītus erat Gabīnam rem rēgī Rōmānō sine ūllō proeliō prōdidit et trādidit.

13: rem: rēs, with a possessive adjective of a city or people, means *power, government,* or *state*

15   Eundem Sex. Tarquinium deī Penātēs, quī iūniōris Tulliae mātris scelere
īrātī sunt, cum et superīs et īnferīs, calamitātis causam et ipsī et domuī suō
tōtī fēcērunt. Nam Sextus, quī in castrīs patrī auxiliō aderat tum cum
Ardeam oppugnābat, ob cupīdinem caecus animī Rōmam clam illinc rediit
et vim fēcit Lūcrētiae, nōbilissimae fēminae, L. Tarquinī Collātīnī coniugī.
20   Quae in cōnspectū Sp. Lucrētī Trīcipītīnī patris et marītī et quōrundam
amīcōrum, inter quōs L. Iūnius Brūtus, postquam vim ā Sextō sibi factam
esse aperuit ipsa suā manū sē gladiō trāiēcit et sīc suprēmō diē fāta clausit.
Illī sē hanc iniūriam ultūrōs iūrāvērunt. Rērum novārum cupidī rēgem urbe
exclūsērunt; exercitus quoque quī cum L. Tarquiniō apud Ardeam aderat,
25   simul atque mīlitēs haec Rōmae gesta esse audīvērunt, rēgem relīquit, quī
fūgit igitur cum uxōre līberīsque, ex quibus duo maiōrēs nātū patrem Caere
in Etrūscōs secūtī sunt. Sex. Tarquinius ille autem Gabiōs tamquam in suum
rēgnum sē contulit, ubi tamen ab eīs quibus nocuerat interfectus est.
    L. Tarquinius Superbus rēgnāvit annōs quīnque et vīgintī. Rōmae rēgnātum
30   est ā tempore quō urbs condita est ad Tarquiniī expulsiōnem annōs dūcentōs
quadrāgintā quattuor.
    Postquam Tarquiniī ēiectī sunt duo Cōnsulēs prō ūnō rēge creārī coeptī
sunt; sīc etsī alter malus esse vīsus est ab alterō coercērī poterat. Eīs annuum
imperium commissum est, nam diūturnitās potentiae quae hominēs inso-
35   lentiōrēs reddit timēbātur. Fuērunt igitur annō prīmō post rēgis fugam
Cōnsulēs L. Iūnius Brūtus, acerrimus lībertātis vindex, et L. Tarquinius
Collātīnus, Lūcrētiae marītus.

▪ READING COMPREHENSION

1. What reply did the messenger get from the king?   **2.** What did the king
do?   **3.** How did Sextus Tarquin interpret this action?   **4.** How did the
Penates get revenge on Tullia, the mother of Sextus Tarquin?   **5.** How
long did the monarchy last?   **6.** What happened after the end of the
monarchy?

---

18. animī: locative, *in his mind*   **22: suprēmō diē:** because the Romans imagined time as
moving upward, **supremus diēs** means *last* or *final day*. *She closed her fates with a final day*
is an idiomatic way of saying *she met her end* or *breathed her last.*   **24. apud Ardeam:**
apud with the name of a town or other geographical term in military language means *near,*
at, or *of.* The Battle of the Ticinus [river] would be **proelium apud Ticīnum.**

LESSON 39

Comparison of Adverbs
Comparison of Adjectives in -eus and -ius
Internal Accusative

A fresco from the house of the Empress Livia

PALACES: THE JULIO-CLAUDIANS

The development of the palace as the official residence of the chief of state proceeded gradually among the Romans. In republican times there was no official state residence as such. However, most of the **nōbilēs,** the class from whom the Consuls were elected, lived on the fashionable Palatine Hill. Residence here became a kind of symbol of membership in this class. Whenever one arrived politically he bought a house on the Palatine. The imperial residence on the Palatine grew larger and larger until eventually the name of the hill had become the word for any elaborate official residence: **Palātium** > **palazzo** > **palais** > *palace.*

Augustus, the first **prīnceps,** prided himself on living in a house no different from other aristocratic residences. But increases in the size of the staff under the emperor's direct control soon made large quarters necessary. Slaves and civil servants, from clerks to cabinet ministers, were all members of the emperor's household and, for convenience and efficiency, lived in the Emperor's house. Tiberius took over the entire northwest quarter of the Palatine for a huge office building surrounding a large courtyard. Caligula enlarged this, building out to the north and west and adding a courtroom and throne room in the Forum, which were reached from the top of the Palatine by a covered ramp through which his carriage or chariot could drive. He also expanded the palace on the Palatine to the east with gardens and some elegantly decorated rooms, one of which survives. Claudius did some more building out over the Forum, bringing the walls of the palace to the boundary of the **Ātrium Vestae,** the house of the Vestal Virgins.

A PHRASE TO USE

Imperium in imperiō
An empire within an empire

Augustus purchased several neighboring dwellings on the Palatine to make his "palace." (*left*) A room from the House of Livia with contemporary fresco decoration (*below*) The room of the masks—House of Augustus

ANCIENT ROME LIVES ON . . .

Compare the residence of a Roman emperor with that of a head of state today.

▬ FORMS ▬

■ COMPARISON OF ADVERBS

The comparative of an adverb is normally the neuter accusative singular of the adjective from which it is derived. The superlative of an adverb is the adverbial form of the superlative of its adjective (i.e. it adds **-ē** to the base of the superlative of the adjective).

POSITIVE	COMPARATIVE	SUPERLATIVE
longē	longius	longissimē
far	*farther*	*farthest*
celeriter	celerius	celerrimē
swiftly	*more swiftly*	*most swiftly*
bene	melius	optimē
well	*better*	*best*
male	peius	pessimē
badly	*worse*	*worst*

Some adverbs have no positive degree:

	COMPARATIVE	SUPERLATIVE
——	magis	maximē
	more, rather	*most, especially*
——	minus	minimē
	less	*least, not at all*

Some adverbs which are not derived from adjectives are compared in the same way.

POSITIVE	COMPARATIVE	SUPERLATIVE
diū	diūtius	diūtissimē
long, for a long time	*longer, for a longer time*	*for the longest time*
saepe	saepius	saepissime
often	*more often*	*most often*

Nōn iam and **nōn diūtius** are both translated *no longer*, but **nōn iam** means *not as formerly* and **nōn diūtius** *not for a longer time*.

Quoniam tam iuvenis quam ōlim fuī nōn iam sum, manēre hīc diūtius nōn valeō.
Since I am no longer so young as I once was, I can remain here no longer.

▪ COMPARISON OF ADJECTIVES ENDING IN -eus AND -ius

To avoid awkwardness in pronunciation, adjectives ending in -eus and -ius are compared by using the adverbs **magis** and **maximē;** just as in English we say *more beautiful* and *most beautiful,* rather than *beautifuller* and *beautifullest.*

idōneus, -a, -um	magis idōneus, -a, -um	maximē idōneus, -a, -um
suitable	*more suitable*	*most suitable*
varius, -a, -um	magis varius, -a, -um	maximē varius, -a, -um
varied	*more varied*	*most varied*

▬ SYNTAX ▬

▪ USE OF ATQUE (AC)

With **alius** and its adverbs *than* is expressed in Latin by **atque (ac).**

Nihil aliud ac nūmen hoc facere potuit.
Nothing other than divine power could have done this.
Lingua Graeca aliter atque Latīna scrībitur.
The Greek language is written otherwise than (differently from) the Latin.

Atque (ac) is translated *as* with **īdem** and with the adverbs **aequē, pariter, similiter** and **dissimiliter,** and **simul** (hence **simul atque,** *at the same time as = as soon as*).

Hoc īdem atque illud est.   *This is the same as that.*
Patriam amō ego aequē ac tū.
I love our country as much (equally) as you do.

▪ QUAM WITH THE SUPERLATIVE

With the superlative of an adjective or adverb **quam** means *as . . . as possible.* Some form of **possum** is implied and sometimes expressed.

Hoc fac quam optimē potes.   *Do this as best you can.*
Hoc fac quam optimē.   *Do this as well as possible.*

■ INTERNAL ACCUSATIVE

The neuter accusative of adjectives, pronouns, and the nouns **nihil, parum, plūs,** and **satis** may be used to modify a noun idea which is in the verb. Hence this construction is called the internal accusative. An internal accusative may be used with transitive or intransitive verbs. If the verb is transitive and active it will also have a direct object.

Multa errat.　　*He makes many mistakes.*

Plūrimum potest.　　*He has the most ability (or power).*

Prīmum mātrem valēre iussit.
　He said his first goodbye to his mother.
　He said goodbye to his mother first.

Tē facile vidēre possum.
　I have an easy ability to see you. I can easily see you.

Quid mihi ista nocent?
　What harm are your actions doing me?

Mihi ista nihil nocent.　　*Your actions do me no harm.*

Plūs valeō quam tū.　　*I have more strength than you.*

Mē nōn satis dīligis. ⎫
Mē parum dīligis.　　⎬　*You don't have enough love for me.*

Distinguish between **multum,** Internal Accusative, and **multō,** Ablative of Degree of Difference.

Tē multum amō.　　*I have much love for you.*

Tē multō plūs quam illam amō.
　I have much more love for you than I do for her.

Also note these uses of **prīmus:**

Prīmus ad oppidum iit.
　He was the first to go to the town.

Prīmō ad oppidum iit.
　At first, he went to the town (Ablative of Time When).

Prīmum ad oppidum iit.
　He went to the town first (Internal Accusative).

VOCABULARY

BASIC WORDS

ars, artis, f. (i-stem) *art, craft, skill*
cāsus, -ūs, m. *fall, accident, event, occasion, chance, fate*
glōria, -ae, f. *glory*
labor, labōris, m. *labor, toil, effort, hardship*
prīnceps, prīncipis, m. *chief, leading man, prince, emperor*
ventus, -ī, m. *wind*

aequus, -a, -um *level; equal; fair, just*
varius, -a, -um *various, varying, varied*

simul (adv.) *at the same time*
vix (adv.) *scarcely, barely*

LEARNING ENGLISH THROUGH LATIN

artifice	*skill, ingenuity; trickery*
artificial	*made as a substitute for something natural; unnatural; affected*
equitable	*fair, just*
inequity	*lack of justice; unfairness*
laborious	*calling for much hard work; difficult*
simultaneously	*at the same time*
variable	*changeable, inconstant*
ventilator	*a device to bring in fresh air and drive out foul air*

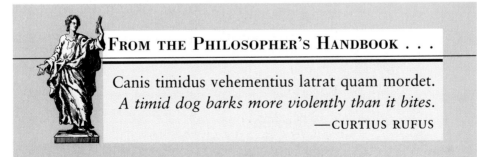

FROM THE PHILOSOPHER'S HANDBOOK . . .

Canis timidus vehementius latrat quam mordet.
A timid dog barks more violently than it bites.

—CURTIUS RUFUS

What English proverb says the same thing in a slightly different way? How would you use this proverb in relation to people?

PRACTICE

A. Fill each blank with an English derivative from this lesson:

1. She seems very friendly, but her smile is rather ___. **2.** The climate in this part of the country is so ___! **3.** This is not an ___ solution for everyone concerned. **4.** Preparing my Latin homework is often a ___ task. **5.** I cannot march and play the trumpet ___. **6.** Such ___ we used to devise to circumvent the rules!

B. Write two original sentences using the words from the list which were not used in A.

C. Find in column B the translation[s] for each expression in column A:

A	B
1. magis	**a.** farther
2. simul atque	**b.** most swiftly
3. diūtius	**c.** least
4. optimē	**d.** well
5. celerrimē	**e.** longer
6. peius	**f.** best
7. maximē idōneus	**g.** especially
8. magis idōneus	**h.** not at all
9. minus	**i.** most suitable
10. bene	**j.** more often
11. minimē	**k.** at the same time as
	l. for a long time
	m. worse
	n. very well
	o. varied
	p. more varied
	q. as soon as
	r. rather suitable
	s. less
	t. far
	u. more
	v. better
	w. rather
	x. more suitable.

D. Compare these adverbs:

1. ācriter   2. bene   3. graciliter   4. longē   5. male   6. miserē
7. nōbiliter   8. similiter   9. simpliciter   10. variē

E. Pronounce and translate:

1. Eōdem ac tū ego eō.   2. Hī aliunde vēnērunt atque illī.   3. Hoc fac pariter atque ego faciō.   4. Indidem Iūlia venit ac Lūcrētia.   5. Mārcus aliō ac Lūcius ībit.

F. Translate:

1. You will learn these things as easily as possible.   2. Tarquin the Proud ruled the city as badly as could be.   3. These are the most favorable circumstances possible.   4. She ran as fast as she could.   5. He was as happy as he could be.

G. Pronounce and translate:

1. Multa eī favēbat.   2. Satis labōrāvimus.   3. Omnia nōbīs paruērunt.
4. Quid mihi prōdest?   5. Nihil eīs parcunt.   6. Parum deōs verēris.
7. Quam maximum clāmāvērunt.   8. Hoc crēde mihi.   9. Multum mē iūvistis.   10. Eum plūrima laudant.

H. Translate:

1. He was the first to cross the sea and arrive at the farther shore.   2. Since I no longer have the fears I once had, I have determined to suffer these things no longer.   3. At first he feared to expose himself to danger, but then he decided to fight for his fatherland.   4. This garment, which I have used much, is much older than that one.   5. What is most preferable, and which of the goddesses ought I to consult first?

I. Pronounce and translate:

1. Etsī vīvere dīcī potest vix vīvus est quī nēminem plūs quam sē dīlēxit nec umquam ūllō amōre aliō ac suī ārsit.   2. Quōcumque ībam miseriōrēs mē humiliōrēsque ubique inveniēbam; deinde igitur mē nōn diūtius dēbēre cāsum meum dolēre sēnsī.

Developing Reading Skills

Latin words which will help: **adeō, aliquam, audeō, circum, clāmō, cum, currō, dīgnus, diū, faciō, fugiō, legō, līber, māter, memor, mōveō, per, prō, sī, spectō, stō, super, trānseō, valeō, vincō,** and **vocō.**

English derivatives: *adit, audacity, clamor, colleague, commotion, community, dignity, exiguous, extinguish, ferrous, impetus, interrupt, intrepid, invade, liberty, lugubrious, matron, migrate, miracle, morbid, obstacle, pontoon, provoke, quasi, recuperate, rescind, stupefy, terror, transit, valid,* and *victor.*

A Solitary Enemy

Ūnī ex duōbus Cōnsulibus paulō post rēgis fugam dīgnitās sublāta est, nam L. Tarquiniō Collātīnō, virō maximā honestāte, nōmen ipsum tamen impedīmentō erat. Omnēs Tarquiniī Rōmā discēdere iussī sunt et postquam is cum familiā ēmigrāvit in eius locum P. Valerius Publicola Cōnsul factus est.
5 Ubi Tarquinius Superbus, quī sē rēgnum quam celerrimē recuperātūrum spērābat, bellum urbī intulit prīmō proeliō Brūtus Cōnsul et Arrūns, maximus nātū Tarquiniī fīliōrum, alius alium interfēcit. Rōmānī tamen ex eō proeliō victōrēs discessērunt. Brūtum quasi commūnem patrem Rōmānae mātrōnae

The ruins of the **Pons Aemilius,** known as the "Broken Bridge", stand not far from the place where stood the wooden **Pons Sublicius** defended by Horatius Cocles.

per annum tōtum lūxērunt. Publicola Sp. Lūcrētium Lūcrētiae patrem sibi
collēgam dēlēgit; quī postquam morbō exstinctus est M. Horātius Pulvillus
Publicolae collēga factus est. Ita prīmus annus novae reī publicae quīnque
Cōnsulēs habuit.

Annō posterō Tarquiniī iam ad Lartem Porsenam Clūsīnum rēgem
perfūgerant, quī sē eīs auxiliō fore prōmīsit. Rōmam ergō cum īnfestō
exercitū vēnit. Nōn umquam aliās ante tantus terror Senātum invāserat, tam
valida rēs tum Clūsina erat magnumque Porsenae nōmen. Ubi hostēs adsunt
omnēs in urbem prō sē quisque ex agrīs migrant, urbem ipsam saepiunt
praesidiīs. Alia moenibus, alia Tiberis flūmine vidēbantur tūta; Pōns autem
Sublicius iter paene hostibus dedit, quod tamen prohibuit ūnus vir cēterīs
fortior, Horātius Coclēs. Positus erat in stātiōne pontis, cum captum
repentīnō impetū Iāniculum esse atque inde celerrimē dēcurrere hostīs vīdit,
trepidamque turbam suōrum arma ordinēsque relinquere. Temptāvit eōs
fugere prōhibēre et "Sī trānsitum ponte ā tergō relīqueritis," clāmābat, "iam
plūrēs hostēs in Palātiō Capitōliōque quam in Iāniculō erunt!" Tum eōs
iussit pontem ferrō, igne, quācumque vī poterant, interrumpere, prōmīsitque
sē impetum hostium quantum corpore ūnō obstārī poterat exceptūrum. Sē
inde contulit ad prīmum aditum pontis ubi ipsō mīrāculō audāciae hostīs
stupēfēcit. Duōs tamen cum eō pudor tenuit, alterum ā dextrā, alterum ā
sinistrā, Sp. Larcium ac T. Herminium, ambōs clārissimōs genere virtūteque.
Cum hīs prīmum impetum sustinuit; deinde eōs quoque ipsōs, ut exigua
modo pars pontis quem cēterī rescindēbant relicta est, cēdere in tūtum coēgit.
Etruscōs quī eum adīre dubitābant nunc singulōs prōvocat, nunc omnīs
increpat servōs rēgum superbōrum suae lībertātis immemorīs aliēnam op-
pugnātum venīre. Illī morātī aliquamdiū sunt et alius alium circumspectant
et proelium incipere iubent. Pudor deinde commōvit aciem, et clāmōrem
tollunt et undique in ūnum hostem tēla coniciunt.

10

15

20

25

30

35

■ READING COMPREHENSION

1. Why did Lucius Tarquinius Collatinus have his rank taken away from
him?   2. Who was Arruns and what did he do?   3. How many Consuls
were there in the first year of the new republic?   4. Who promised to help
the Tarquins?   5. How and why did the Senate react to this?   6. How
did Horatius Cocles prevent the enemy from crossing the Pons Sublicius?

---

17. sē quisque: when a reflexive and a universal with the same antecedent are used in the
same clause they always come together with the reflexive first: prō sē quisque *every man
for himself*

LESSON 40

Expressions of Cause; Review of Case Uses

The octagonal hall of the **Domus Aurea,** lit from above by an oculus. The many rooms off it contained fountains and statuary.

PALACES: DOMUS AUREA

Though the grandeur of the architecture may have been meant to impress the beholder, palaces were at first essentially office buildings. Nero was the first to think of a palace as a luxurious pleasure-house. His first palace, the **Domus Trānsitōria,** was restricted in size by the smallness of the area still available on the Palatine. When the great fire destroyed the slums of inner-city Rome, Nero found that on the land thus vacated he could give free rein to his imagination. The result was the famous **Domus Aurea,** *the Golden House.* The **Domus Aurea,** which covered perhaps 370 acres in the center of the city, consisted primarily of colonnaded buildings, overlaid with semi-precious stone and mother-of-pearl, surrounding a central park. There was a large lake, around which stood a series of pavilions designed to look like villages from the outside. The surrounding land was landscaped to resemble forests, plowed fields, and meadowlands. One of the pavilions has been excavated. It contains many rooms, most of them overlooking the lake, all of them decorated with a riot of fanciful fresco. There are courtyards within the building, and several fountains, one a huge cascade tumbling down several stories to pass through one of the rooms. With the accession of the Flavians, the Golden House was demolished and its site used for public buildings: the Colosseum occupies the position of Nero's lake. But palaces were never again merely office buildings. The third Flavian emperor, Domitian, built the Domus Augustana, the huge palace, both monumental and fanciful in its architecture, which, with a few later additions, occupies most of the Palatine hill today.

(*left*) An elaborate peristyle, or
courtyard, with a complex fountain
base, and (*below*) the so-called
Stadium, an exercise garden and
portico from the **Domus Augustāna**,
the residential palace of the
Emperor Domitian

ANCIENT ROME LIVES ON . . .

Give an example of an old private
building that has been replaced by a new
public one.

SYNTAX

EXPRESSIONS OF CAUSE

The ablative without a preposition is used to express cause. The English translation is *from*, *because of*, or *for*. This is called the Ablative of Cause.

Amōre vestrī id fēcimus.   *We did it* $\left.\begin{array}{l}\textit{because of}\\\textit{from}\\\textit{for the}\end{array}\right\}$ *love of you.*

The genitive of possession is used with the ablative of **causa, -ae,** f., *cause, reason,* to mean *because of, by reason of, for the sake of.*

Virtūtis causā dōna eī data sunt.

Gifts were given him $\left.\begin{array}{l}\textit{because of}\\\textit{by reason of}\\\textit{for the sake of}\end{array}\right\}$ *his courage.*

This accusative is used with the prepositions **ob** and **propter,** *because of, on account of.*

Rēx $\left.\begin{array}{l}\text{ob}\\\text{propter}\end{array}\right\}$ metum mortis discessit.

The king left $\left.\begin{array}{l}\textit{because of}\\\textit{on account of}\end{array}\right\}$ *his fear of death.*

The Ablative of Place from Which is used in the expression **quā dē causā,** *for which reason.*

Imber magnus incipiēbatur, quā dē causā domum abiimus.
A great rainstorm was beginning, for which reason we went home.

REVIEW OF CASE USES

You have now learned the following constructions of substantives. Be sure that you understand each of them. The number of the lesson in which each was presented in the *Syntax* section is provided in case you need to refresh your memory. Additional references are marked with an **F** if the mention occurs in the *Forms* section, with an **H** for *Translation Help*, with a **V** for *Vocabulary Notes*, and with an **R** for *Reading Footnotes*. The constructions in parentheses were used only in the readings and were not to be memorized, but are included for completeness.

■ NOMINATIVE

Subject	1 2H 7R 8H 10H 16R 20H
Predicate Nominative (Subj. Comp.)	1 8H 10H 11
Apposition	2 20H

■ VOCATIVE

Direct Address	6 20H
Apposition	2 20H

■ GENITIVE

Genitive of Possession	1 2H 6H 13 15V 19 25 27F 27R 40
Partitive Genitive (Genitive of the Whole)	6H 16 21 25 26 27F 27V 29V 37
Objective Genitive with Nouns and Adjectives	6H 14 14V 15V 25 27F 27R 33R
Objective Genitive with Verbs	33 35R
Genitive of Description	6H 21
Genitive of Measure	6H 22 26V
(Genitive of Indefinite Value)	(21V 40V)
Apposition	2 20H

■ DATIVE

Dative of the Indirect Object	7 8H 10H 18V 20V
Dative with Compound Verbs	31
Dative with Intransitive Verbs	32
Dative of Possession	19 40V
Dative of Reference	7 17 17V 18V 29
Dative of Purpose	29
Double Dative	29
Dative with Adjectives	13 15V
Apposition	2 20H 26R

This ceiling fresco from the Domus Transitoria is in a style typical of Nero's buildings—Antiquarium of the Palatine, Rome

■ ACCUSATIVE

Direct Object	2 2H 8H 10H 19V
	31 32 32V 33 34V
Double Accusative	29
Internal Accusative	39
Accusative of Extent of Space	25
Accusative of Duration of Time	25
Predicate Accusative (Obj. Comp.)	4 8H 10H
Subject of Infinitive	35
Subjective Complement with Infinitive	35
Accusative of Limit of Motion	30
Accusative of Place to Which	3 4R 11R 18V 31R 36R 38R
(Accusative of Exclamation)	(8R)
(Accusative of Secondary Agent)	(22R 36R)
(Accusative in Apposition with a Clause)	(29R)
Apposition	2 20H

■ ABLATIVE PROPER ("from")

Ablative of Separation	17 40V
Ablative of Cause	40
Ablative of Comparison	38
Ablative of Place from Which	3 17 28V 30 34R 40
Partitive Ablative of Place from Which	16 21 26V 28 29V
Ablative of Personal Agent	11 12H
Apposition	2 20H

■ INSTRUMENTAL/CIRCUMSTANTIAL ABLATIVE ("with")

Ablative of Means or Instrument	8 12H 14V 17R
	18H 20V 27V 40V
Ablative of Means with Deponents	33
Ablative of Price	22
Ablative of Degree of Difference	25 37 39
Ablative of Specification	15 18V 26V 30
Ablative of Description	21
Ablative of Manner	18 18H 20H
Ablative of Accompaniment	2 2H 10V 12H 18H
	20V 25 25R 26F
Apposition	2 2H 20H

◼ LOCATIVE ABLATIVE ("in, on, at")

Ablative of Time When	25
Ablative of Time Within Which	25
Ablative of Place Where	1 2H 3 12H 27R 31R
Apposition	2 20H

◼ LOCATIVE

Showing Location	30 37R 38R
Apposition	2 20H

VOCABULARY

◼ BASIC WORDS

causa, -ae, f. *cause, reason; [legal] case*

honor, honōris, m. *an honor; public office*

iūs, iūris, n. *law; right*

marītus, -ī m. *husband*

opus, operis, n. *work, task*

turba, -ae, f. *crowd; disturbance*

haud (adv.) *by no means, not at all*

procul (adv.) *at a distance*

ob (prep. w. acc.) *because of, on account of*

propter (prep. w. acc.) *because of, on account of*

Notes:

1. The idiom **opus est** with an Ablative of Means (and sometimes with a Dative of Possession) means *there is need*.

   Pecūniā opus est.   *There is need of money.*
   Mihi pecūniā opus est.   *I need money.*

2. **Procul** is sometimes used with an Ablative of Separation.

   Castra hostium haud procul flūmine erant.
   The enemy camp was no great distance from the river.

3. **Quam ob rem**, *on account of which fact, for which reason,* is sometimes written as one word, **quamobrem.**

   Mārcus Lūciō omnibus rēbus praestat,
   quamobrem hic illī invidet.
   *Marcus excels Lucius in every respect,
   for which reason he envies him.*

LEARNING ENGLISH THROUGH LATIN

honorific	*conferring honor; showing respect*
injurious	*harmful, damaging; offensive*
jurisdiction	*range or sphere of authority*
jurisprudence	*the science or philosophy of law*
opus	*a musical composition; a literary work*
perturb	*to cause to be alarmed or agitated*
turbulent	*violently agitated, tumultuous*

PRACTICE

A. Show the relationship of the following common English words to Latin words in the vocabulary of this lesson:

1. cooperate   2. disturb   3. excuse   4. operate

B. Explain the meaning of the following sentences:

1. The senior class conferred an honorific title upon the graduation speaker.
2. The local police could do nothing because the crime was committed outside their jurisdiction.   3. The king attempted to pacify the turbulent mob.   4. The lawyer admonished his client to say nothing that would be injurious to the case.   5. I am so perturbed by the perils that beset me!

C. The sentences in B, in addition to the English derivatives in this lesson, contain eight other words derived from Latin words you have learned. Name five of them and explain their derivation.

D. Say which construction[s] employ[s] each of these prepositions:

1. ā, ab   2. ad   3. cum   4. dē   5. ē, ex   6. in   7. prae   8. sine
9. sub   10. super

E. Translate into Latin each direct object in these English sentences, and name the case use:

1. We lack money.   2. I remember the king.   3. He enjoys life.   4. They will obey the leader.   5. Dangers are pressing the chief.   6. We excel the enemy in courage.   7. They cannot use the gold pieces.   8. Try to forget your mother.   9. The gods favored our enemy.   10. He left (**discessit**) home.

F. Look in the list below for the construction[s] you would need to complete the meaning of each of these verbs:

<table>
<tr><td colspan="2">A</td><td colspan="2">B</td></tr>
<tr><td>1.</td><td>erat
factus est</td><td>a.</td><td>predicate nominative</td></tr>
<tr><td></td><td></td><td>b.</td><td>objective genitive</td></tr>
<tr><td>2.</td><td>vocāverat
dēligent</td><td>c.</td><td>indirect object</td></tr>
<tr><td></td><td></td><td>d.</td><td>dative with compound verbs</td></tr>
<tr><td>3.</td><td>prōdest
parcēbas</td><td>e.</td><td>dative with intransitive verbs</td></tr>
<tr><td></td><td></td><td>f.</td><td>dative of possession</td></tr>
<tr><td>4.</td><td>dabātur</td><td>g.</td><td>direct object</td></tr>
<tr><td>5.</td><td>dīxit
ōstendimus</td><td>h.</td><td>objective complement</td></tr>
<tr><td></td><td></td><td>i.</td><td>double accusative</td></tr>
<tr><td>6.</td><td>rogāvistī</td><td>j.</td><td>retained object</td></tr>
<tr><td>7.</td><td>potītus est</td><td>k.</td><td>accusative of place to which</td></tr>
<tr><td>8.</td><td>docēbitur</td><td>l.</td><td>ablative of means</td></tr>
<tr><td>9.</td><td>dēest</td><td></td><td></td></tr>
<tr><td>10.</td><td>trānsībit
praeteriērunt</td><td></td><td></td></tr>
<tr><td>11.</td><td>vēscor</td><td></td><td></td></tr>
<tr><td>12.</td><td>accēdet</td><td></td><td></td></tr>
</table>

Translation Help

Now that you have learned all but three of the case uses, it would be sensible to make yourself a master list for quick reference. If you want to leave room for the other three, which you will learn in *Second Year Latin,* leave a space each after the Dative of Possession, the Ablative of Separation, and the Ablative of Description. Each entry should include whatever information you will need to recognize the construction in either Latin or its English translation, e.g.

Ablative of Personal Agent:

> English *by,* Latin **ā, ab;** verb must be passive, agent a person.

Prepositions should be marked in some way so that you can quickly find such facts as that an ablative with **ā** or **ab** must be either an Ablative of Place from Which or an Ablative of Personal Agent, while an ablative with **dē, ē,** or **ex** must be either an Ablative of Place from Which or a Partitive Ablative of Place from Which. You may also find it helpful to include a short example of each construction.

READING

Developing Reading Skills

Latin words which will help you in this reading: **ad, bene, circum, cīvis, clāmō, -cumque, dē, dō, domus, dōnum, dūcō, equus, ex, faciō, fortis, fugiō, pareō, redeō, rēx, rogō, scrībō, sedeō, ut,** and **vīvō.**

English derivatives: *adhere, admire, admiration, aggression, appellation, apprehend, arable, beneficial, clamor, consume, custodian, defraud, domestic, donation, equestrian, excruciating, extrude, fortitude, impetus, incendiary, incensed, interrogate, intrude, minatory, pacify, pontoon, private, propitious, restitution, riparian, rupture, sanctity, scribe, statue, terrify,* and *victuals.*

Three Brave Romans

Horātius Coclēs quī Pontem Sublicium dēfendēbat omnia hostium tēla scūtō excipiēbat in quō haerēbant, neque ille minus ingentī pontem obtinēbat gradū. Sed iam impetū temptābant dētrūdere virum cum simul fragor pontis quī ruptus erat, simul clāmor Rōmānōrum pavōre subitō impetum sustinuit. Tum Coclēs "Tiberīne pater," inquit, "tē, sancte, precor: haec arma et hunc mīlitem propitiō flūmine accipe." Itaque sīc cum armīs omnibus in Tiberim dēsiluit incolumisque inter hostium tēla ad suōs trānāvit. Grāta ob tantam virtūtem cīvitās fuit: statua in Comitiō posita est Horātī, cui et tantum agrī quantum ūnō diē circumarāvit datum est. Prīvāta quoque inter publicōs honōrēs studia ostendēbantur: nam in magnā inopiā prō domesticīs copiīs ūnus quisque eī aliquid, etsī sē ipse vīctū suō fraudābat, contulit. 10

Deinde C. Mūcius Scaevola, iuvenis eiusdem virtūtis atque Horātius, in hostium castra sē contulit Porsenam interfectum. At ibi, quod rēgem

The elegant dress of the upper class that so confused Mucius

15 numquam ante vīderat, scrībam rēgis prō ipsō rēge occīdit. Eī ubi ā rēgiīs apparitōribus comprehēnsus adque rēgem adductus et ab hōc interrogātus est Porsena cruciātum flammārum minābātur. Sed Mūcius ipse suam dextram ignī quī in ārā accēnsus erat imposuit, et ibi tenuit dōnec flammīs cōnsumpta est. Fortitūdinem rēx mīrātus est et iuvenem līberāvit. Tum Mūcius "Quon-iam" inquit "est apud tē virtūtī honor, beneficiō ferēs ā mē quod minīs nōn

20 poterās: trecentī iūrāvimus prīncipēs iuventūtis Rōmānae nōs in tē hāc viā aggressūrōs. Mea prīma sōrs fuit; cēterī, utcumque ceciderit, suō quisque tempore aderunt." Porsena quī hāc rē territus est pācem cum Rōmānīs fēcit; sed Iāniculum nōn prius relīquit quam obsidēs cēpit. Patrēs C. Mūciō virtūtis causā trāns Tiberim agrum dōnō dedēre quī posteā Mūcia Prāta appellāta

25 sunt.

Castra Etrūscōrum forte haud procul rīpā Tiberis posita erat. Cloelia virgō igitur, ūna ex obsidibus, custōdēs effūgit et inter tēla hostium Tiberim trānāvit incolumīsque aliās puellās quās multās sēcum dūxerat omnīs Rōmam ad propinquōs restituit. Quod ubi rēgī nūntiātum est prīmō incēnsus īrā est

30 et ōrātōrēs Rōmam mīsit Cloeliam obsidem receptum, nam aliās haud magnī faciēbat.

Deinde autem īra in admīrātiōnem versa est et dīxit Cloeliae virtūtem suprā Coclitēs Mūciōsque esse, et eam passus est dēligere magnum numerum obsidum quōs ipse līberāvit. Rōmānī novam in fēminā virtūtem novō genere

35 honōris, statuā equestrī, dōnāvēre: in summā Sacrā Viā est posita virgō quae equō īnsidēbat.

Post Porsena obsidum quod reliquum erat reddidit atque sīc spem omnem reditūs Tarquiniō dēmpsit quī exsulātum Tusculum abiit.

■ READING COMPREHENSION

1. Who were the three brave Romans? **2.** What is the significance of the following sentence? "Tiberīne pater, tē, sancte, precor: haec arma et hunc mīlitem propitiō flūmine accipe." **3.** What mistake did Scaevola make? **4.** Why did the king relent and set him free? **5.** What is the significance of the following sentence? "Beneficiō ferēs ā mē quod minīs nōn poterās." **6.** What unheard-of honor was bestowed on Cloelia, and why?

---

24. dedēre: The ending -ēre is sometimes used instead of -ērunt. So also **dōnāvēre** in line 35. **30. magnī:** genitive of indefinite value **33. Coclitēs Mūciōsque:** By a figure of speech called *antonomasia*, names of people may be used in the plural when they are used as examples, as we might say *Our country has never had any Napoleons or Hitlers.*

REVIEW 10

A. Give genitive, gender, and meaning of each noun:

aciēs	exercitus	iūs	opus	superī
ars	genus	labor	plēbs	turba
cāsus	glōria	marītus	prīnceps	ventus
causa	honor	mīles	proelium	vōx
dextra	īnferī	numerus	sinistra	

B. Give the other nominative singular endings (or, for adjectives of one termination, the genitive) and the meaning of each adjective:

aequus	dissimilis	īnferus	sinister
caecus	gracilis	nōbilis	superus
dexter	humilis	senex	varius

C. Give the other principal parts and the meaning of **nāscor**.

D. Give the meanings of these adverbs:

ac	haud	quam	vix
atque	procul	simul	

E. Give the meaning of each preposition, and say which case[s] it is used with:

adversus ob propter

DRILL ON FORMS

Compare these adverbs:

1. aequē **2.** bene **3.** celeriter **4.** diū **5.** fēlīciter **6.** male
7. nōbiliter **8.** piē **9.** pulchrē **10.** saepe **11.** similiter **12.** variē

LISTENING AND SPEAKING

A Visit to the Roman Forum

Gnaeus and his son, Titus, now fully recovered from his illness, are spending a few days in Rome. Today they are visiting the Roman Forum. Gnaeus is able to give Titus some excellent background information on all the sites.

1. **templum, -ī, n.**— *sacred precinct*
2. **collis, -is, m.**—*hill*
3. **Rēgia, -ae, f.**— *"Palace", office of the chief priests*
4. **pastor, -is, m.**— *herdsman*
5. **ōrnātus, -a, -um**— *decorated, elaborate*
6. **Pontifex Maximus** —*Supreme Pontiff*
7. **Rēx Sacrificulus**— *Priest King*
8. **aedificium, -ī, n.**— *building*
9. **columna, -ae, f.**— *column*

TĪTUS: Multī, pater, Rōmam pulcherrimam urbem omnium terrārum esse dīcunt. Nunc ego templa[1] et loca nōtissima vidēre cupiō.

GNAEUS: Venī, Tīte. In Forum Rōmānum ambulāmus, nam hic collis[2] Vēlia vocātur et proximus Forō est. In Viā Sacrā Rēgiam[3] videō.

TĪTUS: Nōnne Rēgia domus regum Rōmānōrum antīqua erat? Sunt tamen aedēs, ut ego quidem putō, parvae.

GNAEUS: Rōmānī rēgēs agricolae et pastōrēs[4] erant, itaque aedēs regum nōn ornātae[5] erant. Nunc est locus sacer ubi Pontifex Maximus[6] et Rēx Sacrificulus[7] sacra faciunt. Vidē; hīc nōmina et cōnsulum et victōrum Rōmānōrum legere potes.

TĪTUS: Quod aedificium[8] magnum columnīs[9] ornātum videō? Cūr Rōmānī tantum aedificium fēcērunt?

The actual marble frieze of the abduction of the Sabine women from the Basilica Aemilia in the Roman Forum

GNAEUS: Basilica[10] Aēmilia est, ubi virī in multīs negotiīs versantur. Hīc Praetōrēs[11] causās cognoscunt et hīc nōn modo scrībās[12] actuāriōsque[13] sed etiam argentāriōs[14] mēnsāriōsque[15] invenimus. Quid super portās vidēs?

TĪTUS: Sculptor fābulās dē Romulī vitā caelāvit,[16] nam iuvenēs fēminās Sabīnās auferre videō. Sed sub illō monte aliud aedificium magnum est.

GNAEUS: Mōns Capitōlium, Tīte, est, arx vetera Rōmanōrum. Sub illō est Cūria[17] reī pūblicae Rōmānae, ubi Senātōrēs et cōnsulēs multās ōrātiōnēs[18] et contiōnēs[19] habent. Senātōrēs lēgēs ferunt et in comitiīs[20] cīvēs Rōmānī aut in Senātōrum sententiam[21] aut contrā discēdunt.[22] Rōmānōs ergō virōs līberōs esse dīcimus.

TĪTUS: Maximam aedem, pater, in summō monte videō. Multō maior est quam aedēs deōrum trium in oppidō nostrō. Nōnne deī ipsī hanc aedem pulcherrimam aedificāvērunt?

GNAEUS: Nōn aedificāvērunt deī, fīlī, sed virī Rōmānī, quod rēx septimus Rōmānōrum, Ētruscus quī Tarquinius Superbus vocābātur, cīvīs eam aedificāre coēgit.

TĪTUS: Quis marmōrēs[23] et statuās fēcit? Num Daedalus haec fēcit?

GNAEUS: Daedalus Graecus erat, quī Labȳrinthum Mīnōis aedificāvit. Vulca, sculptor Ētruscus nōtissimus, aedem Iōvis Optimī Maximī prīmus ōrnāvit.[24] Clīvum Capitōlīnum ascendimus.

TĪTUS: Pulcherrimus locus est, unde tōtam urbem Rōmam et septem montīs vidēre possumus. Quanta turba et quantus clāmor in urbe est! Vītam in urbe amō, sed quantō plūribus diēbus ab vīllā et familiā absum, tantō magis illās dēsīderō.

GNAEUS: Bonus fīlius es, Tīte, quem tectī et Laris tuī dēsīderium tenet. Crās domum ībimus nam ego quoque rūrī habitāre amō.

10. **basilica, -ae, f.**—*a Basilica, large hall*
11. **praetor, -ōris, m.**—*praetor, a Roman judge*
12. **scrība, -ae, m.**—*scribe*
13. **actuārius, -ī, m.**—*secretary, scribe, accountant*
14. **argentārius, -ī, m.**—*money-changer*
15. **mensārius, -ī, m.**—*moneylender*
16. **caelō, -āre, caelāvī, caelātum**—*to sculpt, carve*
17. **Cūria, -ae, f.**—*the senate house*
18. **oratio, -iōnis, f.**—*speech, oration*
19. **contio, -iōnis, f.**—*meeting, debate*
20. **comitia, -ōrum, n. pl.**—*elections, assemblies*
21. **sententia, -ae, f.**—*opinion*
22. **discēdo, ēre, descessī, discessum**—*divide*
23. **marmor, -ōris, m.**—*marble*
24. **ōrnō, -āre, -āvī, -ātum**—*to decorate*

After an oral reading of the dialogue, choose a student as translator. The translator will translate various portions of the dialogue and ask for volunteers to find the correct Latin in the dialogue.

TRACES OF ROMAN CIVILIZATION TODAY

England—Hadrian's Wall

Hadrian

Scattered across England at its narrowest point can be found a series of Roman remains. These stretches of walls, ruined buildings, and earthworks once formed the frontier of the Roman province of Britain, and the northernmost limit of the Roman empire.

Hadrian's Wall

This frontier is known today as Hadrian's Wall after the emperor who ordered its construction in the year 122 A.D..

There has always been great interest in the wall. The first Englishman to describe it was the Venerable Bede (675–735 A.D.) who was convinced that the wall was built at the end of the Roman period of occupation to keep out the Picts and Scots who were powerful enemies intent on attacking the Britons and hauling them down from the Wall with long hooks. This legend held the popular imagination for a long time, but it really wasn't the truth.

Why was the wall built? Hadrian followed Trajan as emperor. Trajan had extended the Roman empire enormously and Hadrian spent most of his reign consolidating these gains. However, dangerous rebellions broke out, and one was in Britain. Hadrian felt the time had come to halt expansion. He appointed a governor to construct a permanent and obvious frontier: a wall ten feet thick from sea to sea. It would have milecastles every mile and two turrets between, manned by frontier police who would prevent smuggling, cattle-raiding, and other irregularities. During the building, however, policy had to be modified.

So, the truth of the matter is that Hadrian constructed the wall to separate the Romans from the barbarians.

A milecastle

Other Roman buildings near the wall

Appendix

ENGLISH AND LATIN GRAMMAR COMPARED

Both Latin and English, as well as most modern European languages, the Slavic languages, and some eastern languages (e.g. Iranian and Indic), are descendants of the same parent-language; this parent-language is usually called Indo-European. But although Latin and English are basically similar in structure, the differences between them far outweigh the similarities. There are two reasons for this: one is that Latin represents a much earlier stage of development; the other is that the Latin which we read is not the everyday language which the Romans spoke, but a highly artificial creation developed by the upper classes for literary, social, and political purposes. It is consequently somewhat different in construction from any language used for everyday purposes.

THE PARTS OF SPEECH, ENGLISH AND LATIN

NAME	ATTRIBUTES L = Latin, E = English
Noun	gender, number, case (**L & E**)
Pronoun	person, gender, number, case (**L & E**)
Adjective	gender, number, case (**L**), degree (**L & E**)
Verb	tense, voice, mood, person, number (**L & E**)
Infinitive	tense, voice (**L & E**)
Participle	tense, voice (**L & E**), gender, number, case (**L**)
Supine (**L**)	case
Adverb	degree (**L & E**)
Preposition	case it appears with (**L**)
Conjunction	
Interjection	
Particle (**L**)	

NOUNS

TYPES OF NOUNS

A *noun* is the name of a person, place, thing, or idea.

Common Noun—the name of one of a group of objects:

> picture   story   song   book

Proper Noun—the name of a definite person or place:

> Julius Caesar   Rome   Cicero   Italy

Collective Noun—a singular noun referring to a group:

> family   army   class   audience

Verbal Noun—the name of an action (such nouns often end in *-ing*, *-sion*, or *-tion*):

> Walking is good exercise.
> Studying Latin is a great idea.
> recreation   reaction   motion   omission

Abstract Noun—the name of a quality or condition (such nouns often end in *-ty*, *-ness*, *-hood*, *-dom*, etc.):

> honesty   goodness   wealth   freedom

GENDER

In English the gender of a noun referring to a person or animal is determined by sex: males, masculine; females, feminine. Nouns denoting inanimate objects and sometimes animals are neuter. Gender is not indicated by the form of the noun itself, but by the gender of the pronoun used to refer to it:

> My dog stopped; then she ran ahead.

In Latin the gender of some nouns is indicated by the base plus the nominative singular ending. The following general rules may be a help in determining gender:

1. Names of males, winds, and months, and of most rivers and mountains, are masculine.

2. Names of females and trees, and of most gems, plants, cities, countries, and abstract qualities, are feminine.
3. Infinitives and defective nouns, and phrases and clauses used as nouns, are neuter.
4. A noun which can denote either a male or a female may be masculine or feminine, and is said to be of common gender.

▪ NUMBER

If a word refers to one thing it is *singular* in number. If it refers to more than one thing, it is *plural*. The plural number is shown in both Latin and English by a change in form:

puer puerī   homō hominēs   boy boys   man men

▪ CASE

Case shows the relation of a noun to the other words of the sentence. In English there are three cases: *Nominative, Possessive,* and *Objective.* The Possessive is indicated by the use of an apostrophe; the other two are recognized by their position in the sentence.

1. *The Nominative Case* is used as the subject of a sentence. It is also used in the predicate after a linking verb, or a factitive verb (a verb of making or naming) in the passive, to refer to the subject:

   > The boy ran home.
   > You are a wise person.
   > The man was called General.

2. *The Possessive Case* shows possession:

   > The girls' mother is a very fine singer.
   > The book's title is mysterious.

3. *The Objective Case* is used as the object of a verb or preposition.

   > I am studying Latin.
   > She is going to the city.

In Latin all cases are indicated by changes in the ending of the noun. The Nominative and Genitive in Latin are roughly equivalent to the English Nominative and Possessive. The other cases are represented in English by the Objective. The Accusative is the object of a verb, and it and the other cases do the work usually done by a prepositional phrase in English. A Latin noun has six cases; their basic uses are as follows:

1. *The Nominative* is used as in English.
2. *The Vocative* is the case of direct address: *Look, Marcus!*
3. *The Genitive* enables a noun to qualify another noun in some way; most of its uses are represented in English by prepositional phrases with *of:* the gardens *of Caesar;* part *of the army;* love *of life;* a man *of great distinction.*
4. *The Dative* expresses the object indirectly affected by the action of a verb or by the quality of an adjective: I gave a book *to Lucius.* I gave *Lucius* a book. He did it *for his friend.* She is unfriendly *to my sister.* You are like *my father.*
5. *The Accusative* limits the action of the verb in various ways, i.e. it tells how far the action of the verb extends: She went *home.* I ran *a mile.* He saw *a bird.* We stayed *three days.*
6. *The Ablative,* having taken over the functions of three separate cases of Indo-European, the language from which Latin and English are both descended, has three basic uses:
   a. Ablative Proper (separation: *from*): He comes *from New York.* She fainted *from hunger.* This book was written *by (i.e. comes from) Charles Dickens.*
   b. Instrumental/Circumstantial Ablative (instrument or circumstance: with): She listened *with great eagerness.* We dig *with shovels.* He came *with his father.* She is a woman *of (i.e. with) great influence.*
   c. Locative Ablative (location in space or time: *in, on, at*): *in Italy; in two days; on Thursday; at seven o'clock.*

A few nouns have a seventh case, *the Locative,* which is used instead of the Ablative to show location.

INFLECTION

Inflection is the change in the form of a noun to show its case and number. The inflection of a noun is called *declension.*

CONSTRUCTION

The construction of a word is its use in the sentence. To construe a noun in Latin, name its case and number and explain why it is in that case.

PRONOUNS

A pronoun (Latin **prō**, *instead of*, and **nōmen,** *noun*) is a word used instead of a noun, which is called its antecedent. Like nouns, pronouns have gender, number, and case; they also have person.

Personal Pronoun—refers to the speaker (first person, *I, we*), refers to the person(s) spoken to (second person, *you*); refers to the person or thing spoken of (third person, *he, she, it, they*)

Relative Pronoun—introduces a subordinate clause and has its antecedent in the principal clause. The relative pronouns are *who, which*, and *that*.

> The teacher whom I saw was a Latin major.

Interrogative Pronoun—asks a question. The interrogative pronouns are *who, which*, and *what*.

> What is it?   Who are you?

Demonstrative Pronoun—points out a particular person or thing; *this, that, these, those*:

> Who is that?   What is this?

Indefinite Pronoun—does not have any definite person or thing for its antecedent: *someone, anything, whatever*.

Reflexive Pronoun—has the subject as its antecedent. Reflexives are *myself, ourselves, yourself, yourselves, himself, herself, itself, themselves*.

> The scholar praises himself.

In both languages, a pronoun agrees with its antecedent in gender, number, and person, but not necessarily in case:

> I saw James as he was walking.
> Mary was polite when I spoke to her.
> The students were listening very intently. They wanted to understand.

INFLECTION

Unlike English nouns, some English pronouns have complete declensions in all three genders, both numbers, all three cases, and all three persons.

			NOMINATIVE				
I	we	you	he	she	it	they	who

			POSSESSIVE				
my	our	your	his	her	its	their	whose
mine	ours	yours		hers		theirs	

			OBJECTIVE				
me	us	you	him	her	it	them	whom

All Latin pronouns by their endings show gender, number, and case, and some also show person.

■ CONSTRUCTION

To construe a pronoun in a Latin sentence, give its person, gender, number, and case, show that it agrees with its antecedent in gender, number, and person, and explain why it is in that case.

═══ ADJECTIVES ═══

An adjective is used to limit or describe a noun or other substantive. It may be used merely attributively:

> Five people came.   Industrious students work hard.

It may be used predicatively, to make a statement about the subject:

> The students were industrious.   To forgive is divine.

Rarely in English, but commonly in Latin, it may be used substantively (as a noun):

> the good   the bad   the ugly
> Be generous to the poor.

Articles—The is the *definite article*, referring to a particular person or thing (or persons or things):

the book the animals the class

A or *an* is the *indefinite article*, not referring to a particular person or thing:

a book an animal a class

It is not used with a plural:

books animals classes

Latin has no articles.

Numeral Adjectives—adjectives denoting number.

Cardinals denote *how many:* three, five, ten
Ordinals show *order:* third, fifth, tenth
Multiplicatives show *how manifold:* threefold, triple, fivefold, quintuple, tenfold
Distributives (Latin only) show *how many at a time:* three at a time, five at a time, ten at a time

Interrogative Adjectives—ask a question: *which? what?*

Which way are you going? What time is it?

Demonstrative Adjectives—point out particular persons or things; *this, that, these, those:*

that boy, these books

Indefinite Adjectives—define a noun as not specific (*some, any*)

■ INFLECTION

Unlike English adjectives, Latin adjectives show by their form, gender, number, and case. In both languages, adjectives (not numeral, interrogative, demonstrative, or indefinite adjectives) are compared and show degree.

Comparison of Adjectives—is a change in form by which the degree of the quality is expressed. The degrees of comparison are called *positive, comparative,* and *superlative.*

Positive denotes the quality in the simple state: large, small, good, bad, beautiful

Comparative denotes the quality in a greater or lesser degree (in Latin only in a greater degree): larger, smaller, better, worse, more beautiful, less beautiful

Superlative denotes the quality in the greatest or (in English) least degree: largest, smallest, best, worst, most beautiful, least beautiful

Adjectives are compared regularly in English by adding *-er* for the comparative, and *-est* for the superlative. Some are compared irregularly (e.g. *good, better, best; bad, worse, worst*); some add the words *more, most, less,* and *least* to the positive. Many adjectives of more than one syllables are compared in this last way: *more interesting, less interesting, most intelligent, least intelligent.* Some adjectives have a comparative and a superlative, but no positive: *inner, inmost, former, foremost* (or *first*)

CONSTRUCTION

To construe an adjective in a Latin sentence describe it as demonstrative, interrogative, or indefinite, give its degree (if it is not positive), gender, number, and case, and say whether it is used attributively, predicatively, or substantively. If attributively or predicatively, show that it agrees with the word it modifies in gender, number, and case; if substantively, explain why it is in that case.

VERBS

A verb is a word that shows action or state of being.

The woman sings and dances.   He is very kind.

Transitive Verb—one which requires an object to complete its meaning:

They study Latin.   He plays a violin.

(*Transitive is from the Latin* **trans**, *across, and* **eō**, *go:* the action goes across from the subject to the object of the verb.)

Note: Transitive verbs of *making, naming, choosing,* etc. may take, in addition to the direct object, an objective complement:

We named the dog Spot.
They elected him President.

Such verbs are called *Factitive Verbs.*

Intransitive Verb—does not require an object to complete its meaning.

> She lives in Greece.   He runs fast.

(In English, but not in Latin, very many verbs may be used either transitively or intransitively: They study hard. He plays all the time. He runs the business.)

Impersonal Verb—does not take a personal subject and is used only in the third person singular:

> It rains.   It is forbidden to cross the tracks.

Linking Verb—is not itself the predicate, but links the subject with the predicate:

> My pet is a dog.   The sky is blue.   The castle is on a hill.

A factitive verb in the passive may act as a linking verb:

> My dog is called Spot.   He was elected President.

Modal Verb—needs an infinitive to complete its meaning:

> He dares to go.   She ought to do it.   We can help.

Auxiliary Verb—(Latin **auxilium**, *aid*) a verb which aids in the conjugation of other verbs:

> I was studying. They do not know Latin. Does he read many books?

Verbs have tense, voice, mood, person, and number.

The *tense* of a verb indicates time.

Present Tense—represents an action as taking place at the present time, or at all times. The present tense often uses the verb *to be* to show that the action is taking place right now:

> The scholar is translating the passage.
> He translates very well.

Past Tense—represents an action that occurred, or was occurring, in the past:

> She drove the car to work every day.
> He was driving too fast at the time of the accident.

In Latin there is a separate *Imperfect Tense* for an action that was occurring in the past.

Future Tense—represents an action that will occur in the future:

> She will buy a new house.

Present Perfect Tense—represents an action as completed at the present time:

> They have finished the first revision.

In English, but not in other languages, the present perfect may also represent an action begun in the past and continuing in the present.

> We have sat here for two hours now.

This use is sometimes called *the false perfect*.

Past Perfect Tense—represents an action as having been completed in some past time:

> We had considered many alternatives.

In Latin this tense is called the *Pluperfect* (**plūs**, *more*, + **perfectum**)

Future Perfect Tense—represents an action as having taken place before some definite time in the future:

> She will have finished the report by the end of the course.

The future and future perfect tenses are much more common in Latin than in English: *I'm going when the sun sets* must be changed to *I shall go when the sun will have set* in order to be translated into Latin.

Most verbs have two *voices*. A verb is in the *active voice* when the subject performs the action:

> Caesar fought in Gaul.

A verb is in the *passive voice* when the subject is acted upon:

> The battle was fought in Gaul.

Only transitive and impersonal verbs can be used in the passive voice.

The *Mood* tells the manner of the action of the verb.

A verb is in the *indicative mood* when it states a fact or asks whether something is a fact.

> Ancient Rome was a great city.   Did Virgil write the Aeneid?

The *subjunctive mood* describes the action as wished for or possible.

Things wished for may be expressed as:

WISHES: May the gods help us! God bless you!
COMMANDS: Let there be light.
EXHORTATIONS: Let's go.

Possible actions may be expressed as:

POTENTIAL: I may go. He might do it.
CONDITIONAL: If it should rain they wouldn't go.
DELIBERATIVE: What should I do?
or CONTRARY TO FACT: You would have loved it.

The *imperative mood* expresses a command. The subject is not usually expressed.

> Go to your room!
> Examine the quality of the merchandise carefully.

A verb agrees with its subject in *person* and *number*.

A verb having two or more subjects connected by *and* must be in the plural.

> The man and woman are my friends.

A verb having two or more singular subjects separated by *or* or *nor* must be in the singular.

> Neither the man nor the woman is happy.

A verb having a singular collective noun as its subject may be in the plural if the subject is thought of as a group of individuals:

> My family enjoy holidays by the sea.
> but
> My family is a large one.

The use of a plural verb with a collective-noun subject is common in English, but very rare in Latin.

INFLECTION

Conjugation—The inflection of a verb is called conjugation. Conjugation gives the forms of a verb in all tenses, moods, persons, and numbers:

I am; you are; he, she, it is; we are; you are; they are; I was; you were; etc.

Synopsis—A synopsis of a verb gives its forms in any required person and number through all tenses of different moods:

FIRST PERSON SINGULAR: I am, I was, I shall be. I have been, etc.

■ CONSTRUCTION

To construe a verb in a Latin sentence, give its tense, voice, mood, person, and number; say whether the verb is transitive, intransitive, linking, or modal; and say what it must or may have to complete its meaning (e.g. a direct object, an infinitive, an indirect object, a predicate accusative). Then name the clause of which it is the verb.

INFINITIVES

An infinitive (Latin **īnfinītum,** *unbounded*) has tense and voice, but not mood, person, or number. It is normally preceded by *to*. It can be active or passive, and it has in English only two tenses, the present and the perfect; in Latin it has also a future. An infinitive may be used to complete the meaning of a modal verb:

He ought to go.

It may also be used as a noun:

To forgive is divine. To have loved is to have lived.
I love to read.

In English, but not in Latin, it may be used as an adjective or adverb:

This book is interesting to read. This is the thing to do.

After a verb of *saying, thinking, perceiving,* or *wishing,* the infinitive may have a subject in the objective case (accusative in Latin), making an infinitive phrase:

He considers himself to be perfect. I know it to be true.
He wants me to go.
The teacher prefers us to memorize the vocabulary.

■ CONSTRUCTION

To construe an infinitive in a Latin sentence, give its tense and voice and say whether it is complementary, subjective, objective, or part of an infinitive phrase. In addition, say whether it is transitive, intransitive, linking, or modal, and what it must or may have to complete its meaning (e.g. a direct object, another infinitive, an indirect object, a predicate accusative).

PARTICIPLES

A participle (Latin **particeps,** *sharing*) shares the attributes of a verb and an adjective. Like a verb, it has tense and voice, and may have an object and be modified by adverbial modifiers. Like an adjective, it modifies a noun or other substantive (and, in Latin, has gender, number, case, and even degree). In English the participle has both voices and the present and perfect tenses. In Latin it also has a future tense.

> We watched the students industriously studying Latin in the library.
> I saw the sheep being sheared.
> Having visited Rome, she went on to Pompeii.
> Having been defeated in the fight, he lost his interest in boxing.

■ CONSTRUCTION

To construe a participle in a Latin sentence, give its tense, voice, gender, number, and case (and degree, if it is not positive), and say whether it is used attributively, predicatively, or substantively. If attributively or predicatively, show that it agrees with the word it modifies in gender, number, and case; if substantively, explain why it is in that case. In addition, say whether the participle is transitive, intransitive, linking, or modal, and say what it must or may have to complete its meaning (e.g. a direct object, an infinitive, an indirect object, a predicate accusative).

SUPINES

The supine does not occur in English; in Latin it does some of the work of the English adverbial infinitive:

This is hard to do. He came to see me.

■ CONSTRUCTION

To construe a supine in a Latin sentence, name its case and say whether it is transitive, intransitive, or modal, and say what it must or may have to complete its meaning (e.g. a direct object, an infinitive, an indirect object, a predicate accusative).

ADVERBS

Adverbs modify verbs, infinitives, participles, adjectives, and other adverbs:

VERB: She drove fast.
INFINITIVE: He likes to drive fast.
PARTICIPLE: I saw her driving fast.
ADJECTIVE: He is nearly exhausted.
ADVERB: They struggled very bravely.

Many adverbs derived from adjectives are compared (i.e. have the comparative and superlative degrees).

fast   faster   fastest

Adverbs may express time, place, reason, manner, degree, affirmation, and negation:

TIME: now, then, recently, soon
PLACE: here, there, everywhere, anywhere
REASON: therefore
MANNER: thus, fast, slowly, courageously
DEGREE: so, very, too, more
AFFIRMATION: yes, yea, aye
NEGATION: no, nay

Interrogative Adverb—asks a question about time, place, reason, or manner:

TIME: When will we go?
PLACE: Where will we go?
REASON: Why will we go?
MANNER: How will we go?

Adverbial Conjunction—introduces a subordinate clause:

Where there is life there is hope.

Adverbial conjunctions refer to time, place, reason, manner or condition:

TIME: When I have eaten my breakfast, I go to school.
PLACE: The town where I live is small.
REASON: I went home because it had started to rain.
MANNER: Do as I do.
CONDITION: You won't learn unless you do your work.

CONSTRUCTION

To construe an adverb in a Latin sentence, mention if it is interrogative, relative, or an adverbial conjunction, give its degree (if it is not positive), and say what it modifies.

PREPOSITIONS

A Preposition (Latin **prae**, *before*, and **positiō**, *placement*) is a word placed before a noun or pronoun to show its relation to the rest of the sentence:

The Latin book is *on* the table.

The professor lived *in* Rome.

She hid the homework *under* the bed.

The bird flew *over* the hill.

In English, prepositions are followed by the objective case. In Latin they are used with the accusative or ablative. The work of an English prepositional phrase may also be done by the last four cases in Latin without a preposition. In other words, Latin uses prepositions less than English does.

■ CONSTRUCTION

To construe a preposition in a Latin sentence, say what case or cases it may be used with, and what noun or pronoun it is being used with.

CONJUNCTIONS

A Conjunction (Latin **con**, *together*, and **iunctiō**, *a joining*) is a word used to connect words, phrases, or clauses. A *Coordinating Conjunction* (*and, but, for, or* or *nor*) joins elements of equal rank or importance. An *Adverbial Conjunction* joins elements of unequal rank or importance.

■ CONSTRUCTION

To construe a coordinating conjunction in a Latin sentence, name the two elements which are joined by it.

INTERJECTIONS

An Interjection (Latin **inter**, *between*, and **jactiō**, *a throwing*) is a word thrown into a sentence to express emotion or surprise, and is used independently of the rest of the sentence: Oh! Aha! Alas!

■ CONSTRUCTION

An interjection is independent of the sentence and has no construction.

PARTICLES

English has no particles; in Latin they express what in English would be shown by punctuation or tone of voice. For example, the particle **-ne** attached to the first word of a statement turns it into a question.

| **Adest.** | *He is here.* | **Adestne?** | *Is he here?* |

WORD FORMATION

━━ PREFIXES ━━

On Adjectives (assimilated forms in parentheses)

co-, com-, con- — *completely, very*
dī-, dis-, (dif-) — *not*
ē-, ex-, (ef-) — *completely, very*
in-, (im-) — *not*
per- — *completely, very*
prae- — *completely, very*
sub- — *somewhat*

On Verbs (assimilated forms in parentheses)

ā-, ab-, abs-, au- — *from, off, away*
ad-, (ac-, af-, ag-, al-, am-, an-, ap-, ar-, as-,
    at-) — *to, toward, in addition*
ante- — *before, forward*
co-, com-, con- — *together, forcibly*
dē- — *down, completely*
dī-, dis-, (dif-) — *apart, away, in another
    direction*
ē-, ex-, (ef-) — *out, completely*
in-, (il-, im-, ir-) — *in, on, into, onto*
inter-, (intel-) — *between, at interval, to pieces*
ob-, obs-, (oc-, of-, om-, op-, os-) — *towards,
    to meet, in opposition to*
per-, (pel-) — *through, completely*
por- — *forth, forward*
prae- (English *pre-*) — *ahead, beforehand*
prō- — *forth, forward*
re-, red-, (ret-) — *back, again*
sē- — *apart, to another place*
sub-, (suc-, suf-, sug-, sum-, sup-, sur-, sus-) —
    *under, secretly, up from under, to the aid
    of*
trā-, trāns- — *across, over, through and through*

━━ SUFFIXES ━━

Making nouns from nouns

Denoting the office or function of, or a collected
body of:
    -ātus, -ātūs, m. — *-ate*
Denoting the quality of a noun (English *-ness,
dom, -hood, -ship):*
    -mōnia, -mōniae, f. — *-mony*
    -mōnium, -mōnī, n. — *-mony*
    -tās, -tātis, f. — *-ty*
    -tūs, -tūtis, f. — *-ty*
Denoting a thing connected with something:
    -āria, -āriae, f.
Denoting the place where something is found,
made, or sold:
    -āria, -āriae, f.
    -ārium, -ārī, n. — *-arium*
Denoting the person who deals with something:
    -ārius, -ārī, m. — *-ary*
Meaning the place where something grows:
    -ētum, -ētī, n. — *-et, -etum*
Meaning the act or practice of *"-izing":*
    -isma, -ismatis, n. — *ism*
Meaning one who *"–izes":*
    -ista, istae, m. — *-ist*
Diminutive, meaning small or little:
    -culus, -culī, m. — *-cle, -cule, -culus*
    -cula, -culae, f. — *-cle, -cule*
    -culum, -culī, n. — *-cle, -cule*
    -ellus, -ellī, m. — *-el, -le*
    -ella, -ellae, f. — *-elle, -le*
    -ellum, -ellī, n. — *-el, -le*
    -ōlus, -ōlī, m. — *-ole, -olus*
    -ōla, -ōlae, f. — *-ole*
    -ōlum, -ōlī, n. — *-ole*
    -ulus, -ulī, m. — *-le, -ule*

(Suffixes continued)
   -ula, -ulae, f. — *-le, -ule*
   -ulum, -ulī, n. — *-le, -ule*
Meaning the bearer of:
   -fer, -ferī, m. — *-fer*
Denoting something associated with the noun:
   -āticum, -āticī, n. — *-age*

Making adjectives from nouns:

Meaning provided with, having:
   -ātus, -āta, -ātum — *-ate*
   -tus, -ta, -tum — *-t, -te*
Meaning full of:
   -idus, -ida, -idum — *-id*
   -lēns, -lentis — *-lent*
   -lentus, -lenta, -lentum — *-lent*
   -ōsus, -ōsa, -ōsum — *-ose, -ous*
Meaning belonging to:
   -ānus, -āna, -ānum — *-an, -ane*
   -ārius, -āria, -ārium — *-ary*
   -āticus, -ātica, -āticum — *-atic*
   -ēnus, -ēna, -ēnum — *-ene*
   -ernus, -erna, -ernum — *-ern, -erne, -ern⟨al⟩*
   -icus, -ica, -icum — *-ic*
   -īnus, -īna, -īnum — *-in, -ine*
   -nus, -na, -num — *-n, -n⟨al⟩, -ne*
   -ter, -tris, -tre — *-ter, -tri⟨an⟩*
   -ticus, -tica, -ticum — *-tic*
   -timus, -tima, -timum — *-time*
   -tris, -tre — *-ter, -tri⟨an⟩*
   -urnus, -urna, -urnum — *-urn, -urne, -urn⟨al⟩*
Meaning connected with:
   -āticus, -ātica, -āticum — *-atic*
   -icus, -ica, -icum — *-ic*
   -ticus, -tica, -ticum — *-tic*
Meaning pertaining to:
   -ālis, -āle — *-al, -ale*
   -āris, -āre — *-ar, -ary*
   -īlis, -īle — *-il, -ile*
Meaning bearing:
   -fer, -fera, -ferum — *-ferous*
   -ferus, -fera, -ferum — *-ferous*
Meaning making:
   -ficus, -fica, -ficum — *-fic*
Meaning made of:
   -āceus, -ācea, -āceum — *-aceous*

   -eus, -ea, -eum — *-eous*
   -icius, -icia, -icium — *-icious*
Meaning coming from:
   -āneus, -ānea, -āneum — *-aneous, -ane⟨an⟩*
   -ānus, -āna, -ānum — *-an, -ane*
   -ēnus, -ēna, -ēnum — *-ene*
   -eus, -ea, -eum — *-eous*
   -īnus, -īna, -īnum — *-in, -ine*
   -ius, -ia. -ium — *-ious*
   -nus, -na, -num — *-n, -ne*

Making verbs from nouns:

Meaning to be or perform whatever the noun means:
   -iō, -īre, -īvī, -ītum (on i- stems) — ____, *-ite*
   -ō, -āre, -āvī, -ātum — ____, *-ate*
   -uō, -uere, -uī, -ūtum (on 4th-declension nouns) — ____, *-ute*
Meaning to be bearing, or the bearer of:
   -ferō, -ferāre, -ferāvī, -ferātum — *-ferate*
Meaning to make:
   -ficō, -ficāre, -ficāvī, -ficātum — *-ficate, -fice, -fy*
Meaning to "–ize":
   -izō, -izāre, -izāvī, -izātum — *-ize*

On Adjectives: Making nouns from adjectives

Denoting the quality of an adjective (English *-ness, -dom, -hood):*
   -ia, -iae, f. — *-y*
   -iēs, -iēī, f. — *-y*
   -mōnia, -mōniae, f. — *-mony*
   -mōnium, -mōnī, n. — *-mony*
   -tās, -tātis, f. — *-ty*
   -tia, -tiae, f. — *-ce, -cy, -ty*
   -tiēs, -tiēī, f. — *-ty*
   -tūdō, -tūdinis, f. — *-tude*
   -tūs, -tūtis, f.
Denoting something associated with the adjective:
   -āticum, -āticī, n. — *-age*
Meaning the act or practice of "–izing":
   -isma, -ismatis, n. — *-ism*

Meaning one who "–izes":
  -ista, -istae, m. — *-ist*

Making adjectives from adjectives:

Meaning making:
  -ficus, -fica, -ficum — *-fic*
Meaning connected with:
  -āticus, -ātica, -āticum — *-atic*
  -icus, -ica, -icum — *-ic*
  -ticus, -tica, -ticum — *-tic*
Diminutive, meaning small or slightly:
  -culus, -cula, -culum
  -ellus, -ella, -ellum
  -ōlus, -ōla, -ōlum
  -ulus, -ula, -ulum

Making verbs from adjectives:

Meaning to be or perform whatever the
adjective means:
  -ō, -āre, -āvī, -ātum — *-ate*
  iō, -īre, -īvī, -ītum (on i-stems) — ____, *-ite*
Meaning to make:
  -ficō, -ficāre, -ficāvī, -ficātum — *-ficate, -fice, -fy*
Meaning to "–ize":
  -izō, -izāre, -izāvī, -izātum — *-ize*

On verbs: Making nouns from verbs

Denoting the action of the verb:
  -āticum, -āticī, n. — *-age*
  -iō, -iōnis, f.* — *-ion*
  -ium, -ī, n.* — *-y*
  -or, -ōris, m. — *-or*
  -siō, -siōnis, f. — *-sion*
  -sūra, -sūrae, f. — *-sure*
  -sus, -sūs, m.* — *-se*
  -tiō, -tiōnis, f. — *-tion*
  -tūra, -tūrae, f. — *-ture*
  -tus, -tūs, m.* — *-t, -te*
Denoting the means or instrument of the action:
  -āticum, -āticī, n. — *-age*
  -brum, -brī, n. — ____
  -bula, -bulae, f. — *-ble, -bule*
  -bulum, -bulī, n. — *-ble, -bule*

  -crum, -crī, n. — *-cher, -cre*
  -culum, -culī, n. — *-cle, -cule*
  -men, -minis, n. — *-me, -men, -ment*
  -mentum, -mentī, n. — *-ment*
  -mōnia, -mōniae, f. — *-mony*
  -mōnium, -mōnī, n. — *-mony*
  -trum, -trī, n. — *-ter, -trum*
  -ula, -ulae, f. — *-le, -ule*
Denoting the result of the action:
  -āticum, -āticī, n. — *-age*
  -men, -minis, n. — *-me, -men, -ment*
  -mentum, -mentī, n. — *-ment*
Denoting the abstract quality of the verb:
  -or, -ōris, m. — *-or*
  -sus, -sūs, m.* — *-se*
  -tus, -tūs, m.* — *-t, -te*
Naming the doer or agent of the action:
  -sor, -sōris, m. — *-sor*
  -tor, -tōris, m. — *-tor*
  -trīx, -trīcis, f. — *-tress, -trix*
Denoting the place where the action is
performed:
  -tōrium, -tōrī, n. — *-torium, -tory*

Making adjectives from verbs:

Meaning making:
  -ficus, -fica, -ficum — *-fic*
Meaning connected with the action:
  -āticus, -ātica, -āticum — *-atic*
  -icus, -ica, -icum — *-ic*
  -ticus, -tica, -ticum — *-tic*
Meaning pertaining to the action:
  -sōrius, -sōria, -sōrium — *-sory*
  -tōrius, -tōria, -tōrium — *-tory*
Meaning having an aggressive tendency to ____:
  -āx, -ācis — *-acious*
Meaning performing or able to perform the
action of the verb:
  -bundus, -bunda, -bundum — *-bund*
  -cundus, -cunda, -cundum — *-cund*
  -ēns, -entis — *-ent*
  -idus, -ida, -idum — *-id*

---

* These may also become concrete in their meaning.

-īvus, -īva, -īvum — *-ive*
-ndus, -nda, -ndum — *-nd*
-ns, -ntis — *-nt*
-uus, -ua, -uum — *-uous*

Meaning receiving or able to receive the action of the verb:

-bilis, -bile — *-bile, -ble*
-ilis, -ile — *-ile, -le*
-īvus, īva, -ivum — *-ive*
-tilis, -tile — *-tile, -tle*
-uus, -ua, -uum — *-uous*

Making verbs from verbs:

Meaning to make:

-ficō, -ficāre, -ficāvī, -ficātum — *-ficate, -fice, -fy*

Inceptive, meaning to begin, become, be in the process of:

-scō, -scere, _____, _____ — *-ish, -sce*

Iterative, meaning to do continually or repeatedly:

-itō, -itāre, -itāvī, -itātum — *-itate*
-sō, -sāre, -sāvī, -sātum — *-sate, -se*
-tō, -tāre, -tāvī, -tātum — *-tate*

Diminutive, meaning to do feebly or slightly:
-illō, -iiāre, -illāvī, -illātum — ***-illate***

Meditative, meaning to do eagerly:
-essō, -essere, -essīvī, -essītum

Desiderative, meaning to desire to do:
-suriō, -surīre, -surīvī, -surītum
-turiō, -turīre, -turīvī, -turītum

INFLECTIONS

NOUNS

FIRST DECLENSION

Puella, f., *girl*

	SINGULAR	PLURAL
NOM.	puella, *a girl*	puellae, *girls*
GEN.	puellae, *of a girl*	puellārum, *of girls*
DAT.	puellae, *to a girl*	puellīs, *to girls*
ACC.	puellam, *a girl*	puellās, *girls*
ABL.	puellā, *by* or *with a girl*	puellīs, *by* or *with girls*

SECOND DECLENSION

	Amīcus, m., *friend*	Fīlius, m., *son*	Puer, m., *boy*	Ager, m., *field*
			SINGULAR	
NOM.	amīcus	fīlius	puer	ager
GEN.	amīcī	fīlī	puerī	agrī
DAT.	amīcō	fīliō	puerō	agrō
ACC.	amīcum	fīlium	puerum	agrum
ABL.	amīcō	fīliō	puerō	agrō
			PLURAL	
NOM.	amīcī	fīliī	puerī	agrī
GEN.	amīcōrum	fīliōrum	puerōrum	agrōrum
DAT.	amīcīs	fīliīs	puerīs	agrīs
ACC.	amīcōs	fīliōs	puerōs	agrōs
ABL.	amīcīs	fīliīs	puerīs	agrīs

The vocative is always the same as the nominative, except of nouns and adjectives in **-us** of the second declension, which have **-e** in the vocative. Proper nouns ending in **-ius**, and **filius**, have the vocative ending in **i**.

(Second Declension continued)

Verbum, n., *word*

	SINGULAR	PLURAL
NOM.	verbum	verba
GEN.	verbī	verbōrum
DAT.	verbō	verbīs
ACC.	verbum	verba
ABL.	verbō	verbīs

THIRD DECLENSION

	Frāter, m., *brother*	Soror, f., *sister*	Iter, n., *journey*	Tempus, n., *time*

SINGULAR

	Frāter, m., *brother*	Soror, f., *sister*	Iter, n., *journey*	Tempus, n., *time*
NOM.	frāter	soror	iter	tempus
GEN.	frātris	sorōris	itineris	temporis
DAT.	frātrī	sorōrī	itinerī	temporī
ACC.	frātrem	sorōrem	iter	tempus
ABL.	frātre	sorōre	itinere	tempore

PLURAL

NOM.	frātrēs	sorōrēs	itinera	tempora
GEN.	frātrum	sorōrum	itinerum	temporum
DAT.	frātribus	sorōribus	itineribus	temporibus
ACC.	frātrēs	sorōrēs	itinera	tempora
ABL.	frātribus	sorōribus	itineribus	temporibus

THIRD DECLENSION—I-STEMS

	Ignis, m., *fire*	Urbs, f., *city*	Mare, n., *sea*

SINGULAR

	Ignis, m., *fire*	Urbs, f., *city*	Mare, n., *sea*
NOM.	ignis	urbs	mare
GEN.	ignis	urbis	maris
DAT.	ignī	urbī	marī
ACC.	ignem	urbem	mare
ABL.	igne	urbe	marī

PLURAL

NOM.	ignēs	urbēs	maria
GEN.	ignium	urbium	marium
DAT.	ignibus	urbibus	maribus
ACC.	ignīs	urbīs	maria
ABL.	ignibus	urbibus	maribus

FOURTH DECLENSION

Passus, m., *pace*   Cornū, n., *horn*

	SINGULAR	PLURAL	SINGULAR	PLURAL
NOM.	passus	passūs	cornū	cornua
GEN.	passūs	passuum	cornūs	cornuum
DAT.	passuī	passibus	cornū	cornibus
ACC.	passum	passūs	cornū	cornua
ABL.	passū	passibus	cornū	cornibus

FIFTH DECLENSION

Diēs, m. and f, *day*   Rēs, f., *thing*

	SINGULAR	PLURAL	SINGULAR	PLURAL
NOM.	diēs	diēs	rēs	rēs
GEN.	diēī	diērum	reī	rērum
DAT.	diēī	diēbus	reī	rēbus
ACC.	diem	diēs	rem	rēs
ABL.	diē	diēbus	rē	rēbus

IRREGULAR DECLENSIONS

	Deus, m., *god*	Dea, f., *goddess*	Domus, f., *house*	Vīs, f., *force, strength*
SINGULAR				
NOM.	deus	dea	domus	vīs
GEN.	deī	deae	domūs, -ī	vīs
DAT.	deō	deae	domuī, -ō	vī
ACC.	deum	deam	domum	vim
ABL.	deō	deā	domō, -ū	vī
PLURAL				
NOM.	deī, diī, dī	deae	domūs	vīrēs
GEN.	deōrum, deum	deārum	domuum, -ōrum	vīrium
DAT.	deīs, diīs, dīs	deābus	domibus	vīribus
ACC.	deōs	deās	domōs, -ūs	vīrēs
ABL.	deīs, diīs, dīs	deābus	domibus	vīribus

ADJECTIVES

FIRST AND SECOND DECLENSIONS

Malus, *bad*

	MASC.	FEM.	NEUT.
SINGULAR			
NOM.	malus	mala	malum
GEN.	malī	malae	malī
DAT.	malō	malae	malō
ACC.	malum	malam	malum
ABL.	malō	malā	malō
PLURAL			
NOM.	malī	malae	mala
GEN.	malōrum	malārum	malōrum
DAT.	malīs	malīs	malīs
ACC.	malōs	malās	mala
ABL.	malīs	malīs	malīs

	Miser, *wretched*			Sacer, *sacred*		
		SINGULAR				
	MASC.	FEM.	NEUT.	MASC.	FEM.	NEUT.
NOM.	miser	misera	miserum	sacer	sacra	sacrum
GEN.	miserī	miserae	miserī	sacrī	sacrae	sacrī
ect.	etc.	etc.	etc.	etc.	etc.	etc.

THIRD DECLENSION—THREE ENDINGS

Celer, *swift*

	SINGULAR			PLURAL		
	MASC.	FEM.	NEUT.	MASC.	FEM.	NEUT.
NOM.	celer	celeris	celere	celerēs	celerēs	celeria
GEN.	celeris	celeris	celeris	celerium	celerium	celerium
DAT.	celerī	celerī	celerī	celeribus	celeribus	celeribus
ACC.	celerem	celerem	celere	celerīs	celerīs	celeria
ABL.	celerī	celerī	celerī	celeribus	celeribus	celeribus

THIRD DECLENSION—TWO ENDINGS

Brevis, *short*

	M. AND F.	NEUT.	M. AND F.	NEUT.
NOM.	brevis	breve	brevēs	brevia
GEN.	brevis	brevis	brevium	brevium
DAT.	brevī	brevī	brevibus	brevibus
ACC.	brevem	breve	brevīs	brevia
ABL.	brevī	brevī	brevibus	brevibus

THIRD DECLENSION—ONE ENDING

Audax, *bold*

NOM.	audāx	audāx	audācēs	audācia
GEN.	audācis	audācis	audācium	audācium
DAT.	audācī	audācī	audācibus	audācibus
ACC.	audācem	audāx	audācīs	audācia
ABL.	audācī	audācī	audācibus	audācibus

DECLENSION OF COMPARATIVES

Certior, *more certain*

	SINGULAR		PLURAL	
	M. AND F.	NEUT.	M. AND F.	NEUT.
NOM.	certior	certius	certiōrēs	certiōra
GEN.	certiōris	certiōris	certiōrum	certiōrum
DAT.	certiōrī	certiōrī	certiōribus	certiōribus
ACC.	certiōrem	certius	certiōrēs	certiōra
ABL.	certiōre	certiōre	certiōribus	certiōribus

Plūs *more*

	SINGULAR		PLURAL	
	M. AND F.	NEUT.	M. AND F.	NEUT.
NOM.	——	plūs	plūrēs	plūra
GEN.	——	plūris	plūrium	plūrium
DAT.	——	——	plūribus	plūribus
ACC.	——	plūs	plūrīs	plūra
ABL.	——	plūre	plūribus	plūribus

DECLENSION OF IRREGULAR ADJECTIVES

Alius, *another*   Ūnus, *one*

SINGULAR

	MASC.	FEM.	NEUT.	MASC.	FEM.	NEUT.
NOM.	alius	alia	aliud	ūnus	ūna	ūnum
GEN.	alīus	alīus	alīus	ūnīus	ūnīus	ūnīus
DAT.	aliī	aliī	aliī	ūnī	ūnī	ūnī
ACC.	alium	aliam	aliud	ūnum	ūnam	ūnum
ABL.	aliō	aliā	aliō	ūnō	ūnā	ūnō

The plural of *alius* is regular, of the First and Second Declensions.

Duo, *two*   Trēs, *three*

	MASC.	FEM.	NEUT.	MASC.	FEM.	NEUT.
NOM.	duo	duae	duo	trēs	trēs	tria
GEN.	duōrum	duārum	duōrum	trium	trium	trium
DAT.	duōbus	duābus	duōbus	tribus	tribus	tribus
ACC.	duōs, duo	duās	duo	trīs	trīs	tria
ABL.	duōbus	duābus	duōbus	tribus	tribus	tribus

COMPARISON OF ADJECTIVES

POSITIVE	COMPARATIVE	SUPERLATIVE
fortis	fortior	fortissimus
vēlōx	vēlōcior	vēlōcissimus
miser	miserior	miserrimus
ācer	ācrior	ācerrimus

COMPARISON OF IRREGULAR ADJECTIVES

POSITIVE	COMPARATIVE	SUPERLATIVE
bonus, *good*	melior	optimus
malus, *bad*	peior	pessimus
magnus, *great*	maior	maximus
parvus, *small*	minor	minimus

COMPARISON OF IRREGULAR ADJECTIVES *(continued)*

POSITIVE	COMPARATIVE	SUPERLATIVE
multus, *much*	——	plūrimus
multum, *much*	plūs	plūrimum
multī, *many*	plūrēs	plūrimī
senex, *old*	senior (maior nātū)	maximus nātū
iuvenis, *young*	iūnior (minor nātū)	minimus nātū
idōneus, *suitable*	magis idōneus	maximē idōneus
exterus, *outer*	exterior	extrēmus (*or*) extimus
inferus, *below*	īnferior	īnfimus (*or*) īmus
posterus, *following*	posterior	postrēmus (*or*) postumus
superus, *above*	superior	suprēmus (*or*) summus
(cis, citrā)	citerior, *hither*	citimus
(in, intrā)	interior, *inner*	intimus
(prae, prō)	prior, *former*	prīmus
(prope)	propior, *nearer*	proximus
(ultrā)	ulterior, *farther*	ultimus
facilis, *easy*	facilior	facillimus
difficilis, *difficult*	difficilior	difficillimus
gracilis, *thin*	gracilior	gracillimus
similis, *like*	similior	simillimus
dissimilis, *unlike*	dissimilior	dissimillimus
humilis, *low*	humilior	humillimus

COMPARISON OF ADVERBS

POSITIVE	COMPARATIVE	SUPERLATIVE
lātē (lātus)	lātius	lātissimē
pulchrē (pulcher)	pulchrius	pulcherrimē
miserē (miser)	miserius	miserrimē
fortiter (fortis)	fortius	fortissimē
ācriter (ācer)	ācrius	ācerrimē
facile (facilis)	facilius	facillimē
bene (bonus)	melius	optimē
male (malus)	peius	pessimē
magnopere (magnus)	magis	maximē
parum (parvus)	minus	minimē
diū	diūtius	diūtissimē

NUMERALS

CARDINALS	ORDINALS
1. ūnus, -a, -um	prīmus, -a, -um
2. duo, duae, duo	secundus, alter
3. trēs, tria	tertius
4. quattuor	quārtus
5. quīnque	quīntus
6. sex	sextus
7. septem	septimus
8. octō	octāvus
9. novem	nōnus
10. decem	decimus
11. ūndecim	ūndecimus
12. duodecim	duodecimus
13. tredecim	tertius decimus
14. quattuordecim	quārtus decimus
15. quīndecim	quīntus decimus
16. sēdecim	sextus decimus
17. septendecim	septimus decimus
18. duodēvīgintī	duodēvīcēsimus
19. ūndēvīgintī	ūndēvīcēsimus
20. vīgintī	vīcēsimus
21. vīgintī ūnus	vīcēsimus prīmus
(ūnus et vīgintī)	
29. ūndētrīgintā	ūndētrīcēsimus
30. trīgintā	trīcēsimus
40. quadrāgintā	quadrāgēsimus
50. quīnquāgintā	quīnquāgēsimus
60. sexāgintā	sexāgēsimus
70. septuāgintā	septuāgēsimus
80. octōgintā	octōgēsimus
90. nōnāgintā	nōnāgēsimus
100. centum	centēsimus
200. ducentī, -ae, -a	ducentēsimus
300. trecentī	trecentēsimus
400. quadringentī	quadringentēsimus
500. quīngentī	quīngentēsimus
600. sescentī	sescentēsimus
700. septingentī	septingentēsimus
800. octingentī	octingentēsimus
900. nōngentī	nōngentēsimus
1000. mīlle	mīllēsimus
2000. duo mīlia	bis mīllēsimus

PRONOUNS

PERSONAL

	FIRST PERSON Ego, *I*		SECOND PERSON Tū, *you*	THIRD PERSON Is, *he*; ea, *she* id, *it*
	SINGULAR	PLURAL	SINGULAR	PLURAL *(For declension see p. 505)*
NOM.	ego	nōs	tū	vōs
GEN.	meī	nostrum nostrī	tuī	vestrum vestrī
DAT.	mihi	nōbīs	tibi	vōbīs
ACC.	mē	nōs	tē	vōs
ABL.	mē	nōbīs	tē	vōbīs

REFLEXIVE

FIRST PERSON
Meī, *of myself*

SECOND PERSON
Tuī, *of yourself*

These are declined like the personal pronoun of the same person, except that they have no nominative.

THIRD PERSON
Suī, *of himself, herself, itself*

	SINGULAR	PLURAL
GEN.	suī	suī
DAT.	sibi	sibi
ACC.	sē (*or*) sēsē	sē (*or*) sēsē
ABL.	sē (*or*) sēsē	sē (*or*) sēsē

DEMONSTRATIVE

Hic, *this*

	SINGULAR			PLURAL		
	MASC.	FEM.	NEUT.	MASC.	FEM.	NEUT.
NOM.	hic	haec	hoc	hī	hae	haec
GEN.	huius	huius	huius	hōrum	hārum	hōrum
DAT.	huic	huic	huic	hīs	hīs	hīs
ACC.	hunc	hanc	hoc	hōs	hās	haec
ABL.	hōc	hāc	hōc	hīs	hīs	hīs

Ille, *that*

	SINGULAR			PLURAL		
	MASC.	FEM.	NEUT.	MASC.	FEM.	NEUT.
NOM.	ille	illa	illud	illī	illae	illa
GEN.	illīus	illīus	illīus	illōrum	illārum	illōrum
DAT.	illī	illī	illī	illīs	illīs	illīs
ACC.	illum	illam	illud	illōs	illās	illa
ABL.	illō	illā	illō	illīs	illīs	illīs

Iste, *that, that of yours*   Ipse, *self*

	SINGULAR					
	MASC.	FEM.	NEUT.	MASC.	FEM.	NEUT.
NOM.	iste	ista	istud	ipse	ipsa	ipsum
GEN.	istīus	istīus	istīus	ipsīus	ipsīus	ipsīus
DAT.	istī	istī	istī	ipsī	ipsī	ipsī
ACC.	istum	istam	istud	ipsum	ipsam	ipsum
ABL.	istō	istā	istō	ipsō	ipsā	ipsō

The plural is regular.

Is, *that, he*

	SINGULAR			PLURAL		
	MASC.	FEM.	NEUT.	MASC.	FEM.	NEUT.
NOM.	is	ea	id	eī	eae	ea
GEN.	eius	eius	eius	eōrum	eārum	eōrum
DAT.	eī	eī	eī	eīs	eīs	eīs
ACC.	eum	eam	id	eōs	eās	ea
ABL.	eō	eā	eō	eīs	eīs	eīs

Īdem, *same*

	SINGULAR			PLURAL		
	MASC.	FEM.	NEUT.	MASC.	FEM.	NEUT.
NOM.	īdem	eadem	idem	eīdem	eaedem	eadem
GEN.	eiusdem	eiusdem	eiusdem	eōrundem	eārundem	eōrundem
DAT.	eīdem	eīdem	eīdem	eīsdem	eīsdem	eīsdem
ACC.	eundem	eandem	idem	eōsdem	eāsdem	eadem
ABL.	eōdem	eādem	eōdem	eīsdem	eīsdem	eīsdem

RELATIVE

Quī, *who, which, that*

	SINGULAR			PLURAL		
	MASC.	FEM.	NEUT.	MASC.	FEM.	NEUT.
NOM.	quī	quae	quod	quī	quae	quae
GEN.	cuius	cuius	cuius	quōrum	quārum	quōrum
DAT.	cui	cui	cui	quibus	quibus	quibus
ACC.	quem	quam	quod	quōs	quās	quae
ABL.	quō	quā ✓	quō	quibus	quibus	quibus

INTERROGATIVE

Quis, *who? what?*

	SINGULAR			PLURAL		
	M. AND F.	NEUT.		MASC.	FEM.	NEUT.
NOM.	quis	quid		quī	quae	quae
GEN.	cuius	cuius		quōrum	quārum	quōrum
DAT.	cui	cui		quibus	quibus	quibus
ACC.	quem	quid		quōs	quās	quae
ABL.	quō	quō		quibus	quibus	quibus

The adjective **quī,** *what,* is declined like the relative **quī.**

INDEFINITE

Aliquis, *someone*

	SINGULAR			PLURAL		
	M. AND F.	NEUT.		MASC.	FEM.	NEUT.
NOM.	aliquis	aliquid		aliquī	aliquae	aliqua
GEN.	alicuius	alicuius		aliquōrum	aliquārum	alquōrum
DAT.	alicui	alicui		aliquibus	aliquibus	aliquibus
ACC.	aliquem	aliquid		aliquōs	aliquās	aliqua
ABL.	aliquō	aliquō		aliquibus	aliquibus	aliquibus

The adjective is **aliquī, aliqua, aliquod.**
Quis, *any one,* is declined like **aliquis** without **ali-.**
Quī, qua, quod, the adjective *any,* is declined like **aliquī, aliqua, aliquod** without **ali-.**

Quīdam, *a certain (one)* (the pronoun)

| | SINGULAR | | PLURAL | | |
	M. AND F.	NEUT.	MASC.	FEM.	NEUT.
NOM.	quīdam	quiddam	quīdam	quaedam	quaedam
GEN.	cuiusdam	cuiusdam	quōrundam	quārundam	quōrundam
DAT.	cuidam	cuidam	quibusdam	quibusdam	quibusdam
ACC.	quendam	quiddam	quōsdam	quāsdam	quaedam
ABL.	quōdam	quōdam	quibusdam	quibusdam	quibusdam

Quīdam , quaedam, quoddam, *certain* (the adjective)

SINGULAR

	MASC.	FEM.	NEUT.
NOM.	quīdam	quaedam	quoddam
GEN.	cuiusdam	cuiusdam	cuiusdam
DAT.	cuidam	cuidam	cuidam
ACC.	quendam	quandam	quoddam
ABL.	quōdam	quādam	quōdam

PLURAL

The plural is declined like the plural of the pronoun.

Quisquam, *anyone*

SINGULAR

	M. AND F.	NEUT.
NOM.	quisquam	quidquam (quicquam)
GEN.	cuiusquam	cuiusquam
DAT.	cuiquam	cuiquam
ACC.	quemquam	quidquam (quicquam)
ABL.	quōquam	quōquam

(This is substantive only; there is no plural.)

Quisque, *each*

Quisque, quidque is declined like **quis, quid** with **-que** added.
Quīque, quaeque, quodque, the adjective, is declined like **quī, quae, quod** with **-que** added.

VERBS

FIRST CONJUGATION

PRINCIPAL PARTS: vocō, vocāre, vocāvī, vocātum
STEMS: vocā-, vocāv-, vocāt-

ACTIVE VOICE		PASSIVE VOICE	

INDICATIVE
PRESENT

I call, am calling		*I am called*	
vocō	vocāmus	vocor	vocāmur
vocās	vocātis	vocāris	vocāminī
vocat	vocant	vocātur	vocantur

IMPERFECT

I was calling		*I was being called*	
vocābam	vocābāmus	vocābar	vocābāmur
vocābās	vocābātis	vocābāris	vocābāminī
vocābat	vocābant	vocābātur	vocābantur

FUTURE

I shall call		*I shall be called*	
vocābō	vocābimus	vocābor	vocābimur
vocābis	vocābitis	vocāberis	vocābiminī
vocābit	vocābunt	vocābitur	vocābuntur

PERFECT

I have called, I called		*I have been called, I was called*			
vocāvī	vocāvimus	vocātus { sum	vocātī { sumus
vocāvistī	vocāvistis	(-a, -um) { es	(-ae, -a) { estis
vocāvit	vocāvērunt	{ est	{ sunt

PLUPERFECT

I had called		*I had been called*			
vocāveram	vocāverāmus	vocātus { eram	vocātī { erāmus
vocāverās	vocāverātis	(-a, -um) { erās	(-ae, -a) { erātis
vocāverat	vocāverant	{ erat	{ erant

FUTURE PERFECT

I shall have called   *I shall have been called*

vocāverō	vocāverimus	vocātus	erō	vocātī	erimus
vocāveris	vocāveritis	(-a, -um)	eris	(-ae, -a)	eritis
vocāverit	vocāverint		erit		erunt

IMPERATIVE
PRESENT

Call   *Be called*

vocā	vocāte	vocāre	vocāminī

FUTURE

You, he, they shall call   *You, he, they shall be called*

vocātō	vocātōte	vocātor	——
vocātō	vocantō	vocātor	vocantor

INFINITIVES

PRES. vocāre, *to call*   vocārī, *to be called*
PERF. vocāvisse, *to have called*   vocātus esse, *to have been called*
FUT. vocātūrus esse, *to be about to call* ——

SECOND CONJUGATION

PRINCIPAL PARTS: moneō, monēre, monuī, monitum
STEMS: monē-, monu-, monit-

ACTIVE VOICE   PASSIVE VOICE

INDICATIVE
PRESENT

I advise, am advising   *I was being advised*

moneō	monēmus	moneor	monēmur
monēs	monētis	monēris	monēminī
monet	monent	monētur	monentur

(Second Conjugation continued)

IMPERFECT

I was advising		*I was being advised*	
monēbam	monēbāmus	monēbar	monēbāmur
monēbas	monēbātis	monēbāris	monēbāminī
monēbat	monēbant	monēbātur	monēbantur

FUTURE

I shall advise		*I shall be advised*	
monēbō	monēbimus	monēbor	monēbimur
monēbis	monēbitis	monēberis	monēbiminī
monēbit	monēbunt	monēbitur	monēbuntur

PERFECT

I have advised, I advised		*I have been advised, I was advised*			
monuī	monuimus	monitus	sum	monitī	sumus
monuistī	monuistis	(-a, -um)	es	(-ae, -a)	estis
monuit	monuērunt		est		sunt

PLUPERFECT

I had advised		*I had been advised*			
monueram	monuerāmus	monitus	eram	monitī	erāmus
monuerās	monuerātis	(-a, -um)	erās	(-ae, -a)	erātis
monuerat	monuerant		erat		erant

FUTURE PERFECT

I shall have advised		*I shall have been advised*			
monuerō	monuerimus	monitus	erō	monitī	erimus
monueris	monueritis	(-a, -um)	eris	(-ae, -a)	eritis
monuerit	monuerint		erit		erunt

IMPERATIVE
PRESENT

Advise		*Be advised*	
monē	monēte	monēre	monēminī

FUTURE

You, he, they shall advise		*You, he, they shall be advised*	
monētō	monētōte	monētor	——
monētō	monentō	monētor	monentor

INFINITIVES

PRES.	monēre, *to advise*	monērī, *to be advised*
PERF.	monuisse, *to have advised*	monitus esse, *to have been advised*
FUT.	monitūrus esse, *to be about to advise*	——

THIRD CONJUGATION

PRINCIPAL PARTS: regō, regere, rēxī, rēctum
STEMS: reg-, rēx-, rēct-

ACTIVE VOICE   PASSIVE VOICE

INDICATIVE
PRESENT

I rule, am ruling		*I am ruled*	
regō	regimus	regor	regimur
regis	regitis	regeris	regiminī
regit	regunt	regitur	reguntur

IMPERFECT

I was ruling		*I was being ruled*	
regēbam	regēbāmus	regēbar	regēbāmur
regēbās	regēbātis	regēbāris	regēbāminī
regēbat	regēbant	regēbātur	regēbantur

FUTURE

I shall rule		*I shall be ruled*	
regam	regēmus	regar	regēmur
regēs	regētis	regēris	regēminī
reget	regent	regētur	regentur

(Third Conjugation continued)

PERFECT

I have ruled, I ruled				*I have been ruled, I was ruled*		
rēxī	rēximus	rēctus	sum	rēctī	sumus
rēxistī	rēxistis	(-a, -um)	es	(-ae, -a)	estis
rēxit	rēxērunt		est		sunt

PLUPERFECT

I had ruled				*I had been ruled*		
rēxeram	rēxerāmus	rēctus	eram	rēctī	erāmus
rēxerās	rēxerātis	(-a, -um)	erās	(-ae, -a)	erātis
rēxerat	rēxerant		erat		erant

FUTURE PERFECT

I shall have ruled				*I shall have been ruled*		
rēxerō	rēxerimus	rēctus	erō	rēctī	erimus
rēxeris	rēxeritis	(-a, -um)	eris	(-ae, -a)	eritis
rēxerit	rēxerint		erit		erunt

IMPERATIVE
PRESENT

Rule		*Be ruled*	
rege	regite	regere	regiminī

FUTURE

You, he, they shall rule		*You, he, they shall be ruled*	
regitō	regitōte	regitor	——
regitō	reguntō	regitor	reguntor

INFINITIVES

PRES.	regere, *to rule*	regī, *to be ruled*	
PERF.	rēxisse, *to have ruled*	rēctus esse, *to have been ruled*	
FUT.	rēctūrus esse, *to be about to rule*	——	

FOURTH CONJUGATION

PRINCIPAL PARTS: audiō, audīre, audīvī, audītum
STEM: audī-, audīv-, audīt-

ACTIVE VOICE		PASSIVE VOICE	

INDICATIVE
PRESENT

I hear, am hearing, do hear		*I am heard*	
audiō	audīmus	audior	audīmur
audīs	audītis	audīris	audīminī
audit	audiunt	audītur	audiuntur

IMPERFECT

I was hearing		*I was being heard*	
audiēbam	audiēbāmus	audiēbar	audiēbāmur
audiēbās	audiēbātis	audiēbāris	audiēbāminī
audiēbat	audiēbant	audiēbātur	audiēbantur

FUTURE

I shall hear		*I shall be heard*	
audiam	audiēmus	audiar	audiēmur
audiēs	audiētis	audiēris	audiēminī
audiet	audient	audiētur	audientur

PERFECT

I have heard, I heard			*I have been (was) heard*		
audīvī	audīvimus	audītus (-a, -um) { sum / es / est }	audītī (-ae, -a) { sumus / estis / sunt }		
audīvistī	audīvistis				
audīvit	audīvērunt				

PLUPERFECT

I had heard			*I had been heard*		
audīveram	audīverāmus	audītus (-a, -um) { eram / erās / erat }	audītī (-ae, -a) { erāmus / erātis / erant }		
audīverās	audīverātis				
audīverat	audīverant				

FUTURE PERFECT

I shall have heard			*I shall have been heard*		
audīverō	audīverimus	audītus (-a, -um) { erō / eris / erit }	audītī (ae, -a) { erimus / eritis / erunt }		
audīveris	audīveritis				
audīverit	audīverint				

(Fourth Conjugation continued)

IMPERATIVE
PRESENT

Hear		*Be heard*	
audī	audīte	audīre	audīminī

FUTURE

You, he, they shall hear		*You, he, they shall be heard*	
audītō	audītōte	audītor	____
audītō	audiuntō	audītor	audiuntor

INFINITIVES

PRES.	audīre, *to hear*		audīrī, *to be heard*
PERF.	audīvisse, *to have heard*		audītus esse, *to have been heard*
FUT.	audītūrus esse, *to be about to hear*		____

THIRD CONJUGATION—VERBS IN -iō

PRINCIPLE PARTS: capiō, capere, cēpī, captum
STEMS: capi-, cēp-, capt-

ACTIVE VOICE		PASSIVE VOICE	

INDICATIVE
PRESENT

I take, am taking		*I am taken*	
capiō	capimus	capior	capimur
capis	capitis	caperis	capiminī
capit	capiunt	capitur	capiuntur

IMPERFECT

I was taking	*I was being taken*
capiēbam, etc.	capiēbar, etc.

FUTURE

I shall take		*I shall be taken*	
capiam	capiēmus	capiar	capiēmur
capiēs	capiētis	capiēris	capiēminī
capiet	capient	capiētur	capientur

PERFECT

I have taken, I took	*I have been (was) taken*
cēpī, etc.	captus sum, etc.

FUTURE PERFECT

I shall have taken	*I shall have been taken*
cēperō, etc.	captus erō, etc.

PLUPERFECT

I had taken	*I had been taken*
cēperam, etc.	captus eram, etc.

IMPERATIVE
PRESENT

	Take		*Be taken*
cape	capite	capere	capiminī

FUTURE

You, he, they shall take		*You, he, they shall be taken*	
capitō	capitōte	capitor	____
capitō	capiuntō	capitor	capiuntor

INFINITIVES

PRES.	capere, *to take*	capī, *to be taken*
PERF.	cēpisse, *to have taken*	captus esse, *to have been taken*
FUT.	captūrus esse, *to be about to take*	____

IRREGULAR VERBS

PRINCIPAL PARTS:	PRINCIPAL PARTS:
sum, esse, fuī	possum, posse, potuī

INDICATIVE
PRESENT

I am		*I am able, I can*	
sum	sumus	possum	possumus
es	estis	potes	potestis
est	sunt	potest	possunt

Irregular Verbs (continued)

IMPERFECT

I was			*I was able, I could*	
eram	erāmus		poteram	poterāmus
erās	erātis		poterās	poterātis
erat	erant		poterat	poterant

FUTURE

I shall be			*I shall be able*	
erō	erimus		poterō	poterimus
eris	eritis		poteris	poteritis
erit	erunt		poterit	poterunt

PERFECT

I was, have been			*I have been able, I could*	
fuī	fuimus		potuī	potuimus
fuistī	fuistis		potuistī	potuistis
fuit	fuērunt		potuit	potuērunt

PLUPERFECT

I had been			*I had been able*	
fueram	fuerāmus		potueram	potuerāmus
fuerās	fuerātis		potuerās	potuerātis
fuerat	fuerant		potuerat	potuerant

FUTURE PERFECT

I shall have been			*I shall have been able*	
fuerō	fuerimus		potuerō	potuerimus
fueris	fueritis		potueris	potueritis
fuerit	fuerint		potuerit	potuerint

IMPERATIVE
PRESENT

Be			(lacking)
es	este		

FUTURE

You, he, they shall be			(lacking)
estō	estōte		
estō	suntō		

INFINITIVES

PRES.	esse, *to be*	posse, *to be able*	
PERF.	fuisse, *to have been*	potuisse, *to have been able*	
FUT.	futūrus esse or } *to be about to be* fore	(lacking)	

PRINCIPAL PARTS: ferō, ferre, tulī, lātum, *bear, carry*.

PRESENT INDICATIVE

ACTIVE		PASSIVE	
ferō	ferimus	feror	ferimur
fers	fertis	ferris	feriminī
fert	ferunt	fertur	feruntur

INDICATIVE

ACTIVE		PASSIVE	

IMPERFECT

ferēbam	ferēbar

FUTURE

feram	ferar

PERFECT

tulī	lātus sum

PLUPERFECT

tuleram	lātus eram

FUTURE PERFECT

tulerō	lātus erō

IMPERATIVE

PRESENT

fer	ferte	ferre	feriminī

FUTURE

fertō	fertōte	fertor	——
fertō	feruntō	fertor	feruntor

(Irregular Verbs continued)

INFINITIVES

PRES.	ferre	ferrī
PERF.	tulisse	lātus esse
FUT.	lātūrus esse	——

PRINCIPAL PARTS: eō, īre iī (īvī), itum, *to go.*

	INDICATIVE				INFINITIVES

	PRESENT		PERFECT	PRES.	īre
eō	īmus		iī (īvī)	PERF.	īsse (ivisse)
īs	ītis			FUT.	itūrus esse
it	eunt				

				IMPERATIVE	
	IMPERFECT		PLUPERFECT	PRES.	ī, īte
	ībam		ieram	FUT.	ītō, ītōte
					ītō, euntō

	FUTURE		FUTURE PERFECT		SUPINE
	ībo		ierō		
				ACC.	itum
				ABL.	itū

PRINCIPAL PARTS: fīō, fierī, factus sum, *be made, become.*

	INDICATIVE				INFINITIVES

	PRESENT		PERFECT	PRES.	fieri
fīō	fīmus		factus sum	PERF.	factus esse
fīs	fītis				
fit	fīunt				

	IMPERFECT		PLUPERFECT
	fīēbam		factus eram

	FUTURE		FUTURE PERFECT
	fīam		factus erō

GLOSSARY OF PROPER NAMES

Names are marked with the number of the Lesson in which they first appear. Names that do not have a lesson number occur either in the *If You Lived in Ancient Rome, Listening and Speaking*, or in the *Writing Latin Prose* section included in the Teacher's Resource Binder.

A

Abeōna, -ae, f. *Abeona* ("Goer-Away"; numen which helped a baby in its first steps away from its parents or nurse)

Aborīgīnēs, -um, m. *the Aborigines* (the original inhabitants of Latium, the ancestors of the Latins)

Acestēs, Acestae, m. *Acestes* (a Trojan-descended king in Sicily) 16

Achātēs, -ae, m. *Achates* (a Trojan, faithful friend of Aeneas) 17

Acherōn, Acherontis, m. *Acheron* ("Joyless"; a river of the Lower World) 19

Achillēs, Achillis, m. *Achilles* (greatest Greek hero in the Trojan War) 18

Acca Lārentia, Acca Lārentiae, f. *Acca Larentia* (wife of Faustulus) 27

Ācis, Ācidis, m. *Acis* (a river of Sicily; a handsome shepherd, the son of Faunus)

Actiānus, -a, -um *belonging to Actius*

Actius, -a, -um *Actius, Actia, Actian, of the Actian family* (a Roman **nōmen gentīle**)

Adeōna, -ae, f. *Adeona* ("Goer-Toward"; numen which helped a baby in its first steps towards its parents or nurse)

Aemiliānus, -a, -um *Aemilianus* ("originating from the Aemilian family", a Roman **cognōmen**)

Aemilius, -a, -um *Aemilius, Aemilia, Aemilian, of the Aemilian family* (a Roman **nōmen gentīle**)

Aenēās, Aenēae, m. *Aeneas* 2

Āfrica, -ae, f. *North Africa, Africa* 5

Āfricānus, -a, -um *African* 5; *Africanus* (a Roman **cognōmen**)

Agamemnon, Agamemnonis, m. *Agamemnon* (a Greek name)

Alba Longa, Albae Longae, f. *Alba Longa* (in Roman etymology, "the Long White City") 26

Alexander, Alexandrī, m. *Alexander* (Paris, a son of Priam and Hecuba, was also called Alexander) 4

Amāta, -ae, f. *Amata* (wife of Latinus) 21

Amor, Amōris, m. *Amor* (god of love) 13

Amūlius, -ī, m. *Amulius* (brother of Numitor Silvius) 26

Ancus, -ī, m. *Ancus* (a Sabine **praenōmen**) 33

Andābata, -ae, m. *Andabata* ("Safe-Walker", a type of gladiator)

Andromacha, -ae, f. *Andromache* (widow of Hector and wife of Helenus) 12

Anicētiānus, -a, -um *belonging to Anicetus*

Anicētus, -ī, m. *Anicetus* (a Roman **cognōmen**)

Anna, -ae, f. *Anna* or *Hannah* (Elissa's sister) 5

Antōnius, -a, -um *Antonius, Antony, Antonia, Antonian, of the Antonian family* (a Roman **nōmen gentīle**) 31

Apollō, Apollinis, m. *Apollo* (god of light, music, beauty, and oracular reponses; a savior god) 17

App. abbreviation of *Appius*

Appius, -a, -um *Appian, of Appius*

Appius, -ī, m. *Appius* (a Roman **praenōmen**)

Ardea, -ae, f. *Ardea* (a town of the Rutulians in Latium) 38

Ariadna, -ae, f. *Ariadne* (daughter of King Minos of Crete) 17

Arrūns, Arruntis, m. *Arruns* (an Etruscan name) 35

Asia, -ae, f. *Asia Minor, Asia* 1

Ascanius, Ascanī, m. *Ascanius* (son of Aeneas and Creusa) 8

Athēnae, -ārum, f. *Athens* 30

Ātrium, -ī, n. *Atrium* (a name for several public buildings); **Atrium Vestae** *the Atrium of Vesta* (the House of the Vestals)

Atticus, -a, -um *Attic, Athenian* 17

Augur, Auguris, m. *Augur* ("Teller", a type of soothsayer at Rome)

Augustus, -ī, m. *Augustus* ("Consecrated", the title assumed by Octavian after he came to power, claimed also by later emperors) 23

Aureum see **Milliārium**

Aurōra, -ae, f. *Aurora* (goddess of the dawn) 17

Aventīnus, -a, -um *Aventine, of the Aventine* (one of the hills of Rome) 28

B

Basilica Aemilia, Basilicae Aemiliae, f. *Basilica Aemilia* (a basilica in the Roman Forum, built in 179 B.C. by M. Aemilius Lepidus)

Britannia, -ae, f. *Britain*

Britannus, -a, -um *British;* (as noun) *Briton*

Brutannia, -ae, f. *Brutannia* (original name of **Britannia**)

Brūtus, -ī, m. *Brutus* (eponymous hero of the Britons; also, a **cognōmen** of the Junius family) 37

C

C. (abbreviation for *Gaius*) 36

Cācus, -ī, m. *Cacus* (an evil giant who lived in a cave at the site of Rome) 22

Caere, n. (indecl.) *Caere* (an old town of the Etruscans) 38

Caesar, Caesaris, m. *Caesar* (a **cognōmen** of the Julius family) 26

Camilla, -ae, f. *Camilla* (a Volscian maiden warrior, and ally of Turnus); *a Camilla* (young girl at-tendant on a Roman priest, often the priest's own child)

Camillus, -ī, m. *a Camillus* (young boy attendant on a Roman priest, often the priest's own child)

Campī Luctuōsī, Campōrum Luctuōsōrum, m. *the Fields of Mourning* (a place in the Lower World reserved for the souls of those who had died for love)

Campus, -ī, m. *the Campus* (the *Campus Martius*, a large park, exercise ground, training area, and voting place at Rome) 8

Cānēns, Cānentis, f. *Canens* ("White"; a beautiful nymph, the wife of Picus)

Capitōlīnus, -a, -um *Capitoline* (of the Capitol Hill in Rome) **Clīvus Capitōlīnus** *Clivus Capitolinus* (a street in Rome leading from the Forum to the Capitolium, the upper extension of the Via Sacra)

Capitōlium, -ī, n. *Capitolium* (the Capitoline Hill; the great temple of Jupiter, Juno, and Minerva built there) 29

Carna, -ae, f. *Carna* ("Flesher"; numen of healthy flesh in infants)

Carthāgō, Carthāginis, f. *Carthage* (city in North Africa) 13

Cassandra, -ae, f. *Cassandra* (a daughter of Priam and Hecuba) 8

Celadus, -ī, m. *Celadus* (a Greek name)

Cerēs, Cereris, f. *Ceres* (goddess of agriculture, sister of Jupiter)

Circē, Circae, f. *Circe* (a beautiful witch-goddess who turned men into animals) 22

Circus, -ī, m. *Circus* (the name of several race-tracks) 28; **Circus Maximus** *Circus Maximus* (a chariot-racing track in the valley between the Palatine and Aventine Hills)

Claudius, -a, -um *Claudius, Claudia, Claudian, of the Claudian family* (a Roman **nōmen gentīle**)

Cleopātra, -ae, f. *Cleopatra* (a Macedonian queen of Egypt) 31

Clīvus, -ī, m. *Clivus* ("Slope", part of the name of several Roman streets: **Clivus Urbius** *Clivus Urbius* (a street leading from the Vicus Cyprius up the Esquiline Hill) 37; **Clīvus Capitōlīnus** *Clivus Capitolinus* (a street in Rome leading from the Forum to the Capitolium, the upper extension of the Via Sacra)

Cloāca, -ae, f. *the Cloaca* (a river converted to a sewer by the first Tarquin) 34

Cloelius, -a, -um *Cloelius, Cloelia, Cloelian, of the Cloelian family* (a Roman **nōmen gentīle**) 40

Clūsīnus, -a, -um *Clusian, of Clusium* (modern Chiusi, an Etruscan town) 39

Cn. abbreviation of *Gnaeus*

Coclēs, Coclitis, m. *Cocles* (a Roman **cognōmen**) 39

Cōcytus, -ī, m. *Cocytus* ("Lamentation"; a river of the Lower World) 19

Collātīnus, -a, -um *Collatinus* (a Roman **cognōmen**) 38

Collēgium, -ī, n. *Collegium, College* (a group of magistrates or priests holding the same office); **Collēgium Augurum** *the College of Augurs*; **Collēgium Pontificum** *the College of Pontiffs*

Cōlus, -ī, m. Cole (an early British King)

Cōnsuālia, -ium, n. (i-stem) *Consualia* (Feast of Consus) 28

Cōnsul, Cōnsulis, m. *Consul* (one of the two executive magistrates of Rome) 38

Cōnsus, -ī, m. *Consus* (= *Conditus*, "the buried god", the name of the river which was covered over to make a track for horse racing; the Romans identified Consus with Neptune, the creator of the horse) 28

Corinthius, -a, -um *Corinthian, of Corinth* 33

Cornēlius, -a, -um *Cornelius, Cornelia, Cornelian, of the Cornelian family* (a Roman **nōmen gentīle**)

Crotō, Crotōnis, m. *or* f. *Crotona* (a town of south Italy) 30

Crēta, -ae, f. *Crete* (an island in the eastern Mediterranean) 10

Creūsa, Creūsae, f. *Creusa* 2

Crīmīsus, -ī, m. *Crimisus* (a river in SW Sicily; the god of the river) 16

Cuba, -ae, f. *Cuba* ("Recliner", numen which taught an infant to sleep in a bed rather than a cradle)

Cūmae, Cūmārum, f. *Cumae* (a Greek colony north of Naples) 16

Cupīdō, Cupīdinis, m. *Cupid* (another name for Amor) 14

Cūria, -ae, f. *Curia, Senate House* 36

Cūriātius, -a, -um *Curiatius, Curiatia, Curiatian, of the Curiatian family* (an Alban and Roman **nōmen gentīle**) 32

Cӯprius (see **Vīcus Cӯprius**)

Cytherēa, -ae, f. *Cytherea* (a name for the goddess Venus; she was born from the sea near the island of Cythera) 3

D

Daedalus, -ī, m. *Daedalus* (an Athenian craftsman and inventor) 17

Dēiphoba, -ae, f. *Deiphobe* (the Cumaean Sybil) 17

Dēmarātus, -i, m. *Demaratus* (a Greek name) 33

Diālis, -e *Dialis, of Jupiter*

Diāna, -ae, f. *Diana* (virgin goddess of wild nature, hunting, and childbirth) 30

Dictātor, Dictātōris, m. *Dictator* (an official chosen to take over the government when martial law was declared)

Dīdō, Dīdōnis, f. *Dido* (nickname of Elissa) 13

Dimachaerus, -ī, m. *Dimachaerus* ("Two-Dagger-Man", a type of gladiator)

Dīs, Dītis, m. *Dis* (god of the Lower World, brother of Jupiter) 18

Domus, -ūs, f. *Domus* ("House", the name of several palaces at Rome: **Domus Trānsitōria** *Domus Transistoria* ("Passage House", Nero's first palace); **Domus Aurea** *Domus Aurea* ("Golden House", Nero's great palace)

Duumvir, Duumvirī, m. *Duumvir* (one of the two chief magistrates of a Roman town; at Rome they were called Consuls)

E

Ēduca, -ae, f. *Educa* ("Feeder", numen which helped infants to eat solid food)

Ēgeria, -ae, f. *Egeria* (the nymph of a spring and grove near Rome) 31

Elissa, -ae, f. *Elissa, Eliza* (queen of Tyre and later of Carthage) 5

Ēlysius, -a, -um *Elysian, of Elysium* (a part of the Lower World inhabited by the souls of the good) 20

Ennius, -a, -um *Ennius, Ennia, Ennian, of the Ennian family* (the **nōmen gentīle** of the father of Roman poetry, 239–169 B.C.) 31

Ēpīrus, -ī, f. *Epirus* (a country of Greece, part of modern-day Albania) 12

Eques, Equitis, m. *Eques, Knight* ("Horseman", a member of the second highest of the nine politico-socio-economic classes at Rome; a wealthy businessman)

Erebus, -i, m. *Erebus* (the Lower World, or a god of darkness) 20

Esquiliae, -ārum, f. *the Esquiline* (one of the hills of Rome) 35

Essedārius, -ī, m. *Essedarius* ("Charioteer", a type of gladiator)

Etrūscus, -a, -um *Etruscan, of Etruria* 23

Eurōpa, Eurōpae, f. *Europe* 1

Euryalus, -ī, m. *Euryalus* (a young Trojan)

Eurydicē, Eurydicēs, f. *Eurydice* (wife of Orpheus)

Evander, Evandrī, m. *Evander* (a son of Mercury and Carmenta who led a colony from Pallantium in Arcadia and built a town on the Palatine Hill in Rome) 22

F

Fābulīnus, -ī, m. *Fabulinus* ("Speechful", numen which helped babies learn to speak)

Fāta, Fātōrum, n. *the Fates* 14

Faunus, -ī, m. *Faunus* (a woodland god of prophecy) 21

Faustulus, -ī, m. *Faustulus* (royal herdsman of the Silvian house) 27

Fīdēnātēs, Fīdēnātum, m. *Fidenates* (people of Fidenae, a town in Latium) 30

Flāmen, Flāminis, m. *Flamen* ("Blower of the sacrificial fire", a type of Roman priest)

Flāvius, -a, -um *Flavius, Flavia, Flavian, of the Flavian family* (a Roman **nōmen gentīle**)

Flōra, -ae, f. *Flora* (a goddess of spring and flowers, an important goddess in Campania)

Flōrālia, Flōrālium, n. (pl.) *Floralia* (the feast of Flora)

Fortūna, ae, f. *Fortuna* (the goddess of fortune) 8

Forum, -ī, n. *the Forum* (an open space at Rome used for public and private business) 28

Furia, -ae, f. *a Fury* (the Furies both stirred up and avenged crimes, maddening their victims with the serpents and torches they carried) 22

G

Gabiī, -ōrum, m. *Gabii* (an ancient Latin town near Rome) 37

Gabīnus, -a, -um *Gabinian, of Gabii* 37

Gāius, -i, m. *Gaius* (a Roman **praenōmen**) 36

Galatēa, -ae, f. *Galatea* ("Milk-White"; a sea-nymph)

Genius, -ī, m. *Genius* (the numen of the individual head of a family); **Genius Locī** *Genius of the Place* (the numen of a particular place, perhaps the same as a Lar)

Germānus, -a, -um *German*

Gēryōn, Gēryonis, m. *Geryon* (a three-bodied giant killed by Hercules) 19

Glycō, Glycōnis, m. *Glyco* ("Sweet", a Greek name)

Gnaeus, -ī, m. *Gnaeus* (a Roman **praenōmen**)

Gorgō, Gorgonis, f. *a Gorgon* (a woman-monster with snakes for hair) 19

Graecia, -ae, f. *Greece* 3

Graecus, -a, -um *Greek* 5

H

Hadria, -ae, m. *the Adriatic* 12

Harpȳiae, -ārum, f. *Harpies* 11

Haruspex, Haruspicis, m. *Haruspex* ("Sacred Looker", a type of Etruscan soothsayer)

Hecata, -ae, f. *Hecate* (goddess of the Lower World and of witchcraft) 18

Hecuba, Hecubae, f. *Hecuba* 2

Helena, -ae, f. *Helen* 3

Helenus, -ī, m. *Helenus* (soothsayer, son of Priam) 12

Herculēs, Herculis, m. *Hercules* (most famous of Greek heroes) 18

Herculeus, -a, -um *Herculean, of Hercules*

Herminius, -a, -um *Herminius, Herminia, Herminian, of the Herminian family* (a Roman **nōmen gentīle**) 39

Hersilia, -ae, f. *Hersilia* (the wife of Romulus) 28

Hesperia, -ae, f. *Hesperia* (the Western Land, a poetic name for Italy) 6

Hoplomachus, -ī, m. *Hoplomachus* ("Armor-Fighter", a type of gladiator)

Horātius, -a, -um *Horatius, Horace, Horatia, Horatian, of the Horatian family* (a Roman **nōmen gentīle**) 32

Hostīlius, -a, -um, *Hostilius, Hostilia, Hostilian, of the Hostilian family* (a Roman **nōmen gentīle**) 31

I

Iāniculum, -ī, n. the *Janiculum* (a hill of Rome) 33

Iānus, -ī, m. *Janus* (two-faced god of the year, of gates, and of beginnings) 21

Iarbās, Iarbae, m. *Iarbas* (an African king) 14

Īcarus, -ī, m. *Icarus* (son of Daedalus) 17

Īda, -ae, f. *Ida* (the name of two mountains, one near Troy and one in Crete) 23

Īlia, -ae, f. *Ilia* ("Trojan Woman", another name for Rhea Silvia) 26

Incendium, -ī, n. *The Fire* (title of a famous play)

Ītalia, -ae, f. *Italy* 11

Ītalus, -a, -um *Italian, of Italy* 23

Ithaca, -ae, f. *Ithaca* (an island of Greece, the home of Ulysses) 12

Iūlius, -a, -um *Julius, Julia, Julian, of the Julius family* (a Roman **nōmen gentīle**) 26

Iūlus, -ī, m. (three syllables; the **-i** is not a consonant) *Iulus* (another name for Ascanius, son of Aeneas) 26

Iūnius, -a, -um *Junius, Junia, Junian, of the Junian family* (a Roman **nōmen gentīle**) 38

Iūno, Iūnōnis, f. *Juno* (queen of the gods, sister and wife of Jupiter **13;** also the personal numen of a Roman matron, corresponding to her husband's Genius)

Iuppiter, Iovis, m. *Jove, Jupiter* **14;** **Iuppiter Optimus Maximus** ("*Jupiter Best and Greatest*", Jupiter's title as the chief god of the Romans)

Iūturna, -ae, f. *Juturna* (Nymph of a spring at the site of Rome and sister of Turnus) 24

K

Kalendae, -ārum, f. *the Kalends, the Calends* (the first day of each month)

L

L. (abbreviation for *Lucius*) 33

Labyrinthus, -ī, m. *the Labyrinth* (a large maze-like building built by Daedalus for Minos to imprison the Minotaur) 17

Lacōnica, -ae, f. *Laconia* (land of the Spartans) 3

Laqueārius, -i, m. *Laquearius* ("Noose-Man", a type of gladiator)

Larcius, -a, -um *Larcius, Larcia, Larcian, of the Larcian family* (a Roman **nōmen gentīle**) 39

Lār, Laris, m. *Lar* (the numen of a particular place)

Lars, Lartis, m. *Lars* (an Etruscan first name) 39

Lārentia (see **Acca Lārentia**)

Latīnus, -a, -um *Latin, of Latium* 5

Latīnus, -ī, m. *Latinus* (king of the Laurentines) 21

Latium, -ī, n. *Latium* 5

Laurentius, -a, -um *of Laurentum, Laurentine* 21

Laurentum, -ī, n. *Laurentum* (a town in Latium) 21

Lausus, -ī, m. *Lausus* (young son of Mezentius, the exiled king of the Etruscans) 24

Lāvīnia, -ae, f. *Lavinia* (daughter of Latinus and Amata) 21

Lāvīnium, -ī, n. *Lavinium* (a town in Latium, now Pratica) 26

Lāvīnius, -a, -um *Lavinian, of Lavinium* 26

Leirus, -ī, m. *Lear* (an early British king)

Lerna, -ae, f. *Lerna* (a swamp in Greece, the home of the Hydra, a many-headed serpent) 19

Lethaeus, -a, -um *Lethean, of Lethe* ("Forgetfulness"; a river of the Lower World) 20

Levāna, -ae, f. *Levana* ("Elevator"; numen which helped infants to sit up)

Līber, Līberī, m. *Liber* ("Free One", the god of wine)

Licinius, -ī, m. *Licinius, Licinia, Licinian, of the Licinian family* (a Roman **nōmen gentīle**)

Lictor, Lictōris, m. a *Lictor* (24 Lictors attended the King, carrying the fasces, bundles of rods and axes which symbolized the power of corporal and capital punishment) 34

Līvius, -ī, m. *Livy, Livius, Livia, Livian, of the Livian family* (a Roman **nōmen gentīle**; the most famous Livy was a Roman historian, 59 B.C.– A.D. 16) 36

Locī see **Genius**

Londinium, -ī, n. *London*

Lūcius, -ī, m. *Lucius* (a Roman **praenōmen**) 33

Lūcrētius, -a, -um *Lucretius, Lucretia, Lucretian, of the Lucretian family* (a Roman **nōmen gentīle**) 38

Lucumō, Lucumōnis, m. *Lucumo* (an Etruscan name) 33

Lӯdia, -ae, f. *Lydia* (a country of Asia Minor)

M

M. (abbreviation for *Mārcus*) 31

Mārcius, -a, -um *Marcius, Marcia, Marcian, of the Marcian family* (a Sabine and Roman **nōmen gentīle**) 33

Mārcus, -ī, m. *Marcus* (a Roman **praenōmen**) 31

Mars, Martis, m. *Mars* (god of the growing grain and of war) 26

Martiālis, -e *Martialis, Martial, of Mars* (also a Roman **cognōmen**)

Martius, -a, -um *of Mars, of March*

Maximus see **Iuppiter** and **Pontifex**

Melita, -ae, f. *Malta* 25

Menelāus, Menelāī, m. *Menelaus* (king of the Spartans, husband of Helen) 4

Mercurius, Mercurī, m. *Mercury* (messenger of the gods, god of thieves and merchants) 14

Metabus, -ī, m. *Metabus* (king of the Volscians)

Mezentius, -ī, m. *Mezentius* (a tyrannical king of the Etruscans) 23

Mīlliārium Aureum, Mīlliārī Aureī, n. *The Golden Milestone* (set up in the Forum by Augustus, from which all distances on Roman roads were measured)

Minerva, -ae, f. *Minerva* (virgin goddess of wisdom, war, arts, and crafts) 7

Mīnōs, Mīnōis, m. *Minos* (king of Crete) 17

Mīnōtaurus, -ī, m. *the Minotaur* (monstrous offspring of Minos' wife and a sacred bull) 17

Mūcius, -a, -um *Mucius, Mucia, Mucian, of the Mucian family* (a Roman **nōmen gentīle**) 40

Mūsa, -ae, f. *a Muse* (one of the nine goddesses of music, poetry, and astronomy) 19

Myrmillō, Myrmillōnis, m. *Myrmillo, Gaul* (a type of gladiator)

N

Neptūnus, -ī, m. *Neptune* (god of seas and lakes, brother of Jupiter) 28

Nīsus, -ī, m. *Nisus* (a Trojan)

Numa, -ae, m. *Numa* (a Sabine **praenōmen**) 30

Numīcius, -ī, m. *Numicius* (a river of Latium; the god of the river) 25

Numitor Silvius, Numitōris Silvī, m. *Numitor Silvius* (a king of Alba Longa) 26

Nympha, -ae, f. *a Nymph* (the Nymphs were goddesses of the sea, springs, and streams, of mountains, woodlands, and trees) 23

O

Ocrēsia, -ae, f. *Ocresia* (mother of Servius Tullius)

Optimus see **Iuppiter**

Orcus, -ī, m. *Orcus* (the Lower World, or a god of death) 19

Orpheus, -ī, m. *Orpheus* (a famous singer of Thrace) 18

Ossipaga, -ae, f. *Ossipaga* ("Bone-Joiner", numen of strong bones in infants)

Ostia, -ae, f. *Ostia* (the harbor of Rome) 33

Ovidius, -ī, m. *Ovid* (a Roman poet, 43 B.C.–A.D. 17)

P

P. (abbreviation of Pūblius) 39

Palātium, -ī, n. *the Palatine* (one of the hills of Rome) 22

Palladium, -ī, n. *the Palladium* (an image of Minerva, fallen from heaven, which was kept in Troy, stolen and brought to Italy by Diomedes, who gave it to Aeneas)

Pallās, Pallantis, m. *Pallas* (son of Evander) 23

Patrēs, -um, m. *the Fathers* (a name for the Senators at Rome) 28

Penātēs, -ium, m. *the Penates* ("Dwellers in the Store-Cupboard", the gods of a Roman household) 36

Phlegethōn, Phlegethontis, m. *Phlegethon* ("Flaming"; a river of the Lower World)

Phoenīca, -ae, f. *Phoenicia* 5

Pīcus, -ī, m. *Picus* ("Woodpecker"; son of Saturn, father of Faunus, turned into a woodpecker by Circe)

Poenus, -a, -um *Phoenician, Carthaginian* 5

Pollūx, Pollūcis, m. *Pollux* (a famous boxer, twin brother of Castor) 18

Polydōrus, -ī, m. *Polydorus* (a son of Priam) 10

Polyphēmus, -ī, m. *Polyphemus* (one of the one-eyed Cyclopes, a son of Neptune, blinded by Ulysses) 12

Pompilius, -a, -um *Pompilius, Pompilia, Pompilian, of the Pompilian family* (a Roman **nōmen gentīle**) 30

Pōns Sublicius, Pontis Sublicī, m. *Pons Sublicius* ("Wooden-Pile Bridge", a bridge across the Tiber built by Ancus Marcius) 39

Pontifex, Pontificis, m. *Pontifex, Pontiff* ("Bridge-Maker", a type of priest at Rome); **Pontifex Maximus** *Pontifex Maximus* (the chief priest at Rome)

Porsena, -ae, m. *Porsena* (an Etruscan name) 39

Porta Triumphālis, Portae Triumphālis, f. *Porta Triumphalis, Triumphal Gate* (the eastern gate of the Circus Maximus)

Pōta, -ae, f. *Pota* ("Drinker", numen which helped infants to be weaned from breast feeding to a drinking cup)

Praetor, Praetōris, m. *Praetor* (Roman magistrate next in rank to the Consuls; in charge of legal hearings)

Prāta Mūcia, Prātōrum Mūciōrum, n. *Prata Mucia* ("Mucius' Meadows", an area of Rome on the right bank of the Tiber, now called Prati) 39

Priamus, Priamī, m. *Priam* (king of Troy) 4

Prīscus, -a, -um *Priscus* (a Roman **cognōmen**) 33

Prōserpina, -ae, f. *Proserpina* (daughter of Ceres and wife of Dis) 18

Publicola, -ae, m. *Publicola* (a Roman **cognōmen**) 39

Pūblius, -ī, m. *Publius* (a Roman **praenōmen**) 39

Pulvillus, -ī, m. *Pulvillus* (a Roman **cognōmen**) 39

Pūnicus, -a, -um *Punic* (Carthaginian) 13

Pygmaliōn, Pygmaliōnis, m. *Pygmalion* (Dido's brother) 25

Pyriphlegethōn, Pyriphlegethontis, m. *Pyriphlegethon* ("Flaming with Fire"; a river of the Lower World)

Pȳthagorās, -ae, m. *Pythagoras* (a Greek philosopher)

Q

Q. (abbreviation for **Quīntus**) 31

Quīntus, -ī, m. *Quintus* (a Roman **praenōmen**) 31

Quirīnālis, -e *Quirinal,* of [the god] Quirinus, of the Quirinal (one of the hills of Rome) 35

R

Rēgia, -ae, f. *the Regia* (the King's official residence, near the temple of Vesta in the Forum)

Remus, -ī, m. *Remus* (son of Mars, one of the twin founders of Rome) 23

Rētiārius, -ī, m. *Retiarius* ("Net-Man", a type of gladiator)

Rēx Sacrificulus, Rēgis Sacrificulī, m. *Rex Sacrificulus* ("Sacrificing King"; a priest at Rome who carried out the religious duties of the kings after the monarchy was overthrown)

Rhēa Silvia, Rhēae Silviae, f. *Rhea Silvia* (daughter of Numitor Silvius, mother of Romulus and Remus) 26

Rōmānus, -a, -um *Roman, of Rome* 10

Rōmulus, -ī, m. *Romulus* (son of Mars, one of the twin founders of Rome) 23

Rūpēs Tarpēia, Rūpis Tarpēiae, f. *the Tarpeian Rock* (a cliff of the Capitoline Hill from which those guilty of treason were hurled to their deaths) 29

Rutulus, -a, -um *Rutulian* (of a tribe of the Latins) 21

S

Sabīnus, -a, -um *Sabine* 28

Sacra (see **Via Sacra**)

Sacrificulus see **Rēx Sacrificulus**

Samnis, Samnītis, m. *Samnite* (also a type of Gladiator)

Samus, -ī, f. *Samos* (a small island in the Aegean Sea) 30

Sardēs, -ium, f. *Sardis* (the capital of Lydia, in Asia Minor) 30

Sāturnus, -ī, m. *Saturn* (a god of planting, father of Jupiter) 21

Scaevola, -ae, m. *Scaevola* ("Lefty", a Roman **cognōmen**) 40

Scelerātus (see **Vīcus Scelerātus**)

Scīpiō, Scīpiōnis, m. *Scipio* (a Roman **cognōmen**)

Scylla, -ae, f. *Scylla* (a monster, woman above, six long dog-headed serpents below) 19

Secūtor, Secūtōris, m. *Secutor* ("Pursuer", a type of gladiator)

Segesta, -ae, f. *Segesta* (a Trojan woman sent to Sicily to escape the war; a town in Sicily named for her) 16

Senātor, Senātōris, m. *Senator* (a member of the Senate) 28

Senātus, -ūs, m. *Senate* (a legislative body made up of the heads of families) 34

Ser. (abbreviation of **Servius**) 34

Servius, -ī, m. *Servius* (a Roman **praenōmen**) 34

Sex. (abbreviation of **Sextus**) 37

Sextus, -ī, m. *Sextus* (a Roman **praenōmen**) 37

Sibylla, -ae, f. *a Sybil* (an oracular priestess of Apollo) 17

Sicilia, -ae, f. *Sicily* 12

Siciliānus, -a, -um *Sicilian, of Sicily* 12

Silvius, -a, -um *Silvius, Silvia, Silvian, of the Silvian Family* ("of the forest" not only a Latin family name but also the dynastic name of the kings of Alba Longa) 22

Sōl, Sōlis, m. *Sol* ("Sun"; the sun-god) 22

Somnus, -ī, m. *Somnus* (the god of sleep) 7

Sp. (abbreviation of **Spurius**) 29

Spurius, -ī, m. *Spurius* (Roman **praenōmen**) 29

Statānus, -ī, m. *Statanus* ("Standingful", numen which helped infants to stand)

Stygius, -a, -um *Stygian, of the Styx* 19

Styx, Stygis, f. *Styx* ("Hatred", a river of the Lower World; the goddess of the river) 19

Sulla, -ae, m. *Sulla* (a Roman **cognōmen**; L. Cornelius Sulla was Dictator 81–79 B.C.)

Sublicius (see **Pōns Sublicius**)

Superbus, -a, -um *Superbus* ("Haughty, Proud", **cognōmen** of King L. Tarquinius II) 37

Sychaeus, -ī, m. *Sychaeus* (Dido's husband) 5

T

T. (abbreviation of **Titus**) 29

Tanaquil, Tanaquilis, f. *Tanaquil* (an Etruscan name) 33

Tarpēius, -a, -um *Tarpeius, Tarpeian* (a Roman **nōmen gentīle**) 29

Tarquiniī, -ōrum, m. *Tarquinii* (an Etruscan city, sixty miles from Rome) 33

Tarquinius, -a, -um *Tarquinian, of Tarquinii; Tarquinius, Tarquin, Tarquinia, Tarquinian, of the Tarquin family* (a Roman **nōmen gentīle**) 33

Tartara, -ōrum, n. *Tartarus* 20

Tartarus, -ī, m. *Tartarus* (a place under the Lower World set aside for punishment of the wicked) 18

Tatius, -a, -um *Tatius, Tatia, Tatian, of the Tatian family* (a Sabine **nōmen gentīle**) 29

Tenedus, -ī, f. *Tenedos* (an island near Troy) 7

Terminālis, -e *of Terminus*; (as noun) **Terminālia, -ium**, n. *Terminalia* (the Feast of Terminus)

Terminus, -ī, m. *Terminus* (god of boundary stones)

Thēseus, -ī, m. *Theseus* (an Athenian hero) 17

Thrācia, -ae, f. *Thrace* 9

Thrāx, Thrācis, m. *a Thracian* (also a kind of gladiator)

Ti. abbreviation of **Tiberius** 40

Tiberīnus, -a, -um *Tiberine, of the Tiber* 40

Tiberis, Tiberis (Tiberī, Tiberim, Tiberī), m. *the Tiber* 22

Tiberius, -ī, m. *Tiberius* (a Roman **praenōmen**)

Titus, -ī, m. *Titus* (a Sabine and Roman **praenōmen**) 29

Trīcipitīnus, -a, -um *Tricipitinus* (a Roman **cōgnomen**) 38

Triumphālis see **Porta Triumphālis**

Trōia, Trōiae, f. *Troy* 1

Trōiānus, -a, -um *Trojan* 5

Tullius, -a, -um *Tullius, Tullia, Tullian, of the Tullian family* (a Roman **nōmen gentīle**) 34

Tullus, -ī, m. *Tullus* (an old Roman **praenōmen**) 31

Turnus, -ī, m. *Turnus* (chief of the Rutulians) 21

Tusculum, -ī, n. *Tusculum* (an old town of Latium) 40

Tyrus, -ī, f. *Tyre* (a city of Phoenicia)

U

Ulpius, -a, -um *Ulpius, Ulpia, Ulpian, of the Ulpian family* (a Roman **nōmen gentīle**)

Urbius see **Clīvus Urbius**

V

Valerius, -a, -um *Valerius, Valeria, Valerian, of the Valerian family* (a Roman **nōmen gentīle**) 39

Vēientēs, -um, m. *Veientes, Veientines* (people of Veii) 30

Vēiī, -ōrum, m. *Veii* (an Etruscan town near Rome) 30

Velia, -ae, f. *the Velia* (a low hill just above the Roman Forum to the east)

Venus, Veneris, f. *Venus* (goddess of love) 13

Vergilius, Vergilī, m. *Vergilius, Virgil* 6

Vesta, -ae, f. *Vesta* (goddess of the hearth fire) **Ātrium Vestae** *Atrium of Vesta* (House of the Vestals)

Vestālis, Vestālis, f. (i-stem) *a Vestal* (maiden dedicated to the service of Vesta) 26

Vestālis, -e *Vestal, of Vesta* 26

Via, -ae, f. *Via, Way, Street, Road* (part of the name of many Roman streets and highways): **Via Sacra, Viae Sacrae,** f. *Via Sacra* ("Sacred Way", a street leading from the east end of the Circus Maximus around the Palatine and through the Forum to the foot of the Capitoline) 40; **Via Appia, Viae Appiae,** f. *Via Appia, Appian Way* (Rome's first highway)

Vīcus Cӯprius, Vīcī Cӯprī, m. *Vicus Cyprius* ("Cyprian Street", a street between the Forum and the Esquiline Hill) 37

Vīcus Scelerātus, Vīcī Scelerātī, m. *the Vicus Sceleratus* ("Wicked Street", a street at the foot of the Esquiline Hill) 37

Vīcus Tuscus, Vīcī Tuscī, m. *the Vicus Tuscus* ("Etruscan Street", the street between the Palatine and Capitoline Hills where lived the Etruscan workmen who helped to build the Capitoline Temple)

Vīminālis, -e *Viminal, of the Viminal* (one of the hills of Rome) 35

Volscī, -ōrum, m. *the Volscians* (a tribe of the Latins)

Vulca, -ae, m. *Vulca* (an Etruscan name)

LATIN—ENGLISH VOCABULARY

Words which appear in the Lesson Vocabularies (Basic Words) are followed by the number of the Lesson in which each occurs. They must be memorized for active use. Words without a lesson number are for recognition and occur in the other sections of the text such as: *If You Lived in Ancient Rome; A Phrase to Use; From the Philosopher's Handbook*, and *Listening and Speaking*.

A

a (interj.) *ah! oh!*

ā, ab (prep. w. abl.) *from, away from* 3

ab See ā, ab.

abacus, -ī, m. *sideboard*

abdūcō, -ere, abdūxī, abductum *lead away*

abeō, abīre, abiī (abīvī), abitum *go away* 32

abhorreō, -ēre, -uī, -itum *shrink away from;* (w. abl. of place from which) *be inconsistent with*

absēns, absentis *absent*

absum, abesse, āfuī, āfutūrus *be away, be absent* 26

ac See atque.

accēdō, -ere, accessī, accessum *go to, go toward, approach* 18, 31

accendō, -ere, accendī, accensum *kindle*

accidō, -ere, accidī, ___ *fall to, happen*

accipiō, -ere, accēpī, acceptum *receive* 19

ācer, ācris, ācre *sharp, fierce, keen, shrill* 15

āciēs, -ēī, f. *sharp edge; straight line; eyeshot; line of battle* 38

actuārius, -ī, m. *secretary, scribe, accountant*

ad (prep. w. acc.) *to, towards, for* 3

addō, -ere, addidī, additum *put to, add* 22

addūcō, -ere, addūxī, adductum *lead to*

adeō, adīre, adiī, (adīvī) aditum *go to, approach* (trans.) 32

adferō, adferre, attulī, allātum *bring up;* (w. dat.) *bring to, report* 31

adfīnitās, adfīnitātis, f. *relationship by marriage*

adiciō, -ere, adiēcī, adiectum *throw to, add* 24, 31

aditus, -ūs, m. *approach, access*

adiuvō, -āre, adiūvī, adiūtum *help, assist*

adloquium, -ī, n. *exhortation, encouragement*

adloquor, -ī, adlocūtus sum *address, exhort, encourage*

admīrātiō, admīrātiōnis, f. *admiration, wonder*

admonitus, -ūs, m. *warning, advice*

adolēscō, -ere, adolēvī, adultum *come to maturity, grow up*

adsum, adesse, adfuī, adfutūrus *be present;* (w. dat.) *be present at, be present to help* 31

adulēscēns, adulēscentis, m. or f. *young man, young woman*

advena, -ae, m. or f. *stranger, foreigner*

adversus (prep. w. acc.) *against, opposed to, opposite to* 37

advolō, -āre, -āvī, -ātum *fly towards*

aedificium, -ī, n. *building*

aedificō, -āre, -āvī, -ātum *build* 5

aedēs, aedis, f. *temple;* (plural) *house* 26

aedicula, -ae, f. *[household] shrine*

aeger, aegra, aegrum *sick, ill*

aequitās, aequitātis, f. *fairness, justice*

aequō, -āre, -āvī, -ātum *level, equal, equate*

aequus, -a, -um *fair, just; level, calm; equal* 39

aeternus, -a, um *eternal, everlasting* 27

aetās, aetātis, f. *age; lifetime* 26

ager, agrī, m. *field, territory* 4

aggredior, -ī, aggressus sum *approach, attack*

agitō, -āre, -āvī, -ātum *agitate; harass; practise*

agnus, -ī, m. *[male] lamb*

agō, -ere, ēgī, actum *drive;* **rem agō** *carry on one's business;* **grātiās agō** (w. dat. of ref.) *thank*

agricola, -ae, m. *farmer* 1

alā, -ae, f. *wing;* **ala** (*a side alcove in an atrium*)

albus, -a, -um *white*

aliās (adv.) *at another time* 27

alibi (adv.) *elsewhere* 27

alicubi (indef. adv.) *somewhere, anywhere* 28

alicunde (indef. adv.) *from somewhere, from anywhere* 28

aliēnus, -a, -um *another's, someone else's; foreign* 27

aliō (adv.) *to another place* 27

aliquamdiū (adv.) *for some time, for a little while*

aliquandō (indef. adv.) *at some time, sometimes, at any time* 28

aliquantus, -a, -um (indef. adj.) *some little, of some size* 28

aliquī, aliqua, aliquod (indef. adj.) *some; any* 28

aliquis, aliquid (indef. pron.) *someone, something, anyone, anything* 28

aliquō (indef. adv.) *[to] somewhere, [to] anywhere* 28

aliquot (indecl. indef. adj.) *several, some number of* 28

aliquotiēns (indef. adv.) *several times* 28

aliter (adv.) *otherwise, else* 27

aliunde (adv.) *from another place* 27

alius, alia, aliud (pron. decl.) *another;* **alius . . . alius,** *one . . . another,* (pl.) *some . . . others* 27

alter, altera, alterum (pron. decl.) *the other [of two];* **alter . . . alter,** *the one . . . the other* 27

altitūdō, altitūdinis, f. *height, depth* 21

altum, -ī, n. *the deep [sea]*

altus, -a, -um *high, deep* 6

ambitiōsus, -a, -um *eager for public office, seeking popularity*

ambō, -ae, -ō *both* 21

ambulō, -āre, -āvī, -ātum *walk* 3

amīcitia, -ae, f. *friendship* 10

amictus, -a, -um *dressed, clothed*

amīcus, -a, -um *friendly* 5

amīcus, -ī, m. *friend* 4

āmigrō, -āre, -āvī, -ātum *move [one's place of residence] away*

āmittō, -ere, āmīsī, āmissum *let go away, lose* 18

amnis, amnis, m. (i-stem) *river* 16

amō, -āre, -āvī, -ātum *love, like* 2; **amābō** *please, if you please*

amor, amōris, m. *love* 13

amphitheātrum, -ī, n. *amphitheatre*

amphora, -ae, f. *amphora* (a large conical jar used for the transportation of liquids; also, a liquid measure of about 5¾ gallons)

amplificō, -āre, -āvī, -ātum *enlarge*

ampliō, -āre, -āvī, -ātum *enlarge*

an (conj.) *or* (in disjunctive questions)

ancilla, -ae, f. *maidservant, maid*

angina, -ae, f. *sore throat* (or any disease with this symptom)

anguis, anguis, m. or f. (i-stem) *snake* 19

anima, -ae, f. *breath, life, soul* 12

animal, animālis, n. (i-stem) *animal*

animus, -ī, m. *spirit, mind, soul;* (plural) *morale* 12

annōn (conj. + adv. in disjunctive questions) *or not* 9

annus, -i, m. *year* 7

annuus, -a, -um *annual, yearly, year-long*

ante (prep. w. acc.) *before, in front of, facing* 8

ante (adv.) *before, earlier, in front* 8

antiquus, -a, -um *ancient; old-fashioned; former*

ānulus, -ī, m. *finger-ring*

appāritor, appāritōris, m. *servant, attendant; public slave*

appellō, -āre, -āvī, -ātum *address; appeal to; name*

aper, aprī, m. *wild boar*

aperiō, -īre, aperuī, apertum *open, uncover, make known* 20

aptus, -a, -um *fit, fitting, neat*

apud (prep. w. acc.) *among, at the house of, in the presence of, in the works of* 27

aqua, -ae, f. *water* 12; *a water supply, aqueduct;* **caput aquārum** *source of a water supply*

aquila, -ae, f. *eagle*

āra, -ae, f. *altar* 10

arbiter, arbitrī, m. *witness*

arbor, arboris, f. *tree*

arca, -ae, f. *box, chest*

arceō, -ēre, -uī, ___ *keep at a distance; prevent*

arcera, -ae, f. *[ambulance] cart*

ardeō, -ēre, ārsī, ārsum *burn* 26

arēna, -ae, f. *sand; arena* (sand was put on the arena floor to absorb blood)

argentārius, -ī, m. *banker, money-changer*
arma, -ōrum, n. (no singular) *arms* 23
armārium, -ī, n. *cupboard*
armilla, -ae, f. *bracelet*
arō, -āre, -āvī, -ātum *plow*
arripiō, -ere, arripuī, arreptum *snatch, appropriate, seize with violence*
ārs, artis, f. *art, skill, craft* 39
arx, arcis, f. (i-stem) *citadel, castle* 16
ascendō, -ere, ascendī, ascēnsum *mount, climb, go up*
asper, aspera, asperum *rough, harsh*
aspiciō, -ere, aspexī, aspectum *look at, behold, see* 19
astrum, -ī, n. *constellation*
asylum, -ī, n. *asylum, place of refuge*
at (conj.) *but, yet, but yet* 10
atque or **ac** (conj.) *and, and even, and also; than; as* 10, 39
ātrium, -ī, n. *atrium* (chief reception room in a Roman house)
auctor, auctōris, m. *originator, founder, author* 14
auctōritās, auctōritātis, f. *authority, approval*
audācia, -ae, f. *boldness, rashness, daring*
audax, audācis *bold, rash, daring*
audeō, -ēre, ausus sum *dare* 35
audiō, -īre, -īvī, -ītum *hear, listen to* 20
auferō, auferre, abstulī, ablātum *carry off, steal* 31
augeō, -ēre, auxī, auctum *increase, enlarge, enrich, strengthen*
augurium, -i, n. *omen, augury*
aureus, -a, -um *golden, of gold* 22
aurīga, -ae, m. *[racing] charioteer*
auris, auris, f. (i-stem) *ear*
aurum, -ī, n. *gold* 20
auspicium -ī, n. *auspice* (religious interpretation of the behavior of birds)
aut (conj.) *or* 9
aut . . . aut . . . *either . . . or . . .* 9
autem (postpositive conj.) *but, however, on the other hand* 10
autumnus, -ī, m. *autumn*
auxilium, auxilī, n. *help, aid* 4
ave (interjection) *hail! farewell!*
āvertō, -ere, āvertī, āversum *turn away*
avis, avis, f. (i-stem) *bird* 22
avītus, -a, -um *of a grandfather*

āvolō, -āre, -āvī, -ātum *fly away*
avus, -ī, m. *grandfather*

B

baculum, -ī, n. *staff, walking-stick*
basilica, -ae, f. *basilica* (a large hall in a Forum, used for public and private business)
bellicōsus, -a, -um *warlike*
bellum, bellī, n. *war* 4
belua, -ae, f. *large animal, monster*
bene (adv.) *well* 6
beneficium, -ī, n. *kindness, good deed*
benīgnus, -a, -um *kind, kindly*
bestia, -ae, f. *beast, animal*
bibliothēca, -ae, f. *library*
biformis, -e *of double form*
bīnī, -ae, -a *two by two, two at a time* 21
bis (adv.) *twice* 21
bonus, -a, -um *good* 6
bōs, bovis (dat. and abl. plur. **bōbus**), m. or f. *ox, cow*
brācchium, -ī, n. *arm, lower arm* [from elbow to wrist]
brevis, -e *short*
brūma, -ae, f. *winter solstice, winter*
bucca, bucca *buck, buck; buckshee, buckshee* (a nonsense word in a children's game)
bulla, -ae, f. *locket* [containing talismans]

C

C *100* 22
cadō, -ere, cecidī, cāsum *fall*
caecō, -āre, -āvī, -ātum *blind, darken*
caecus, -a, -um *blind; dark; invisible* 38
caedēs, caedis, f. *slaughter, murder* 16
caelestis, -e *heavenly*
caelō, -āre, -āvī, -ātum *carve*
caelum, -ī, n. *sky, heaven* 8
calamitās, calamitātis, f. *disaster, calamity*
calceus, -ī, m. *[heavy] sandal, shoe, boot*
caldārium, -ī, n. *caldarium* (hot room of a bath)
caliga, -ae, f. *[military hobnailed] boot*
calor, calōris, m. *heat*
calvus, -a, -um *bald*

campus, -ī, m. *plain, meadow* 8

candēns, candentis *glowing*

candidus, -a, -um *white, shining white;* **toga candida** [*unbordered*] *toga of political candidates*

canis, canis, m. or f. (not an i-stem) *dog, bitch*

canō, -ere, cecinī, cantum *sing*

capillus, -ī, m. *a hair*

capiō, -ere, cēpī, captum *take, capture;* (with **cōnsilium**) *form, make* 19

captīvus, -a, -um *captive* 12

caput, capitis, n. *head* 26; **caput aquārum** *source of a water supply*

carbō, carbōnis, m. *charcoal*

carcer, carceris, m. *prison, jail;* [*race-track*] *starting-box, starting-gate*

careō, -ēre, -uī, ___ *lack* (w. abl. of sep.) 17

carmen, carminis, n. *song, poem* 19

caro, carnis, f. *meat, flesh*

carpentum, -ī, n. [*light two-wheeled*] *carriage*

carrūca, -ae, f. [*covered four-wheeled traveling*] *carriage*

carrus, -ī, m. [*light freight*] *cart*

cārus, -a, -um *dear, expensive* 13

casa, -ae, f. *hut, cabin*

castellum, -ī, n. *fortress;* [*water*] *reservoir*

castra, castrōrum, n. (plural only) *camp* 23

cāsus, -ūs, m. *fall; event; chance, accident, fate* 39

cauda, -ae, f. *tail*

caupōna, -ae, f. *wine-shop*

causa, -ae, f. *cause, reason;* [*legal case*] 40; **causam cognōscō** *hear a case*

caveō, -ēre, cautus sum *be on one's guard, beware*

cēdō, -ere, cessī, cessum *move, yield* (w. dat. of ref.) 18

celebrō, -āre, -āvī, -ātum *visit in large numbers, celebrate*

celer, celeris, celere *swift* 15

cella, -ae, f. *store-room, storehouse; servant's room; sanctuary* [*of a temple*]

cēlō, -āre, -āvī, -ātum *conceal*

cēna, -ae, f. *dinner*

cēnō, -āre, -āvī, -ātum *dine*

cēnseō, -ēre, -uī, cēnsum *estimate; hold a census; give an opinion; vote*

cēnsus, -ūs, m. *census*

centēsimus, ā, -um *hundredth* 21

centum (indecl.) *a hundred* 21

centumgeminus, -a. -um *hundredfold*

cēra, -ae, f. *wax*

cernō, -ere, crēvī, crētum or certum *perceive, determine* 36

certāmen, certāminis, n. *contest, struggle, rivalry*

certātim (adv.) *competitively*

certus, -a, -um *sure, certain* 36

cervus, -ī, m. *stag*

cessō, -āre, -āvī, -ātum *cease; loiter; rest; pause, hesitate* 35

cēterī, -ae, -a *the other, the rest* [*of*] 25

cholē, cholae, f. *yellow, bile*

cibus, -ī, m. *food*

cingulum, -ī, n. *belt, girdle*

circā (prep. w. acc.) *around, about, at the side of* 28

circā (adv.) *about, round about, approximately* 28

circēnsis, -e *of the Circus;* [*ludī*] **circēnsēs** *chariot-races*

circum (prep. w. acc.) *around* 12

circum (adv.) *around, round about, on all sides* 12

circumarō, -āre, -āvī, -ātum *plow around*

circumdō, circumdāre, circumdedī, circumdatum *put around*

circumeō, circumīre, circumiī (circumīvī), circumitum (circuitum) *go around, go round*

circumfundō, -ere, circumfūdī, circumfūsum *pour around*

circumsaepiō, -īre, circumsaepsī, circumsaeptum *hedge about*

circumspectō, -āre, -āvī, -ātum *look around at*

circus, -ī, m. [*chariot*] *race-track*

cisium, -ī, n. [*light two-wheeled traveling*] *wagon*

cito, -āre, -āvī, -ātum *summon*

cīvīlis, -e *civil, of a citizen, of the citizens*

cīvis, cīvis, m. or f. (i-stem) *citizen, fellow-citizen* 25

cīvitas, cīvitātis, f. *citizenship; citizenry, city, state*

clabulāre, clabulāris, n. (i-stem) [*military transport*] *wagon*

clam (prep. w. acc.) *without the knowledge of*

clam (adv.) *secretly, in private*

clāmō, -āre, -āvī, -ātum *shout* 11

clāmor, clāmōris, m. *clamor, shouting*

clangor, clangōris, m. *noise, clang, blare*

clārus, -a, -um *clear; bright; famous* 23

claudō, -ere, clausī, clausum *shut, close* 28

claudus, -a, -um *lame*

cliēns, clientis, m. *protegé, dependent* [*of a* **patrōnus**]

clipeus, -ī, m. [*round metal*] *shield*

clīvus, -ī, m. *slope, ascent, sloping street*

coctus, -a, -um *cooked*

coepī, coepisse, coeptum *began* 34

coerceō, -ēre, -uī, -itum *check, curb*

cōgitātiō, cōgitātiōnis, f. *thought, plan, meditation*

cognātus, -a, -um *related [by blood]*

cognōmen, cognōminis, n. *cognomen (a third name)*

cognōscō, -ere, cognōvī, cognitum *come to know, find out, learn* (perf.) *know* 36; **causam cognōscō** *hear a case*

cogō, -ere, coēgī, coactum *collect* (w. acc.); *compel* (w. inf. phrase) 35

cohors, cohortis, f. *cohort; bodyguard*

collēga, -ae, m. *colleague*

colligō, -ere, collēgī, collēctum *collect* 26

collis, collis, m. (i-stem) *hill*

collocō, -āre, -āvī, -ātum *put, place*

colloquium, -ī, n. *conversation, conference*

colō, -ere, coluī, cultum *cultivate; worship* 26

colossus, -ī, m. *colossus, colossal statue, giant*

columba, -ae, f. *dove, pigeon*

columbarium, -ī, n. *dove-cote; columbarium* (large communal burial chamber)

columna, -ae, f. *column*

coma, -ae, f. *hair [of the head]*

comātus, -a, -um *having hair on the head*

comes, comitis, m. or f. *companion*

comitātus, -ūs, m. *retinue*

comitia, -ōrum, n. *assembly [of the Roman people]*

commendō, -āre, -āvī, -ātum *commend; introduce, present*

commīgrō, -āre, -āvī, ātum *move [one's place of residence]*

committō, -ere, commīsī, commissum *combine; entrust* 18

commoveō, -ēre, commōvī, commōtum *move violently, upset*

commūnis, -e *common, shared*

comparō, -āre, -āvī, ātum *prepare; furnish; get; buy*

complector, ī, complexus sum *embrace*

compluvium, -ī, n. *compluvium* (a rain-collecting funnel-shaped roof)

compōnō, -ere, composuī, compositum *collect, arrange, quiet* 18

compositus, -a, -um *arranged, settled; pretended;* **ex compositō** *by prearrangement, as prearranged*

comprehendō, -ere, comprehendī, comprehēnsum *arrest, apprehend*

conciliō, -āre, -āvī, -ātum *win over*

concipiō, -ere, concēpī, conceptum *take together, contain, receive, conceive, feel*

conclāmō, -āre, -āvī, -ātum *shout together*

concors, concordis *of one mind, harmonious*

concurrō, -ere, concurrī, concursum *run together*

concursus, -ūs, m. *a running together*

condemnō, -āre, -āvī, -ātum *condemn, sentence*

condīciō, condīciōnis, f. *condition, terms*

condō, -ere, condidī, conditum *put together, collect, bury, conceal; found [a city]* 22

cōnfarreātiō, cōnfarreātiōnis, f. *[formal] marriage*

cōnferō, cōnferre, contulī, collātus *bring together, collect;* (reflexive) *betake oneself, proceed, go;* (w. dat.) *compare* 31

cōnficiō, -ere, cōnfēcī, cōnfectum *finish, accomplish; use up, weaken, kill* 19

cōnfirmō, -āre, -āvī, -ātum *strengthen; establish; encourage; assert* 12

congerō, -ere, congessī, congestum *bring together, heap*

coniciō, -ere, coniēcī, coniectum *throw together, hurl* 24

coniunx, coniugis, m. or f. *spouse, wife, husband* 27

conquiēscō, -ere, conquiēvī, conquiētum *rest, get rest*

consecrātiō, consecrātiōnis, f. *consecration; deification*

cōnsentēs, -ium *agreeing;* **deī (dī) cōnsentēs** *the agreeing gods* (the twelve chief gods of the Romans)

consequor, -ī, consecūtus sum *follow closely; catch up with; obtain*

cōnsīdō, -ere, cōnsēdī, cōnsessum *sit down, settle, rest*

cōnsilium, -ī, n. *plan; advice, counsel* 12

cōnsistō, -ere, cōnstitī, cōnstitum *halt, stop; take a stand*

cōnsociō, -āre, -āvī, -ātum *share; associate*

cōnspectus, -ūs, m. *sight, view*

cōnspicuus, -a, -um *visible, remarkable, conspicuous*

cōnstituō, -ere, cōnstituī, cōnstitūtum *establish; decide* 34

cōnsulō, -ere, cōnsuluī, cōnsultum (w. acc.) *consult;* (w. dat.) *take counsel for, consult the interests of* 32

cōnsūmō, -ere, consumpsī, consumptum *consume*

contactus, -ūs, m. *contact, touching*

contendō, -ere, contendī, contentum *strive, struggle, hasten*

contineō, -ēre, -uī, contentum *hold together, restrain, bound* 17

contiō, contiōnis, f. *public meeting, assembly*

contrā (prep. w. acc.) *against* 4

contrā (adv.) *on the contrary; on the other hand; in return* 4

contrahō, -ere, contrāxī, contractum *draw together; unite; reduce*

contumēlia, -ae, f. *insult, outrage*

cōnūbium, -ī, n. *legal marriage; right of intermarriage*

conveniō, -īre, convēnī, conventum *come together, meet; agree* 20

convertō, -ere, convertī, conversus *turn round; direct the attention of*

convīvium, -ī, n. *feast, entertainment, party*

convocō, -āre, -āvī, -ātum *call together, assemble* 8

cōpia, -ae, f. *supply; plenty; opportunity* 11

coqua, -ae, f. *or* coquus, -ī, m. *cook*

cor, cordis, n. *heart* 29

cornū, -ūs, n. *horn; wing [of an army]* 29

corpus, corporis, n. *body* 24

cotīdiē (adv.) *daily, every day*

crambē, -ēs (dat. crambae, acc. crambēn, abl. crambē) f. *cabbage*

crās (adv.) *tomorrow* 9

crēdō, -ere, crēdidī, crēditum (w. dat.) *believe;* (w. acc.) *entrust* 32

crēdulus, -a, -um *credulous, believing*

creō, -āre, -āvī, -ātum *create, make, elect*

crepundia, -ōrum, n. *[baby's] rattle*

crēscō, -ere, crēvī, crētum *grow*

crīmen, crīminis, n. *charge, accusation*

croceus, -a, -um *of saffron; saffron-colored, yellow*

cruciātus, -ūs, m. *torture*

crūdēlis, -e *cruel*

crūdēlitās, crūdēlitātis, f. *cruelty*

cruentus, -a, -um *bloody, gory*

crusta, crusta, -ae, f. *rind, shell;* summa crusta *surface [of a Roman road]*

cubiculum, -ī, n. *bedroom*

cucullus, -ī, m. *hood*

culīna, -ae, f. *kitchen*

culpa, -ae, f. *guilty, fault*

cultūra, -ae, f. *cultivation*

cum (prep. w. abl.) *with* 2

cum (adv. conj.) *when* 24

cupiditās, cupiditātis, f. *desire, greed, lust*

cupīdō, cupīdinis, f. *longing, desire, eagerness* 14

cupidus, -a, -um *desirous, eager* (w. obj. gen.)

cupiō, -ere, cupīvī, cupītum *want, desire* 34

cūr (interrogative adv.) *why?* 8

cūra, -ae, f. *care, carefulness, anxiety* 14

cūrō, -āre, -āvī, -ātum *care for, take care of, watch over, manage*

currō, -ere, cucurrī, cursum *run* 28

cursus, -ūs, m. *a running, course* 29

curtus, -a, -um *shortened, cut short*

custōs, custōdis, m. *guard*

D

D *500* 22

damnum, -ī, n. *loss, damage*

dē (prep. w. abl.) *from, down from; about, concerning* 3

dea, -ae, f. *goddess* 3

dēbeō, -ēre, -uī, -itum *owe; ought* 34

decem (indecl.) *ten* 21

decimus, -a, -um *tenth* 21

dēcurrō, -ere, dēcurrī, dēcūrsum *run down*

decus, decoris, n. *ornament, honor, glory;* (plural) *honorable exploits* 14

dēcutiō, -ere, dēcussī, dēcussum *shake down; knock off*

dēdō, -ere, dēdidī, dēditum *give up, surrender, devote*

dēdūcō, -ere, dēdūxī, dēductum *lead down, escort* 18

dēductiō, dēductiōnis, f. *honorific escort [to the Forum, of a patron, by clients]*

dēficiō, -ere, dēfēcī, dēfectum *fail, run out, fall short, be deficient* 19

dehinc (adv.) *hereafter*

dēiciō, -ere, dēiēcī, dēiectum *throw down*

deinceps (adv.) *one after another, successively*

deinde (adv.) *next, then; henceforth, hereafter, thereafter* 27

dēlīberābundus, -a, -um *thinking things over, deliberating*

dēligō, -ere, dēlēgī, dēlēctum *pick out, choose* 26

dēmentia, -ae, f. *madness, insanity*

dēmittō, -ere, dēmīsī, dēmissum *let go down, lower, let fall*

dēmō, -ere, dēmpsī, dēmptum *take away, subtract* 22

dēmōnstrō, -āre, -āvī, -ātum *point out, show* 11

dēnique (adv.) *finally, at last, in short* 19

dēnsus, -a, -um *dense, thick*

dēns, dentis, m. *tooth, fang, tusk*

dēpōnō, -ere, deposuī, depositum *put down, lay aside*

dēsīderium, -ī, n. *longing, desire*

dēsīderō, -āre, -āvī, -ātum *long for, miss, desire*

dēsiliō, -īre, dēsiluī, dēsultum *leap down*

dēsinō, -ere, dēsiī, dēsitum *stop, cease* 34

dēsistō, -ere, dēstitī, dēstitum *leave off, cease*

dēsum, dēesse, dēfuī, dēfutūrus *be missing, be lacking* 19

dētrūdō, -ere, dētrūsī, dētrūsum *push away, push down, dislodge*

deus, -ī, m. *god* 6; deī (dī) cōnsentēs *the agreeing gods* (the twelve chief gods of the Romans)

dēvolō, -āre, -āvī, -ātum *fly down*

dēvorō, -āre, -āvī, -ātum *devour*

dexter, dextera, dexterum (or dextra, dextrum) *on the right; handy, dexterous, skillful* 38

dextimus, -a, -aum (superl. of dexter) 38

dīcō, -ere, dīxī, dictum *say* 36

diēs, -ēī, m. *day* 30; diēs lustricus, diēī lustricī, m. *naming-day*

difficilis, -e *difficult, hard* 19

dīgnitās, dīgnitātis, f. *worth, reputation, honor, rank*

dīgnus, -a, -um *worthy* 15

dīiūdicātiō, dīiūdicātiōnis, f. *adjudication, decision*

dīligō, -ere, dīlēxī, dīlēctum *prize, love, feel affection for* 26

dīmidius, -a, -um *half;* dīmidia pārs *one-half*

dīmittō, -ere, dīmīsī, dīmissus *let go away, send away, dismiss*

dīrus, -a, -um *dire, horrible, frightful*

discēdō, -ere, discessī, discessum *go away, depart* 18; in sententiam discēdō *go over to an[other's] opinion, vote [with someone]*

discerpō, -ere, discerpsī, discerptum *pluck to pieces, dismember*

disciplīna, -ae, f. *instruction, teaching, training*

discipulus, -ī, m. *pupil, student*

discō, -ere, didicī, ___ *learn*

discrīmen, discrīminis, n. *distinction; crisis*

dispār, disparis *unequal, disparate*

disputandus, -a, -um *to be discussed*

dissimilis, -e *unlike* 37

dissimulō, -āre, -āvī, -ātum *dissemble, dissimulate, conceal*

distribuō, -ere, distribuī, distribūtum *distribute, divide*

diurnus, -a, -um *of a day, of the daytime*

diū (adv.) *for a long time* 10

diūturnitās, diūturnitātis, f. *long duration*

dīves, dīvitis *rich, wealthy*

dīvidō, -ere, dīvīsī, dīvīsum *divide, separate, share*

dīvīnitus (adv.) *by divine influence, by divine inspiration*

dīvīnus, -a, -um *divine, of the gods*

dīvitiae, -ārum, f. *wealth, riches*

dō, dare, dedī, datum *give;* sē in fugam dare *take to flight* 9

doceō, -ēre, -uī, doctum *teach, inform* 29

doleō, -ēre, -uī, -itum *suffer pain; cause pain* (w. dat.); *lament* (w. acc.); *be sorry* (w. inf. phrase) 35

dōlium, -ī, n. *[large earthenware] jar, vat [for new wine]*

dolor, dolōris, m. *pain, grief* 18

dolōsus, -a, -um *crafty, cunning*

dolus, -ī, m. *trick, deception, trickery*

domesticus, -a, -um *domestic, household*

domina, -ae, f. *lady, mistress [of a household], [female] ruler*

dominātiō, dominātiōnis, f. *domination, tyranny*

dominus, -ī, m. *lord, master [of a household, of a political unit]* 10

domō, -āre, domuī, domitum *tame, subdue*

domus, -ūs, f. *home* 29; domus equestris *horseback house* (an apartment opening both on the street and on a courtyard)

dōnum, -i, n. *gift* 7

dōnec (adv. conj.) *until*

dōnō, -āre, -āvī, -ātum *present*

dormiō, -īre, -īvī, -ītum *sleep*

dorsum, -ī, n. *back; hide;* summum dorsum *surface [of a Roman road]*

dōs, dōtis, f. *dowry*

dōtālis, -e *belonging to a dowry*

dubitō, -āre, āvī, -ātum *doubt, hesitate* 35

dubius, -a, -um *doubtful, hesitating, at a loss;* rēs dubiae *dangerous or critical situation* ducentēsimus, -a, -um *two hundredth* 22

ducentī, -ae, -a, *two hundred* 22

dūcō, -ere, dūxī, ductum *lead* 18; spiritum dūcō *draw breath*

dulcis, -e *sweet*

dum (adv. conj.) *while*

duo, duae, duo *two* 21

duodecim (indecl.) *twelve* 21; duodecim scrīpta, duodecim scrīptōrum, n. *Twelve Lines* (a game like backgammon)

duodecimus, -a, -um *twelfth* 21

duodēvīcēsimus, -a, -um *eighteenth* 21

duodēvīgintī (indecl.) *eighteen* 21

duplex, duplicis *double, twofold; two-faced* 21

dux, ducis, m. *leader, guide* 18

E

ē, ex (prep. w. abl.) *from, out of* 3

ecce (interjection) *see here!* ecce nōs *here we are*

ēditor, ēditōris, m. *publisher, producer;* ēditor mūnerum *sponsor of gladiatorial games*

ēdō, -ere, ēdidī, ēditum *give out, publish;* mūnera ēdere *sponsor gladiatorial games*

ēducō, -āre, āvī, -ātum *bring up, rear, educate*

ēdūcō, -ere, ēdūxī, ēductum *lead out, raise up* 18

efferō, efferre, extulī, ēlātum *bring out, bring forth, raise up*

efficiō, -ere, effēcī, effectum *produce, effect, make* 19

effugiō, -ere, effūgī, effugitum *escape, elude*

egeō, -ēre, -uī, ⸺ *need* (w. abl. of sep.)

egestās, egestātis, f. *need, poverty*

ego, meī (pers. & refl. pron.) *I* 25

ēgregius, -a, -um *outstanding*

ēiciō, -ere, ēiēcī, ēiectum *throw out* 24

ēlectiō, ēlectiōnis, f. *choice, election*

ēmittō, -ere, ēmīsī, ēmissum *let go out, send out, emit*

emō, -ere, ēmī, emptum *buy* 22

emptiō, emptiōnis, f. *purchase; [marriage by] purchase*

ēnarrō, -āre, -āvī, -ātum *narrate in full*

enim (postpositive conj.) *for* 10

eō (adv.) *[to] here, there, to this [that] place* 23

eō, īre, iī (īvī), itum *go* 32

eōdem (adv.) *to the (this, that) same place* 27

equester, equestris, equestre *of horsemen; of knights; of horses; on horseback;* domus equestris *horseback house (an apartment opening both on the street and on a courtyard)*

equus, -ī, m. *horse* 7

ergastērium, -ī, n. *[slave] workshop, factory*

ergō (adv.) *therefore, consequently, then, accordingly* 23

ērigō, -ere, ērēxī, ērectum *raise up. encourage*

ēripiō, -ere, ēripuī, ēreptum *snatch away, tear out; rescue*

errō, -āre, āvī, -ātum *wander, stray, go wrong, be wrong* 20

essedum, -ī, n. *[heavy traveling or light fighting] chariot*

et (conj.) *and* 2

et (adv.) *also, even* 2

et . . . et . . . *both. . .and. . .* 9

etiam (adv.) *even, yet, still, also* 24

etsī (adv.) *even if* 24

ēveniō, -īre, ēvēnī, ēventum *come out; happen*

ēventus, -ūs, m. *outcome*

ēversus, -a, -um *overturned*

ēvītō, -āre, -āvī, -ātum *avoid*

ēvocō, -āre, -āvī, -ātum *call out*

ēvolō, -āre, -āvī, -ātum *fly out, fly up, leap out*

ex see ē, ex

exanimis, -e *lifeless*

excelsus, -a, -um *high, lofty*

excipiō, -ere, excēpī, exceptum *take, take out, catch* 19

excītō, -āre, -āvī, -ātum *rouse up, stir up*

exclūdō, -ere, exclūsī, exclūsum *shut out* 28

exedra, -ae, f. *[garden] alcove*

exemplum, -ī, n. *example*

exerceō, -ere, -uī, -itum *weary; practice, manage*

exercitus, -ūs, m. *army* 37

exigō, -ere, exēgī, exactum *complete, demand, require*

exiguus, -a, -um *small, thin, scanty;* toga exigua *single toga*

eximō, -ere, exēmī, exemptum *take out, exempt* (w. abl. of separation) 22

exīstimō, -āre, -āvī, -ātum *suppose, consider* 36

expellō, -ere, expulī, expulsum *drive out, banish*

experientia, -ae, f. *experience*

expōnō, -ere, exposuī, expositum *put out, expose, explain* 28 expulsiō, expulsiōnis, f. *expulsion*

exspectō, -āre, -āvī, -ātum *look for, wait for, await* 8

exspīrō, -āre, -āvī, -ātum *breathe out, exhale*

exstinguō, -ere, exstīnxī, exstīnctum *extinguish, destroy*

exsulō, -āre, -āvī, -ātum *go into exile, live in exile*

extemplō (adv.) *immediately, straightway*

externus, -a, -um *external, foreign*

extrā (prep. w. acc.) *outside of*

extrā (adv.) *on the outside*

extrēmus, -a, -um *end of, outermost* 16

F

faba, -ae, f. *[broad] bean*

faber, fabrī, m. *worker, workman, craftsman*

fābula, fābulae, f. *story* 2

faciēs, -ēī, f. *appearance; face* 30

facilis, -e, *easy;* facile *easily* 19

facinus, facinoris, n. *crime*

faciō, ere, fēcī, factum *make, do* 19

factiō, factiōnis, f. *faction; chariot-racing team*

facultās, facultātis, f. *ease, facility; opportunity, faculty*

fallāx, fallācis *deceptive*

fāma, -ae, f. *rumor, report; reputation* 11

famēs, famis, f. (i-stem) *hunger, famine*

familia, familiae, f. *household* 2

familiāris, -e *belonging to a household;* rēs familiāris *entailed property*

falsus, -a, -um *feigned, false*

famula, -ae, f. *handmaid*

fanāticus, -a, -um *fanatical;* (as noun) *fanatic, fan*

farīna, -ae, f. *flour*

farreum, -ī, n. *spelt-cake*

fātidicus, -a, -um *fate-speaking, prophetic*

fātum, -ī, n. *fate* 22

fautor, fautōris, m. *favorer, promoter, supporter, applauder*

faveō, -ere, fāvī, fautum (w. dat.) *favor* 32; favēte linguīs *keep silent*

fēbris, fēbris (i-stem: acc. sing. fēbrim, abl. fēbrī), f. *fever* (or any disease with this symptom)

fēlix, fēlīcis *fertile, lucky, successful, happy* 25

fēmina, -ae, f. *woman* 1

fenestra, -ae, f. *window*

fera, -ae, f. *wild beast*

ferculum, -ī, n. *tray; course;* (pl.) *main course*

ferē (adv.) *almost, nearly, about*

feriae, -ārum, f. *holidays*

ferō, ferre, tulī, lātum *bear, bring, take; relate, say, report* 31; lēgem ferō *pass a law*

ferox, ferōcis *warlike, high-spirited; unbridled, wild*

ferrum, -ī, n. *iron, steel; sword, dagger;* ferrō et igne *with fire and sword*

ferus, -a, -um *wild, savage* 5

ferveō, -ēre, ferbuī, ___ *be hot, boil*

fessus, -a, -um *weary, tired*

festīnō, -āre, -āvī, -ātum *hasten, hurry*

fibula, -ae, f. *fibula (safety pin)*

fidēs, -eī, f. *faith, trust, belief; trustworthiness; pledge; safe conduct; protection* 30

fidus, -a, -um *faithful, trusty, reliable*

figūra, -ae, f. *figure, form, shape*

filia, -ae, f. *daughter* 2

filius, filī, m. *son* 6

findō, -ere, fīdī, fissum *split*

fīnis, fīnis, m. or f. *boundary, limit, border; end*

fīnitimus, -a, -um *adjacent, neighboring* 13

fīō, fierī, ___, ___ *become, be made*

flamma, -ae, f. *flame* 13

flammeus, -ā, -um *flame-colored, yellow;* (as n. noun) flammeum, -ī, n. *wedding veil*

flēbiliter (adv.) *tearfully*

flōs, flōris, m. *flower, blossom*

flūmen, flūminis, n. *stream* 27

fluō, -ere, fluxī, fluxum *flow*

focus, -ī, m. *hearth, stove*

foedus, -a, -um *foul, filthy, horrible, detestable* 12

foedus, foederis, n. *league; treaty, agreement*

fōns, fontis, m. *spring*

fonticulus, -ī, m. *small fountain*

forās (adv.) *out, [to] outdoors*

fore future active infinitive of sum

forma, -ae, f. *form, shape; beauty* 21

fors (defective; abl. forte), f. *chance, luck* 25

forsan (adv.) *perhaps, maybe*

fortis, -e *brave* 21

fortitūdō, fortitūdinis, f. *bravery*

fortūna, ae, f. *fortune* 8

foveō, -ēre, fōvī, fōtum *warm, cherish, support*

fragor, fragōris, m. *crashing sound*

frāter, frātris, m. *brother* 13

fraudō, -āre, -āvī, -ātum *cheat, defraud, deceive*

fraus, fraudis, f. *deceit, deception, fraud*

frēnī, -ōrum, m. *reins*

frēnum, -ī, n. *bridle, bit*

fretum, -ī, n. *strait, sound, channel*

frigidārium, -ī, n. *frigidarium* (cold room of a bath)

frīgus, frigoris, n. *cold*

frūmentum, -ī, n. *grain* 10

fruor, -ī, frūctus sum (w. abl. of means) *enjoy* 33

frūstrā (adv.) *in vain*

fuga, -ae, f. *flight, a running away, escape, exile;* in fugam dare *put to flight* 5

fugiō, -ere, fūgī, fugitum *flee, flee from* 25

fugitīvus, -a, -um *fugitive, runaway*

fulcrum, -ī, n. *headrest; elbow-rest*

fulmen, fulminis, n. *thunderbolt*

fundus, -ī, m. *farm, country property*

fungor, -ī, functus sum (w. abl. of means) *perform* 33

funus, funeris, n. *funeral, death*

furnus, -ī, m. *oven*

G

galērus, -ī, m. *neck-protector* (a high one-sided collar strapped to the shoulder)

garriō, -īre, -īvī, -ītum *chatter, prattle; talk, chat*

garum, -ī, n. *garum, fish sauce*

gaudeō, -ēre, gāvīsus sum *rejoice* 33

gaudium, -ī, n. *joy* 18

geminō, -āre, -āvī, -ātum *double*

geminus, -a, -um *twin*

gemma, -ae, f. *gem, jewel*

gemmātus, -a, -um *jeweled*

gener, generī, m. *son-in-law*

genetrix, genetrīcis, f. *mother, ancestress*

gēns, gentis, f. (i-stem) *family, clan, nation* 20

gentīlis, -e *of a family;* nōmen gentīle *family name*

genus, generis, n. *birth; offspring; kind* 37

germāna, -ae, f. *sister*

germānus, -ī, m. *brother*

gerō, -ere, gessī, gestum *bear; carry on; wear; wage*

gignō, -ere, genuī, genitum *beget, give birth to*

gladiātor, gladiātōris, m. *gladiator*

gladiātōrius, -a, -um *gladiatorial, of gladiators, of a gladiator;* mūnera gladiātōria *gladiatorial games*

gladius, -ī, m. [*Roman short*] *sword*

glōria, -ae, f. *glory, fame* 39

gracilis, -e *thin, slim, scrawny* 37

gradus, -ūs, m. *step*

grātia, -ae, f. *pleasantness; influence; gratitude;* (pl.) *thanks* 14; grātiās agō (w. dat. of ref.) *thank*

grātus, -a, -um *pleasing, welcome; grateful* 12

gravis, -e *heavy, serious* 24

gremium, gremī, n. *lap*

gubernō, -āre, -āvī, -ātum *steer, guide*

gustātiō, gustātiōnis, f. *appetizer course*

gustō, -āre, -āvī, -ātum *taste, eat*

gustus, -ūs, m. *taste*

H

habeō, -ēre, -uī, -itum *have, hold, consider; wear* 17; ōrātiōnem habēre *deliver a speech*

habitō, -āre, -āvī, -ātum *live, dwell* 2

habitus, -ūs, m. *condition, appearance; dress*

haereō, -ēre, haesī, haesum *stick, cling*

haud (adv.) *not at all, by no means* 40

herba, -ae, f. *grass* 19

hērēs, hērēdis, m. or f. *heir*

herī (adv.) *yesterday* 9

heu (interj.) *alas!*

heus (interj.) *hey!*

hic, haec, hoc *this; he, she, it; the latter* 23

hīc (adv.) *here, in this place* [*near me*] 23

hiems, hiemis, f. *winter*

hinc (adv.) *from here, from this place* [*near me*] 23

hinc . . . hinc . . . *from one side . . . from another side . . .*

hodiē (adv.) *today* 9

holus, holeris, n. *vegetable*

homō, hominis, m. or f. *human being, person,* (plural) *people* 18

honestās, honestātis, f. *honor, honesty*

honor, honōris, m. *an honor; public office* 40; in honōrem (w. gen.) *to honor, in honor* [*of*]

hōra, -ae, f. *hour* 25

horreum, -ī, n. *barn, granary*

horridus, -a, -um *rough, shaggy, uncouth, savage, dreadful*

hortus, -ī, m. *garden, vegetable garden*

hospes, hospitis, m. *or* f. *stranger; guest-friend, [house] guest, host* 28

hospitium, -ī, n. *hospitality; guest-friendship; inn*

hostis, hostis, m. (i-stem) *[public] enemy* 15

hūc (adv.) *(to) here, to this place [near me]* 23

hūmānus, -a, -um *human; humane*

humilis, -e *low, humble, insignificant* 37

hūmor, hūmōris, m. *moisture, liquid, [bodily] fluid*

humus, -ī, f. *ground, earth, soil* 30

hypocaustum, -ī, n. *hypocaust* (under-floor hot air heating channel)

I

I *1* 21

iaceō, -ēre, -uī, -itum *lie, be situated* 17

iaciō, -ere, iēcī, iactum *throw* 24

iam (adv.) *now, already;* nōn iam *no longer* 8

iānus, -ī, m. *gate-arch; janus* (a magical bridge over the pomerium)

ibi (adv.) *here, there, in this place, in that place* 9

ibidem (adv.) *in the (this, that) same place* 27

iciō, -ere, īcī, ictum *strike, hit*

īdem, eadem, idem *same* 27

idōneus, -a, -um *suitable* 13

ientāculum, -ī, n. *breakfast*

igitur (adv.) *therefore* 27

ignāvia, -ae, f. *laziness; cowardice*

ignis, ignis, m. (i-stem) *fire* 15

ignōrō, -āre, -āvī, -ātum *not know, be ignorant*

ignōscō, -ere, ignōvī, ignōtum (w. dative) *overlook, forgive, pardon*

ille, illa, illud *that; he, she, it* (not near the speaker or the person spoken to); *the former;* (after its noun) *the famous, the well-known* 23

illīc (adv.) *there, in that place* 23

illinc (adv.) *from there, from that place* 23

illūc (adv.) *[to] there, to that place* 23

imāgō, imāginis, f. *image, likeness, portrait, statue* 26; *death mask*

imber, imbris, m. (i-stem) *rainstorm, shower* 15

immātūrus, -a, -um *unripe; untimely*

immemor, immemoris *unmindful, forgetful*

immō (particle expressing disagreement with what has been said or implied) *Oh, yes! Oh, no!*

immortālitās, -tātis, f. *immortality*

impār, imparis *unequal; uneven* (of a number); pār impār *Odd or Even?* (children's game)

impedīmentum, -ī, n. *hindrance* 29

impellō, -ere, impulī, impulsum *set in motion, push forward*

imperitō, -āre, -āvī, -ātum (w. dat.) *give orders to*

imperium, -ī, n. *command, right to command, empire* 14

impetus, -ūs, m. *onrush, attack*

impiger, impigra, impigrum *not lazy, active, energetic*

impius, -a, -um *undutiful, godless, unpatriotic, disloyal*

impleō, -ēre, implēvī, implētum *fill*

impluvium, -ī, n. *impluvium* (pool for collecting rainwater)

impōnō, -ere, imposuī, impositum (w. acc. & dat.) *put in, put on;* (w. dat.) *deceive* 31

īmus, -a, -um *bottom of* (also used as superl. of inferus) 16, 38

in (prep. w. acc. or abl.) *into, onto, against, for* (w. acc.); *in, on* (w. abl.) 1, 3

inambulō, -āre, -āvī, -ātum *stroll*

inānis, -e *empty, useless*

incēdō, -ere, incessī, incessum *come on, go on, advance*

incendō, -ere, incendī, incensum *set on fire*

incidō, -ere, incidī, ___ *fall upon, happen to* (w. dat. w. compound verbs)

incipiō, -ere, incēpī, inceptum *begin* 19

inclūdō, -ere, inclūsī, inclūsum *shut in* 28

incolumis, -e *unharmed*

increpō, -āre, increpuī, increpitum *shout out insultingly; reproach, rebuke*

incubātiō, incubātiōnis, f. *incubation* (the practice of spending the night in the temple of a god)

inde (adv.) *from here, from there, from this place, from that place* 23

index, indicis, m. *or* f. *informer; sign, token*

indīcō, -ere, indīxī, indictum *proclaim, appoint, declare*

indidem (adv.) *from the (this, that) same place* 27

indīgnitās, indīgnitātis, f. *unworthiness, baseness, indignity*

indīgnus, -a, -um *undeserved; unworthy, base, shameful*

indō, -ere, indidī, inditum *put on, give to*

indūcō, -ere, indūxī, inductum *lead on, influence*

indulceō, -ēre, -uī, -itum *sweeten, make pleasant*

ineō, inīre, iniī, (inīvī), initum *go into, enter*

ineptus, -a, -um *foolish*

īnfēlīx, īnfēlīcis *unfortunate, unhappy*

īnfero, īnferre, intulī, illātum *carry onward;* (w. dat.) *bring upon, inflict;* bellum alicui īnferre *make war on;* sīgna īnferre *advance to the attack* 31

īnferī, -ōrum, m. *the gods below, the gods of the Lower World* 38

īnferus, -a, -um *below* 38

īnfestus, -a, -um *hostile; dangerous*

īnfimus, -a, -um (superl. of īnferus) 38

ingenium -ī, n. *nature, character; talent, genius*

ingēns, ingentis *huge, vast* 16

ingrātus, -a, -um *unpleasant; ungrateful*

ingredior, -ī, ingressus sum *enter, walk in*

inhibeō, -ēre, -uī, -itum *hold in, restrain*

inhumānus, -a, -um *inhuman*

iniciō, -ere, iniēcī, iniectum *throw in, throw on*

inimīcitia, -ae, f. *enmity, hostility*

inimīcus, -a, -um *unfriendly, hostile* 5

initium, -ī, n. *beginning*

iniūria, -ae, f. *wrong, injustice*

inopia, -ae, f. *lack, need* 10

inquam (defective verb: forms are inquam, inquis, inquit, inquiunt) *say, said* 25

inrumpō, -ere, inrūpī, inruptum (irruptum) *burst in*

insideō, -ēre, insēdī, insessum *sit on*

īnsolēns, īnsolentis *extravagant, arrogant*

īnspiciō, -ere, īnspexī, īnspectum *look into, inspect*

īnstituō, -ere, īnstituī, īnstitūtum *establish, institute, arrange* 34

īnstō, -āre, īnstitī, ___ *stand in, stand on; follow closely, press* 31

īnsula, -ae, f. *island* 9; *city block, apartment house, apartment building, tenement*

integer, integra, integrum *whole, untouched, unharmed*

intentus, -a, -um *intent, attentive*

inter (prep. w. acc.) *between, among;* inter nōs, vōs, sē *each other, one another* 12, 25

intercipiō, -ere, intercēpī, interceptum *intercept; steal*

interficiō, -ere, interfēcī, interfectum *destroy, kill* 19

interim (adv.) *in the meantime, meanwhile* 8

interrogō, -āre, -āvī, -ātum *question, interrogate*

interrumpō, -ere, interrūpī, interruptum *break in the middle; interrupt*

intersum, interesse, interfuī, interfutūrus *be between; be different; be involved in*

intervallum, -ī, n. *interval*

interveniō, -īre, intervēnī, interventum *come between, intervene, interrupt*

intrō (adv.) *inward, turned toward the inside*

intrō, -āre, -āvī, -ātum *enter*

invādō, -ere, invāsī, invāsum *go in; go into, invade*

invehō, -ere, invexī, invectum *bring in;* (passive) *travel on, travel into*

inveniō, -īre, invēnī, inventum *come upon, find* 20

invideō, -ēre, invīdī, invīsum (w. dat.) *envy* 32

invidia, -ae, f. *envy, hatred, unpopularity*

invītāta, -ae, f. *or* invītātus, -ī, m. *guest*

invītus, -a, -um *unwilling*

ipse, ipsa, ipsum *myself, ourselves, yourself, yourselves, himself, herself, itself, themselves* 27

īra, -ae, f. *anger, rage* 11

īrāscor, -ī, īrātus sum *become angry*

īrātus, -a, -um *angry*

is, ea, id *this, that; he, she, it* (the one[s] being spoken of) 23

iste, ista, istud *that; he, she, it* [near you] 23

istīc (adv.) *there, in that place* [near you] 23

istinc (adv.) *from there, from that place* [near you] 23

istūc (adv.) [to] *there, to that place* [near you] 23

ita (adv. modifying verbs) *so, thus, in such a manner;* (modifying adjectives and adverbs) *so, to such a degree;* (it is so) = *yes* 23

itaque (conjunction) *and so, therefore* 4

iter, itineris, n. *way, route, journey* 16

iterum (adv.) *again, a second time* 23

iūba, -ae, f. *mane, crest*

iubeō, -ēre, iussī, iussum *bid, order* 35

iūdex, iūdicis, n. *judge, juror*

iūdicium -ī, n. *trial, judgment*

iūdicō, -āre, -āvī, -ātum *judge*

iūmentum, -ī, n. *draft animal; beast of burden*

iungō, -ere, iūnxī, iūnctum *join*

iūnior (comp. of iuvenis) 38

iūrō, -āre, -āvī, -ātum *swear* 35

iūs, iūris, n. *broth, soup, sauce*

iūs, iūris, n. *right, law* 40

iussus, -ūs, m. *command, bidding*

iūstitia, -ae, f. *justice*
iūstus, -a, -um *just, right, fair*
iuvenis, iuvenis (no neuter) *young* 23
iuvenis, -is, m. or f. (not an i-stem) *young man, young woman* 23
iuvō, -āre, iūvī, iūtum *help, assist; delight, please, gratify* 12

L

labor, labōris, m. *labor, toil, effort, hardship* 39
labōrō, -āre, -āvī, -ātum *toil; suffer; be in difficulties* 11
lacerna, -ae, f. *[felt outdoor] cloak*
lacrima, -ae, f. *tear, teardrop*
laetus, -a, -um *joyful, glad* 11
laevus, -a, -um *left, lefthand*
lāna, -ae, f. *wool*
later, lateris, m. *brick*
laterāria, -ae. f. *brick factory*
laterārius, -ī, m. *brick-maker*
lātifundium, -ī, n. *large estate, big farm or ranch*
lātitūdō, lātitūdinis, f. *width* 21
latrīna, -ae, f. *toilet*
latrō, -āre, -āvī, -ātum *bark*
lātrō, lātrōnis, m. *bandit, robber*
latrunculī, -ōrum, m. *Little Bandits* (a game like chess)
lātus, -a, -um *wide, broad* 7
laudātiō, laudātiōnis, f. *eulogy*
laudō, -āre, -āvī, -ātum *praise* 2
laus, laudis, f. *praise, fame, glory* 14
lectica, -ae, f. *litter*
lectus, -ī, m. *couch, bed*
lēgātiō, lēgātiōnis, f. *embassy, delegation*
lēgātus, -ī, m. *legate, envoy* 4
legō, -ere, lēgī, lēctum *pick; read* 26
lentus, -a, -um *clinging, lingering, slow*
lepra, -ae, f. *scaliness [of the skin]* (or any disease with this symptom)
levis, -e *light; fickle*
lēx, lēgis, f. *law, rule* 19; **lēgem ferō** *pass a law*
līber, lībera, līberum *free* 6
liber, librī, m. *book*
līberī, līberōrum, m. *children* 6
līberō, -āre, -āvī, -ātum *free, set free* 11

lībertās, lībertātis, f. *liberty, freedom*
lībertus, -ī, m. *freedman*
ligneus, -a, -um *wooden*
lignum, -ī, n. *wood, log*
līmen, līminis, n. *threshold*
lingua, -ae, f. *tongue, language* 9; **favēte linguīs** *keep silent*
liquāmen, liquāminis, n. *garum* (a sauce made of fish trimmings and strong brine)
lītus, lītoris, n. *seashore, coast* 25
locus, -ī, m. (pl. **loca**, -ōrum, n.) *place* 10
longitūdō, longitūdinis, f. *length* 21
longus, -a, -um *long* 6; **navis longa** *warship*
lūcerna, -ae, f. *lamp*
lūcrum, -ī, n. *profit*
lūctuōsus, -a, -um *mournful, lamentable*
lūdībrium, -ī, n. *derision, mockery, sport, joke; laughingstock*
lūdō, -ere, lūsī, lūsum *play, sport;* (trans.) *mock*
lūdus, -ī, m. *game, sport; school;* (pl.) *religious festival;* **ludī circēnsēs** *chariot races;* **ludī scaenicī** *theatrical productions*
lūgeō, -ēre, lūxī, lūctum *mourn, bewail*
lūna, -ae, f. *moon*
lupa, -ae, f. *she-wolf*
lupus, -ī, m. *wolf*
lustricus, -a, -um *expiatory, sacrificial;* **diēs lustricus** *naming-day*
lūx, lūcis, f. *light;* **prīma lux** *dawn*
lychnus, -ī, m. *lamp*

M

macellum, -ī, n. *macellum* (a central food market)
magicus, -a, -um *magical*
magis (adv.) *more, rather* 39
magister, magistrī, m. *master [of a school, of a ship, etc.]* 10
magnus, -a, -um *great, large;* **magna pars** *the majority* 5
magnitūdō, magnitūdinis, f. *greatness, size* 21
maior, -ius (comp. of **magnus**) 38
male (adv.) *badly, ill* 6
malignus, -a, -um *malicious, grudging, stingy*
mālum, -ī, n. *apple*
malus, -a, -um *bad, evil, wicked* 5

mamma, -ae, f. *teat*

mandō, -āre, -āvī, -ātum *entrust*

māne, ___, n. (defective: sing., nom. māne, acc. māne, & abl. māne, only) *early morning;* multō māne *very early in the morning*

maneō, -ēre, mānsī, mānsum *stay, remain, last* 17

manifestus, -a, -um *clear, evident, manifest*

mānsiō, mānsiōnis, f. *stopover; stopping-place*

mansuētus, -a, -um *tame*

manus, -ūs, f. *hand; band* [*of men*] 29; *power* [*of a father over his daughter or a husband over his wife*]

mare, maris, n. (i-stem) *sea* 15

marītus, -ī, m. *husband* 40

marmor, marmoris, n. *marble;* (pl.) *marble objects*

māter, mātris, f. *mother* 13

māteria, -ae, f. *matter, material*

mātrimōnium, -ī, n. *marriage*

mātrōna, -ae, f. *matron, married woman*

maximus, -a, -um (superl. of magnus) 38

medicāmentum, -ī, n. *medicine*

medicātus, -a, -um *drugged; medicinal*

medicus, -ī, m. *doctor, physician*

medius, -a, -um *middle of, middle* 16

mēhercule (interjection) *by Hercules! so help me Hercules!*

mel, mellis, n. *honey*

melancholia, -ae, f. *black bile*

melior, melius (comp. of bonus) 38

meminī, meminisse, ___ (w. obj. gen.) *remember* 33

memor, memoris *mindful, remembering* 16

memoria, -ae, f. *memory* 14

mendāx, mendācis *untruthful, lying*

mēns, mentis, f. *mind, opinion* 26

mēnsa, -ae, f. *tabletop;* secunda mēnsa *or* secundae mēnsae *dessert course*

mēnsārius, -ī, m. *banker, moneylender*

mercēs, mercēdis, f. *pay, wages*

mēta, -ae, f. *turning-post* [*in a circus*]

metō, -ere, messuī, messum *reap, mow, harvest*

metus, -ūs, m. *fear, dread* 31

meus, -a, -um *my, mine* 6

micātiō, micātiōnis, f. *Flickering* (a game like mora)

migrō, -āre, -āvī, -ātum *move* [*one's place of residence*]

mīles, mīlitis, m. *soldier* 37

mīlia, mīlium, n. (pl. only) *thousands* 29

mīlia passuum, mīlium passuum, n. *miles* 29

mīlitāris, -e *military, of a soldier, of soldiers*

mīlitia, -ae, f. *military service;* (locative) mīlitiae *on military service*

mīlle (indecl. adj.) *a thousand, one thousand* 22

mīlle passūs, mīlle passuum, m. *mile* (= 1.48 km., 4850 English ft.) 29

mīllēsimus, -a, -um *thousandth* 22

mīlliārium, -ī, n. *milestone*

mīmus, -ī, m. *comic opera*

minae, -ārum, f. *threats*

minimus, -a, -um (superl. of parvus) 38

minor, -ārī, -ātus sum *threaten*

minor, minus (comp. of parvus) 38

mīrābilis, -e *amazing, wonderful*

mīrāculum, -ī, n. *a wonder, miracle*

mīror, -ārī, mīrātus sum *wonder, be amazed; wonder at, admire*

mīrus, -a, -um *amazing, wonderful* 23

misceō, -ēre, -uī, mixtum *mix* 20

miser, misera, miserum *poor, wretched, unhappy* 5

miserē (adv.) *wretchedly, pitiably; desperately* 5

misericordia, -ae, f. pity, mercy

mītis, -e *mild, gentle*

mittō, -ere, mīsī, missum *let go, send* 18

mixtūra, -ae, f. *mixture*

modo (adv.) *only, just; just now* 9

modus, -ī, m. *measure, degree; manner, way* 26

moenia, moenium, n. (i-stem) *fortifications, walls* 28

mollis, -e *soft, tender, gentle*

moneō, -ēre, -uī, -itum *warn, advise* 36

mōns, montis, m. (i-stem) *hill, mountain* 21

mōnstrum, -ī, n. *portent; monster*

morbus, -ī, m. *disease*

mordeō, -ēre, mōrsī, mōrsum *bite*

moribundus, -a, -um *dying*

moritūrus, -a, -um *destined to die*

moror, -ārī, morātus sum *delay* 33

mors, mortis, f. (i-stem) *death* 16

mortālis, -e *mortal*

mortuus, -a, -um *dead*

mōs, mōris, m. *custom;* (pl.) *morals; character*

mōveō, -ēre, mōvī, mōtum *move* 20

mox (adv.) *soon* 12

mūgiō, -īre, -īvī, -ītum *moo, bellow*

muliēbris, -e *of a woman, womanly, feminine*

mulier, mulieris, f. (the -i is a consonant) *woman*

mulsum, -ī, n. *mulsum* (wine flavored with honey)

multitūdō, multitūdinis, f. *large number, number, multitude* 16

multus, -a, -um *much;* (pl.) *many* 5

mundus, -ī, m. *world, universe, cosmos*

mūniō, -īre, -īvī, -ītum *fortify, build [a fortification]*

mūnitiō, mūnitiōnis, f. *fortification*

mūnus, mūneris, n. *duty; favor; funeral; gift* 14; (pl.) mūnera [gladiatōria] *gladiatorial show*

mūrus, -ī, m. *wall*

mūtō, -āre, -āvī, -ātum *change* 20

N

nam (conj.) *for* 10

narrātiō, narrātiōnis, f. *narration*

narrō, -āre, -āvī, -ātum *tell, narrate* 2

nāscor, -ī, nātus sum *be born* 38

nātūra, -ae, f. *birth, nature* 25

nauta, -ae, m. *sailor* 3

nāvigium, -ī, n. *sailing, navigation; a sailing vessel, ship*

nāvigō, -āre, -āvī, -ātum *sail* 3

nāvis, nāvis, f. (i-stem) *ship* 15 nāvis onerāria *transport ship, merchant ship;* nāvis longa *warship*

-ne (interrogative enclitic particle) ? 3

nē . . . quidem (adv.) *not even* 25

nec see neque 10

nec . . . nec . . . see neque . . . neque . . . 10

necesse (defective adj., nom. & acc. neut. sing.) *necessary*

necessitās, necessitātis, f. *necessity; inevitability; need*

negō, -āre, -āvī, -ātum (w. acc.) *deny, refuse;* (w. indirect statement) *say . . . not* 36

negōtium, -ī, n. *trouble; business*

nēmō, nēminis, m. *no one, nobody* 21

nemus, nemoris, n. *grove*

nēnia, -ae, f. *dirge; lullaby*

neō, -ēre, nēvī, nētum *spin, weave*

nepōs, nepōtis, m. or f. *grandson, granddaughter* 13

nēquāquam (adv.) *in no way, by no means*

neque (conj.) *nor, and . . . not . . .* 10

neque . . . neque . . . *neither . . . nor . . .* 10

nesciō, -īre, -īvī, ___ *not know* 36

neuter, neutra, neutrum (pron. decl.) *neither* 27

niger, nigra, nigrum *black*

nihil, nihilī (no dat.), nihil, nihilō (no pl.), n. *nothing* 16

nīl a contraction of nihil

nimbus, -ī, m. *cloud, mist; rain-storm, storm*

nimium, -ī (no pl.), n. *too much*

nisi (adv. conj.) *if . . . not, unless* 10

nō, -āre, -āvī, -ātum *swim*

nōbilis, -e *well-known; noble* 37

noceō, -ēre, -uī, -itum (w. dat.) *harm* 32

nōdus, -ī, m. *knot;* nōdus Herculeus *knot of Hercules* (special wedding-knot for a belt)

nōmen, nōminis, n. *name* 15; nōmen gentīle *family name*

nōmenclātor, nōmenclātōris, m. *receptionist*

nōminō, -āre, -āvī, -ātum *name*

nōn (adverb) *not* 3

nōnāgēsimus, -a, -um *ninetieth* 21

nōnāgintā (indecl.) *ninety* 21

nōngentēsimus, -a, -um *nine hundredth* 22

nōngentī, -ae, -a *nine hundred* 22

nōnus, -a, -um *ninth* 21

nōs, nostrum (nostrī) (pers. & refl. pron.) *we* 25

nōscō, -ere, nōvī, nōtum *come to know, find out, learn;* (perf.) *know* 36

noster, nostra, nostrum *our, ours* 6

nota, -ae, f. *mark, brand; quality*

nōtus, -a, -um *famous, well-known* 13

novem (indecl.) *nine* 21

noverca, -ae, f. *stepmother*

novitās, novitātis, f. *novelty, newness*

novus, -a, -um *new* 11

nox, noctis, f. (i-stem) *night* 25

nūbēs, nūbis, f. *cloud*

nūbō, -ere, nūpsī, nūptum (w. dat.) *be married*

nucleus, -ī, m. *nut, pine-nut, kernel; [concrete] grading level [of a Roman road]*

nūdus, -a, -um *naked*

nūllus, -a, -um (pron. decl.) *no, not any, none* 27

num (interrogative particle expecting the answer no) ?! 9

nūmen, nūminis, n. *divine will, divine spirit, divinity* 14

numerus, -ī, m. *number; group* 38

nummus, -ī, m. *coin*

numquam (adv.) *never* 34

nunc (adv.) *now, at this time* 8

nūntiō, -āre, -āvī, -ātum *announce, report* 10

nūntius, -a, -um *serving as a messenger*

nūntius, nūntī, m. *message, news; messenger* 4

nūbō, -ere, nūpsī, nūptum *veil;* (w. dat. of ref.) *be married*

nugae, -ārum, f. *trifles, nonsense*

nuptiae, -ārum, f. *nuptials, wedding*

nusquam (adv.) *nowhere*

O

ō (interj.) *O, oh* (usually followed by vocative or acc. of exclamation)

ob (prep. w. acc.) *because of, on account of* 40

obdūrō, -āre, -āvī, -ātum *become hard; hold out*

obeō, obīre, obiī (obīvī), obitum *go to, go to meet, take part in* (transitive) 32

oblīvīscor, -ī, oblītus sum (w. obj. gen.) *forget* 33

obloquor, -ī, oblocūtus sum *speak against, contradict*

obscūrus, -a, -um *dark, in the dark, obscure*

obsēs, obsidis, m. or f. *hostage*

obsōnium, -ī, n. *food, provisions, shopping*

obstō, -āre, obstitī, -ātum *stand in the way of*

obstrepō, -ere, obstrepuī, obstrepitum *shout against*

obtineō, -ēre, -uī, obtentum *hold on to*

obtruncō, -āre, -āvī, -ātum *assassinate*

occīdō, -ere, occīdī, occīsum *cut down, kill*

occupō, -āre, -āvī, -ātum *seize* 3

octāvus, -a, -um *eighth* 21

octingentēsimus, -a, -um *eight hundredth* 22

octingentī, -ae, -a *eight hundred* 22

octō (indecl.) *eight* 21

octōgēsimus, -a, -um *eightieth* 21

octōgintā (indecl.) *eighty* 21

oculus, -ī, m. *eye* 27

odium, -ī, n *hatred*

offa, -ae, f. *morsel, fritter, hushpuppy*

officīna, -ae, f. *shop, workshop*

officium, -ī, n. *duty*

oleum, -ī, n. *olive oil*

ōlim (adv.) *once, at one time, at some time* 7

olīva, -ae, f. *olive*

olīvētum, -ī, n. *olive grove*

olla, -ae, f. [*earthenware*] *jar, pot*

omnis, omne *all, every* 15

onerārius, -a, -um *for carrying freight;* nāvis onerāria *transport ship, merchant ship*

onus, oneris, n. *burden, load*

opera, -ae, f. *work, task*

operiō, -īre, operuī, opertum *cover, conceal*

opēs, opum, f. *might, power, influence, resources, assistance*

opīniō, opīniōnis, f. *opinion; expectation*

oportet, -ēre, oportuit *it is necessary, it is proper*

oppidānus, -a, -um *of the town*

oppidānus, -ī, m. *townsman*

oppidum, -ī, n. *town* 4; *gate-tower* [*of a circus*]

oppugnō, -āre, -āvī, -ātum *attack* [*a fortified position*]

optimus, -a, -um (superl. of **bonus**) 38

optō, -āre, -āvī, -ātum *choose, wish for; wish* 34

opus, operis, n. *work, task* 40

ōra, -ae, f. *shore, coast*

ōrāculum, -ī, n. *oracle*

ōrātiō, ōrātiōnis, f. *speech;* ōrātiōnem habēre *deliver a speech*

ōrātor, ōrātōris, m. *speaker, spokesman*

orbitās, orbitātis, f. *bereavement, orphanhood, childlessness*

orbus, -a, -um *bereft, orphaned, childless*

ordior, -īrī, orsus sum *begin;* rem ordīrī *open a case* [*at law*]

ordō, ordinis, m. *order, rank, class*

orior, -īrī, ortus sum (oritūrus) *rise, arise*

oriundus, -a, -um *arising* [*from*]

ornātus, -a, -um *decorated, ornate, elaborate; equipped*

ornō, -āre, -āvī, -ātum *decorate; honor; equip*

ōs, ōris, n. *mouth, face* 24

ostendō, -ere, ostendī, ostentum *display, show* 31

ostiārius, -ī, m. *doorkeeper*

ostium, -ī, n. *entrance, door; river mouth*

ōtium, -ī, n. *leisure, idleness, peace, rest*

ōvum, -ī, n. *egg*

P

paedagōgus, ī, m. *pedagogue* (a schoolboy's personal slave)

paene (adv.) *almost* 19

paenula, -ae, f. [large traveling] cloak

pagina, -ae, f. page

palaestra, -ae, f. wrestling-ground

palla, -ae, f. [woman's] himation

pallium, -ī, n. [man's] himation

palūdāmentum, -ī, n. [commander's military] cloak

palūs, palūdis, f. swamp, marsh

pānis, pānis, m. (i-stem) bread, loaf, piece of bread

pantomīmus, -ī, m. ballet

papāver, papāveris, n. poppy

pār, paris equal; even (of a number); as m. noun peer; as n. noun pair 16;

pār impār Odd or Even? (children's game)

parātus, -a, -um ready, prepared 11

parcō, -ere, pepercī, pārsum (w. dat.) spare 32

parēns, parentis, m. or f. parent 16

pāreō, -ēre, -uī, -itum (w. dat.) obey 32

parma, -ae, f. [small round] shield

parō, -āre, -āvī, -ātum prepare 4

pars, partis, f. part, share; role; magna pars the majority 16

parum, n. (only in nom. and acc. sing.) too small an amount, too little 16

parvulus, -a, -um very little, very small, tiny, little tiny

parvus, -a, -um little, small 9

passus, passūs, m. pace (as unit of measure = 1.48 m., 4.85 English ft.) 29

pāstor, pāstōris, m. shepherd, herdsman

pateō, -ēre, -uī, ___ be open, lie open

pater, patris, m. father 13

paternus, -a, -um paternal, of a father

patior, -ī, passus sum endure, experience; allow 33

patria, -ae, f. fatherland, native land 1

patrōnus, -ī, m. patron (protector of dependent clients or former owner of a freed slave)

paucī, paucae, pauca (no sing.) few, a few 5

paulum (def. noun, abl. paulō) a little

pauper, pauperis, paupere poor, needy

pavidus, -a, -um trembling, in a panic

pavīmentum, -ī, n. pavement; [mortar] base [for a Roman road]

pavor, pavōris, m. panic

pax, pācis, f. peace, peace treaty

pectus, pectoris, n. breast, heart 14

pecūnia, -ae, f. money 22

pecus, pecoris, n. herd, flock

peior, peius (comp. of malus) 38

penitus (adv.) in (into) the inmost part, deeply

penna, -ae, f. feather

per (prep. w. acc.) through 7

peregrīnus, -a, -um foreign

perferō, perferre, pertulī, perlātum carry through; report; endure

perfidus, -a, -um treacherous

perfugiō, -ere, perfūgī, perfugitum flee, flee for refuge

perīculum, -i, n. danger 5

peristȳlum, -ī, n. peristyle, colonnaded court

perītus, -a, -um (w. obj. gen.) skilled

pereō, perīre, periī (perīvī), peritum perish, be lost 32

persuādeō, -ēre, persuāsī, persuāsum (w. dat.) persuade

pertinax, pertinācis stubborn, tenacious

perveniō, -īre, pervēnī, perventum come all the way, arrive 20

pēs, pedis, m. foot (as measure, 11.65 English inches) 21

pessimus, -a, -um (superl. of malus) 38

pessum (adv.) downwards, to the bottom; pessum dō destroy, ruin

pestilentia, -ae, f. pestilence, epidemic

petō, -ere, petīvī, petītum aim at, seek, attack 18

pīcus, -ī, m. woodpecker

pietās, pietātis, f. dutifulness towards gods, parents, or country

pila, -ae, f. ball

pīlentum, -ī, n. [small four-wheeled traveling] carriage

pilleus, -ī, m. [close-fitting felt] cap

piscīna, -ae, f. swimming pool

pistor, pistōris, m. miller, baker

pistrīna, -ae, f. mill, bakery

pius, -a, -um loyal, dutiful [to gods, country, or relatives] 20

placeō, -ēre, -uī, -itum (w. dat.) please 32

plānus, -a, -um flat, level; plain, clear

plaustrum, -ī, n. [heavy-duty farm] wagon

plēbs, plēbis, f. the multitude, the common people 37

plēnus, -a, -um full (w. abl. of means or gen. of the whole) 27

plūrēs, plūra (comp. of multī) 38

plūrimus, -a, -um (superl. of multus) 38

plūs, plūris, n. (no dat. sing, no pl.) a larger amount, more 16 podagra, -ae, f. *foot pain* (or any disease with this symptom)

poena, -ae, f. *punishment, penalty*

poēta, -ae, m. *poet* 2

pollex, pollicis, m. *thumb;* pollice versō *with up-turned thumb* (signalling the killing of a gladiator)

pōmērium, -ī, n. *pomerium* (the magical boundary of a city)

pompa, -ae, f. *parade, procession*

pondus, ponderis, n. *weight*

pōnō, -ere, posuī, positum *put, place, lay down* 18

pōns, pontis, m. *bridge*

populus, -i, m. *a nation, a people* 10

porta, -ae, f. *gate* 7

portendō, -ere, portendī, portentum *forebode, portend*

portitor, portitōris, m. *ferryman*

portō, -āre, āvī, -ātum *carry, bring* 4

posco, -ere, poposcī, ___ *demand, require*

possideō, -ere, possēdī, possessum *possess*

possum, posse, potuī, ___ *can, be able* 35

post (prep. w. acc.) *after, behind, in back of* 7

post (adv.) *afterward, behind* 7

posteā (adv.) *afterward*

posterus, -a, -um *subsequent, following* 28

posterī, -ōrum, m. *posterity, descendants* 28

posterum, -ī, n. *the future* 28

postquam (adv. conj.) *after* 24

postrēmō (abl. of time when of postrēmum) *at the last, last of all* 38

postrēmus, -a, -um (superl. of posterus) 38

postulō, -āre, -āvī, -ātum *demand*

postumus, -a, -um (superl. of posterus) 38

potēns, potentis *powerful*

potentia, -ae, f. *power*

potior, -īrī, potītus sum (w. obj. gen. or abl. of means) *get possession of* 33

potior, -ius *preferable* 38

potissimus, -a, -um *most important* 38

prae (prep. w. abl.) *before, in front of, ahead of; in comparison with* 17

praebeō, -ēre, -uī, -itum *offer* 17, 31

praeceptor, praeceptōris, m. *teacher, instructor*

praecipiō, -ere, praecēpī, praeceptum *receive in advance; instruct, teach* 19, 31

praecipuē (adv.) *especially*

praecō, praecōnis, m. *herald, town crier*

praeda, -ae, f. *prey, booty*

praeficiō, -ere, praefēcī praefectum *put in charge of*

praemittō, -ere, praemīsī, praemissum *send ahead*

praemium, -ī, n. *reward*

praenōmen, praenōminis, n. *praenomen* (first name)

praeparō, -āre, āvī, -ātum *prepare in advance*

praesidium, -ī, n. *protection, defense; garrison*

praestō, -āre, praestitī, praestitum (w. dat.) *stand before, excel* 31

praesum, praeesse, praefuī, praefutūrus *be at the head of, be in charge of*

praeter (prep. w. acc.) *besides, beyond*

praetereō, praeterīre, praeteriī (praeterīvī) praeteritum *go by* (transitive) 32

praetextus, -a, -um *bordered;* toga praetexta *purple-bordered toga*

prandium, -ī, n. *midday meal, lunch*

precor, -ārī, -ātus sum *pray*

prēlum, -ī, n. *olive press, wine press*

premō, -ere, pressī, pressum *press, crush, follow closely*

prēnsus, -a, -um *caught, arrested*

pretium, -ī, n. *price*

prex, precis, f. *prayer*

prīmus, -a, -um *first, foremost* 21; prīma lux *dawn*

prīnceps, prīncipis, m. *chief, chieftain, leading man, prince, emperor* 39

prīncipātus, -ūs, m. *principate, princedom, emperorship*

prior, prius *former, earlier* 38

prīscus, -a, -um *former, original; ancient*

pristinus, -a, -um *former, previous, early*

prīvātus, -a, -um *private;* rēs prīvāta *private property*

prīvātus, -ī, m. *private citizen*

prō (prep. w. abl.) *before, in front of; for* (on behalf of, in exchange for, in proportion to) 17

probō, -āre, -āvī, -ātum *approve, recommend*

prōcēdō, -ere, prōcessī, prōcessum *go forth, go forward*

procella, -ae, f. *storm, gust, squall*

procul (adv.) *at a distance* 40

prōdigium, -ī, n. *prodigy, portent, omen; monster*

prōditiō, prōditiōnis, f. *betrayal, treachery*

prōdō, -ere, prōdidī, prōditum *put forth, betray* 22

proelium, -ī, n. *battle* 37

profectō (adv.) *for a fact, in fact, actually*

profugus, -ī, m. *exile, fugitive*

profundus, -a, -um *deep*

prōgredior, -ī, prōgressus sum *move forward*

prohibeō, -ēre, -uī, -itum *hold off, keep away; prevent, prohibit* 17

prōlēs, prōlis, f. *offspring*

prōmittō, -ere, prōmīsī, prōmissum *send forth; promise* 31

prōmō, -ere, prōmpsī, prōmptum *bring forth* 22

prōnuba, -ae, f. *maid of honor*

prope (prep. w. acc.) *near* 12

prope (adv.) *nearby; nearly* 12

properō, -āre, -āvī, -ātum (intrans.) *hasten, make haste;* (trans.) *hasten, accelerate* 34

propinquus, -a, -um *near, close* 13

propinquus, -ī, m. *kinsman, relative* 13

propior, -ius *nearer* 38

propitius, -a, -um *propitious, favorable*

proprius, -a, -um *[one's] own*

propter (prep. w. acc.) *because of, on account of* 40

prōsum, prōdesse, prōfuī, prōfutūrus *be useful, be advantageous, be profitable* 31

prōvincia, -ae, f. *province* 1

prōvocō, -āre, -āvī, -ātum *call forth, challenge*

proximus, -a, -um *nearest, next* 38

publicānus, -ī, m. *tax collector*

publicus, -a, -um *public, belonging to the people* (populus) 30

pudor, pudōris, m. *shame, sense of honor*

puella, -ae, f. *girl* 1

puer, puerī, m. *boy, slave boy* 4

pugillāris, pugillāris, n. *notebook (small wax tablet)*

pugna, -ae, f. *fight*

pugnō, -āre, -āvī, -ātum *fight* 10

pulcher, pulchra, pulchrum *beautiful, handsome, fine* 5

pullus, -a, -um *dark-colored;* vestis pulla *mourning garment*

pultō, -āre, -āvī, -ātum, *knock on, strike*

pūpa, -ae, f. *doll*

pūpillus, -ī, m. *[legal] ward*

puteus, -ī, m. *well*

putō, -āre, -āvī, -ātum *think* 36

Q

quadrāgēsimus, -a, -um *fortieth* 21

quadrāgintā (indecl.) *forty* 21

quadrīgae, -ārum, f. or quadrīga, -ae, f. *a team of four horses; a chariot drawn by four horses*

quadringentēsimus, -a, -um *four hundredth* 22

quadringentī, -ae, -a *four hundred* 22

quadruplex, quadruplicis *fourfold* 21

quaerō, -ere, quaesīvī, quaesītum *seek, ask for*

quālis, -e *of which kind* (rel.); *of what kind?* (interr.) 26

quāliscumque, quālecumque (indef. rel adj.) *of whatever kind* 28

quam (adv. conj. modifying adjectives and adverbs) *as;* (interr. adv.) *how?* (w. comp.) *than;* (w. superl.) *as . . . possible* 24, 38, 39

quamquam (indef. adv.) *however* 28

quamquam (adv. conj.) *although*

quandō (inter. adv.) *when?* 28

quandōcumque (indef. adv.) *whenever* 28

quantus, -a, -um *of which size* (rel.); *how big? how large? how much* (interr.) 26

quantuscumque, quantacumque, quantumcumque (indef. rel. adj.) *of whatever size; however big, however large, however much* 28

quartus, -a, -um *fourth* 21

quasi (adv.) *as if, just as if, as it were*

quater (adv.) *four times* 21

quaternī, -ae, -a *four by four, four at a time* 21

quattuor (indecl.) *four* 21

quattuordecim (indecl.) *fourteen* 21

-que (enclitic conjunction) *and* 7

quemadmodum (adv.) *as* (rel.); *how?* (interr.) 26

queror, -ī, questus sum *complain*

quī, quae, quod (rel & interr. pron.) *who, which, that; which?* 26

quī, quae, quod (rel. & interr. adj.) *which; which?* 26

quī, qua, quod (indef. adj.) *some; any* 28

quia (adv. conj.) *because* 24

quīcumque, quaecumque, quodcumque (indef. rel. adj.) *whichever* 28

quīdam, quiddam (indef. pron.) *someone, something; a certain person, a certain thing* 28

quīdam, quaedam, quoddam (indef. adj.) *some; a certain* 28

quidem (postpositive adv.) *in fact; to be sure, at any rate;* nē . . . quidem *not even* 25

quiēs, quiētis, f. *rest, repose, sleep*

quiētus, -a, -um *quiet, calm, peaceful*

quīndecim (indel.) *fifteen* 21

quīngentēsimus, -a, -um *five hundredth* 22

quīngentī, -ae, -a *five hundred* 22

quīnī, -ae, -a *five by five, five at a time* 21

quīnquāgēsimus, -a, -um *fiftieth* 21

quīnquāgintā (indecl.) *fifty* 21

quīnque (indecl.) *five* 21

quīnquerēmis, quīnquerēmis, f. (i-stem) quinque-reme (a ship with five banks of oars)

quīnquiēns *or* quīnquiēs (adv.) *five times* 21

quīnquiplex, quinquiplicis *fivefold* 21

quīntus, -a, -um *fifth* 21

quīque, quaeque, quodque (universal adjective) *each* 27

quis, quid (interr. pron.) *who?, what?* 26

quis, quid (indef. pron.) *someone, something; any-one, anything* 28

quisquam, quidquam (indef. pron.) *anyone, any-thing* 28

quisque, quidque (universal pron.) *each one* 27

quisquis, quidquid (indef. rel. pron.) *whoever, what-ever* 28

quō (interrogative adverb) *where [to]?* 3

quō (relative adverb) *to which place, to which* 3

quō (indef. adverb) *to any place, to some place* 28

quōcumque (indef. rel. adv.) *[to] wherever* 28

quod (adv. conj.) *because* 10

quōmodo (adv.) *as* (rel.); *how?* (interr.) 26

quoniam (adv. conj.) *since, whereas* 24

quōquam (indef. adv.) *[to] anywhere* 28

quoque (adv.) *too, also* 24

quōquō (indef. rel. adv.) *[to] wherever* 28

quot (indecl.) *of which number* (rel.); *how many?* (interr.) 26

quotcumque (indecl. indef. rel. adj.) *however many* 28

quotiēns (adv.) *as often* (rel.); *how often?* (interr.) 26

quotiēnscumque (indef. rel. adv.) *however often* 28

quotquot (indecl. indef. rel. adj.) *however many* 28

R

rādix, rādicis, f. *root, root vegetable*

raeda, -ae, f. *[large four-wheeled traveling] coach*

rāmus, -ī, m. *branch, bough, twig*

rapidē (adv.) *hurriedly, rapidly*

rapiō, -ere, rapuī, raptum *snatch*

ratiō, ratiōnis, f. *account; reason; method, system*

recipiō, -ere, recēpī, receptum *take back, accept* 19

recuperō, -āre, -āvī, -ātum *recover*

reddō, -ere, reddidī, redditum *give back; render*

redeō, redīre, rediī (redīvī), reditum *go back, come back, return* 32

reditus, -ūs, m. *return*

referō, referre, rettulī, relātum *bring back, report back;* pedem referre *go back, return, give ground;* grātiam alicui referre *show gratitude to someone* 31

reflō, -āre, -āvī, -ātum *blow back, blow contrary*

refugiō, -ere, refūgī, refugitum *escape, avoid, take refuge*

rēgālis, -e *regal, royal*

rēgia, -ae, f. *palace*

rēgīna, rēgīnae, f. *queen* 2

rēgiō, rēgiōnis, f. *region; direction*

rēgius, -a, -um *royal, of a king*

rēgnō, -āre, -āvī, -ātum *reign*

rēgnum, -ī, n. *kingdom, kingship* 8

rēgō, -ere, rēxī, rēctum *rule* 18

religiō, religiōnis, f. *scrupulousness, religious feeling, superstition*

relinquō, -ere, relīquī, relictum *leave behind, leave, abandon* 26

reliquus, -a, -um *rest of, remaining* 16

repentīnus, -a, -um *sudden, unexpected*

reperiō, -īre, repperī, repertum, *find, discover* 20

repetō, -ere, repetīvī, repetītum *demand back, seek to recover*

repōnō, -ere, reposuī, repositum *put back*

repudiō, -āre, -āvī, -ātum *refuse, reject; divorce*

res. -eī, f. *thing, affair, fact, circumstances, situation, reality; property; benefit; lawsuit; business, art, science* 30

rescindō, -ere, rescidī, rescissum *cut off, cut away; rescind*

reservō, -āre, -āvī, -ātum *keep back, save*

respiciō, -ere, respexī, respectum *look back at;* (of a god) *look with favor upon* 19

respondeō, -ēre, respondī, respōnsum *respond, an-swer, reply*

respōnsum, -ī, n. *response, answer, reply*

restituō, -ere, restituī, restitūtum *restore*

retineō, -ēre, -uī, retentum *hold back* 17

reverentia, -ae, f. *reverence, respect*

rēx, rēgis, m. *king* 18

rīdeō, -ēre, rīsī, rīsum *laugh; laugh at*

rīpa, -ae, f. *bank [of a river]*

rixa, -ae, f. *quarrel, brawl, fight*

rogō, -āre, -āvī, -ātum *ask, ask for* 29

rogus, -ī, m. *funeral pyre*
rosa, -ae, f. *rose*
roseus, -a, -um *rosy, rose-colored, pink, reddish*
rūdus, rūderis, n. *rubble;* [*concrete*] *fill* [*of a Roman road*]
ruīna, -ae, f. *collapse, downfall;* (plural) *ruins*
rumpō, -ere, rūpī, ruptum *burst, break*
rūs, rūris, n. *country, countryside; country place* 30
rūrsus (adv.) *back; again* 11
rūsticus, -a, -um *of the country, of farming* 30

S

sacellum, -ī, n. *chapel*
sacer, sacra, sacrum *sacred; accursed* 10
sacerdōs, sacerdōtis, m. *or* f. *priest, priestess*
sacrificium, -ī, n. *sacrifice*
saeculum, -ī, n. *age, generation, century* 22
saepe (adv.) *often* 7
saepiō, -īre, saepsī, saeptum *hedge in, enclose*
saevitia, -ae, f. *ferocity*
saevus, -a, -um *fierce, cruel*
sagum, -ī, n. [*soldier's*] *cloak*
salūs, salūtis, f. *health, safety, salvation* 29
salūtātiō, salūtātiōnis, f. *greeting, salutation; morning greeting* [*of patron by clients*]
salūtō, -āre, -āvī, -ātum *greet, salute*
salvātor, -tōris, m. *savior*
salveō, -ēre, ——, —— *be safe, be well in health;* (imperative) salvē, salvēte *hello*
salvus, -a, -um *safe*
sanctus, -a, um *sacred, holy, sanctified*
sanguis, sanguinis, m. *blood* 25
sānō, -āre, -āvī, -ātum *cure, heal*
sānus, -a, -um *sound, healthy, sane*
sarrācum, -ī, n. [*heavy-duty freight*] *wagon*
satis, n. (only in nom. and acc. sing.) *a sufficient amount, a sufficient number, enough* 16
satisfactiō, satisfactiōnis, f. *satisfaction*
saxum, -ī, n. *rock*
scamnum, -ī, n. *footstool*
scelus, sceleris, n. *wickedness, crime*
schola, -ae, f. *lounge, lecture hall; park bench*
scientia, -ae, f. *knowledge*
sciō, -īre, -īvī, -ītum *know*
scrība, -ae, m. *scribe, secretary*

scrībō, -ere, scrīpsī, scrīptum *write* 36
scrīnium, -ī, n. *book box*
scrīptum, -ī, n. *writing; line;* duodecim scrīpta *Twelve Lines* (a game like backgammon)
sculpōnea, -ae, f. *wooden shoe*
sculptor, sculptōris, m. *sculptor*
scūtum, -ī, n. [*large leather-covered semicylindrical rectangular*] *shield*
sēcrētum, -ī, n. *retirement, solitude; secret*
sēcrētus, -a, -um *secret*
secundus, -a, -um *following; favorable; second* 21
secunda mēnsa *or* secundae mēnsae *dessert course*
secūris, secūris, f. (i-stem; acc. secūrim, abl. secūrī) *axe*
sed (conjunction) *but* 5
sēdecim (indecl.) *sixteen* 21
sedeō, -ēre, sēdī, sessum *sit* 28
sēdēs, sēdis, f. *seat;* (pl.) *residence* 28
sēditiō, sēditiōnis, f. *sedition, insurrection, revolt, mutiny*
segniter (adv.) *lazily, sluggishly, slowly*
sēgregō, -āre, -āvī, -ātum *segregate, separate*
sella, -ae, f. *seat, stool, bench, chair; sedan chair*
semel (adv.) *once* 21
sēmentis, sēmentis, f. (i-stem) *a sowing*
sēmihomo, sēmihominis, m. *a half-human creature*
semper (adv.) *always, continually* 11
senectūs, senectūtis, f. *old age*
senex, senis (masc. only) *old* 38
senior (comp. of senex) 38
sententia, -ae, f. *opinion, vote;* in sententiam discēdō *go over to an*[*other's*] *opinion, vote* [*with someone*]
sentiō, -īre, sēnsī, sēnsum *feel, perceive* 36
sepeliō, -īre, -īvī, sepultum *entomb, bury*
septem (indecl.) *seven* 21
septendecim (indecl.) *seventeen* 21
septimus, -a, -um *seventh* 21
septingentēsimus, -a, -um *seven hundredth* 22
septingentī, -ae, -a *seven hundred* 22
septuāgēsimus, -a, -um *seventieth* 21
septuāgintā (indecl.) *seventy* 21
sepulcrum, -ī, n. *grave, tomb*
sequor, -ī, secūtus sum *follow*
serēnus, -a, -um *clear, bright, fair, serene*
sermō, sermōnis, m. *conversation*
serva, -ae, f. *slave-woman*
serviō, -īre, -īvī, -ītum (w. dat.) *serve; be a slave* 32
servō, -āre, -āvī, -ātum *keep, save, guard* 11

servus, -ī, m. *slave* 6

sescentēsimus, -a, -um *six hundredth* 22

sescentī, -ae, -a *six hundred* 22

sestertius, -i, m. *sesterce* (a silver coin, 1/100 of an aureus)

seu See sīve.

seu. . .seu. . . See sīve. . .sīve. . .

sex (indecl.) *six* 21

sexāgēsimus, -a, -um *sixtieth* 21

sexāgintā (indecl.) *sixty* 21

sextus, -a, -um *sixth* 21

sī (adv. conj.) *if* 10

sīc (adv. modifying verbs) *so, thus, in such a manner; (it is so)* = *yes* 24

sīca, -ae, f. *sickle;* [*short curved*] *sword*

siccus, -a, -um *dry*

sīcut (adv. conj. modifying verbs) *just as, just as if* 24

sīdus, sīderis, n. *constellation, heavenly body*

signum, -ī, n. *sign, signal;* [*military*] *standard* 28

silentium, -ī, n. *silence*

silva, -ae, f. *a wood, forest* 1

simia, -ae, f. *monkey*

similis, -e *like* 15

similitūdō, similitūdinis, f. *likeness*

simul (adv.) *at the same time* 39

simul ac See simul atque.

simul atque or ac (adv. conj.) *as soon as* 24

simulō, -āre, -āvī, -ātum *simulate, feign, pretend*

simplex, simplicis *single, simple* 21

sīn (adv. and coord. conj.) *but if;* sīn autem *but if, on the other hand* 24

sine (prep. w. abl.) *without* 17

singulī, -ae, -a *one by one, one at a time* 21

sinister, sinistra, sinistrum *on the left, lefthand* 38

sinus, -ūs, m. *fold; bosom* [*of a toga*]

sīve (adv. and coord. conj.) *or if* 24

sīve. . .sīve. . . *whether. . .or. . ., if. . .or if. . .* 24

socer, socerī, m. *father-in-law*

societās, societātis, f. *companionship; partnership, company; alliance*

socius, socī, m. *ally, comrade* 10

sōl, sōlis, m. *sun* 27

sōlātium, sōlātī, n. *consolation, comfort*

soleō, -ēre, solitus sum *be accustomed, do usually* 35

solium, -ī, n. *throne; bathtub*

sollemnis, -e *festive; solemn; customary; annual*

solea, -ae, f. [*light*] *sandal*

sōlus, -a, -um (pron. decl.) *alone, sole* 27

solvō, -ere, solvī, solūtum *loosen, untie, undo*

somnus, -ī, m. *sleep* 7

soror, sorōris, f. *sister* 13

sors, sortis, f. (i-stem) *lot*

spatha, -ae, f. [*broad two-edged*] *sword*

spatium, -ī, n. *space; length of time*

speciēs, -ēī, f. *sight, appearance, show; kind* 30

speciōsus, -a, -um *beautiful, good-looking, attractive; well-sounding, plausible*

spectāculum, -ī, n. *spectacle, show, a viewing*

spectō, -āre, -āvī, -ātum *look at, watch* 3

spēlunca, -ae, f. *cave, cavern*

spērō, -āre, -āvī, -ātum *hope, hope for* 35

spēs, -eī, f. *hope, expectation* 30

spīna, -ae, f. *thorn; backbone;* [*central*] *barrier* [*of a circus*]

spiritus, -ūs, m. *breath;* spiritum dūcō *draw breath*

spolium, -ī, n. *the skin stripped from an animal, arms and clothing taken from an enemy*

spōnsus, -ī, m. *betrothed, fiancé; bridegroom*

stadium, -ī, n. *stadium, running track*

statim (adv.) *immediately, at once* 19

statua, -ae, f. *statue*

statūmen, statūminis, n. *support;* [*flagstone*] *foundation* [*of a Roman road*]

stercorārius, -ī, m. *manure-wagon driver*

stilus, -i, m. *stylus* (a Roman instrument for writing on wax)

stimulō, -āre, -āvī, -ātum *goad, incite*

stirps, stirpis, f. *stock*

stō, stāre, stetī, stātum *stand* 9

stola, -ae, f. *stola* (the long outer garment of a Roman lady)

stolidus, -a, -um *foolish, dull*

stringō, -ere, strīnxī, strīctum *draw*

strophium, -ī, n. *brassiere* (girdle tied under the bosom)

studium, -ī, n. *eagerness, zeal, enthusiasm; study, hobby* 27

stultus, -a, um *stupid, foolish*

stupefaciō, -ere, stupefēcī, stupefactum *stupefy, stun*

sub (prep. w. acc. or abl.) *to under, up to, to the foot of* (w. acc.); *under, at the foot of* (w. abl.) 3

subeō, subīre, subiī (subīvī), subitum *go under, go up to* (transitive) 32 subitus, -a, -um *sudden;* **subitō** (abl.) *suddenly*

sublīmis, -e *on high, elevated, uplifted*

submoveō, -ēre, submōvī, submōtum *remove gradually*

succēdō, -ere, successī, successum *go under; succeed to, come after*

sūcus, -ī, m. *juice*

suffrāgium, -ī, n. *vote, suffrage*

suī (no nom.) (refl. pron.) *himself, herself, itself, themselves* 25

sum, esse, fuī, futūrus *be* 3

summus, -a, -um *top of* (also used as superl. of **superus**, *highest*) 16, 38

supellex, supellectilis, f. *[household] furniture*

super (prep. w. acc.) *over, above* 3

superbia, -ae, f. *haughtiness, pride*

superbus, -a, -um *haughty, proud, overbearing*

superō, -āre, -āvī, -ātum *surpass, overcome, defeat* 7

supersum, superesse, superfuī, superfutūrus *be left, be left over, survive*

superī, -ōrum, m. *the gods above, the heavenly gods* 38

superus, -a, -um *above*

suprā (adv. & prep. w. acc.) *above*

supremus, -a, -um (superl. of **superus**) 38

suspiciō, -ere, suspexī, suspectum *look up to*

suspēnsūra, -ae, f. *hypocaust* (under-floor, hot-air heating channel)

suspirium, -ī, n. *sigh*

sustineō, -ēre, -uī, sustentum *hold up, withstand* 17

suus, -a, -um (refl. poss. adj.) *his [own], her [own], its [own], their [own]* 25

synthesis, synthesis, f. *synthesis* (a man's dinner suit)

T

tabella, -ae, f. *notebook* (wax tablet)

tābeō, -ēre, -uī, ___ *waste away, melt*

taberna, -ae, f. *booth; shop; tent*

tablinum, -ī, n. *tablinum* (master bedroom and office of a Roman house)

taceō, -ēre, -uī, -itum *be silent*

tacitus, -a, -um *silent*

tālis, -e *such, of such a kind* 23

tālus, -ī, m. *knucklebone* (used for games)

tam (adv. modifying adjectives and adverbs) *so, to such a degree* 24

tamen (adv.) *nevertheless, yet, still* 24

tamquam (demonst. and rel. adv.) *just as; as if* 24

tandem (adv.) *at length, at last*

tantus, -a, -um *so great, so large* 23

tardus, -a, -um *slow, late*

taurus, -ī, m. *bull*

tectum, -ī, n. *roof*

tēlum, -ī, n. *weapon, spear* 11

temeritās, temeritātis, f. *rashness, irresponsibility*

temperāmentum, -ī, n. *proper mixture, correct proportion*

tempestās, tempestātis, f. *weather; storm*

templum, -ī, n. *holy precinct, sacred area*

temptō, -āre, -āvī, -ātum *test; try, attempt* 34

tempus, temporis, n. *time* 23

teneō, -ēre, -uī, tentum *hold, grasp* 17

tendō, -ere, tetendī, tentum (tēnsum) *stretch*

tepidārium, -ī, n. *tepidarium* (warm room of a bath)

ter (adv.) *thrice, three times* 21

tergum, -ī, n. *back*

terminālis, -e *of a boundary;* **lapis terminalis** *boundary stone*

terra, terrae, f. *earth, land* 1

terreō, -ēre, -uī, -itum *frighten*

terror, terrōris, m. *terror*

tertius, -a, -um *third* 21

testāmentum, -ī, n. *will, testament*

thermae, -ārum f. *[large] baths* (community center, health club, etc.)

thermopōlium, -ī, n. *thermopolium* (a snack bar or fast-food restaurant)

timeō, -ēre, -uī, ___ *fear, be afraid* 17

timidus, -a, -um *timid, fearful*

timor, timōris, m. *fear* 14

toga, -ae, f. *toga* (male Roman citizen's official outer garment); **toga praetexta** *purple-bordered toga;* **toga virilis** *[unbordered] toga of manhood;* **toga candida** *[unbordered] toga of political candidates;* **toga exigua** *single toga*

tollō, -ere, sustulī, sublātum *lift up, raise, remove* 31

tonītrus, -ūs, m. *thunder*

torreō, -ēre, -uī, tōstum *burn, parch; bake*

tot (indecl. adj.) *so many* 23

totiēns (adv.) *so often* 23

tōtus, -a, -um (pron. decl.) *whole, entire* 27

trādō, -ere, trādidī, trāditum *hand over, hand down* 26

trahō, -ere, trāxī, trāctum *drag, draw*

trāiciō, -ere, trāiēcī, trāiectum *throw across, pierce* 24

trānō, -āre, -āvī, -ātum *swim across*

tranquīllō, -āre, -āvī, -ātum *calm*

tranquillus, -a, -um *tranquil, calm*

trāns (prep. w. acc.) *across* 8

trānseō, trānsīre, trānsiī (trānsīvī), trānsitum *go over, go across, cross* (transitive) 32

trānsferō, trānsferre, trānstuli, trānslātus *carry across, transfer, translate*

trānsfugiō, -ere, trānsfūgī, trānsfugitum *desert to the enemy*

trānsiliō, -īre, trānsiluī, ____ *leap across, leap over*

trānsitus, -ūs, m. *crossing*

trecentēsimus, -a, -um *three hundredth* 22

trecentī, -ae, -a, *three hundred* 22

tredecim (indecl.) *thirteen* 21

trepidus, -a, -um *alarmed; alarming*

trēs, tria *three* 21

trīceps, trīcipitis *three-headed*

trīcēsimus, -a, -um *thirtieth* 21

trīclīnium, -ī, n. *triclinium, dining room*

tricorpor, tricorporis *three-bodied*

trīgeminus, -a, -um *triplet*

trīgintā (indecl.) *thirty* 21

trigōn, trigōnis, m. *Triangle* (a ball game)

trīnī, -ae, -a *three by three, three at a time* 21

triplex, triplicis *triple, threefold* 21

trirēmis, trirēmis, f. (i-stem) *trireme* (a ship with three banks of oars)

tristis, triste *mournful, grim, gloomy* 20

trītus, -a, -um *worn, rubbed*

triumphus, -ī, m. *triumph* (a solemn procession awarded by the Senate to some victorious generals)

trochus, -ī, m. *hoop* (child's toy)

tū, tuī (pers. & refl. pron.) *you* (sing.) 25

tuba, -ae, f. *[straight] war trumpet*

tum or tunc (adv.) *then, at that time* 8

tumultuōsus, -a, -um *disquieted, tumultuous, confused*

tumultus, -ūs, m. *uproar, confusion, tumult*

tunc (see **tum**)

tunica, -ae, f. *tunic* (male and female undergarment)

turba -ae, f. *crowd; disturbance* 40

turbidus, -a, -um *confused, wild, troubled, disturbed*

turbō, turbinis, m. *top* (child's toy); *hurricane, whirlwind, tornado, cyclone*

turpis, -e *ugly; disgraceful*

tussis, tussis (i-stem: acc. sing. **tussim**, abl. **tussī**), f. *cough* (or any disease with this symptom)

tūtēla, -ae, f. *guardianship, protection*

tūtor, tūtōris, m. *[legal] guardian*

tūtus, -a, -um *safe*

tuus, -a, -um *your, yours* (one person's) 6

tyrannus, -ī, m. *despot, tyrant*

U

ubi (interrogative adverb) *where [at]?* 3

ubi (relative adverb) *where, when* 3

ubicumque (indef. rel. adv.) *wherever* 28

ubique (adv.) *everywhere* 27

ubiubi (indef. rel. adv.) *wherever* 28

ulcīscor, -ī, ultus sum *avenge*

ūllus, -a, -um (pron. decl.) *any* 27

ulterior, -ius *farther* 38

ultimus, -a, -um *farthest*

umbra, -ae, f. *shade, shadow, ghost* 9

umbriferus, -a, -um *shade-bearing, shady*

umerus, -ī, m. *shoulder*

umquam (adv.) *ever* 34

unctōrium, -ī, n. *massage room*

unda, -ae, f. *wave*

unde (interrogative adverb) *where from?* 3

unde (rel. adverb) *from which place, from which* 3

ūndecim (indecl.) *eleven* 21

ūndecimus, -a, -um *eleventh* 21

undecumque (indef. rel. adv.) *from wherever* 28

undeunde (indef. rel. adv.) *from wherever* 28

ūndēvīcēsimus, -a, -um *nineteenth* 21

ūndēvīgintī (indecl.) *nineteen* 21

undique (adv.) *from all sides, on all sides* 27

ūniversī, -ae, -a *all together*

ūnus, -a, -um *one* 21

urbs, urbis, f. (i-stem) *city* 16

usque *all the way, continuously*

ūsus, -ūs, m. *usefulness, advantage; habit, practice* 29; *[marriage by] usufruct* ut (adv. conj. modifying verbs) *as;* (interr. adv.) *how?* 10

utcumque (indef. rel. adv.) *however*

uter, utra, utrum (pron. decl.) *which [of two]?*

uterque, utraque, utrumque (pron. decl.) *each [of two]* 27

uterus, -i, m. *womb*

ūtor, -ī, ūsus sum (w. abl. of means) *use* 33

utrimque (adv.) *from both sides, on both sides*

utrum (interrog. particle introducing a disjunctive question) 9

ūva, -ae, f. *grape*

uxor, uxōris, f. *wife* 19

V

V *5* 21

vacuus, -a, -um *empty, free*

vae (interj.) *alas! woe!*

valeō, -ēre, -uī, -itum *be strong, be well* 35

validus, -a, -um *strong*

vallēs, vallis, f. *valley*

varius, -a, -um *various, varying, varied* 39

vātēs, vātis, m. or f. (not an i-stem) *soothsayer, seer, prophet; bard* -ve (enclitic conj.) *or, or possibly* 24

vehemēns, vehementis *vehement, impetuous, violent, strong*

vehiculum, -ī, n. *vehicle*

vehō, -ere, vexī, vectum *transport;* (passive) *travel, ride*

vel (conj.) *or, or even, or in fact, or if you please* 9 vel. . .vel. . . *either. . .or. . .* 9

vēlōx, vēlōcis *swift, speedy*

velut (adv.) *just as, just as if, as for example*

vēnātiō, vēnātiōnis, f. *the hunt, hunting*

vēndō, -ere, vēndidī, vēnditum *sell* 22

veneror, -ārī, -ātus sum *venerate, respect*

veniō, -īre, vēnī, ventum *come* 20

vēnor, -ārī, -ātus sum *hunt*

ventus, -ī, m. *wind* 39

verbum, verbī, n. *word* 4

vereor, -ērī, veritus sum *stand in awe of; fear* 33

versō, -āre, -āvī, -ātum *keep turning, occupy,* (passive) *be employed* 27

versus, -a, -um *turned, upturned;* pollice versō *with upturned thumb* (signalling the killing of a gladiator)

versus, -ūs, m. *a turning; a verse [of poetry]; a line [of prose]* 31

vertō, -ere, versī, versum *turn* 27

vērus, -a, -um *true, real* 12

vērō in *truth, indeed, really*

vēscor, -ī, ___ (w. abl. of means) *feed upon* 33

vester, vestra, vestrum *your, yours (more than one person's)* 6

vestibulum, -ī, n. *entrance-court, vestibule, antechamber*

vestīgium, -ī, n. *foot-sole, footstep, footprint, trace*

vestīmentum, -ī, n. *clothing; (pl.) clothes*

vestis, vestis, f. (i-stem) *garment, clothing; (pl.) clothes* 28;

vestis pulla *mourning garment*

veterrimus, -a, -um (superl. of vetus) 38

vetō, -āre, -āvī, -ātum *forbid*

vetulus, -a, -um (not an i-stem) *oldish, little old* 16

vetus, veteris (not an i-stem) *old* 15

vetustior, -ius (comp. of vetus) 38

via, -ae, f. *way, road, street* 1

viātor, viātōris, m. *traveler*

vīcēsimus, -a, -um *twentieth* 21

vīcīnus, -a, -um *near, neighboring* 13

victor, victōris, m. *conqueror, winner (in apposition = victorious)*

victoria, -ae, f. *victory*

victus, -a, -um *conquered*

vīctus, -ūs, m. *living, victuals*

videō, -ēre, vīdī, vīsum *see;* (passive) *seem* 17

viduus, -a, -um *bereft, widowed*

vīgintī (indecl.) *twenty* 21

vīlla, -ae, f. *farmhouse, villa* 1

vinciō, -īre, vinxī, vinctum *tie, bind* 24

vincō, -ere, vīcī, victum *conquer* 24

vindex, vindicis, m. *defender, champion*

vīnea, -ae, f. *vineyard*

vīnum, -ī, n. *wine*

violēns, violentis *violent*

vir, virī, m. *man; husband; hero* 4

vireō, -ēre, -uī, -itum *be green; be healthy, flourish*

virgō, virginis, f. *maiden, girl* 24

virgulta, -ōrum, n. *thicket*

virīlis, -e, *manly, of a man, of manhood;* toga virīlis [unbordered] *toga of manhood*

viritim (adv.) *man by man*

virtūs, virtūtis, f. *manliness, virtue, worth, courage* 14

vīs, vīs, f. (i-stem) *force, violence;* (pl.) vīrēs, vīrium *strength* 15

vīta, -ae, f. *life* 2

vītō, -āre, -āvī, -ātum *avoid*

vitta, -ae, f. [*unspun white wool*] *fillet*

vīvō, -ere, vīxī, vīctum *live, be alive* 24

vīvus, -a, -um *alive, living* 24

vix (adv.) *scarcely, barely, with difficulty* 39

vōciferor, -ārī, -ātus sum *cry loudly, shout, vociferate*

vocō, -āre, -āvī, -ātum *call* 2

volēns, volentis *willing*

volō, velle, voluī, ___ *wish, want, be willing*

volō, -āre, -āvī, -ātum *fly, move swiftly, speed, rush* 7

volūmen, volūminis, n. *book*

vorō, -āre, -āvī, -ātum *devour, eat*

vōs, vestrum (vestrī) (pers. & refl. pron.) *you* (pl.) 25

vōtīvus, -a, -um *votive, promised by a vow*

vōtum, -ī, n. *vow*

vōx, vōcis, f. *voice* 38

vulgō, -āre, -āvī, -ātum *spread, make common*

vulgus, -ī, n. *the public, the mob;* vulgō *commonly*

vulnerātus, -a, um *wounded*

vulnerō, -āre, -āvī, -ātum *wound*

vulnus, vulneris, n. *wound*

vulpes, vulpis, f. *fox, vixen*

X

X 10 21

ENGLISH—LATIN VOCABULARY

Latin words are almost never exact synonyms. When there are more than one Latin word given for an entry, you will need to check them in the Latin-to-English list to see which one you want. Vocabulary forms and Lesson references are given only in the Latin-to-English list.

A

a: no Latin equivalent
abandon: *relinquō*
[ability] have __: *possum*
[able] be __: *possum*
about: *circā, dē,* see Lesson 29; __ to: see Lesson 34; round __: *circā, circum*
above: *superus, super;* gods __: *superī*
[absent] be __: *absum*
accept: *recipiō*
accident: *cāsus*
accomplish: *cōnficiō*
account: *nōmen;* on __ of: *ob, propter;* on __ of which fact: *quam ob rem, quamobrem*
accursed: *sacer*
[accustomed] be __: *soleō*
across: *trāns;* go __: *trānseō;* throw __: *trāiciō*
act: *faciō,* see Lesson 29
[actual] in __ fact: *rē vērā*
add: *addō, adiciō;* be __ ed: *accēdō*
adjacent: *fīnitimus*
advance, advance to the attack: *signa īnferō;* receive in __ *praecipiō*
advantage: *ūsus;* to one's own __: *ex* ⟨possessive⟩ *rē*
advantageous: see Lesson 29; be __: *prōsum*
advice: *cōnsilium*
advise: *moneō*
affair: *rēs*
[affection] feel __ for: *dīligō*
[afraid] be __, be __ of: *timeō*
after: *post, postquam*

afterward: *post*
afterwards: *post*
again: *iterum, rūrsus*
against: *adversus, contrā, in* + acc.
age: *aetās, saeculum*
ago: *ante*
ahead of: *prae*
aid: *auxilium*
aim at: *petō*
alike: *similēs*
alive: *vīvus;* be __: *vīvō*
all: *omnis;* __ over: *tōtō, tōta, tōtīs;* __ of: *omnis;* come __ the way: *perveniō;* from __ sides: *undique;* in __ respects: *omnibus rēbus;* not at __: *haud, male, minimē;* on __ sides: *undique*
allow: *patior*
ally: *socius*
almost: *paene*
alone: *sōlus*
along: *per*
already: *iam*
also: *et, etiam, quoque*
altar: *āra*
always: *semper*
[am] see be & Lesson 2
amazing: *mīrus*
among: *inter, apud*
[amount] a larger __: *plūs;* a sufficient __: *satis;* too small an __: *parum*
and: *ac, atque, et, -que;* __ he, __ she, etc.: *quī;* __ so: *itaque*
anew: *dē novō*
anger: *īra*

announce: *nūntiō*

another: *alius;* at ___ place: *alibi;* at ___ time: *aliās;* from ___ place: *aliunde;* of ___: *alterīus;* one ___: *inter nōs, inter vōs, inter sē, alius* or *alter* repeated in a different case, see Lesson 22; one . . . ___ *alius . . . alius, hic . . . hic;* to ___ place *aliō*

another's: *aliēnus*

anxiety: *cūra*

any: *aliquantus, aliquī, quī, ūllus;* at ___ rate: *quidem;* at ___ time *aliquandō,* quandō; not ___ *nihil, nūllus*

anyone: *aliquis, quis, quisquam*

anything: *aliquid, quid, quidquam*

anywhere: *alicubi, aliquō, quō, quōquam;* from ___: *alicunde*

appearance: *faciēs, speciēs*

apply: *adferō*

approach: *accēdō, adeō*

approximately: *circā*

arms: *arma, tēla;* set of ___: *arma*

army: *exercitus*

around: *circā, circum*

arrange: *compōnō*

arrive: *perveniō*

art: *ars, rēs*

as: *ac, atque, quam, quemadmodum, quōmodo, ut,* see Lessons 2 & 29; ___ . . . ___: *sīc* or *ita . . . ut, tam* or *ita . . . quam;* ___ . . . ___ possible: *quam* + superlative; ___ big ___, ___ large ___: *tantus . . . quantus;* ___ many ___: *tot . . . quot;* ___ much ___: *tantus . . . quantus, pariter atque, pariter ac;* ___ often ___: *totiēns . . . quotiēns;* ___ soon ___: *simul ac* or *atque;* just ___: *tam . . . quam, tamquam, ita . . . quam, sīc . . . ut, sīcut, ita . . . ut, sīc . . . quemadmodum, ita . . . quōmodo, sīc . . . quōmodo;* just ___ if: *sīcut, tamquam;* of the same kind ___: *tālis . . . quālis;* offer ___ a pretext: *prae se ferre*

ask, ask for: *rogō*

assemble: *convocō*

assist: *iuvō*

at: *ad, apud,* see Lessons 25 & 30; ___ a distance: *procul;* ___ another place: *alibi;* ___ another time: *aliās;* ___ any rate: *quidem;* ___ any time: *aliquandō, quandō;* ___ last, ___ length: *dēnique;* ___ once: *statim;* ___ one time: *ōlim;* ___ some time: *aliquandō, ōlim, quandō;* ___ that time: *tum, tunc;* ___ the foot of: *sub;* ___ the house of: *apud;* ___ the same time: *simul;* ___ the side of: *circā;* ___ this moment: *nunc iam;* ___ this time: *nunc;* ___ which place: *ubi;* aim ___: *petō;* be present ___: *adsum;* five ___ a time: *quīnī;* four ___ a time: *quaternī;* look ___: *aspiciō, spectō;* look back ___: *respiciō;* not ___ all: *haud, male, minimē;* one ___ a time: *singulī;* three ___ a time: *trīnī;* two ___ a time: *bīnī*

attack: *petō;* advance to the ___: *sīgna īnferō*

aureus: *aureus*

author: *auctor*

await: *exspectō*

[away] ___ from: *ā, ab;* be ___: *absum;* go ___: *abeō;* keep ___: *prōhibeō;* let go ___: *āmittō;* running ___: *fuga;* take ___: *dēmō*

[awe] stand in ___ of: *vereor*

B

back: *rūrsus;* bring ___: *referō;* come ___, go ___: *pedem referō, redeō;* hold ___: *retineō;* in ___ of: *post;* look ___ at: *respiciō;* report ___: *referō;* take ___: *recipiō*

bad: *malus;* badly: *male*

band: *manus*

barely: *vix*

[basis] on the ___ of: *e, ēx*

battle: *proelium;* line of ___: *aciēs*

be: *sum,* see Lessons 2 & 11; ___ a slave: *serviō;* ___ able: *possum;* ___ absent: *absum;* ___ accustomed: *soleō;* ___ added: *accēdō;* ___ advantageous: *prōsum;* ___ afraid, ___ afraid of: *timeō;* ___ alive: *vīvō;* ___ away: *absum;* ___ better than: *praestō, superō;* ___ born: *nāscor;* ___ deficient: *dēficiō;* ___ distant: *absum;* ___ favorable: *faveō;* ___ glad: *gaudeō;* ___ important: *valeō;* ___ in difficulties: *labōrō;* ___ lost: *pereō;* ___ pleasing: *placeō;* ___ present, ___ present at, ___ present to help: *adsum;* ___ profitable: *prōsum;* ___ situated: *iaceō;* ___ sorry: *doleō;* ___ strong: *valeō;* ___ useful: *prōsum;* ___ well: *valeō;* ___ wrong: *errō;* to ___ sure: *quidem*

bear: *ferō*

beautiful: *pulcher*

beauty: *forma*

because: *causā, quia, quod;* ___ of: *ob, propter*

before: *ante, prae, prō;* **just __:** *sub* + acc.; **stand __:** *praestō*

begin: *incipiō;* **began:** *coepī*

[behalf] on __ of: *prō*

behave: *faciō*

behind: *post;* **leave __:** *relinquō*

behold: *aspiciō*

[being] human __: *homo*

belief: *fidēs*

believe: *crēdō*

[belonging] __ to the people: *publicus*

below: *īnferus, sub;* **gods __:** *īnferī*

benefit: *rēs*

best: *optimus;* **seems __:** *vidētur*

betake: *cōnferō*

betray: *prōdō*

better: *melior;* **be __ than:** *praestō, superō*

between: *inter*

bid: *iubeō*

big: *magnus;* **as __ as:** *tantus . . . quantus;* **how __:** *quantus;* **however __:** *quantuscumque;* **so __:** *tantus*

bind: *vinciō*

bird: *avis*

birth: *nātūra, genus;* **by __:** *nātū*

blind: *caecus*

blood: *sanguis*

body: *corpus*

[born] be __ *nāscor*

both: *ambō;* **__ . . . and . . . :** *et . . . et . . .*

[bottom] __ of: *īmus;* **__ line:** *summa rēs, summa*

boy: *puer*

brave: *fortis*

breadth: *lātitūdō*

breast: *pectus*

breath: *anima*

bright: *clārus*

bring: *portō, ferō;* **__ back:** *referō;* **__ forth:** *prōmō;* **__ to:** *adferō;* **__ together:** *cōnferō;* **__ up:** *adferō;* **__ upon:** *īnferō*

broad: *lātus* & see Lesson 22

brother: *frāter*

build: *aedificō*

burn: *ardeō*

business: *res;* **mind you own __:** *fac tuam rem*

bury: *condō*

but: *at, autem, sed;* **__ if:** *sīn;* **__ yet:** *at, at tamen*

buy: *emō*

by: *per* & see Lessons 8, 11, 22, & 25; **__ far:** *longē;* **__ land and sea:** *terrā marīque;* **__ no means:** *haud;* **five __ five:** *quīnī;* **four __ four:** *quaternī;* **go __:** *praetereō;* **one __ one:** *singulī;* **pass __:** *praetereō;* **three __ three:** *trīnī;* **two __ two:** *bīnī*

bypass: *praetereō*

C

call: *vocō*

call together: *convocō*

camp: *castra*

can: *possum*

captain: *magister*

captive: *captīvus*

capture: *capiō*

care: *cūra;* **take __ of:** see Lesson 29

carry: *portō;* **__ off:** *auferō;* **__ onward:** *īnferō*

case (legal): *causa*

castle: *arx*

catch: *excipiō*

cause: *causa, efficiō:* **__ pain:** *doleō*

cease: *dēsinō*

century: *saeculum*

certain: *certus, quīdam:* **a __ person:** *quīdam;* **a __ thing:** *quiddam*

chance: *cāsus, fors*

change: *mūtō;* **political __:** *rēs novae*

[charge] take __: *rērum potior;* **take __ [of]:** *potior*

chief: *prīnceps*

children: *līberī*

choose: *dēligō, optō*

circumstances: *rēs;* **favorable __:** *rēs secundae*

citadel: *arx*

citizen: *cīvis*

city: *urbs*

clan: *gēns*

clear: *clārus*

close: *propinquus, claudō*

[closely] follow __: *īnstō*

clothes: *vestēs*

clothing: *vestis*

coast: *lītus*

[coin] gold __: *aureus*

collect: *cogō, colligō, compōnō, condō, cōnferō*

combine: *committō*

come: *veniō;* ___ all the way: *perveniō;* ___ back: *redeō;* ___ in handy: see Lesson 29; ___ to know: *cognōscō, nōscō;* ___ together: *conveniō;* ___ upon: *inveniō*

command: *imperium*

common people: *plebs*

commonwealth: *rēs pūblica*

compare: *cōnferō*

[comparison] in ___ with: *prae*

compel: *cogō*

comrade: *socius*

conceal: *condō*

concern(ed): see Lesson 29

concerning: *dē*

conquer: *vincō*

consequently: *ergō*

consider: *exīstimō, habeō*

consult: *cōnsulō;* ___ the interests of: *cōnsulō*

contain: *contineō*

continually: *semper*

[contrary] ___ to: *contrā;* on the ___: *contrā*

[control] take ___ of, get ___ of: *potior*

counsel: *cōnsilium;* take ___ for: *cōnsulō*

country: *patria, rūs, terra;* ___ place: *rūs;* of the ___: *rūsticus*

countryside: *rūs*

courage: *virtūs*

course: *cursus*

craft: *ars, rēs*

cross: *trānseō*

crowd: *turba*

cry: *clāmō*

cultivate: *colō*

D

danger: *perīculum*

dare: *audeō*

daughter: *fīlia*

day: *diēs;* from ___ to ___, from one ___ to the next: *in diēs*

dear: *cārus, cordī*

death: *mors*

deceive: *impōnō*

decide: *cōnstituō, īnstituō,* I ___d: *mihi visum est, mihi certum est*

deed of valor: *decus*

deep: *altus,* see Lesson 22; the ___ ⟨sea⟩: *altum*

defeat: *superō*

[deficient] be ___: *dēficiō*

definite: *certus*

degree: *modus;* to such a ___: *ita, tam*

delay: *moror*

delight: *iuvō*

deny: *negō*

depart: *discēdō*

depth: *altitūdō*

descendants: *posterī*

desire: *cupīdō, cupiō*

desperately: *misere*

destroy: *interficiō*

determine: *cernō*

detestable: *foedus*

differently from: *aliter ac, aliter atque*

difficult: *difficilis*

[difficulties] be in ___: *labōrō*

direction: *pars*

discover: *reperiō*

display: *ōstendō*

[distance] at a ___: *procul;* no great ___: *haud procul*

[distant] be ___: *absum*

disturbance: *turba*

divine spirit, divine will: *nūmen*

divinity: *nūmen*

do: *faciō,* see Lessons 2 & 9; ___ harm: *noceō;* ___ usually: *soleō;* harm is done: *nocētur*

[domestic] in ___ policy: *domī*

double: *duplex*

doubt: *dubitō*

[down] ___ from: *dē;* hand ___: *trādō;* lay ___: *pōnō;* lead ___: *dēdūcō*

dread: *metus*

[dream] in a ___: *in somnīs*

dutiful: *pius*

duty: *mūnus*

dwell: *habitō*

E

each: *quisque, quīque;* ___ [of two]: *uterque;* ___ one: *quisque;* ___ other: *inter nōs, inter vōs, inter sē, alius* or *alter* repeated in a different

case; **five** ___: *quīnī;* **four** ___: *quaternī;* **one**
___: *singulī;* **three** ___: *trīnī;* **two** ___: *bīnī*

eagerness: *studium*

earlier: *ante*

earth: *terra, humus*

easy: *facilis*

[edge] sharp ___: *aciēs*

effect: *efficiō*

effort: *labor*

eight: *octō;* ___ **hundred:** *octingentī;* ___
hundredth: *octingentēsimus;* ___ **times:** *octiēns*

eighteen: *duodēvīgintī*

eighteenth: *duodēvīcēsimus*

eighth: *octāvus*

eightieth: *octōgēsimus*

eighty: *octōgintā*

[either] ___ **... or ...** : *aut ... aut ... ,* ___ **one:**
alter

elder: *senior*

eldest: *maximus nātū*

eleven: *ūndecim*

eleventh: *ūndecimus*

else: *aliter;* **someone** ___**'s:** *aliēnus*

elsewhere: *alibi, aliō*

emperor: *prīnceps*

empire: *imperium*

[employ] be ___**ed:** *versor*

encourage: *cōnfirmō*

end of: *extrēmus*

endure: *patior*

enemy: *hostis, inimīcus*

enjoy: *fruor*

enough: *satis*

enthusiasm: *studium*

entirely: *tōtus*

entrust: *committō, crēdō*

envoy: *lēgātus*

envy: *invideō*

equal: *aequus, pār*

equanimity: *aequus animus*

escape: *fuga*

escort: *dēdūcō*

especially: *in prīmīs, maximē, potissimum*

establish: *cōnfirmō, constituō, īnstituō*

eternal: *aeternus*

even: *et, etiam;* ___ **if:** *etsī;* **not** ___: *nē ...
quidem;* **or** ___: *vel*

event: *cāsus*

ever: *umquam*

everlasting: *aeternus*

every: *omnis, quīque*

everyone: *omnēs, quisque*

everything: *omnia, quidque*

everywhere: *ubique;* ___ **in the world:** *ubique
terrārum, ubique gentium:* **from** ___: *undique*

evil: *malum, malus*

excel: *praestō*

exchange: *mūtō;* **in** ___ **for:** *prō*

exempt: *eximō*

exile: *fuga*

exist: *sum*

expect: *spērō*

expectation: *spēs*

expensive: *cārus*

experience: *patior*

explain: *expōnō*

[exploits] honorable ___: *decora*

expose: *expōnō*

eye: *oculus*

F

face: *ōs, faciēs*

fact: *rēs;* **in actual** ___: *rē vērā;* **in** ___: *quidem;*
on account of which ___: *quam ob rem, qua-
mobrem*

fail: *dēficiō*

fair: *aequus*

faith: *fidēs*

fall: *cāsus*

fame: *laus*

family: *gēns*

famous: *clārus;* **that** ___: *ille*

far, far off, by far: *longē;* see also **farther, farthest**

farewell: *valē, valēte;* **bid** ___**, say** ___: *valēre
iubeō*

farmer: *agricola*

farmhouse: *villa*

[farming] of ___: *rūsticus*

farther: *ulterior, longius*

farthest: *ultimus, longissimē*

fate: *cāsus, fātum*

father: *parēns, pater*

fatherland: *patria*

favor: *faveo;* **look with** ___ **on, upon:** *respiciō*

favorable: *secundus;* **be** ___: *faveō*

fear: *timor, metus, timeō, vereor*
feed upon: *vēscor*
feel: *sentiō;* ___ affection for: *dīligō*
fellow-citizen: *cīvis*
few: *paucī*
field: *ager*
fierce: *ācer*
fifteen: *quīndecim*
fifth: *quīntus*
fiftieth: *quīnquagēsimus*
fifty: *quīnquāgintā*
fight: *pugnō*
[fighting] there is ___, ___ is: *pugnātur*
filthy: *foedus*
final: *suprēmus*
finally: *dēnique*
find: *inveniō, reperiō;* ___ out: *cognōscō, nōscō*
fine: *pulcher*
finish: *cōnficiō, fungor*
fire: *ignis;* set ___ to: *ignem (ignīs) īnferō*
first: *prīmus*
five: *quīnque;* ___ at a time, ___ by ___, ___ each: *quīnī;* ___ hundred: *quīngentī;* ___ hundredth: *quīngentēsimus;* ___ times: *quīnquiēns*
fivefold: *quīnquiplex*
flame: *flamma*
flee, flee from: *fugiō*
flight: *fuga;* put to ___: *in fugam dō;* take to ___: *sē in fugam dare*
fly: *volō*
[follow] ___ closely: *īnstō*
following: *posterus, secundus;* the ___: *ille*
foot: *pes;* at, to the ___ of: *sub*
for: *ad, dē, in, prō, enim, nam;* ___ the sake: *causā, grātiā;* ___ which reason: *quam ob rem, quamobrem;* feel affection ___: *dīligō;* hope ___: *spērō;* in exchange ___: *prō;* take counsel ___: *cōnsulō;* wait ___: *exspectō;* wish ___: *optō*
force: *vīs*
foremost: *prīmus*
forest: *silva*
forget: *oblīvīscor*
form: *forma;* ___ a plan: *cōnsilium capiō*
former: *ille, prior*
[forth] bring ___: *prōmō;* put ___: *prōdō;* send ___: *prōmittō;* take ___: *prōmō*
fortieth: *quadrāgēsimus*

fortifications: *moenia*
fortune: *fortūna*
forty: *quadrāgintā*
foul: *foedus*
founder: *auctor*
four: *quattuor;* ___ at a time, ___ by ___, ___ each: *quaternī;* ___ hundred: *quadringentī;* ___ hundredth: *quadringentēsimus;* ___ times: *quater*
fourfold: *quadruplex*
fourteen: *quattuordecim*
fourth: *quartus*
free: *līber, līberō;* set ___: *līberō*
friend(ly): *amīcus;* in a ___ manner: *amīcē*
friendship: *amīcitia*
from: *ā, ab, dē, ē, ex;* ___ all sides: *undique;* ___ another place: *aliunde;* ___ anywhere: *alicunde;* ___ day to day: *in diēs;* ___ everywhere: *undique;* ___ here: *inde, hinc;* ___ one day to the next: *in diēs;* ___ somewhere: *alicunde;* ___ that place: *inde, illinc;* ___ that place of yours: *istinc;* ___ that same place, ___ the same place: *indidem;* ___ there: *inde, illinc;* ___ there near you: *istinc;* ___ this place: *inde, hinc;* ___ this same place: *indidem;* ___ which, ___ which place: *unde;* differently ___: *aliter ac, aliter atque;* flee ___: *fugiō;* prevent ___: see Lesson 35; where ___: *unde;* wherever ___: *undecumque, undeunde*
[front] in ___, in ___ of: *ante;* out in ___ of: *prō*
full: *plēnus*
funeral: *mūnus*
future: *posterum*

G

garment: *vestis*
generation: *saeculum, saeculum hominum*
[get] ___ control of: *potior;* ___ in the way: see Lesson 29; ___ lost: *amittor, errō, pereō;* ___ possession of: *potior*
ghost: *umbra*
gift: *dōnum, mūnus*
girl: *puella, virgō*
give: *dō;* ___ a name: *nōmen impōnō;* ___ ground: *pedem referō*

glad: *laetus;* **be ___:** *gaudeō*
gladiatorial show: *mūnus*
glory: *decus, glōria, laus*
go: *eō, sē conferre;* **___ across:** *trānseō;* **___ away:** *abeō, discedo;* **___ back:** *pedem referō, redeō;* **___ by:** *praetereō;* **___ on . . .ing:** see **went;** **___ over:** *trānseō;* **___ to:** *accēdō, adeō, obeō;* **___ to meet:** *obeō;* **___ toward:** *accēdō, adeō, obeō;* **___ under, ___ up to:** *subeō;* **___ wrong:** *errō;* **let ___:** *mittō;* **let ___ away:** *āmittō*
god: *deus;* **___s above:** *superī;* **___s below:** *īnferī*
goddess: *dea*
gold: *aurum;* **___ piece, ___ coin:** *aureus;* **of ___:** *aureus*
golden: *aureus*
good: *bonus*
goodbye: *valē, valēte;* **say ___:** *valēre iubeō*
government: *rēs, rēs pūblica*
grain: *frūmentum*
granddaughter: *nepōs*
grandson: *nepōs*
grasp: *teneō*
grass: *herba*
grateful: *grātus*
gratify: *iuvō*
gratitude: *grātia;* **show ___:** *grātiam referō*
great: *magnus;* **as ___ as** *tantus . . . quantus;* **how ___:** *quantus;* **no ___ distance:** *haud procul;* **so ___:** *tantus*
greet: *salutem dare*
grief: *dolor*
grim: *tristis*
ground: *humus;* **give ___:** *pedem referō*
group: *numerus*
guard: *servō*
guest: *hospes*
guest-friend: *hospes*

H

habit: *usus*
had: see Lesson 10
hand: *manus;* **___ down, ___ over:** *trādō;* **but on the other ___:** *autem;* **left ___:** *sinistra;* **on the other ___:** *contrā;* **right ___:** *dextra*
handy: *dexter;* **come in ___:** see Lesson 29
happy: *laetus, fēlīx*
hard: *difficilis*
hardship: *labor*
harm, do harm: *noceō;* **___ is done:** *nocētur*
hasten: *properō*
have: *habeō,* see Lessons 9 & 19; **___ ability, ___ power:** *possum;* **___ strength:** *valeō*
he: *hic, ille, is, iste, se,* see Lesson 2; **and ___:** *quī*
head: *caput*
health: *salūs*
healthful: *salūtī* (see Lesson 29)
hear: *audiō*
heart: *cor, pectus;* **lose ___:** *animō dēficiō*
heaven: *caelum*
heavy: *gravis*
height: *altitūdō*
help: *auxilium, iuvō;* **be present to ___:** *adsum*
henceforth: *deinde*
her: *eius, huius, illīus, istīus, suus;* **and ___:** *cuius*
here: *eō, hīc, hūc, ibi;* **from ___:** *inde, hinc;* **to ___:** *eō, hūc*
hereafter: *deinde*
hero: *vir*
hers: *eius, huius, illīus, istīus, suus*
herself: *suī, ipsa;* **to ___:** *sēcum, sibi*
hesitate: *cessō, dubitō*
high: *altus,* see Lesson 22; **on ___:** *altē*
hill: *mōns*
himself: *suī, ipse;* **to ___:** *sēcum, sibi*
hindrance: *impedīmentum*
his: *eius, huius, illīus, istīus, suus;* **and ___:** *cuius*
hobby: *studium*
hold: *habeō, teneō;* **___ back:** *retineō;* **___ off:** *prōhibeō;* **___ together:** *contineō;* **___ up:** *sustineō,* see Lesson 29
holy: *sacer*
home: *domus*
honor: *decus, honor*
hope: *spēs, spērō;* **___ for:** *spērō*
horn: *cornū*
horrible: *foedus*
horse: *equus*
host: *hospes*
hostile: *inimīcus*
hour: *hōra*
house: *aedes, domus;* **at the ___ of:** *apud*
household: *familia*

how: *quam, quemadmodum, quōmodo;* ___ **big,** ___ **large:** *quantus;* ___ **many:** *quot;* ___ **much:** *quantus;* ___ **often:** *quotiēns*

however: *autem, quamquam;* ___ **big,** ___ **large:** *quantuscumque;* ___ **many:** *quotcumque, quotquot;* ___ **much:** *quantuscumque;* ___ **often:** *quotiēnscumque*

huge: *ingēns*

human being: *homo*

humble: *humilis*

hundred: *centum;* **eight** ___**:** *octingentī;* **five** ___**:** *quīngentī;* **four** ___**:** *quadringentī;* **nine** ___**:** *nōngentī;* **seven** ___**:** *septingentī;* **six** ___**:** *sescentī;* **three** ___**:** *trēcentī;* **two** ___**:** *ducentī*

hundredth: *centēsimus;* **eight** ___**:** *octingentēsimus;* **five** ___**:** *quīngentēsimus;* **four** ___**:** *quadringentēsimus;* **nine** ___**:** *nōngentēsimus;* **one** ___**:** *centēsimus;* **seven** ___**:** *septingentēsimus;* **six** ___**:** *sescentēsimus;* **three** ___**:** *trēcentēsimus;* **two** ___**:** *ducentēsimus*

hurl: *coniciō*

husband: *coniunx, marītus, vir*

difficulties: *labōrō;* **come** ___ **handy:** see Lesson 29; **everywhere** ___ **the world:** *ubique gentium, ubique terrārum;* **get** ___ **the way:** see Lesson 29; **out** ___ **front of:** *prō;* **put** ___**:** *impōnō;* **receive** ___ **advance:** *praecipiō;* **shut** ___**:** *inclūdō;* **stand** ___**:** *īnstō;* **take part** ___**:** *obeō;* **throw** ___**:** *iniciō*

inflict: *īnferō*

influence: *grātia*

inform: *doceō*

instruct *praecipiō*

[interests] consult the ___ **of:** *cōnsulō*

into: *in;* **throw** ___**:** *iniciō*

invisible: *caecus*

is: see be, Lesson 2

island: *īnsula*

it: *hoc, id, illud, istud,* see Lesson 2; **and** ___**:** *quod*

its: *eius, huius, illīus, istīus, suus;* **and** ___**:** *cuius*

itself: *suī, ipse, ipsa, ipsum*

I

I: *ego,* see Lesson 2

if: *sī;* ___ **...not,** ___ **not:** *nisi;* **but** ___**:** *sīn;* **even** ___**:** *etsī;* **just as** ___**:** *sīcut, tamquam*

ill: *male*

image: *imāgō*

immediately: *statim*

[important] be ___**:** *valeō;* **most** ___**:** *potissimus*

in: *in,* see Lessons 1, 3, 8, 15, 22, 25, & 30; ___ **a dream:** *in somnīs;* ___ **a friendly manner:** *amīce;* ___ **actual fact:** *rē vērā;* ___ **all respects:** *omnibus rēbus;* ___ **back of:** *post;* ___ **comparison with:** *prae;* ___ **exchange for:** *prō;* ___ **fact:** *quidem;* ___ **front,** ___ **front of:** *ante;* ___ **proportion to:** *prō;* ___ **return:** *contrā;* ___ **such a manner:** *ita, sīc;* ___ **that place:** *ibi, illīc;* ___ **that place of yours:** *istīc;* ___ **that same place:** *ibidem;* ___ **the meantime:** *interim;* ___ **the presence of:** *apud;* ___ **the same place:** *ibidem;* ___ **the works of:** *apud;* ___ **the world:** *in terrīs;* ___ **this place:** *hīc, ibi;* ___ **this same place:** *ibidem;* **be** ___

J

journey: *iter*

joy: *gaudium*

joyful: *laetus*

just: *aequus, modo;* ___ **as:** *ita...quam, ita...ut, sīc...quemadmodum, sīc...quōmodo, sīc...ut, sīcut, tam...quam, tamquam, ita...quōmodo;* ___ **as if:** *sīcut, tamquam;* ___ **before:** *sub* + acc.; ___ **now:** *modo*

K

keen: *ācer*

keep: *servō;* ___ **away:** *prōhibeō;* ___ **turning:** *versō*

kill: *interficiō*

kind: *genus, speciēs;* **of such a** ___**:** *tālis;* **of the same** ___ **as:** *tālis...quālis;* **of what** ___**:** *quālis;* **of whatever** ___**:** *quāliscumque;* **what** ___ **of:** *quālis, quī*

king: *rēx*

kingdom: *rēgnum*

kingship: *rēgnum*
kinsman: *propinquus*
know: *cognōvī, nōvī, sciō;* come to ___: *cognōscō, nōscō;* not ___: *nesciō*
known: *nōtus;* make ___: *aperiō*

L

labor: *labor*
lack: *inopia, careō;* be ___ing: *dēficiō*
lament: *doleō*
land: *terra;* by ___ and sea: *terrā marīque;* father-___, native ___: *patria*
language: *lingua*
large: *magnus;* ___ number: *multitūdō;* a larger amount: *plūs;* as ___ as: *tantus ... quantus;* how ___: *quantus;* however ___: *quantuscumque;* so ___: *tantus*
last: *postumus, suprēmus, maneō;* at ___: *dēnique*
later: *posterior, post*
latter: *hic, posterior*
law: *iūs, lēx*
lawsuit: *rēs*
lay down: *pōnō*
lead: *dūcō;* ___ down: *dēdūcō;* ___ out: *ēdūcō*
leader: *dux*
leading man: *prīnceps*
learn: *cognōscō, nōscō*
least: *minimus*
leave: *discēdō, relinquō;* ___ behind: *relinquō*
left: *sinister;* ___ hand: *sinistra;* on the ___: *sinister, ā sinistrā*
legate: *lēgātus*
length: *longitūdō;* at ___: *dēnique*
less: *minor*
let go: *mittō;* let go away: *āmittō*
level: *aequus*
lie: *iaceō*
life: *anima, vīta*
lifetime: *aetās*
lift, lift up: *tollō*
like: *similis, amō*
likeness: *imāgō*
line: *versus;* ___ of battle: *aciēs;* bottom ___: *summa rēs, summa;* straight ___: *aciēs*
listen to: *audiō*

little: *parvus;* some ___: *aliquantus;* too ___: *parum*
live: *habitō, vīvō*
living: *vīvus*
long: *longus, diū,* & see Lesson 22; for a ___ time: *diū;* no longer: *nōn diūtius, nōn iam*
longing: *cupīdō*
[look] ___ at: *aspiciō, spectō;* ___ back at, ___ with favor upon: *respiciō*
lord: *dominus*
lose: *āmittō;* ___ heart: *animō dēficiō*
[lost] be ___: *pereō;* get ___: *āmittor, errō, pereō*
love: *amor, amō, dīligō*
low: *humilis, īnferus*
loyal: *pius*
luck: *fors, fortūna*
lucky: *fēlīx*

M

maiden: *virgō*
majority: *magna pars*
make: *efficiō, faciō;* ___ a mistake: *errō;* ___ a plan: *cōnsilium capiō;* ___ known: *aperiō;* ___ mistakes: *errō;* ___ war on: *bellum īnferō*
man: *vir,* & see Lesson 5; leading ___: *prīnceps;* young ___: *iuvenis*
manliness: *virtūs*
manner: *modus;* in a friendly ___: *amīcē;* in such a ___: *ita, sīc*
many: *multī;* as ___ as: *tot ... quot;* how ___: *quot;* however ___: *quotcumque, quotquot;* so ___: *tot*
master: *dominus, magister*
meadow: *campus*
means: see Lesson 8; by no ___: *haud*
[meantime] in the ___: *interim*
meanwhile: *interim*
measure: *modus*
meet: *conveniō, obeō;* go to ___: *obeō*
memory: *memoria*
message: *nūntius*
messenger: *nūntius*
middle of: *medius*
mile: *mīlle passūs*
military standard: *signum*

mind: *animus, mēns;* —— your own business: *fac tuam rem*

mindful: *memor*

mine: *meus*

[mistake] make a ——, make ——s: *errō*

mix: *mīsceō*

[moment] at this ——: *nunc iam*

money, sum of money: *pecūnia*

morale: *animī*

more: *plūs, plūrēs, magis,* & see Lessons 37–39

most: *plūrimus, maximē,* & see Lessons 37–39

mother: *māter, parēns*

mountain: *mōns*

mournful: *tristis*

mouth: *ōs*

move: *cēdō, mōveō;* —— swiftly: *volō*

much: *multus;* as —— as: *tantus . . . quantus, pariter atque, pariter ac;* how ——: *quantus;* however ——: *quantuscumque*

multitude: *multitūdō, plebs*

murder: *caedēs*

my, my own: *meus*

myself: *meī, ipse, ipsa;* to ——: *mēcum, mihi*

N

name: *nōmen*

narrate: *narrō*

nation: *populus, gēns*

native land: *patria*

nature: *nātūra*

near: *propinquus, vicinus, apud, prope;* nearer : *propior;* nearest: *proximus;* from there —— you: *istinc;* there —— you: *istīc, istūc;* to there —— you: *istūc*

nearby: *prope*

nearly: *prope*

need: *inopia;* I ——: *mihi opus est* + abl.; there is —— of: *opus est* + abl.

neighbor: *fīnitims, vīcīna, vīcinus*

neighboring: *fīnitimus, vīcinus*

neither: *neuter;* —— . . . nor . . .: *nec . . . nec . . . , neque . . . neque . . .*

never: *numquam*

nevertheless: *tamen*

new: *novus*

news: *nūntius*

next: *proximus, deinde;* from one day to the ——: *in diēs*

nicely: *pulchrē*

night: *nox*

nine: *novem;* —— hundred: *nōngentī;* —— hundredth: *nōngentēsimus;* —— times: *nōniēns*

nineteen: *ūndēvīgintī*

nineteenth: *ūndēvīcēsimus*

ninth: *nōnus*

ninetieth: *nōnāgēsimus*

ninety: *nōnāgintā*

no: *nūllus,* + see Lesson 3 & 16; —— great distance: *haud procul;* —— longer: *nōn diūtius, nōn iam;* —— one: *nemō;* by —— means: *haud*

noble: *nōbilis*

nobody: *nemō*

nod: *nūmen*

none: *nūllus*

nor: *nec, neque*

not: *nōn;* —— any: *nūllus,* + see Lesson 16; —— at all: *haud, male, minimē;* —— even: *nē . . . quidem;* —— know: *nesciō;* if ——: *nisi;* or ——: *annōn;* say . . . ——: *negō*

nothing: *nihil*

now: *autem, iam, nunc;* just ——: *modo;* right ——: *nunc iam*

number: *multitūdō, numerus;* a large ——: *multitūdō;* a sufficient ——: *satis;* of which ——: *quot;* some —— of: *aliquot*

O

obey: *pareō*

occasion: *cāsus*

occupy: *versō*

of: *apud, dē, ē, ex,* & see Lessons 1, 2, 14, 15, 16, 21, 22, 27, & 29; —— farming: *rūsticus;* —— gold: *aureus;* —— some size: *aliquantus;* —— such a kind: *tālis;* —— such a size: *tantus;* —— the country: *rūsticus;* —— the same kind as: *tālis . . . quālis;* —— what kind: *quālis;* —— whatever kind: *quāliscumque;* —— whatever size: *quantuscumque;* —— which number: *quot;* —— which size: *quantus;* —— which kind: *quālis;* ahead ——: *prae;* at the house ——: *apud;* at the side ——: *circā;* be afraid ——: *timeō;* because ——: *ob, propter,* see Lesson 40; consult the interests __: *cōnsulō*; each __ the two: *uterque*; from that place __ yours: *istinc*; in that place __ yours: *istīc*; in the presence __: *apud*; in the works __: *apud*; on account __: *ob, propter*; on account __ which fact: *quam ob rem, quamobrem*; on behalf __: *prō*; on the basis __: *ē, ex*; out in front __: *prō*; set __ arms: *arma*; some number __: *aliquot*; sum __ money: *pecūnia*; take care __: see Lesson 29; that __ yours: *iste*; the other __ two: *alter*; the rest __: *ceterī, reliquus*; to that place __ yours: *istūc*; what kind __: *quālis, quī*; which __ the two: *uter*

[off] carry __: *auferō*; hold __: *prōhibeō*

offer: *praebeō*; __ as a pretext: *prae sē ferre*

[office] public __: *honor*

offspring: *genus*

often: *saepe*; as __: *quotiēns*; as __ as: *totiēns . . . quotiēns*; how __: *quotiēns*; however __: *quotiēnscumque*; so __: *totiēns*

old: *senex, vetus*, + see Lesson 26; oldest: *maximus nātū*

on: *in*, & see Lessons 1, 3, 8, 25, & 30; __ account of: *ob, propter*; __ account of which fact: *quam ob rem, quamobrem*; __ all sides: *undique*; __ behalf of: *prō*; __ high: *altē*; __ the basis of: *ē, ex*; __ the contrary: *contrā*; __ the left: *sinister, ā sinistrā*; __ the other hand: *contrā*; but __ the other hand: *autem*; make war __: *bellum īnferō*; put __: *impōnō*; stand __: *īnstō*; throw __: *iniciō*

once: *ōlim, semel*; at __: *statim*

one: *ūnus*; great __, little __, etc.: use adjective substantively; __ . . . another: *alius . . . alius, ūnus . . . ūnus*; __ another: *inter nōs, inter vōs, inter sē, alius* or *alter* repeated in a different case, & see Lesson 22; __ at a time, __ by __, each: *singulī*; __ hundred: *centum*; __ hundredth: *centēsimus*; __ thousand: *mīlle*; thousandth: *mīllēsimus*; at __ time: *ōlim*; either __: *alter*; from __ day to the next: *in diēs*; no __: *nemō*; the __ . . . the other: *alter . . . alter*; the __s . . . the others: *alterī . . . alterī*; which __s: *quī*

only: *sōlus, modo*

onto: *in*; throw __: *iniciō*

[onward] carry __: *īnferō*

open: *aperiō*

opportunity: *cōpia*

or: *an, aut, seu, sīve, -ve, vel*; __ even: *-ve, vel*; __ not: *annōn*; __ possibly: *-ve, vel*

order: *iubeō*

ordinary people: *humiliōrēs*

ornament: *decus*

other: *alius*; but on the __ hand: *autem*; each __: *inter nōs, inter vōs, inter sē, alius* or *alter* repeated in a different case; on the __ hand: *contrā*; some . . . __s: *aliī . . . aliī*; the __ [of two]: *alter*; the __s: *ceterī*; the one . . . the __: *alter . . . alter*; the one or the __: *alter*; the ones . . . the __s: *alterī . . . alterī*

otherwise: *aliter*

ought: *dēbeō*

our: *noster*

ours: *noster*

ourselves: *nostrum, nostrī, ipsī, ipsae*; to __: *nōbīs, nōbīscum*

[out] __ of: *ē, ex*; __ in front of: *prō*; find __: *cognōscō, nōscō*; lead __: *ēdūcō*; pick __: *dēligō*; point __: *dēmōnstrō*; put __: *expōnō*; run __: *dēficiō*; shut __: *exclūdō*; take __: *eximō*; throw __: *ēiciō*; over: *super*; go __: *trānseō*; hand __: *trādō*; all __: *tōtā, tōtō, tōtīs*

overcome: *superō*

owe: *dēbeō*

[own] her __, his __, its __: *suus*; my __: *meus*; our __: *noster*; their __: *suus*; your __: *tuus, vester*

P

pace: *passus*

pain: *dolor*; cause __, suffer __: *doleō*

parent: *parēns*

part: *pars*; take __ in: *obeō*

party: *partēs, rēs* (pl.)

pass by: *praetereō*

pause: *cessō*

people: *hominēs, populus*, + see Lesson 5; belonging to the __: *pūblicus*; common __: *plebs*; ordinary __: *humiliōrēs*

perceive: *cernō, sentiō*

perform: *fungor*

perish: *pereō*

person: *homō*, + see Lesson 5; a certain ___: *quīdam*

personal enemy: *inimīcus*

pick: *lēgō*; ___ out: *dēligō*

[piece] ___ of luck: *fortūna*; gold ___: *aureus*

pierce: *trāiciō*

pitiable: *miser*

place: *locus, pōnō*; ___ together: *compōnō*; at another ___: alibi; at that ___: *ibi, illīc*; at that ___ of yours: *istīc*; at that same ___, at the same ___: *ibidem*; at this ___: *hīc, ibi*; at this same ___: *ibidem*; at which ___: *ubi*; from another ___: *aliunde*; from that ___: *illinc, inde*; from that ___ of yours: *istinc*; from that same ___, from the same ___: *indidem*; from this ___: *hinc, inde*; from this same ___: *indidem*; from which ___: *unde*; in another ___: *alibi*; in that ___: *ibi, illīc*; in that ___ of yours: *istīc*; in that same ___, in the same ___: *ibidem*; in this ___: *hīc, ibi*; in this same ___: *ibidem*; to another ___: *aliō*; to that ___: *eō, illūc*; to that ___ of yours: *istūc*; to that same ___, to the same ___: *eōdem*; to this ___: *eō, hūc*; to this same ___: *eōdem*; to which ___: *quō*

plain: *campus*

plan: *cōnsilium*

pleasantness: *grātia*

please: *iuvō, placeō*

pleasing: *grātus*; be ___: *placeō*

pledge: *fidēs*

plenty: *cōpia*

poem: *carmen*

poet: *poēta*

point out: *dēmōnstrō*

[policy] in domestic ___: *domī*

political change: *rēs novae*

poor: *miser*

portrait: *imāgō*

[possession] get ___ of: *potior*

[possible] as . . . as ___, the . . . est ___: *quam* + superlative

[possibly] or ___: *vel, -ve*

posterity: *posterī*

power: *rēs* (sing.); have ___: *possum, valeō*; ruling ___: *imperium*

practice: *ūsus*

praise: *laus, laudō*

preferable: *potior*

prepare: *parō*

prepared: *parātus*

[presence] in the ___ of: *apud*

[present] be ___, be ___ at, be ___ to help: *adsum*

press: *īnstō*

[pretext] offer as a ___: *prae sē ferre*

prevent: *prōhibeō*

prince: *prīnceps*

prize: *dīligō*

proceed: *sē conferre*

produce: *efficiō*

[profitable] be ___: *prōsum*

prohibit: *prōhibeō*

promise: *prōmittō*

property: *rēs*

[proportion] in ___ to: *prō*

prosperity: *rēs secundae*

protection: *fidēs*

province: *prōvincia*

public: *pūblicus*; ___ enemy: *hostis*; ___ office: *honor*

put: *pōnō*; ___ forth: *prōdō*; ___ in, ___ on: *impōnō*; ___ out: *expōnō*; ___ to: *addō*; ___ to flight: *in fugam dō*; ___ together: *condō*

Q

quadruple: *quadruplex*

queen: *rēgīna*

question: *rogō*

quiet: *compōnō*

quintuple: *quīnquiplex*

R

rage: *īra*

rainstorm: *imber*

raise: *ēdūcō, tollō*; ___ up: *ēdūcō*

[rate] at any ___: *quidem*

rather: *magis, potius*, & see Lesson 38

read: *legō*

ready: *parātus*

real: *vērus*

reality: *rēs*

really: *rē vērā*

reason: *causa;* by ___: *causā;* for which ___: *quā dē causā, quam ob rem, quamobrem*
receive: *accipiō;* ___ in advance: *praecipiō*
refuse: *negō*
rejoice: *gaudeō*
relate: *ferō*
relative: *propinquus*
remain: *maneō*
remember: *meminī*
remembering: *memor*
remove: *tollō*
report: *fāma, nūntiō, adferō;* ___ back: *referō*
republic: *rēs pūblica*
reputation: *fāma*
residence: *sedēs*
[respects] in all ___: *omnibus rēbus*
[rest] the ___ of: *cēterī, reliquus*
restrain: *contineō*
return: *pedem referō, redeō;* in ___: *contrā*
revolution: *rēs novae*
right: *iūs, dexter;* ___ hand: *dextrā;* ___ now: *nunc iam;* on the ___: *dexter, ā dextrā*
river: *amnis*
road: *via*
role: *pars*
round about: *circā, circum*
route: *iter*
rule: *lēx, rēgō*
ruling power: *imperium*
rumor: *fāma*
run: *currō;* ___ out: *dēficiō*
running: *cursus;* ___ away: *fuga*
rush: *volō*

S

sacred: *sacer*
sacrifice: *sacra faciō*
sad: *tristis*
safe-conduct: *fidēs*
safety: *salūs*
sail: *nāvigō*
sailor: *nauta*
[sake] for the ___: *causā, grātiā*
salvation: *salūs*
same: *īdem;* at that ___ place, at the ___ place: *ibidem;* at the ___ time: *simul;* at this ___ place:

ibidem; from that ___ place, from the ___ place, from this ___ place: *indidem;* in that ___ place, in the ___ place, in this ___ place: *ibidem;* of the ___ kind as: *tālis ... quālis;* that ___, this ___: *īdem;* to that ___ place, to the ___ place, to this ___ place: *eōdem*
savage: *ferus*
save: *servō,* & see Lesson 29
say: *dīcō, inquam;* ___ farewell, ___ goodbye: *valēre iubeō;* ___ ... not: *negō*
scarcely: *vix*
science: *rēs*
scrawny: *gracilis*
sea: *mare;* by land and ___: *terrā marīque*
seashore: *lītus*
seat: *sedēs*
second: *alter, secundus;* a ___ time: *iterum*
see: *aspiciō, videō*
seek: *petō*
seem: *videor;* it ___s best: *vidētur*
seize: *occupō*
sell: *vēndō*
send: *mittō;* ___ forth: *prōmittō*
serious: *gravis*
serve: *serviō,* & see Lesson 29
[set] ___ fire to: *ignem (ignīs) īnferō*
seven: *septem;* ___ hundred: *septingentī;* ___ hundredth: *septingentēsimus;* ___ times: *septiēns*
seventeen: *septendecim*
seventh: *septimus*
seventieth: *septuāgēsimus*
seventy: *septuāgintā*
several: *aliquot;* ___ times: *aliquotiēns*
shade: *umbra*
shadow: *umbra*
shape: *forma*
share: *pars*
sharp: *ācer;* ___ edge: *aciēs*
she: *ea, haec, illa, ista, sē,* & see Lesson 2; and ___: *quae*
ship: *nāvis*
shout: *clāmō*
show: *speciēs, dēmōnstrō, ōstendō;* ___ gratitude: *grātiam referō;* gladiatorial ___: *mūnus*
shower: *imber*
shut: *claudō;* ___ in: *inclūdō;* ___ out: *exclūdō*
side: *rēs (pl.);* at the ___ of: *circā;* on all ___s, from all ___s: *undique*
sight: *speciēs*

sign: *sīgnum*
signal: *sīgnum*
simple: *simplex*
since: *quoniam*
single: *simplex*
sit: *sedeō*
[situated] be __: *iaceō*
situation: *rēs* (pl.)
six: *sex;* __ hundred: *sescentī;* __ hundredth: *sescentēsimus;* __ times: *sexiēns*
sixteen: *sēdecim*
sixth: *sextus*
sixtieth: *sexāgēsimus*
sixty: *sexāgintā*
[size] of some __: *aliquantus;* of whatever __: *quantuscumque;* of which __: *quantus*
skill: *ars*
skillful: *dexter*
sky: *caelum*
slaughter: *caedēs*
slave: *servus;* be a __: *serviō*
sleep: *somnus*
slim: *gracilis*
small: *parvus;* too __ an amount: *parum*
sister: *soror*
snake: *anguis*
so: *ita, sīc, tam:* __ big, __ great, __ large: *tantus;* __ many: *tot;* __often: *totiēns;* and __: *itaque*
soil: *humus*
soldier: *mīles*
some: *aliquī, quī, quīdam;* __ . . . others: *aliī. . .aliī;* __ little: *aliquantus;* __ number of: *aliquot;* at __ time: *aliquandō, ōlim, quandō;* of __ size: *aliquantus*
someone: *aliquis, quīdam, quis;* __ else's: *aliēnus*
something: *aliquid, quid, quiddam*
sometimes: *aliquandō*
somewhere: *alicubi, aliquō:* from __: *alicunde;* to __: *aliquō*
son: *fīlius*
song: *carmen*
soon: *mox;* as __ as: *simul ac, simul atque*
[sorry] be __: *doleō*
soul: *anima, animus*
spare: *parcō*
spear: *tēlum*
speed: *volō*
spirit: *animus;* divine __: *nūmen*

spouse: *coniunx*
stand: *stō;* __ before: *praestō;* __ in: *īnstō;* __ in awe of: *vereor;* __ on: *īnstō;* __ still: *stō*
standard, military standard: *sīgnum*
state: *rēs* (sing.)
statue: *imāgō*
stay: *maneō*
steal: *auferō*
steersman: *magister*
still: *etiam, semper, tamen;* stand __: *stō*
stop: *dēsinō*
story: *fābula*
straight line: *aciēs*
stranger: *hospes*
stray: *errō*
stream: *flūmen*
street: *via*
strength: *vīrēs* (pl. of *vīs*); have __: *valeō*
strengthen: *cōnfirmō*
[strong] be __: *valeō*
study: *studium*
subsequent: *posterus*
subtract: *dēmō*
successful: *fēlīx*
such: *tālis;* in __ a manner: *ita, sīc;* of __ a kind: *tālis;* to __ a degree: *ita, tam*
suffer: *patior;*__ pain: *doleō*
[sufficient] a __ amount, a __ number: *satis*
suitable: *idōneus*
sum: *summa rēs, summa;* __ of money: *pecūnia*
sum total: *summa rēs, summa*
sun: *sōl*
supply: *copia*
suppose: *exīstimō*
sure: *certus;* to be __: *quidem*
surely: see Lesson 9
surpass: *superō*
suffer: *labōrō, patior*
swear: *iūrō*
swift: *celer*
[swiftly] move __: *volō*

━━━━━━ **T** ━━━━━━

take: *capiō, ferō;* __ away: *dēmō;* __ back: *recipiō;* __ care of: see Lesson 29; __ charge: *rērum potior;* __ charge of, __ control of: *potior;*

___ counsel for: *cōnsulō;* ___ forth: *prōmō;* ___ out: *excipiō, eximō;* ___ part in: *obeō;* ___ to flight: *sē in fugam dare*

task: *opus*

teach: *doceō, praecipiō*

teacher: *magister*

tell: *narrō*

temple: *aedēs*

ten: *decem;* ___ times: *deciēns*

tenth: *decimus*

territory: *ager*

test: *temptō*

than: *ac, atque, quam,* & see Lesson 38; be better ___: *praestō, superō*

that: *ille, is, iste, qui,* & see Lesson 36; ___ famous: *ille;* ___ of yours: *iste;* ___ same: *idem;* ___ well-known: *ille;* at ___ place: *ibi, illīc;* at ___ place of yours: *istīc;* at ___ same place: *ibidem;* at ___ time: *tum, tunc;* from ___ place: *illinc, inde;* from ___ place of yours: *istinc;* from ___ same place: *indidem;* in ___ place: *ibi, illīc;* in ___ place of yours: *istīc;* in ___ same place: *ibidem;* to ___ place: *eō, illūc;* to ___ place of yours: *istūc;* to ___ same place: *eōdem*

the: no Latin equivalent; and ___: *quōrum, quārum*

theirs: *eārum, eōrum, hārum, hōrum, illārum, illōrum, istārum, istōrum, suus*

themselves: *ipsa, ipsae, ipsī, suī;* to ___: *sēcum, sibi*

then: *deinde, ergō, tum, tunc*

there: *eō, ibi, illīc, illūc,* & see Lessons 1 & 3; ___ near you: *istīc, istūc;* from ___: *illinc, inde;* from ___ near you: *istinc;* to ___: *eō, illūc;* to ___ near you: *istūc*

thereafter: *deinde*

therefore: *ergō, igitur*

they: *eī, hī, illī, istī, suī,* & see Lesson 2; and ___: *quī, quae*

thin: *gracilis*

thing: *rēs,* & see Lesson 5; a certain ___: *quiddam*

think: *putō*

third: *tertius*

thirteen: *trēdecim*

thirtieth: *trīcēsimus*

thirty: *trīgintā*

this: *hic, is;* ___ same: *īdem;* at ___ place: *hīc, ibi;* at ___ same place: *ibidem;* at ___ time: *nunc;* from ___ place: *hinc, inde;* from ___ same place: *indidem;* in ___ place: *hīc, ibi;* in

___ same place: *ibidem;* to ___ place: *eō, hūc;* to ___ same place: *eōdem*

thousand, one thousand: *mīlle*

thousands: *mīlia*

thousandth: *mīllēsimus*

three: *trēs;* ___ at a time, ___ by ___, ___ each: *trīnī;* ___ hundred: *trēcentī;* ___ hundredth: *trēcentēsimus;* ___ times: *ter*

threefold: *triplex*

thrice: *ter*

through: *per*

throughout: *per*

throw: *iaciō;* ___ across: *trāiciō;* ___ in, ___ into, ___ on, ___ onto: *iniciō;* ___ out: *ēiciō;* ___ to: *adiciō;* ___ together: *coniciō*

tie: *vinciō*

time: *tempus;* a second ___: *iterum;* at another ___: *aliās;* at any ___: *aliquandō, quandō;* at one ___: *ōlim;* at some ___: *aliquandō, ōlim, quandō;* at this ___: *nunc;* at that ___: *tum, tunc;* at the same: ___ *simul;* eight ___s: *octiēns;* five at a ___: *quīnī;* five ___s: *quīnquiēns;* four at a ___: *quaternī;* four ___s: *quater;* nine ___s: *noviēns;* one at a ___: *singulī;* seven ___s: *septiēns;* several ___s: *aliquotiēns;* six ___s: *sexiēns;* ten ___s: *deciēns;* three at a ___: *trīnī;* three ___s: *ter;* two at a ___: *bīnī*

to: *ad,* & see Lessons 3, 7, 13, 17, 29, 30, 34; ___ ⟨one's own⟩ advantage: *ex* ⟨possessive⟩ *rē;* ___ another place: *aliō;* ___ anywhere: *aliquō, quōquam;* ___ be sure: *quidem;* ___ here: *eō, hūc;* ___ herself, ___ himself: *sēcum, sibi;* ___ myself: *mēcum, mihi;* ___ ourselves: *nōbīs, nōbīscum;* ___ somewhere: *aliquō, quō;* ___ such a degree: *ita, tam;* ___ that place: *eō, illūc;* ___ that place of yours: *istūc;* ___ that same place: *eōdem;* ___ the foot of: *sub;* ___ the same place: *eōdem;* ___ themselves: *sēcum, sibi;* ___ there: *eō, illūc;* ___ there near you: *istūc;* ___ this place: *eō, hūc;* ___ this same place: *eōdem;* ___ under: *sub;* ___ which, ___ which place: *quō;* ___ yourself: *tēcum, tibi;* ___ yourselves: *vōbīs, vōbīscum;* advance ___ the attack: *signa īnferō;* be added ___: *accēdo;* be present ___ help: *adsum;* belonging ___ the people: *pūblicus;* bring ___: *adferō;* go ___: *adeō, obeō;* go ___ meet: *obeō;* go up ___: *subeō;* in proportion ___: *prō;* listen ___: *audiō;* put ___: *addō;* put ___ flight: *in*

(continued)

fugam dō; set fire ___: *ignem (ignīs) īnferō;* take ___ flight: *sē in fugam dare;* throw ___: *adiciō;* wherever ___: *quōcumque, quōquō*

today: *hodiē*

[together] bring ___: *cōnferō;* call ___: *convocō;* come ___: *conveniō;* hold ___: *contineō;* place ___: *compōnō;* put ___: *condō;* throw ___: *coniciō*

toil: *labor, labōrō*

tomorrow: *crās*

tongue: *lingua*

too: *et, quoque,* & see Lesson 38; ___ little, ___ small an amount: *parum*

top of: *summus*

toward: *ad*

towards: *ad, sub*

town: *oppidum*

triple: *triplex*

true: *vērus*

trust: *fidēs*

trustworthiness: *fidēs*

turn: *vertō*

turning: *versus;* keep ___: *versō*

try: *temptō*

twelfth: *duodecimus*

twelve: *duodecim*

twentieth: *vīcēsimus*

twenty: *vīgintī*

twice: *bis*

two: *duo;* ___ at a time, ___ by ___, ___ each: *bīnī;* ___ hundred: *ducentī;* ___ hundredth: *ducentēsimus;* each of ___: *uterque;* the other of ___: *alter;* which of ___: *uter*

twofold: *duplex*

U

uncover: *aperiō*

under: *sub;* ___ the protection: *in fidē, in fidem;* go ___: *subeō;* to ___: *sub*

unfriendly: *inimīcus*

unhappy: *miser, tristis*

universe: *rēs*

unless: *nisi*

unlike: *dissimilis*

[up] ___ to: *sub;* bring ___: *adferō;* go ___ to: *subeō;* hold ___: *sustineō,* & see Lesson 29; lift ___: *tollō;* raise ___: *ēdūcō;* use ___: *cōnficiō*

[upon] bring ___: *īnferō;* come ___: *inveniō;* feed ___: *vēscor;* look with favor ___: *respiciō*

use: *ūsus, ūtor;* ___ up: *cōnficiō*

used to: see Lesson 7

useful: *ūsuī;* be ___: *prōsum*

usefulness: *ūsus*

[usually] do ___: *soleō*

V

[valor] deed of ___: *decus*

value: see Lesson 21

varied: *varius*

various: *varius*

varying: *varius*

vast: *ingēns*

verse: *versus*

very: see Lesson 38

villa: *vīlla*

violence: *vīs*

voice: *vox*

W

wait for: *exspectō*

walk: *ambulō*

walls: *moenia*

wander: *errō*

want: *inopia, cupiō,* & see Lesson 29

war: *bellum;* make ___ on: *bellum īnferō*

warn: *moneō*

was: see be was . . . ing (use imperfect)

watch: *spectō*

water: *aqua*

way: *iter, modus, via;* come all the ___: *perveniō;* get in the ___: see Lesson 29

we: *nōs,* & see Lesson 2

weaken: *cōnficiō*

weapon: *tēlum*

welcome: *grātus*

welfare: *salūs*

well: *bene;* be __: *valeō*

well-known: *nōbilis, nōtus;* that __: *ille*

were: see be; were . . . ing (use imperfect)

what: *quī, quid;* __ kind of: *quālis, quī;* of __ kind: *quālis*

whatever: *quidquid;* of __ kind: *quāliscumque;* of __ size: *quantuscumque*

when: *cum, quandō, ubi*

whenever: *quandōcumque*

where: *quō, ubi;* __ from: *unde;* __ to: *quō*

wherever: *quōcumque, quōquō, ubicumque, ubiubi;* __ from: *undecumque, undeunde;* __ to: *quōcumque, quōquō*

whether: *seu, sive;* __ . . . or: *seu . . . seu, sive . . . sive*

which: *qui, uter;* __ of two: *uter;* at __ place: *ubi;* for __ reason: *quam ob rem, quamobrem;* from __, from __ place: *unde;* of __ kind: *quālis;* of __ number: *quot;* of __ size: *quantus;* on account of __ fact: *quam ob rem, quamobrem;* to __, to __ place: *quō*

whichever: *quīcumque*

who: *quī, quis*

whoever: *quisquis*

whole: *tōtus*

why: *cūr*

wicked: *malus*

wide: *lātus,* & see Lesson 22

width: *lātitūdō*

wife: *coniunx, uxor*

wild: *ferus*

[will] divine __: *nūmen*

wind: *ventus*

wing: *cornū*

wish, wish for: *optō*

with: *apud, cum,* & see Lessons 2, 8, 18, & 27; in comparison __: *prae;* look __ favor upon: *respiciō*

within: see Lesson 25

withstand: *sustineō*

without: *sine*

woman: *fēmina,* see Lesson 5; young __: *iuvenis*

wonderful: *mīrus*

wood: *silva*

woods: *silva*

word: *verbum*

work: *opus,* & see Lesson 29; in the __s: *apud*

[world] everywhere in the __: *ubique gentium, ubique terrārum;* in the __: *in terrīs*

worried: see Lesson 29

worry: *cūra*

worse: *pēior*

worship: *colō*

worst: *pessimus*

worth: *virtus,* & see Lesson 21

worthy: *dīgnus*

would: use imperfect

wretched: *miser*

write: *scrībō*

[wrong] be __, go __: *errō*

Y

year: *annus*

yes: see Lesson 3

yesterday: *herī*

yet: *at, etiam, tamen*

yield: *cēdō*

you: *tū, vōs,* & see Lesson 2; from there near __: *istinc;* there near __: *istīc, istūc;* to there near __: *istūc*

young, young man, young woman: *iuvenis;* youngest: *minimus nātū*

your: *tuus, vester*

yours: *tuus, vester;* from that place of __: *istinc;* in that place of __: *istīc;* that of __: *iste;* to that place of __: *istūc*

yourself: *ipsa, ipse, tuī;* to __: *tēcum, tibi*

yourselves: *ipsae, ipsī, vestrī, vestrum;* to __: *vōbīs, vōbīscum*

youth: *iuvenis*

GRAMMATICAL INDEX

Alinari—24, 326T, 349BL, 371, 418B

Jim Anderson—226B

Art Resource—9, 48T (Vincent de Florio), 54, 100L, 121T&B, 136B, 143, 154L, 180 (Ann Chwatsky), 240L, 249, 272–273 (all photos), 276L, 311T, 359B, 373B, 384, 441, 470B

Art Resource/SEF Torino—121M, 215, 251L, 261M, 272B

R. Bartoccini—184, 465

Borromeo/Art Resource—34L, 48BL, 126

A.E. Burgess—42, 70, 108, 170, 173, 400

Paul Conklin—87TR, MR, BR

John Curtis/Photosynthesis—all photos of background marble, 427B

Fototeca Unione—4, 186T&B

Robert Frerck/Odyssey—17, 44–45 (all photos), 75, 132–133 (all photos), 176–177 (all photos), 227BR, 230B, 240R, 322–323 (all photos), 340, 365, 376R, 386B, 418T, 419T, 420, 422L, 427T

Giraudon—90

Giraudon/Art Resource—139, 277, 357, 377, 396B, 442L

Madeline Grimoldi—428

Robert Harding Assoc.—43

Jefferson's Fine Arts Library, University of Virginia—86

Bemporad Marzocco—356R

Erwin Meyer—164B

Courtesy Museum of Fine Arts, Boston—204

Photo Heermance—349T&R

Burt Rush—27, 372T&B, 373T, 418M, 419TR&BR, 470T, 471T&B

Scala—22

Scala/Art Resource—i, ii, xvi, 1, 3, 11, 13, 16R&L, 19, 25, 31, 32, 34R, 37, 39R, 42, 48R, 51, 56, 58, 65, 74, 77L, 77R, 79, 88, 98, 100R, 102, 109, 111L, 117, 119, 134, 136T, 138, 145, 154R, 157, 162, 164T&M, 182, 188, 189, 191, 192, 193, 195, 203T&B, 211, 213R, 217, 238, 251R, 259, 261B, 266, 274, 276R, 285, 286, 288R, 293, 298, 300, 301, 305, 307, 321, 335, 346, 347, 352, 359T, 363, 374, 376L, 383, 394, 396T, 404, 416L&R, 431, 433, 435, 445, 447T&B, 456, 458T&B, 460

Ronald Sheridan/Ancient Art and Architecture Collection—10 (G. Tortoli), 39L, 41, 46 (John Ormerod), 64 (Michael David Sheridan), 67T&B, 83, 104, 111R, 118, 151, 166, 178, 201 (all photos), 210, 213L, 225, 228, 230T, 248, 261T, 288L, 296, 309, 311B, 324, 326B, 333, 337L&R, 339, 356L, 368, 386T&M, 389, 399, 407, 414, 422R, 439, 454 (J.P. Stevens), 468

Royal Ontario Museum, Toronto—101

Texa Stock—87BL, 227TL, TR, BL

Susan Van Etten—226TR, 227TM&M

Vision Publications, Rome—442R

Bill Weems—86B

Woodfin Camp—152 (Robert Frerck), 252 (Mike Yamashita)

Marble tiles supplied by Tiles: A Refined Selection, Boston